# VIOLENCE AND WARFARE AMONG HUNTER-GATHERERS

# VIOLENCE AND WARFARE AMONG HUNTER-GATHERERS

**Mark W. Allen**
**Terry L. Jones**

Editors

LONDON AND NEW YORK

First published 2014 by Left Coast Press, Inc.

Published 2016 by Routledge
2 Park Square, Milton Park, Abingdon, Oxon OX14 4RN
711 Third Avenue, New York, NY 10017, USA

*Routledge is an imprint of the Taylor & Francis Group, an informa business*

Copyright © 2014 Taylor & Francis

All rights reserved. No part of this book may be reprinted or reproduced or utilised in any form or by any electronic, mechanical, or other means, now known or hereafter invented, including photocopying and recording, or in any information storage or retrieval system, without permission in writing from the publishers.

Notice:
Product or corporate names may be trademarks or registered trademarks, and are used only for identification and explanation without intent to infringe.

Library of Congress Cataloging-in-Publication Data:

Violence and Warfare among Hunter-Gatherers / edited by Mark W. Allen and Terry L. Jones.
     pages cm
Includes bibliographical references and index.
ISBN 978-1-61132-939-1 (hardback)
ISBN 978-1-61132-941-4 (institutional eBook)
ISBN 978-1-61132-942-1 (consumer eBook)
1. Hunting and gathering societies. 2. Warfare, Prehistoric. I. Allen, Mark W., author, editor of compilation. II. Jones, Terry L., author, editor of compilation.
GN388.V56 2014
306.3´64—dc23

2014005346

ISBN 978-1-61132-939-1 hardback

# Contents

| | |
|---|---|
| List of Illustrations | 7 |
| Preface | 11 |

**PART I: A Neglected Anthropology: Hunter-Gatherer Violence and Warfare**

1. Hunter-Gatherer Conflict: The Last Bastion of the Pacified Past?　15
   *Mark W. Allen*

2. Forager Warfare and Our Evolutionary Past　26
   *Steven A. LeBlanc*

**PART II: Violence and Warfare among Mobile Foragers**

3. Violence and Warfare in the European Mesolithic and Paleolithic　49
   *Virginia Hutton Estabrook*

4. Wild-Type Colonizers and High Levels of Violence among Paleoamericans　70
   *James C. Chatters*

5. Hunter-Gatherer Violence and Warfare in Australia　97
   *Mark W. Allen*

6. Conflict and Territoriality in Aboriginal Australia: Evidence from Biology and Ethnography　112
   *Colin Pardoe*

7. Conflict and Interpersonal Violence in Holocene Hunter-Gatherer Populations from Southern South America　133
   *Florencia Gordón*

8. Warfare and Expansion: An Ethnohistoric Perspective on the Numic Spread　149
   *Mark Q. Sutton*

9. Wait and Parry: Archaeological Evidence for Hunter-Gatherer Defensive Behavior in the Interior Northwest  168
*Kenneth C. Reid*

10. Scales of Violence across the North American Arctic  182
*John Darwent and Christyann M. Darwent*

11. The Spectre of Conflict on Isla Cedros, Baja California, Mexico  204
*Matthew R. Des Lauriers*

## PART III: Violence and Warfare among Semisedentary Hunter-Gatherers

12. Foragers and War in Contact-Era New Guinea  223
*Paul ("Jim") Roscoe*

13. Middle and Late Archaic Trophy Taking in Indiana  241
*Christopher W. Schmidt and Amber E. Osterholt*

14. The Bioarchaeological Record of Craniofacial Trauma in Central California  257
*Marin A. Pilloud, Al W. Schwitalla, and Terry L. Jones*

15. Archaic Violence in Western North America: The Bioarchaeological Record of Dismemberment, Human Bone Artifacts, and Trophy Skulls from Central California  273
*Al W. Schwitalla, Terry L. Jones, Randy S. Wiberg, Marin A. Pilloud, Brian F. Codding, and Eric C. Strother*

16. Stable Isotope Perspectives on Hunter-Gatherer Violence: Who's Fighting Whom?  296
*Jelmer W. Eerkens, Eric J. Bartelink, Karen S. Gardner, and Traci L. Carlson*

17. The Technology of Violence and Cultural Evolution in the Santa Barbara Channel Region  314
*James M. Brill*

18. Updating the Warrior Cache: Timing the Evidence for Warfare at Prince Rupert Harbour  333
*Jerome S. Cybulski*

## PART IV: Synthesis and Conclusion

19. The Prehistory of Violence and Warfare among Hunter-Gatherers  353
*Terry L. Jones and Mark W. Allen*

Index  372

About the Editors and Contributors  385

# Illustrations

## Figures

| | | |
|---|---|---|
| 4.1 | Patterns of traumatic defects in the skeletons of Paleoamerican males and females | 76 |
| 4.2 | Examples of traumatic defects in Paleoamerican skeletons | 77 |
| 4.3 | The pattern of violent trauma in Late Prehistoric hunter-gatherers from the Columbia Plateau | 81 |
| 4.4 | Mortality distribution of Paleoamerican males and females | 84 |
| 4.5 | Sexual dimorphism in Paleoamerican female and male skulls | 87 |
| 6.1 | The Central Murray River region | 113 |
| 6.2 | Parrying fractures by regional group Australia-wide, sides combined | 123 |
| 6.3 | Cranial depression fractures by group | 126 |
| 7.1 | Patagonian region and northeastern Patagonia study area | 135 |
| 7.2 | Traumatic variables with types of artificial cranial deformation | 140 |
| 8.1 | Location of Numic-language and other groups in the late 1800s | 151 |
| 9.1 | Johnson Bar South, a probable battlefield cemetery in Hells Canyon, Idaho | 176 |
| 10.1 | The North American Arctic | 184 |
| 10.2 | Slat-armor piece carved from caribou antler recovered from Cape Espenberg, Alaska | 189 |
| 10.3 | Large knife or dagger (*savik*) carved of polar bear bone used in close-contact fighting | 190 |
| 11.1 | Baja California and Isla Cedros | 205 |
| 11.2 | Punta Norte Village aerial view | 207 |
| 11.3 | Aerial view of village at Campo Quintero | 208 |
| 12.1 | Variation of intercentroid distance with density for polities of sizes 25 and 50 | 230 |
| 13.1 | Indiana sites: Bluegrass, Kramer Mound, Meyer, 12Hr6, 12F173, and Firehouse | 242 |
| 13.2 | Cache of forelimbs from site 12F173 | 246 |

| | | |
|---|---|---|
| 13.3 | Scalping marks on cranial fragment from Kramer Mound | 247 |
| 13.4 | Mandible from B.42 at the Meyer Site | 248 |
| 14.1 | Location of sites used in study by geographic region | 259 |
| 14.2 | Adult male with antemortem depressed cranial fracture to the right parietal | 260 |
| 14.3 | Adult male exhibiting multiple perimortem depressed cranial fractures | 261 |
| 14.4 | Distribution of craniofacial trauma divided by age and sex | 262 |
| 14.5 | Correspondence analysis of craniofacial trauma location and sex | 263 |
| 14.6 | Distribution of craniofacial trauma by region and sex | 265 |
| 15.1 | Archaeological sites in the Central California Bioarchaeological Database | 275 |
| 15.2 | Butchering marks as evidence of scalping from CA-MRN-67 | 280 |
| 15.3 | Modified right and left ulnae from CA-SOL-364 | 280 |
| 15.4 | Burial 44, an adult male, in situ, with a trophy skull at CA-ALA-42 | 281 |
| 15.5 | A young adult female interred as an isolated skull and deliberately oriented on a rock platform in association with other individuals that exhibited evidence of perimortem trauma | 282 |
| 15.6 | Burial 137, adult male, interred with a trophy skull at CA-CCO-548 | 282 |
| 15.7 | Sites with skeletal evidence for trophy taking in central California | 285 |
| 15.8 | Trends through time in trophy-taking–related features/artifacts in central California | 291 |
| 16.1 | Location of three central California case studies | 299 |
| 16.2 | Mass burial pit from CA-YOL-117, reconstructed from 1964 field sketch | 300 |
| 16.3 | Comparison of Sr and O stable isotopes from CA-YOL-117 and CA-ALA-554 samples | 302 |
| 16.4 | $\delta^{13}C$ and $\delta^{15}N$ in bone collagen for pit burials ("nonlocals") and "locals," and expected ranges for central California environmental zones | 302 |
| 16.5 | Seven males from CA-ALA-554 and intrusive housepit | 303 |
| 16.6 | Excavation photo of B141, B142, B143, and B144 from CA-SCL-38 | 306 |
| 17.1 | Study sites | 316 |
| 17.2 | Continuum of innovation | 318 |
| 17.3 | Point measurements | 324 |
| 17.4 | Total $CV$ percentages with weight removed for each Malaga Cove sample divided by time | 328 |
| 17.5 | Sex distribution of people with projectile wounds | 329 |
| 18.1 | Archaeological sites in the Prince Rupert Harbour region | 335 |

| | | |
|---|---|---|
| 18.2 | Two of three headless individuals found at the Lachane site | 339 |
| 18.3 | Calibrated calendar ages for six Prince Rupert Harbour middens | 344 |

## Tables

| | | |
|---|---|---|
| 3.1 | Mesolithic injuries potentially attributable to violence | 53 |
| 3.2 | Middle Paleolithic trauma possibly related to interpersonal violence | 59 |
| 3.3 | Middle Paleolithic trauma possibly related to violence | 60 |
| 3.4 | Mesolithic trauma possibly related to violence | 61 |
| 3.5 | Number of instances of injury by degree of severity | 64 |
| 3.6 | Counts of projectile/blade versus blunt force injuries | 65 |
| 3.7 | Number of instances of antemortem injury possibly related to violence by degree of severity | 65 |
| 4.1 | Paleoamerican skeletons in this study | 72 |
| 4.2 | Traumatic injuries in Paleoamerican males and females | 75 |
| 4.3 | Frequency of evidence for interpersonal violence in skeletal populations of North America | 80 |
| 6.1 | Parrying fractures by side, sex, and group | 124 |
| 6.2 | Incidence of depression fractures by sex | 125 |
| 6.3 | Regional contrasts in head dents by sex | 127 |
| 7.1 | Age and sex distribution of the analyzed sample | 139 |
| 7.2 | Trauma distribution by area, sex, and age | 141 |
| 10.1 | Incidences of male violence recorded by Knud Rasmussen in the settlement of Kunajuk on the Ellice River (*Kuunnuaq*) | 186 |
| 12.1 | Fry's "simple" nomadic forager file | 229 |
| 12.2 | The hunter-gatherers of contact-era New Guinea | 229 |
| 13.1 | Dates from Indiana sites | 242 |
| 14.1 | Demographic profile of the skeletal sample | 258 |
| 14.2 | Distribution of antemortem craniofacial trauma by sex | 262 |
| 14.3 | Distribution of perimortem craniofacial trauma by sex | 262 |
| 14.4 | Distribution of craniofacial trauma by location and sex | 263 |
| 14.5 | Distribution of fracture types | 264 |
| 14.6 | Temporal distribution of craniofacial trauma | 265 |
| 14.7 | Temporal and regional distribution of craniofacial trauma | 266 |
| 14.8 | Dimensions of antemortem depressed fractures by element in central California | 266 |
| 14.9 | Dimensions of antemortem depressed fractures by element in southern California | 267 |
| 14.10 | One-way ANOVA of dimensions of antemortem depressed fractures between southern and central California | 267 |

| | | |
|---|---|---|
| 15.1 | Geographic and ethnographic distribution of burials in the Central California Bioarchaeological Database with evidence of trophy taking | 277 |
| 15.2 | Summary of central California archaeological sites with evidence of trophy taking | 278 |
| 15.3 | Demographic breakdown of burials in the Central California Bioarchaeological Database by ethnographic territory | 284 |
| 15.4 | Human bones with evidence of butchering over time in central California | 286 |
| 15.5 | Human bone artifacts by burial association over time in central California | 287 |
| 15.6 | Burials with missing or repositioned cranial or postcranial skeletal elements | 289 |
| 15.7 | Summary of crania and postcranial elements found as isolates or in other context suggesting use as trophies from central California | 290 |
| 17.1 | Summary of the projectile point sample | 321 |
| 17.2 | Definitions of projectile point measurements | 325 |
| 17.3 | Chronology of the Santa Barbara Channel | 325 |
| 18.1 | Laboratory provided radiocarbon dates and calibrated calendar ages for individuals in the Prince Rupert Harbour sites | 342 |

# Preface

The concept for this volume was developed several years ago in consultation with Mitch Allen of Left Coast Press, Inc. The original plan was for Mark Allen to compare a limited number of cases of forager violence and warfare, including those of California and the Great Basin, Australia, and a region to be named later. The Australian research was accomplished through a month-long research trip spent mostly at the Australian Institute of Aboriginal and Torres Strait Islander Studies in June of 2008 to gather materials. The project then languished in the face of the daunting scale of work involved in compiling the material for additional cultural areas.

Wisely, it turns out; the decision was made to transform the project into an edited volume. A symposium held at the 2013 Society for American Archaeology Annual Meeting in Honolulu brought most of the contributors together, and a few more were recruited to expand the volume's regional coverage. Our editorial team of Allen and Jones proved that the two polytechnic universities of the California State University could come together to produce more than Rose Parade floats. We wish to express our thanks to the volume contributors for agreeing to produce their chapters in a relatively short period of time and for enduring our final push over the last months of the project. Nancy Allen provided crucial assistance in production of the volume's index.

Finally, we are very grateful for the extensive support and guidance that we received from Mitch Allen and Caryn Berg, as well as the editorial expertise of Michelle Treviño.

# PART I

# A Neglected Anthropology: Hunter-Gatherer Violence and Warfare

# 1

# Hunter-Gatherer Conflict:
# The Last Bastion of the Pacified Past?

*Mark W. Allen*

When I arrived in New Zealand in the 1980s to begin dissertation research on the roles of warfare and economic power in the development of Maori chiefdoms, there was no shortage of recent scholarly research on cultural evolution, ecology, and social power, but there was little being written at the time about indigenous or prehistoric warfare. American archaeology was then in the midst of a multi-decadal moratorium on violence research that emphasized instead the ingenuity, ecological balance, and intergroup harmony of traditional, nonwestern subsistence adaptations. My research design relied heavily on a masterful and widely known ethnographic summary of Maori warfare by Andrew Vayda (1960) that had been penned before the anthropological pendulum had swung away from recognition of violence and warfare in traditional cultures. Because that work (and others) had established unequivocally the role of violent conflict in the evolution of Polynesian chiefdoms, New Zealand was one of the few places at the time where the archaeology of warfare could be investigated without raising anthropological eyebrows.

This situation changed dramatically in the 1990s due largely to Lawrence Keeley's influential 1996 book, *War before Civilization: The Myth of the Peaceful Savage*, along with other seminal anthropological studies (e.g., Ember and Ember 1992; Ferguson 1992; Milner et al. 1991; Otterbein 1999; Wrangham and Peterson 1996). These works, particularly Keeley's, put forward a persuasive call for archaeologists to take a fresh look at the evidence for warfare in their respective regional records. Of course, anthropologists, other social scientists,

---

*Violence and Warfare among Hunter-Gatherers*, edited by Mark W. Allen and Terry L. Jones, 15–25. ©2014 Taylor & Francis. All rights reserved.

**16** | Mark W. Allen

and philosophers had been studying and theorizing about warfare, albeit with only limited input from archaeologists, for centuries. Indeed, the two basic views on warfare and the human condition that continue to permeate writing on the subject were established centuries ago: one was promoted by Thomas Hobbes, who argued that civilization essentially rescued humanity from a situation of "war of all against all" in which lives were "nasty, brutish and short," while the alternative was developed by Jean-Jacques Rousseau, who suggested that civilization brought increases in oppression, conflict, and violence, and that simpler, noncivilized societies were marked by greater levels of peace and harmony. Although archaeological evidence of various types has been used to support both views (see discussions by Kim [2012] and Lawler [2012]), most of the twentieth-century anthropological attempts to support one or the other side of this debate were based on ethnographic data, a tradition that continues today (see Fry 2013; Kim 2012). Keeley, however, persuasively argued that cultural anthropologists and archaeologists had frequently "pacified the past" by ignoring evidence of violence and warfare, and further argued that in cases where prehistoric or traditional war was undeniable, there had been a strong tendency to classify it as mere ritual, game-like, or otherwise unserious. He also took aim at Ferguson's (1992) influential argument that tribal warfare in Amazonia and other areas was largely a product of colonial infiltration into previously peaceful regions.

Keeley's book unleashed a torrent of in-depth archaeological and bioarchaeological studies of prehistoric violence and warfare in a wide range of cultural areas, including those by Arkush (2011), Arkush and Allen (2006), Chacon and Dye (2007), Chacon and Mendoza (2007a, 2007b), Dye (2009), Lambert (2002), LeBlanc (1999), LeBlanc and Register (2003), Martin et al. (2012), Rice and LeBlanc (2001), and Snead and Allen (2010), among others, as well as hundreds of journal articles, far too many to be cited here.

Despite this wealth of research, there has been one glaring omission in considerations of the archaeology and prehistory of warfare. Many of the comprehensive works summarizing indigenous warfare and violence consider some hunter-gatherer societies (e.g., Chacon and Mendoza 2007a; Lambert 2002), but have not emphasized the distinction between forager societies and farmers. In many cases this omission simply comes from a desire to demonstrate the levels and intensity of indigenous warfare without regard to the underlying type of precivilized adaptation. Moreover, evidence for conflict among foragers (Ember 1978; Ember and Ember 1992; Keeley 1996; Otterbein 2004) has often been neglected. Anthropologists often perpetuate the long-cherished notion that small-scale societies of foragers (especially the most mobile hunter-gatherers) are inherently peaceful with low levels of violence and extremely rare warfare. While more complex hunter-gatherer groups with greater sedentism, storage, organizational capacity, and population density are now routinely acknowledged as having considerable violence and war, there continues to be a widely held belief that less complex, mobile foragers conform with the ideal of the noble savage, at least in regard to their proclivity (or lack thereof) for intergroup conflict.

The lack of attention to conflict within the full range of hunter-gatherer adaptations is all the more curious since it is a potential key to the heavily debated questions of when and why war originated. Some argue for a violent propensity in our genes that can be triggered under certain material conditions (Wrangham and Peterson 1996); others claim that its roots are in social competition inherent in even small populations; and still others propose that war did not arise until dependence on agriculture led to increased competition between groups. Psychological and enculturation models are also widespread. Thus far, there is little agreement. The cultural anthropologist Keith Otterbein (1997, 2004) created a colorful dichotomy of two "species" of scholars from diverse fields with firm views on this subject. "Hawks" believe that war has always been with us, right back to the first hominins. "Doves" believe that warfare is fairly recent, and is mainly associated with the spread of more complex societies such as chiefdoms, early states, and especially colonial empires. Another way to conceptualize the polarity of views on the prehistory of violence and warfare is to distinguish a long chronology of war versus a short chronology (Allen 2012:198–200; Roscoe, this volume).

## The Long Chronology of War

Perhaps the most visible proponent of the long chronology of war is Richard Wrangham. Apart from his scholarly writings, his general-audience book, *Demonic Males: Apes and the Origins of Human Violence,* touched many nerves (Wrangham and Peterson 1996). His view is that the group violence exhibited by chimpanzees is an accurate glimpse of the distant hominin past as well. His argument is that humans are adapted for violence, and in particular that male humans are selected for coalition-based fighting:

> That chimpanzees and humans kill members of neighboring groups of their own species is . . . a startling exception to the normal rule for animals. Add our close genetic relationship to these apes and we face the possibility that intergroup aggression in our two species has a common origin. This idea of a common origin is made more haunting by the clues that suggest modern chimpanzees are not merely fellow time-travelers and evolutionary relatives, but surprisingly excellent models of our direct ancestors. It suggests that chimpanzee-like violence preceded and paved the way for human war, making modern humans the dazed survivors of a continuous, 5-million-year habit of lethal aggression (Wrangham and Peterson 1996:63).

Most cultural anthropologists still shy away from any suggestion that humans are biologically driven to violence despite the fact that many human

**18** | Mark W. Allen

behaviors related to aggression are highly advantageous in conflict, such as alliance formation, wariness of strangers, perception of in-group versus out-group, and altruism. These behaviors likely have some genetic component and thus could have been selected for under conditions of extreme competition (see LeBlanc and Chatters, this volume). Nevertheless, many advocates of the long chronology prefer to attribute human aggression and conflict to ecology and resource stress rather than biology, or to see both at work. For Roscoe (2007), warfare is a rational calculation of risk and benefit that could exist well before the short chronology would have it appear.

The most influential long-chronology archaeologists are Keeley and Steven LeBlanc. LeBlanc's (1999) treatise on warfare in the American southwest is perhaps the most detailed study yet of the evidence for prehistoric warfare in one particular cultural area. He, like Wrangham, wrote a book for general audiences summarizing his views, aptly titled *Constant Battles: The Myth of the Peaceful, Noble Savage* (LeBlanc and Register 2003). Scholars interested in arguing that war has been around for a long time rely heavily on Wrangham, Keeley, and LeBlanc, whose views are often cited in popular works directed at diverse audiences. A good example of their influence can be seen in Gat's (2006) book *War in Human Civilization*, in which the author reviews the available evolutionary, archaeological, and ethnographic evidence to conclude that violent aggression has been with us for at least two million years (the origin of the genus *Homo*) and that it is primarily caused by resource scarcity. He also points out that violence and war have many proximate causes such as prestige, revenge, sorcery, use of narcotics, and so on, but that the most prevalent underlying cause is competition for resources. Even the simplest hunter-gatherer societies, he argues, have high rates of mortality resulting from competition for reproductive success and territory.

Another example of a "hawkish" view written for a popular audience is David Livingstone Smith's (2007) *The Most Dangerous Animal: Human Nature and the Origins of War*. Smith accepts innate aggression in humans as a consequence of competition for reproductive success and resources, which ultimately causes humans to be naturally aggressive, xenophobic, and nepotistic. But he also claims that humans dread killing and are inherently self-deceptive, and that this internal conflict must be understood to solve "the puzzle of war" (Smith 2007:161). In *The Better Angels of Our Nature*, Steven Pinker (2011) argues for a deep history of human violence and warfare that is decreasing through time. His work draws heavily on an analysis of forager societies conducted by Bowles (2009) in an influential article in *Science* that advocates for the long chronology and makes the case that severe Late Pleistocene and Early Holocene intergroup conflict could have affected the evolution of group-beneficial behaviors.

Though members of the public as well as specialists from many disciplines seem to favor the long-chronology theory, it is not the majority view among anthropologists. This discrepancy is due to many causes (Keeley 1996), but an especially significant one is the tendency for anthropology texts and courses to continue to equate hunter-gatherers with peace. In anthropology, the default position is advocacy of a short chronology of war.

## The Short Chronology of War

Perhaps the most ardent "dove" is cultural anthropologist Douglas P. Fry, whose books *The Human Potential for Peace: An Anthropological Challenge to Assumptions about War and Violence* (2006), *Beyond War: The Human Potential for Peace* (2007), and *War, Peace, and Human Nature* (2013) are attempts to counter the popularity of the long chronology. He accepts that warfare—which he defines as lethal conflict between communities—has been common in the past 6,000 to 4,000 years in both agricultural and complex hunter-gatherer societies. In contrast, he argues that non-complex foragers are/were characterized by low levels of violent intergroup conflict, but high rates of homicide and moderate levels of feuding among descent groups. Importantly, he does not recognize kin-based organizations as polities, and is adamant that feuding among them should not be conflated with warfare. He reanalyzes the available ethnographic material from foragers, and concludes that they were peaceful societies with very little warfare. He makes a spirited attack on Wrangham's work, which he calls the "Pervasive Intergroup Hostility Model," attempting to show that many of its tenets are incorrect. In Fry's view, "nomadic foragers, living in a weakly partitioned or unpartitioned social world, perceive homicides and lesser disputes in terms of individual grievances, not as occasions for making war, group against group" (Fry 2006:234).

Most recently, Fry and Söderberg (2013) question the research of Wrangham, Pinker, and Bowles that found evidence of warfare in samples of forager societies. Fry and Söderberg developed their own sample of 21 mobile forager band societies (MFBS) and used it to examine lethal aggression through data drawn from "only the principle authority sources . . . as the earliest high-quality ethnographic descriptions available" (Fry and Söderberg 2013:271). Their conclusion is that the research citing warfare in forager societies suffers from flaws such as ethnographic case self-selection, reliance on secondary sources, and inflated lethality due to colonial encounters. They argue:

> most incidents of lethal aggression can aptly be called homicides, a few others feud, and only a minority warfare. The findings do not lend support to the coalitionary model. The predictions are substantiated that MFBS, as a social type, possess many features that make warfare unlikely. The actual reasons for lethal aggression are most often interpersonal, and consequently, the particulars of most of the lethal events in these societies do not conform to the usual conceptualization of war (Fry and Söderberg 2013:272).

**20** | Mark W. Allen

Perhaps most archaeologists and cultural anthropologists working on warfare are "dove"-like in the sense that they accept the position that warfare is mainly a recent phenomenon, dating only to the development of complex hunter-gatherers and/or agriculturalists. R. Brian Ferguson, a cultural anthropologist with a body of work on warfare that spans several decades, contends that much tribal warfare can be attributed to changes wrought by European encroachment over the last few centuries (Ferguson 1992; Ferguson and Whitehead 1992). As noted earlier, this position drew criticism from Keeley (1996), and Ferguson (2006, 2013) has subsequently critiqued the archaeological data used to argue for a long chronology of violence and warfare. Most recently, he has assailed Pinker's research (Ferguson 2013).

Some archaeologists also self-identify with Fry's camp. Jonathan Haas (2001) has long argued that warfare is rare before the last few thousand years of prehistory, and recently declared "there is extremely limited empirical evidence of any warfare among past hunters and gatherers" (Haas and Piscitelli 2013:184). Eastern Woodlands archaeologist David Dye (2009, 2013) is also an advocate of the short chronology. His view is "that for nearly half the time that Native Americans lived in eastern North America—approximately six thousand years—peaceful relations characterized these family-level hunter-gathers, and that violent conflict among social groups emerged only with increasingly complex forms of social and political organization" (Dye 2009:17). Both Haas (Haas and Piscitelli 2013) and Dye (2013) are included in Fry's latest book as archaeological critics of the long chronology of war. It is worth noting that a renowned specialist of hunter-gather societies, Robert Kelly, has a far more equivocal view in the same volume, noting that, "it is not useful to ask whether hunter-gatherers (inclusive of egalitarian and nonegalitarian types) are peaceful or warlike; we find evidence for both among them. . . . [T]he better question is: when do foragers resort to war?" (Kelly 2013:158).

Proponents of the short view of war often rely on tenuous definitions that are often tautological, inconsistent, or idiosyncratic. War is commonly defined as potentially lethal combat between different polities, but short-chronology proponents often define war in such a way that it would be impossible for small-scale societies to meet the proffered standard, such as the number of participants, level of leadership, or some other organizational capacity. Likewise, the definition of homicide is frequently stretched to mean much more than is generally accepted (i.e., that it is unsanctioned killing within a society). In other words, killings between kin-based groups are often classified as homicides rather than intergroup conflict. Similarly, "feuding" is often the label applied to tribal warfare by the argument that it is between kin-militias, but not different communities. As Roscoe (this volume) points out, in the tribal world kin groups often, and in some areas *always*, are communities. This semantic sleight of hand is not constructive.

## Raymond Kelly's Theory of the Origin of Warfare

One of the most significant recent anthropological theories on violence and warfare is that of Raymond Kelly (2000). Certainly he is the cultural anthropologist who has most influenced archaeologists working on these issues. In his book *Warless Societies and the Origin of War*, he developed "a general model for the initial evolution of war that is grounded in the comparative analysis of ethnographic data and then applied to the interpretation of pertinent data in the archaeological record" (Kelly 2000:ix). He uses case societies from the limited set of ethnographically identified "peaceful" or "warless" societies, as well as those from societies with frequent incidence of warfare, to identify key differences or thresholds in a sociocultural context. It was this change in context, according to Kelly, that pushed societies toward warfare in the human past. He believes that warfare was rare until the development of fairly complex segmented societies in which group members perceive the killing of one of their own as an attack on the entire group. Kelly views the "calculus of social substitutability" as key to the transformation of violence into an instrument of the social group. Since he classifies human societies during the Upper Paleolithic (ca. 35,000 years ago) as unsegmented societies, he concludes that warfare was rare until later in human history.

More recently, Kelly (2005) has further developed his arguments about the origins of "lethal intergroup violence." He agrees with the view that early hominins probably had competitive social groups, but he sees the origin of the thrown spear as a turning point since it provided defensive advantages for hunters in their own territories that could not be overcome. He thinks that warfare was put on hold until the evolution of complex societies that used organization and specialized weapons to overcome defensive advantages. He thus acknowledges a long chronology of violence among hominins, but believes that the level of warfare has a short chronology. This position is widely cited and is potentially testable with archaeological data. Some areas of concern with the model include the small number of ethnographic cases Kelly used, and the ambiguity of social organization during the Upper Paleolithic (Allen 2003). The capacity of the thrown spear to be a deterrent to offensive action among hunter-gatherers is also questionable as surprise attacks, particularly fierce fighters, or other random variables could easily overcome the defensive benefits of spears.

## Purpose and Organization of This Volume

This volume was developed with the view that the best way to understand the origins of violence and warfare and how each changed through time and space is to conduct more detailed and systematic analyses of hunter-gatherer conflict. With such cases in hand, a comparative approach has the potential to

## 22 | Mark W. Allen

examine patterns of how violence and warfare vary according to variables such as ecology, social organization, climatic instability, stress, and culture contact. Reliance on twentieth-century ethnography alone is rife with problems such as the biases of post–World War II anthropologists who avoided research on conflict, the marginal nature of places where foragers survived into modern times (that hardly represent most human environments of the past), and drastic changes that affected hunter-gatherers well before recent ethnographic material was collected.

Evaluating the archaeology of hunter-gatherer warfare, especially among mobile foraging bands, is, without question, challenging. The first steps are recognizing the limitations of the archaeological record and avoiding the pitfall of arguing from negative evidence. This volume is a compilation of research that turns to multiple lines of evidence, including archaeological data, ethnography, ethnohistory, skeletal analyses, trace element analyses, and linguistic information. The contributions reveal useful approaches, some never before attempted, to fill a significant gap in the anthropology and archaeology of warfare and conflict in pre-state societies: hunter-gatherer violence and warfare.

The first section focuses on theoretical issues of hunter-gatherer violence and warfare and includes this chapter as well as the one by LeBlanc. He further develops his case that not just violence but also warfare characterized most forager societies. He takes umbrage with studies relying on ethnographic cases that define warfare in such a way that precludes it from applying to foragers. LeBlanc also points out that much of the ethnographic material assembled to support the view that foragers were peaceful is highly questionable since it was recorded after major population or technological changes that may have drastically lowered levels of stress. He sees forager war as very risky, and very deadly. In his view, stress was nearly constant because human populations grow rapidly to carrying capacity. One result of this, he claims, is that marginal areas often functioned as population sinks for the more productive areas. LeBlanc argues that genetic and ecological models for the origin of violence and warfare are not mutually exclusive, and that it is quite possible that selection shaped human behaviors that were adaptive for groups in competition for resources (altruism, protecting group members, suspicion of strangers, and alliance formation). Yet another key point LeBlanc makes is that warfare appears to be rational behavior, and he points out how quickly it often ceased in areas after European contact when the equations of resources and competition were shifted by demographic changes and access to new economic networks.

As noted earlier, it is commonly held that there is a significant difference in the types, levels, or intensities of violence and warfare between mobile foraging societies characterized by small-band level of organization, and more complex hunter-gatherers who live in larger, more sedentary groups with higher degrees of social differentiation supported by surplus or stored resources (see Kelly 2013). The case studies are therefore separated into these two types to facilitate comparison. Following the introductory comments in Part I, Part II of the volume takes up studies of mobile hunters and gatherers, including ethnographic treatments of Australian Aborigines, Numic speakers of the Great Basin, the North American Arctic, and Baja California arrayed with other types of evidence. Primarily archaeological data are used to consider the European Paleolithic and Mesolithic, North American Paleoindians, Patagonia, and the interior of northwestern North America.

The studies in Part II document that violence was common in the earliest occupations of *Homo sapiens* in Europe (Estabrook), North America (Chatters), and Australia (Allen, Pardoe). Several of the chapters note that evidence from the Early and Middle Holocene is sketchy at best, but may be due to preservation issues. Though warfare is even more difficult to detect than violence, it is clear from these cases that it was not a rare anomaly in forager societies.

In Part III, we consider the ethnography and archaeology of semi-sedentary hunter-gatherers characterized by stored food supplies, hierarchy, organizational complexity, and group sizes more in line with small tribes than bands. This includes Roscoe's ethnographic treatment of foragers in contact-era New Guinea and archaeological studies of the Middle and Late Archaic in the American Midwest, four chapters on southern and central California, and recent findings from the American northwest coast. These cases, not unexpectedly, reveal the presence of significant violence and frequently warfare. Part IV of the volume has a concluding chapter that explores the themes of the three previous sections.

The contributors to this volume use a wide variety of methodologies and theoretical approaches in their consideration of the regional case studies. Some focus on the details of a particular region or culture; others are continental in scope and focus on long cultural sequences. One key finding resounds throughout the volume: violence and warfare are not always present. Even in regions where they commonly occur, the long-term view afforded by archaeology and history shows that violence and war can change rapidly as well as decline drastically. Comparison of such cases is a promising path to better understand violent conflict. We hope that the range of perspectives in this volume will do much to stimulate further research in the same regions examined here, as well as in other areas that are not included due to limitations of space.

## Acknowledgments

I am grateful to Terry Jones and Elizabeth Arkush for their numerous suggestions, which greatly improved this chapter.

**24** | Mark W. Allen

## References

Allen, Mark W. 2003. Review of *Warless Societies and the Origin of War*, by Raymond C. Kelly. *American Anthropologist* 105:432–4.

——— 2012. A Land of Violence. In *Contemporary Issues in California Archaeology*, edited by Terry L. Jones, and Jennifer E. Perry, pp. 93–114. Left Coast Press, Walnut Creek, CA.

Arkush, Elizabeth N. 2011. *Hillforts of the Ancient Andes: Colla Warfare, Society, and Landscape.* University Press of Florida, Gainesville.

Arkush, Elizabeth N., and Mark W. Allen (editors) 2006. *The Archaeology of Warfare: Prehistories of Raiding and Conquest.* University of Florida Press, Gainesville.

Bowles, Samuel 2009. Did Warfare among Ancestral Hunter-Gatherers Affect the Evolution of Human Social Behaviors? *Science* 324:1293–98.

Chacon, Richard J., and Rubén G. Mendoza 2007a. *North American Indigenous Warfare and Ritual Violence.* University of Arizona Press, Tucson.

——— 2007b. *Latin American Indigenous Warfare and Ritual Violence.* University of Arizona Press, Tucson.

Chacon, Richard J., and David H. Dye (editors) 2007. *The Taking and Displaying of Human Body Parts by Amerindians.* Springer, New York.

Dye, David H. 2009. *War Paths, Peace Paths: An Archaeology of Cooperation and Conflict in Native Eastern North America.* Altamira Press, Lanham, MD.

——— 2013. Trends in Cooperation and Conflict in Native Eastern North America. In *War, Peace, and Human Nature*, edited by Douglas P. Fry, pp. 132–50. Oxford University Press, New York.

Ember, Carol R. 1978. Myths about Hunter-Gatherers. *Ethnology* 17:439–48.

Ember, Carol R., and Melvin R. Ember 1992. Resource Unpredictability, Mistrust, and War: A Cross-Cultural Study. *Journal of Conflict Resolution* 36:242–62.

Ferguson, R. Brian 1992. Tribal Warfare. *Scientific American* 266:108–16.

——— 2006. Archaeology, Cultural Anthropology, and the Origins and Intensifications of War. In *The Archaeology of Warfare: Prehistories of Raiding and Conquest*, edited by Elizabeth N. Arkush and Mark W. Allen, pp. 469–523. The University Press of Florida, Gainesville.

——— 2013. Pinker's List: Exaggerating Prehistoric War Mortality. In *War, Peace, and Human Nature,* edited by Douglas P. Fry, pp. 112–31. Oxford University Press, New York.

Ferguson, R. Brian, and Neil L. Whitehead 1992. *War in the Tribal Zone.* School of American Research Press, Santa Fe, NM.

Fry, Douglas P. 2006. *The Human Potential for Peace: An Anthropological Challenge to Assumptions about War and Violence.* Oxford University Press, New York.

——— 2007. *Beyond War: The Human Potential for Peace.* Oxford University Press, New York.

——— (editor) 2013. *War, Peace, and Human Nature.* Oxford University Press, New York.

Fry, Douglas P., and Patrik Söderberg 2013. Lethal Aggression in Mobile Forager Bands and Implications for the Origins of War. *Science* 341:270–2.

Gat, Azar 2006. *War in Human Civilization.* Oxford University Press, New York.

Haas, Jonathan 2001. Warfare and the Evolution of Culture. In *Archaeology at the Millennium: A Sourcebook*, edited by Gary M. Feinman and T. Douglas Price, pp. 329–50. Kluwer Academic/Plenum Publishers, New York.

Haas, Jonathan, and Matthew Piscitelli 2013. The Prehistory of Warfare: Misled by Ethnography. In *War, Peace, and Human Nature*, edited by Douglas P. Fry, pp. 168–90. Oxford University Press, Oxford, United Kingdom.

Keeley, Lawrence H. 1996. *War before Civilization.* Oxford University Press, New York.

Kelly, Raymond C. 2000. *Warless Societies and the Origin of War.* University of Michigan Press, Ann Arbor.

——— 2005. The Evolution of Lethal Intergroup Violence. *Proceedings of the National Academy of Sciences* 102:15294–8.

## Hunter-Gatherer Conflict: The Last Bastion of the Pacified Past? | **25**

Kelly, Robert L. 2013. From the Peaceful to the Warlike: Ethnographies and Archaeological Insights into Hunter-Gatherer Warfare and Homicide. In *War, Peace, and Human Nature*, edited by Douglas P. Fry, pp. 151–67. Oxford University Press, Oxford, United Kingdom.

Kim, Nam C. 2012. Angels, Illusions, Hydras, and Chimeras: Violence and Humanity. *Reviews in Anthropology* 41:239–72.

Lambert, Patricia M. 2002. The Archaeology of War: A North American Perspective. *Journal of Archaeological Research* 10:207–41.

Lawler, Andrew 2012. The Battle Over Violence. *Science* 336:829–30.

LeBlanc, Steven A. 1999. *Prehistoric Warfare in the American Southwest*. University of Utah Press, Salt Lake City.

LeBlanc, Steven A., and Kathleen E. Register 2003. *Constant Battles: The Myth of the Peaceful, Noble Savage*. St. Martin's Press, New York.

Martin, Debra L., Ryan P. Harrod, and Ventura R. Pérez (editors) 2012. *The Bioarchaeology of Violence*. University Press of Florida, Gainesville.

Milner, George R., Eve Anderson, and Virginia G. Smith 1991. Warfare in Late Prehistoric West-Central Illinois. *American Antiquity* 56:581–603.

Otterbein, Keith F. 1997. The Origins of War. *Critical Review* 11:251–77.

———— 1999. A History of Research on Warfare in Anthropology. *American Anthropologist* 101:794–805.

———— 2004. *How War Began*. Texas A&M University Press, College Station.

Pinker, Steven 2011. *The Better Angels of Our Nature: Why Violence Has Declined*. Viking Press, New York.

Rice, Glen E., and Steven A. LeBlanc (editors) 2001. *Deadly Landscapes: Case Studies in Prehistoric Southwestern Warfare*. University of Utah Press, Salt Lake City.

Roscoe, Paul 2007. Intelligence, Coalitional Killing, and the Antecedents of War. *American Anthropologist* 109:485–95.

Smith, David Livingstone 2007. *The Most Dangerous Animal: Human Nature and the Origins of War*. St. Martin's Press, New York.

Snead, James E., and Mark W. Allen (editors) 2010. *Burnt Corn Pueblo: Conflict and Conflagration in the Galisteo Basin A.D. 1250–1325*. The Anthropological Papers of the University of Arizona, No. 74. The University of Arizona Press, Tucson.

Vayda, Andrew P. 1960. *Maori Warfare*. Polynesian Society Monograph No. 2, Wellington, New Zealand.

Wrangham, Richard, and Dale Peterson 1996. *Demonic Males: Apes and the Origins of Human Violence*. Hougton Mifflin, Boston.

# 2

# Forager Warfare and Our Evolutionary Past

*Steven A. LeBlanc*

On approaching the enemy's quarters, they laid themselves down in ambush until all was quiet, and finding most of them asleep, laying about in groups, our party rushed upon them, killing three on the spot and wounding several others. The enemy fled precipitately, leaving their war implements in the hands of their assailants and their wounded to be beaten to death by boomerangs, three loud shouts closing the victors triumph.

The bodies of the dead they mutilated in a shocking manner, cutting the arms and legs off, with flints, and shells, and tomahawks.

When the women saw them returning, they also raised great shouts, dancing about in savage ecstasy. The bodies were thrown upon the ground, and beaten about with sticks—in fact, they all seemed to be perfectly mad with excitement... (William Buckley describing south Australian Aborigines in 1852 in *The Life and Adventures of William Buckley* [Morgan [1852] 1979:43-44]).

The next morning the raiders attack the camp and killed all the women and children remaining there....

After shoving sheefish into the vaginas of all the Indian women they had killed, the Noatakers...retreated toward the upper Noatak River....

Some weeks later, the Kobuk caribou hunters returned home to find the rotting remains of their wives and children and vowed revenge. A year or two after that, they headed north to the upper Noatak to seek it. They soon located a large body of Nuataagmiut and secretly followed them. One morning the men in the Nuataagmiut camp spotted a large band of caribou and went off in pursuit.

---

*Violence and Warfare among Hunter-Gatherers*, edited by Mark W. Allen and Terry L. Jones, 26–46. ©2014 Taylor & Francis. All rights reserved.

Forager Warfare and Our Evolutionary Past | **27**

While they were gone, the Kobuk raiders killed every woman in the camp. Then they cut off their vulvas, strung them on a line, and headed quickly toward home (Burch 2005:110).

The peaceful forager is a myth. But we need to do more than dispel this myth, and we need to go beyond questions and concepts like peaceful societies or warlike societies. We can ask potentially more interesting questions: What was the nature of forager warfare? Can it tell us anything about our evolutionary past? The literature is filled with studies, interpretations, and conclusions that result from using inconsistent definitions of *warfare*, of *foragers*, of *hunter-gatherers*, and the like. As a result, scholars talk past each other or miss key points. Trying to find a perfect definition for such terms is of limited utility, but discussing these terms and what the various definitions imply has considerable value.

What is meant by *warfare* is particularly relevant to studies of foragers, for some scholars have defined the term in such a way that it would be impossible for foragers to have warfare. If *raiding* and *ambush* are not warfare, and *conflict within linguistic groups* is not warfare (because it is termed *feuding*), then, intentionally or not, most forager conflict is excluded from warfare discussions. Yet foragers did have warfare that was just as real, deadly, and impacting as other types of societies, and we need to understand it. There are various more useful definitions of warfare. *Socially sanctioned lethal conflict between independent polities* seems to be useful, although even this is not broad enough for some purposes as it precludes comparisons with other primates. With such a definition, *murder, dispute-settling intergroup fights that are not lethal*, and *intragroup violence* are excluded. So, warfare is not equated with lethal violence. This is the approach I take, but it is not necessarily the correct one for all questions.

## What Do We Mean by Foragers, and Who Were They?

I have used the term *foragers*, but it is not easy to determine what we mean by foragers, nor how appropriate recent examples of foragers are as models for our deep past. The "standard anthropological model" of foragers equates them with small, rather egalitarian groups that are highly mobile and do not store food. Usually men hunt and women collect plants, often contributing more than half the group's calories. This concept of *foragers* is in contrast to the concept of *hunter-gatherers* conceived broadly, which includes all societies that do not have domesticated plants or animals.

Of course, nothing is simple. Are people hunter-gatherers if they trade for domesticates or use domesticated horses for hunting? What if they only grow a small fraction of what they need for subsistence? In many cases, such peoples were in contact with farmers, often in symbiotic relationships with

**28** | Steven A. LeBlanc

them. I believe many contemporary and historic hunter-gatherers are poor analogs for the deep past. It is a very different world when farmers surround hunter-gatherers (and foragers), in contrast to foragers surrounding other foragers.

Another issue is that many of these hunter-gatherers specialized in using particular plants or animals as a staple food and were sometimes quite sedentary and lived in large settlements. They often stored food and were sometimes not egalitarian: that is, they behaved very much like farmers, except that their staple "crops" were not domesticated. To frame a discussion that lumps Northwest Coast salmon fishers with foragers is purposeless. However, the historic record of foragers is not set in the deep past, and so we must view ethnographic examples of foragers as useful but imperfect analogs for the deep past.

Thus, when I say "foragers," I mean people who used no domesticated plants or animals; lived in small, mobile groups; moved several times a year; did not store substantial amounts of food; and were relatively egalitarian. Archetypical examples of foragers include Australian Aborigines, !Kung Bushmen, Aeta, Andamanese, and Iñupiaq (Eskimo). These are the classic highly mobile peoples living in small groups with low social complexity. Another type of forager includes the Pygmies of central Africa, the Semang and Agta of southeast Asia, and the Paliyan and Nayaka of south India, who, when studied, were in highly symbiotic relationships with farmers (Lee and Daly 1999). I believe these symbiotic foragers are very poor analogs and provide confusion, not enlightenment.

Examples of hunter-gatherers that I would not classify as foragers include numerous groups in California who lived in permanent villages, stored acorns, and in some cases focused on marine resources, such as the Chumash. I also exclude societies, such as those along the Sepik River in New Guinea, who used wild palms as a staple and who had substantial permanent villages. The people of the Northwest Coast with their focus on salmon are perhaps the most complexly organized of the hunter-gatherers. Some Eskimo groups who focused on whaling should also not be considered foragers, as they also stored quantities of food and had permanent, relatively large villages. Archaeologically, the Jōmon of Japan, the Natufians of the Levant, and the Calusa of south Florida were also people who did not farm but had permanent villages and/or stored food. These various hunter-gatherers who are not foragers are sometimes called complex hunter-gathers, among other appellations.

Conversely, there are farmers such as the Yanomami and some New Guinea peoples who farmed but otherwise behaved much like foragers in terms of mobility, the level of hunting, group size, and social complexity. I believe we can, judiciously, consider them relevant in some sense as deep-past analogs, but it is a slippery slope.

## The Nature of Forager Warfare Data

A problem we face in dealing with the information about these peoples is when the data were collected. I believe the best data relevant to warfare come from early ethnographies and missionary or explorer accounts, but timing is everything. If, as I believe, resource stress and carrying capacity limitations are important determinants of warfare behavior (directly and indirectly), then any changes in the resources and carrying capacity will affect the behaviors in which we are interested.

Thus, increases in carrying capacity derived from new tools (especially metal tools), new sources of food (e.g., livestock), and interactions with farmers or herders who may provide buffering mechanisms against resource variability all serve to increase carrying capacity, thereby lowering potential resource-induced stress. Declines in population have the same effect. Population declines from diseases (including those sexually transmitted), from incorporating part of the population into farmer/herder societies, and from slave raiding all serve to reduce population density and growth and thereby change the carrying capacity balance. Changes in terms of access to trade and the need to form new alliances due to the new presence of Westerners or other indigenous foragers also affect the warfare environment, sometimes increasing it, sometimes reducing it.

Finally, female capture was sometimes an important component of conflict. The desire to capture females may result from a sex ratio imbalance due to female infanticide, which in turn can derive from carrying capacity limitations. (It also may be due to the male propensity to have as many wives as possible, which is a different issue.) Changing the carrying capacity may change the sex ratio in even a generation or two, thereby changing the environment for warfare. These problems with much of the data do not preclude obtaining useful information; they just mean that many of the classic ethnographies were made too late for our purposes.

A classic example of the impact of such changes may be found among the western Alaska Eskimos. In the early 1800s, the Iñupiaq of western Alaska (also known as the Kotzebue Sound Eskimo) described by Burch (2005) experienced very significant warfare. Fifty years later, after population decline and access to rifles, they had essentially none. As a consequence, the later ethnographies from this area have little resemblance to the early accounts in terms of warfare. I consider the "peaceful" Netsilik Inuit of Canada later in this chapter as another example of this data problem.

Another perhaps more dramatic example of the problem of timing is from Australia. The first permanent British settlement was founded near present-day Sydney in 1788. In less than two years, epidemics had reduced the local Aboriginal population by half (Dowling 1992), and their carrying capacity relationship was changed almost immediately. The apparent change in the

**30** | Steven A. LeBlanc

intensity of warfare in less than a generation is remarkable. Similar changes can be seen among other Australian Aborigines, in the Great Basin, and in South Africa.

To summarize, at least two important things happen to nonfarmers, but especially foragers, when they come into contact with farmers: (1) their numbers decline and (2) they acquire new technologies that have the effect of raising their carrying capacity. To the extent that warfare relates to carrying capacity pressure, or any other factor that is either density dependent or simply requires a minimum number of people, the underlying conditions for warfare will then be changed. This does not mean that warfare does not have other causes and will necessarily not exist. Moreover, under such changed conditions, what might originally have been classed as warfare in the presence of farmers may then be considered homicide or feuding. To simply ignore the data time frame is to lump very different situations into meaningless buckets.

## The Prevalence and Basis of Forager Warfare

Prehistoric warfare was pervasive, constant, and deadly. There is ample evidence this applies to tribal farmers and to complex hunter-gatherers. While the evidence is not as overwhelming, it applies to foragers as well. The following is a brief synopsis of my argument for a carrying capacity limitations basis for forager warfare. It is not meant to be the only reason for warfare, but I believe it is a core reason that could have resulted in biological selection for warfare behaviors and could have residual effects even when carrying capacities changed. This argument is greatly expanded in *Constant Battles* (LeBlanc 2003).

No nonmodern societies ever successfully controlled their population growth; this includes all foraging societies. No social methods have ever been shown to maintain populations well below the carrying capacity, nor has anyone ever come up with a theoretical model of how this could work (see Read and LeBlanc [2003] for a more extended discussion). Moreover, if any local group did succeed in controlling growth and neighboring groups did not, the nongrowth group would be eliminated by the fast-growing one. This is rather like "The Grasshopper and the Ant" in reverse. It does not pay to plan for tomorrow by not growing your population today. The suggestion that foragers like the !Kung were at zero growth is simply wrong. Most foragers seem to have been able to grow at 2 percent when the carrying capacity allowed for it, and even a fraction of 1 percent growth would exceed any improvement in carrying capacity in 300 years or less. Moreover, the carrying capacity would have never been constant due to rapid, even minor, changes in climate. In other words, societies, including essentially all foraging societies, would have found themselves resource-stressed most of the time. Warfare can reduce stress by taking resources (land) from adjacent groups. It is interesting to note that big-game hunting and warfare are essentially the same adaptation. If you are good at one, you are good at the other, so every foraging society was focused on big-game hunting if such game was available. Rodent hunters would be relatively disadvantaged when it comes to warfare behaviors, and there are no foragers that are specialized that way.

People certainly do take resources from other groups. Do they recognize that they are resource-stressed, and can they see that taking resources from others is a solution? Do people consciously decide to fight before they starve, or do they fight whenever there is resource stress, regardless of how dire it is? These are very difficult questions.

My argument is that from a distance, forager warfare behavior is rational. Behaviors that promote successful warfare are adaptive. Good fighters get more women, more food, and more resources. Indoctrination that the "other" is the enemy is good business. Does this lead to group selection for "warlike" behavior? At the same time, allies are important, which may lead to mechanisms that promote cooperation. Does this lead to group selection for "peaceful" behavior?

One takes care of one's own children, but killing the children of others can happen at the same time. One fears some "others," but one also needs some "others." Resource competition warfare does not need to rely on instinct for an explanation, but that does not mean that instinct is not involved. Do foragers actually calculate the benefits versus costs of warfare? Does appealing to instinct explain anything? Conversely, if we are adapted to have aggressive hair-trigger responses to threats, the desire to win, and the desire for revenge, these would certainly make it much easier to fight successfully. Can we explain warfare by instinct alone? Explanations given by the people themselves very rarely invoke a rational calculation of resource gains, and ethnography does not seem to provide answers.

These are very important questions for our understanding of the evolutionary consequences of warfare. The purpose here is not to resolve them but to demonstrate the value and importance of the study of forager warfare.

## Foragers in a Land of Foragers

The presumed human condition up until the last 10,000 years or so, and even more recently for much of the world, was foragers in a land of foragers. This would have been the world in which most selection for any relevant behavioral traits in humans would have taken place. In the historic past, most foragers did not live in a land of foragers, but lived in lands dominated by farmers and herders. For example, the Bushmen of South Africa lived near or they themselves were herders of goats and/or cattle. More recently, almost all of them live immediately adjacent to and are economically and socially

**32** | Steven A. LeBlanc

involved with Bantu-speaking herders. Similarly, the Pygmies of central Africa are in even more symbiotic relationships with farmers, to the extent they speak the farmers' languages. The Hadza also are completely surrounded by herders. The same is true for all foragers in southern and southeast Asia, except for the Andamanese.

In the ethnographic present, mobile foragers live in Australia, Tasmania, the Arctic and subarctic (especially Eskimos), the Great Basin (Numic speakers including Paiute, Ute, and Shoshone), Tierra del Fuego, and the Andaman Islands. This is not an adequate sample. It is not large, and these people tend to live in very marginal environments. Farmers or complex hunter-gatherers began to occupy richer environments a long time ago, but in the deep past most foragers would have lived in those richer environments. Nevertheless, there are some generalities we can identify among the ethnographic examples of foragers. We have a much better sample if we include the not-quite-foragers of California for which we have some good warfare information (e.g., the Wintu [Chase-Dunn and Mann 1998] and the Atsugewi [Garth 1953]; Eerkens et al.; Pilloud et al.; Schwitalla et al. [all this volume]; see also Allen 2012) and marginal farmers in Amazonia (Chagnon 1968a, 1968b; Wilbert 1972) and New Guinea (Roscoe, this volume). Some of the patterns I describe here include evidence from such groups.

## Patterns of Forager Warfare

Some patterns are more or less general among foragers. The information about them tends to correlate with the quality of the data in that the better the data, the more likely we find the patterns, so they are probably more general than presence-absence information alone would predict.

*They kill vulnerable strangers on sight.* This seems to be the case even when the stranger is not a threat. This is sometimes seen indirectly by the presence of elaborate mechanisms to enable strangers to signal their intent to interact peacefully.

*They make high investments in warfare.* This includes building and maintaining special weapons, such as shields, armor, or daggers, which are—or almost are—used only for conflict, and boats. Boats are an interesting example. There are specialized kayaks for warfare among the Aleut. Investment in warfare (defense) also involves locating structures or villages that are expensive to build and use and that are not optimal for other functions but good for defense. Villages on tops of hills or points of land, and cactus fences that act like defensive walls around refuges in southern California are examples of time and effort investments in village defenses. Another investment by foragers is carrying weapons almost all the time. Tribal farmers do not need to carry weapons when in or close to their villages. Carrying weapons would be a high cost to foragers because weapons are heavy and bulky, and many

Forager Warfare and Our Evolutionary Past | **33**

weapons, such as daggers or shields, are not useful for hunting. Armor is quite common among the Eskimo (Burch 2005:85; Darwent and Darwent, this volume), Andamanese (Kelly 2000:Plate 5, 2005:15295; Sarkar 1962:675), and California Indian (Allen 2012:208) examples. Andamanese Islanders apparently wore body armor even when they went out hunting, presumably because they feared meeting enemies (Kelly 2000).

*They involve large numbers of warriors in conflicts, requiring considerable coordination in deployment and timing.* In the Andaman Islands, one group apparently invaded and took over part of another island. Essentially all the males on one island were able to put aside their differences and come together at the same place and time to attack the British. High numbers were also involved in some described battles among the southern Australian Aborigines: Buckley (Morgan [1852] 1979) said his group was attacked by 300 men. Several pre–horse-era battles are known in the North American Mountain West, especially involving Numic speakers, where 50 to 100 men per side were involved (Secoy 1953). Numbers in that range also seem possible for Andamanese based on claims of 100, 150, and even 1,500 men in various battles with the British in the 1800s (Kelly 2000). The Yaghans of Tierra del Fuego were apparently able to muster large forces. At Nassau Bay in 1624, 17 men from L'Hermite's ships were killed in a single attack, implying a large Yaghan attack force (Lothrop 1928). Western Eskimos were able to deploy 300 to 400 men at a time (Burch 2005), and Hottentot herders, who were in many ways culturally similar to the desert-dwelling Bushmen, successfully attacked a Portuguese party of 150 men in 1510, killing the viceroy of India and at least 50 men. That attack party must have been in the hundreds. Given that a typical forager band would have no more than 10 to 15 men, these numbers are substantial and imply the ability to coordinate efforts among numerous bands.

*They engage in highly risky behavior beyond the fighting itself.* Eskimos provide examples of building a raft to more quickly get at an enemy, with the entire attack party drowning as a consequence (Burch 2005). Raiding parties were discovered before they engaged the enemy and were then in turn massacred. There is always a risk of treachery when trying to build and maintain alliances (Wadley 2003). Through significant miscalculation, overeagerness to engage the enemy, or other mistakes, foragers took considerable risks in warfare. How much more risk they took for this than for hunting is hard to determine, but warfare was definitely not undertaken only when the real risks were very low. The problem is, in all these instances, the level of risk is assessed after the fact. Did the instigators of these behaviors recognize how risky they were? It is clear that people felt meeting to form alliances was very risky, and they were typically wary. Men were known to drop out of parties planning surprise attacks. Did they see risk the other members did not, and so dropped out? I know of no one who has looked at this important question systematically.

34 | Steven A. LeBlanc

One form of risky behavior is using boats in warfare. Boats were used by people of Tierra del Fuego to either fight from or for raiding (Gusinde 1961). Boats were attacked by other boats among the Aleut and Eskimo (Zimmerly 2000), and were used for raiding (Lantis 1984). There must have been a boat-based invasion force that was successful in the Andaman Islands, and Takic speakers must have engineered a similar invasion to take over Catalina Island in California. Among hunter-gatherers, the Asmat, who populated several large rivers on the southwest coast of New Guinea, had large war canoes (Eyde 1967), and of course there were the great war canoes of the Northwest Coast (Suttles 1990). At least some of these boats were purpose-built for warfare or designed with it in mind, although most boats used in forager warfare were built and used for other purposes as well.

Naval warfare has always been one of risk of catastrophic loss, because nature in the form of weather and tides can be treacherous. In a warfare situation, it may not be possible to wait out bad weather or properly detect tides if one needs to flee or approach an enemy in the dark Moreover, most battle deaths occur when the losers try to flee. All individuals in a boat are likely to be killed if things go wrong and they try to flee. Thus, the consequences of things going wrong would seem to be higher in warfare involving boats than otherwise. Thus, using boats in warfare demonstrates the level of risk that was undertaken by foragers in some circumstances.

*They are likely to engage in ambush or hit-and-run warfare.* In contrast, farmers and hunter-gatherers are more likely to have actual battles. The belief that ambushes and surprise attacks are not warfare has led to the conclusion that some foragers were peaceful. The ambush form of warfare is probably nothing more than the effect of group size on the nature of conflict and does not mean that forager warfare was somehow not deadly. Ambush can be effective in several ways. If a raid kills two people, and one raids almost continually, in a few years, if one group gets the upper hand, they can annihilate or force the other group to permanently disperse.[1] However, the attackers can also get lucky. If everything goes according to plan, the people under attack are caught completely by surprise, or many of the men are off hunting, the results can be complete annihilation of the raided group. This did happen with foragers, although it is particularly common with simple farmers.

*They select defensive locations for their camps and villages.* In contrast, farmers and some hunter-gatherers build defenses. Examples of selecting defensive locations are documented among Eskimo, Andamanese, and California Indians. Since most of these same people did not invest heavily in their houses, this is not surprising. Eskimos did at times build stockades and other defenses, including fields of sharpened sticks that would impale an attacker's foot, apparently like the *punji* or sharpened bamboo sticks of the Viet Cong (Burch 2005). A particularly common defensive location is a

Forager Warfare and Our Evolutionary Past | **35**

headland or bluff along the ocean and between river courses. As noted here, the use of these locations came at a cost. It is the lack of built fortifications or strongpoints that makes it appear that archaeologically documented foragers did not use defenses. We would not be able to see that they had used vegetation as a defense, and archaeologists do not ask why particular locations were chosen for camps.

*They experience high death rates in warfare.* Perhaps as many as 25 percent of the men and 5 percent of women died from warfare among foragers (Keeley 1996; LeBlanc 2003), so the biological consequences would have been significant. It has been argued that warfare was lethal enough to result in group selection (Choi and Bowles 2007). Children were also killed, but it is hard to quantify these numbers. From an individual selection perspective, the accuracy of these numbers is irrelevant. Even death rates of 5 percent should have presented ample opportunity for trait selection to take place.

*Their behavior in warfare is territorial.* Territories—tracts of land that were used more or less intensively, were reasonably static, and were defined by known boundaries—seem to exist wherever we have good data. While there may not have been clear and sharp boundaries within macrogroups, and there were often mechanisms to allow some groups to use the territory of others, territories were clearly defended, and other's territories were taken over when the opportunity presented itself. Examples exist for the Eskimo (Burch 2005), Andamanese (Kelly 2000), and groups in northern Australia, Tierra del Fuego (Lothrop 1928), California (James and Graziani 1975), and the Plateau area of North America (Chatters 2004). Closely related to territories are buffer zones or empty zones between territories. They are better documented for farmers (see DeBoer [1981] for South American examples), but a good example is a 20-mile-wide buffer zone between the Chippewa (foragers) and the Sioux (some farming) that lasted at least from 1750 to 1850 (Hickerson 1965).

*They kill with clubs, knives, and axes.* Close combat was the norm for forager and leaderless society warfare, and archaeological evidence confirms it (Jurmain 2001; Knuckley 1992; Walker 1989; Walker and Lambert 1989; Webb 1995). Carrying clubs, knives/daggers, and a willingness to get close to the enemy are typical of accounts of forager warfare, and for that matter, all warfare until very recently. This does not mean that spears, atlatls, and bows were not used when available. Instead, even when such distant weapons were used, ambush, close-quarter fighting, and dispatching of wounded still involved hand weapons.

*They are less inclined to take body-part trophies, such as scalps, heads, or hands, than farmers.* However, mutilation of enemies does occur (e.g., Eskimo [Burch 2005], Australian Aborigines [Horne and Aiston 1924], central California [Andrushko et al. 2005; also see chapters in this volume]), but again, perhaps not with the frequency we find with farmers (Chacon and Dye 2007).

## Related Generalizations on Forager Warfare

We can make some generalizations on a few topics closely related to forager warfare behaviors. Alliances are ubiquitous, and they can take several forms. Groups can combine for planned raids or pitched battles. For farmers, having allies come to help for defense is common, but forager raids are so quick that allies rarely could help in an attack. These alliances were more for sharing information and for offensive actions. There can also be an agreement that one group can pass unmolested through the territory of a second group for the purpose of attacking a third group. Obviously, such negotiations require a high level of trust because the second group can warn the people about to be attacked with dire consequences for the attackers. So, such arrangements imply some form of alliance and common cause against the group to be attacked.

Woman capture or disputes over women are constants among the reasons given for particular wars, raids, disputes, and the desire for revenge. This is a very complicated topic because infanticide, especially female infanticide, was quite prevalent among foragers (Balikci 1967; Cowlishaw 1978; see also Divale and Harris 1976). If the shortage of women reflects a shortage of resources, as it appears, then fighting for women may simply be part and parcel of fighting for resources. However, to the extent fighting to obtain women is done to increase the number of mates, regardless of resource limitations, a different factor is at work. Walker and Bailey's (2013) study on warfare and woman capture is particularly useful. Their sample is essentially simple farmers, and there is really nothing like it from other parts of the world for comparisons. They found that a typical raid resulted in about 0.7 woman abducted per raid. Given that the probability of a male attacker dying in these raids was 0.025 or less, raiding to capture women seems to have been very rational and effective. In general, women are certainly captured, but they are also killed. In the same study, about 1 of every 3 individuals killed in raids were women. Why each alternative is selected in various instances is not clear. What is clear, however, is that women are captured and taken as wives at times, but they are also sometimes killed. There is ample opportunity to see instinctive behavior involved in these behaviors.

Revenge is a commonly given motive for warfare. Revenge killing can take months or years to carry out. It is certainly a strongly held motivation as the two quotes at the beginning of this chapter imply. In spite of evidence for competition over resources and territory, the predominant explanations for warfare given by those involved are disputes over women and revenge. The problem with revenge as an explanation for warfare is that members of any group are likely to have reasons for revenge with all their neighbors. Yet they form alliances with some, and are not fighting all of them at the same time. So, revenge is selective. Or, to put it another way, revenge seems to be a motivator for conflict, but it is tempered by other factors. Again, the potential of a genetic basis for such revenge is obvious.

## The Rule of 10

The realization that foragers can form very large groups for offensive actions encouraged me to look at war group sizes of other types of social organizations. There seems to be a very rough and broad generalization that can be made. This is not the venue to explore this topic fully, but it is useful to mention it here, as it puts forager warfare both in perspective and shows that it fits a broader pattern. I refer to the generalization as the "Rule of 10." The typical group size for an attacking party of foragers is probably around 10 men; yet, as I have noted here, party size can be 10 times that number. Thus, there is about a factor of 10 between the usual and maximal number of men in an attack group. It turns out that such a factor of 10 seems to hold for other types of social organizations: if tribal organizations can regularly muster 100 men, they can on occasion muster 1,000. And the same factor of 10 seems to hold for chiefdoms. Incidentally, the normal group size for attacking forces tends to be about a tenfold increase for each jump in social complexity, so the rule might be called the "10-10 Rule." The point here is that foragers are like other social systems in that they could increase the attack party by a factor of 10 times normal under extraordinary circumstances. This is additional evidence that forager warfare was not fundamentally different than other warfare: it was very serious business if such large groups could be formed and managed.

### Non-Warfare Violence among Foragers

Another factor for consideration is the presence of lethal violence that is not technically warfare among foragers. In the case of several forager groups that do not recently have any meaningful warfare, there is a high incidence of intragroup violence. I believe these are all groups that previously would have had warfare, but recent circumstances eliminated it. This violence shows that not having warfare does not make people "peaceful," and so these examples are of some theoretical interest. I present some brief statistics of a few of the better-known examples but do not pursue this topic further here. Among the Aché of eastern Paraguay, roughly 40 percent of children and a bit more than 10 percent of adult deaths were from intragroup violence (Hill and Hurtado 1995). It is even higher for the South American Hiwi (Hill et al. 2007). Although intragroup lethal violence is lower for the African Hadza or !Kung, it is still significant. Among Bushmen, one study (Lee 1979) reported 22 known murders; essentially all victims were males, including some over 50 years old. With a group size of approximately 400 people—or 100 adult males—and a generation time span, the homicide rate was about 0.5 percent per year.

**38** | Steven A. LeBlanc

## Patterns of Peace among Foragers

The entire literature on peaceful foragers essentially misses the point. These authors universally argue that peaceful societies existed and show that people can be peaceful. However, the implication is that these people were *always* peaceful, for which there is no evidence (see below). Instead, what is far more interesting (and accurate) is that people can stop engaging in warfare (but not violence) quite quickly. Examples include Eskimo, Australian Aborigines, California acorn gatherers, Bushmen, and south Indian and southeast Asian foragers. The best documented case of a rapid transition is the western Eskimo, who went from very significant warfare affecting all parts of their lives to universal peace in less than 50 years, and perhaps in half that time. Many examples of the same rapid transition are known for farmers, but that is not the topic here.

The repeated suggestion that there were peaceful foragers in the past warrants discussion. Some of the more vocal promoters of this thinking are Fry (2007, 2012) and Ferguson (1992). I believe a strong motivation for such a position derives from a Pollyanna-ish attitude that if there is not a genetic component to warfare, it will be easier to eliminate. Thus, somehow showing there were peaceful societies demonstrates the absence of a genetic component. Of course, such logic is invalid, and no one makes such a bold claim. Nevertheless, it seems implicit in the argument. The primary difficulty with the peaceful societies in the past is that most were not actually peaceful, or their circumstances were so unique that they are not relevant to the general question of how peaceful foragers were in the past. If foragers are the primary relevant social type from an evolutionary perspective, then one must exclude hunter-gatherers in general as well as foragers such as the Mbuti who are embedded in farmer societies. Once these peoples are excluded, the number of forager societies that have been proposed as peaceful becomes very small. Some, as noted, are considered peaceful by definition, as Kelly (2000) seems to classify the Andamanese, when clearly they are not.

The Bushmen are a very complex and difficult case. Here the problem is twofold. First, the Bushmen were part of a population gradient from richer to more marginal environments. While there is ample evidence that these other peoples, including foragers in the richer areas, did engage in warfare, there is also some evidence even for the most marginal groups (Eibl-Eibesfleldt 1975; Parkington 1984; Schapera 1930; Schire 1980). However, it is possible that the most marginal areas were really population sinks (as described below) until the government drilled boreholes for water. If these populations did not engage in warfare, it tells us little about the general human condition. In addition, the evidence for conflict derives from early accounts, which are scarce, and we probably have a good case of carrying capacity changes brought on by the introduction of herd animals and metal long before any ethnographers were present.

The failure to consider the early literature also exists for another oft-cited case of a peaceful society, the Netsilik Eskimo. There is plenty of evidence that the Netsilik were not peaceful in the past and were like all their neighbors, who had ample warfare (Melbye and Fairgreive 1994; Smith and Burch 1979). The classic ethnographies of Rasmussen (1931) and Balikci (1967) were recorded long after the carrying capacity balance had changed. I discuss this in more detail elsewhere (LeBlanc 2013), but one does have to question the motivation of those who claim such societies were peaceful when evidence to the contrary is so easy to find.

## Complex Foragers, Forager Replacement, and Biology

There are both archaeological and ethnographic hunter-gatherers that are far different from the classic Bushmen or Australian Aborigines that we consider to be analogs for the deep past. These include the Natufians of the Middle East, the Jōmon of Japan, the Chumash of southern California, some coastal Eskimo groups, and Northwest Coastal people such as the Tlingit, as well as numerous coastal people in New Guinea, the Calusa of southwest Florida, and possibly people along the lower Murray-Darling River in Australia.

As mentioned, for the most part such peoples had permanent villages, stored food, and had complex social organizations. They invested in equipment such as boats, fish traps, temple mounds, and village defenses. That is, their behaviors were much more like what we think of as tribally organized farmers or even chiefdoms rather than mobile foragers. Peter Rowley-Conwy (2001) challenges the notion that all humans lived as simple foragers throughout the Pleistocene. Rather, based on archaeological evidence, he suggests that complex hunter-gatherers could have appeared as early as 90,000 years ago. He further argues that foraging groups could shift from simple to complex foraging and back based on climate change and food availability, especially in coastal areas directly affected by glacial melting. Sassaman (2004) provides other North American examples.

To the extent complex hunter-gatherers have a greater time depth than is usually considered, there are several factors of importance. Their potential growth rates would have been higher than we find for contemporary foragers. This would result in more resource competition and more warfare among such groups. As a result of this competition we would expect some of these groups to have been pushed into more marginal environments, such as we find, for example, among egalitarian farmers in the New Guinea highlands or the Yanomami of South America, or among more complex foragers. When defeated groups flee, they move into more marginal areas. And we can see from present day linguistic distributions that some nonfarmers moved into and replaced other nonfarmers (e.g., northern Australia [Dixon 2002; Tindale

**40** | Steven A. LeBlanc

1974] and California [Moratto 1984]). Since this level of warfare is in the long run attritional, the group with the greatest growth rate is most likely to prevail. Thus, just as farmers replace foragers (Bellwood 2005), complex hunter-gatherers replace foragers. We would expect resource competition among more complex hunter-gatherers to result in their spreading into more marginal areas, replacing the foragers they encounter, but this in turn would eventually put pressure on the foragers in the most marginal areas, where people moving away from more successful competitors would "spill" into even the most marginal of areas.

There are a couple of somewhat analogous examples involving farmers and malaria. In these cases, growth in optimal areas results in conflict and the eventual spillover into an area that is so malarial that the population does not seem capable of reproducing itself; it is instead maintained by a steady flow of people from areas where growth did take place. This seems to be the case for the Nunu farmers of equatorial Africa, where conflict pushes people into the high-malaria environment (Harms 1987). A similar situation seems to have taken place among the Gidra of the south coast lowlands of Papua New Guinea, who are sago collectors and hunters, but did grow bananas and other garden crops. Here the population originally lived in the hinterland with an effective growth rate of 0.5 percent, but when they were forced to move to the malarial coast, they subsequently had a negative growth rate (Ohtsuka 1996). This would be a process not unlike that found in early cities such as London, which was so unhealthy that the population did not did not biologically reproduce itself but actually grew as the result of others moving in from the fecund hinterland.

Thus, for example, we might have a productive river valley, where population growth was high. Competition would exist between groups living along the river, and there would be a tendency for some of the defeated riverine groups to flee away from the river. Over time, these people would replace those groups who had occupied the territory away from the river, but that conflict would have also resulted in defeated groups, who in turn would replace those farther away from the river. Eventually this process would push some people into areas where they were unable to biologically replace themselves (population sinks). Over time, genes would flow from the rich riverine environment, but not the reverse. Over a very long time, essentially all the genes would derive from riverine people in spite of the population distribution at any particular time. So, even if the people in the extreme environment did not have warfare, genetically they would derive from people—the riverine people—who had considerable warfare. Examples of this principle may be seen in the Darling River area of Australia in contrast to the western desert (Lourandos 1985); the Netsilik Eskimo in contrast to the western Eskimo; the !Kung in contrast to the coastal people (so-called Hottentots) of southern Africa; and the Northwest Coast salmon fishers in contrast to the interior bracken fern root collectors. So, what appear to us as very marginal societies, possibly with minimal warfare, might

Forager Warfare and Our Evolutionary Past | **41**

really be the descendants of highly competitive and more complexly organized people. This would be the opposite of a world made up of lots of low-density, rather peaceful foragers, with small islands of denser, more complex hunter-gatherers with considerable warfare. This would be a world of a gradient of the level of density, growth, and warfare intensity, but biologically, one derived from those who had the most warfare.

## An Ecological Basis for Warfare?

There are several possible explanations for forager warfare. In my opinion, the two that are the most interesting are ecology and genetics. I summarize again the argument for ecology here and genetics in the next section. They are by no means mutually exclusive.

The ecological basis for warfare is that foragers, like all other human groups and all other mammalian species, had positive growth rates except under the most extreme and rare conditions. This does not mean that their populations grew; they clearly usually did not. It means that if they were not at the carrying capacity of their environment, their rate of growth was substantial until they reached carrying capacity. Thus, in essence, foragers were at their carrying capacities almost all the time, and competition for scarce resources would have been adaptive and rational. The justification for these statements is long and involved and can be found in Read and LeBlanc (2003) and LeBlanc (2003). The key point is the ideas that foragers were able to maintain their populations well below the carrying capacity, or that people like the !Kung had zero population growth in the presence of ample resources, are simply myths: widely believed, but nevertheless myths.

This is in essence an argument for rational behavior with respect to warfare. It is strengthened by evidence that warfare stopped very quickly in many instances when it ceased being useful. The Iñupiaq of western Alaska went from the people of serious warfare evidenced in the quote at the beginning of this chapter to the friendly, peaceful people we think of today in one generation. Similar rapid changes occurred among the Australian Aborigines, the !Kung of South Africa, and many other examples among nonforagers. Of course, warfare does not always end so abruptly when it is no longer useful, but that it does frequently is an argument for its having a strong rational component.

## A Genetic Basis for Warfare

A good argument can also be made for a genetic basis for warfare, which leads to the question: Has there been enough time for selection to have taken place for warfare-related traits? Even if one considers only the Late Stone Age, there were at least 50,000 years, and more realistically at least 10 times that long, available for human foragers to evolve behaviors selected by warfare. But even the last 50,000 years is 1,000 to 2,000 generations, and this is plenty of time for selection.

There has also been enough potential for selection. With death rates from warfare of at least 5 percent and often 15 percent or even higher for men and perhaps half to a third of that for women, this is more than enough selection pressure for excelling at warfare. This does not mean that violent behavior was specifically selected for, but that any behavior that has gone on that long and results in that much differential survival can have resulted in strong selection for whatever relevant traits were adaptive. Such traits as a desire for revenge, a desire to win, fear of strangers, and the ability to see the world in terms of "them versus us" could all have been selected for. Again, not all selection would necessarily have been for what we might call aggressive behavior. There could also have been selection for the ability to form strong alliance groups or the desire to protect group members. It may be almost impossible to survive on your own as a forager, but with constant warfare it is almost impossible to survive without being in a group roughly the size of adjacent groups. Nevertheless, even though there was surely selection for cooperative behaviors, we should not expect there to be an absence of a genetic component in warfare-related behavior. All we know about warfare among foragers and hunter-gatherers in general points to the opposite. Warfare was pervasive, constant, and deadly: a formula for selection.

## A Missing Piece

Given this strong selective pressure for adaptive responses to warfare, the field of evolutionary psychology seems to have almost completely missed it. Most anthropologists have also missed the implications of pervasive warfare, but that is a different topic. The standard textbooks in the field do not even discuss the evolutionary implications of warfare. Their authors do not seem to think the close-to-human-universals of revenge or fear of strangers could derive from a past filled with warfare. Evolutionary psychologists focus on differences between males and females based on their different reproductive strategies, for example, but they fail to see that if men engaged in warfare and women did not, then one would expect different evolutionary outcomes. But this is changing (see Browne [2001] and especially Benenson and Markovits [2014]). The point is that other disciplines seem to have accepted the false idea of a peaceful deep human past, which has led them down some false paths. Getting the story right is important, and the study of forager warfare is critical to that goal.

## Conclusions

Evidence about forager warfare supports its being rational, highly patterned, and very significant from social and demographic points of view. At the same time, there was ample time and selective pressure for a potentially strong genetic component to warfare. Warfare was high cost in terms of investments for weapons and the time cost for defense. Warfare was also lethal, with the consequences not evenly distributed. Warfare would have enabled people in more resource-rich environments to expand at the expense of those living in more marginal localities. Patterns, such as killing strangers on sight and a desire for revenge, seem to be almost universal, suggesting they have existed for a very long time. There is no reason to believe that significant warfare did not exist throughout the time of foragers, and it is very relevant to our understanding of human history and human behavior today.

## Note

1. The only systematic study I am aware of that provides the number of people killed in raids is Walker and Bailey (2013) for lowland South America, but the sample was composed of farmers. Their most likely number killed was close to two, but the average was closer to seven because of the occasional massacre.

## References

Allen, Mark W. 2012. A Land of Violence. In *Contemporary Issues in California Archaeology*, edited by Terry L. Jones and Jennifer E. Perry, pp. 197–215. Left Coast Press, Walnut Creek, CA.

Andrushko, Valerie A., K. A. S. Latham, D. L. Grady, A. G. Pastron, and Philip L. Walker 2005. Bioarchaeological Evidence for Trophy-taking in Prehistoric Central California. *American Journal of Physical Anthropology* 127:375–84.

Balikci, A. 1967. Female Infanticide on the Arctic Coast. *Man* 2:615–25.

Bellwood, Peter 2005. *First Farmers: The Origins of Agricultural Societies*. Blackwell Publishers, Oxford, United Kingdom.

Benenson, Joyce F., and Henry Markovits 2014. *Warriors and Worriers: The Survival of the Sexes*. Oxford University Press, New York.

Browne, K. R. 2001. Women at War: An Evolutionary Perspective. *Buffalo Law Review* 49:51–247.

Burch, Ernest S. Jr. 2005. *Alliance and Conflict: The World System of the Iñupiaq Eskimos*. University of Nebraska Press, Lincoln.

Chacon, Richard J., and David H. Dye (editors) 2007. *The Taking and Displaying of Human Body Parts as Trophies by Amerindians*. Springer, New York.

Chagnon, Napoleon 1968a. Yanomamo Social Organization and Warfare. In *War: The Anthropology of Armed Conflict and Aggression*, edited by Morton Fried, Marvin Harris, and Robert Murphy, pp. 109–59. Natural History Press, New York.

——— 1968b. *Yanomamo: The Fierce People*. Holt, Reinhart and Winston, New York.

Chase-Dunn, Christopher, and Kelly M. Mann 1998. *The Wintu and their Neighbors*. The University of Arizona Press, Tucson.

Chatters, James C. 2004. Safety in Numbers: The Influence of the Bow and Arrow on Village Formation on the Columbia Plateau. In *Complex Hunter-Gatherers: Evolution and Organization of Prehistoric Communities on the Plateau of Northwestern North America*, edited by William C. Prentiss and Ian Kujit, pp. 67–83. University of Utah Press, Salt Lake City.

Choi, J.-K., and Samuel Bowles 2007. The Coevolution of Parochial Altruism and War. *American Association for the Advancement of Science* 318:636–40.

**44** | Steven A. LeBlanc

Cowlishaw, Gillian 1978. Infanticide in Aboriginal Australia. *Oceania* 48:262–83.

DeBoer, Warren R. 1981. Buffer Zones in the Cultural Ecology of Aboriginal Amazonia: An Ethnohistorical Approach. *American Antiquity* 46:364–77.

Divale, William T., and Marvin Harris 1976. Population, Warfare and the Male Supremacist Complex. *American Anthropologist* 78:521–38.

Dixon, Robert M. W. 2002. *Australian Languages: Their Nature and Development.* Cambridge University Press, Port Chester, NY.

Dowling, P. J. 1992. When Urban Dwellers meet Hunter-gatherers: Impact of Introduced Infectious Disease on Aboriginal Australians. *Proceedings of the Australasian Society for Human Biology* 5:39–46.

Eyde, David Bruener 1967. Cultural Correlates of Warfare among the Asmat of South-west New Guinea. Unpublished Ph.D. dissertation, Department of Anthropology, Yale University, New Haven, CT.

Eibl-Eibesfleldt, I. 1975. Aggression in the !Ko-Bushmen. In *War, Its Causes and Correlates*, edited by Martin A. Nettleship, R. Dale Givens, and Anderson Nettleship, pp. 281–96. Mouton, The Hague, the Netherlands.

Ferguson, R. Brian 1992. A Savage Encounter: Western Contact and the Yanomami War Complex. In *War in the Tribal Zone: Expanding States and Indigenous Warfare*, edited by R. Brian Ferguson and Neil L. Whitehead, pp. 199–227. School of American Research Press, Santa Fe, NM.

Fry, Douglas P. 2007. *Beyond War: The Human Potential for Peace.* Oxford University Press, Oxford, United Kingdom.

———— 2012. Life without War. *Science* 336:879–84.

Garth, Thomas R. 1953. Atsugewi Ethnography. *University of California Anthropological Records* 14:129–212.

Gusinde, Martin 1961. *The Yamana: The Life and Thought of the Water Nomads of Cape Horn.* Human Relations Area Files, New Haven, CT.

Harms, Robert 1987. *Games Against Nature: An Eco-cultural History of the Nunu of Equatorial Africa.* Cambridge University Press, New York.

Hickerson, Harold 1965. The Virginia Deer and Intertribal Buffer Zones in the Upper Mississippi Valley. In *Man, Culture, and Animals*, edited by Anthony Leeds and Andrew P. Vayda, pp. 43–65. American Association for the Advancement of Science, Washington, D.C.

Hill, Kim, and A. Magdalena Hurtado 1995. *Ache Life History: The Ecology and Demography of a Foraging People.* Aldine de Gruyter, New York.

Hill, Kim, A. Magdalena Hurtado, and R. S. Walker 2007. High Adult Mortality among Hiwi Hunter-Gatherers: Implications for Human Evolution. *Journal of Human Evolution* 52:443–54.

Horne, George, and G. Aiston 1924. *Savage Life in Central Australia.* Macmillan and Co., London.

James, Steven R., and S. Graziani 1975. California Indian Warfare. *Contributions of the University of California Archaeological Research Facility* 23:47–109.

Jurmain, Robert 2001. Paleoepidemiological Patterns of Trauma in a Prehistoric Population from Central California. *American Journal of Physical Anthropology* 115:13–23.

Keeley, Lawerence. H. 1996. *War Before Civilization.* Oxford University Press, New York and Oxford.

Kelly, Raymond C. 2000. *Warless Societies and the Origin of War.* University of Michigan Press, Ann Arbor.

———— 2005. The Evolution of Lethal Intergroup Violence. *Proceedings of the National Academy of Sciences* 102:15294–8.

Knuckey, G. 1992. Patterns of Fracture upon Aboriginal Crania from the Recent Past. *Proceedings of the Australasian Society for Human Biology* 5:47–58.

Lantis, Margaret 1984. Nunivak Eskimo. In *Arctic*, edited by David Damas, pp. 209–23. Handbook of North American Indians, Vol. 5, William C. Sturtevant, general editor. Smithsonian Institution, Washington, D.C.

LeBlanc, Steven A. 2003. *Constant Battles*. St. Martin's Press, New York.

—— 2013. Warfare and Human Nature. In *The Evolution of Violence*, edited by Todd K. Shackelford and Ranald D. Hansen, pp. 73–97. Springer, New York.

Lee, Richard B. 1979. *The !Kung San: Men, Women, and Work in a Foraging Society*. Cambridge University Press, Cambridge, United Kingdom.

Lee, Richard B., and Richard H. Daly (editors) 1999. *The Cambridge Encyclopedia of Hunters and Gatherers*. Cambridge University Press, Cambridge, United Kingdom.

Lothrop, Samuel Kirkland 1928. *The Indians of Tierra de Fuego*. Museum of the American Indian, New York.

Lourandos, Harry 1985. Intensification and Australian Prehistory. In *Prehistoric Hunter-Gatherers: The Emergence of Cultural Complexity*, edited by T. D. Price and J. A. Brown, pp. 385–423. Academic Press, Orlando, FL.

Melbye, Jerry, and Scott I. Fairgreive 1994. A Massacre and Possible Cannibalism in the Canadian Arctic: New Evidence from the Saunaktuk Site (NgTn-1). *Arctic Anthropology* 31:57–77.

Moratto, Michael J. 1984. *California Archaeology*. Academic Press, Orlando, FL.

Morgan, John [1852] 1979. *The Life and Adventures of William Buckley: Thirty Two Years a Wanderer Amongst the Aborigines*. Australia National University Press, Canberra.

Ohtsuka, R. 1996. Long-Term Adaptation of the Gidra-Speaking Population of Papua New Guinea. In *Redefining Nature: Ecology, Culture, and Domestication*, edited by Roy Ellen and Katsuyoshi Fukui, pp. 515–30. Berg, Oxford, United Kingdom.

Parkington, John E. 1984. Soaqua and Bushmen: Hunters and Robbers. In *Past and Present in Hunter Gatherer Studies*, edited by Carmel Schire, pp. 151–74. Academic Press, Orlando, FL.

Rasmussen, Knud 1931. *The Netsilik Eskimos: Social Life and Spiritual Culture*. Report of the Fifth Thule Expedition 1921–1924, Vol. 8(1–2). Copenhagen, Denmark.

Read, Dwight W., and Steven A. LeBlanc 2003. Population Growth, Carrying Capacity, and Conflict. *Current Anthropology* 44:59–86.

Rowley-Conwy, Peter 2001. Time, Change and the Archaeology of Hunter-Gatherers: How Original is the "Original Affluent Society"? In *Hunter-Gatherers: An Interdisciplinary Perspective*, edited by Catherine Panter-Brick, Robert H. Layton, and Peter Rowley-Conwy, pp. 39–72. Cambridge University Press, Cambridge, United Kingdom.

Sarkar, S. S. 1962. The Jarawa of the Andaman Islands. *Anthropos* 57:670–77.

Sassaman, Kenneth E. 2004. Complex Hunter-Gatherers in Evolution and History: A North American Perspective. *Journal of Archaeological Research* 12:227–80.

Schapera, Isaac 1930. *The Khoisan Peoples of South Africa: Bushmen and Hottentots*. George Routledge & Sons, London.

Schire, Carmel 1980. An Inquiry into the Evolutionary Status and Apparent Identity of San Hunter-Gatherers. *Human Ecology* 8:9–32.

Secoy, Frank Raymond 1953. *Changing Military Patterns on the Great Plains: 17th Century through Early 19th Century*. Monographs of the American Ethnological Society XXI. University of Washington Press, Seattle.

Smith, James G. E., and Ernest S. Burch, Jr. 1979. Chipewyan and Inuit in the Central Canadian Subarctic. *Arctic Anthropology* 16:76–101.

Suttles, Wayne (editor) 1990. *Northwest Coast*. Handbook of North American Indians, Vol. 7, William C. Sturtevant, general editor. Smithsonian Institution, Washington, D.C.

Tindale, Norman B. 1974. *Aboriginal Tribes of Australia: Their Terrain, Environmental Controls, Distribution, Limits, and Proper Names*. University of California Press, Berkeley.

Wadley, Reed L. 2003. Lethal Treachery and the Imbalance of Power in Warfare and Feuding. *Journal of Anthropological Research* 59:531–54.

**46** | Steven A. LeBlanc

Walker, Philip L. 1989. Cranial Injuries as Evidence of Violence in Prehistoric Southern California. *American Journal of Physical Anthropology* 80:313–23.

Walker, Philip L., and Patricia Lambert 1989. Skeletal Evidence for Stress during a Period of Cultural Change in Prehistoric California. In *Advances in Paleopathology*, edited by Luigi Capasso, pp. 207–12. Marino Solfanelli, Chieti, Italy.

Walker, Robert S., and Drew H. Bailey 2013. Body Counts in Lowland South American Violence. *Evolution and Human Behavior* 34:29–34.

Webb, Stephen 1995. *Palaeopathology of Aboriginal Australians*. Cambridge University Press, Cambridge, United Kingdom.

Wilbert, Johannes 1972. *Survivors of Eldorado: Four Indian Cultures of South America*. Praeger, New York.

Zimmerly, David W. 2000. *Qayaq: Kayaks of Alaska and Siberia*. University of Alaska Press, Fairbanks.

# PART II

## Violence and Warfare among Mobile Foragers

# 3

# Violence and Warfare in the European Mesolithic and Paleolithic

Virginia Hutton Estabrook

## The Mesolithic: Dawn of Human Violence?

The Mesolithic period has been defined as a time of transition since Westropp (1866) coined the term to distinguish an intermediate technology between the Paleolithic and the Neolithic in Europe. Because the term "Mesolithic" describes technological transitions rather than chronology, latitude has been taken in the use of the term, as well as its disuse, in describing contemporary sites in other parts of the world. An example of this decoupling of "Mesolithic" from chronological or geographical ties is Roksandić's (2004:1) definition the term as "a combination of economic practices (hunter-gatherers) and mobility patterns (semi-sedentary or sedentary), irrespective of the geographic area and temporal framework" to encompass not only early Holocene Europeans but also later sites from Uruguay and China. Others criticize the definition of Mesolithic to be anything other than chronological because in terms of ecology, technology, economy, and social system, "there is no shared attribute (except for chronology) that could safely be used to define the entire Mesolithic" (Kozlowski 2003:xxi). In general practice, the Mesolithic refers to a (mostly) European technology produced during a time spanning the transition from the Pleistocene into the significantly warmer Holocene and the accompanying global changes in the distributions of flora and fauna.

In the past few decades, there has been a great deal of academic debate about the role violence played in prehistory and its implications for our understandings

---

*Violence and Warfare among Hunter-Gatherers*, edited by Mark W. Allen and Terry L. Jones, 49–69. ©2014 Taylor & Francis. All rights reserved.

## 50 | Virginia Hutton Estabrook

of human warfare (as thoroughly reviewed by Ferguson 2013a:112–31). In discussions about the role of violence in the Mesolithic, skeletal evidence of injury has been used by proponents of both sides of the debate: one side argues that *Homo sapiens* are warlike and vicious as part of our evolutionary trajectory and that human prehistory as characterized by the Mesolithic highlights these attributes (Keeley 1996; Pinker 2011; Vencl 1991). The opposite pole contends economic complexity and social stratification produce the primary provocation for war and interpersonal violence; although as a species we are relatively peaceful, we start to see the roots of these preconditions in the Mesolithic (Ferguson 2013b). Because of the European Mesolithic confluence of regional specificity, increased sedentism and aggregation, improvements in projectile technology, climate change, dietary shifts, and, most important, better skeletal preservation showing compelling evidence of interpersonal violence, there are many plausible ways to interpret injuries in human skeletal remains from the Mesolithic.

However, the question of whether there was an intensification of violence during the Mesolithic compared with earlier periods proves difficult to address from a comparative skeletal perspective. Examination of the skeletal record from the European Mesolithic reveals instances of injury certainly attributable to interpersonal violence such as embedded projectiles, as well as other injuries to the cranium and lower arms that are likely due to violence. However, there are instances of embedded projectiles and injuries to the cranium and lower arms in the skeletal records from the Middle Paleolithic and the Upper Paleolithic. Although there are fewer cases of injury from the Paleolithic compared with the Mesolithic, there are exponentially fewer individuals preserved and generally a much higher level of fragmentation. Comparative study of the frequency of trauma—especially trauma that might be attributed to violence—in the European Mesolithic, Upper Paleolithic, and Middle Paleolithic is difficult because of variations in the reporting of trauma, in the attribution of violence to an injury, and in the level of preservation of the remains themselves, all of which hamper conventional bioarchaeological comparative methods.

The observation of trauma in human skeletal remains is a rare event and noteworthy in that it contains information about activity patterns in the past as well as surrounding cultural practices such as interpersonal violence or care. There are two main approaches to the study of the trauma of human skeletal remains: descriptive and comparative. Descriptive approaches to trauma generally address patterns of injury in specific individuals and include detailed description all injuries on the individual as well as details about sex, age at death, and other demographic or occupational details. Comparative approaches address frequencies of injuries on a bone-by-bone basis by counting the total number of elements in a sample and the number of those elements with trauma to determine percentages by bone that can be compared with other populations. However, this comparative approach requires knowing the number of bones

# Violence and Warfare in the European Mesolithic and Paleolithic | 51

without trauma, which becomes problematic in the comparison of Mesolithic with Middle Paleolithic and Upper Paleolithic skeletal remains because it is often difficult to determine how many total elements are represented.

Many studies of Paleolithic trauma have focused on descriptive approaches rather than comparative approaches. This is partially because the samples from individual sites are too small to lend themselves to comparative study with the exception of Krapina, a Neandertal site (Estabrook and Frayer 2013). The higher levels of fragmentation in skeletal elements from the Paleolithic sites also render the counts of bones difficult to determine and unusable under many standard collection protocols (Grauer and Roberts 1996; Lovejoy and Heiple 1981). Although there is generally a very high level of preservation in Mesolithic skeletal remains, some reports of Mesolithic trauma only focus on the injuries without much context of the total number of remains recovered, or list only the number of individuals present at the site without specificity about skeletal completeness for each individual.

There is also a great deal of variation in how different researchers attribute an etiology to a specific injury. A blunt force cranial injury during the Middle Paleolithic is much more likely to be attributed to accidental injury than a similar injury during the Mesolithic, even though the causes of the injuries are equally unknown.

To comparatively address whether violence intensified during the European Mesolithic compared with previous periods, somewhat novel methodology must be used. First, the Mesolithic, Upper Paleolithic, and Middle Paleolithic samples need to be pooled so that there are enough instances of trauma to have statistically significant weight because a majority of the sites showing trauma only contain one or two cases. Also, a measure of standardization in the reporting of trauma needs to be applied: some studies of European Mesolithic skeletal remains report all trauma; some focus on trauma attributed to violence; and others focus only on projectile injury related to violence. For the comparisons in this study, I compared trauma that could possibly be attributed to violence. Because it is impossible to directly compare frequencies (number of injured skeletal elements/ total number of elements in the sample) of trauma from the Mesolithic, Middle Paleolithic and Upper Paleolithic, I compared the admittedly novel measure of distribution of injuries by "degrees of severity" instead, so that is possible to meaningfully compare these three periods, specifically to determine if there are statistically significant differences in patterns of injury.

## Materials and Methods

Detecting violence in the human skeletal record, defined as injury caused by external human agency intended to do harm to the victim, is often difficult in prehistoric contexts and involves interpretive comparisons with modern

**52** | Virginia Hutton Estabrook

injuries. With the exception of projectile injuries, it is less clear whether most of the trauma observed in skeletal elements is violent or accidental. The possibility of violence can be inferred from human skeletal remains in three main ways: the location of the injury on the body, the type of injury, and the taphonomic context of the skeletal remains. Traumatic injuries to the cranium, face, and forearm ("parry fracture") are the injuries most consistently, although not exclusively, associated with skeletal manifestations of violence both in the past and in the present (Rogers 2004; Walker 2001). Projectiles embedded in bone clearly show human agency, which is generally considered malicious in intent (Jurmain 1999:214). Injuries that occurred during the perimortem interval are associated with the cause of death and are often attributed to human agency unless otherwise demonstrated (Rogers 2004). Antemortem injuries may also represent past instances of violence and/ or ritualized nonlethal violence (Tyson 1977; Walker 1989; Webb 1995). Taphonomic indications of the disposal of bodies in mass graves also mostly point to a violent etiology (Frayer 1997; Rogers 2004).

Because of the difficulty of differentiating injuries that are accidental from those due to violence, extreme caution should be exercised in attributing specific injuries to violence. However, this conservatism often may lead to the underinterpretation of violence in deep prehistory (Estabrook and Frayer 2013), where the remains are fragmentary and the taphonomic context is often harder to assess. Until very recently (Estabrook and Frayer 2013), researchers did not attribute a violent etiology to Neandertal injuries because Neandertals' "undoubtedly low population densities probably made dispersal a far more viable alternative to conflict resolution than the interpersonal violence" (Berger and Trinkaus 1995:849). Although a violent etiology has been attributed to a few Upper Paleolithic injuries, such as the remains from Grimaldi and San Teodoro (Bachechi et al. 1997), few of the blunt force injuries have been linked to violence. As a way of circumventing the limitations to definitive interpretations of violence, I propose considering a measure of the distribution of the degree of severity of trauma as a way to make comparisons of injury patterns among groups. This provides a means by which to contextualize each incidence of injury based on the functional severity of the area of the body injured and its subsequent level of impairment. In this way, it is possible to quantitatively compare the distribution of the severity of injuries in the Middle Paleolithic, Upper Paleolithic, and Mesolithic.

## Instances of Trauma Potentially Related to Violence from the Mesolithic

A comprehensive list of injuries to Mesolithic human skeletal remains that possibly have a violent etiology is provided in Table 3.1. This list is organized alphabetically by name of site with country, source, and the date attributed to the

**Table 3.1**  Mesolithic injuries potentially attributable to violence

| Site Name and ID No. | Date | Country | Reference | Age/Sex, M/F | Injury |
|---|---|---|---|---|---|
| Birsmatten–Bassisgrotte 1 | 6000–5530 BC | Switzerland | Newell et al. 1979:104 | Prime M | Two antemortem depressions in calotte |
| Bøgebakken 3 | 4100–3860 BC | Denmark | Newell et al. 1979:50 | Prime F | Antemortem frontal depression |
| Bøgebakken 7 | 4100–3860 BC | Denmark | Newell et al. 1979:50 | Young M | Perimortem projectile in femur |
| Bøgebakken 19A | 4100–3860 BC | Denmark | Newell et al. 1979:50 | Young M | Perimortem projectile between T2 –T3 vertebrae |
| Colombres 1 | 6959–5054 BC | Spain | Newell et al. 1979:154 | Old F | Antemortem injury right frontal at supraorbital torus |
| Culoz sous Balme 1a | 7200–6000 BC | France | Newell et al. 1979:113 | Young M | Antemortem small depression right parietal |
| Donkalnis Grave 3 | 5785 BC | Lithuania | Jankauskas 2012 | Prime F | Antemortem blunt injury to skull vault |
| Donkalnis Grave 6 | 5785 BC | Lithuania | Jankauskas 2012 | Prime F | Antemortem left ulna fracture |
| De Bruin 2 | 5250–4500 BC | Netherlands | Smits 2012 | Prime M | Antemortem large depression on rear right parietal |
| Franchthi 001 | 7550–6050 BC | Greece | Papathanasiou 2012; Cullen 1995 | Young M | Perimortem two fractures to frontal and antemortem single depression fracture to frontal |
| Gøngehusvej 7 | 5000 BC | Denmark | Brinch Petersen et al. 1993 | Prime F | Antemortem large depression to right rear parietal |
| Gough's Cave 1 | 7130 BC | England | Newell et al. 1979:97 | Young M | Perimortem fractures to left parieto-temporal region and left maxilla |
| Hoëdic 5 | 4625 BC | France | Newell et al. 1979:122 | Prime M | Antemortem right ulna fracture |
| Iron Gates: Lepinski Vir 69 | 7949–7585 BC | Serbia-Romania | Roksandić 2004; Roksandić et al. 2006 | Prime M | Antemortem large frontal depression and antemortem small frontal depression |

*(Continued)*

**Table 3.1** *(Continued)*

| Site Name and ID No. | Date | Country | Reference | Age/Sex, M/F | Injury |
|---|---|---|---|---|---|
| Iron Gates: Vlasac 4a | 7949–7585 BC | Serbia-Romania | Roksandić 2004; Roksandić et al. 2006 | Young M | Perimortem bone projectile in innominate |
| Iron Gates: Vlasac 51a | 7949–7585 BC | Serbia-Romania | Roksandić 2004; Roksandić et al. 2006 | Prime F | Antemortem ulna fracture |
| Iron Gates: Vlasac 69 | 7949–7585 BC | Serbia-Romania | Roksandić 2004; Roksandić et al. 2006 | Prime M | Perimortem frontal depression |
| Iron Gates: Vlasac 82a | 7949–7585 BC | Serbia-Romania | Roksandić 2004; Roksandić et al. 2006 | Old M | Antemortem large frontal depression |
| Korsør Nor 1 | 5000–3200 BC | Denmark | Newell et al. 1979:71 | Old M | Antemortem two depressions on calotte |
| Mannlefelsen I | 6280–5860 BC | Germany | Newell et al. 1979:125 | Prime M | Antemortem small depression on occipital |
| Møllegabet II boat | After 5000 BC | Denmark | Skaarup and Grøn 2004 | Prime M | Antemortem large depression on right parietal |
| Muge: Amoreira n.n | 6800–7240 BC | Portugal | Cunha et al. 2004 | Prime M | Antemortem fracture to right radius |
| Muge: Cabeço da Arruda 1 | 6800–7240 BC | Portugal | Cunha et al. 2004 | Adult F | Antemortem facture to left ulna |
| Muge: Cabeço da Arruda 2 | 6800–7240 BC | Portugal | Cunha et al. 2004 | Adult F | Antemortem depression to right parietal |
| Muge: Cabeço da Arruda 3 | 6800–7240 BC | Portugal | Cunha et al. 2004 | Old M | Antemortem TMJ dislocation (temporal) |
| Muge: Cabeço da Arruda n.n | 6800–7240 BC | Portugal | Cunha et al. 2004 | Adolescent | Antemortem trauma to left radius and ulna |

*(Continued)*

**Table 3.1** *(Continued)*

| Site Name and ID No. | Date | Country | Reference | Age/Sex, M/F | Injury |
|---|---|---|---|---|---|
| Muge: Case 5 | 6800–7240 BC | Portugal | Cunha et al. 2004 | Prime F | Antemortem right parietal depression |
| Muge: Cova da Onça n.n. | 6800–7240 BC | Portugal | Cunha et al. 2004 | Adult | Antemortem fracture to left ulna |
| Muge: Moita do Sebastião 2 | 6800–7240 BC | Portugal | Jackes 2004 | Prime M | Antemortem bladelet in right calcaneus |
| Muge: Moita do Sebastião 3 | 6800–7240 BC | Portugal | Cunha et al. 2004 | Prime M | Antemortem left parietal depression |
| Muge: Moita do Sebastião 10 | 6800–7240 BC | Portugal | Jackes 2004 | Adult F | Antemortem right ulna pseudoarthrosis |
| Muge: Moita do Sebastião 20 | 6800–7240 BC | Portugal | Cunha et al. 2004 | Old M | Antemortem left frontal depression |
| Muge: Moita do Sebastião 25 | 6800–7240 BC | Portugal | Jackes 2004 | Adult F | Antemortem fracture to right ulna |
| Ofnet 2475.2 | 7360–7560 BC | Germany | Frayer 1997 | Prime M | Perimortem cranial trauma and antemortem wound on left parietal |
| Ofnet 2477.4 | 7360–7560 BC | Germany | Frayer 1997 | Prime F | Perimortem cranial trauma |
| Ofnet 2481.8 | 7360–7560 BC | Germany | Frayer 1997 | Young M | Perimortem cranial trauma |
| Ofnet 2486.13 | 7360–7560 BC | Germany | Frayer 1997 | Young F | Perimortem cranial trauma |
| Ofnet 2490.18 | 7360–7560 BC | Germany | Frayer 1997 | Prime F | Perimortem cranial trauma |
| Ofnet 2490.21 | 7360–7560 BC | Germany | Frayer 1997 | Young M | Perimortem cranial trauma |
| Ofnet 2496.24 | 7360–7560 BC | Germany | Frayer 1997 | Old M | Perimortem cranial trauma |
| Ofnet 2504.32 | 7360–7560 BC | Germany | Frayer 1997 | Young M | Perimortem cranial trauma |
| Ofnet 2497.25 | 7360–7560 BC | Germany | Frayer 1997 | Subadult/15–16 y | Perimortem cranial trauma |
| Ofnet 2489.17 | 7360–7560 BC | Germany | Frayer 1997 | Subadult/2–3 y | Perimortem cranial trauma |
| Ofnet 2476.3a | 7360–7560 BC | Germany | Frayer 1997 | Subadult/5 y | Perimortem cranial trauma |
| Ofnet 2492.20 | 7360–7560 BC | Germany | Frayer 1997 | Subadult/9–10 y | Perimortem cranial trauma |
| Ofnet 2480.7 | 7360–7560 BC | Germany | Frayer 1997 | Subadult/7–8 y | Perimortem cranial trauma |
| Ofnet 2479.6 | 7360–7560 BC | Germany | Frayer 1997 | Subadult/<2 y | Perimortem cranial trauma |
| Ofnet 2498.26 | 7360–7560 BC | Germany | Frayer 1997 | Subadult/7 y | Perimortem cranial trauma |

*(Continued)*

**Table 3.1** *(Continued)*

| Site Name and ID No. | Date | Country | Reference | Age/Sex, M/F | Injury |
|---|---|---|---|---|---|
| Ofnet 2483.11 | 7360–7560 BC | Germany | Frayer 1997 | Subadult/11 y | Perimortem cranial trauma |
| Ofnet 2505.33 | 7360–7560 BC | Germany | Frayer 1997 | Subadult/2–4 y | Antemortem two depressions on left frontal |
| Schela Cladovei 42 | 7307–7545 BC | Romania | Boroneant et al. 1999 | Adult F | Antemortem blunt force trauma to skull |
| Schela Cladovei 46 | 7307–7545 BC | Romania | Boroneant et al. 1999 | Adult M | Antemortem fracture to lower arm |
| Schela Cladovei 47 | 7307–7545 BC | Romania | Boroneant et al. 1999 | Adult | Perimortem flint projectile |
| Schela Cladovei 48 | 7307–7545 BC | Romania | Boroneant et al. 1999 | Adult M | Perimortem bone projectile and blunt force trauma to skull |
| Schela Cladovei 49 | 7307–7545 BC | Romania | Boroneant et al. 1999 | Adult F | Antemortem fracture to lower arm |
| Schela Cladovei 50 | 7307–7545 BC | Romania | Boroneant et al. 1999 | Adult M | Perimortem bone projectile to innominate |
| Skateholm I, Grave 13 | 5250–4900 BC | Sweden | Larsson 1989 | Adult M | Perimortem arrowhead in innominate |
| Stora Bjers 1 | 6200–4000 BC | Norway | Newell et al. 1979:39 | Prime M | Perimortem bone point in pelvis |
| Tågerup | 6500–5000 BC | Sweden | Karsten and Knarrström 2003 | Subadult/10 y | Perimortem arrowhead in pelvis |
| Téviec 1 | 4725 BC | France | Newell et al. 1979:133 | Young F | Antemortem fracture to right radius |
| Téviec 2 | 4725 BC | France | Newell et al. 1979:133 | Young M | Antemortem trauma to left parietal and frontal |
| Téviec 16 | 4725 BC | France | Newell et al. 1979:133 | Young M | Perimortem microliths in T6 and T1 and antemortem mandibular fracture |

*(Continued)*

**Table 3.1** *(Continued)*

| Site Name and ID No. | Date | Country | Reference | Age/Sex, M/F | Injury |
|---|---|---|---|---|---|
| Le Trou Violet B | 7000–3200 BC | France | Newell et al. 1979:138 | Prime M | Antemortem parietal depression |
| Tybrind Vig B | 4490 BC | Denmark | Newell et al. 1979:62 | Adult | Antemortem 2 injuries to right parietal |
| Valle di Zambana | 6050–5790 BC | Italy | Newell et al. 1979:42 | Prime F | Antemortem injury to radius and ulna |
| Vasilyevka I 17 | 10,080–9980 BC | Ukraine | Lillie 2004 | Adult M | Perimortem multiple projectile injuries |
| Vasilyevka I 10 | 10,080–9980 BC | Ukraine | Lillie 2004 | Adult | Perimortem rib fracture associated with projectile |
| Vasilyevka III 5 | 10,080–9980 BC | Ukraine | Lillie 2004 | Adult | Perimortem arrow and spear embedded in body |
| Vasilyevka III 33 | 10,080–9980 BC | Ukraine | Lillie 2004 | Prime F | Perimortem projectile found with ribs |
| Vasilyevka III 34 | 10,080–9980 BC | Ukraine | Lillie 2004 | Prime F | Perimortem projectile in lumbar vertebrae |
| Vasilyevka III 36 | 10,080–9980 BC | Ukraine | Lillie 2004 | Prime F | Perimortem projectile found with ribs |
| Vasilyevka III 37 | 10,080–9980 BC | Ukraine | Lillie 2004 | Prime M | Perimortem projectile embedded in lumbar vertebra |
| Voloshkoe 3 | 10,080–9980 BC | Ukraine | Lillie 2004 | Adult | Perimortem projectile in atlas |
| Voloshkoe 5 | 10,080–9980 BC | Ukraine | Lillie 2004 | Adult M | Perimortem projectile in sternum |
| Zvejnieki Grave 154 | 8000–6550 BC | Latvia | Jankauskas 2012 | Prime M | Antemortem nasal fracture |

**58** | Virginia Hutton Estabrook

site at time of publication, as well as information about the individual by skeletal identification number, known demographic variables, and a short description of the trauma. For age at death, I use the following fairly broad categories to allow comparison to the Paleolithic remains: subadult (0–18 years), young adult (18–30 years), prime adult (30–50 years), and old adult (50+ years).

## Degree of Severity of Trauma

Because of variation in the way in which injuries from the Mesolithic were reported and levels of preservation of skeletal remains in the Mesolithic, Middle Paleolithic, and Upper Paleolithic, comparisons of frequencies of trauma by skeletal element are not directly possible. It is also often not possible, especially in the case of poorly preserved skeletal remains, to definitively attribute a specific cause to an injury.

Previously, I created five categories (e.g., an ordinal scale showing degree of severity) to describe severity of injury based on impact to mobility and level of care necessary for recovery (Estabrook 2009). For the purposes of this chapter, I have slightly modified these categories down to four that reflect intensities of injuries that may be related to violence, deleting a category for postcranial injuries related to impaired mobility that were unlikely to have a violent etiology.

First-degree injuries involve antemortem trauma to the postcranial skeleton. These are injuries that are least likely to affect the mobility of an individual or involve any injury to the skull that would affect the brain. They include injuries to the forearm such as midshaft ulnar fractures and clearly healed projectile postcranial injury. Radial shaft injuries (without concomitant ulnar involvement) are also included in counts because of the possibility that they might represent a Galeazzi fracture, which may also be the result of a direct blow (Jurmain 1999:221).

Second-degree injuries represent minor cranial trauma. Although these injuries may not be as problematic to their sufferers as first degree injuries, because they involve the cranium, there is always the possibility of some loss of consciousness or mental impairment. All of these cranial injuries are either small cranial depression fractures involving only the outer table or some other superficial periosteal reaction related to a traumatic impact.

Third-degree injuries represent serious antemortem cranial trauma such as penetrating scalp wounds or large depression fractures to the side of the head. It is possible that many of the third-degree injuries also contributed to the weakening of the individuals and were indirect causes of death; however, all third-degree injuries show some sign of healing.

Fourth-degree injuries are defined as trauma that contributed as a direct cause of death. Any perimortem trauma is included in this category. All instances of projectiles embedded in bone are included; instances of projectiles in association with skeletal remains, but not embedded, are not. Instances of

Violence and Warfare in the European Mesolithic and Paleolithic | 59

postmortem dismemberment are also not included in this category because they are not the direct cause of death.

## List of Injuries by Degree of Severity

Tables 3.2, 3.3, and 3.4 summarize the distributions of injuries recorded for the Middle Paleolithic, Upper Paleolithic, and Mesolithic into the four categories of "Degree of Severity" related to potentially violent trauma.

## Analysis of Contingency Tables Using Simulations

The ACTUS program (Analysis of Contingency Tables Using Simulation; Estabrook and Estabrook 1989; Estabrook 2011) was designed to address

**Table 3.2** Summary of Middle Paleolithic trauma possibly related to interpersonal violence

| Degree of Severity | No. Individuals | Area of Trauma | By Age Class | By Sex |
|---|---|---|---|---|
| First Degree | 4 | | | |
| *Nonlethal trauma to* | Feldhofer 1 | Ulna | Old | Male |
| *postcranial skeleton* | Krapina 180 | Ulna | Adult | Unknown |
| | Krapina 188.8 | Ulna | Adult | Unknown |
| | Le Moustier 1 | Mandible | Adolescent | Male |
| Second Degree | 10 | | | |
| *Minor cranial trauma* | Feldhofer 1 | Occipital | Old | Male |
| | Krapina 4 | Frontal | Adult | Male |
| | Krapina 5 | Parietal | Adult | Male |
| | Krapina 20 | Frontal | Adult | Female |
| | Krapina 31 | Frontal | Adult | Female |
| | Šala 1 | Frontal | Adolescent | Female |
| | Shanidar1 | Frontal | Old | Male |
| | Shanidar 5 | Frontal | Old | Male |
| | Skhul 1 | Frontal | Child | Unknown |
| | Skhul 1 | Temporal/ Mandible | Child | Unknown |
| Third Degree | 5 | | | |
| *Major cranial trauma,* | Krapina 34.7 | Parietal | Adult | Unknown |
| *probably involving a* | Shanidar 1 | Frontal/Parietal | Old | Male |
| *loss of consciousness* | St. Césaire | Parietal | Adolescent | Male |
| | Cova Negra 1 | Parietal | Unknown | Unknown |
| | Qafzeh 11 | Frontal | Adolescent | Male? |
| Fourth Degree | 2 | | | |
| *Fatal trauma* | Shanidar 3 | Rib | Old | Male |
| | Skhul IX | Innominate | Prime | Male |

**Note:** For references to site publications, see Estabrook (2009:105–65) and Wu et al. (2011).

**60** | Virginia Hutton Estabrook

**Table 3.3**  Summary of Middle Paleolithic trauma possibly related to violence

| Degree of Severity | No. Individuals | Area of Trauma | By Age Class | By Sex |
|---|---|---|---|---|
| First Degree | 3 | | | |
| *Nonlethal trauma to* | Dolni Vestonic 15 | Ulna | Adolescent | Male |
| *postcranial skeleton* | San Teodoro 2 | Innominate | Prime | Female |
| | Caviglione 1 | Radius | Prime | Male |
| Second Degree | 8 | | | |
| *Minor cranial trauma* | Dolni Vestonice 3 | Frontal | Prime | Female |
| | Dolni Vestonice 13 | Frontal/Parietal | Prime | Male |
| | Dolni Vestonice 16 | Frontal | Prime | Male |
| | Pavlov 1 | Parietal | Prime | Male |
| | Mladeč 5 | Frontal | Prime | Male |
| | Chancelade | Frontal/Parietal | Old | Male |
| | Sourde 2 | Parietal | Adult | Unknown |
| | Cro Magnon II | Frontal | Prime | Female |
| Third Degree | 2 | | | |
| *Major cranial trauma,* | Dolni Vestonice 3 | Frontal/Maxilla | Prime | Female |
| *probably involving a* | Dolni Vestonice | Frontal | Prime | Male |
| *loss of consciousness* | 11/12 | | | |
| Fourth Degree | 3 | | | |
| *Fatal trauma* | Sunghir 1 | Innominate | Old | Male |
| | Grotte des Enfants | Thoracic 2 | Child | Unknown |
| | Montfort-sur-Lizier | Thoracic | Adult | Unknown |

**Notes:** References for Upper Paleolithic instances of trauma: Dolni Vestonic and Pavlov remains (Trinkaus and Svoboda 2006); San Teodora and Grotte des Enfants (Bachechi 1997); Caviglione (Verneau 1906); Monfort-sur-Lizier (Begouen et al. 1922); Mladeč (Teschler-Nicola 2006); Chancelade, Sourde, and Cro-Magnon (Brennan 1991); and Sunghir (Trinkaus and Buzhilova 2010).

the problem of statistical analyses of two-way tables from small samples in determining whether to reject a null hypothesis of independence. Such analyses are especially important in fields such as history and other social sciences (the context for which this program was created) or in any instance where counts of differing character states are being compared. Because the approximation to classical statistical distributions (such as chi-square) is poor when only a few cases are involved, the minimum number of cases expected under the hypothesis of independence must exceed four for tabulated probabilities to be accurate using classical statistical methods (Estabrook and Estabrook 1989:5). With a small sample, when the null hypothesis of independence is rejected using classical statistics, it is difficult to tell which cells to interpret as being more and/or less frequent than predicted under the null hypothesis, because the co-occurrences that merit a more substantive interpretation are not necessarily the largest or smallest counts (Estabrook 2002:23).

## Violence and Warfare in the European Mesolithic and Paleolithic | **61**

**Table 3.4**  Summary of Mesolithic trauma possibly related to violence

| Degree of Severity | No. Individuals | Area of Trauma | By Age Class | By Sex |
|---|---|---|---|---|
| First Degree | 14 | | | |
| *Nonlethal trauma* | Muge: Sebastião 2 | Calcaneus | Prime | Male |
| *to postcranial* | Muge: Sebastião 10 | Ulna | Adult | Female |
| *skeleton* | Muge: Sebastião 25 | Ulna | Adult | Female |
| | Muge: Cabeço 1 | Ulna | Adult | Female |
| | Muge: Cabeço n.n | Radius/Ulna | Subadult | Unknown |
| | Muge: Cova n.n | Ulna | Adult | Unknown |
| | Muge: Amoreira n.n | Radius | Prime | Male |
| | I.G.: Vlasac 51a | Ulna | Adult | Female |
| | Schela Cladovei 46 | Lower Arm | Adult | Male |
| | Schela Cladovei 49 | Lower Arm | Adult | Female |
| | Hoëdic 5 | Ulna | Prime | Male |
| | Téviec 1 | Radius | Young | Female |
| | Valle di Zambana | Radius and Ulna | Prime | Female |
| | Donkalnis 6 | Ulna | Prime | Female |
| Second Degree | 19 | | | |
| *Minor cranial* | Muge: Moita 3 | Parietal | Prime | Male |
| *trauma* | Muge: Case 5 | Parietal | Prime | Female |
| | Muge: Moita 20 | Frontal | Old | Male |
| | Muge: Cabeço 2 | Parietal | Adult | Female |
| | Muge: Cabeço 3 | Temporal | Old | Male |
| | I.G.: Lepinski Vir 69 | Frontal | Prime | Male |
| | Bøgebakken 3 | Frontal | Prime | Female |
| | Offnet 2505.33 | Frontal | Subadult | Unknown |
| | Offnet 2475.2 | Parietal | Adult | Male |
| | Korsør Nor 1 | Skull | Old | Male |
| | Tybrind Vig B | Parietal | Adult | Unknown |
| | Mannlefelsen I | Occipital | Prime | Male |
| | Birsmatten-Bass. | Skull | Prime | Male |
| | Culoz 1a | Parietal | Prime | Male |
| | Téviec 16 | Mandible | Young | Male |
| | Trou Violet B | Parietal | Young | Male |
| | Franchthi 001 | Frontal | Young | Male |
| | Zvejnieki | Nasal | Prime | Male |
| | Donkalnis 3 | Skull | Prime | Female |
| Third Degree | 7 | | | |
| *Major cranial* | I.G.:Vlasac 82a | Frontal | Old | Male |
| *trauma, probably* | I.G.:Lepinski Vir 69 | Frontal | Prime | Male |
| *involving a loss* | Téviec 2 | Frontal and Parietal | Young | Male? |
| *of consciousness* | Colombres 1 | Frontal | Old | Female |
| | De Bruin 2 | Parietal | Prime | Male |
| | Møllegabet: boat | Parietal | Prime | Male |
| | Gøngehusvej 7 | Parietal | Prime | Female |

*(Continued)*

## 62 | Virginia Hutton Estabrook

**Table 3.4** *(Continued)*

| Degree of Severity | No. Individuals | Area of Trauma | By Age Class | By Sex |
|---|---|---|---|---|
| Fourth Degree | 37 | | | |
| *Perimortem* | I.G. Vlasac 4a | Innominate | Prime | Unknown |
| *(fatal) trauma* | I.G. Vlasac 69 | Frontal | Prime | Male |
| | Schela Cladovei 47 | Unknown | Adult | Unknown |
| | Schela Cladovei 48 | Skull/projectile in body | Adult | Male |
| | Schela Cladovei 50 | Innominate | Adult | Male |
| | Voloshkoe 3 | Atlas (C1) | Adult | Unknown |
| | Voloshkoe 5 | Sternum | Adult | Male |
| | Vasilyevka I.17 | Multiple projectiles | Adult | Male |
| | Vasilyevka I.10 | Rib | Adult | Unknown |
| | Vasilyevka III.5 | Arrow and Spear | Adult | Unknown |
| | Vasilyevka III.33 | Rib | Prime | Female |
| | Vasilyevka III. 34 | Lumbar Vertebra | Prime | Female |
| | Vasilyevka III.36 | Rib | Prime | Female |
| | Vasilyevka III.37 | Lumbar Vertebra | Prime | Male |
| | Offnet 2475.2 | Skull | Prime | Male |
| | Offnet 2477.4 | Skull | Prime | Female |
| | Offnet 2481.8 | Skull | Young | Male |
| | Offnet 2486.13 | Skull | Young | Female |
| | Offnet 2490.18 | Skull | Prime | Female |
| | Offnet 2490.21 | Skull | Young | Male |
| | Offnet 2496.24 | Skull | Old | Male |
| | Offnet 2504.21 | Skull | Young | Male |
| | Offnet 2497.25 | Skull | Subadult | Unknown |
| | Offnet 2489.17 | Skull | Subadult | Unknown |
| | Offnet 2476.3a | Skull | Subadult | Unknown |
| | Offnet 2492.20 | Skull | Subadult | Unknown |
| | Offnet 2480.7 | Skull | Subadult | Unknown |
| | Offnet 2479.6 | Skull | Subadult | Unknown |
| | Offnet 2498.26 | Skull | Subadult | Unknown |
| | Offnet 2483.11 | Skull | Subadult | Unknown |
| | Stora Bjers 1 | Innominate | Prime | Male |
| | Bøgebakken 7 | Femur | Young | Male |
| | Bøgebakken 19A | Thoracic Vertebrae | Young | Male |
| | Gough's Cave 1 | Parietal, temporal and maxilla | Young | Male |
| | Franchthi 001 | Frontal | Young | Male |
| | Skateholm I-13 | Innominate | Adult | Male |
| | Tågerup | Innominate | Subadult | Unknown |

**Note:** See Materials section for sources.

ACTUS calculates estimates of realized significance of each cell from small data sets. It does this by comparing two classifications under the null hypothesis that they are independent. Counts of both classifications are arrayed in a contingency table. The program then uses a random number generator to simulate thousands of comparable data sets whose counts are known to be

Violence and Warfare in the European Mesolithic and Paleolithic | **63**

samples of the null hypothesis, and counts the number of simulated tables with entries that are larger or smaller than the corresponding entries input by the user. The results of an ACTUS analysis show not only whether the entire contingency table rejects the null hypothesis, but also which cells are larger or smaller than predicted. ACTUS uses direct comparison of the value of a statistic calculated from the observed table with a value calculated in the same way from a simulated table to estimate its realized significance with the fraction of simulated tables not less or not greater. This method works for any statistic, not just those that approximate a known precalculated distribution. It provides an easy-to-understand, direct measure of the extent to which an observed table differs from what might be predicted by a hypothesis of independence.

# Results

The distribution in the severity of trauma observed in the Mesolithic sample was compared with the Middle Paleolithic and Upper Paleolithic samples in two ways. The first way addresses distributions of the degrees of severity of trauma observed within the pooled context of all the known traumas from each of the groups to address the issue of whether injuries are more likely to be relatively more severe or fatal during any of these periods. In the second approach, the distribution of cases of blunt force trauma and projectile trauma was compared for all of the traumas of known etiology from each of the populations to address the hypothesis that projectile technology during the Mesolithic is driving any differences in patterns of trauma.

## Comparative Analysis of Severity of Trauma

For the comparisons of the distribution of severity of trauma, the null hypothesis of independence was tested using data from the Mesolithic, Middle Paleolithic, and Upper Paleolithic samples listed in Tables 3.2, 3.3, and 3.4. For each degree of severity, prevalence of trauma is hypothesized to be independent of the population observed. Each of these columns represents a table used in the ACTUS simulation run. The number of times out of the 10,000 simulated tables that the chi-square values calculated from F-simulated tables were equal to or exceeded the chi-square value calculated from the observed table was counted. These counts represent the significance ($p$ value) of the comparisons over the group. For each degree of severity, the null hypothesis of independence of prevalence of trauma and population observed was rejected if $p \leq 0.05$. Any of the individual counts of trauma in a population that are significantly higher or lower than predicted under the null hypothesis ($p \leq 0.05$) are marked with a plus or minus sign, respectively. The testing of independence of individual cells as well as the group as a whole shows which cells represent statistically significant higher or lower trauma

**64** | Virginia Hutton Estabrook

**Table 3.5** Distribution of instances of injury for known samples with trauma

| Population | First Degree | Second Degree | Third Degree | Fourth Degree |
|---|---|---|---|---|
| Middle Paleolithic | 4 | 10 | 5 | $2 - (p=0.01)$ |
| Upper Paleolithic | 3 | 8 | 2 | 3 |
| Mesolithic | 14 | 19 | 7 | $37 + (p=0.03)$ |

counts than would be predicted within the context of the pooled group of Mesolithic, Middle Paleolithic, and Upper Paleolithic injuries. In this way, we can observe whether the Mesolithic severity of injury distributions counts are significantly smaller or larger for each degree of severity than would be predicted at random given the sample size compared with Middle Paleolithic and Upper Paleolithic samples.

The results of the group comparisons are shown in Table 3.5. The distribution of instances of severity of trauma was inconsistent with the null hypothesis of independence of degree of severity of trauma and population observed. The chi-square values calculated from F-simulated tables were equal to or exceeded 15.662, the chi-square value calculated from the data table, 143 times out of 10,000 simulations ($p=0.01$). This indicates a rejection of the null hypothesis of independence in the distribution of severity of trauma and time period for the whole table. In addition, individual counts that represent extreme outliers are indicated with plus or minus signs. The observed number of two instances of fourth-degree injuries (perimortem trauma) in the Middle Paleolithic was significantly small ($p=0.01$), and out of the 10,000 simulated data sets, the simulated count did not exceed the observed count only 130 times. The observed number of 37 instances of fourth-degree trauma injuries observed in the Mesolithic was significantly large ($p=0.03$) and out of the 10,000 simulated data sets, the simulated count exceeded the observed count only 330 times. All the other counts of instances of severity of trauma were not significantly small or large.

## Comparative Analysis of Frequencies of Blunt Force versus Projectile Trauma

For the comparison of instances of blunt force and projectile trauma, the counts for each trauma of known etiology was compared for each of the populations (Mesolithic, Middle Paleolithic, and Upper Paleolithic) using ACTUS as previously described. The distribution of counts of blunt force and projectile injuries are listed in Table 3.6 for the Middle Paleolithic, the Upper Paleolithic, and the Mesolithic.

The distribution of instances of severity of trauma was consistent with the null hypothesis of independence of type of injury and population observed. The chi-square values calculated from F-simulated tables were equal to or exceeded

Violence and Warfare in the European Mesolithic and Paleolithic | **65**

**Table 3.6** Projectile/blade versus blunt force injuries

| Population | Non-Projectile Injury, no. | Projectile Injury, no. |
|---|---|---|
| Middle Paleolithic | 20 | 1 |
| Upper Paleolithic | 13 | 3 |
| Mesolithic | 60 | 17 |

3.294, the chi-square value calculated from the data table, 1,946 times out of 10,000 simulations ($p$=0.19). The null hypothesis that frequency of type of injury is independent of time period is not rejected. Although there are many more projectile injuries observed during the Mesolithic, the relative frequency of their observation compared with that of blunt force injuries is not higher than what is observed during the Middle Paleolithic and Upper Paleolithic.

## The Mesolithic: Does Trauma Get More Lethal?

When the distributions of instances of trauma into the four degrees of severity of injuries were compared for the Middle Paleolithic, Upper Paleolithic, and Mesolithic, there was shown to be a statistically significant difference in the distributions of trauma by degree of severity. Most of that statistical significance was driven by the significantly low number of instances of fourth-degree (perimortem) trauma in the Middle Paleolithic and the significantly high number of instances of fourth-degree trauma in the Mesolithic. If we remove the "fourth-degree" severity of injury category and only compare antemortem injuries identified for the three time periods (Table 3.7), the chi-square values calculated from F-simulated tables were equal to or exceeded 2.094, the chi-square value calculated from the data table, 7,368 times out of 10,000 ($p$=0.73), and the null hypothesis of independence of distribution of severity of injury and time period is not rejected. No individual counts were significantly large or small. It becomes fairly clear that fourth-degree injuries that occurred during the perimortem interval and likely contributed to the cause of death are what is driving the significant differences in the distribution of traumatic injuries possibly related to violence during the Mesolithic, Upper Paleolithic, and Middle Paleolithic as shown in Table 3.5.

**Table 3.7** Distribution of antemortem injury possibly related to violence for known samples with trauma

| Population | First Degree, no. | Second Degree, no. | Third Degree, no. |
|---|---|---|---|
| Middle Paleolithic | 4 | 10 | 5 |
| Upper Paleolithic | 3 | 8 | 2 |
| Mesolithic | 14 | 19 | 7 |

**66** | Virginia Hutton Estabrook

There are several possibilities that may explain the statistically significantly greater amount of fourth-degree trauma observed during the Mesolithic compared with the Middle Paleolithic and Upper Paleolithic: (1) more lethal violence during the Mesolithic; (2) underrepresentation of perimortem trauma in the Middle and Upper Paleolithic due to differences in levels of preservation; and (3) one anomalous site (Ofnet) driving this difference.

The first explanation seems the most intuitively obvious: we see more perimortem trauma in the Mesolithic because of an escalation in the level of interpersonal violence. Lillie (2004) suggested that changes in projectile technology increased rates of homicide because it is easier to inflict lethal damage remotely; however the results in this study (Table 3.6) do not demonstrate a statistically significant change in the distribution of projectile injuries relative to blunt force injuries in the Mesolithic compared with the Middle Paleolithic and Upper Paleolithic. Increases in lethal injuries during the Mesolithic cannot be explained only by an increased number of projectiles because blunt force injuries are also common during the Mesolithic. Ecological pressures due to rapid climate change may have contributed to increased levels of interpersonal aggression during the Mesolithic, as this has been postulated to explain similar patterns in ethnographic studies (Ember and Ember 1997). Rapid changes in foraging territory may also have brought relatively nonaffiliated groups much closer together, which also may have skewed intergroup dynamics toward homicide rather than nonlethal forms of conflict.

The significantly larger number of perimortem injuries observed during the Mesolithic may also be the result of better preservation of human skeletal remains from the this period relative to the Upper Paleolithic and Middle Paleolithic. The human skeletal remains from the Mesolithic period are much better preserved than most remains from the Middle Paleolithic and Upper Paleolithic and show much smaller levels of fragmentation, which may influence the number of perimortem injuries observed. Taphonomic differences in the preservation of skeletal remains may manifest themselves in two ways: greater preservation in the Mesolithic sample of some of the more fragile axial elements such as ribs, sternum, and innominates (Mays 1991), which are close to major internal organs, where injury might likely produce a fatality; and greater levels of preservation of all skeletal elements in the Mesolithic may result in better preservation of perimortem trauma from effects of taphonomic processes such as weathering and postmortem fragmentation. If the results are being driven by sampling biases, it is our ability to observe perimortem injury during the Mesolithic that has changed rather than interpersonal behaviors.

Another aspect of possible sampling bias is the high number of perimortem traumas observed at a single site, Ofnet, relative to all other Mesolithic sites. Although the "skull nest" composition of the site is not unique to Ofnet, many more individuals are represented there, and Ofnet is the only collection of

Violence and Warfare in the European Mesolithic and Paleolithic | **67**

decapitated skulls that show perimortem injury beyond the decapitation (Frayer 1997:189). Of the 37 perimortem injuries observed during the Mesolithic, 16 (43 percent) come from this single site, which is likely a low estimation for the number of individuals from Ofnet who died from perimortem injury because only the crania and cervical vertebra were preserved. The decapitations themselves were not included as perimortem injury because decapitation could have happened after death during some form of ritual collection of "trophy skulls" or other form of burial rite (Orschiedt 2005); however, given the prevalence of head injuries alone, there was likely postcranial perimortem injury in some, if not all, of the other 22 individuals represented at the site and possibly the other "skull nest" sites as well.

Clearly, there is a great deal of variability in the levels of injury manifested in European Mesolithic sites; however, pooling the data about trauma potentially related to violence allows this range of variability to be directly compared with earlier Paleolithic groups where individual sites are too small to have any comparative statistical relevance on their own. What these comparisons show is that the distribution of injuries changes significantly during the Mesolithic compared with the Middle Paleolithic and Upper Paleolithic in an increased amount of perimortem injuries that show no sign of healing and are likely related to the cause of death.

## References

Bachechi, Luca, Francesco Mallegni, and Pier-Francesco Fabbri 1997. An Arrow-Caused Lesion in a Late Upper Palaeolithic Human Pelvis. *Current Anthropology* 38:135–40.

Begouen, Henri, [?] Cugulieres, and Henri Miquel 1922. Vertebre Humaine Traversee par une Lame en Quartzite. *Revue Anthropologique* 1922:230–2.

Berger, Thomas, and Erik Trinkaus 1995. Patterns of Trauma among the Neandertals. *Journal of Archaeological Science* 22:841–52.

Boroneant, Vasile, Clive Bonsall, Kath McSweeny, Robert Payton, and Mark Macklin 1999. A Mesolithic Burial Area at Schela Cladovei, Romania. In *L'Europe des Derniers Chasseurs: Epipaleolithique et Mesolithique*, edited by Andre Thevien, pp. 385–90. Editions du Comite des Travaux Historiques et Scientifiques, Paris.

Brennan, Mary U. 1991. Health and Disease in the Middle and Upper Paleolithic of Southwestern France: A Bioarcheological Study. Unpublished Ph.D. dissertation, Department of Anthropology, New York University, New York.

Brinch Petersen, Erik, Verner Alexandersen, and Christopher Meiklejohn 1993. Vedbaek, Graven Midt i Byen. *Nationalmuseets Arbejdsmark* 1993:61–9.

Cullen, Tracey 1995. Mesolithic Mortuary Ritual at Franchthi Cave, Greece. *Antiquity* 69:270–89.

Cunha, Eugenia, Claudia Umbelino, and Francisca Cardoso 2004. About Violent Interactions in the Mesolithic: The Absence of Evidence from the Portuguese Shell Middens. In *Violent Interactions in the Mesolithic: Evidence and Meaning*, edited by Mirjana Roksandic, pp. 41–46. B.A.R. International Series Volume 1237. Archaeopress, Oxford, United Kingdom.

Ember, Carol R., and Melvin L. Ember 1997. Violence in the Ethnographic Record: Results of Cross-Cultural Research on War and Aggression. In *Troubled Times: Violence and Warfare in the Past*, edited by Debra L. Martin and David W. Frayer, pp. 1–20. Gordon and Breach, Amsterdam.

## 68 | Virginia Hutton Estabrook

Estabrook, Carl B., and George F. Estabrook 1989. ACTUS: A Solution to the Problem of Small Samples in the Analysis of Two-Way Contingency Tables. *Historical Methods* 22:5–8.

Estabrook, George F. 2002. Two Hypotheses of Independence for the Recognition of Qualitative Co-Occurrences in Small Amounts of Data. *Historical Methods* 35:21–31.

——— 2011. *A Computational Approach to Statistical Arguments in Ecology and Evolution.* Cambridge University Press, Cambridge, United Kingdom.

Estabrook, Virginia H. 2009. Sampling Biases and New Ways of Addressing the Significance of Trauma in Neandertals. Unpublished Ph.D. dissertation, Department of Anthropology, University of Michigan, Ann Arbor.

Estabrook, Virginia H., and David W. Frayer 2013. Trauma in the Krapina Neandertals: Violence in the Middle Paleolithic? In *The Routledge Handbook of the Bioarchaeology of Human Conflict,* edited by Martin J. Smith and Christopher J. Knusel, pp. 67–89. Routledge, New York.

Ferguson, R. Brian 2013a. Pinker's List: Exaggerating Prehistoric War Mortality. In *War, Peace and Human Nature: The Convergence of Evolutionary and Cultural Views,* edited by Douglas P. Fry, pp. 112–31. Oxford University Press, Oxford, United Kingdom.

——— 2013b. The Prehistory of War in Europe and the Near East. In *War, Peace, and Human Nature,* edited by Douglas P. Fry, pp. 473–7. Oxford University Press, Oxford, United Kingdom.

Frayer, David W. 1997. Ofnet: Evidence for a Mesolithic Massacre. In *Troubled Times: Violence and Warfare in the Past,* edited by Debra L. Martin and David W. Frayer, pp. 181–216. Gordon and Breach Publishers, Amsterdam.

Grauer, Anne L., and Charlotte A. Roberts 1996. Paleoepidemiology, Healing and Possible Treatment of Trauma in the Medieval Cemetery Population of St. Helen-on-the-Walls, York, England. *American Journal of Physical Anthropology* 100:531–44.

Jackes, Mary K. 2004. Osteological Evidence for Mesolithic and Neolithic Violence: Problems of Interpretation. In *Violent Interactions in the Mesolithic,* edited by Mirjana Roksandic, pp. 23–40. B.A.R. International Series Volume 1237. Archaeopress, Oxford, United Kingdom.

Jankauskas, Rimantas 2012. Violence in the Stone Age from an Eastern Baltic Perspective. In *Sticks, Stones, and Broken Bones: Neolithic Violence in a European Perspective,* edited by Rick J. Schulting and Linda Fibiger, pp. 35–50. Oxford University Press, Oxford, United Kingdom.

Jurmain, Robert 1999. *Stories from the Skeleton.* Gordon and Breach, Amsterdam.

Karsten, Per, and Bo Knarrström 2003. *The Tågerup Excavations.* National Heritage Board, Lund, Sweden.

Keeley, Lawrence H. 1996. *War Before Civilization: The Myth of the Peaceful Savage.* Oxford University Press, Oxford, United Kingdom.

Kozlowski, Stefan K. 2003. The Mesolithic: What do We Know and What do We Believe? In *Mesolithic on the Move,* edited by Lars Larsson, Hans Kindgren, Kjel Knutsson, David Loeffler, and Agneta Akerlund, pp. xvii–xxi. Oxford University Press, Oxford, United Kingdom.

Larsson, Lars 1989. Late Mesolithic Settlements and Cemeteries in Skateholm, Southern Sweden. In *The Mesolithic in Europe,* edited by Clive Bonsall, pp. 367–78. John Donald, Edinburgh, Scotland.

Lillie, Malcom C. 2004. Fighting for Your Life? Violence at the Late-Glacial to Holocene Transition. In *Violent Interactions in the Mesolithic: Evidence and Meaning,* edited by Mirjana Roksandic, pp. 89–96. B.A.R. International Series Volume 1237. Archaeopress, Oxford, United Kingdom.

Lovejoy, C. Owen, and Kingsbury G. Heiple 1981. The Analysis of Fractures in Skeletal Populations with an Example from the Libben Site, Ottawa County, Ohio. *American Journal of Physical Anthropology* 55:529–41.

Mays, Simon 1991. Taphonomic Factors in a Human Skeletal Assemblage. *Circaea* 9:54–8.

Newell, Raymond R., Trinette S. Constandse-Westermann, and Christopher Meiklejohn 1979. The Skeletal Remains of Mesolithic Man in Western Europe: An Evaluative Catalogue. *Journal of Human Evolution* 8:1–288.

## Violence and Warfare in the European Mesolithic and Paleolithic | **69**

Orschiedt, Jorg 2005. The Head Burials from Ofnet Cave: An Example of Warlike Conflict in the Mesolithic. In *Warfare, Violence, and Slavery in Prehistory: Proceedings of a Prehistoric Society Conference at Sheffield University*, edited by Michael P. Pearson and Ian J. N. Thorpe, pp. 67–73. B.A.R. International Series Volume 1374. Archaeopress, Oxford, United Kingdom.

Papathanasiou, Anastasia 2012. Evidence of Trauma in Neolithic Greece. In *Sticks, Stones and Broken Bones: Neolithic Violence in a European Perspective*, edited by Rick J. Schulting and Linda Fibiger, pp. 249–63. Oxford University Press, Oxford, United Kingdom.

Pinker, Steven 2011. *Angels of Our Better Nature: Why Violence Has Declined*. Viking, New York.

Rogers, Tracy 2004. Recognizing Inter-Personal Violence: A Forensic Perspective. In *Violent Interactions in the Mesolithic*, edited by Mirjana Roksandic, pp. 9–21. B.A.R. International Series Volume 1237. Archaeopress, Oxford, United Kingdom.

Roksandić, Mirjana 2004. Contextualizing the Evidence of Violent Death in the Mesolithic: Burials Associated with Victims of Violence in the Iron Gates Gorge. In *Violent Interactions in the Mesolithic: Evidence and Meaning*, edited by Mirjana Roksandic, pp. 53–74. B.A.R. International Series Volume 1237. Archaeopress, Oxford, United Kingdom.

Roksandić, Mirjana, Marija Djuric, Zoran Rakocevic, and Kimberly Seguin 2006. Interpersonal Violence at Lepenski Vir Mesolithic/Neolithic Complex of the Iron Gates Gorge (Serbia-Romania). *American Journal of Physical Anthropology* 129:339–48.

Skaarup, Jorgen, and Ole Grøn 2004. *Mollegabet II: a Submerged Mesolithic Settlement in Southern Denmark* 1328. B.A.R. International Series, Oxford, United Kingdom.

Smits, Elisabeth 2012. Interpersonal Violence in the Late Mesolithic and Middle Neolithic in the Netherlands. In *Sticks, Stones and Broken Bones: Neolithic Violence in a European Perspective*, edited by Rick J. Schulting and Linda Fibiger, pp. 191–206. Oxford University Press, Oxford, United Kingdom.

Teschler-Nicola, Maria 2006. *Early Modern Humans at the Moravian Gate: The Mladec Caves and their Remains*. Springer, New York.

Trinkaus, Erik, and Alexandra P. Buzhilova 2010. The Death and Burial of Sunghir 1. *International Journal of Osteoarchaeology* 22:655–66.

Trinkaus, Erik, and Jiri Svoboda 2006. *Early Modern Human Evolution in Central Europe: The People of Dolní Věstonice and Pavlov*. Oxford University Press, Oxford, United Kingdom.

Tyson, Rose A. 1977. Historical Accounts as Aids to Physical Anthropology: Examples of Head Injury in Baja California. *Pacific Coast Archaeological Society Quarterly* 13:52–8.

Vencl, Slavomil 1991. Interpretation des Blessures Causees par les Armes au Mesolithique. *L'Anthropologie* 95:219–28.

Verneau, Rene 1906. Les Grottes de Grimaldi. *L'Anthropologie* 17:291–320.

Walker, Philip L. 1989. Cranial Injuries as Evidence of Violence in Prehistoric Southern California. *American Journal of Physical Anthropology* 80:313–23.

——— 2001. A Bioarchaeological Perspective on the History of Violence. *Annual Review of Anthropology* 30:573–96.

Webb, Steve 1995. *Palaeopathology of Aboriginal Australians*. Cambridge University Press, Cambridge, United Kingdom.

Westropp, Hodder 1866. *Prehistoric Phases; or Introductory Essays on Prehistoric Archaeology*. Bel and Daldy, London.

Wu, Xiu-Jie, Lynne A. Schepartz, Wu Liu, and Erik Trinkaus 2011. Antemortem Trauma and Survival in the Late Middle Pleistocene Human Cranium from Maba, South China. *Proceedings of the National Academy of Sciences* 108:19558–62.

# 4

# Wild-Type Colonizers and High Levels of Violence among Paleoamericans

James C. Chatters

The first people who arrived in North America south of the Laurentide and Cordilleran ice sheets entered a land free from competitors of their own species. Their number would have been small (e.g., West 1996). Even within the first few millennia after their arrival, human population densities are likely to have remained well below the land's carrying capacity, even for people lacking the technologies needed to use much of the resource base the continent ultimately offered. Populations were in most cases highly mobile (Chatters 2010a; Wallthal 1999) and, if lithic raw material sources are a good indicator of range (e.g., Jones et al. 2003), apparently lacked a strong sense of territoriality. Given the limited level of competition, anthropological theories of human conflict would lead us to expect little evidence of interpersonal violence (Fry and Söderberg 2013). War is expected to be the result of competition, primarily for resources, and thus to be precipitated by an ecological imbalance between a population and the land's capacity to support it (Keeley 1996; LeBlanc 1999). If there was ever a period without such an imbalance, it would have been during these early millennia of human occupation. Perhaps only then was Rousseau's image of the "noble savage" a reality. In this chapter, I review the archaeological evidence for interpersonal violence among the Paleoamericans, occupants of North America between the earliest identifiable arrivals and approximately 9,000 years (calibrated) before present (cal BP); consider that record in the light of the morphology,

---

*Violence and Warfare among Hunter-Gatherers*, edited by Mark W. Allen and Terry L. Jones, 70–96. ©2014 Taylor & Francis. All rights reserved.

health, and demography of those people; and offer potential explanations for
the pattern that emerges.

## The Archaeological Record

Assessing conflict among highly mobile hunter-gatherers is difficult at
best. The archaeological record consists almost exclusively of lithic and
bone concentrations—campsites, kills, or graves—with no evidence for
constructions of any kind; even evidence for dwellings is extremely rare. Thus
most archaeological indicators of conflict, including defensive works, defensive
forms of house construction, or militaristic art (e.g., Reid, this volume), are
unavailable. Even the defensive positioning of settlements is problematic
because geologic processes are likely to have biased the archaeological record
toward open, lowland settlements and natural stone shelters. Weapons appear
to have been made primarily for hunting; variability in projectile points
forms that might indicate specialization for war is lacking. The only piece of
evidence available for analysis is the skeletons of the people themselves, and
even those are rare.

Remains of no more than 50 individuals have been found that can be
said with confidence to predate 9,000 years cal BP. Of these, many, like
the Arlington Springs man (Johnson et al. 2002), the Marmes skeletons
(Krantz 1979), or many individuals from the Eastern North American Early
Archaic (Wallthal 1999), consist of only a few partial elements or highly
fragmented assemblages of cremated bone. Even many of the more complete
skeletons lack any portions of the axial skeleton, which are some of the most
likely parts to reveal evidence of skeletal trauma due to violence. When the
study is limited to skeletal remains that include at least a neurocranium or
axial skeleton, which are most likely to contain evidence of violence, only 28
individuals—12 males and 16 females—are available for this analysis. Two
males that could be included based on their completeness, Chamalhuacan
from the Valley of Mexico and J. C. Putnam from Texas, have not been
sufficiently documented for inclusion. Table 4.1 lists these 28 individuals,
along with the remaining individuals for which sex, and age or stature, are
available (see Discussion).

Although small, the sample is geographically extensive and culturally
diverse. Individuals are distributed across most of temperate and subtropical
North America, from Prince of Wales Island, Alaska, and southern British
Columbia in the northwest to the Yucatan Peninsula in the southeast and
from the California and Alaskan coasts in the west to Minnesota, Alabama,
and Kentucky in the east. They represent cultures including components
of the Western Stemmed Tradition (e.g. Kennewick, Marmes, Buhl, Spirit
Cave, Wizard Beach, and possibly Arlington Springs) and descendants

**Table 4.1**   Paleoamerican skeletons in this study

| Skeleton | State Found | Sex | Age, Years | Stature, cm | Nutr. | Traumatic Defects | Death | References |
|---|---|---|---|---|---|---|---|---|
| | | | | | FEMALES | | | |
| Horn Shelter II, No 2 | TX | F[a] | 11–13 | — | Unk | — | — | Young et al. 1987; Owsley p.c. 1999 |
| Pelican Rapids | MN | F | 13–15 | — | HL, CO | FR: rib(s) | — | Jenks 1938; direct observation |
| Hoyo Negro | QR | F | 15–16 | 148.6 | Unk. | FR: radius | Misadv: fall | Chatters et al. 2012; updated 2013 |
| La Brea | CA | F | 16–18 | 143.0 | CO | — | — | Kroeber 1962; direct observation |
| Spirit Cave Cremation | NV | F | 17–21 | — | — | — | — | Dansie 1997; direct observation |
| Buhl | ID | F | 17–21 | 157.5 | HL | — | — | Green et al. 1998 |
| Arch Lake | NM | F | 17–20 | 165.5 | — | — | — | Owsley et al. 2010 |
| Marmes I | WA | F | 18–25 | — | — | — | — | Krantz 1979 |
| Wilson-Leonard | TX | F | 18–25 | 158.1 | — | — | — | Steele 1998 |
| Penon III | MX | F | 25 | 150.5 | — | — | — | Jiménez-López et al. 2006 |
| Dust Cave | AL | F | 24–28 | 154.1 | — | — | — | Hogue 1994 |
| Gordon Creek | CO | F | 26–30 | 149.5 | — | — | — | Breternitz et al. 1971 |
| Naharon | QR | F | 20–30 | 141.0 | — | — | — | González González et al. 2006 |
| Ashworth Shelter No 4 | KY | F | 27–30 | 155.4 | Unk | PE: 3rd thoracic | Homicide | DiBlasi 1981 |
| Whitewater Draw | AZ | F | 25–35 | — | — | — | — | Waters 1986 |
| Las Palmas | QR | F | 44–50 | 152.0 | Unk | — | — | González González et al. 2006 |
| | | | | | MALES | | | |
| Grimes Point | NV | M | 16–18 | — | — | PE: rib | Homicide | Owsley and Jantz 2000; direct observation |
| Marmes III | WA | M | Young adult | — | — | FR: skull | — | Krantz 1979 |
| On-Your-Knees Cave | AK | M | 23 | — | — | Too incomplete | Misadv. (bear) | Dixon 1999 |

*(Continued)*

**Table 4.1** *(Continued)*

| Skeleton | State Found | Sex | Age, Years | Stature, cm | Nutr. | Traumatic Defects | Death | References |
|---|---|---|---|---|---|---|---|---|
| Gore Creek | BC | M | 23–39 | 166.5 | — | — | Misadv. (landslide) | Cybulski et al. 1981 |
| Brown's Valley | MN | M | 25–35 | 165.1 | — | — | Infection | Jenks 1937; Barbara O'Connell p.c. 1999 |
| Marmes CH I | WA | M | Mature adult | — | — | Too incomplete | — | Krantz 1979 |
| Tlapacoya I | MX | M | 30–35 | — | — | — | — | González González et al. 2006 |
| Chamalhuacan | MX | M | 33–35 | 172 | — | Not assessed | — | Jiménez-López p.c. 2013 |
| Wizards Beach | NV | M | 32–42 | 171.8 | — | — | Infection | Edgar 1997 |
| Horn Shelter II, no 1 | TX | M | 35–44 | 165.4 | HL | FR: foot, clavicle | — | Young et al. 1987; direct observation |
| Kennewick | WA | M | 35–45 | 173.1 | None | multiple FR, PE | — | Chatters 2000 |
| San Miguel Is. | CA | M | 34–44 | — | — | FR: right ulna | — | Kuzminsky 2013; direct observation |
| J.C. Putnam | TX | M | 40 | 166 | — | (not assessed) | — | Stewart 1945 |
| Hourglass Cave | WY | M | 35–45 | 161.6 | None | — | Misadv. (lost) | Mosch and Watson 1996 |
| Spirit Cave mummy | NV | M | 40–44 | 164.2 | — | FR: skull, metacarpal | Infection | Jantz and Owsley 1997 |
| Stick Man | WA | M | 40–60 | — | — | Skull fracture | — | Chatters et al. 2000 |
| Arlington Springs | CA | M | Adult | 164.2 | — | Too incomplete | — | Johnson et al. 2002; Johnson p.c. 2013 |

**Notes:** QR and MX are Quintana Roo and Mexico states in the Estados Unidos de Mexico (EUM); Nutr indicates nutrition indicators; misadv, misadventure; HL, Harris line; CO, cribra orbitalia; FR, fracture(s); PE, penetrating wound; unk., unknown; p.c., personal communication.
[a]Young et al. tentatively identify this as a male, but Owsley strongly believes it to be female. The only associated grave good was a small, eyed needle, which supports this assertion.

**74** | James C. Chatters

of Clovis (e.g., Brown's Valley, Horn Shelter, Ashworth Shelter, Wilson-Leonard, and Dust Cave), and others for whom no cultural affiliation is known (the Mexican group). The sample is a good window into the lives of the earliest Americans.

This study uses the kind and distribution of skeletal defects in this group of skeletons as clues to the prevalence and nature of violence among Paleoamericans. Defects caused by trauma (either wound or injury) are abundant in these skeletons; at least one such defect has been observed in seven males and three females. I have directly inspected all of the traumas discussed here, with the exception of the projectile wound in the woman from Ashworth Shelter. In this study, I consider defects to be consistent with interpersonal violence if they include projectile or stab wounds, or consist of damage that could have resulted from inflicting, defending, or receiving a blow from a fist or club, or could have resulted from rough handling, as in a person being forcibly gripped or yanked about by the arms or hands. These injuries include depressed cranial fractures, fractures of the nasal bones or other bones of the face, clavicle fractures, parry fractures of the forearm, fractures of the lateral metacarpals, rib fractures (in a limited sense), and projectile wounds (Cybulski 2006; see also Walker 1997). I refer to these as "violent traumas." This is not to be taken as an assertion that violence is the only possible cause for the observed defects, only that it could have been the cause.

It is important to note that although I accept 28 individuals as appropriate for this study because of their degree of completeness and the level of analysis they have received, the number is actually something of an overestimate. Not every individual included in this group has a complete skull and complete axial skeleton. Many crania are incomplete, as are most axial skeletons. Among the males, 10 individuals have at least partial skulls, but the Marmes III and Hourglass Cave have only partial neurocrania; Stick Man and Tlapacoya lack faces. Nasal bones, which might include fractures due to conflict, are absent in all but three. Bones of the axial skeleton are present in only five males. Just six have forearm elements, which could hold evidence of parry fractures. Females tend to be somewhat more complete, but still only 11 of the 16 have at least partial axial skeletons. Forearms are present in 10, but two of these have only one radius. Documented evidence for violent trauma is therefore an underestimate of its true extent in this skeletal population.

## Patterns of Injury in Males

Traumatic defects in male skeletons include both fractures and stab wounds (Table 4.2). Traumas have been documented in the skull, ribs, arm, hand, shoulder, pelvis, and foot (Figure 4.1). Fifteen are observable among the seven individuals. Occurrence of multiple traumas in a single individual is

## Wild-Type Colonizers and High Levels of Violence | 75

**Table 4.2** Traumatic injuries in Paleoamerican males and females

| Skeleton | Age, y | Skeletal Trauma | Fatal? | Reference |
|---|---|---|---|---|
| | | MALES | | |
| Grimes Point Cave | 16–18 | **Two adjacent stab wounds, right 2nd rib** | Yes | Owsley and Jantz 2000; direct observation |
| Horn Shelter II, Burial 1 | 44 | **Healed fractures of left clavicle**; left 5th metacarpal | No | Young et al. 1987; direct observation |
| Kennewick Man | 40–45 | **Healed projectile wound in right ilium, depressed fracture left frontal**, multiple rib fractures, scapula (glenoid) fracture | No | Chatters 2000 |
| Marmes III | Young adult | **Healed depressed fracture, left frontal** | No | Krantz 1979 |
| San Miguel Island | 36–46 | **Healed fracture, right ulna** | No | Kuzminsky 2013; direct observation |
| Spirit Cave Mummy | 40–44 | **Healing depressed fracture, left frontal; healed fracture, right 4th and 3rd(?) metacarpal(s)** | No | Jantz and Owsley 1997; direct observation |
| Stick Man | 40–60 | **Healed depressed fracture, right frontal** | No | Chatters et al. 2000 |
| | | FEMALES | | |
| Ashworth Shelter | Adult | **Projectile point in 3rd thoracic** | Yes | DiBlasi 1981 |
| Hoyo Negro | 15–16 | **Greenstick fracture, left radius** | No | Direct observation |
| Pelican Rapids | 13–15 | **Healed fracture of right rib 8** | No | Direct observation |

**Note:** Bold indicates injuries consistent with interpersonal violence.

not uncommon. Kennewick Man presents a long-healed spear wound in his right ilium, along with multiple rib fractures, and single fractures of the scapula and skull. The man from Spirit Cave had skull and hand fractures. The one from Horn Shelter had a healed fracture of the foot, reported by the original investigators (Young et al. 1987), but in a later study of this skeleton, I found an additional defect in a clavicle that appears to have resulted from trauma. Both clavicles are well preserved. The right clavicle is normal, but the left presents a group of three large openings in the superior mid shaft at a location where foramina do not normally occur (Figure 4.2A). Having the appearance of fistulae (drainage channels), these openings are surrounded by an area of shiny, sclerosed cortical bone and a slight elevation of the bone surface. Apparently, much earlier in life this middle-aged man's clavicle was traumatized—either fractured or severely bruised—by a blow from above.

With the exception of the foot fracture in Horn Shelter skeleton, and the shoulder and rib injuries of Kennewick Man, the traumas to the Paleoamerican

76 | James C. Chatters

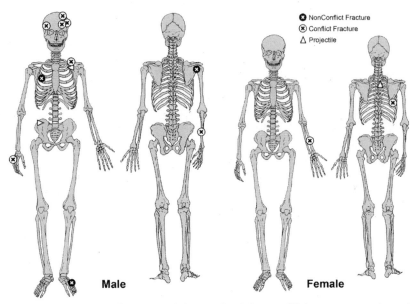

**Figure 4.1** Patterns of traumatic defects in the skeletons of Paleoamerican males and females. Most injuries are consistent with interpersonal violence. On the males, such injuries are entirely on the anterior surface of the body with the exception of the ulnar parry fracture, which would be frontal when the arm was held up in defense. In the females, trauma was more often posterior, as if the women were fleeing an attacker.

male skeletons are consistent with violence. The rib fractures in Kennewick Man are excluded from this group because the aligned fractures of six adjacent ribs constitute a trauma too massive to have been inflicted by another person. A fall from height or a blow from a large prey animal is more likely. Kennewick Man, Marmes III, Stick Man (Figure 4.2D), and Spirit Cave have skull fractures. Three of these are on the frontal and one (Marmes III) on the parietal, near the parietal boss. All are small (less than 10 mm in diameter), shallow (approximately 2 mm), circular depressions of the sort that could be inflicted by a small-headed club. All are to the front or side of the skull and could have been inflicted by a blow from an assailant who was facing the victim. Three are on the left side, one on the right, consistent with the proportion of right- and left-handed people. The clavicle injury to the Horn Shelter male could also have been inflicted by a misdirected blow to the head. Again, the assailant would have been right-handed. The ulna fracture on the San Miguel skeleton is a classic parry fracture (Figure 4.2B), resulting from warding off a blow like those that landed on the other men's skulls. The right metacarpal fracture to the Spirit Cave man could have been caused by a blow from his own fist on another male. It is a classic "boxer's fracture" (Cybulski 2006).

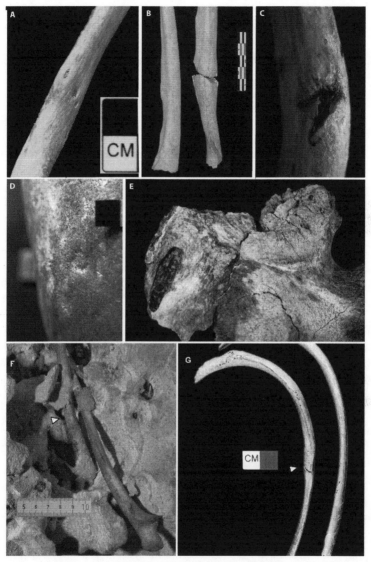

**Figure 4.2** Examples of traumatic defects in Paleoamerican skeletons. Male examples are (A) the healed injury to Horn Shelter II, Burial 2's left clavicle (note the three fistulae); (B) healed parry fracture of the San Miguel skeleton's right ulna (at right); (C) perimortem stab wounds in the left second rib of the Grimes point male; (D) healed, depressed fracture of Stick Man's left frontal; and (E) healed projectile wound in the right ilium of Kennewick Man. Female examples are (F) the healed green stick fracture of the Hoyo Negro girl's left radius and (G) fractured eighth rib of the Pelican Rapids girl. The Hoyo Negro radius is seen with its proximal end out of view at top; the adjacent ulna has the opposite orientation.

**78** | James C. Chatters

Penetrating wounds received by Kennewick Man and the Grimes Point youth were certainly inflicted by other people. The large, leaf-shaped, serrated-edged dart point that healed inside the right ilium of Kennewick man (Figure 4.2E) entered from the front right. Although it is possible the man could have received the wound in a hunting accident, malice is more likely. Malice is certain in the Grimes Point case. Inflicted in the upper surface of the second rib, around mid-body, it includes two side-by-side cuts containing tiny chips of obsidian, penetrating from only slightly different angles (Figure 4.2C). At least one of the cuts shows indications the blade that inflicted it was extracted before the second wound was inflicted. This man was stabbed near the clavicle twice in quick succession with the same blade. The cuts are so close to each other that they are not likely to be from a spear, with which it would be difficult to hit the same spot twice on a living victim. They represent something more akin to a dagger wielded from close quarters by a right-handed assailant who was facing the victim.

The violent traumas in the males are markedly patterned (Figure 4.1). All (in fact all but one of any kind of trauma in the males) are in the upper body, and all but one are on the ventral side of the body. Even the single exception, the parry fracture, would have been received when the ulna was held in front of the body. If we presume that this fracture was received in protecting the head or face, all conflict-consistent fractures resulted from blows directed at the head. This includes even the fracture of Spirit Cave man's fourth metacarpal, which may be from striking a skull or the dense body of someone's mandible. An assailant who stood no more than an arm's length from the victim inflicted most of the violent traumas. This almost certainly includes the Grimes Point youth, who we can envision being wounded in a knife fight. Only the assailant who hurled the dart at Kennewick inflicted his damage at a distance. This pattern indicates that conflict experienced by the males represents hand-to-hand fights, with clubs or fists the usual weapon of choice. In one case, the fight escalated to knives. One can almost hear the music from *West Side Story*.

Another important pattern in the traumas to males is the fact that all but one of the traumas healed. The Grimes Point youth is the only one who died of, or at least at the time of, his injury. None of the head injuries led to death, although the blows that inflicted them are likely to have decided the altercation in favor of the assailant. Kennewick Man even survived the spear wound, which would certainly have left him vulnerable during a lethal attack.

## Patterns of Injury in Females

Females were less frequently injured than the males. Only three skeletal traumas occur, all of them consistent with interpersonal violence. An adult female discovered in Early Archaic levels of Ashworth Shelter, Kentucky, had a spear point embedded in her third thoracic vertebra. The young teenage girl from Pelican Rapids (the "Minnesota Woman") had at least one broken rib, expressed as a thickened callus in the eighth rib, near its angle (Figure 4.2G) approximately beneath the inferior end of the right scapula. The teenaged girl from Hoyo Negro exhibits an odd bowing in the shaft of her left radius that is matched in neither the right radius nor distal left ulna (Figure 4.2F). Although this skeleton has not yet been extracted from its location 140 feet below sea level, photographs show no distinct ridge of callus, indicating this defect probably represents a green bone fracture that had occurred well before her death by age 16. The spear wound is almost certainly evidence of interpersonal conflict. The rib fracture could result from a blow or kick to the back of what was a very gracile child. Too firm a grip and twist on the wrist of a pubescent girl or a grab-and-shake action on the arm of a child is a possible cause for the greenstick fracture in the forearm of the teenager from Hoyo Negro.

In contrast to the males, two of the three violent traumas in the females are in the back of the body, inflicted by force directed from behind. The Ashworth shelter woman was fleeing her assailant. The Pelican Rapids girl was facing away from her attacker, perhaps to minimize injury to the abdomen or face. If the Hoyo Negro girl was assaulted by a right-handed person, that individual could have stood facing her. As with the males, however, the Paleoamerican females also rarely received fatal injuries. Only the projectile wound to the Ashworth shelter woman occurred at the time of her death.

## Evidence of Frequent Conflict

To summarize the evidence, skeletal trauma consistent with interpersonal conflict is present in 10 (38 percent) of the 28 Paleoamerican skeletons complete enough to exhibit it. Most of that trauma was experienced by males (58 percent). Only three (18 percent) of the females were similarly injured. When we take into account the potential for observing types of trauma, based on the presence of appropriate skeletal elements, this image of frequent trauma is emphasized, particularly for the males. Skull fractures occur in 4 of 10 male skulls; penetrating wounds occur in two of five axial skeletons. When male and female axial skeletons are considered together, 3 (18 percent) of 16 have penetrating wounds.

These are particularly high frequencies for prehistoric North America, especially when we look at the records that cover similarly long time spans (Table 4.3). Investigators report that during the Middle and Late Archaic of the American Midwest and the entire Archaic of the Great Plains, evidence for interpersonal violence was "rare" (Myster and O'Connell 1997; Owsley and Bruwelheide 1997; Scheiber and Gill 1996). For Tennessee

**80** | James C. Chatters

**Table 4.3** Frequency of evidence for interpersonal violence in skeletal populations of North America

| Region | Period | Violent Trauma, % | Reference |
|---|---|---|---|
| American Midwest | Mid-Late Archaic | Rare | Myster and O'Connell 1997 |
| Tennessee | Mid-Late Archaic | 2.3 | Smith 1997 |
| North and central Plains | Archaic | Rare | Owsley and Rose 1997; Scheiber and Gill 1996 |
| Northwest Coast | 5,450–1,450 years BP | 21 | Cybulski 1994 |
| Central California coast | 3,450–570 years BP | 25 | Lambert 2002 |
| Wyoming | Nineteenth century | 82 (mostly males) | Gill 1994; Scheiber and Gill 1996 |
| North America | 9,000 years BP | 38 (58% males) | This chapter |

alone, Smith (1997) gives a value to "rare," placing the frequency of violent trauma at 2.3 percent. This is a considerable decline from nearly 40 percent for the Paleoamericans. Even if the Midwestern and Plains assessments counted only projectile wounds, the groups differ by a factor of 10. Higher levels of violent trauma are documented by Lambert (2002) for the central California coast and by Cybulski (1994) for the Northwest Coast; both consider a comparable range of traumas to those discussed here, but these levels are only 25 percent and 21 percent, respectively. These western examples are similar to the Paleoamericans in that most of the trauma in the centuries before the introduction of the bow and arrow was nonlethal, appearing primarily as healed, depressed skull fractures and parry fractures of the forearms.

The one American case shown in Table 4.3 that exceeds the level of violent trauma seen in the Paleoamericans is that of the nineteenth-century pioneers of Wyoming. In that population, Gill (1994; Scheiber and Gill 1996) observed violent trauma, including gunshot and stab wounds, in more than 80 percent of all skeletons and more than 90 percent of the males. I return to this group in the Discussion section of this chapter, as it is particularly germane to understanding why violent trauma is so common among the Paleoamericans.

## Discussion

Violent trauma is more common in the Paleoamericans than in any later North American hunter-gather group for which figures are available. The levels of violent trauma are nearly twice as high as those seen in any later group. Two key questions about this pattern beg to be answered: What was the nature of the conflict? Why were the Paleoamericans so violent? I address each in turn.

## Nature of the Conflict

The violence inflicted on the Paleoamericans is primarily frontal, primarily inflicted at close quarters, and primarily nonlethal. It would appear that the intent of the conflict was rarely, if ever, to kill the victim. If that were the case, Kennewick Man with his dart wound, or Kennewick, Stick Man, Spirit Cave, and Marmes III with their skull fractures are likely to have been dispatched while debilitated or unconscious. Comparison with a skeletal population in which violent trauma almost always ended in fatality is instructive.

The Columbia Plateau is not an area known for conflict (see references in Reid, this volume), but over the past 30 years, 21 victims of single and mass killings have been recovered from both cemeteries and isolated graves dating to the last 2,000 years of prehistory (Chatters 1989, 2003, 2004). Except for the fact that most violent trauma is seen in males (77 percent of the Plateau group), the distribution of violent trauma in these skeletons is markedly different from that seen in the Paleoamericans (Figure 4.3). Whereas the Paleoamerican injuries were sustained about the head or in targeting or defending the head, wounds in the Plateau group are concentrated on the torso. All but six are in the chest and upper arms. In

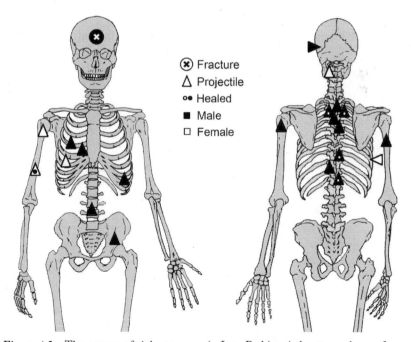

**Figure 4.3** The pattern of violent trauma in Late Prehistoric hunter-gatherers from the Columbia Plateau. Example of violence with lethal intent (Based on Chatters [1989, 2003]).

# 82 | James C. Chatters

the Paleoamericans, 77 percent of violent trauma is to the front of the body, and perimortem wounds are equally distributed front and back. All violent traumas to the males, including projectile wounds, were effectively frontal. Only one of the female wounds was frontal; the sole projectile wound was to the back. In the Plateau example, wounds to females (five of the total) were almost equally distributed front and back, with three anterior and two posterior. Male wounds (17) were predominantly posterior (64 percent). Most wounds (77 percent) were received in lethal encounters. One anterior arrow wound, four posterior arrow wounds, and the skull fracture were the only nonlethal traumas.

Violence among the Paleoamericans was pervasive, but typically nonlethal. When the intent of the conflict was to kill, as it was in the Plateau example, the assailant aimed for the heart and lungs and usually, especially with male victims, attacked his victim from behind or shot at a fleeing adversary. Paleoamerican violence, which so strongly differs in its skeletal manifestation from the pattern formed by lethal intent, clearly had a different cause or purpose. It consisted of two forms: frontal attacks on males who stood and fought, and attacks on the backs of fleeing females. Rarely, as in the case of the Grimes Point youth and the Ashworth Shelter woman, did that conflict escalate and lead to a death. This is not the pattern expected either of warfare or of retributive feud, as I have previously labeled the Plateau pattern (Chatters 1989). The pattern of injury in the males is more in line with a contest for dominance. The pattern of healed head wounds, which is similar to what Lambert reports among the prehistoric Chumash, and what Cybulski reports for the Northwest Coast, may represent a sort of ritualized combat like that recorded for the Yanomami (Chagnon 1968); however, the clavicle injury and parry fracture indicate a somewhat higher level of intensity than expected from men alternately directing blows to each other's heads.

The injuries to the females serve to clarify the meaning of male violence. Inflicted on a fleeing woman and two girls who could barely have been pubescent at the time of their injuries (if they were even that), the female injuries, assuming they are due to violent encounters, fit more comfortably in the category of abuse. Greenstick fracture consistent with gripping too hard or twisting a child or young girl's forearm, a kick or fist blow to a fleeing girl who is unlikely to have been over 14 at the time, and the killing of a fleeing woman with a spear or atlatl dart all point to abusive males.

To review, violence was pervasive but usually nonlethal, even when the victim would have been vulnerable to being killed after a blow or projectile rendered him helpless. The absence of lethality indicates the conflict was usually between members of the same social group, not between competing groups.[1] Overall, the pattern of face-to-face violence between males and abuse of females portrays Paleoamerican males as unusually violent, fighting their fellows probably for dominance or for access to females.

## Wild-Type Colonizers and High Levels of Violence | **83**

# Reasons for the High Level of Violence

To understand the high level of violence enacted by Paleoamerican males, it is necessary to first understand the Paleoamerican population structure, physical condition, manner of death, and physical characteristics of the members of this group. The differences between males and females are of particular importance. Table 4.1 includes data on four important variables for females and males: age at death, stature, indicators of nutritional stress, and manner of death. Data are based primarily on work of the original investigators of each find, although in some cases my own observations are included. Age at death is reported as a range, and mean ages at death are computed as mean age minima and maxima. Stature is computed in all cases using Genovés (1967) to make the estimates comparable, so the value seen here may differ from that reported in the cited authority. Manner of death is as reported or based on condition and context of the remains if no manner has been reported. These latter cases are discussed individually.

## Mortality Profiles

Paleoamerican males lived much longer than their female counterparts. Mean ages at death range from 27.5 to 34 years for males, but only 20.7 to 25.2 years for females. The female means are strongly skewed by the Las Palmas woman from Yucatan, whose actual radiocarbon age is in question because investigators have failed to report its source.[2] In addition, her age at death of 44 to 50 years is based strictly on dental attrition, a less than wholly reliable basis because of its environmental and cultural relativity. Without the Las Palmas woman, the age at death for the Paleoamerican females averages only 19.1 to 23.5 years. The longevity gap between the sexes is even more evident when the mortality profile is considered (Figure 4.4). A total of 66 percent of females, but only 19 percent of males, died before age 26. In stark contrast, 50 percent of the males, but only 6 percent of females (if Las Palmas is included), lived beyond 35 years. Breaking down the categories shown in Figure 4.4 and considering individual estimates, 11 of 16 males and only 2 of 16 females lived past the age of 30. This marked disparity indicates not only that reproductive-age females would have been in short supply for the long-lived males, but also that population recruitment would have been particularly low (Chatters 2010a).

The stark difference in longevity is probably due in part to the impact of childbearing exacerbated by the stresses placed on women's physiology by constant mobility and an uncertain food supply (see nutritional stress later in this chapter). A woman nursing a small child while on the move would rapidly deplete her fat reserves and increase her vulnerability to infection. Postmenarchal girls and early postpartum women would have an increased

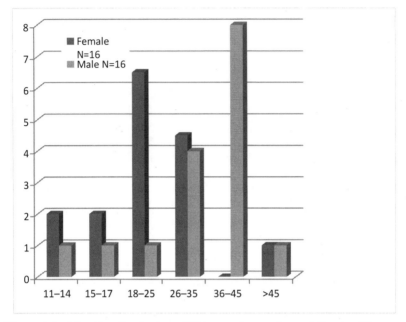

**Figure 4.4** Mortality distribution of Paleoamerican males and females. If an age distribution from Table 4.1 intersects more than one range, it is placed according to the median of its distribution. Nahjaron, estimated at 20 to 30 years old, is split between the 18- to 25-year and 26- to 35-year ranges. Individuals categorized as "young adult" are placed in the 18- to 25-year range; middle adult, the 26- to 35-year range.

risk of urogenital infection under conditions of variable hygiene and constant movement.

## Manner of Death

Manner of death can be assessed for seven males and two females. Misadventure, homicide, and infection are identified. One male and one female—the youth from Grimes Point and the Ashworth Shelter woman—died of penetrating wounds; they were homicides. Three men are likely to have died of systemic infections most likely related to dental abscess. In the cases of Brown's Valley and Wizard Beach, infection was severe enough to elicit periosteal reaction in long bones. Four individuals, three males and one adolescent female, died through misadventure. The Hoyo Negro girl, who was walking about in a dark cave, fell more than 30 meters into a deep underground chamber (Chatters et al. 2012). The man from On-Your-Knees Cave was killed (or at least eaten) by a bear. The Gore Creek man died in a landslide. The man found in Hourglass Cave appears to have become lost in the darkness of what became his underground tomb.

Altogether, six of nine individuals for which manner of death can be assessed died of homicide or misadventure. These were, in fact, the primary causes of death for young men, accounting for the only three under 30 years old for whom manner can be discerned. This frequency of death by misadventure indicates either a very hazardous environment or a strong tendency for risk taking, particularly, but not exclusively, among the young. Kennewick Man, although he did not die of his many injuries, came close to death at least twice from the spear wound and multiple rib fractures, indicating he too was inclined to take risks.

## Nutritional Stress

Part of the difference in size and longevity between males and females could be due to differences in access to food, particularly protein. Evidence of nutritional stress is more often recorded for females than males, although the record is far from clear. Indications of nutritional stress considered in this analysis are Harris lines (growth interruptions in long bone diaphyses) and cribra orbitalia (a spongy appearance to the upper inner surface of the eye socket). Where nutritional stress is not mentioned in a source, it is often unclear whether radiographs have not been taken at all, or taken, reviewed, and—found to be negative—left unreported. Some reports, such as Mosch and Watson's (1996) brief paper on Hourglass Cave, state that no signs of poor nutrition were evident, but do not report how that conclusion was reached. What can be said is that we have information on nutrition on three males (Kennewick, Hourglass Cave, Horn Shelter) and three females (Buhl, Pelican Rapids, La Brea). Two of the females exhibited cribra orbitalia and two presented Harris lines in radiographs of their long bones. In the Buhl case, at least 15 lines were visible in the distal femur. Among the males, only Horn Shelter exhibits Harris lines, although radiography of additional skeletons might increase the frequency of stress indicators in members of this sex.

## Stature

Males not only lived longer than females, but also grew to be much larger. Stature can be computed for 10 males and 11 females. Using only the modal values for stature, males ranged from 161.1 to 173.1 cm in height (5'4" to 5'8") with a mean of 167.0 cm (5'6"). Females ranged from 141.0 to 165.5 cm (4'8" to 5'5"), with a mean of only 152.3 cm (5'0"). This disparity computes to a sexual dimorphism index (mean male value/mean female value) of 1.10. The Middle Archaic hunter-gatherer population at Indian Knoll (351 individuals) had a sexual dimorphism index of 1.05 (based on data in Snow 1948); based on reconstructed statures, recent Native American populations are typically around 1.06 to 1.08 (Auerbach and Ruff 2010). Modern populations worldwide

**86** | James C. Chatters

typically have sexual dimorphism indices of around 1.2 to 1.3 (Steele 1998). Paleoamericans were strongly sexually dimorphic.

## Robusticity and Cranial Morphology

Sexual dimorphism is also expressed in skeletal robusticity as well as in cranial size and rugosity. Metric attributes of long bones are too few for an adequate comparison within or between sexes, but analysts frequently describe female skeletons as gracile (e.g., Breternitz et al. 1971; Chatters 2010a; Chatters et al. 2012; Steele 1998) and the males as robust (Chatters 2000; Jiménez-López, personal communication 2013) or at least well-muscled (Young et al. 1987). Some males, though, are described as slender (Cybulski et al. 1981) or gracile (Kuzminsky 2013).

Dimorphism is prominently displayed in Paleoamerican crania. In general terms, when compared with later Native Americans, Paleoamericans exhibit larger skulls that are proportionately long, narrow, and low vaulted, with lower, narrower faces, lower orbits, broader interorbital space, and marked facial forwardness and/or moderate alveolar prognathism (e.g., Chatters 2000; González-José et al. 2005; Jantz and Owsley 1997; Steele and Powell 2002). Palates tend to be broad and parabolic, and the teeth are large. In proportion to females, male skulls are robust and often distinctly rugose, as befits their large size (Lahr and Wright 1996). Many, most notably Horn Shelter No. II, Brown's Valley, and Chamalhuacan, exhibit prominent supraorbital ridges, depressed nasal roots, prominent nuchal crests and occipital lines, and large mastoid processes marked by crests and angular tori. Zygomatic trigones and tuberosities are not unusual. They were, in today's parlance, "manly" men: hypermasculine. The females, in contrast, despite their large size, have weakly developed mastoids and nuchal lines, sharply bordered upper orbital rims, and virtually nonexistent glabellar eminences. Many, such as those from Wilson-Leonard, Pelican Rapids, and Hoyo Negro, have high, rounded foreheads. All have either moderate alveolar prognathism or strongly forward-positioned upper faces. In no Paleoamerican case is sex of the individual in doubt when the skull is recovered. This marked dimorphism is well illustrated in Figure 4.5, which displays two approximately coeval individuals from central Texas.

## The Paleoamerican Pattern

Paleoamerican males were strongly sexually dimorphic, with large, robust males and small, gracile females. In cranial development, males were prominently masculine, females just as prominently feminine; they occupied the extremes. The males were violent, often extremely so. They directed their aggression not

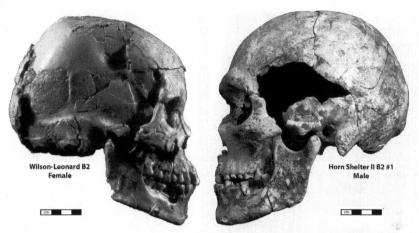

**Figure 4.5** Sexual dimorphism in Paleoamerican female and male skulls is well illustrated by the Wilson Leonard adult female and Horn Shelter adult male. Both date from approximately 10,000 years BP and come from central Texas, making them candidates for members of the same breeding population. Note the massive supraorbital ridge, depressed nasal root, large, rugose mastoids, and distinct occipital line in the male and complete lack of rugosity in the female.

only at other males, whom they faced in hand-to hand combats that occasionally turned lethal, but also toward weaker members of their communities. Intermale fights may have been for dominance or access to females. Females dying at an early age put mate access at a premium for the longer-lived males, lending credence to such an explanation. Males appear to have been better fed than the females (although the evidence is limited), which could indicate that males had preferential access to food because their contribution to the community was considered more critical to its survival. These people were also risk-takers, males more so than females.

In sum, Paleoamerican males were highly valued risk-takers who were prone to aggression and violence. If the stronger males were more successful at mating, these characteristics of temperament were being selected for under the cultural milieu of late Pleistocene and Early Holocene North America.

## The Human Wild Type

The Paleoamerican pattern of sexual dimorphism and robust, aggressive males is not unique. It is repeated across the northern hemisphere during the human diaspora. In her survey of late Pleistocene *Homo sapiens*, Lahr (1996) observed that the earliest members of our species in Europe, Asia, and Australia shared

**88** | James C. Chatters

a common morphology that is reflected in the Paleoamericans. She describes European skeletons of the late Aurignacian and the Gravettian as having large, long, low vaults with acute occipital angles and short, broad, forward-positioned upper faces with prominent supraorbital ridges; low, widely spaced orbits; a depressed nasal root; pinched nasal bones; and wide palates with large teeth. Females reflect these characteristics, but are more gracile. East Asian and southeast Asian skeletal material, although extremely rare (approximately 13 individuals), is similar with robust, long, low crania with marked occipital angles; short, wide, moderately prognathic faces; depressed nasal roots; prominent supraorbital tori; and low, square orbits (Brown 1999). When these early skulls of both regions are compared morphometrically with other ancient and modern populations, males most often group with Australoids or Polynesians, and females with modern European males (Howells 1995), as do many of the Paleoamericans. Lahr (1996) links all of these groups as manifestations of an early, generalized form of *Homo sapiens* that expanded outside of Africa.

Early Upper Paleolithic European *Homo sapiens* shared other characteristics with the Paleoamericans. Skeletal populations exhibit the same marked degree of sexual dimorphism in stature (Formicola and Giannecchini 1999). In the period before 15,000 years BP, males averaged an estimated 175 cm tall and 76 kg in weight, while the females averaged 164 cm and 68 kg, for dimorphism ratios of 1.08 for stature and 1.25 for mass (Holt and Formicola 2008). Cranial morphology of the sexes also often diverged strongly, as best expressed in populations from Combe Capelle and Brno (Lahr 1996). A recent study of hand stencils in Upper Paleolithic European cave paintings echoes this difference, demonstrating that the hands of males and females diverged in the ratios of digit lengths much more than the hands of modern Europeans (Snow 2013). Among these early Upper Paleolithic people, there was also a high level of interpersonal violence, as seen particularly among the Czech skeletal populations (Keeley 1996). Cranial injuries are common.

The skeletal assemblage from eastern Asia consists primarily of the three crania (two female, one male) from Upper Cave Zhoukoudian, up to nine highly fragmented individuals (two males, up to seven females), and the Liujiang specimen (Brown 1999; Suzuki 1982). The Upper Cave 101 skull from Zhoukoudian and the one nearly complete male skull from Minatogawa are much larger and more robust than their associated, apparently female, counterparts (see Suzuki 1982: Tables 2.2, 2.3). Mean statures for the Minatagawa skeletons are 155 cm for the males and 144 cm for females, for a sexual dimorphism index of 1.08. The American Museum of Natural History cast of Upper Cave 101, a second-generation reproduction, shows a small, shallow, rounded depression near the left temporal line where it crosses the coronal suture. It is sharp edged, and cracks extend from it along the coronal suture line. Although this is likely the mark of hasty excavation (a pick perhaps), its similarity in size and location might identify it as the sort of depressed skull fracture seen in the Paleoamericans, although this one would have been fatal.

The earliest modern *Homo sapiens* we encounter in Europe, eastern Asia, and the Americas share robust cranial morphology, pronounced sexual dimorphism, and a propensity for violent behavior. This may be thought of, in terms common in the biology of other species, as the human "wild type." The behavioral characteristics indicated by skeletal injuries are reminiscent of those reported for chimpanzee males. Wrangham and Peterson (1996) document violence within the community for hierarchical dominance and coercion of females among chimpanzees in their native habitat. The human wild type's manifestation is time transgressive; it occurs first in western Eurasia, later in eastern Eurasia, and finally in the Americas. Redevelopments of human forms similar to this wild type can be seen later in the robust, large-headed, aggressive populations of Polynesia. The Wyoming male pioneers who exhibit such a high frequency of violent trauma are described by Gill (1994:119) as "a select and unique group. Skeletal size appears to be above average and male robustness . . . was well developed. Cranial sizes are large and the skulls and faces long." In his final words, Gill alludes to an explanation for this wild-type human. It could, he suggests, be explained by selective migration into and/or differential survival in a new land.

The populations of wild-type humans all lived as mobile hunter-gatherers whose ancestors had recently expanded their species' range into new territory. At the time of their existence or that of their progenitors (in the case of most Paleoamericans), these populations faced large, dangerous prey and large, even more dangerous predators on a regular basis. They competed for scarce females and perhaps group dominance through physical contests. In this context the robust, aggressive males had selective advantage. In this context, too, before plant foods and the technology to effectively exploit them were known, males would have been valued over females as the primary food providers.

Testosterone was probably a primary determinant of the hypermasculine cranial characteristics of the wild-type males (e.g., Walker 1995), but genes that regulate psychotropic compounds are also implicated in the men's behavior. Humans are polymorphic for two genes that regulate serotonin and dopamine: monoamine oxidase A (MAOA) and dopamine regulator D4 (DRD4). Each is characterized by base pair repeats that associate with variations in behavior. The 7-repeat version of DRD4 (DRD4-7R) is associated with novelty seeking, hyperactivity, and aggression. The low-repeat versions of MAOA (MAOA-L, the so-called "warrior gene") cause carriers to be more willing to take risks while enabling them to better assess the chances of success from risky behavior (Frydman et al. 2010). They are also, however, predisposed to aggression and

**90** | James C. Chatters

violence, particularly when provoked (McDermott et al. 2009). There is also a strong synergistic effect between MAOA-L and testosterone on the propensity for aggression and violence (Sjoberg et al. 2008). Linkage-segment length analysis indicates DRD4-7R underwent rapid positive selection around 40,000 years ago, as humans were beginning their expansion out of Africa and possibly entered the human genome through early interbreeding with Neanderthals (Ding et al. 2002). MOAA-L also appears to have had selective advantage in the last 10,000 to 40,000 years. It is most common in South America and Polynesia (Cochran and Harpending 2009). The genetically compelled desire for novelty and the willingness to take well-reasoned risks would have been strongly advantageous, if not necessary, for humans colonizing new lands, and was probably common in the wild-type populations of early Eurasia and America. Males with these characteristics—risky, aggressive, violent—along with high testosterone likely had a high success rate in contests for dominance and female attention.

The disappearance of the human wild type is also time transgressive. During the Magdalenian and Mesolithic, Europeans became more gracile. Skulls became higher, shorter, and rounder; projecting faces receded and were tucked under the cranium; palates and teeth became smaller. People became shorter, less robust, and less sexually dimorphic. This pattern is repeated in every other continent except Australia (Lahr 1996; Lahr and Wright 1996). In eastern Asia, the pattern, which is represented in the "Mongoloid" morphology, included longer faces than seen in Europe, but changes were more profound, including proportionate shortening of the limbs. In the Americas, the Paleoamerican morphology was almost universally replaced by the mongoloid-like Amerindian form.[3] In all cases, the change entails feminization of the males through the process of neotenization (Lahr 1996; see Gould 1977).

The changes seen in *Homo sapiens* during the latest Pleistocene and early Holocene closely mirror the differences between the wild-type and domestic forms of other mammalian species. The process by which these changes occur has been well illustrated by the work of Baleev on Siberian silver foxes (Trut 1999). After only a few dozen generations, selecting strictly for docility, Baleev's team achieved not only tame foxes, but also saw profound changes in physical characteristics. Skulls became shorter and narrower, muzzles shorter and wider. Male skulls became "feminized." Cranial volumes between the sexes remained different, but in other respects the male skulls became more female-like. Surprisingly, their pelage also began to change, appearing in new colors and patterns, and developing wavy and even curly forms. Changes that occur in humans during their Mesolithic/Archaic phases of cultural development might be explained just as simply.

Violence declined in America when the populations became less mobile and occupied more static, predictable environments. By 9,000 years ago they had obtained technologies, particularly hot rock cooking (Thoms 2003), that reduced the dependence on hunting and enhanced the status and longevity of females. At this same time, we tend to see the appearance or development of more gracile males in populations who much more closely resemble modern Native Americans (Chatters 2010b). This is when violent skeletal trauma declines markedly, largely disappearing in eastern North America and dropping by more than half in the west. I suspect that, like Baleev, Archaic American females were selecting against the hyper-male, aggressive mates, who no longer promoted community welfare.

## Conclusion

The sample of Paleoamerican skeletons is small and incomplete, but the evidence for interpersonal violence in that sample is ubiquitous and extensive. The pattern it presents is almost exclusively one of nonlethal fights between males within their own community and abuse of women and children by those same males. This pattern of violence is associated with a high level of sexual dimorphism and a marked robusticity in the crania of males. In a population in which males long outlived females, it is likely that much of the violence entailed competition for mates, but spillover of aggression onto weaker members of the social group indicates that the males' aggressiveness was in part biochemically determined. During the human disapora, novelty seeking and risk taking, which are both genetically influenced, drove the expansion and would have been strongly selected for. This combination of robusticity, sexual dimorphism, and violence is repeated in early *Homo sapiens* populations across the northern hemisphere and may be characterized as the *Homo sapiens* wild type. When risk taking, novelty seeking, and aggression ceased to be advantageous to the population, I suspect that females, particularly those who were abused, selected for docility. They domesticated the men.

## Acknowledgments

The ideas about the human wild type and domestication of males grew out of a 2008 brainstorming session with the late Phil Walker, although he preferred to call it the "female revolution." Access to skeletons was courtesy of the Paige Museum (La Brea), Barbara O'Connell and Susan Myster (Browns Valley and Pelican Rapids), Al Redder (Horn Shelter), The Nevada State Museum (Wizard Beach, Spirit Cave, and the Grimes Point skeleton), Phil Walker (San Miguel), Central Washington University (Stick Man), and the Texas Archaeological Research Laboratory (Wilson Leonard). Edward Mallon assisted with preparation of Figures 4.1 and 4.3.

# 92 | James C. Chatters

## Notes

1. The spear wound in Kennewick Man's pelvis could be an exception. It is of the Olcott variety of Cascade Point, which was in widespread use across the Cascade Mountain Range from where Kennewick Man met his death, at the time of his death, but does not appear on the east side of that range until several hundred years later.
2. This skeleton comes from a submerged cave in a tropical environment. In that context, bone protein is readily decomposed. Because dating of bone proteins is unlikely and the research does not report the dated medium, the age remains in question.
3. The Yaghan and related peoples of southern Patagonia were an exception, retaining the large, rugged skull of Paleoamericans (Lahr 1995). These were extremely violent people and occupied one of the regions that still has a high frequency of MAOA-L.

## References

Auerbach, Benjamin M., and Christopher B. Ruff 2010. Stature Estimation Formulae for Indigenous Native American Populations. *American Journal of Physical Anthropology* 141:190–207.

Brown, Peter 1999. The First Modern East Asians? Another Look at Upper Cave 101, Liujiang and Minatogawa 1. In *Interdisciplinary Perspectives on the Origins of the Japanese*, edited by K. Omoto, pp. 105–30. International Research Center for Japanese Studies, Kyoto, Japan.

Breternitz, David. A., Alan C. Swedlund, and David C. Anderson 1971. An Early Burial from Gordon Creek, Colorado. *American Antiquity* 36:170–82.

Chagnon, Napoleon A. 1968. Yanomamö Social Organization and Warfare. In *War: The Anthropology of Armed Conflict and Aggression*, edited by Morton Fried, pp. 109–59. Natural History Press, Garden City, NJ.

Chatters, James C. 1989. Pacifism and the Organization of Conflict on the Plateau of Northwestern America. In *Cultures in Conflict: Current Archaeological Perspectives*, edited by Diana C. Tkaczuk and Brian C. Vivian, pp. 241–52. University of Calgary Press, Alberta.

—— 2000. Recovery and First Analysis of an Early Holocene Human Skeleton from Kennewick, Washington. *American Antiquity* 65:291–316.

—— 2003. Osteoarchaeology and Mortuary Practices of the Sinkaietk. Report to Douglas County PUD, by Applied Paleoscience, Bothell, WA.

—— 2004. Safety in Numbers: Influence of the Bow and Arrow on the Development of Villages in the Southern Plateau. In *Evolution of Social Complexity in the Plateau of Northwest America*, edited by Willam C. Prentiss and Ian Kiujt, pp. 67–83. University of Utah Press, Salt Lake City.

—— 2010a. Patterns of Death and the Peopling of the Americas. In *Symposio International III: El Hombre Temprano en America,* edited by J. C. Jiménez López, C. S. Sánchez, A. González González, and F. J. Aguilar Arellano, pp. 53–74. Instituto National de Antropología y Historia, Mexico City.

—— 2010b. Peopling of the Americas via Multiple Migrations from Beringia: Evidence from the Early Holocene of the Columbia Plateau. In *Human Variation in the Americas*, edited by Benjamin Auerbach, pp. 51–76. Southern Illinois University Press, Carbondale.

Chatters, James C., Steven A. Hackenberger, Alan J. Busacca, Linda S. Cummings, Richard A. Jantz, Thomas W. Stafford, and Royal E. Taylor 2000. A Possible Second Early Holocene Skull from Central Washington. *Current Research in the Pleistocene* 17:93–4.

Chatters, James C., Dominique Rizzolo, Pilar Luna-Erreguerena, and Alberto Nava-Blank 2012. A Potential Late Pleistocene Human Skeleton in Hoyo Negro, a Submerged Cave Site in Quintana Roo, Mexico. *American Journal of Physical Anthropology* 54(Supplement):114.

Wild-Type Colonizers and High Levels of Violence | **93**

Cochran, Gregory, and Henry Harpending 2009. *The 10,000 Year Explosion: How Civilization Accelerated Human Evolution.* Basic Books, New York.

Cybulski, Jerome S. 1994. Culture Change, Demographic History, and Health and Disease on the Northwest Coast. In *In the Wake of Contact: Biological Responses to Conquest,* edited by C. Seth Larsen and George R. Milner, pp. 75–85. Willey-Liss, New York.

——— 2006. Skeletal Biology: Northwest Coast and Plateau. In *Environment, Origins, and Population,* edited by David H. Ubelaker, pp. 532–47. Handbook of North American Indians, Vol. 3, William C. Sturtevant, general editor. Smithsonian Institution, Washington, D.C.

Cybulski, Jerome S., Donald E. Howes, James A. Haggarty, and Morley Eldridge 1981. An Early Human Skeleton from South-Central British Columbia: Dating and Bioarchaeological Inference. *Canadian Journal of Archaeology* 5:49–59.

Dansie, Amy 1997. Early Holocene Burials in Nevada: Overview of Localities, Research, and Legal Issues. *Nevada Historical Society Quarterly* 40:1–14.

DiBlasi, Philip J. 1981. A New Assessment of the Archaeological Significance of the Ashworth Site (11BU236): A Study of the Dynamics of Archaeological Investigations in Cultural Resource Management. Unpublished Master's thesis, Department of Anthropology, University of Louisville, Kentucky.

Ding, Yuan-Chen, Han-Chang Chi, Deborah L. Grady, Atsuyuki Morishimi, Judith K. Kidd, Kenneth K. Kidd, Pamela Flodman, M. Anne Spence, Sabrina Schuck, James M. Swanson, Ya-Ping Zhang, and Robert Moyzis 2002. Evidence of Positive Selection Acting at the Human Dopamine Receptor D4 Gene. *Proceedings of the National Academy of Sciences* 99:309–14.

Dixon, E. James 1999. *Bones Boats and Bison.* University of New Mexico Press, Albuquerque.

Edgar, Heather J. H. 1997. Paleopathology of the Wizards Beach Man and Spirit Cave Mummy. *Nevada Historical Society Quarterly* 40:57–61.

Formicola, Vincenzo, and Monica Giannecchini 1999. Evolutionary Trends of Stature in Upper Paleolithic and Mesolithic Europe. *Journal of Human Evolution* 36:319–33.

Fry, Douglas P., and Patrik Söderberg 2013. Lethal Aggression in Mobile Forager Bands and Implications for the Origins of War. *Science* 341:270–73.

Frydman, Cary, Colin Camerer, Peter Bossearts, and Antonio Rangel 2010. MAOA-L Carriers Are Better at Making Optimal Financial Decisions under Risk. *Proceedings of the Royal Society B* 278:2053–9.

Genovés, Santiago 1967. Proportionality of the Long Bones and Their Relation to Stature among Native Americans. *American Journal of Physical Anthropology* 26:67–77.

Gill, George W. 1994. Skeletal Injuries of Pioneers. In *Skeletal Biology of the Great Plains: Migration, Warfare, Health, and Subsistence,* edited by Douglas W. Owsley and Richard L. Jantz, pp. 159–72. Smithsonian Institution Press, Washington, D.C.

González González, Arturo C., Carmen Rojas Sandoval, Alejandro Terrazas Mata, Marta Benivente Sanvicente, and Wolfgang Stinnesbeck 2006. Poblamiento Temprano en la Península de Yucatán: Evidencias Localizadas en Cuevas Sumergidas de Quintana Roo, Mexico. In *2° Simposio Internacional El Hombre Temprano en América,* edited by José C. Jimenéz Lopez, Oscar K. Polaco, Gloria Martínez Sosa, and Rocío Hernández Flores, pp. 73–90. INAH, Mexico City.

González-José, Renaldo, Walter Neves, Marta Mirazón Lahr, Silvia González, Hector Pucciarelli, Miquel Hernández Martínez, and Gonzalo Correal 2005. Late Pleistocene-Holocene Cranial Morphology in Mesoamerican Paleoindians: Implications for the Peopling of the New World. *American Journal of Physical Anthropology* 128:772–80.

Gould, Steven J. 1977. *Ontogeny and Phylogeny.* Belknap Press, Cambridge, United Kingdom.

Green, Thomas J., Bruce Cochran, Todd W. Fenton, James C. Woods, Gene L. Titmus, Larry Tieszen, Mary Anne Davis, and Suzanne J. Miller 1998 The Buhl Burial: A Paleoindian Woman from Southern Idaho. *American Antiquity* 63:4378–456.

Hogue, S. Homes 1994. Human Skeletal Remains from Dust Cave. *Journal of Alabama Archaeology* 40:173–91.

## 94 | James C. Chatters

Holt, Brittite M., and Vincenzo Formicola 2008. Hunters of the Ice Age: The Biology of Upper Paleolithic People. *Yearbook of Physical Anthropology* 47:70–99.

Howells, W. W. 1995. *Who's Who in Skulls: Ethnic Identification of Crania from Measurements.* Papers of the Peabody Museum of Archaeology and Ethnology, Harvard University, Vol. 82.

Jantz, Richard L., and Douglas W. Owsley 1997. Pathology, Taphonomy, and Cranial Morphometrics of the Spirit Cave Mummy. *Nevada Historical Society Quarterly* 40:62–84.

Jenks, Albert E. 1937. *Minnesota's Browns Valley Man and Associated Burial Artifacts.* Memoirs of the American Anthropological Association No 49.

———— 1938. *Pleistocene Man in Minnesota: A Fossil Homo sapiens.* University of Minnesota Press, Minneapolis.

Jiménez-López, José C., Rocío Hernández Flores, Gloria Martínez Sosa, and Gabriel Saucedo Arteaga 2006. La Mujer del Peñon III. In *El Hombre Temprano en América y sus Implicaciones en el Poblamienbto de la Cuenca de Mexico*, edited by José C. Jiménez-López, Silvia González, José A. Pompa y Padilla, and Francisco Ortiz Pedraza, pp. 49–66. INAH, Mexico City.

Johnson, John R., Thomas W. Stafford, Jr., Henry O. Ajie, Don P. Morris 2002. Arlington Springs Revisited. In *Proceedings of the Fifth California Islands Symposium*, edited by D. R. Brown, K. C. Mitchell, and H. W. Chaney, pp. 541–5. U.S. OCS Study MMS 99-0038. Department of the Interior Minerals Management Service, Pacific OCS Region.

Jones, George T., Charlotte Beck, Erik E. Jones, and Richard E. Hughes 2003. Lithic Source Use and Paleoarchaic Foraging Territories in the Great Basin. *American Antiquity* 68:5–38.

Keeley, Laurence 1996. *War Before Civilization.* Oxford University Press, New York.

Krantz, Grover S. 1979. Oldest Human Remains from the Marmes Site. *Northwest Anthropological Research Notes* 13:159–73.

Kroeber, A. L. 1962. The Rancho La Brea Skull. *American Antiquity* 27:416–17.

Kuzminsky, Susan C. 2013. Human Craniofacial Variation among Pacific Rim Populations throughout the Holocene: A Test of the Coastal Migration Hypothesis using 3D Morphometric Methods. Unpublished Ph.D. dissertation, Department of Anthropology, University of California, Santa Barbara.

Lahr, Marta M. 1995. Patterns of Modern Human Diversification: Implications for Amerindian Origins. *Yearbook of Physical Anthropology* 38:163–98.

———— 1996. *The Evolution of Modern Human Diversity.* Cambridge University Press, Cambridge, United Kingdom.

Lahr, Marta M., and Richard V. S. Wright 1996. The Question of Robusticity and the Relationship between Cranial Size and Shape in *Homo sapiens. Journal of Human Evolution* 31:157–91.

Lambert, Patricia M. 2002. The Archaeology of War: A North American Perspective. *Journal of Archaeological Research* 10:208–41.

LeBlanc, Steven 1999. *Prehistory of Warfare in the American Southwest.* University of Utah Press, Salt Lake City.

McDermott, Rose, Dustin Tingley, Jonathan Cowden, Giovanni Frazzetto, and Dominic D. P. Johnson 2009. Monamine Oxidase A Gene (MAOA) Predicts Behavioral Aggression Following Provocation. *Proceedings of the National Academy of Sciences* 106:2118–23.

Mosch, Cynthia, and Patty Jo Watson 1996. The Ancient Explorer of Hourglass Cave. *Evolutionary Anthropology* 5:111–15.

Myster, Susan M. T., and Barbara H. O'Connell 1997. Bioarchaeology of Iowa, Wisconsin, and Minnesota. In *Bioarchaeology of the North Central United States,* edited by Douglas W. Owsley and Jerome C. Rose, pp. 147–241. Arkansas Archaeological Survey Research Series No. 49, Fayetteville.

Owsley, Douglas W., and Karen L. Bruwelheide 1997. Bioarchaeological Research in Northeastern Colorado, Northern Kansas, Nebraska, and South Dakota. In *Bioarchaeology of the North*

*Central United States*, edited by Douglas W. Owsley and Jerome C. Rose, pp. 7–57. Arkansas Archaeological Survey Research Series No. 49, Fayetteville.

Owsley, Douglas W., and Richard L. Jantz 2000. Biography in the Bones. *Scientific American Discovering Archaeology* 2000(January/February):56–8.

Owsley, Douglas W., Margaret A. Jodry, Thomas W. Stafford, C. Vance Haynes, Jr., and Dennis J. Stanford 2010. *Arch Lake Woman*. Texas A&M Press, College Station.

Owsley, Douglas W., and Jerome C. Rose 1997. *Bioarchaeology of the North Central United States*. Arkansas Archaeological Survey Research Series No. 49, Fayetteville.

Scheiber, Laura L., and George W. Gill 1996. Bioarchaeology of the Northwestern Plains. In *Archaeological and Bioarchaeological Resources of the Northwestern Plains*, edited by Geoge C. Frison and Robert C. Mainfort, pp. 91–119. Arkansas Archaeological Survey Research Series No. 47, Fayetteville.

Sjoberg, Rickard L., Francesca Ducci, Christina S. Barr, Timothy K. Newman, Lilliana Dell'Osso, Matti Virkkunen, and David Goldman 2008. A Non-Addictive Interaction of a Functional MOA VNTR and Testosterone Predicts Antisocial Behavior. *Neuropsychopharmacology* 33:425–30.

Smith, Maria O. 1997. Osteological Indications of Warfare in the Archaic Period of the Western Tennessee Valley. In *Troubled Times: Violence and Warfare in the Past*, edited by Debra Martin and David Frayer, pp. 241–65. Gordon and Breach, Amsterdam.

Snow, Charles E. 1948. Indian Knoll Skeletons of Sites OH2, Ohio County, Kentucky. *The University of Kentucky Reports in Anthropology* IV(3):Part 1, Lexington.

Snow, Dean R. 2013. Sexual Dimorphism in European Upper Paleolithic Cave Art. *American Antiquity* 78:746–61.

Steele, D. Gentry 1998. Human Biological Remains from the Wilson Leonard Site (41WM235). In *Wilson Leonard: an 11,000 Year Record of Hunter-Gatherers in Central Texas*, edited by Michael Collins, pp. 1141–58. Texas Archaeological Research Laboratory, Austin.

Steele, D. Gentry, and Joseph F. Powell 2002. Facing the Past: A View of the North American Fossil Record. In *The First Americans: The Pleistocene Colonization of the New World*, edited by Nina G. Jablonski, pp. 93–122. Memoirs of the California Academy of Sciences No. 27, San Francisco.

Stewart, T. Dale 1945. Report on the J. C. Putman Skeleton from Texas. *Bulletin of the Texas Archaeological and Paleontological Society* 16:31–8.

Suzuki, Hisashi 1982. Skulls of the Minatogawa Man. In *The Minatogawa Man: The Upper Pleistocene Man from the Island of Okinawa*, edited by Hisashi Suzuki and Kazuro Hanihara, pp. 7–47. The University Museum, University of Tokyo Bulletin No. 19, Tokyo.

Thoms, Alston V. 2003. Cook Stone Technology in North America: Evolutionary Changes in Domestic Fire Structures during the Holocene. In *Le Feu Domestique en Ses Structures au Néolithique et aux Ages des Tetaux*, edited by Marie-Chantal Ferére-Sautot, pp. 87–96. Collection Prehistories No. 9, Editions Monique Mergoil, Montagnac, France.

Trut, Lyudmila 1999. Early Canid Domestication: The Farm-Fox Experiment. *American Scientist* 87:160.

Walker, Phillip L. 1995. Problems of Preservation and Sexism in Sexing: Some Lessons from Historical Collections for Paleodemographers. In *Grave Reflections: Portraying the Past through Skeletal Studies*, edited by Shelley R. Saunders and Anne Herring, pp. 31–47. Canadian Scholars' Press, Toronto.

———— 1997. Wife Beating, Boxing, and Broken Noses: Skeletal Evidence for the Cultural Patterning of Interpersonal Violence. In *Troubled Times: Violence and Warfare in the Past*, edited by Debra Martin and David Frayer, pp. 145–75. Gordon and Breach, Amsterdam.

Wallthal, J. A. 1999. Mortuary Behavior and Early Holocene Land Use in the North American Mid-Continent. *North American Archaeologist* 20:1–30.

Waters, Michael R. 1986. Sulphur Springs Woman: An Early Human Skeleton from South-Eastern Arizona. *American Antiquity* 51:361–5.

## 96 | James C. Chatters

West, Frederick H. 1996. Beringia and New World Origins. In *American Beginnings: The Prehistory and Paleoecology of Beringia,* edited by Frederick H. West, pp. 525–59. University of Chicago Press, IL.

Wrangham, Richard, and Dale Peterson 1996. *Demonic Males: Apes and the Origins of Human Violence.* Houghton-Mifflin, Boston.

Young, Dianne, Suzanne Patrick, and D. Gentry Steele 1987. An Analysis of the Paleoindian Double Burial from Horn Shelter No. 2, in Central Texas. *Plains Anthropologist* 32:275–98.

# 5

# Hunter-Gatherer Violence and Warfare in Australia

*Mark W. Allen*

Studying hunter-gatherer violence and warfare is not an easy task. One promising option is to focus on cultural areas characterized by diverse geography and sociopolitical organization that have rich archaeological, ethnographic, and ethnohistoric sources. As I have argued for California, these allow for comparative studies of ecological or social variables compared against different scales of conflict (Allen 2012). Australia similarly holds great promise for research on violence and warfare among hunter-gatherer cultures. It is a vast continent with extreme ecological variation that has been inhabited by highly diverse foraging and collecting societies for more than 40,000 years. A breadth and depth of data and evidence for prehistoric, contact-era, and early historic violence and warfare is available to those who look for them. Unfortunately, there has thus far been a remarkable lack of interest in this topic among Australian anthropologists. As an illustration, the majority of recent syntheses of Australia written by archaeologists simply do not address warfare or violence (e.g., Hiscock 2008; Keen 2004; Lourandos 1997). They do briefly address weapons or note increasing "competition" leading to the need to control resources, but how such control would be secured is not discussed. This omission and neglect are holdout perceptions of a "pacified past" that has not yet given way to resurgence in the archaeology of warfare (Keeley 1996). Likely, and understandably, this reticence is due at least in part to modern political sensitivity.

Nevertheless, the evidence of violence and warfare in Aboriginal Australia is rich and detailed. It reveals tremendous variation across vast spaces and deep periods of time, but nonetheless shows clear patterns of conflict that date back

---

*Violence and Warfare among Hunter-Gatherers*, edited by Mark W. Allen and Terry L. Jones, 97–111. ©2014 Taylor & Francis. All rights reserved.

**98** | Mark W. Allen

to at least the late Pleistocene. In this chapter, I argue that Australia has much to add to the discussion of conflict in nonagricultural societies, particularly through the comparison of multiple lines of evidence.

## An Archaeological Foundation for the Study of Violence and Warfare in Australia

While the study of violence and warfare in Australia has been quite limited to date, a survey of the anthropological and archaeological literature for the continent reveals three topics that form a crucial foundation for deeper investigation. These include an influential theoretical perspective in Australian archaeology, a unique stone tool industry that may have functioned in part as specialized weaponry against human targets, and important insights on the surprising antiquity of conflict from rock art studies.

Intensification theory is a major theoretical school in Australian archaeology (Lourandos 1977, 1997; Lourandos and Ross 1994; also see papers in David et al. 2006); proponents have developed neo-Marxist models that compare ethnohistorical sources with the archaeological record. While the theory overtly acknowledges "competition," neither warfare nor violence is explicitly discussed. Intensification theory emphasizes a wide range of economic and settlement pattern changes that occurred between the mid-Holocene and the late Holocene, and further argues that various resources were intensified during this time span, including eels, moths, fish, seeds, and toxic cycad palms that required heavy processing. It further posits that such intensified economic practices spurred on changes in social and political organization, albeit not those involving violence or warfare. A good recent example of this perspective is by Pate (2006:229):

> The social dynamics generated by intergroup competitive relations provided a catalyst for further changes or "complexification" in hunter-gatherer societies, including the establishment of extensive exchange and alliance networks, craft specialists, ritual leaders, polygyny, more complex economic strategies and facilities, territorial boundaries, and semi-sedentism.

Pate's study is one of many in a recent volume (David et al. 2006) on social archaeology in Australia. While nearly every contributor discusses competition and the need for groups to protect resources, only one mentions warfare. According to the volume's index, "warfare" appears just one time. The word "violence" is more common in the volume, appearing on a total 5 of 318 pages of text.

Despite this apparent reluctance to come to grips with conflict, intensification theory commonly acknowledges that territoriality was marked in much of Australia. Territories have been most clearly documented by Pardoe (1988, 1990, this volume) for the highly productive Murray River region, where he has found evidence of cemeteries with established lineal descent extending back 13,000 years ago. A less distinct pattern of clustered burials was reported by Littleton (2002) in the Hay Plain along the Murrumbidgee River, also in southeastern Australia, which seem to date from the mid- to late Holocene. In coastal southern New South Wales, Lampert and Hughes (1974) identified substantial economic changes and population increase between 7,000 and 5,000 years ago in response to an extension of the tidal and intertidal zones. Lourandos (1977), Ross (1985), and Williams (1987) have examined mounds in southwest Victoria, along with other evidence for complexity. Similarly sized *Anadona* shellmounds as large as 100 meters long and 10 meters high are common in northern Australia, and appear to have been formed by fairly sedentary populations between 3,000 and 600 years ago (Hiscock 2008:175). There is thus a great deal of work that infers maintenance of territoriality and potential conflict over resources. The next (but so far largely absent) step is to consider the roles of violence or warfare in the widely appreciated competition. Pardoe's work in the Central Murray region thus far stands alone as an explicit study of these issues.

A second foundation for further archaeological research on violence and warfare in Australia is a decades-old focus on the introduction and spread of microlithic flake tools and small backed blades dubbed the Australian Small Tool Tradition (ASTT) by Gould (1969). It has long been argued that this technology, as well as the dingo, may have been introduced from India or Indonesia given morphological similarities and other types of evidence (including genetic). Hiscock (2008:154–7) recently argued that while flake tools and backed blades increased around 5,000 to 4,500 years before present (BP), they were present in Australia as far back as 15,000 years ago. Australian archaeologists such as Lampert (1971), McCarthy (1967), and Noone (1943) have long suggested that microliths and (probably at an earlier time) backed blades may have been used, among other functions, as insets for specialized composite weapons known in the ethnohistorical and ethnographic literature for Western Australia, South Australia, and New South Wales as "Death Spears" (Davidson 1934; Davidson and McCarthy 1957; Kamminga 1980, 1982; Mulvaney 1975:108). These spears have small blades inset in a wooden shaft and attached with a fixative that dislodge inside wounds and are extremely difficult to remove from victims. Others have argued that they were not necessarily specialized weapons of warfare (Hiscock 2008:159; McDonald et al. 1994). However, the ethnographic distribution of the "Death Spear" matches well with that of the mid-Holocene microliths (Lampert 1971; Noone 1943).

Recently, a skeleton of a male aged between 30 and 40 years at the time of death was excavated at Narrabeen in northern Sydney in a dune near the coast (McDonald et al. 2007). The individual was clearly killed by weapons consistent with "Death Spears" and perhaps other composite weapons. One injury, demonstrated by the presence of backed flakes inside the body, was caused by a barbed spear thrust through his back just above his left hip. He also had two perimortem head wounds, one a cut and the other a puncture.

**100** | Mark W. Allen

The excavators noted other backed artifacts in association with the skeleton and concluded that a second barbed spear caused one of the head wounds; the other was caused by either another spear, or perhaps a stone-headed club. The man also had a healed cranial fracture from an earlier violent episode. The burial dates to around 4,000 years ago, contemporary with the proliferation of backed blades and microliths, as well as the evidence of increasing territoriality throughout Australia, including the Sydney region (McDonald and Veth 2006). This would seem to be a smoking gun that firmly links microliths with at least occasional use as weapons against humans.

The third foundation for further investigation of conflict in Australia is the widespread presence of rock art, which appears to graphically depict both individuals and groups engaged in combat. What makes this particularly interesting is the antiquity of the art. The earliest of these are associated with the Dynamic Phase dating to the Pleistocene. They include small numbers of individuals throwing boomerangs and spears at human targets, as well as others who are attempting to aid or finish off speared victims (Chippendale et al. 2000). Figures are often shown dodging thrown spears as well. There are also Dynamic Phase images of part-human and part-animal individuals killing humans with war picks or boomerang blows to the head. Taçon and Chippendale (1994) have argued that somewhat later Holocene-period rock art in the region shows conflict between larger groups of individuals. Other Australian rock art studies have been less concerned with the meanings of these images, even when discussing human figures holding clubs and shields (Morwood 2002:28). Scholars have also noted that rock art increases dramatically in many parts of Australia during the mid-late Holocene (David and Chant 1995; David and Lourandos 1998; McDonald and Veth 2006; Veth 2006). This has been interpreted as evidence of increased territoriality and social identity formation as another aspect of intensification.

## Neglected Evidence of Violence and Warfare

A wide variety of rich data, information, and perspectives is available to examine violence and warfare in Australia representing the entire sequence of the continent's long prehistory, as well as the tumultuous contact period and the era of historic colonization during the second half of the nineteenth century. Each type of data is described in turn.

### Paleopathology

As noted by Pardoe (this volume), there are three types of pathologies that are fairly common in Australian skeletal populations from the entire span of human occupation: depressed fractures on the crania of skeletons

(Brown 1987, 1989; Haglund 1976; Jurisich and Davies 1976; Pretty and Kricun 1989; Prokopec 1979; Sandison 1973a; Webb 1995; Wood 1968); parry fractures of the ulna, radius, or both (Dinning 1949; Freedman 1985; Jurisich and Davies 1976; Mackay 1938; Macintosh 1967a, 1967b; Pretty and Kricun 1989; Prokopec 1979; Sandison 1973b; Webb 1995); and other traumas, including perforations of long bones, ribs, and crania most likely caused by spears, epitomized by the study of the Narabeen skeleton with multiple wounds discussed in this chapter, but with numerous other examples (Haglund 1976; Jurisich and Davies 1976; Prokopec 1979; Sandison 1973a, 1973b; Wood 1968; also see a few more examples in Pardoe, this volume). Pardoe has compiled the data for the Central Murray region to examine the nature of violence and warfare through time, and Webb (1995) has produced some regional data, but there is great potential for paleopathology to contribute much more detailed analyses in other regions. The existing studies show skeletal trauma likely caused by human action is fairly common through both time and space in Australia. Moreover, the types of injuries observed accord well with the ethnographic and ethnohistoric accounts of conflict.

## The Ethnohistory of the Contact Period

Five "First Fleeters" from the original colonies at Botany Bay and Port Jackson kept journals that were published. Despite the usual need to be wary of ethnocentrism, these have two key advantages: they were made by colonial officials trained to make rather full descriptions of indigenous societies as part of their duties, and they describe initial contact. Moreover, as they are often describing the same events, they can be directly compared. Those of the Marine officer Tench ([1789, 1793] 1961) and the surgeon White ([1790] 1962) are the most useful for interpretations of violence and warfare during the first months of contact. Tench noted that several of the fleet convict runaways were killed by thrown spears:

> we have found that these spears are not invariably alike, some of them being barbed like a fish gig, and others simply pointed . . . nor are their weapons of offence confined to the spear only, for they have besides long wooden swords, shaped like a saber, capable of inflicting a mortal wound, and clubs of an immense size. Small targets made of the bark of trees, are likewise now and then to be seen among them. . . . from circumstances which have been observed, we have sometimes been inclined to believe these people at war with each other. They have more than once been seen assembled, as if bent on an expedition. An officer one day met fourteen of them marching along in a regular Indian file through the woods, each man armed with a spear in his right hand, and a large stone in his left: at their head appeared a chief, who was distinguished by being painted (Tench [1789, 1793] 1961:50–1).

# 102    Mark W. Allen

In addition, he gives a graphic account of the wound that Governor Phillip sustained: a 10-foot-long barbed spear went through his right shoulder. This is also described by the judge advocate Collins ([1798] 1975:111) and by Hunter ([1793] 1968:209–10). Tench ([1789, 1793] 1961:206) also provides an interesting account of the death of convict McEntire by a "Death Spear." Visiting Aboriginals advised the surgeon to not pull out the 7.5 inches of spear embedded in his left side (the implication being this was no new thing to them), but they did so anyway, and McEntire died. They opened him up later and found several barbs from the spear lodged inside him. One was wooden and the others were stone, according to both Tench and Hunter, but Collins reported that they were shell. All agree that they were affixed to the spear with yellow gum.

White ([1790] 1962:110) describes men with shields and spears with barbs of fish bone, as well as various forms of clubs ([1790] 1962:151–2, 201; Plate 37), boomerangs, and *woomera* (spear throwers) used as weapons. Hunter ([1793] 1968:53) notes that spears could be thrown from 60 to 70 yards and that he measured one throw at 90 yards. He also notes that they saw shields with the broken tips of spears stuck in them (Hunter [1793] 1968:55).

There are other accounts by other Europeans during the early days of the colony. A Spanish commander, Malaspina, made notes about Aboriginal conflict observed during his visit in 1793 (King 1990:162). Bellingshausen was a Russian commander who visited New South Wales between 1814 and 1822 and notes both mock fights and extreme xenophobia between different groups of Aboriginals even after the Sydney area had been pacified (Barratt 1981:39, 92). A Frenchman named Baudin ([1801–1802] 1974:324) recorded what he saw as an attempt by three men with spears to cover a fourth who was trying to snatch a steel sword in New South Wales.

Two decades later, Scott Nind was a medical officer at the Western Australia Swan River Colony in King George's Sound from 1827 to 1829. He made some excellent observations of weapons (Nind 1831:26–7), including "Death Spears." He noted that such "war spears" were longer and heavier than the 8-foot-long versions used for hunting. Another interesting observation he made was that dances were only held at camps during times of peace because the inhabitants were afraid to advertise their positions during times of war (Nind 1831:40). Nind also argues that the groups in the area of the colony were:

> very jealous as to encroachments on their property, and the land is divided into districts, which is the property of families or individuals . . . when a man is killed, his tribe instantly sets about revenging his death; but they are not particular whether they kill the principle [sic] offender or any other of his tribe . . . their quarrels most frequently arise about their women. For depredations on each other's ground, or any slight cause, they are contended with spearing through the legs or thighs, and do not attempt to kill each other; and the moment one of the party is wounded the engagement ceases . . . their attacks when intended to

Hunter-Gatherer Violence and Warfare in Australia | **103**

be fatal, are most frequently made at night, and always by stealth. We have more than once witnessed their common rencontres (Nind 1831:44).

The missionary Threlkeld related descriptions of weapons and violent episodes dating from 1824 to 1859 in his diaries (Gunson 1974:67–71), while those of John Bulmer date to 1855 to 1908 (Campbell and Vanderwal 1994:31–4).

Perhaps the best-known later account is that of William Buckley, an escaped convict who wandered out of the bush in 1835 after 32 years spent with the Wathaurung of the Melbourne area in Victoria. His memoirs of this experience were published some years later, and many have questioned their accuracy. However, there are details that seem to corroborate much of what he related (Flannery 2002). He recorded at least 14 different episodes where he witnessed combat between his group and others that resulted in deaths, sometimes including nighttime assaults on camps that resulted in considerable loss of life.

## Expansion of Languages in Australia

At least one anthropologist has argued for quick expansions of several languages or related languages that seem linked to expansion into new territories and replacement of others. McConvell (1996:143) argues that several were on the move around 6,000 years ago. This would correlate well with the expansion of the Small Tool Tradition. In particular, the Western Desert languages are mutually intelligible and correlate with numerous societies that are closely related socially and cosmologically in that they are closely bound by Dreamtime paths (Berndt 1972:181; Hamilton 1982:96; Veth 2006). Kestevan (1984:53) discusses evidence for similar language changes on a smaller scale in western Arnhem Land. In California, language shifts has often been cited as indirect evidence of conflict (Allen 2012).

## Nineteenth- and Early Twentieth-Century Ethnography

Given the relatively late colonization of much of Australia, there are a large number of early anthropological accounts of traditional Aboriginal society and culture, too vast to be comprehensively summarized here. These, of course, have significant problems given that considerable change may well have occurred due to contact (even far inland), and given the ethnocentric biases of the early pioneers. Nevertheless, they share similar descriptions of conflict and violence during the nineteenth century. They are particularly rich in detail in their descriptions of weapons and shields, but many of them describe similar patterns in conflict involving two types of combat. The first is more common and is a means of settling disputes. Two groups face off

**104** | Mark W. Allen

and trade spears, or sometimes there are individual hand-to-hand combats. These often would stop when serious injury was sustained with the conflict being judged as settled, but sometimes they led to more serious engagements with several or more killed (Basedow 1925; Flanagan 1888; Mann 1883; Ross 1899; Rudder 1899; Wheeler 1910). A second type is various forms of deadly sneak attack at night or dawn, sometimes executed by groups that covered hundreds of miles to strike enemies (Basedow 1925; Howitt [1904] 1996; Wheeler 1910). Sometimes conflicts escalated beyond bands to include entire-dialect tribal groups (Basedow 1925; Howitt [1904] 1996). Descriptions of attacks on groups traveling long distances to procure red ochre from sources in other territories are fairly common (Howitt [1904] 1996:711–13). Another common theme discussed is parties that attack to avenge insults or offenses such as breaching Dreamtime prohibitions.

## More Recent Ethnographic Research

Probably the most detailed ethnographic description of Aboriginal violence and warfare dating from after the first quarter century of the twentieth century is by Warner ([1937] 1969), who devotes an entire chapter to "warfare" in northeastern Arnhem Land caused by "the killing of a clansman by a member of another clan, and interclan rivalry for women . . . an isolated killing, owing to the strength of the kinship structure, usually results in the whole of northeastern Arnhem Land becoming a battle ground at fairly frequent intervals" (Warner [1937] 1969:144). Much of his original fieldwork dates to the 1930s. Warner ([1937] 1969:147) estimated about 200 young men had been killed in fighting in a 20-year period (1909–1929). He describes several distinctly different types of war ranging from formalized battles to sneak attacks designed to kill as many as possible.

Many original or synthetic ethnographic works deal to a more limited extent with violence or warfare in Australia. These include remembered events from the past as well as violent encounters observed directly by the researchers during the twentieth century. They commonly cite stories of particular battles or fights of renown in their particular area, often over a water hole or ochre source (for example, Berndt and Berndt [1964] 1988:356–9; Blainey [1975] 1982:102–13; Falkenberg 1962:141, 149; Gould 1969:210–11; Hart and Pilling 1960:83; Hiatt 1965:127–47; Jones 1984:8–9; Lourandos 1977:209–11; Meggitt 1962:42, 245–7; Myers 1986; O'Rourke 2005:146; Reid 1978:54, 201; Strehlow 1970:123–6, 1978:38–45; Tindale 1972:219, 221, 236, 1974:10; Tonkinson 1966:290–9).

The essential points seem to be that important resources were clearly owned by groups and defended against outsiders. Hostility to strangers was the norm, and smoke on the horizon from unexpected quarters was a cause of fear. Tindale (1972:221) points out that the Pitjandjara of the Western Desert often expressed this fear in song, with lyrics such as "strange people looking down deadly, silently, death, stealing, sneaking."

Disputes were settled by formalized battles or duels with fairly light fatalities despite extreme violence. This included both thrown spears and club fights. However, these could erupt into fierce melees on occasion. Even a few deaths would have been a huge impact to such small societies. However, as described by the early anthropologists, there were also periodic night or dawn raids on camps that could result in massacres. Warfare and violence were still common in the early twentieth century in more remote areas, and violence continued to be a mechanism for solving disputes into the late twentieth century. The one key exception was in the Western Desert, where territorial boundaries were permeable among groups speaking mutually intelligible dialects and linked closely to Dreamtime pathways (Berndt 1972; Hamilton 1982; Tonkinson 1991; Veth 2006). One other important point that some make is that ownership was often not really correlated with boundaries, but with sacred places in the Dreamtime (Hamilton 1982; Keen 1991; Myers 1991). These, of course, are often water sources or the locations of other important resources. One last point is that warfare was probably most intense in the north of Australia, particularly in the Torres Strait area (McNiven 1998). It often included hostilities against groups from New Guinea, and was the other side of the coin of extensive trade connections across the strait.

## Historical Sources of Frontier Warfare

Historical sources from Indonesia attest to expeditions sent to Northern Australia to harvest sea slugs between 1720 and 1907 (Campbell 2002; Flood 1995:258; Hart and Pilling 1960:97; Hiscock 2008). These accounts often include descriptions of assaults and massacres perpetrated on the intruders by the inhabitants of the Kimberley and Arnhem Land regions. Archaeological work supports these sources (Macknight 1986).

Finally, there is a substantial literature available on the nature of frontier warfare and violence during the late eighteenth and nineteenth centuries (Broome 1988; Connor 2002; Nance 1981). Connor (2002) notes that the conflict was less severe before 1838, at which point the task of establishing colonial authority was transferred from the British Army to police and armed citizen groups. Aboriginal resistance was most effective when it was directed toward raiding farmhouses and farms for food supplies. They were able to slow expansion of settlers for significant periods of time in some areas. More than 800 settlers were killed by Aboriginals in Queensland between 1841 and 1897, but only about 59 were killed in Victoria, considerably fewer than an estimated 400 Aboriginals killed by whites in the area during the same period (Nance 1981:532–3). Nance (1981:550) also cites numerous examples of intertribal warfare in Victoria between 1836 and 1850. A recent

**106** | Mark W. Allen

volume edited by Atwood and Foster (2003) contains several detailed studies of frontier conflict. All of these sources demonstrate that Aboriginals altered their traditional warfare and attempted to defend their territories, and that the loss of life during this period was substantial.

## Conclusion

Despite the wide range of evidence summarized in this chapter, recent archaeological research and syntheses in Australia for the most part do not consider the roles of violence or warfare. It is important to note, however, that Douglas Fry (2006:146–61, 2007:113–30) has published several analyses of the evidence for violence and warfare in Australia, taking the position that:

> events that could be considered warfare were extremely few and far between in the ethnographic record of Aboriginal Australia, and in some exceptional cases may have been prompted by territorial loss and other changes caused by the arrival of Europeans. At contact, the Aboriginal hunting-and-gathering societies on this island continent were functioning within a "peace system" wherein each society generally respected the territorial rights of its neighbors. Whereas it probably would be an exaggeration to claim that warfare never happened before European contact, the evidence clearly supports the conclusion that *warfare was a very rare anomaly among native Australian societies* (emphasis original) Fry (2007:119).

He acknowledges that violence was fairly common, but argues that it was between individuals and not groups. Of course what he sees as individual actions by a small number of participants might really be groups given the small size of bands, particularly in the more arid regions. Judging from his citations and end notes, Fry bases his assessment on a fairly small set of ethnographies and early anthropological works on Australia. Other types of data are not included in his analysis, other than a dismissal of rock art as representing punished individuals. Fry is of course not the only anthropologist to see Australian Aboriginal societies as highly peaceful.

The more thorough examination of ethnographic sources cited here indicates that resources were very much defended, and entire groups were sometimes eliminated because of conflicts over them: mostly sacred places (often water holes, also economically vital, of course) rather than fixed territorial boundaries. The Pitjandjara song about "strange people looking down deadly, silently, death, stealing, sneaking" does not accord well with a peace system based solely on mutual respect of territorial rights.

Moreover, the archaeological data, skeletal trauma, and ethnohistorical evidence that Fry neglects in his analyses demonstrate that violent conflict, including warfare, predate European contact in Australia, probably back to the late Pleistocene at least. There is tremendous potential to look at how it varies across time, space, and sociopolitical organization by looking at multiple lines of evidence. The need for more research on this topic is all the more important given the prominence of Australia in anthropological literature.

## Acknowledgments

Funds to support this research were provided by Cal Poly Pomona. The assistance of the staff at the Australian Institute of Aboriginal and Torres Strait Islander Studies in Canberra is gratefully acknowledged. Colin Pardoe is thanked for comments on a draft of this paper.

## References

Allen, Mark W. 2012. A Land of Violence. In *Contemporary Issues in California Archaeology*, edited by Terry L. Jones and Jennifer E. Perry, pp. 197–216. Left Coast Press, Walnut Creek, CA.

Atwood, Bain, and S. G. Foster (editors) 2003. *Frontier Conflict: The Australian Experience*. The Australian National Museum Press, Canberra.

Barratt, Glynn 1981. *The Russians at Port Jackson, 1814–1822*. Australian Institute of Aboriginal Studies, Canberra.

Basedow, Herbert 1925. *The Australian Aboriginal*. F. W. Pierce and Sons, Adelaide.

Baudin, Nicolas (1801–1802) 1974. *The Journal of Post Captain Nicolas Baudin, Commander-in-Chief of the Corvettes Geographe and Naturaliste, Assigned by Order of the Government to a Voyage of Discovery*. Translated from the French by Christine Cornell. Libraries Board of South Australia, Adelaide.

Berndt, Ronald M. 1972. The Walmadjeri and Gugadja. In *Hunters and Gatherers Today: A Socioeconomic Study of Eleven Such Cultures in the Twentieth Century*, edited by M. G. Bicchieri, pp. 177–216. Holt, Rinehart, and Winston, Inc., New York.

Berndt, Ronald M., and Catherine H. Berndt (1964) 1988. *The World of the First Australians: Aboriginal Traditional Life Past and Present* (5th edition). Canberra: Aboriginal Studies Press. Ure Smith, Sydney.

Blainey, Geoffrey (1975) 1982. *Triumph of the Nomads: A History of Ancient Australia* (revised edition). MacMillan, Sydney.

Broome, Richard 1988. The Struggle for Australia: Aboriginal-European Warfare, 1770–1930. In *Australia: Two Centuries of War and Peace*, edited by M. McKernan and M. Bronwne, pp. 99–120. Australian War Memorial in association with Allen and Unwin, Canberra.

Brown, Peter 1987. Pleistocene Homogeneity and Holocene Size Reduction: The Australian Human Skeletal Evidence. *Archaeology in Oceania* 22:41–67.

———— 1989. Cobol Creek: A Morphological and Metrical Analysis of the Crania, Mandibles and Dentitions of a Prehistoric Australian Human Population. *Terra Australis* No. 13. Department of Prehistory, Research School of Pacific Studies, The Australian National University, Canberra.

Campbell, Judy 2002. *Invisible Invaders: Smallpox and other Diseases in Aboriginal Australia 1780–1880*. Melbourne University Press, Melbourne.

Campbell, Alastair (compiler), and Ron Vanderwal (editor) 1994. *John Bulmer's Recollection of Victorian Aboriginal Life 1855–1908*. Occasional Papers, Anthropology and History, No. 3. Museum Victoria, Melbourne.

**108** | Mark W. Allen

Chippendale, Christopher, B. Smith, and Paul S. C. Taçon 2000. Visions of Dynamic Power: Archaic Rock-Paintings, Altered States of Consciousness and "Clever Men" in Western Arnhem Land (NT), Australia. *Cambridge Archaeological Journal* 10:63–101.

Collins, David (1798) 1975. *An Account of the English Colony in New South Wales* (Volume I). A. H. and A.W. Reed, Sydney. Originally published by T. Cadell Jun and W. Davies, London.

Connor, John 2002. *The Australian Frontier Wars, 1788–1838.* University of New South Wales Press, Sydney.

David, Bruno, Bryce Barker, and Ian J. McNiven (editors) 2006. *The Social Archaeology of Australian Indigenous Societies.* Aboriginal Studies Press, Canberra.

David, Bruno, and David Chant 1995. Rock Art and Regionalisation in North Queensland Prehistory. *Memoirs of the Queensland Museum* 37:357–528.

David, Bruno, and Harry Lourandos 1998. Rock Art and Socio-Demography in Northeastern Australian Prehistory. *World Archaeology* 30:193–219.

Davidson, D. S. 1934. Australian Spear-Traits and Their Derivations. *Journal of the Polynesian Society* 43:41–72, 143–62.

Davidson, D. S., and F. D. McCarthy 1957. The Distribution and Chronology of Some Important Types of Stone Implements in Western Australia. *Anthropos* 52:390–458.

Dinning, T. A. R. 1949. A Study of Healed Fractures in the Australian Aboriginal. *The Medical Journal of Australia* 2:712–13.

Falkenberg, Johannes 1962. *Kin and Totem: Group Relations of Australian Aborigines in the Port Keats District.* Allen and Unwin Ltd., Oslo, Norway.

Flanagan, Roderick J. 1888. *The Aborigines of Australia.* Edward F. Flanagan and George Robertson and Co., Sydney.

Flannery, Tim (editor) 2002. *The Life and Adventures of William Buckley: Thirty-Two Years a Wanderer Amongst the Aborigines of the then Unexplored County Round Port Phillip.* The Text Publishing Company, Melbourne.

Flood, Josephine 1995. *Archaeology of the Dreamtime: The Story of Prehistoric Australia and its People.* Revised edition. Angus and Robertson, Sydney.

Freedman, L. 1985. Human Skeletal Remains from Mossgiel, N.S.W. *Archaeology in Oceania* 20:21–31.

Fry, Douglas P. 2006. *The Human Potential for Peace: An Anthropological Challenge to Assumptions about War and Violence.* Oxford University Press, New York.

——— 2007. *Beyond War: The Human Potential for Peace.* Oxford University Press, New York.

Gould, Richard 1969. *Yiwara: Foragers of the Australian Desert.* Collins, London-Sydney.

Gunson, Neil (editor) 1974. Australian *Reminiscences and Papers of L. E. Threlkeld, Missionary to the Aborigines, 1824–1859* (2 volumes). Australian Institute of Aboriginal Studies, Canberra.

Haglund, Laila 1976. Dating Aboriginal Relics from the Contact Period. *Archaeology & Physical Anthropology in Oceania* 9:163–74.

Hamilton, Annette 1982. Descended from Father, Belonging to Country: Rights to Land in the Australian Western Desert. In *Politics and History in Band Societies,* edited by Eleanor Leacock and Richard Lee, pp. 85–108. Cambridge University Press, Cambridge, United Kingdom.

Hart, C. W. M., and Arnold R. Pilling 1960. *The Tiwi of North Australia.* Holt, Rinehart, and Winston, New York.

Hiatt, L. R. 1965. *Kinship and Conflict: A Study of an Aboriginal Community in Northern Arnhem Land.* The Australian National University, Canberra.

Hiscock, Peter 2008. *Archaeology of Ancient Australia.* Routledge, London.

Howitt, A. W. (1904) 1996. *The Native Tribes of South-East Australia.* Aboriginal Studies Press, Canberra. Originally published by MacMillan and Co., London.

Hunter, John (1793) 1968. *An Historical Journal of the Transactions at Port Jackson and Norfolk Island.* J. Stockdale, London.

Jones, Phillip 1984. Red Ochre Expeditions: An Ethnographic and Historical Analysis of Aboriginal Trade in the Lake Eyre Basin. *Journal of the Anthropological Society of South Australia* 22:3–10.

Jurisich, M., and D. Davies 1976. The Paleopathology of Prehistoric Aboriginal Skeletal Remains Excavated by the Victoria Archaeological Survey. *The Artefact* 1:194–218.

Kamminga, Johan 1980. A Functional Analysis of Austalian Microliths. *The Artefact* 5:1–18.

––––––– 1982. *Over the Edge: Functional Analysis of Australian Stone Tools*. Occasional Papers in Anthropology No. 12. Anthropology Museum, University of Queensland.

Keeley, Lawrence 1996. *War Before Civilization*. Oxford University Press, Oxford, United Kingdom.

Keen, Ian 1991. Yolngu Religious Property. In *Hunters and Gatherers 2: Property, Power, and Ideology*, edited by Tim Ingold, David Riches, and James Woodburn, pp. 272–91. Cambridge University Press, Cambridge, United Kingdom.

––––––– 2004. *Aboriginal Economy and Society*. Oxford University Press, Oxford, United Kingdom.

Kestevan, Sue 1984. Linguistic Consideration of Land Tenure in Western Arnhem Land. In *Further Applications of Linguistics to Australian Aboriginal Contexts*, edited by G. R. Mckay and B. A. Sommer, pp. 47–64. Applied Linguistics Association of Australia, Occasional Papers, No. 8, Melbourne.

King, Robert J. 1990. *The Secret History of the Convict Colony: Alexandro Malaspina's Report on the British Settlement of New South Wales*. Allen and Unwin, Sydney.

Lampert, R. J. 1971. *Burrill Lake and Currarong: Coastal Sites in Southern New South Wales. Terra Australis 1*. The Australian National University, Canberra.

Lampert, R. J., and P. J. Hughes 1974. Sea Level Change and Aboriginal Coastal Adaptations in Southern New South Wales. *Archaeology and Physical Anthropology in Oceania* 9:226–35.

Littleton, Judith 2002. Mortuary Behavior on the Hay Plain: Do Cemeteries Exist? *Archaeology in Oceania* 37:105–22.

Lourandos, Harry 1977. Aboriginal Spatial Organization and Population: South Western Victoria Reconsidered. *Archaeology and Physical Anthropology in Oceania* 12:202–25.

––––––– 1997. *Continent of Hunter Gatherers: New Perspectives in Australian Prehistory*. Cambridge University Press, Cambridge, United Kingdom.

Lourandos, Harry, and Anne Ross 1994. The Great "Intensification Debate": It's History and Place in Australian Archaeology. *Australian Archaeology* 39:54–63.

Macintosh, N. W. G. 1967a. "Fossil Man" in Australia. *Australian Journal of Science* 30:86–98.

––––––– 1967b. Recent Discoveries of Early Australian Man. *Annals of the Australian College of Dental Surgery* 1:104–26.

Mackay, Charles V. 1938. Some Pathological Changes in Australian Aboriginal Bones. *The Medical Journal of Australia* 2:536–55.

Macknight, C. C. 1986. Maccassans and the Aboriginal Past. *Archaeology in Oceania* 21:69–75.

Mann, John F. 1883. Notes on the Aborigines of Australia. *Proceedings of the Royal Geographical Society of Australasia* 1:27–63.

McCarthy, F. D. 1967. *Australian Aboriginal Stone Implements: Including Bone Shell, and Teeth Implements*. Government Printer, Sydney.

McConvell, Patrick 1996. Backtracking to Babel: The Chronology of Pama-Nyungan Expansion in Australia. *Archaeology in Oceania* 31:125–44.

McNiven, Ian J. 1998. Enmity and Amity: Reconsidering Stone-Headed Club (*gabagaba*) Procurement and Trade in Torres Strait. *Oceania* 69:94–115.

McDonald, Josephine, and Peter Veth 2006. Rock Art and Social Identity: A Comparison of Holocene Graphic Systems in Arid and Fertile Environments. In *The Archaeology of Oceania, Australia, and the Pacific Islands*, edited by Ian Lilley, pp. 96–115. Blackwell, Oxford, United Kingdom.

McDonald, Josephine, Elizabeth Rich, and Huw Barton 1994. The Rouse Hill Infrastructure Project (Stage 1) on the Cumberland Plain, Western Sydney: Recent Research and Issues. In *Archaeology in the North: Proceedings of the 1993 Australian Archaeological Association Conference*, edited by Marjorie Sullivan, Sally Brockwell, and Ann Webb, pp. 259–93. Australian National University, Darwin.

McDonald, Josephine J., Denise Donlon, Judith H. Field, Richard L. K. Fullagar, Joan Brenner Coltrain, Peter Mitchell, and Mark Rawson 2007. The First Archaeological Evidence for Death by Spearing in Australia. *Antiquity* 81:877–85.

Meggitt, Mervyn J. 1962. *Desert People: A Study of the Walbiri Aborigines of Central Australia.* Angus and Robertson, Sydney.

Morwood, M. J. 2002. *Vision from the Past: The Archaeology of Australian Aboriginal Art.* Allen and Unwin, Crows Nest, NSW, Australia.

Mulvaney, D. J. 1975. *The Prehistory of Australia.* 2nd edition. Penguin, Melbourne.

Myers, Fred R. 1986. *Pintupi Country, Pintupi Self: Sentiment, Place, and Politics among Western Desert Aborigines.* Australian Institute of Aboriginal Studies, Canberra.

―――― 1991. Burning the Truck and Holding the Country: Property, Time, and the Negotiation of Identity among Pintupi Aborigines. In *Hunters and Gatherers 2: Property, Power, and Ideology,* edited by Tim Ingold, David Riches, and James Woodburn, pp. 52–74. Cambridge University Press, Cambridge, United Kingdom.

Nance, Beverly 1981. The Level of Violence: Europeans and Aborigines in Port Phillip, 1835–1850. *Historical Studies* 19:532–52.

Nind, Scott 1831. Description of the Natives of King George's Sound (Swan River Colony) and Adjoining Country. *Journal of the Royal Geographical Society* 1:21–51.

Noone, H. V. V. 1943. Some Aboriginal Stone Implements of Western Australia. *Records of the South Australian Museum* 7:271–80.

O'Rourke, Michael 2005. *"Sung for Generations": Tales of Red Kangaroo, War Leader of Gunnedah.* Michael O'Rourke, Braddon, ACT, Australia.

Pardoe, Colin 1988. The Cemetery as Symbol: The Distribution of Prehistoric Aboriginal Burial Grounds in Southeastern Australia. *Archaeology in Oceania* 23:1–16.

―――― 1990. The Demographic Basis of Human Evolution in Southeastern Australia. In *Hunter-Gatherer Demography: Past and Present.* Oceania Monograph, No. 39, edited by Betty Meehan, and Neville White, pp. 59–70. University of Sydney Press, Sydney.

Pate, F. Donald 2006. Hunter-Gatherer Social Complexity at Roonka, South Australia. In *The Social Archaeology of Australian Indigenous Societies,* edited by Bruno David, Bryce Barker, and Ian J. McNiven, pp. 242–53. Aboriginal Studies Press, Canberra.

Pretty, Graeme L., and Morrie E. Kricun 1989. Prehistoric Health Status of the Roonka Population. *World Archaeology* 21:198–224.

Prokopec, Miroslav 1979. Demographical and Morphological Aspects of the Roonka Population. *Archaeology and Physical Anthropology in Oceania* 14:11–26.

Reid, Janet C. 1978. *Sorcery and Healing: The Meaning of Illness and Death to an Australian Aboriginal Community.* Unpublished Ph.D. dissertation, Department of Anthropology, Stanford University, California.

Ross, Andrew D. 1899. Aboriginal Tribal Fight. *Science of Man and Australasian Anthropological Journal* 2:77–8.

Ross, Anne 1985. Archaeological Evidence for Population Change in the Middle to Late Holocene in Southeastern Australia. *Archaeology in Oceania* 20:81–9.

Rudder, Eugene F. 1899. An Aboriginal Battle in Queensland. *Science of Man and Australasian Anthropological Journal* 1:264–5, 2:8–9.

Sandison, A. T. 1973a. *Paleopathology of Human Bones from Murray River Region between Mildura and Renmark, Australia.* Memoirs of the National Museum of Victoria 34:173–4.

―――― 1973b. Disease Changes in Australian Aboriginal Skeletons. *Australian Institute of Aboriginal Studies Newsletter* 3:20–2.

Strehlow, T. G. H. 1970. Geography and the Totemic Landscape in Central Australia: A Functional Study. In *Australian Aboriginal Anthropology: Modern Studies in the Social Anthropology of the Australian Aborigine,* edited by Ronald M. Berndt, pp. 92–140. University of Western Australia Press, Nedlands.

Strehlow, T. G. H. 1978. *Journey to Horseshoe Bend*. 2nd edition. Rigby Ltd., Adelaide, Australia.

Taçon, Paul, and Christopher Chippendale 1994. Australia's Ancient Warriors: Changing Depictions in the Rock Art of Arnhem Land, N. T. *Cambridge Archaeological Journal* 4:211–48.

Tench, Watkin (1789, 1793) 1961. *Sydney's First Four Years: Being a Reprint of a Narrative of the Expedition to Botany Bay and a Complete Account of the Settlement at Port Jackson*, edited by L. F. Fitzhardinge. Angus and Robertson, Sydney.

Tindale, Norman B. 1972. The Pitjandjara. In *Hunters and Gatherers Today: A Socioeconomic Study of Eleven Such Cultures in the Twentieth Century*, edited by M. G. Bicchieri, pp. 217–68. Holt, Rinehart, and Winston, Inc., New York.

——— 1974. *Aboriginal Tribes of Australia*. University of California Press, Berkeley.

Tonkinson, Robert 1966. Social Structure and Acculturation of Aborigines in the Western Desert. Unpublished Master's thesis, Department of Anthropology, Western Australian University, Perth.

——— 1991. "Ideology and Domination" in Aboriginal Australia: A Western Desert Test Case. In *Hunters and Gatherers 2: Property, Power and Ideology*, edited by Tim Ingold, David Riches, and James Woodburn, pp. 150–64. Berg, New York.

Veth, Peter 2006. Social Dynamism in the Archaeology of the Western Desert. In *The Social Archaeology of Australian Indigenous Societies*, edited by Bruno David, Bryce Barker, and Ian J. McNiven, pp. 242–53. Aboriginal Studies Press, Canberra.

Warner, W. Lloyd (1937) 1969. *A Black Civilization: A Study of an Australian Tribe* (revised edition). Harper Torchbooks, New York.

Webb, Stephen 1995. *Paleopathology of Aboriginal Australians: Health and Disease across a Hunter-Gatherer Continent*. Cambridge University Press, Cambridge, United Kingdom.

Wheeler, Gerald C. 1910. *The Tribe, and Intertribal Relations in Australia*. John Murray, London.

White, John (1790) 1962. *Journal of a Voyage to New South Wales*. Angus and Robertson, Sydney.

Williams, Elizabeth 1987. Complex Hunter-Gatherers: A View from Australia. *Antiquity* 61:310–21.

Wood, W. B. 1968. An Aboriginal Burial Ground at Broadbeach, Queensland: Skeletal Material. *Mankind* 6:681–6.

# 6

## Conflict and Territoriality in Aboriginal Australia: Evidence from Biology and Ethnography

Colin Pardoe

This chapter examines both skeletal and ethnographic evidence for warfare and violence in Aboriginal Australia, focusing principally on the Central Murray River, a rich and densely populated area approximately 500 km long in the Murray-Darling Basin (Figure 6.1). Historical evidence from the 1850s is compared with skeletal evidence covering 10,000 years. This allows us to assess the value and limitations of both sources, following a long tradition of applying ethnographic analogy to the archaeological record.

The historical accounts used in this chapter were written by a number of initial European settlers taking up land in the Central Murray region in the 1840s. They give insights into traditional life among the Barapa Barapa (Wemba Wemba) as well as their Yorta Yorta neighbors upstream and the Wadi Wadi downstream. These eyewitness accounts were based on diaries written at the time but published several decades later, so it is important to allow for historical revisionism. Despite this, the descriptions are remarkably consistent in details of material culture or Aboriginal daily life, including descriptions of what they invariably describe as "warfare." In this study, I distinguish between categories of violence based on this ethnographic record.

The skeletal evidence for warfare and violence in the Central Murray area comes from a variety of sources, including first-hand field research and data gathered from museum collections as well as data from published sources.

---

*Violence and Warfare among Hunter-Gatherers*, edited by Mark W. Allen and Terry L. Jones, 112–132. ©2014 Taylor & Francis. All rights reserved.

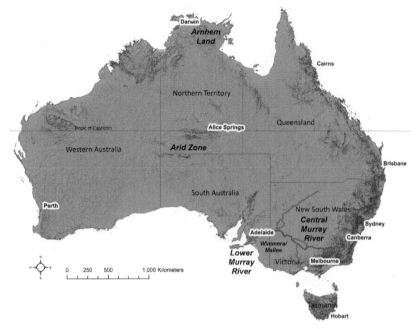

**Figure 6.1** Map of the Central Murray River region and other places named in text.

The number of skeletal remains collected and excavated along the Murray River is as great as those from rest of the country combined. Preservation of bone is good because the region is characterized by carbonate-rich soils, and some of the first ancient remains that date to more than 10,000 years were found here. The imbalance in sample sizes may well skew our view of biological variation, but at the same time has allowed a detailed examination of this region.

This skeletal evidence from the Central Murray region is then compared with skeletal indicators of trauma across the whole of Australia, allowing us to examine regional variation in patterns of violence across different ecological zones to test the hypothesis that levels of warfare and conflict in the Central Murray area can be related to demographic pressure in an area of rich resources (Pardoe 1988a, 1990, 1995, 2006).

## The Central Murray River Region

This brief overview of the Central Murray demonstrates the relationship between environment, demography, biology, and social organization that is central to this regional model. Levels of warfare and violence form part of this model and are critically examined in this chapter.

## Environment

The Murray River has experienced climatic and geomorphological change from the beginning of the Holocene Epoch, with increasing temperatures and rainfall, changes to the nature and flow of rivers, and greater environmental stability. At the same time, the Murray River and the people living along it have been subject to enduring and stable aspects of environment and ecology.

The Murray River environment is not the hard desert inhabited by true nomads so common in the Australian literature, but rather is characterized by good-quality food resources: fish and fowl that are high in protein and fats, and massed amounts of staple carbohydrates in yams and rhizomes. Water is always available, and this obviously has great importance for carrying capacity (Birdsell 1953). String, wood, and shell are available for tool manufacture, although the region is lacking in stone. All these factors have contributed to the river's reputation as "the most favoured area of Australia" (Brown 1918:231, 1923). An important feature of the Murray River corridor is its contrast to the semiarid plains that surround it, which may best be characterized in terms of resource predictability and distribution. This has implications for group relations and evolutionary processes (Pardoe 1988a, 2006).

## Demography

Although it is difficult to estimate population size in the past, the pattern of population relationships along the Murray River contrasted with the rest of the continent points to large and dense populations (Pardoe 1994, 2006). The linear nature of the Murray River, a lifeline of reliable water flowing through a semiarid land, means large populations with fewer neighbors and smaller territories than their back-country compatriots. These rich territories need strategies for defense and boundary maintenance against intruders (Wobst 1974). Population size and density differentials between river and back-country also serve as a barrier to intermarriage and gene flow, and the Murray River corridor acts as a population center where reproductive isolation is maintained by a demographic rather than physical barrier (Pardoe 1994, 2006).

## Biology

Environmental changes in the Murray Basin that occurred during the early Holocene between 10,000 and 6,000 years ago have been mirrored in some aspects of biology, in particular size decrease, reduction in robusticity, and the morphological changes in facial and vault size and shape that have fueled colonization theories for decades (Brown 1987, 1989; Pardoe 1991a). I have demonstrated previously that changes due to selection may occur within a stable gene flow network (Pardoe 2010a).

Biological variation across the continent is patterned by gene flow and the demography of populations, structured in turn by environmental patterns of resource availability and barriers to interaction with neighbors. Isolation by distance is a major structuring agency over continental scales (Pardoe 1991b). While regional biological variation is evident across the continent, the particular linear environment of the Murray River drives extreme differentiation and biological diversification that distinguishes the region from the rest of the continent (Pardoe 1994). The difference between populations at either end of the Murray River is as great as the difference between populations in southwest Western Australia and Cape York in the far northeast.

On a smaller scale, the Central Murray River region shows stability in patterning of variation over time and space among samples within a 200-km radius (Pardoe 2010a). The difference among riverine groups as well as between river and back-country groups is well-patterned, demonstrating the interaction of selection and gene flow.

## A Model of Social Organization in the Central Murray

Ecological theory has been used to good effect in the analysis of social organization in the archaeological record, where territoriality is related to resources and demography (Cashdan 1983; Dyson-Hudson and Smith 1978; Smith 1988). The early Holocene (between about 9,000 and 6,000 years ago) was a time of change in both the environment and the archaeological record. A pattern emerges from several strands of evidence of societies framed on principles of "exclusion" as opposed to desert groups that have been defined as "inclusive."

Biological evidence shows highly differentiated, but stable, populations along the Murray River, both created and maintained by gene flow and inter-marriage patterns in a linear context (Pardoe 2006). Population increase is accompanied by decrease in body size and increased rates of disease, particularly "diseases of overcrowding" (Webb 1984). Burial archaeology shows people increasingly burying their dead in large cemeteries over the last 7,000 years, a visible expression of territoriality, land ownership, and group identification (Pardoe 1988a).

The rise of cemeteries is followed in the archaeological record by large earthen mounds indicating village sites and a more sedentary pattern of resource exploitation. Ground ovens are used on a more industrial scale for the production of string for nets up to 50 meters long for hunting ducks, emu, and kangaroo. Elaborate weirs are constructed for catching quantities of fish.

Vigorous boundary maintenance was inferred from the stability over millennia of the biological patterning, items of material culture related to violence and warfare, and an increase in cranial blunt force trauma over time. It is this aspect of the model that is discussed in this chapter.

116 | Colin Pardoe

## Ethnographic Accounts of Warfare in Aboriginal Australia

Documentary records of warfare and violence can provide important, but limited, information. Whether collected by early settlers or trained anthropologists, the evidence is invariably subject to an ethnographic present that may have no relevance to an archaeological past. It is also subject to observer bias, ideology, or theoretical perspective. Warner ([1937] 1969), for instance, who recorded the most detailed account of warfare among the Murngin of northeastern Arnhem Land in the late 1920s, interpreted his findings according to the functionalist theories popular at the time.

In the 1950s and 1960s, anthropologists became more keenly aware of Aboriginal spiritual links to country, and an individual's relationship to the Dreaming ancestors who created features in the landscape (Berndt [1964] 1992; Elkin [1938] 1974). In this context, they argued that no wars were deliberately designed to take over a stretch of country, or as conquest over neighboring groups. This very static view of Aboriginal territorial organization does not allow for original Aboriginal colonization of the continent or variation in climate or changing resource distribution over millennia. While relationship to territory represents an ideal, there is considerable documentation of the processes that allow outsiders to move into a neighbor's territory following demographic change as a result of disease, a dearth of male children, or a decline in fertility. Many ideologies are honored in the breach, and evidence from the Central Murray clearly suggests that "sham fights" and other forms of more serious conflict are processes that operate as boundary maintenance.

Half a century on, discussions of violence among recently invaded hunter-gather societies risked being caught up in an ideological perspective that contrasted an idealized, harmonious pre-colonial life with the brutality of the invaders, individually and collectively. We know from skeletal and ethnographic evidence, as well as items of material culture, that warfare and conflict were important aspects of life in the Aboriginal past. Arguments have been made for an increase in conflict between groups as population pressure increased from 7,000 years ago (Pardoe 1995).

## Historical Accounts of Violence and Warfare from the Central Murray Region

These remarkably consistent accounts of violence and warfare are an important resource for understanding the archaeological record in this region. Items of material culture are generally perishable, since most of them were made of wood or string, but some have been preserved in museum collections, where clubs (*waddy* or *nulla-nulla*), hafted fighting implements and boomerangs, kidney-fatting cords, and death spears are to be seen. Women's digging or yam

## Conflict and Territoriality in Aboriginal Australia | **117**

sticks, used to dig out tubers and small game, were also used in fighting. They were typically a stout stick about 1.5 meters long, taken from one of the small trees whose wood is iron-hard.

Linguistic research in the area (Hercus 1992; Stone 1911) includes vocabulary associated with warfare, such as the word *liya-wil*, meaning "battle axe." The word *parn-parn*, "war party," was important enough to classify as a small or large *parntya-parntya* ("vengeance party"). The names of the peoples themselves—*Barapa Barapa*, *Wemba Wemba*, *Wadi Wadi*, and *Yorta Yorta*— all translate as "No-No" in their respective languages, underscoring their unwelcoming attitude to outsiders.

In this chapter, violence documented in the historical accounts is divided into six broad categories to assist interpretation of the skeletal record from the area.

### Domestic Violence or Camp Fights

There were several kinds of domestic violence. Arguments between men in a camp often led to fights that resulted in an exchange of blows. Usually, though, these were stopped by older men and, if serious, a formal trial by ordeal might be arranged (see the next section).

Ill treatment of women, though, was common, as women were generally considered the property of men to treat as they liked (Curr [1883] 2001:243). This included hitting, giving away, or even killing. Beveridge (1889:13) provides similar evidence. Since a woman always came from a different tribe or clan, her only recourse was to her own brothers, who might avenge ill treatment. Since sister exchange between different groups was common, vengeance might take the form of a woman's brother beating his own wife to express his displeasure!

Fights between women were also common. Since they had married into the group from different tribes or clans, this often caused conflict, as did jealousy, particularly if a man had a number of wives (Curr [1883] 2001: 268). Women settled disagreements by fighting with their yam sticks, which were solid, hardwood poles that could cause serious injury. Women might also collectively punish another woman for inappropriate behavior. It would be wrong to assume that all the parrying fractures found on women's skeletal remains were caused by men.

### Conflict Settled through Trial by Ordeal (between Individuals, or between an Individual and a Group)

Trial by ordeal was a common way of dispute resolution both between individuals within a group or between members of different groups. Curr ([1883] 2001:317–22), a settler who spent almost 10 years in the Central Murray region, gives a detailed account of formal single combat between a young Bangerang (Yorta Yorta) warrior and a Ngooraialum man from a neighboring tribe who had insulted him. This took the form of a stylized duel, each combatant in turn throwing several reed spears or boomerangs until the old men in the camp intervened, inviting the combatants to conclude the business with shields and waddies (clubs). After an appropriate time had elapsed, friends on both sides intervened and stopped the fight, as both fighters had suffered blows to the head, and blood was flowing freely.

Intergroup conflict was often settled by agreement that the offending individual be submitted to trial by ordeal. The individual presented himself, with only a shield for protection, before six men from the opposing tribe or clan, each armed with a number of spears, *nulla-nullas* (or cudgels), and boomerangs, all of which would be thrown at him over a 20-minute period. If he managed to dodge these or deflect them with his shield, honor was satisfied, and the offender might escape with only minor flesh wounds.

Hinkins (1884) discusses in detail an occasion he observed in the 1840s when ritual conflict took place between a gathering of over a 100 members of two neighboring tribes in the Central Murray over a woman.

A blackfellow of the Murray tribe had stolen a woman from the Goulburn tribe, though it was quite with the woman's consent. . . . The chief and friends of the captured girl, who was remarkably pretty, came to demand her from the hands of her captor. . . . On arriving at the plain we found that upwards of a hundred of the two tribes had met. As far as I could understand their talk, it was decided that the young woman was to be given up to her friends, unless the captor, her intended husband, could stand an "ordeal" of six of her friends—her nearest relatives—endeavouring to wound or even kill him by throwing a certain number of each of their war instruments at him. He was to use no weapons to defend himself against these attacks but a shield. This ordeal seems to have been customary with them on such occasions. Six able young men were chosen, and each of them was supplied with a certain number of "spears", "nulla nullas", a kind of club, "boomerangs", and other implements of war. The captor was to stand about fifty yards distant from the warriors, and these instruments were hurled at him one at a time by the six men. If he was either killed or wounded, the young woman was to return with her friends to her own tribe, but if by his dexterity her would-be husband was able to evade all their weapons he would then rightly claim her as his bride, and she would be delivered up to him accordingly. . . . A greater sight of agility and cleverness on the part of this young aboriginal [sic] I never witnessed. Every weapon was hurled at him with unerring aim, but he cleverly disposed of them all by turning them off with his shield, stooping down or stepping aside, lifting an arm of a leg, showing how good and steady his sight must have been. One "nulla nulla" was thrown with such force that it broke his shield, which was made from the bark of a tree. He was immediately supplied with another, for they would have scorned to take advantage of his undefended state, and then with the same success he avoided all the rest of the weapons that were cast at him, not receiving a single wound. There was a great shout raised

Conflict and Territoriality in Aboriginal Australia | **119**

for the victor, and he was allowed to carry off his prize, who seemed greatly pleased, for she had evidently been watching the scene anxiously. Indeed all parties appeared completely satisfied, and her friends returned home.

Beveridge (1889:121) describes similar punishment by ordeal carried out within groups if a member is found guilty of murder. According to his estimates, murder is common: 20 percent of men in his area of the Central Murray had committed murder, and all then experienced this punishment. The murderer is immediately condemned to stand within easy spearing distance, protected by only a shield, while the young men of the tribe try out their marksmanship. Most flesh wounds occur, according to Beveridge, in the right arm, between the elbow and the point of the shoulder. Fatalities occur rarely and only when the offender is too exhausted to handle his shield.

## Stylized Conflict, or "Sham Fights"

Battles between opposing groups, perhaps over a territorial transgression or theft of women, were common. Such battles often formed a prelude to large meetings for trade, feasting, or marriage arrangements. Although fiercely fought, resulting in numerous injuries and an occasional death, the major purpose seems to have been conflict resolution to deal with any outstanding grievances between groups before ceremony and trade began. The public and performatory nature of such battles came to their being widely called "sham fights" by a number of early authors.

Stainthorpe ([1925] 1983:4–5) described "a big fight between the Swan Hill blacks and blacks at Dimboola [in the Mallee to the south-west]" that lasted for nearly a week. He was impressed by the way injuries were treated by putting soft clay on the wound, over which a strip of bark was tied with kangaroo tail sinews.

Blandowski (1838:136) described "the Loddon tribe or Gunbowers" as collecting in large numbers in January "to enjoy the fishing season on the Murray. Playing at sham-fights is their amusement. In February they commence to fight in earnest with the neighboring tribes, and have several hard combats."

## More Serious Warfare between Groups or Tribes

In historical accounts, there seems to be a fine line between the "sham fights" and more serious battles that might result in a number of deaths. Some researchers have argued that there was frequent conflict between groups. According to Hofmaier (1960:63): "The Millegundeet or Murray blacks . . . were greatly feared by the others, and the Mallee blackfellow could always be given a thorough good fright by the words, 'The Murray blacks are coming.'"

**120** | Colin Pardoe

Curr ([1883] 2001:301) writes: "When a tribe in our neighbourhood had a substantial grievance against another ... such as the violation of their territory or the abduction of some of their women, it was usually fought out in broad daylight with spears, boomerangs, and waddies" in battles that might involve scores of people. Women would often run on to the battlefield to give the combatants new weapons. Despite his referring to these clashes as "warfare," apparently people were seldom killed, suffering only ugly gashes and other injuries. He notes, though (1883:299), that a whole tribe, or coalition of language groups, often considered themselves "in a chronic state of war" with surrounding tribes who were seen as enemies.

## Revenge Killings, Socially Sanctioned "Payback" by a Group on the Death of One of their Members by Sorcery

Whereas public battles or the settlement of disputes by ordeal seldom resulted in death, secret revenge attacks and night raids by stealth were a major cause of death, both of individuals and groups (Curr 1883:301). Except in very old age, deaths were rarely considered natural. Most were attributed to sorcery by a neighboring group, and vengeance, or "payback," needed to be carried out if the dead were to be at peace. Depending on the age and status of the person who died, whether by accident, or by falling sick, vengeance would be carried out against the supposed perpetrators (Phillips 1893:74–7.)

An inquest was always carried out to identify the direction of those responsible. This might include watching the direction of smoke from a funeral fire, or footprints found near the grave. Four or more of the dead men's relatives would head off, fully armed, often taking with them a special strangling cord. Usually the first lone stranger encountered in the right direction was the guilty party. Death invariably followed the excision of the kidney fat of the victim, which is the source of an individual's spiritual strength. According to Curr ([1883] 2001:302), "for every adult male who died from any cause save old age, a corresponding victim was anxiously desired."

Hinkins (1884:32–4) describes seeing an unfortunate young woman still alive after she had been operated on in this way, but people never survived for long afterwards. At one time he endeavored to prevent two young men from going on a revenge attack, telling them how wrong it was, but he failed to persuade them to turn them back. Beveridge (1889:124) and Phillips (1893:74–7) also give detailed descriptions of this manner of death showing that it was widespread in the Central Murray. Phillips commented that those carrying out such attacks either anointed themselves with the kidney fat or formed it into a bracelet or necklace that they wore as a protective charm. Hercus (1992:31), who did most of her linguistic research in the Central Murray in the 1960s working with Barapa Barapa and Wemba Wemba people, records the expression "*yukwek mambulin*," meaning "I wish I had your kidney fat."

Curr ([1883] 2001:303–12) gives a detailed description of a revenge or "payback" expedition that resulted in the murder of a whole clan from a neighboring tribe. Following the death of an important young warrior who fell from a tree while hunting possum, the inquest pointed in a north-westerly direction. As a result, a war party of 15 men traveled several days through friendly country until they encountered an encampment of strangers. Painted in white clay, they attacked the group while they slept, killing first the men and then the women and children, tearing out the kidney fat from their victims.

## Violence against Europeans

Violence against Europeans was widespread and demonstrated planning and coordination. If warfare among Aboriginal groups gave the appearance of "sham fights," warfare against many (but by no means all) of the early settlers was sustained and deadly. In the early years of European settlement on the Murray River, settlers had to rely on muzzle-loading muskets; Aboriginal warriors were adept at counting the time between shots to support their advance. One of the first settlers on the Central Murray, at Perricoota, was driven off his proposed settlement several times, and finally installed "a swivel gun" so that he could direct repeated fire through his slit windows. Hinkins (1884:17), who was the first manager of Gunbower Station on the Murray, and moved there in 1850, also describes the slit-holes cut into the walls of all the huts, which were made for defence in case of any attacks by "the natives."

Phillips (1893:66), one of the first settlers to take up land in the 1840s in Barapa Barapa country on the banks of the Edward River, a tributary north of the Murray, describes a property 30 miles downstream from his coming under sustained attack by Aborigines. Their slab hut with a bark roof, like many early settler huts, was perforated with square-cut holes in the sides for firing their muskets. Eventually, approximately 200 local Aborigines advanced with firebrands attached to the end of their spears, intending to set fire to the bark roof and burn them out. The Aboriginal force was routed and driven into dense reed beds by a troop of native mounted police under their captain, deputized as a superintendent of police, whose job was to protect outlying stations from attack.

This area was settled before breech-loading guns appeared in the 1860s and became widespread in the 1870s, although powder and shot was still cheaper and more accessible in the bush. The outlaw, or bush ranger Ned Kelly, for example, was still using muskets when arrested in 1880. Given this, the successful settlers were those who negotiated terms with the Aboriginal landowners and entered into reciprocal relations, providing meat, flour, axes, and other valuable items as payment for land and labor.

## 122 | Colin Pardoe

## Comparative Ethnographic Evidence from Northern Australia

The evidence provided from early settlers on the Murray in the 1850s is often considered anecdotal compared with evidence from trained anthropologists. The categories defined here have been compared with research in the late 1920s in northeastern Arnhem Land, prior to any significant European contact (Warner [1937] 1969). Despite a time difference of 80 years and a distance of 3,000 km, the categories are almost identical. His enumeration of the number of deaths documented over a two-year period is particularly instructive. Out of 67 deaths, only two resulted from domestic violence and three from what are considered "sham fights" in this chapter. A total of 62 deaths, though, were attributed to "payback" or revenge killing by stealth at night. Of these, 27 were individual killings and 35 were group killings. A final category that Warner described but did not observe was pitched battles between two groups. According to his sources, only two such battles had occurred over the previous 20 years, resulting in the death of 29 people.

## Skeletal Evidence

The study of skeletal material, buried over many thousands of years, can give important information about warfare, conflict, and violence in the Aboriginal Australian past. This information, though, has serious limitations. Our stories are restricted only to those individuals given burial, subject to preservation, and later excavated. Burial is also only one form of disposition of the dead in Australia, biasing the archaeological record. Whole family groups who may have been killed in night raids may well not have been buried. And finally, the potential of skeletal studies to give any insight into flesh wounds or cause of death beyond that evident on the bones is limited.

It should also be noted that most observed fractures had healed, with the person dying and being buried at a later date. Perimortem fractures occurring at or near death, which are difficult to determine, have rarely been identified. Skeletal evidence of violence is largely restricted to three classes of damage in which we can attribute traumatic injury to human aggression: cranial depression fractures, parrying fractures, and occasional pathologies directly attributable to traumatic origin. Not only is there a reasonable cause and effect, the frequency of occurrence can only be interpreted as violent in origin. The patterning of these categories of trauma—differences between regions, groups, and sexes—may allow for inferences of cause not possible with single events.

Here, I present the evidence for trauma among Central Murray populations by class of damage, then compare that trauma with evidence from across the continent to look for variation between regions. Finally, I assess the skeletal data against the historical evidence to look for any correlations between the two.

## Parrying Fractures

Parrying fractures are transverse breaks of the distal ulna, above the wrist, resulting from raising the arm in defense against attack by a club, digging stick, or the like. The prevalence of these fractures between sexes and groups provides an indication of personal violence.

The incidence of parrying fractures is greater among the tribes of the Central Murray River region than most other areas (Figure 6.2, Table 6.1). When calculated by individual, regardless of side, the percentages for women are exceeded only by the east coast sample. For men, only the Arid zone group has more.

The Central Murray sample shows more consistent left-side preference for both sexes, clearly related to handedness. Samples downstream (the general Murray River sample and that from the Rufus River) have similar incidences for men, but the sides are more equally affected.

Samples from other parts of Australia, including the eastern and southern coast and the Arid zone, vary in incidence. Parrying fractures are more common among women than men (Figure 6.1) on the Murray River generally and along the east coast. Differences between men and women are generally small. In his continental survey, Webb (1984) recorded totals of 3.9 percent parrying fractures among men and 5.0 percent among women (sides combined; n=618 and n=321, respectively). These numbers vary by side and region. Women

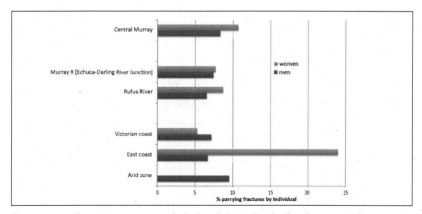

**Figure 6.2** Percent occurrence (calculated by individual) of parrying fractures by regional group Australia-wide, sides combined (data from Webb 1984).

**124** | Colin Pardoe

**Table 6.1** Parrying fractures by side, sex, and group

| | Men | | | | Women | | | |
|---|---|---|---|---|---|---|---|---|
| | % Parrying | | N | | % Parrying | | N | |
| Group | L | R | L | R | L | R | L | R |
| Central Murray River | 5.3 | 3.3 | 57 | 60 | 5.6 | 3.6 | 36 | 28 |
| Murray River (Echuca–Darling River junction) | 4.9 | 2.8 | 102 | 108 | 3.4 | 3.8 | 59 | 52 |
| Rufus River | 4.7 | 2.2 | 43 | 46 | 4.5 | 4.3 | 22 | 23 |
| Victorian coast | 4.8 | 3.6 | 21 | 28 | 4.8 | 0 | 21 | 19 |
| Arid zone | 10.5 | 0 | 19 | 21 | 0 | 0 | 5 | 5 |
| NSW and Queensland coast | 5.7 | 1.7 | 53 | 60 | 19.2 | 4.0 | 26 | 25 |
| Totals | 5.4 | 2.5 | 295 | 323 | 6.5 | 3.3 | 169 | 152 |

**Note:** Data from Webb (1984).

typically suffered more fractures than men among groups on the Murray River and east coast, and fewer on the Victorian coast and in the Arid zone samples. The greater incidence for desert men is obscured by the very small sample for women, and so it is difficult to interpret this data point. It should be noted, however, that Webb's Victorian coast sample included the Ngarrindjeri and other groups of the Lower Murray River as well as the Kaurna of the Adelaide Plains. None of the sex differences by group are significant.

There is a consistent excess of parrying fractures on the left side among all groups and both sexes except for the combined Murray River sample. This may indicate face-to-face combat, where a direct blow, or an indirect blow off a shield from a right-handed assailant, would hit the victim's left arm. There are, of course, a number of fractures of the right side, possibly indicating left-handed assailants in face-to-face combat, or an unexpected blow toward the victim's right side. Among the women, there is more variation in side.

One can interpret parrying fractures as the result of face-to-face combat or as a reflex action to ward off an unexpected or sudden blow. The incidence by side confirms a supposition that most would result from a direct blow from a right-handed assailant who would generally be in the victim's line of sight. This could be the result of a direct blow on an unprotected arm or by glancing off a shield. The data do not allow us to distinguish between domestic violence (within or between the sexes). Nor does it assist us to distinguish between camp fights or trial by ordeal, which can result in formal hand-to-hand combat. While both "sham fights" and more serious warfare could result in parrying fractures, the use of spears makes it appear less likely. It would seem least likely that parrying fractures would result from revenge killings of individuals or night raids on a sleeping group. These are invariably planned assassinations with an element of surprise that few people survive.

## Cranial Depression Fractures

Cranial depression fractures are a common feature of Australian skeletal biology. They are small, circular to oval depressions in the outer table of the vault typically measuring 20 mm by 15 mm and a few millimeters deep. There is rarely any infection in the form of periostitis (but see Pardoe 1988b), nor is there evidence of radial fracture lines. Most do not disrupt the inner table. The depressions are caused by a sharp rap on the head with a club or stick that collapses the outer part of the skull and leaves a dent.

There is tremendous variation in the proportion of dents among groups on the Central Murray River, nearly as much as the rest of the country (Table 6.2), ranging from 12 percent to 71 percent. Differences between the sexes also vary from many more among women in two groups, with a slight excess among Barapa Barapa men.

There is considerable variation in incidence of cranial depression fractures across the continent (Figure 6.3, Table 6.2). Women generally suffered more hits than men, with an overall incidence of 36.1 percent for women and 21.6 percent for men. When the Murray River groups are examined in more detail (these are the first 10 samples in Figure 6.3 and Table 6.2), it becomes

**Table 6.2**  Incidence of depression fractures by sex

| Region | Location | % | | N | | Source |
|---|---|---|---|---|---|---|
| | | Men | Women | Men | Women | |
| Central Murray River | Yorta | 43 | 50 | 21 | 8 | Pardoe 2004 |
| | Pangerang | 29 | 71 | 7 | 7 | Pardoe 2004 |
| | Barapa | 19 | 18 | 31 | 17 | Webb 1984 |
| | Wemba | 12 | 21 | 41 | 28 | Webb 1984 |
| | Coobool Pleistocene | 11 | 19 | 28 | 16 | Webb 1984 |
| Rest of Murray River | Swan Hill | 25 | 28 | 56 | 40 | Webb 1984 |
| | Lake Benanee | 14 | 27 | 119 | 66 | Webb 1984 |
| | Lake Victoria | 34 | 39 | 122 | 83 | Webb 1984 |
| | Swanport | 25 | 58 | 57 | 53 | Webb 1984 |
| | Murray River mouth | 8 | 21 | 12 | 19 | Pardoe 2003 |
| Southeastern Australia | Adelaide | 73 | 60 | 11 | 10 | Pardoe 2005 |
| | South coastal Victoria | 17 | 18 | 48 | 38 | Webb 1984 |
| | Wimmera Mallee | 29 | 32 | 17 | 19 | Webb 1984 |
| | NSW coast | 42 | 52 | 59 | 44 | Webb 1984 |
| | Tasmania | 19 | 17 | 27 | 35 | Webb 1984 |
| Other Regions | Central Australia | 27 | 53 | 94 | 40 | Webb 1984 |
| | WA | 24 | 24 | 54 | 21 | Webb 1984 |
| | Larrakia (NT) | 29 | 28 | 42 | 32 | Pardoe 2002 |
| | All NT | 19 | 32 | 94 | 62 | Webb 1984 |
| | Broadbeach | 19 | 20 | 21 | 5 | Webb 1984 |
| | South coastal Queensland | 25 | 57 | 44 | 28 | Webb 1984 |
| | Cairns | 5 | 41 | 64 | 39 | Webb 1984 |

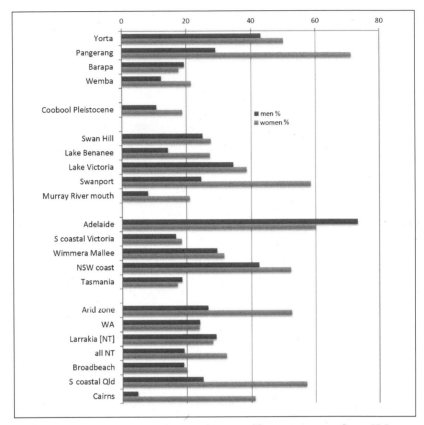

**Figure 6.3** Cranial depression fractures by group. The groupings are Central Murray, the single Pleistocene sample from the same region, rest of the Murray River, rest of southeastern Australia, and rest of the country (data in Table 6.2).

clear that there is as wide a range as the rest of the continent. Some groups appear to have suffered much more violence. The Kaurna of the Adelaide Plains have among the highest incidences for both men and women. Women of the Queensland coast (Broadbeach, south coastal Queensland, and Cairns) show some of the highest incidences. This is similar to the findings of parrying fractures.

A summary regional comparison between the Central Murray River and groups of the Arid and Semiarid zones (Table 6.3) shows almost no difference in incidence by sex. There are minimal differences between regions but considerable variety within each region. The incidence of multiple cranial depression fractures overall is greater among women. Across the country, 21.6 percent of men suffered dents, of which 16.6 percent were single and

# Conflict and Territoriality in Aboriginal Australia | 127

**Table 6.3** Regional contrasts in head dents by sex

| Region | Men | | | Women | | |
|---|---|---|---|---|---|---|
| | % | Dents, no. | N | % | Dents, no. | N |
| Central Murray River | 22.7 | 127 | 559 | 35.7 | 138 | 387 |
| Arid and Semiarid zones | 23.6 | 61 | 259 | 36.6 | 52 | 142 |

5.0 percent multiple. For women, the numbers are 36.1 percent, 26.2 percent, and 9.9 percent, respectively. Although not numerous, twice the proportion of women would suffer multiple attacks.

The variation in occurrence of blunt force trauma to the head in the Central Murray River region is considerable. Like most other places, women have the greater proportion of these injuries, both single and multiple. The placement of these blows on the head indicates that there is little difference in the placement of injuries between the sexes. Multiple occurrences are more common among women, but men are also likely to have suffered more than one. The cause of such blows is therefore most likely to be from domestic disputes (within and between the sexes), sham fights, formal battle, or trial by ordeal.

It has also been considered that the dents are the result of "dueling," where two individuals engage in formalized combat, or trial by ordeal as it is termed here (Brown 1989; Knuckey 1992). It has also been suggested that the dents might be the result of "sorry business" at a funeral, where the bereaved, both men and women, may strike themselves in an expression of sorrow. On the Central Murray River in the 1850s, "the men beat their heads with the butts of their iron tomahawks until the blood streamed over their faces and backs" (Curr 1883:311–13). Similar scenes were recorded on the Darling River, where "warriors slid quietly into the grave, each bearing a sharp-edged boomerang, with which he struck and cut his companion's head until from each the blood flowed freely down on to the leaves covering the dead body" (Stockdale 1905). It seems unlikely that "sorry business," which is a public demonstration of grief often resulting in spectacular flows of blood, would inflict such serious blunt force trauma.

## Individual Trauma

The third class of osteological data relevant to violence and warfare is traumatic damage from a variety of sources. These sorts of trauma are rare and it is often difficult to differentiate perimortem from postmortem damage. Individual cases may provide a clear insight into kinds of violence, but of themselves are no more than anecdotal. Examples include a spear point embedded in a knee

# 128 | Colin Pardoe

around which bone had grown following the injury (Pardoe 2003). Another case (Octavia Man) shows embedded stone barbs that are clearly a cause of death (McDonald et al. 2007). The excavated remains of a young man in the Northern Territory revealed a bone point (part of a larger composite spear) in his ribcage (Pardoe 2013). In the same cemetery, another young man had suffered a broken hand bone and a well-defined crease on the left iliac or hip bone, which gave further evidence of fighting but not cause of death.

Although rare, such individual cases lend themselves to interpretation. Historical illustrations of trial by ordeal, for example, show that the stance of someone about to throw a spear or holding a shield for defense would readily result in a spear point in the side of the knee. In the case of Octavia man, he had received multiple spear wounds, was dismembered and burned, then abandoned without burial. This clearly suggests a revenge or "payback" attack. Given the location of the spear point, the young man in the Northern Territory almost certainly had been speared in his sleep in what could only be a night raid on a sleeping camp. In this context, it is relevant to note the role of watchdogs. The dingo, the native Australian dog, has no bark. The first settlers at Botany Bay in 1798 reported that "sensible of the danger they ran in the night," local Aborigines were keen to acquire spaniel and terrier puppies from Europeans as watch dogs (David Collins quoted in Fletcher 1975:460–1).

## Discussion

In this chapter, I present historical evidence for violence in the Central Murray River region of Australia from eyewitness accounts documented in the mid-1800s along with skeletal evidence from the same region from people who died over several thousand years.

The analysis has sought to test two hypotheses. The first evaluates the extent to which historical and ethnographic evidence over a short period of time can be correlated with indicators of skeletal trauma over many thousands of years. In other instances, historical documentation in the Central Murray area has given useful insights assisting interpretation of the archaeological record that have proven testable: the construction of earthen mounds and the use of bulrush in string manufacture, for example (Pardoe 2010b).

Documentary evidence has given important insights into patterns of warfare and violence in the region. None of this, though, could be inferred from the archaeological record. There are limits to what can be inferred from the skeletal pathological data in terms of social organization.

The second proposition tested is part of the model that includes high levels of warfare and violence in the Central Murray as one piece of evidence for boundary maintenance and competition between defined groups. To test this model, skeletal evidence of violence and warfare in the Central Murray is assessed against evidence from other groups across the continent. Although the numbers of individuals showing indicators of skeletal trauma in this core area is high, the analysis has demonstrated that there is little proportional difference across the continent. The territorial model used to bring together patterns of biology, archaeological residence, material culture, and historical data is still persuasive. Some territorial adjustments, no doubt assisted by warfare between groups, would follow from the ebb and flow of lineages. While minor variations in numbers of parrying fractures and cranial depressions between groups and sexes can be demonstrated, they do not allow us to infer a higher degree of warfare and violence in the Central Murray based on skeletal evidence alone.

## Conclusions

What is the evidence for violence and warfare? This case study has brought together skeletal and historical data. The historical record provides a detailed view of violence that may be categorized in a manner that is supported by ethnographic studies from the rest of the continent. Violence was common across the country, taking the form of domestic disputes, revenge killings, and larger battles. The Central Murray River region was typical in this regard. There are only a few osteological markers of trauma accessible for analysis. Parrying fractures and cranial depression fractures attest to high levels of violence in the Central Murray River region, but these incidences are not the highest in the country. There is a wide range of variation in occurrence that does not appear to be correlated with ecological regions or size of the tribal areas. Cranial depression fractures occur more commonly among women, and while we may be confident that most of these are the result of domestic violence, the distribution of dents on the head is similar for both sexes, and so we are not able to differentiate likely causes among the men. Night raids, the major cause of death by violence according to the historical evidence and Warner's data, may not show up in the archaeological record because these victims have a slighter chance of burial. Skeletal evidence of trauma and killing in night raids would result in perimortem damage occurring at or near death, thus being excluded from the samples considered here.

Although some of the results appear negative, there are several useful contributions to be made. There is no compelling evidence that any of the densely populated regions suffered any more warfare or violence than other areas. Is my original view of warfare as boundary maintenance supported? From the skeletal pathological evidence, the answer must be no. The evidence of population biology, though, where stable populations and highly structured gene flow, or intermarriage, have created systematic patterning, is still best

# 130 | Colin Pardoe

explained by groups that are strongly territorial and maintain boundaries over long periods of time. The evidence suggests, as is often the case today, that threat and intimidation played a larger role than physical assault.

The historical record of Australian hunter-gatherers may not be transportable in some global ethnographic analogy, but principles arising from these observations should be given credence for the simple fact that these are observations of hunter-gatherer societies in their core territory, unaffected by agriculture and domestication (always excepting the dog). This takes on an importance relevant to hunter-gatherers everywhere.

## Acknowledgments

I welcome the Barapa Barapa Nation Aboriginal Corporation's support of these investigations. Neville Whyman and Norman Moore, in particular, have been positive in promoting the ancient history of their people. I thank Mark Allen for inviting me to participate in the SAA session "Violence and Warfare among Hunter-Gatherer Societies," and for the opportunity to investigate further the data on which our models and interpretations are based. My dear wife Penny threw herself into the study with typical zest, not allowing pesky illness or car crash to get in the way.

## References

Berndt, Ronald M. (1964) 1992. *The World of the First Australians.* Aboriginal Studies Press, Canberra.

Beveridge, Peter 1889. *The Aborigines of Victoria and Riverina as Seen by Peter Beveridge.* M. L. Hutchinson, Melbourne.

Birdsell, Joseph B. 1953. Some Environmental and Cultural Factors Influencing the Structuring of Australian Aboriginal Populations. *The American Naturalist* 87:171–207.

Blandowski, William 1838. Recent Discoveries in Natural History on the Lower Murray. *Transactions of the Philosophical Institute Victoria* 2:124–37.

Brown, A. R. Radcliffe 1918. Notes on the Social Organization of Australian Tribes Part I. *Journal of the Royal Anthropological Institute* 48:222–53.

——— 1923. Notes on the Social Organization of Australian Tribes Part II. *Journal of the Royal Anthropological Institute* 53:424–47.

Brown, Peter 1987. Pleistocene Homogeneity and Holocene Size Reduction: The Australian Human Skeletal Evidence. *Archaeology in Oceania* 22:41–67.

——— 1989. *Coobool Creek: A Morphological and Metrical Analysis of the Crania, Mandibles and Dentitions of a Prehistoric Australian Human Population.* Terra Australis Monograph No. 13, Prehistory. Research School of Pacific Studies, the Australian National University, Canberra.

Cashdan, Elizabeth 1983. Territoriality among Human Foragers: Ecological Models and an Application to Four Bushman Groups. *Current Anthropology* 24:47–66.

Curr, Edward M. (1883) 2001. *Recollections of Squatting in Victoria, then Called the Port Phillip District, from 1841 to 1851.* Reproduction, Rich River Printers, Echuca, 1968 facsimile edition. Libraries Board of South Australia, Adelaide.

Dyson-Hudson, Rada, and Eric Alden Smith 1978. Human Territoriality: An Ecological Reassessment. *American Anthropologist* 80:21–41.

## Conflict and Territoriality in Aboriginal Australia | **131**

Elkin, Adolphus P. (1938) 1974. *The Australian Aborigines.* Angus and Robertson, Melbourne.

Fletcher, B. H. (editor) 1975. *An Account of the English Colony in New South Wales, David Collins [1798–1802].* A. H. & A. W. Reed, Sydney.

Hercus, Luise Anna 1992. *Wemba Wemba Dictionary.* Australian Institute of Aboriginal and Torres Strait Islander Studies, Canberra.

Hinkins, J. 1884. *Life amongst the Native Race: With Extracts from a Diary.* Haase, McQueen and Co., Melbourne.

Hofmaier, K. 1960. Aborigines of the Southern Mallee of Victoria. *Victorian Historical Magazine* 31:63–81.

Knuckey, G. 1992. Patterns of Fracture upon Aboriginal Crania from the Recent Past. *Proceedings of the Australasian Society for Human Biology* 5:47–58.

McDonald, Josephine J., Denise Donlon, Judith H. Field, Richard L. K. Fullagar, Joan Brenner Coltrain, Peter Mitchell, and Mark Rawson 2007. The First Archaeological Evidence for Death by Spearing in Australia. *Antiquity* 81:877–85.

Pardoe, Colin 1988a. The Cemetery as Symbol: The Distribution of Aboriginal Burial Grounds in Southeastern Australia. *Archaeology in Oceania* 23:1–16.

———— 1988b. The Mallee Cliffs Burial (Central River Murray) and Population Based Archaeology. *Australian Archaeology* 27:45–62.

———— 1990. The Demographic Basis of Human Evolution in Southeastern Australia. In *Hunter-Gatherer Demography, Past and Present*, edited by Betty Meehan and N. White, pp. 59–70. Oceania Monograph No. 39, University of Sydney.

———— 1991a. Competing Paradigms and Ancient Human Remains: The State of the Discipline [review]. *Archaeology in Oceania* 26:79–85.

———— 1991b. Isolation and Evolution in Tasmania. *Current Anthropology* 32:1–21.

———— 1994. Bioscapes: The Evolutionary Landscape of Australia. *Archaeology in Oceania* 29:182–90.

———— 1995. Riverine, Biological and Cultural Evolution in Southeastern Australia. *Antiquity* 69:696–713.

———— 2002. *Expert Assessment and Documentation of Larrakia Skeletal Remains Collected by W. R. Smith in 1906.* Report to the Repatriation Unit, National Museum of Australia, Canberra, Australian Capital Territory.

———— 2003. *Return of Ngarrindjeri Skeletal Remains. Expert Assessment and Documentation of Ngarrindjeri Skeletal Remains, collected by W. R. Smith in 1906, and Held by the National Museum of Australia, Canberra.* Report to the Repatriation Unit, National Museum of Australia, Canberra, Australian Capital Territory.

———— 2004. Skeletal Remains from the Berry Collection. Report to the Anatomy Department, University of Melbourne, Victoria.

———— 2006. Becoming Australian: Evolutionary Processes and Biological Variation from Ancient to Modern Times. *Before Farming* [online version] 1(article 4):1–21.

———— 2010a. Global Human Variation: Polarised Positions and Alternative Perspectives. *Before Farming* [online version] 3(article 3):1–21.

———— 2010b. Earthen Mounds in South-Eastern Australia: Distribution, Residential Patterning, Soul Food, and String. Paper presented at the Australian Archaeological Association Conference, Batemans Bay, NSW, Australia, December 1–4, 2010.

———— 2013. *Report on the Study in Jabiru of the Skeletons Excavated from the Madjedbebe Rock Shelter.* Report to Gundjeihmi Aboriginal Corporation, Jabiru, Northern Territory, Australia.

Phillips, J. 1893. *Reminiscences of Australian Early Life by a Pioneer.* A. P. Marsden, London.

Smith, Eric Alden 1988. Risk and Uncertainty in the "Original Affluent Society": Evolutionary Ecology of Resource-Sharing and Land Tenure. In *Hunters and Gatherers 1: History, Evolution and Social Change*, edited by Tim Ingold, David Riches, and James Woodburn, pp. 222–51. Berg Publishers, New York.

Stainthorpe, R. (1925) 1983. *Early Reminiscences of the Wimmera and Mallee*. Published privately, Warracknabeal, Victoria. Republished by the Warracknabeal Historical Society.

Stockdale, H. 1905. By the Way. *Australian Town and Country Journal* (NSW), April 19, p. 35.

Stone, A. C. 1911. The Aborigines of Lake Boga. *Royal Society of Victoria, Proceedings* 23:433–68.

Warner, William Lloyd (1937) 1969. *A Black Civilization: A Study of an Australian Tribe*. Peter Smith, Gloucester, MA.

Webb, S. G. 1984. *Prehistoric Stress in Australian Aborigines*. Unpublished Ph.D. thesis, Department of Prehistory, Australian National University, Canberra.

Wobst, Martin 1974. Boundary Conditions for Paleolithic Social Systems: A Simulation Approach. *American Antiquity* 39:147–78.

# 7

## Conflict and Interpersonal Violence in Holocene Hunter-Gatherer Populations from Southern South America

Florencia Gordón

Southern South America is an important area to examine the nature of hunter-gatherer violence and warfare. In recent years, there has been increased interest among regional specialists in the investigation of skeletal remains and other evidence in the Patagonia region, which covers much of the southernmost area of the continent across Chile and Argentina. This chapter deals with the Argentine section, which is delimited by the Andes Mountains on the west, the Colorado River on the north, and the coast along the south and east (Figure 7.1A). I briefly describe the culture history of the region, examine patterns of documented conflict, summarize a limited number of published studies of prehistoric and ethnohistory violence in the region, and present an analysis of traumas from skeletal populations from northeastern Patagonia. Many argue that the paucity of systematic studies on interpersonal violence in Patagonia helps to promote the idea of a peaceful past in the region, making isolated recorded cases anecdotal. The aim of this study is to demonstrate that conflict was characteristic of Patagonian hunter-gatherers during the late Holocene (Gordón 2011).

---

*Violence and Warfare among Hunter-Gatherers,* edited by Mark W. Allen and Terry L. Jones, 133–148. ©2014 Taylor & Francis. All rights reserved.

**134** | Florencia Gordón

# The Prehistory of Patagonia

The peopling of Patagonia was characterized by periods of population expansion and contraction associated with climatic fluctuations and subsequent changes in the distribution and availability of resources (Borrero 2001). Episodes of glacial retraction and temperature increase can be dated back to 14,000 years before present (BP), clearly illustrating an improvement of climatic conditions (Clapperton et al. 1995). The arrival of humans in Patagonia dates back to the Pleistocene-Holocene transition (ca. 12,500–10,000 years BP) (Borrero 2001). Archaeological sites are discontinuously scattered across the Patagonian steppe, the central plateau, the Magellan area, and Chilean central Patagonia. Borrero (1989–1990) claims that this level of discontinuity, distributed across large territories, was the result of exploration and colonization of unknown areas by highly mobile groups with wide home ranges and low demographic densities. During the Early Holocene (ca. 10,000–8,000 years BP), climatic conditions continued to improve (Bianchi 1999). In northeastern Patagonia, the climate was arid, while in the northwest, conditions favored the development of *Nothofagus* forests and grasslands (Markgraf 1983; Schäbitz 2003). During this time human groups expanded, population density increased, and home ranges decreased (Borrero 2001). Human presence has been recorded in northwestern Patagonia near the Andes and in periglacial areas (Aschero 1996; Franco and Borrero 2003). The oldest skeletal remains come from northwestern Patagonia (Epullán Grande Cave, 9,900–7,500 years BP; Crivelli Montero et al. 1996).

The Middle Holocene (ca. 8,000–4,000 years BP) was a period of increasing aridity and temperature (Grimm et al. 2001), with glacial re-advances in the Andes (Rabassa et al. 2000). Also at this time, marine transgressions resulted in the displacement of the Atlantic coast inland. The changes in the coastline influenced the use of space and archaeological visibility. The first human occupations on the Atlantic coast occur during the Middle Holocene; however, the skeletal data for human occupation during the Middle Holocene are scarcer than in previous periods. This phenomenon is attributed to regional depopulation, demographic retraction, and even local extinctions of populations that occurred between 8,000 and 4,000 years BP in close association with climate changes (Barrientos and Perez 2004; Neme and Gil 2001).

Finally, the Late Holocene (ca. 4,000–400 years BP) is characterized by climatic variability in the short term. This has been mainly related to water availability associated with temperature and precipitation (Agosta et al. 2005; Schäbitz 2003; Stine 1994). Near the end of the Late Holocene aridity increased, reaching a maximum level between 1,150 and 600 years BP that corresponds with the Medieval Climatic Anomaly (Stine and Stine 1990). A significant increase in the number of sites, more occupational redundancy, and the effective incorporation of new habitats by hunter-gatherers, such as mountain forests (Bellelli et al. 2000) and elevated plateaus (Goñi 2000), can be verified only for the Late Holocene. Moreover, the bioarchaeological record from the last 2,000 years is more robust given a high density of human burials in certain regions (Figure 7.1A) (Barrientos 1997; Bórmida 1953–1954; Castro and Moreno 2000; Della Negra and Novellino 2005; Flensborg 2012;

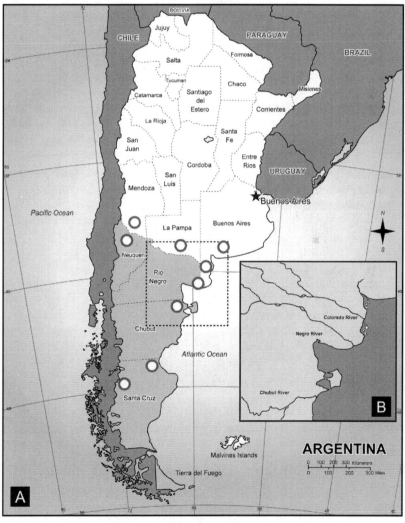

**Figure 7.1** (A) Patagonian region (in medium gray). Circles mark the areas with high concentration of human burials. (B) Northeastern Patagonia. Study area for systematic research on patterns of violence discussed herein.

# 136 | Florencia Gordón

García Guraieb 2010; Gómez Otero and Dahinten 1997–1998; Imbelloni 1923; Luna 2009). The demographic change is interpreted as evidence of an increase in population density (Barrientos 1997; Gómez Otero 2007). Given the arid conditions recorded near the end of the Late Holocene it is logical that human groups would have tended to concentrate around water resources such as rivers, lakes, and water basins. It is highly likely that at this time extensive networks of exchange in regional and supraregional scales were established. These circumstances might have generated favorable conditions for an increase in interpersonal violence, although this hypothesis has never been systematically explored.

## The Ethnohistorical Context of Patagonia

The western European expansion that began in the fifteenth century affected pre-existing violence patterns in small-scale societies in southern South America. Ferguson (1990) proposes the existence of disruptive aspects such as demographic alterations caused by the use of gunfire and more lethal warfare techniques, and the emergence of situations of violence and competition for access to western goods. Elsewhere, within a few decades after contact, some groups went from raids to organized battles, as was the case for the Nuer and the Dinka in northern Africa after contact with the English, as well as the Maori of New Zealand. The new weapons forced violence patterns in small-scale societies from adaptive to maladaptive in a very short time, thus contributing to the rapid and total destruction of certain groups (Vayda 1970).

This was the case for the Onas of Tierra del Fuego in insular Patagonia. They were subjected to overcrowding from the advance of mining and cattle activities after the 1880s, which increased hostilities among groups (Borrero 1991). This situation, together with the increase in infectious diseases, disrupted the Onas' way of life and led to their extinction in less than 40 years. In continental Patagonia, a series of coastal European settlements, known as *fuertes* (forts), acted as meeting and exchange points. These *fuertes* facilitated the procurement of goods that were indispensable to Indians. Natives, who provided goods to the European colonists, were key to colonial society as they knew the routes and resources, and were familiar with neighboring groups. Nacuzzi (1998) points out that exchange between groups has very old roots, like the important and crucial commercial relationships that were established with local "guanaco hunters" from Patagonia. Archaeological evidence from the Late Holocene supports this idea. For example, Chilean ceramics are recorded east of the Andes, and some common motifs in movable goods, leathers, and in rock art were found in the Pampa and Patagonian regions, and even west of the Andes. This has been interpreted as evidence for the exchange of information between the groups in the area

Conflict and Interpersonal Violence in Holocene Hunter-Gatherers | **137**

during the final Late Holocene (Belardi 2004; Berón 2007; Bonomo 2006). Furthermore, studies in craniofacial morphology suggest intergroup contact during this period, particularly in northern Patagonia and southeastern Pampas (Barrientos and Pérez 2004).

After the founding of Valdivia, Chile, in 1552, hostilities became common in northwestern sections of Argentine Patagonia. Chilean conquerors took prisoners from native groups to the east to meet labor demands in the Chilean mines and fields. Bandieri (2005) argues for the existence of a quasi-permanent state of war in the area beginning around 1600. Toward the end of the eighteenth century, the effective management of herd animals such as cattle and horses brought "another source of conflict and concord among indigenous groups" (Bechis 1998:10). The use of horses introduced profound changes in war practices; for instance, battles on foot gave way to organized actions by cavalry (Ratto 2007).

Ethnographic descriptions describe the political structure of the native groups during the contact period as chiefdoms, evidently created through negotiations and alliances with colonial society (Nacuzzi 1998). However, the groups would have retained their flexible nature of competitive leaderships regardless of the state's presence. This dynamic structure has been called "segmental" due to the presence of fusion and fission mechanisms and its manner of reproduction.

To the south of the Chubut River, colonial presence was not so intense. In 1780, the presence of the San Julian *fuerte* became an attractive place for southern groups to exchange goods. Moving closer to the fort would have increased the distance from those groups to the north. Economic complementarity existed among the native groups of northern Patagonia, especially those groups along the east-west corridor formed by the Colorado and Negro rivers (Mandrini 1985) that had different settlement patterns and diverse management systems of natural resources (Nacuzzi 1998; Villarino [1782–1783] 1972). Moreover, deserters of the state seeking refuge status as well as interethnic marriages between native groups are well documented (Claráz [1865–1866] 1988; Musters [1869–1870] 1997; Ratto 2007).

## Previous Studies of Interpersonal Violence in Patagonia

Several human skeletons with evidence of interpersonal violence have been described for northeastern Patagonia (Flensborg 2012) and for Argentina's Pampean region (Barrientos 1997; Luna 2009; Scabuzzo 2010). In northwestern Patagonia, sites with a putative defensive function have been described (Goñi 1986–1987), in addition to cases of individuals presenting evidence of trauma (Gordón 2013a). Further south, in the Chubut province,

**138** | Florencia Gordón

skeletons were found in association with spearheads (Gómez Otero and Dahinten 1997–1998; Vignati 1947). Likewise, García Guraieb et al. (2007) describe another case in northwestern Santa Cruz province, and L'Heureux and Amorosi (2009) present bioarchaeological evidence of violence in the Magallanes region of Chile. A human skull with an embedded spearhead was found on the northern coast of Magellan's Strait (Constantinescu 2003). All of these examples correspond to the Late Holocene, with the exception of a case in the Pampean region (Arroyo Seco 2 site) that corresponds to the Early to Middle Holocene (Barrientos 1997).

Together, these findings suggest violent relations among Holocene hunter-gatherer groups in Patagonia. However, most of these cases are isolated and poorly contextualized, with some exceptions (Flensborg 2012; García Guraieb 2010; Luna 2009). The scarcity of systematic tests and comparative studies of violence for the Late Holocene, in contrast to the extensive focus on conflict in postcolonial societies (Bandieri 2005; Nacuzzi 1998; Ratto 2007), gives the impression of a virtually pacific past among the late prehistoric populations of Patagonia.

## Bioarchaeological Studies in Northeastern Patagonia

Hypotheses on the patterns of variation in interpersonal violence from northeastern Patagonia have been tested recently, and full methods and results have already been published (Gordón 2009a, 2009b, 2011, 2013b; Gordón and Bosio 2012; Gordón and Ghidini 2006). These studies identify criteria for the interpretation of changes in conflict from the early occupation (4,500–5,000 years BP; Gómez Otero and Dahinten 1997–1998) until contact with colonial society (ca. 400 years BP), with an emphasis on the bioarchaeological record. A series of 797 crania was analyzed, representing a temporal sequence of approximately 4,000 years (Figure 7.1B). The series are from collections housed at the Museo de La Plata (UNLP) and the Museo Etnográfico "Juan B. Ambrosetti" (UBA). The crania were collected toward the end of the nineteenth century and the beginning of the twentieth century. At the time of collection, it was common practice to separate the cranium from the postcranium; hence, for most cases it was not possible to put together the remains from an individual.

The total series (N=797) was divided by geographic groups, sex, age categories, and period. First, it was divided into a northern group (NG), formed by those individuals from sites around the Colorado River and the Negro River valley; and a southern group (SG), formed by individuals from sites around the lower valley of the Chubut River. Sex categories, established by a previous study on the same collection, were estimated using geometric morphometrics (Perez 2006) and dimorphic traits of the cranium (Buikstra and

## Conflict and Interpersonal Violence in Holocene Hunter-Gatherers | **139**

**Table 7.1**  Age and sex distribution of the analyzed sample

|  | Female | Male | Undetermined | Totals |
| --- | --- | --- | --- | --- |
| Subadults | — | — | 65 | 65 |
| Young adults | 81 | 52 | 8 | 141 |
| Middle-aged adults | 140 | 202 | 18 | 360 |
| Senile adults | 38 | 71 | 6 | 115 |
| Undetermined adults | 50 | 40 | 26 | 116 |
| Totals | 309 | 365 | 123 | 797 |

Ubelaker 1994). Subadult individuals were not sexed. The series was classified into adults and subadults, according to dental eruption patterns and the degree of closure of the sphenobasilar suture (Buikstra and Ubelaker 1994). According to the degree of closure of the sutures of the lateral-anterior system (Meindl and Lovejoy 1985), adult individuals were subdivided into young (20–34 years), middle-aged (35–49 years) and senile (>50 years) (Table 7.1). The different types of artificial cranial modifications are reliable chronological indicators in the study area (Gordón 2011). On the basis of 45 radiocarbon dates (see full references in Gordón 2011) and the mode of artificial cranial deformation, three chronological periods were established:

(1) 4,000 to 2,500 years BP, a time period during which the annular deformation predominated (n=55) (Figure 7.2B);
(2) 2,500 to 1,500 years BP, characterized by the artificial tabular oblique deformation (n=66) (Figure 7.2C); and
(3) 1,500 to 400 years BP, characterized by a tabular erect deformation in the lambda-plane (n=287) (Figure 7.2D) (Dembo and Imbelloni 1938).

A large part of the sample did not present any artificial deformation (n=348), and a group presented an undetermined type of deformation (n=41). The cranial modifications were previously estimated by geometric morphometrics (Perez 2006) and by a more traditional method (Dembo and Imbelloni 1938). To evaluate diachronic trends, only those individuals with an artificial modification were considered.

Prior to registering traumas, the state of preservation of specimens was assessed through completeness indices and the record of taphonomic variables (Gordón 2009a). The presence, distribution, type, location, and healing of traumas were recorded. The types of trauma are also shown in Figure 7.2.

The classification of certain traumas can be ambiguous; therefore, frequencies of trauma were statistically analyzed twice: a broad level (L1), which considered all lesions as potentially positive, even those that are not necessarily the product of violence (e.g., healed fractures); and a second level (L2), which considered as positive traumas those cases with low level to

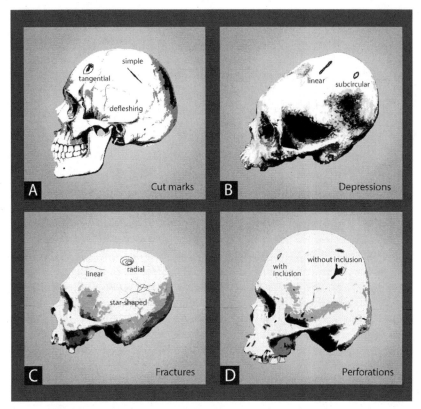

**Figure 7.2** Traumatic variables recorded for this study along with types of artificial cranial deformation found in the sample: (A) nondeformed; (B) circular deformation; (C) tabular oblique deformation; (D) tabular erect deformation in the lambda-plane.

zero ambiguity in their identification (e.g., embedded spearheads, multiple associated lesions). Thus, maximum and minimum thresholds for estimation of interpersonal violence were established. Only significant deviations from a background level were interpreted in population terms. Frequencies were assessed using 2×2 tables with Yates continuity correction to calculate $\chi^2$.

## Results: Interpersonal Violence Patterns

Table 7.2 shows percentages of trauma distribution by area, by sex within area, and by age within area. All results are presented at the two levels of analysis. Results indicate that for the northern group, the percentage of individuals with signs of violence is higher than in the southern group, although these differences are statistically significant only for level 1 ($p$=0.002). There are

# Conflict and Interpersonal Violence in Holocene Hunter-Gatherers | **141**

**Table 7.2** Trauma distribution by area, sex, and age

|  | Level 1, % | Level 2, % |
| --- | --- | --- |
| NG/SG | 21.8/13.3* | 4.3/2.2 |
| F (NG/SG) | 14.9/14.7 | 1.6/4.1 |
| M (NG/SG) | 25.6/18.6 | 7.8/2.2* |
| NG (M/F) | 25.6/14.9* | 7.8/1.6* |
| SG (M/F) | 18.6/14.7 | 2.2/4.1 |
| AD / SA | 22.7/10.7* | 3.7/1.5 |
| NG (AD / SA) | 25.1/15.8 | 4.4/5.2 |
| SG (AD /SA) | 19.7/8.7 | 2.8/0.0 |

NG indicates Northern Group; SG, Southern Group; F, female; M, male; AD, adults; and SA, subadults.
*Statistically significant difference ($p>0.05$).

no statistically significant differences in relation to sex distribution among females from the northern and southern groups, while the difference between the males from both groups is statistically significant ($p=0.029$ for level 2). In the northern section, males evidenced a higher percentage of traumas than females with significant differences at both levels (level 1: $p=0.010$; level 2: $p=0.011$). In the southern group, the differences between sexes are not statistically significant, though slightly higher among females in level 2. In relation to age groups, there are statistically significant differences when comparing all adult categories grouped to subadults, and only for the first level of analysis (i.e., considering the whole sample, northern and southern groups) (level 1: $p=0.036$). However, when samples are analyzed separately, the differences are not statistically significant; the general trend shows that adults presented a higher percent of traumas than subadults. It is possible that some percentages are skewed to the differences in sample size. When the three categories of adults (i.e., young, middle-aged, and senile) are compared, differences are not statistically significant.

The percentage of incidence of lesions is significantly increased for the latest group. Considering the whole sample, there is an increase from 14.3 percent to 25 percent in level 1 ($p=0.009$) and from 1.7 percent to 7.8 percent in level 2 ($p=0.019$). These differences are more marked for the northern group (level 1: northern group, $p=0.055$; southern group, $p=0.096$; level 2: northern group, $p=0.009$; southern group, $p=0.610$), in concordance with the ethnohistorical frame. From an experimental complementary approach (Gordón and Bosio 2012), it could be established that a certain type of lesion present only in the latest group corresponded to use of cold-steel weapons. This type of weapon was not present in the area until the mid-seventeenth century (Bechis 1998).

Once the individuals whose lesions were produced by cold-steel weapons were identified, the statistical analyses were repeated without including them, with the aim of exploring patterns of pre-contact violence. Even if the trend

**142** | Florencia Gordón

showed an increase of violence (from 14.3 percent to 22.6 percent in level 1; and from 1.7 percent to 6.1 percent in level 2), the differences are not statistically significant (northern group: level 1, $p$=0.146; level 2, $p$=0.223, southern group: level 1, $p$=0.107; level 2, $p$=0.584). However, the spatial pattern was maintained, with higher frequencies in the northern section (level 1: northern group, 19.7 percent versus southern group, 12.3 percent; level 2: northern group, 1.8 percent versus southern group, 1.1 percent). This difference is statistically significant for level 1 ($p$=0.006).

## Discussion: Patagonia as an Example of Conflict and Interpersonal Violence in Small-Scale Societies

The results indicate that in the northernmost sections (NG), the patterns of violence correspond to a state of frequent conflict, involving adult males in higher proportions than females, both in pre- and post-Hispanic indigenous contact times. This interpretation is congruent with the intergroup relationships that have been suggested for populations from northern Patagonia during the Late Holocene, especially along the Colorado and Negro rivers. The southern group showed a different pattern, which could be thought of in the context of domestic violence, surprising attacks or raids, in which both sexes are involved (e.g., Gat 1999). The proportion of nonlethal violence among women supports this idea (Walker 1997).

In recent decades, studies based upon small-scale societies (Keeley 1996; Lambert 2002; Milner 1995; Walker 2001) demonstrate the existence of higher levels of violence than those usually proposed. In Patagonia, despite the record of individuals with traumatic lesions, no reference frameworks have been developed for the interpretation of such cases at a population scale. For this reason, interpretations of the signs of violence recorded in Patagonia have been limited. The case study from northeastern Patagonia represents a first step toward more systematic bioarchaeological analysis of the variability of violence. Such studies must also rely on ethnohistorical accounts and cross-cultural studies.

The verification of traumatic lesions throughout the chronologic sequence investigated from northeastern Patagonia, together with the description of isolated cases in other areas of continental and insular Patagonia, considered alongside the ethnohistorical record, point to a threshold level of interpersonal violence. This finding challenges traditional interpretations of small-scale societies in southern South America as being inherently pacific. An example from Patagonia presents a record of 13 percent of violent deaths among the Kaweskar from Tierra del Fuego as a result of violence perpetrated in most cases by adult males (Emperarire 1963). On the one hand, Prieto and Cárdenas (2007) maintain that during the decades of European expansion, the levels of intergroup violence may have increased. Conversely, other authors propose that since the beginning of the twentieth century, violence levels

# Conflict and Interpersonal Violence in Holocene Hunter-Gatherers | **143**

might have decreased as a consequence of fewer conflict situations due to a dramatic decline in population density (Gusinde 1982). This is in accordance with the disruptive situation created by the European expansion, which has been recorded by cross-cultural studies. Surprise attacks and ambushes might have been the most common forms of attack both among Fuegian tribes (Gusinde 1982) and in continental Patagonia (De La Cruz [1835] 1969), as in other small-scale societies (Keeley 1996). It is worth noting that, despite the vast information available today, the Rousseaunian notion of a pacific state within this kind of societies still prevails (Fry and Söderberg 2013).

It has been suggested that in northern Patagonia coexistence, complementarities, and exchange relationships were maintained among diverse groups across the Pampean region, Patagonia, and even the Andes (Berón 2007; Martínez 2008–2009; Prates 2008). Morphological evidence from bioanthropological studies suggests population displacements during the final stages of the Late Holocene, possibly comprising expansions and retractions (Barrientos and Perez 2004). Curtoni (2004) suggests that during the Holocene, the lower stretches of the Colorado River valley constituted a "soft" boundary of permeable territories, inhabited and negotiated by groups from different areas. The bioarchaeological pattern indicating higher violence levels in the northern sections of Patagonia before and after Spanish contact supports this idea. At the time of European arrival, the population dynamic in Patagonia was complex, and the flexible structure of these groups was probably exacerbated, enabling the interaction with the Western world for at least two centuries (Nacuzzi 1998).

In addition to the changes that arose from contact with Europeans, it is possible that certain internal factors might have had some influence in the collapse of the hunter gatherer system. At least in southern Patagonia, these processes cannot be explained solely by the expansion of capitalism. External factors can accelerate or exacerbate previous situations. Instead of single-factor explanations, it is interesting to consider alternative answers, taking into account internal organizational factors that might respond to an external impact (Goñi 2000). In this chapter, I emphasize the multifactor character of conflict (Gat 2000), and support the idea that ecological, economic, or material causes are implied at the root of conflicts. Demographic factors might be important in explaining violence patterns in Patagonia. There is evidence of migration, interethnic marriages, exchange networks, and violence that predates the arrival of Europeans; in other words, there were both pacific and conflicting relationships among groups. This situation suggests that the mobility and the segmented system of the groups from Patagonia lent itself to strategies based upon fusion and fission mechanisms, avoiding elevated violence levels that might have resulted in malfunctioning systems. Violence in the region might have been an evolutionary adaptation playing an important role in the maintenance and reinforcement of social liaisons in the form of more contacts, exchanges, alliances, and conflict (de Waal 2000; Roscoe 2007). Therefore, even if the nineteenth-century military campaigns

**144** | Florencia Gordón

were disruptive, they represented the end of a process that might have begun at least two centuries before, and that was characterized by peace and conflict lapses. This situation seems to have been adaptive prior to European military campaigns in line with the cross-cultural and ethnohistorical studies.

## Final Considerations

The purpose of this contribution is to reiterate the need to overcome the stages of mere record of cases of violence, and to start interpreting and integrating the information into a regional scale within Patagonian archaeology. Also, it is useful to demonstrate how a data set can be interpreted within the wide context of small-scale societies to elucidate the conditions under which variable levels of interpersonal violence are to be expected. The studies conducted in northeastern Patagonia need to be expanded in several different directions. On the one hand, the fact that conflict resolution is not exhausted in the exertion of violence proposes a basis for further studying the alternatives stated here, such as the mechanisms and implications of population fusion and fission. Demographically, it is informative to compare the results from this area with other regions in Patagonia. In that sense, northwestern Patagonia represents an interesting area where studies of this genre are now under way. Certain factors indicate that in this zone, violence levels might have been higher than in northeastern Patagonia (Gordón 2011, 2013a). This would allow us to specify more precisely under which conditions variations in violence patterns took place. Even when this latter point is fundamental, further development of this research line in Patagonia depends upon the existence of adequate conceptual frameworks that give meaning to the observations.

From the case study in northeastern Patagonia, and also from the available cross-cultural, archaeological, and ethnohistorical information, it is apparent that the isolated findings throughout the rest of Patagonia do not necessarily reflect an isolated behavior, but rather a skewed interpretation associated with a skewed methodological approach. The case study for northeastern Patagonia constitutes a systematic, population, and regional study on the prevalence of violence in small-scale societies from Argentina. Even so, it is just the start of a research line in southern South America that will continue to be explored further.

## Acknowledgments

It is an honor to participate as an author in this book; I wish to express my deepest gratitude to its editors, Mark W. Allen and Terry Jones, for their invitation. I would also like to thank Diego Rindel, who made relevant comments on the manuscript. Jerónimo Pan and Tyler O'Brien helped me

Conflict and Interpersonal Violence in Holocene Hunter-Gatherers | **145**

to translate the manuscript into English. Héctor Pucciarelli, head of the Anthropology Division at Museo de La Plata (UNLP), and the authorities at Museo Etnográfico (UBA) granted me access to the collections. This work is a part of my Ph.D. thesis financed by Consejo Nacional de Investigaciones Científicas y Técnicas (CONICET, Argentina).

## References

Agosta, Eduardo A., Cristian Favier Dubois, and Rosa Compagnucci 2005. *Anomalías Climáticas en la Patagonia Durante el Calentamiento Vikingo y la Pequeña Edad de Hielo.* Actas IX Congreso Argentino de Meteorólogos, Buenos Aires.

Aschero, Carlos 1996. Al Área Río Belgrano–Lago Posadas (Santa Cruz): Problemas y Estado de Problemas. In *Arqueología: Solo Patagonia*, edited by Julieta Gómez Otero, pp. 17–26. Centro Nacional Patagónico, Puerto Madryn.

Bandieri, Susana 2005. *Historia de la Patagonia.* Editorial Sudamericana, Buenos Aires.

Barrientos, Gustavo 1997. Nutrición y Dieta de las Poblaciones Aborígenes Prehispánicas del Sudeste de la Región Pampeana. Unpublished Ph.D. dissertation, Facultad de Ciencias Naturales y Museo, Universidad Nacional de la Plata, Buenos Aires.

Barrientos, Gustavo, and Sergio I. Pérez 2004. La Expansión y Dispersión de Poblaciones del Norte de Patagonia Durante el Holoceno Tardío: Evidencia Arqueológica y Modelo Explicativo. In *Contra Viento y Marea: Arqueología de la Patagonia*, edited by Teresa Civalero, Pablo Fernández, and Gabriela Guraieb, pp. 179–95. Instituto Nacional de Antropología y Pensamiento Latinoamericano. Sociedad Argentina de Antropología, Buenos Aires.

Bechis, Marta 1998. Preface. In *Identidades Impuestas. Tehuelches, Aucas y Pampas en el Norte de la Patagonia*, edited by Lidia R. Nacuzzi, pp. 9–14. Sociedad Argentina de Antropología, Buenos Aires.

Belardi, Juan Bautista 2004. Más Vueltas que una Greca. In *Contra Viento y Marea: Arqueología de la Patagonia*, edited by Teresa Civalero, Pablo Fernández, and Gabriela Guraieb, pp. 591–603. Instituto Nacional de Antropología y Pensamiento Latinoamericano. Sociedad Argentina de Antropología, Buenos Aires.

Bellelli, Cristina, Vivian Scheinsohn, Pablo Fernández, Fernando Pereyra, Mercedes Podestá, and Mariana Carballido 2000. Arqueología de la Comarca Andina del Paralelo 42º. Localidad de Cholila. Primeros resultados. In *Desde el País de los Gigantes*, edited by Juan Bautista Belardi, Flavia Carballo Marina, and Silvana Espinosa, pp. 587–602. Río Gallegos, Universidad Nacional de la Patagonia Austral.

Berón, Mónica A. 2007. Circulación de Bienes como Indicador de Interacción entre las Poblaciones de la Pampa Occidental y sus Vecinos. In *Arqueología en las Pampas*, Tomo I, edited by Cristina Bayón, Alejandra Pupio, María Isabel González, Nora Flegenheimer, and Magdalena Frere, pp. 345–64. Sociedad Argentina de Antropología, Buenos Aires.

Bianchi, María Martha 1999. Registros Polínicos de la Transición Glacial Postglacial en el Parque Nacional Nahuel Huapi, Noroeste de Patagonia, Argentina. *Asociación Paleontológica Argentina* 6(Special Issue):43–8.

Bonomo, Mariano 2006. Un Acercamiento a la Dimensión Simbólica de la Cultura Material en la Región Pampeana. *Relaciones de la Sociedad Argentina de Antropología* XXXI:89–115.

Bórmida, Marcelo 1953–1954. Los Antiguos Patagones. Estudio de Craneología. *Runa* 6:55–96.

Borrero, Luis Alberto 1989–1990. Evolución Cultural Divergente en la Patagonia Austral. *Anales del Instituto de la Patagonia* 19:133–40.

——— 1991. *Los Selk'nam (Onas): Su Evolución Cultural.* Búsqueda yuchán, Buenos Aires.

——— 2001. *El Poblamiento de la Patagonia. Toldos, Milodones y Volcanes.* Emecé, Buenos Aires.

## 146 | Florencia Gordón

Buikstra, Jane. E., and Douglas. H. Ubelaker 1994. *Standards for Data Collection from Human Skeletal Remains.* Arkansas Archeological Survey Research Series No. 44, Fayetteville.

Castro, Alicia, and Eduardo Moreno 2000. Noticia Sobre Enterratorios Humanos en la Costa Norte de Santa Cruz. *Anales de Instituto de la Patagonia Serie Ciencias Humanas* 28:225–33.

Clapperton, Chalmers M., David E. Sugden, Darrell S. Kaufman, and Robert D. McCulloch 1995. The Last Glaciation in Central Magellan Strait, Southernmost Chile. *Quaternary Research* 44:133–48.

Claráz, Jorge (1865–1866) 1988. *Diario de Viaje de Exploración al Chubut.* Marymar, Buenos Aires.

Constantinescu, Florence 2003. Obsidiana Verde Incrustada en un Cráneo Aónikenk: ¿Tensión Social Intraétnica. . . . o Interétnica? We'll Never Know! *Magallania* 31:149–53.

Crivelli Montero, Eduardo, Ulyses Pardiñas, Mabel Fernández, Micaela Bogazzi, Adriana Chauvin, Viviana Fernández, and Maximiliano Lezcano 1996. La Cueva Epullán Grande (Provincia del Neuquén, Argentina). Informe de Avance. *Præhistoria* 2:185–265.

Curtoni, Rafael 2004. Territorios y Territorialidad en Movimiento: la Dimension Social del Paisaje. *Etnía* 46 47:87–104.

De La Cruz, Luis (1835) 1969. Viaje Desde el Fuerte de Ballenar hasta Buenos Aires. In *Colección de Obras y Documentos Relativos a la Historia Antigua y Moderna de las Provincias delrío de La Plata,* edited by Pedro de Ángelis Tomo II, pp. 7–491. Plus Ultra, Buenos Aires.

Della Negra, Claudia, and Paula Novellino 2005. "Aquihuecó": un Cementerio Arqueológico, en el Norte de la Patagonia, Valle del Curi Leuvú–Neuquén, Argentina. *Magallania* 33:165–72.

Dembo, Adolfo, and José Imbelloni 1938. *Deformaciones Intencionales del Cuerpo Humano de Carácter Étnico.* J. Anesi, Buenos Aires.

de Waal, Frans B. 2000. Primates: A Natural Heritage of Conflict Resolution. *Science* 289:586–90.

Emperaire, Joseph 1963. *Los Nómades del Mar.* Ediciones de la Universidad de Chile, Santiago de Chile.

Ferguson, R. Brian 1990. Blood of the Leviathan: Western Contact and Warfare in Amazonia. *American Ethnologist* 17:237–57.

Flensborg, Gustavo 2012. Análisis Paleopatológico en el Curso Inferior del río Colorado (Pcia. de Buenos Aires): Exploración y Evaluación del Estado de Salud de Sociedades Cazadoras-Recolectoras en el Holoceno Tardío. Unpublished Ph.D. dissertation, Department of Anthropology, Universidad Nacional del Centro de la Provincia de Buenos Aires.

Franco, Nora, and Luis Alberto Borrero 2003. Chorrillo Malo 2: Initial Peopling of the Upper Santa Cruz Basin. In *Where the South Winds Blow: Ancient Evidences of Paleo South Americans,* edited by Laura Miotti, Monica Salemme, and Nora Flegenheimer, pp. 149–52. Center for the Studies of the First Americans (CSFA) and Texas A&M University Press, College Station, TX.

Fry, Douglas P., and Patrik Söderberg 2013. Lethal Aggression in Mobile Forager Bands and Implications for the Origins of War. *Science* 341:270–73.

García Guraieb, Solana 2010. Bioarqueología de Cazadores Recolectores del Holoceno Tardío de la Cuenca del Lago Salitroso (Santa Cruz): Aspectos Paleodemográficos y Paleopatológicos. Unpublished Ph.D. dissertation, Department of Anthropology, Universidad de Buenos Aires.

García Guraieb, Solana, Rafael Goñi, and Luis A. Bosio 2007. Lesiones Traumáticas en un Entierro del Lago Salitroso (Santa Cruz, Argentina). In *Arqueología de Fuego Patagonia: Levantando Piedras, Desenterrando Huesos . . . y Develando Arcanos,* edited by Flavia Morello, Mateo Martinic, Alfredo Prieto, and Gabriel Bahamonde, pp. 375–80. Ediciones CEQUA, Punta Arenas, Chile.

Gat, Azar 1999. The Pattern of Fighting in Simple, Small Scale, Prestate Societies. *Journal of Anthropological Research* 55:563–83.

——— 2000. The Human Motivational Complex: Evolutionary Theory and the Causes of Hunter Gatherer Fighting. *Anthropological Quarterly* 73:20–34.

Gómez Otero, Julieta 2007. *Dieta, Uso del Espacio y Evolución de las Poblaciones Cazadoras Recolectoras de la Costa Centro Septentrional de Patagonia durante el Holoceno Medio y Tardío.* Unpublished Ph.D. dissertation, Facultad de Filosofía y Letras, Universidad de Buenos Aires.

## Conflict and Interpersonal Violence in Holocene Hunter-Gatherers | **147**

Gómez Otero, Julieta, and Silvia Dahinten 1997–1998. Costumbres Funerarias y Esqueletos Humanos: Variabilidad y Poblamiento en la Costa Nordeste de la Provincia de Chubut (Patagonia Argentina). *Relaciones de la Sociedad Argentina de Antropología* (N.S.) 22–23:101–24.

Goñi, Rafael 1986–1987. Arqueología de Sitios Tardíos en el valle del Río Malleo, Provincia del Neuquén. *Relaciones de la Sociedad Argentina de Antropología* (N.S.) 17:37–66.

———— 2000. Arqueología de Momentos Históricos Fuera de los Centros de Conquista y Colonización: un Análisis de Caso en el Sur de la Patagonia. In *Desde el País de los Gigantes*, edited by Juan Bautista Belardi, Flavia Carballo Marina, and Silvana Espinosa, pp. 283–96. Río Gallegos, Universidad Nacional de la Patagonia Austral.

Gordón, Florencia 2009a. Tafonomía Humana y Lesiones Traumáticas en Colecciones de Museos: Evaluación de Cráneos del Noreste de Patagonia. *Intersecciones en Antropología* 10:27–41.

———— 2009b. Atribución Causal a Traumas Craneofaciales en Muestras del norte de Patagonia (República Argentina): una Perspectiva Experimental. *Magallania, Anales del Instituto de la Patagonia.* 37(2):57–76.

———— 2011. Dinámica Poblacional, Conflicto y Violencia en el Norte de Patagonia durante el Holoceno Tardío: un Estudio Arqueológico. Unpublished Ph.D. dissertation, Anthropology Division, Universidad Nacional de La Plata, Buenos Aires.

———— 2013a. Violencia Interpersonal en Cazadores-Recolectores del Noroeste Patagónico: Perspectiva Comparativa con el Noreste de la Región. *XI Jornadas Nacionales de Antropología Biológica*, p. 43.

———— 2013b. Bioarchaeological Patterns of Violence in North Patagonia (Argentina) during the late Holocene: Implications for the Study of Population Dynamics. *International Journal of Osteoarchaeology* July 1. DOI: 10.1002/oa.2325.

Gordón, Florencia, and Luis A. Bosio 2012. An Experimental Approach to the Study of Interpersonal Violence in Northeastern Patagonia (Argentina), during the late Holocene. *Journal of Archaeological Science* 39:640–7.

Gordón, Florencia, and Gabriela Ghidini 2006. Análisis Bioarqueológico de la Violencia Interpersonal: El Valleinferir del Río Negro (República Argentina) durante el Holoceno Tardío. *Revista Werken* 9(2):27–45.

Grimm, Eric, Socorro Lozano García, Hermann Belhing, and Vera Markgraf 2001. Holocene Vegetation and Climate Variability in the Americas. In *Interhemispheric Climate Linkages*, edited by Vera Markgraf, pp. 325–63. Academic Press, San Diego.

Gusinde, Martín 1982. *Los Indios de Tierra del Fuego. Los Selk'nam.* Tomo I. Vol. I. Centro Argentino de Etnología Americana, Buenos Aires.

Imbelloni, José 1923. Introducción a Nuevos Estudios de Craneotrigonometría. *Anales del Museo Nacional de Historia Natural* 31:31–94.

Keeley, Lawrence H. 1996. *War before Civilization.* Oxford University Press, New York.

Lambert, Patricia M. 2002. The Archaeology of War: A North American Perspective. *Journal of Archaeological Research* 10:207–41.

L'Heureux, Gabriela L., and Tomás Amorosi 2009. El Entierro 2 del Sitio Cañadón Leona 5 (Región de Magallanes, Chile). Viejos Huesos, Nuevos Datos. *Magallania* 37(2):41–55.

Luna, Leandro 2009. *Estructura Demográfica, Estilo de Vida y Relaciones Biológicas de Cazadores-Recolectores en un Ambiente de Desierto: Sitio Chenque I (Parque Nacional Lihué Calel, Provincia de La Pampa).* BAR International Series 1886. Archaeopress, Oxford, UK.

Mandrini, Raúl J. 1985. La Sociedad Indígena de las Pampas en el Siglo XIX. In *Antropología*, edited by Marta Lischetti, pp. 205–30. EUDEBA, Buenos Aires.

Markgraf, Vera 1983. Late and Postglacial Vegetational and Paleoclimatic Changes in Subantarctic, Temperate and Arid Environments in Argentina. *Palynology* 7:43–70.

Martínez, Gustavo 2008–2009. Arqueología del Curso Inferior del Río Colorado: Estado Actual del Conocimiento e Implicaciones para la Dinámica Poblacional de Cazadores Recolectores Pampeano Patagónicos. *Cazadores Recolectores del Cono Sur. Revista de Arqueología* 3:71–92.

## 148 | Florencia Gordón

Meindl, Richard S., and C. Owen Lovejoy 1985. Ectocranial Suture Closure: A Revised Method for the Determination of Skeletal Age at Death Based on the Lateral–Anterior Sutures. *American Journal of Physical Anthropology* 68:57–66.

Milner, George 1995. An Osteological Perspective on Prehistoric Warfare. In *Regional Approaches to Mortuary Analysis*, edited by Lane A. Beck, pp. 221–44. Plenum Press, New York.

Musters, George (1869–1870) 1997. *Vida entre los Patagones*. El Elefante Blanco, Buenos Aires.

Nacuzzi, Lidia R. 1998. *Identidades Impuestas: Tehuelches, Aucas y Pampas en el Norte de la Patagonia*. Colección Tesis Doctorales, Sociedad Argentina de Antropología, Buenos Aires.

Neme, Gustavo, and Adolfo Gil 2001. El Patrón Cronológico en las Ocupaciones Humanas del Holoceno Medio del sur Mendocino: Implicancias para el Poblamiento Humano en Áreas Áridas y Semiáridas. *XIV Congreso Nacional de Arqueología Argentina* pp. 253–4, Rosario.

Perez, Sergio I. 2006. El Poblamiento Holocénico del Sudeste de la Región Pampeana: Un Estudio de Morfometría Geométrica Craneofacial. Unpublished Ph.D. dissertation, Facultad de Ciencias Naturales y Museo, Universidad Nacional de La Plata, Buenos Aires.

Prates, Luciano 2008. *Los Indígenas del Río Negro: Un Enfoque Arqueológico*. Sociedad Argentina de Antropología, Colección Tesis Doctorales, Buenos Aires.

Prieto, Alfredo, and Rodrigo A. Cárdenas 2007. The Struggle for Social Life in Fuego–Patagonia. In *Latin American Indigenous Warfare and Ritual Violence*, edited by Richard. J. Chacon and Ruben G. Mendoza, pp. 212–33. The University of Arizona Press, Tucson.

Rabassa, Jorge, Andrea Coronato, Gustavo Bujalesky, Mónica Salemme, Claudio Roig, Andrés Meglioli, Calvin Heusser, Sandra Gordillo, Fidel Roig, Ana Borromei, and Mirta Quatrocchio 2000. Quaternary of Tierra del Fuego, Southernmost South America: An Updated Review. *Quaternary International* 68 71:217–40.

Ratto, Silvia 2007. *Indios y Cristianos: Entre la Guerra y la Paz en las Fronteras*. Editorial Sudamericana, Buenos Aires.

Roscoe, Paul 2007. Intelligence, Coalitional Killing and the Antecedents of War. *American Anthropologist* 109:485–95.

Scabuzzo, Clara 2010. Actividades, Patologías y Nutrición de los Cazadores Recolectores Pampeanos. Unpublished Ph.D. dissertation, Facultad de Ciencias Naturales y Museo, Universidad Nacional de La Plata, Buenos Aires.

Schäbitz, Frank 2003. Estudios Polínicos del Cuaternario en las Regiones Áridas del Sur de Argentina. *Revista del Museo Argentino de Ciencias Naturales* 5:291–9.

Stine, Scott 1994. Extreme and Persistent Drought in California and Patagonia during Mediaeval Time. *Nature* 369:546–9.

Stine, Scott, and Mary Stine 1990. A Record from Lake Cardiel of Climate Change in Southern South America. *Nature* 345:705–8.

Vayda, Andrew P. 1970. Maoris and Muskets in New Zealand: Disruption of a War System. *Political Science Quarterly* 85:560–84.

Vignati, Mircíades A. 1947. Contribuciones al Conocimiento de la Paleopatología Argentina I XIII. *Notas del Museo de La Plata Antropología* 36–48:19–81.

Villarino, Basilio (1782–1783) 1972. Diario del Piloto de la Real Armada D. Basilio Villarino del Reconocimiento que Hizo del Río Negro en la Costa Oriental de la Patagonia. In *Colección de Obras y Documentos Relativos a la Historia Antigua y Moderna de las Provincias de lrío de La Plata*, edited by Pedro de Ángelis Tomo VIII (B), pp. 967–1138. Plus Ultra, Buenos Aires.

Walker, Philip L. 1997. Wife Beating, Boxing, and Broken Noses: Skeletal Evidence of the Cultural Patterning of Violence. In *Troubled Times: Violence and Warfare in the Past, War and Society*, edited by Debra L. Martin and David W. Frayer, pp. 145–79. Gordon and Breach Publishers, Amsterdam.

——— 2001. A Bioarchaeological Perspective on the History of Violence. *Annual Review of Anthropology* 30:573–96.

# 8

# Warfare and Expansion: An Ethnohistoric Perspective on the Numic Spread

Mark Q. Sutton

(*Originally published as "Warfare and Expansion: An Ethnohistoric Perspective on the Numic Spread" in the* Journal of California and Great Basin Anthropology 8(1):65–82. *It appears here with permission from Malki Press.*)

In 1958, Sydney Lamb proposed that Numic populations had spread across the Great Basin in comparatively recent times (after ca. AD 1000), presumably supplanting earlier inhabitants (Lamb 1958). Since its proposal, the spread hypothesis has received considerable attention (e.g., Taylor 1961; Gunnerson 1962; Euler 1964; Miller, Tanner, and Foley 1971; Fowler 1972; Goss 1977; Bettinger and Baumhoff 1982; Sutton 1984; Aikens and Witherspoon 1986). While linguists have generally accepted the Lamb hypothesis, archaeologists still have reservations, although recently the idea seems to have gained some tacit acceptance (cf. Bettinger and Baumhoff 1982).

One of the major questions inherent in the analysis of the hypothesis is how, in what many view as a marginal environment, could one hunter-gatherer population expand and replace another. Recently, several attempts have been made to explain this "replacement." Bettinger and Baumhoff (1982) proposed a model in which dietary competition was emphasized, while Sutton (1984) suggested a physical occupation of important resource patches by Numic groups, thereby denying pre-Numic populations access to those resources.

---

*Violence and Warfare among Hunter-Gatherers,* edited by Mark W. Allen and Terry L. Jones, 149–167. ©2014 Taylor & Francis. All rights reserved.

**150** | Mark Q. Sutton

One line of evidence regarding both the merit and method of a Numic spread are the ethnographic and ethnohistoric data, a consideration of which forms the basis for this chapter. The data were gathered from various sources, including explorers' diaries, government records, oral traditions, culture element distribution lists, ethnographies, and other researchers' analyses of similar data. Two basic questions were asked: (1) Were Numic populations expanding at contact? (2) What was the method by which such expansions, if any, were accomplished?

As a result of this analysis (detailed in this chapter), I suggest that Numic populations were indeed expanding at contact, that this expansion was a consistent pattern all along the periphery of the territory occupied by Numic groups (Figure 8.1), and that military force was a key method by which these expansions were accomplished. Further, it is suggested that these data support the Lamb (1958) hypothesis of a Numic spread late in time and that force may have been an important factor in any expansions of Numic groups in antiquity.

## Ethnohistoric Accounts

The importance of the ethnohistoric data relating to movements of Numic peoples and their neighbors just prior to direct (substantial) Euroamerican contact has not been totally neglected (e.g., Nichols 1981). Recent movements of Numic populations onto the Plains were discussed by Malouf (1968) and Wright (1978), and Kroeber (1959) noted recent ethnic spreads for the Monache, Chemehuevi, and Northern Paiute. A review of relevant ethnohistoric accounts of these and other groups on the periphery of Numic territory (Figure 8.1) is presented below.

### Kawaiisu

Zigmond (1986) reported that the Kawaiisu were peaceful and nonviolent, although there may have been some hostility with the Southern Yokuts. The Kawaiisu do not appear to have been expanding or militarily active at the time of historic contact.

### Monache

Although data are scant, it appears that the Monache, in east-central California, moved west across the crest of the Sierra Nevada within the last 200 to 300 years, displacing some Yokuts groups (Kroeber 1959:266), although Kroeber did not discuss the method by which this may have been accomplished. Bennyhoff (1956:7 and references therein) suggested that the Monache may have pushed the Miwok out of Yosemite by force, but friendly contacts were

An Ethnohistoric Perspective on the Numic Spread | 151

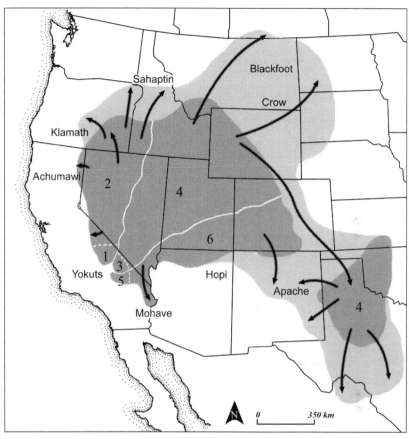

**Figure 8.1** Location of Numic-language and other groups noted in the late 1800s (the ethnographic present): (1) Monache; (2) Northern Paiute-Paviotso; (3) Panamint; (4) Northern Shoshone–Comanche; (5) Kawaiisu; (6) Ute-Chemehuevi. Areas where various Numic groups appear to have controlled and/or heavily raided before being pushed back to their ethnographically recorded boundaries are represented by light shading. (Adapted from Malouf 1968: Fig. 1; Hyde 1959; and other sources cited in text.)

also noted. Bettinger (1982:84) supported the recency of such an expansion and suggested that it may have been of a military nature. In contrast with their non-Numic neighbors, the Monache apparently conducted war for adventure, as a group rather than as individuals, employed surprise attacks, and viewed the abduction of women and children as a cause for war (Driver 1937:94). Powers (1877:453) reported that the Monache had crossed into California west of the Sierra "and pushed their invasion of California nearly down to the edge of the great San Joaquin plains." The time frame and method of this "invasion" is not clear from Powers' statement. Robert Spier (1978:427)

**152** | Mark Q. Sutton

disputed Powers' assessment, stating that hostilities initiated by the Monache usually stemmed from injuries attributed to the malevolent shamans, and that these problems rarely led to tribal hostilities (such as invasions).

James and Graziani (1975:68–81) summarized the ethnographic data on the relationships between the "Paiutes" and Sierran California groups (Washo, Maidu, Miwok, and Yokuts). While hostilities certainly did exist, and some appear to have been rather intense (e.g., Gayton 1948:159–60), James and Graziani (1975) did not report instances of territory being taken.

## Northern Paiute

Kelly (1932:186) reported that Northern Paiute groups had pushed the Klamath out of Surprise and Warner valleys within the last several hundred years:

> The Klamath are said to have held Warner and Surprise valleys prior to the occupancy by the Gidu'tikadu [Surprise Valley Paiute]. At that time, the latter were living the other side of Steens Mountain, southeast of Burns, Oregon. Although outnumbered, the Paiute "got the best of them all the time" and finally drove them out and took possession.

The description of the Surprise Valley Paiute (Kelly 1932) may have been based on data obtained from individuals who entered Surprise Valley after the establishment of Fort Bidwell in the 1860s (Voegelin 1956:4; Layton 1981:130–1). However, Layton (1981:130) suggested that Surprise Valley had previously been occupied by "pedestrian Paiute" groups who abandoned the area about 1820 due to pressure from mounted predatory bands (possibly other Paiute) from the north.

While there is no mention of lost territory in Leslie Spier's (1930) ethnography of the Klamath, it seems that the Klamath continually were at war with the Paiute north and east of them, apparently well into the 1800s (Layton 1981). It was also explicitly stated by the Surprise Valley Paiute that they were never at war with other Paiutes and even received military assistance from the Bannock in fighting the Klamath (Kelly 1932), although these data may reflect a very late situation. Another Northern Paiute group (from Pyramid Lake) apparently moved into Honey Lake Valley in comparatively recent times, displacing Maidu-speakers (Nichols 1981).

Powers (1877:452) observed that Northern Paiute had occupied a portion of eastern Washo territory. Powers had the impression that the Paiute "seem to be later arrivals [than the Washo]." The Washo situation is confused, however, by the presence of Northern Paiute loan words in Washo (Michael J. P. Nichols, personal communication, 1985). These consist of about a dozen words for various plants and animals from the desert area and may indicate a recent movement of the Washo eastward, into the Basin. The Northern Paiute seem to have had fairly peaceful relations with the Washo since the mid-1800s.

# An Ethnohistoric Perspective on the Numic Spread | 153

The Achumawi, south of the Klamath, also were enemies of the Northern Paiute. According to Curtis (1924:130), the earliest wars related in Achumawi oral tradition were with Northern Paiute, who were portrayed as invading Achumawi territory sometime near the end of the 1700s. The Northern Paiute were said to have taken no prisoners and mutilated the bodies of their victims (Curtis 1924:130). A confederation of Achumawi, Atsugewi, Modoc, and Warm Springs Indians (Klamath?) were reported to have finally defeated the Northern Paiute in a large battle, and the hostilities ended (Curtis 1924:130). Northern Paiute (Paviotso) oral tradition does not note such a defeat, but instead relates a victory over the "Pitt River" (Achumawi) in which all but two of the Achumawi, who were left to spread the word, were killed in a pitched battle (Lowie 1924:242).

The Northern Paiute have a legend of a "small tribe of barbarians" (Hopkins 1883:73) being driven out of the Humboldt Sink area of west-central Nevada and exterminated by the Northern Paiute several hundred years ago. According to the story, the Northern Paiute tried to assimilate these other people by taking some of them "into their families, but they could not make them [the other people] like themselves. So at last they [the Northern Paiute] made war on them" (Hopkins 1883:73–4).

The Northern Paiute referred to these people as *Sai-i*, or *sai-duka'a*, "tule-eaters," the same name the Northern Paiute called the Achumawi (Loud and Harrington 1929:1,166), although Hopkins (1883:73–5) stated that these "other people" spoke a Northern Paiute language (see Hattori [1982] and Aikens and Witherspoon [1986] for discussions of the possibility of Penutian speakers in the Humboldt Sink). In other studies, the *Sai-i* are identified as Achumawi (Hokan speakers) (e.g., Loud 1929:162; Steward 1938:271; O. Stewart 1941:440–1).

Hopkins (1883:75) noted that:

> all of the people round us [the Paviotso] called us Say-do-carah [similar to sai duka'a, "tule-eaters"; see Loud and Harrington 1929:166]. It means conqueror; it also means "enemy." I do not know how we came by the name of Piutes.

A similar story was related by Harry Openheim, a Northern Paiute, to John Reid (Reid 1973) (also see Loud and Harrington [1929:Appendix 4], and Lowie [1924]). Openheim related stories of at least several other battles with (presumably) the same group that Hopkins discussed. From Openheim's narration, it appears that the Paiute were the intruders and eventually killed or drove the other group into Oregon.

In southeastern Oregon, Teit (1928:101) recorded a large number of tribal and/or group movements from south to north:

> The pressure from the Snake [Northern Paiute[1]] seems to have resulted in, first, a displacement of Sahaptian by them; second, in a displacement of the Waiilatpuan tribes (the Sahaptian Cayuse and Molale) either by Sahaptian

or Snake or both; third, in a displacement of Salish tribes by Sahaptian and
Waiilatpuan, but chiefly by the former.

The extent of such a Northern Paiute move into Oregon is uncertain (see
Teit 1928; Berreman 1937; Murdock 1938; Ray 1938; and O. Stewart 1938 for
the arguments). Teit (1928) dated the majority of the movements of Northern
Paiute into Oregon to after AD 1750. Berreman (1937) agreed and argued that
the use of horses were a major factor in their success, although the entry of
horses into the northwestern Basin is poorly dated (Layton 1978).

The military balance began to shift in favor of the Sahaptian when they got
both horses and firearms, and were able to push the Northern Paiute (who did
not have firearms) south, reclaiming some territory lost to the Northern Paiute
in earlier conflicts (Ray 1938:391) (a pattern repeated by the Blackfoot against
the Northern Shoshoni). While the specifics of these various movements are
poorly known, it appears reasonably certain that the Northern Paiute did move
into southeastern Oregon late in time and disrupted the groups then there.

## Northern Shoshoni

Northern Shoshoni expansion onto the Plains is reasonably well documented
(e.g., Hewes 1948; Malouf 1968; Shimkin 1938, 1939; Wright 1978). Malouf
(1968) discussed Shoshonean movements northward into the Plains, and
suggested that they had moved as far north as Canada and as far east as the
Dakotas (see Malouf 1968:Fig. 1). Malouf (1968) further noted that the
Northern Shoshoni had been repelled by the Nez Perce and had remained
enemies with them until the nineteenth century. Shimkin (1939:20) believed
that the Northern Shoshoni entered the Plains just after AD 1500, certainly
pre-horse. Hewes (1948:54) supported this dating and suggested that the
Northern Shoshoni reached as far east as the Black Hills and the western-
most portion of Nebraska.

While the acquisition of the horse has traditionally been viewed as the major
factor enabling the Northern Shoshoni to move onto the Plains, it appears
that the Northern Shoshoni had unfriendly contacts with the Blackfoot and
Flathead prior to the introduction of the horse (Haines 1938; Hyde 1959;
Malouf 1968; Wright 1978). The early ethnohistoric accounts (see below)
suggest that the Northern Shoshoni were organized for foot warfare on the
Plains, and that their incursions onto the Plains predated their acquisition of
horses (also see Keyser 1979).

Secoy (1953) discussed two patterns of warfare in what he called the
Pre-horse–Pre-gun period: surprise attacks against small targets and formal
large-scale battles, both using infantry. Secoy used an early account (after
Thompson 1916) of a Northern Shoshoni–Blackfoot[2] battle (in about 1730) as
his example of the military technique of the Pre-horse–Pre-gun period. Secoy

# An Ethnohistoric Perspective on the Numic Spread | **155**

(1953:34) described the 1730 battle as the "first Snake-Blackfoot battle" and later (1953:36) described the "second Snake-Blackfoot battle," which apparently occurred about 1740. In the original account (Thompson 1916:328–32), there is no indication of the battles being the "first" or "second"; on the contrary, one gets the impression that the animosity had been longstanding. The story was related to Thompson (in about 1790) by a Cree named Saukamappee ("Young Man"), who had joined the Blackfoot and had participated in the hostilities in 1730:

> The Peeagans [Blackfoot] were always the frontier Tribe, and upon whom the Snake Indians made their attacks, these latter were very numerous, even without their allies . . . when we had crossed [a river in preparation for the battle] and numbered our men, we were about 350 warriors . . . they [the Shoshoni] had their scouts out, and came to meet us [on foot]. Both parties made a great show of their numbers, and I thought they were more numerous than ourselves. After some singing and dancing, they sat down on the ground, and placed their large shields before them. . . . We did the same. . . . Theirs were all placed touching each other . . . [after some exchanges of arrows in which several men on both sides were wounded] . . . night put an end to the battle, without a scalp being taken on either side, and in those days [pre-horse] such was the result . . . the great mischief of war then, was as now, by attacking and destroying small camps of ten to thirty tents, which are obliged to separate for hunting (Thompson 1916:328–30).

Secoy stated (1953:35) that "during the first phase of their life on the Plains," the Northern Shoshoni "retained the old Pre-horse–Pre-gun military technique pattern" and did not risk their few horses in battle. Secoy did not speculate where the Northern Shoshoni learned this "old" pattern, but if they were proficient in it, as they appeared to be from Thompson's account, it may be that they had been practicing it for some time. Shimkin (1939:21) believed that this battle took place in Saskatchewan and that the Northern Shoshoni did not have horses. If so, the pedestrian expansion of the Northern Shoshoni must have been well advanced.

Another battle was fought between the Northern Shoshoni and Blackfoot about 10 years later (Secoy 1953:36) in which horses were again not used, although the Northern Shoshoni apparently possessed them in small numbers and the Blackfoot had heard of them (Thompson 1916:330). The usual infantry battle lines were formed (as described here), and the fighting was initially similar to the earlier battle. This time, however, the Blackfoot had several firearms and succeeded in routing the Northern Shoshoni, chasing them on foot (Thompson 1916:332). Secoy (1953:37) noted that by 1742 or 1743, the Northern Shoshoni were well supplied with horses and were using cavalry in their military operations.

While the antiquity of the pattern is not established, it seems clear that the Northern Shoshoni first entered the Plains on foot and in force. This expansion seems to have been under way prior to their receiving horses, or

**156** | Mark Q. Sutton

at least prior to horses becoming an important military factor. However, the importance of the acquisition of horses should not be underestimated. Although the Northern Shoshoni appear to have already been expanding on foot (e.g., Shimkin 1939:21), they "expanded explosively in all favorable directions" (Secoy 1953:33) when they got horses in quantity.

The Northern Shoshoni probably obtained horses about 1690 from the south and are responsible for their introduction onto the northern Plains (Haines 1938:436). The Northern Shoshoni apparently made full use of their advantage in being mounted against their northern and eastern neighbors who were not. They pushed farther out onto the Plains, displacing the Blackfoot and Crow, although the Crow were fairly successful in resisting their incursions. The Northern Shoshoni attacked in large war parties and preferred to attack small camps or villages at dawn (a pattern noted by Secoy [1953]), killing the men and taking the women and children.

In 1742, the explorer Chevalier de la Verendrye noted the effect of Northern Shoshoni incursions in North Dakota:

> we reached a village of the Gens des Chevaux [identified as probably Cheyenne or Arikara]. They were in a state of great desolation. There was nothing but weeping and howling, all their village having been destroyed by the Gens du Serpent (Snake Indians) and only a few members of their tribe having escaped. These Snake Indians are considered very brave. They are not satisfied in a campaign merely to destroy a village, according to the custom of all other Indians. They continue their warfare from spring to autumn, they are very numerous, and woe to those whom they meet on their way!

> They are friendly to no tribe. We are told that in 1741 they had entirely destroyed seventeen villages, had killed all the old men and old women, and made slaves of the young women and had traded them at the seacoast for horses and merchandise (Blegen 1925:118).

While the Northern Shoshoni were very successful on the Plains for a while, the Blackfoot received help from the Cree and Assiniboine in their fight with them (e.g., Thompson 1916; Secoy 1953). Moreover, the Blackfoot soon obtained horses too and, in addition, they received firearms prior to the Northern Shoshoni, firearms having come into the region from the north. These factors, coupled with a larger population and larger, more defensible camps, were probably great advantages for the Blackfoot who, with the Gros Ventres (Secoy 1953), were able to push the Northern Shoshoni back out from most of the Plains area.

After having pushed the Northern Shoshoni out of the Plains, the Blackfoot seem to have held them in contempt: "The Snakes are a miserable, defenseless nation who never venture abroad. The Piegans call them old women, whom they can kill with sticks and stones" (Henry and Thompson 1897:726; written about 1811).

An Ethnohistoric Perspective on the Numic Spread | **157**

Zenas Leonard (1934:80) alluded to the Blackfoot/Shoshoni hostilities in his observations of the Northern Shoshoni in 1831:

> The Snake Indians, or as some call them, the Shoshonies, were once a powerful nation, possessing a glorious hunting ground on the east side of the [Rocky] mountains; but they, like the Flatheads, have been almost annihilated by the revengeful Blackfoot, who, being supplied with firearms were enabled to defeat all Indian opposition.

Leonard's use of the term "revengeful Blackfoot" may support the thesis that the Northern Shoshoni had taken Blackfoot territory earlier (also see Morse 1822:34n; Odgen 1950:145). The observations of Hale (1846:224) in 1841 also support this idea: "The Shoshonees formerly inhabited the country of the Blackfoot, and there are old men among the former who are better acquainted with the defiles and secret passes of the country than the Blackfoot themselves."

After being pushed south and west by the Blackfoot, the Northern Shoshoni were left with only the marginal Plains environment (see discussions in Fox [1976] and Wright [1978]). To the south, the Crow and Cheyenne, and later the Arapaho, having the same advantage (firearms) over the Northern Shoshoni, began to push them west, out of the central Plains (Malouf 1968). From about 1727 on, the Comanche (then only recently separated from the Northern Shoshoni) supplied limited numbers of French firearms to the Northern Shoshoni (Hyde 1959) that were used in an attempt to counter the Blackfoot advantage, but the guns were too few to stem the tide.

Although the Northern Shoshoni did not generally appear to be hostile or aggressive at the time of Euroamerican contact (Hale [1846:199] did call them "warlike"), it is possible that they had been so badly mauled by the Blackfoot (as noted by Odgen [1950:145]) that they were disorganized and demoralized. If this were so, it may help explain the general ethnographic perception of the Northern Shoshoni as being peaceful and destitute (cf. Steward 1938).

Keyser (1975), in an analysis of the shield-bearing warrior motif in the rock art of the northwestern Plains, suggested that the Northern Shoshoni borrowed the motif from the Fremont and spread it onto the Plains during the Late Prehistoric–Historic periods. Keyser (1975:210) noted that the shield motif is also present in the southern Plains, within the Comanche area, and includes horses, an indication that they are late. Keyser (1979) argued that the (apparent) absence of horses in the northern examples indicates that the Northern Shoshoni were on the Plains prior to the acquisition of horses.

## Comanche

The Comanche incursion into the Plains is reasonably well known and is only summarized briefly here (following Hyde [1959] and Wallace and Hoebel [1952]). The Comanche split from the Northern Shoshoni somewhere in

**158** | Mark Q. Sutton

eastern Idaho and/or western Wyoming and entered the Plains around 1700 (e.g., Wallace and Hoebel 1952), just after acquiring horses. They entered the southern Plains in two large divisions, with the Yamparikas moving south prior to the Kwqaharis (Hyde 1959:55). They were in New Mexico by about 1705, where they entered into trade and warfare with the Spanish (Casagrande 1954). Even while the Comanche were trading with the Spanish, they were "overbearing" (Bolton 1917:392) and raided the settlements.

Prior to the arrival of the Comanche, the Apache controlled the southern Plains, but were pushed out in the early 1700s by the Comanche and Ute from the north (Hyde 1959) and the Caddoans from the east (Secoy 1953:80). The Comanche would wait until the Apache were in their rancherias (during the agricultural season) and then attack the rancherias one by one in overwhelming strength (Secoy 1953:31). It should be noted that although the Comanche had horses, so did the Apache. The Comanche appear to have been able to defeat the Apache because they were able to concentrate greater strength at particular spots at times of their choosing and did not let the Apache gain the initiative.

> ... the Comanche and Utes [also pushing out onto the Plains] did not let up on their defeated enemies. They followed the fleeing Apaches and Padoucas, driving them in on the New Mexican border and continuing to raid them. They probably then extended their attacks to the Apaches of the Canadian River (Hyde 1959:96).

The Comanche started raiding Pecos in 1744 (Hyde 1959:103), and while the Spanish counterattacked in 1748, they met with only moderate success. With French encouragement and arms, the Comanche pushed south to the Red River from 1748 to 1750 (Hyde 1959:107–8). The French and Indian War (1755) resulted in the cutoff of arms and supplies to the Comanche, and secondarily, to the Northern Shoshoni.

The Comanche resumed raids into New Mexico from 1760 to 1780. About the same time, they began expanding their military operations into Old Mexico (Hyde 1959:116). A smallpox epidemic in 1780 and 1781 severely affected the Comanche and Northern Shoshoni, disrupted their military operations, and forced the Northern Shoshoni to retreat even further south and west under pressure from the Blackfoot. It took many years for the population to recover from the epidemic. The Comanche were subdued by the United States military about 1875.

## Ute

The Ute were also active on the southern Plains during the early 1700s. Hyde (1959:63) noted that the Ute appear to have entered the Southwest "through the Colorado mountains, poor, all afoot" sometime prior to 1680

An Ethnohistoric Perspective on the Numic Spread | **159**

(Secoy 1953:28; also see Tyler 1951, 1954). The northern limit of horses did not include Ute territory north of New Mexico at that time (Secoy 1953:104), so they probably did not have access to horses (Secoy 1953:28–9).

Hyde (1959:53, 63) noted that the Ute entered northern New Mexico in a nonhostile manner, intermarried with Navajos and Apaches, and gained a position in the San Luis Valley, at the head of the Rio Grande. Later (for reasons not understood, perhaps related to obtaining horses), the Ute began raiding their neighbors, with the assistance of the recently arrived Comanche (Hyde 1959:64). By the time the Americans entered the New Mexico area, the Ute were "well-defined and warlike . . . [and an] effective war leadership and organization was in evidence among all the Ute bands" (Zingg 1938:148).

The Ute and Comanche had driven the Apache from southern Colorado by 1718 (Hyde 1959:71), using a hit-and-run military technique. Although the Apache mounted punitive military expeditions against the Ute, the latter were able to elude the Apache due to their high mobility (cf. Tyler 1951:161), keeping the choice of battle to themselves. The Ute were apparently raiding Taos, New Mexico, from 1680 on and started raiding the Navajo about 1690 (Hyde 1959:56). The Ute drove the Apache south of the Arkansas River prior to 1718 (Hyde 1959:71) while the Comanche were operating north of the river.

Opler (1940:164) argued that the Ute interest in warfare centered on obtaining loot and reported that the Ute and Comanche were often enemies, although being allied at certain times. Opler (1940:162) noted that to the Ute: "Warfare, then, was more the result of horse raiding and buffalo hunting than any desire on the part of the Ute to win prestige. . . . There were no war honors institutionalized in the culture." Smith (1974) generally agreed with this assessment.

The peace and cooperation that had existed between the Ute and Comanche (but see Opler 1940) came to an end about 1749. It is not clear why this happened, but the Comanche having firearms and the Ute not having them may have caused some jealousy among the Ute (Hyde 1959:96). At about the same time that the Comanche began receiving firearms from the French, the Comanche suddenly attacked the Ute and drove them from the Plains into the mountains (Hyde 1959:106). The Ute were heavily engaged in warfare with the Navajo at the time and were unable to cope with the attacks. They even made defensive alliances with some Apache groups that they and the Comanche had recently defeated (Hyde 1959:106). The Ute and Comanche have been unfriendly ever since.

Escalante recorded "Cumanches" northeast of the Great Salt Lake in 1776 (Bolton 1950:171) and noted that the Ute were afraid of the Comanche, perhaps as a result of their earlier dispute (1950:153). Escalante recorded Comanche in both western Colorado and New Mexico but distinguished them from the group in northeast Utah by calling the former "Cumanches Yamparicas" (Bolton 1950:153).

**160** | Mark Q. Sutton

The term "Yamparicas" probably refers to the Yamparikas group of Comanche, the first to split from the Northern Shoshoni and move south (Hyde 1959:55). The Ute reference to "Cumanches" to their north may reflect a general Ute term for the Northern Shoshoni, or an ethnic lumping by Escalante. Nevertheless, it appears that the Comanche occupied much of central and western Colorado as late as 1776 and the Ute entry into that area (their ethnographically recorded territory) may post-date that time.

## Southern Paiute

Both Steward (1938:185) and Manners (1974:192) argued that warfare was unimportant to the Southern Paiute. The analysis of Southern Paiute oral tradition relating to Southwestern groups by Pendergast and Meighan (1959) suggested that there was peaceful contact between the Mukwitch (Anasazi and/or Fremont) and the Southern Paiute. The informants noted, however, that the Mukwitch were being raided by the Ute and Shoshoni from the north (Pendergast and Meighan 1959:130; also see Fowler and Fowler 1981).

However, such peacefulness was not characteristic of all Southern Paiute groups. During the last 200 years or so, the Chemehuevi, a Southern Paiute group in the Mojave Desert (Kelly 1934:549) (Chemehuevi is a Mohave word for Southern Paiute [Kroeber 1959:261]), appear to have displaced the Mohave (a Yuman group) from the Mojave Desert in eastern California and along portions of the western bank of the Colorado River (Lerch 1985). Kroeber (1959:262 [following Garces]) had placed the Chemehuevi in the Mojave Desert west of the Colorado River by 1776 (also see K. Stewart 1968:13), and suggested that they moved into the desert areas that had been abandoned due to other population movements along the Colorado River (also see Rogers 1936:38; Kelly 1934:556; Van Valkenburgh 1976:2). Kroeber (1959:294) contended that the Chemehuevi had recently moved (in the late 1700s [perhaps after Rogers 1936:38]) south from the Las Vegas area (also see Kelly 1934:556), and that this movement had occurred "within the desert." The Chemehuevi were not living on the Colorado River in 1776 (K. Stewart 1968:13). Only later (1830–1840), owing to disruptions caused by warfare between the Mohave and the Halchidhoma, did the Chemehuevi occupy portions of the western bank of the Colorado River and become farmers (Kroeber 1959).

Open hostilities broke out between the Chemehuevi and Mohave from 1865 to 1867, but were indecisive (Kroeber 1959:294; Kroeber and Kroeber 1973:39–46, 82–9). Kroeber (1959:295) felt (apparently from a Mohave source) that the Chemehuevi originally moved onto the Colorado River as "poor relations or hungry friends" and were "tolerated" by the Mohave. However, it seems that the Chemehuevi and Mohave may have been hostile to each other prior to the "war" of 1865–1867, since Chemehuevi traders would

An Ethnohistoric Perspective on the Numic Spread | **161**

not enter Mohave territory (actively guarded by the Mohave) as early as 1854 (K. Stewart 1968:16).

An analysis of the Chemehuevi-Mohave hostilities by Kroeber and Kroeber (1973) (from Mohave sources) does not greatly clarify the situation. They did suggest, however, that the Chemehuevi may have taken advantage of a Mohave decline to further their interests.

In a Mohave account of the fighting, an informant stated: "I don't know why the Chemehuevis attacked. Maybe it was just meanness. The Mohaves were pretty generous to them and gave them all they needed, so I don't see why they came and fought" (K. Stewart 1968:20). A Chemehuevi informant held a slightly different view: "The Chemehuevis didn't like to fight, but their enemies kept on bothering them. . . . The Chemehuevis didn't like war" (K. Stewart 1968:21).

Roth (1977:273) generally agreed with the concept of a recent Chemehuevi incursion into Mohave territory: "This [Blythe, California, on the west bank of the Colorado River] was the southernmost penetration of Chemehuevis, who, in the centuries before American settlement, had been gradually pushing south and west [east?] from out of the desert." Roth (1977:282) further suggested that as Mohave fortunes declined, the Chemehuevi "had grown stronger, aggressively taking advantage of new economic opportunities and moving into new areas."

During a confrontation with United States troops over the killing of a white man in 1880, the Chemehuevi (including families) fled into the mountains west of the Colorado River and threatened the entire population of the area (Roth 1977). The military took the threat seriously as the Chemehuevi were heavily armed and willing to fight. Roth (1977:277) noted that the military considered the Chemehuevi women to be very able fighters as well. The incident was ended peacefully.

In a more recent paper using data probably not available to Kroeber, Lerch (1985) argued that the portion of the Mojave Desert west of the Colorado River had not been abandoned by the Mohave but was inhabited by a group of "Desert Mohave." He then contended that the Chemehuevi invaded the Mojave Desert, and after much warfare, the Chemehuevi succeeded in killing nearly all of the Desert Mohave, thus gaining control of the desert west of the Colorado River:

> The Chemehuevi originally came from the north—they must have for the country up by nevagant? Mtn. [Spring Mountains, Charleston Peak] is their story country. They used to be mountain people but kept drifting down south, drifting down south. The Desert-Mohaves lived at Providence Mts., Old Woman Mountain and clear out to Soda Lakes [about 80 miles west of the Colorado River]. The Chemehuevis fought these Desert Mohaves in a long warfare of many years and killed nearly all of them, but a few of them escaped and lived among the river Mohaves. The reason for this fight was that the

**162** | Mark Q. Sutton

Desert Mohaves held the springs and the Chern. [Chemehuevi] wanted them (Harrington 1986:reel 146, frame 144).

The Chemehuevi appear to have then moved east to the Colorado River, gaining control of a portion of the west bank from the Mohave (Kroeber 1959:294). The River Mohave were still fighting the Chemehuevi at contact (also see Kroeber and Kroeber 1973), who apparently received aid from the Southern Paiute to the north (Kroeber 1959:262).

In the meantime, however, the Chemehuevi had succeeded in moving even further south, partly due to the decline of the Halchidhoma, whose military power had blocked their progress earlier (Kroeber 1959:262). K. Stewart (1968) argued that the Chemehuevi did not coalesce as a tribal unit until they occupied a portion of the west bank of the Colorado River. At that time, "an incipient national consciousness began to stir among [them]" (1968:26). Whether Stewart's assessment implies a lack of unity and ethnic recognition among the Chemehuevi prior to their gaining the west bank of the Colorado is questionable. If anything, it would appear that the Chemehuevi were quite "nationalistic" prior to the 1850s.

## Military Force as a Factor in Numic Expansions

It is the general view that warfare was rarely practiced in the Great Basin, especially with those groups lacking horses (e.g., Steward 1938:185, 238; Manners 1974:192–3). Linton (1944) argued that small "nomadic" populations could not be a military threat to settled groups, a thesis that seemingly ignores the disruptive power of raiding (e.g., the Comanche and Ute against the Apache [Wallace and Hoebel 1952:288], the Apache against the Spanish [cf. Spicer 1962:238]).

The present review reveals several apparent consistencies for the ethnohistoric period:

(1) Numic populations on the periphery of their territory were usually at war with, and expanding against, their non-Numic neighbors.
(2) The application of military force was consistently employed in the known expansions.
(3) Numic groups rarely fought among themselves (the late Ute-Comanche enmity being a notable exception).
(4) Until unilaterally armed with guns, other groups did not expand at the expense of Numic groups (the Washo example being a possible, but very uncertain, exception).

Where such data exist, they often illustrate a similar military method on the part of Numic populations: isolated groups of the enemy were attacked with overwhelming force and destroyed when possible. This tactic is also mentioned in Numic myth (e.g., Lowie 1924:80–1, 242) and indeed (e.g., Blegen 1925:118; Wallace and Hoebel 1952:288). Personal prestige does not

An Ethnohistoric Perspective on the Numic Spread | **163**

appear to have been as much of a factor as the destruction of enemy populations and habitations (e.g., Opler 1940), although this may not have been as true in southeastern Oregon (e.g., Ray 1938).

The Numic groups seem to have enjoyed a military superiority over other groups, including those with larger total populations. Their ability to disperse their own population and then gather a large number of men together for military actions (fission-fusion, a well-documented economic tactic in the Great Basin [Steward 1938]) may have been an important factor.

To be sure, the acquisition of horses was an important factor in some of the expansions of Numic groups, most notably that of the Comanche. However, the Northern Shoshoni appear to have been already expanding onto the Plains prior to getting horses, and their obtaining horses may have only speeded up an already ongoing process (Shimkin 1939:21). The Monache did not have horses when they (apparently) crossed the Sierra Nevada, nor did the Chemehuevi when they (apparently) invaded the eastern Mojave Desert.

Secoy (1953:23) noted that early Apache raiding may have been motivated by the lure of captives, which they sold to the Spanish as a "cash crop." As it appears that the Northern Shoshoni conducted a similar trade in captives with groups on the Pacific coast (e.g., Blegen 1925:53), it may be that a similar motivation was in operation there.

In pre-horse times, the settlement pattern on the Plains was probably somewhat similar to that of the Great Basin, with most of the population being concentrated near water sources (rivers) with much of the area being inhabited only seasonally (cf. Wedel 1963). Such a situation would have been very familiar to the Northern Shoshoni, who would have encountered large areas without permanent populations. The Numic basketry technology (specifically twined water bottles) may have enabled the Numic groups to more efficiently exploit the rather arid High Plains.

## Conclusions

The purpose of this study is to document population movements by Numic peoples during the ethnohistoric period. That they appear to have been expanding at the time of historic contact all along their perimeter may reflect a continuation of a general expansion through the Great Basin that may have begun in antiquity (within the last millennia; cf. Lamb 1958). Further, it appears that Numic populations of the ethnohistoric period (at least on their perimeter) were militarily aggressive and inclined to exploit their non-Numic neighbors. The fact that the Numic groups did not generally fight among themselves but were at war with virtually all their neighbors supports this contention. This territorial expansion appears to have predated the acquisition of the horse, although horses were a very important factor in some of the expansions of Numic populations, especially the Comanche.

**164** | Mark Q. Sutton

The presence or absence of horses is not the crucial point. The pattern of territorial expansion was not limited to those groups that were mounted; Numic groups were expanding onto the Plains (much of which was sparsely populated) prior to the introduction of the horse, and other pedestrian Numic groups were also expanding. Horses only meant that Numic populations could expand more rapidly. Other non-Numic groups also had horses (e.g., the Apache), but did not expand at the expense of Numic populations (except the better-armed Blackfoot and Sahaptian apparently taking back lost territory).

Numic populations seem to have consistently applied force and were only halted or pushed back by coalitions of greater size and/or better weapons (e.g., firearms). Since the use of force was apparently so important in the ethnohistorically documented expansions, it is possible that force may have been an important factor in the postulated replacement of the predecessors of the Numic peoples throughout the Great Basin over the past millennium.

## Acknowledgments

This is an expanded and revised version of a paper presented at the 50th Annual Meeting of the Society for American Archaeology, Denver.

I extend my thanks to C. Melvin Aikens, J. Richard Ambler, E. N. Anderson, Jr., Michael K. Lerch, Carling Malouf, Michael J. P. Nichols, Philip J. Wilke, and the reviewers for the Journal for their helpful comments and criticism. They have all graciously insisted, however, that they take no credit for the thesis of this paper.

## Notes

1. The term "Snake" was broadly used by early explorers, immigrants, and United States Government personnel (cf. Voegelin 1955:note 2) to refer to various groups of Northern Paiute and Northern Shoshoni. Use of the term is avoided here except in direct quotes.
2. Hyde (1959:121) suggested that this group of Shoshoni was ancestral to the Lemhi Shoshoni called *Tukuarika*, or "Mountain Sheep Eaters." He did not cite the source of his data.

## References

Aikens, C. Melvin, and Younger T. Witherspoon 1986. Great Basin Prehistory: Linguistics, Archaeology, and Environment. In *Anthropology of the Desert West: Papers in Honor of Jesse D. Jennings*, edited by Carol Condie and Don D. Fowler, pp. 7–20. University of Utah Anthropological Papers No. 110, Salt Lake City.

Bennyhoff, James A. 1956. *An Appraisal of the Archaeological Resources of Yosemite National Park*. University of California Archaeological Survey Reports No. 34, Berkeley.

Berreman, Joel V. 1937. *Tribal Distributions in Oregon*. American Anthropological Association Memoir No. 47, Arlington, VA.

An Ethnohistoric Perspective on the Numic Spread | **165**

Bettinger, Robert L. 1982. *Archaeology East of the Range of Light: Aboriginal Human Ecology of the Inyo-Mono Region, California.* Monographs in California and Great Basin Anthropology No. 1, Davis, CA.

Bettinger, Robert L., and Martin A. Baumhoff 1982. The Numic Spread: Great Basin Cultures in Competition. *American Antiquity* 47:485–503.

Blegen, Anne 1925. Journal of the Voyage made by Chevalier De La Verendrye with one of his Brothers in Search of the Western Sea. *Oregon Historical Quarterly* 26:116–29.

Bolton, Herbert E. 1917. French Intrusions into New Mexico, 1749–1752. In *The Pacific Ocean in History,* edited by H. Morse Stephens and Herbert E. Bolton, pp. 389–407. Macmillan, New York.

————— 1950. Pageant in the Wilderness: The Story of the Escalante Expedition to the Interior Basin, 1776. *Utah Historical Quarterly* 18:1–265.

Casagrande, Joseph B. 1954. Comanche Linguistic Acculturation: I. *International Journal of American Linguistics* 20:140–51.

Curtis, Edwards 1924. *The North American Indian,* Vol. 13. Plimpton Press Norwood, Massachusetts.

Driver, Harold E. 1937. *Culture Element Distributions: VI, Southern Sierra Nevada.* University of California Anthropological Records 1(2), Berkeley.

Euler, Robert C. 1964. Southern Paiute Archaeology. *American Antiquity* 29:379–81.

Fowler, Catherine S. 1972. Some Ecological Clues to Proto-Numic Homelands. In *Great Basin Cultural Ecology: A Symposium, Don D. Fowler,* pp. 105–22. Desert Research Institute Publications in the Social Sciences No. 8, Reno, Nevada.

Fowler, Catherine S., and Don D. Fowler 1981. The Southern Paiute: A.D. 1400–1776. In *The Protohistoric Period in the North American Southwest, A.D. 1450–1700,* edited by David R. Wilcox and W. Bruce Masse, pp. 129–62. Archaeological Research Papers No. 24, Arizona State University, Phoenix.

Fox, Steven J. 1976. *Cultural Ecological Patterns of the Eastern Shoshoni.* Tebiwa: Miscellaneous Papers of the Idaho State University Museum of Natural History No. 2. Idaho State University, Pocatello.

Gayton, Anna H. 1948. *Yokuts and Western Mono Ethnography II: Northern Foothill Yokuts and Western Mono.* University of California Anthropological Records 10(2), Berkeley.

Goss, James A. 1977. Linguistic Tools for the Great Basin Prehistorian. In *Models and Great Basin Prehistory: A Symposium,* edited by Don. D. Fowler, pp. 49–70. Desert Research Institute Publications in the Social Sciences No. 12, Reno, Nevada.

Gunnerson, James H. 1962. Plateau Shoshonean Prehistory: A Suggested Reconstruction. *American Antiquity* 28:41–5.

Haines, Francis 1938. The Northward Spread of Horses Among the Plains Indians. *American Anthropologist* 40:429–37.

Hale, Horatio 1846. *Ethnology and Philology.* United States Exploring Expedition During the Years 1838, 1839, 1840, 1841, 1842 Under the Command of Charles Wilkes, U.S.N., Vol. 6. Lea and Blanchard, Philadelphia.

Harrington, John P. 1986. *Ethnographic Field Notes, Vol. 3, Southern California/Basin.* Smithsonian Institution, National Anthropological Archives, Washington, D.C. (Microfilm edition, Millwood, NY: Kraus International Publications).

Hattori, Eugene M. 1982. *The Archaeology of Falcon Hill, Winnemucca Lake, Washoe County, Nevada.* Nevada State Museum Anthropological Papers No. 18, Carson City, NV.

Henry, Alexander, and David Thompson 1897. New Light on the Early History of the Greater Northwest, Elliott Coues, ed. (2 vols). Minneapolis: Ross and Haines, Inc.

Hewes, Gordon 1948. Early Tribal Migrations in the Northern Great Plains. *Plains Archaeological Conference Newsletter* 1(4):49–61.

Hopkins, Sarah Winnemucca 1883. *Life Among the Paiutes: Their Wrongs and Claims.* G. P. Putnam, New York.

Hyde, George E. 1959. *Indians of the High Plains.* University of Oklahoma Press, Norman.

## 166 | Mark Q. Sutton

James, Steven R., and Suzanne Graziani 1975. California Indian Warfare. *Contributions of the University of California Archaeological Research Facility* 23:47–109.

Kelly, Isabel T. 1932. *Ethnography of the Surprise Valley Paiute*. University of California Publications in American Archaeology and Ethnology 31(3), Berkeley.

——— 1934. Southern Paiute Bands. *American Anthropologist* 36:548–60.

Keyser, James D. 1975. A Shoshonean Origin for the Plains Shield Bearing Warrior Motif. *Plains Anthropologist* 20:207–15.

——— 1979. The Plains Indian War Complex and the Rock Art of Writing-on-Stone, Alberta, Canada. *Journal of Field Archaeology* 6:41–8.

Kroeber, Alfred L. 1959. *Ethnographic Interpretations 7–11*. University of California Publications in American Archaeology and Ethnology 47(3), Berkeley.

Kroeber, Alfred L., and C. B. Kroeber 1973. *A Mohave War Reminiscence, 1854–1880*. University of California Publications in Anthropology 10, Berkeley.

Lamb, Sydney 1958. Linguistic Prehistory in the Great Basin. *International Journal of American Linguistics* 25:95–100.

Layton, Thomas N. 1978. From Pottage to Portage: A Perspective on Aboriginal Horse Use in the Northern Great Basin Prior to 1850. *Nevada Historical Society Quarterly* 11:243–57.

——— 1981. Traders and Raiders: Aspects of Trans-Basin and California Plateau Commerce, 1800–1830. *Journal of California and Great Basin Anthropology* 3:127–37.

Leonard, Zenas 1934. *Narrative of the Adventures of Zenas Leonard*, The Lakeside Press, Chicago.

Lerch, Michael K. 1985. Desert Mojave: A Review of Ethnohistoric Data and Archaeological Implications. Manuscript on file at the Department of Anthropology, University of California, Riverside.

Linton, Ralph 1944. Nomad Raids and Fortified Pueblos. *American Antiquity* 10:28–32.

Loud, Llewellyn L. 1929. Notes on the Northern Paiute. In *Lovelock Cave*, by Llewellyn L. Loud and Mark R. Harrington, Appendix 2. University of California Publications in American Archaeology and Ethnology 25(1), Berkeley.

Loud, Llewellyn L., and Mark R. Harrington 1929. *Lovelock Cave*. University of California Publications in American Archaeology and Ethnology 25(1), Berkeley.

Lowie, Robert H. 1924. Shoshonean Tales. *Journal of American Folklore* 37:1–242.

Malouf, Carling 1968. The Shoshonean Migrations Northward. *Archaeology in Montana* 9:1–19.

Manners, Robert A. 1974. Southern Paiute and Chemehuevi: An Ethnohistorical Report. In *Paiute Indians I*, edited by David A. G. Horr, pp. 29–300. Garland Publishing Company, New York.

Miller, Wick R., James L. Tanner, and Lawrence P. Foley 1971. A Lexicostatistical Study of Shoshoni Dialects. *Anthropological Linguistics* 13:142–64.

Morse, J. 1822. *A Report to the Secretary of War of the United States on Indian Affairs, Comprising a Narrative of a Tour Performed in the Summer of 1820, Under a Commission from the President of the United States, for the Purposes of Ascertaining, for the Use of the Government, the Actual State of the Indian Tribes in Our Country*. New Haven.

Murdock, George P. 1938. Notes on the Tenino, Molala, and Paiute of Oregon. *American Anthropologist* 40:395–402.

Nichols, Michael J. P. 1981. Old Californian Uto-Aztecan. *Survey of California Indian Languages Report* 1:5–41.

Odgen, Peter S. 1950. *Odgen's Snake Country Journals 1824–26*. Publications of the Hudson's Bay Record Society, Vol. 13. The Hudson's Bay Record Society, London.

Opler, Marvin K. 1940. The Southeastern Ute of Colorado. In *Acculturation in Seven American Indian Tribes*, edited by Ralph Linton, pp. 119–206. D. Appleton-Century, New York.

Pendergast, David M., and Clement W. Meighan 1959. Folk Traditions as Historic Fact: A Paiute Example. *Journal of American Folklore* 72:128–33.

Powers, Stephen 1877. *Centennial Mission to the Indians of Western Nevada and California*. Smithsonian Institution Annual Report for 1876, pp. 449–60. Government Printing Office, Washington, D.C.

## An Ethnohistoric Perspective on the Numic Spread | **167**

Ray, Vern F. 1938. Tribal Distributions in Eastern Oregon and Adjacent Regions. *American Anthropologist* 40:384–415.

Reid, John 1973. Story of Harry Openheim Recited to John Reid, In Person, October 10, 1934. *Nevada Historical Review* 1:88–90.

Rogers, Malcolm J. 1936. *Yuman Pottery Making.* San Diego Museum Papers No. 2, San Diego.

Roth, George 1977. The Calloway Affair of 1880: Chemehuevi Adaptation and Chemehuevi-Mohave Relations. *The Journal of California Anthropology* 4:273–86.

Secoy, Frank R. 1953. *Changing Military Patterns on the Great Plains.* Locust Valley, New York.

Shimkin, D. B. 1938. Wind River Shoshone Geography. *American Anthropologist* 40:413–15.

———— 1939. Shoshone-Comanche Origins and Migrations. *Proceedings of the 6th Pacific Science Conference* 4:17–25.

Smith, Anne M. 1974. *Ethnography of the Northern Utes.* Museum of New Mexico Papers in Anthropology No. 17, Santa Fe.

Spicer, Edward H. 1962. *Cycles of Conquest.* University of Arizona Press, Tucson.

Spier, Leslie 1930. Klamath Ethnography. *University of California Publications in American Archaeology and Ethnology* 30:1–338.

Spier, Robert F. G. 1978. Monache. In *California,* edited by Robert F. Heizer, pp. 426–36. Handbook of North American Indians, Vol. 8, William C. Sturtevant, general editor. Smithsonian Institution, Washington, D.C.

Steward, Julian H. 1938. *Basin-Plateau Aboriginal Sociopolitical Groups.* Bureau of American Ethnology Bulletin 120, Washington, D.C.

Stewart, Kenneth M. 1968. A Brief History of the Chemehuevi Indians. *The Kiva* 34:9–27.

Stewart, Omer C. 1938. Northern Paiute. *American Anthropologist* 40:405–7.

———— 1941. *Culture Element Distributions: XIV, Northern Paiute.* University of California Anthropological Records 4(3), Berkeley.

Sutton, Mark Q. 1984. Short-Term and Long-Term Optimal Foraging Strategies: A Mechanism of Numic Expansion in the Great Basin. Paper presented at the Biennial Meetings of the Great Basin Anthropological Conference, Boise, ID.

Taylor, Walter W. 1961. Archaeology and Language in Western North America. *American Antiquity* 27:71–81.

Teit, James H. 1928. The Middle Columbia Salish. *University of Washington Publications in Anthropology* 2:83–128.

Thompson, David 1916. *David Thompson's Narrative of his Explorations in Western America, 1784–1812.* The Champlain Society, Toronto.

Tyler, S. Lyman 1951. The Yuta Indians Before 1680. *The Western Humanities Review* 5:153–63.

———— 1954. The Spaniard and the Ute. *Utah Historical Quarterly* 12:343–61.

Van Valkenburgh, Richard F. 1976. Chemehuevi Notes. In *Paiute Indians II,* edited by David A. G. Horr, pp. 225–53. Garland Publishing Company, New York.

Voegelin, Erminie W. 1955. The Northern Paiute of Central Oregon: A Chapter in Treaty Making (Part 1). *Ethnohistory* 2:95–132.

———— 1956. The Northern Paiute of Central Oregon: A Chapter in Treaty Making (Part 3). *Ethnohistory* 3:1–10.

Wallace, Ernest, and E. Adamson Hoebel 1952. *The Comanches: Lords of the South Plains.* University of Oklahoma Press, Norman.

Wedel, Waldo R. 1963. The High Plains and Their Utilization by the Indians. *American Antiquity* 29:1–16.

Wright, Gary A. 1978. The Shoshonean Migration Problem. *Plains Anthropologist* 23:113–37.

Zigmond, Maurice L. 1986. Kawaiisu. In *Great Basin,* edited by Warren L. d'Azevedo, pp. 398–411. Handbook of North American Indians, Vol. 11, William C. Sturtevant, general editor. Smithsonian Institution, Washington, D.C.

# 9

# Wait and Parry: Archaeological Evidence for Hunter-Gatherer Defensive Behavior in the Interior Northwest

*Kenneth C. Reid*

Ethnographic accounts of "plateau pacifism" have come under growing criticism from archaeologists working in the Columbia and Snake River basins of the Interior Northwest. Ray (1933, 1939) contrasted a warlike northern or Canadian plateau pattern with an originally pacifistic southern plateau pattern, the latter stamped by recent military influences from the east, and set the Columbia basin as a whole apart from the more violent Northwest Coast and Plains culture areas.

Given recent interest in prehistoric social and economic inequalities in the same area (Prentiss and Kujit 2004), any evidence for collective violence here deserves closer attention. For example, we have been recently reminded that links between organized warfare and hereditary leadership and the sustained exploitation of non-kin labor remain neglected in this region (Arnold 2004:108). Many theorists of Late Holocene complexity might agree with Hayden (1997:22) that "trade, exchange, and the wealth that resulted from them seem to have been more important than warfare, and these wealthy, complex groups were noted for their non-warlike attitudes."

While evidence comparable to the community massacres, cannibalism, human trophy taking, and "pincushionings" (Kelly 2000:149–50) unearthed from neighboring areas has yet to be recorded for the Interior Northwest, the defensive functions of fortified mesas in the channeled scablands of central Washington (Kent 1980; Smith 1977; Suttles 1981) and recent reviews

---

*Violence and Warfare among Hunter-Gatherers,* edited by Mark W. Allen and Terry L. Jones, 168–181. ©2014 Taylor & Francis. All rights reserved.

Hunter-Gatherer Defensive Behavior in the Interior Northwest | **169**

linking skeletal trauma, the bow and arrow, food caching, fortifications, and island refuges to patterns of regional conflict (Chatters 1989, 2004) invite us to reconsider how pacific the Interior Northwest has really been during the past 2,000 years.

Challenges to Ray's thesis first emerged as linguists and archaeologists examined the dynamics of Interior Salishan and Chinookan expansion into the Interior Northwest. For example, Smith (1977:80–1) saw a very different prehistory at the Sanpoil core of Ray's "plateau pacifism," arguing that several of the fortified and barricaded mesas in the channeled scablands offered refuge and defense for root-harvesting parties during the spring season of food shortages. He attributed the mesa refuges to the late prehistoric southeastern expansion of the Interior Salish into the middle Columbia region.

Archaeological evidence for violence continued to emerge, along with attempts to find appropriate terms for it. Chatters (1989:243–4) interpreted the orientations of cranial and arrow wounds to indicate feuds over resources rather than interethnic warfare. A subsequent review broadened the argument and recognized indirect evidence for increasing warfare in the form of changing settlement and food-caching patterns, triggered in turn by the adoption of the bow and arrow (Chatters 2004).

Here I will offer a partial defense of Ray's early recognition of the comparatively nonbelligerent character of the region, without slighting the emerging evidence for collective violence in the same area. I think Ray's generalization for the southern plateau is consistent with subsequent research, especially Anastasio's (1975) model of intergroup economic collaboration and Ackerman's (1994) analysis of nonunilineal kinship in the Interior Northwest. I also argue that Kelly's (2000) theory for the origin of war among warless societies illuminates all three arguments.

## Segmentation and Social Substitution

Kelly observed that nonsegmentary social organization restrained interpersonal violence at the level of homicides and sanctioned executions (2000:3–6). Occasional outbursts of collective violence occur in these societies, but lacking a mechanism of social substitution, they subside quickly. For example, when a killing occurred among the Klamath tribelets, the victim's relatives demanded the murderer's life or appropriate compensation (Spier 1930:26–7). Similar affronts in a segmental society would be resolved by killing *any* member of the murderer's descent group. Among clans or lineages, segments retain equivalence within a hierarchy, and retaliation becomes inclusive and self-perpetuating instead of individualized and episodic. With the emergence of segmentation and social substitution, feuding escalates to raids, ambushes, and massacres. Such social violence is occasionally formalized and ritualized as battle.

**170** | Kenneth C. Reid

Segmented societies are conspicuously absent in regional ethnographic surveys. Bilateral kindreds prevailed throughout the Interior Northwest, with Hawaiian kinship norms presumably emerging out of an earlier Eskimo system without ever straying toward Crow/Omaha unilinearity. Daughters and sons could marry into either parent's descent group, or into another unrelated group. Parents maintained permanent links with dispersed children, and siblings and sibling-pairs with one another. Both sexes maneuvered within consanguineal kin networks to ensure the movement of labor and goods, to retain access to alternate locations when local circumstances changed, and to arrange marriages, adoptions, formalized and rule-bound friendships, and trade partnerships (Marshall 1977:104–9).

Nevertheless, even among these unsegmented societies, as Spier (1930) found for the Klamath, spontaneous eruptions of violence might occur. Kelly's cross-cultural review found such outbreaks became most predictable ". . . in environments that are rich in naturally occurring subsistence resources, that are characterized by high resource density, diversity, and reliability, and that support population densities in excess of 0.2 persons per square mile. The incidence and severity of conflict is amplified by higher population densities and/or environmental circumscription" (Kelly 2000:136).

To cite one of several examples on the southern plateau, the Nez Perce met these conditions. Fish, game, and roots were abundant, diverse, dense, and dependable, and the pre-contact population density hovered at the specified threshold. Boyd (1985:371) estimates the Nez Perce population at 8,329 in 1750. Their territory included 69,930 square km (Marshall 1977:1) for a population density of one person in every 8.4 square km (0.3/sq. mi.).

In this context, we should not be surprised by spontaneous, intraethnic disputes prompted by brief local scarcities. There are sound theoretical reasons for expecting archeological traces of such violence in the Interior Northwest, and at least one family-scale massacre involving men, women, and children has been documented (Chatters 1989:244). Nevertheless, the scarcity of such evidence, certainly by comparison with neighboring areas, underscores the regional lacunae of organizational features of warfare. Nowhere do we see mechanisms for recruitment, ranking or grading, ritual, and logistics carry over to the intervals between wars, leaving legible traces of permanently increased social and economic inequalities. Instead we find episodic outbreaks within or among local communities prompted by temporary resource stress. Social violence conforms to a defensive rather than aggrandizing frame, and fails to achieve the organizational properties of warfare proper.

In light of this admittedly homicidal defense of plateau pacifism, we can now address the emerging evidence for violence along ethnolinguistic edges or borderlands between speech communities. The appearance of such indicators as fortifications, shifts in weaponry, battlefield cemeteries, and rock art and heraldic imagery probably reflects tensions and frictions fueled by the

# Hunter-Gatherer Defensive Behavior in the Interior Northwest | **171**

southeastern expansion of the Interior Salish, the northern movements of the Numa, and western incursions of Algonkians in the past 2,000 years.

## Fortifications

Although defensive works in the Interior Northwest have received little attention from archaeologists, early ethnographers recorded several examples. In fact, detailed descriptions of fortifications found among the very tribes listed as exemplars of "plateau pacifism" remain the biggest embarrassment to the Ray thesis. Thus, a siege-proofed refuge above a Southern Okanogan village was ". . . fortified by piles of rocks behind which trenches were dug. . . . The women stayed hidden in the trenches during battle. . . . This refuge was . . . on the tableland. . . . Here were trenches for defense and food stored in underground cellars. They would flee up the steep slopes by ladders which were pulled up after them" (Walters 1938:80).

Comparable fortifications and enclosed refuges are reported among neighboring Sahaptin, Interior Salishan, Numic, and Algonkian tribes. An example on the lower Yakima River described in 1855 included two concentric circles of earth about 1 meter high enclosing 20 "cellars" 10 meters in diameter and a meter deep. "It is well posted for defense in warfare, being on the edge of a terrace about fifteen feet high, a short distance from the river, and flanked on either side by a gully" (Gibbs 1978:15). His Indian guide said it was made long ago by an unknown people. The description suggests a cluster of housepit depressions enclosed by circular ramparts, probably separated by a ditch or moat.

However, the most revealing ethnographic accounts of native fortifications come from the Interior Salishan tribes. Apart from the Okanogan example already cited, Teit's descriptions of Coeur d'Alene and Thompson defensive works are especially detailed (Teit and Boas 1928:117–18). They included stockades, log-and-earth bunkers, and breastworks. Stockades were erected from deeply set posts about 3 meters in height with loopholes for archers. The larger stockades were rimmed on the interior with mat shelters, while the smaller ones were roofed over completely with mats. Some stockades included pits and trenches to shelter noncombatants. All were circular in plan and included baffled or zigzagged entrances wide enough for only one person to pass at a time. The entrances were also barred. Some served as defensive fighting positions, others as sanctuaries for noncombatants.

A second type of fortification was built from logs laid horizontally to an oblong or square floor plan. Walls were raised to a height of 2 meters, included loopholes or firing slits, and were externally banked with earth. The roof was also of logs, layered with brush and capped with earth. Some of these fortifications included internal pits or escape tunnels leading to bank edges or

**172** | Kenneth C. Reid

concealed exits among rocks or trees. Entrances were low and narrow so that movement in and out required crawlways. Such structures must have been safe from missiles fired on both flat and plunging trajectories, and fireproofed by their earthen mantles.

A third variant comprised quickly erected temporary fieldworks. These included breastworks in the form of circles, semicircles, straight lines, and zigzags. Typically about 1 meter in height, they were made from the materials at hand: logs, brush, bark, earth, or rocks, sometimes accompanied by an interior crawl trench. Similar improvisations appear among their Nez Perce neighbors to the south, including a valley-wide breastwork of stones and earth erected during an eighteenth-century war with the Spokane (Sappington et al. 1995:201). A Nez Perce place name from the upper end of Meadows Valley, an area contested with the northward-pressing Numa, translates as "barricade" (Aoki 1994:776).

To the south, Numic fortifications took the form of rock alignments positioned on high or broken ground. An example inspected in 1864 on the Crooked River is typical:

> ... above their camp was a semicircular ledge of rocks that had been turned into a fortification with a good deal of labor and skill. The upper side of the ledge was protected by a low wall hastily thrown up along its entire length. ... The place was large enough to contain with ease sixty or seventy men, nearly inaccessible on account of the extremely rugged character of the surrounding country (Drake 1897:337).

Finally, along the eastern approaches of the study area, Algonkian raiders harassing the upper Snake and Salmon country in the early nineteenth century operated from the log- or rock-walled "war lodge" (Ewers 1944). These structures provided patrol bases for winter raiding campaigns in hostile country. While able to function as sleeping quarters, supply depots, or fighting bunkers, war lodges served primarily as rally points during staged withdrawals to the east, as captives, horses, and booty were conveyed back to the Missouri headwaters.

How much time depth do these fortifications have? The available dates fall within the last two millennia, though there are not many of them. In general, archaeologists remain reluctant to analyze earthworks or other traces of extradomestic engineering as potential fortifications. For example, an earthwork 60 meters long at the Slocan Narrows fishery on the upper Columbia, together with elevated earthen platforms at a nearby site, have been tentatively identified as defensive features (Goodale et al. 2004:187–8). They date to within the past 800 years and presumably relate to the nearby salmon fishery, but how they functioned and in response to what threat await further study.

As noted earlier, a more emphatic challenge to Ray's plateau pacifism came from the fortified Mesa Complex in Washington's channeled scablands (Smith 1977). Stacked rock features numbering in the hundreds rim at least

Hunter-Gatherer Defensive Behavior in the Interior Northwest | **173**

50 of these isolated and elevated landforms. They include linear, lunate, circular, and rectangular walls, alignments, depressions, and isolated cairns. Eleven radiocarbon ages range from 200 to 2,000 radiocarbon years before present (rcybp) (Smith 1977:67). A critique of Smith's interpretation stressed the distances between fortifications and water sources or villages, and noted their failure to align in any defensively coherent layout (Lothson 1989:365–7). However, rock alignments invite realignment, and there is probably a significant time-averaging problem in how these feature complexes present themselves for analysis and interpretation. A rubble field-wall barricade might be reformed a few generations afterward into a game pound and still later into a rancher's property line.

Stacked rock refuges built immediately above a camp or village have the greatest reported time depth on the upper Snake River plain. Five examples, each comprising a camp, a point water source, and an elevated stacked rock enclosure associated with Desert Series points and Intermountain Ware sherds have been identified (Henrikson and Pace 2006). At one camp a hearth provided a late seventeenth-century date. A circular rock wall nearly 1.5 meters in height enclosing an area of 177 square meters on a low basalt knob overlooking the entrance to an ice cave provides another example (Henrikson 2002). These lava tubes served as food larders, and the site recorded as the "Fortress" may represent a defensive post protecting a meat cache. An antler pick dated to 1,430 ± 40 rcybp from within the lava tube may also refer to the rock alignment (Henrikson 2002:77).

Here as elsewhere, the links between fortifications and combat, between preparation and performance, remain ambiguous (Wileman 2009:142). Did the fort forestall, withstand, or succumb to the attack? Without associated data sets such as skeletal trauma or interpretable iconography, perhaps our best course is to expand the scale of inquiry. Thus, fortifications do offer the "deterrence leverage" that might facilitate a village's participation in regional interaction spheres (Keeley et al. 2007:81), and their appearance at a regional scale certainly marks collective anticipation and readiness for conflict. The evidence for fortifications among the Yakama and Interior Salish corresponds geographically with the skeletal trauma data mapped by Chatters (2004:82) and summarized by Schulting (1995). Similarly, late prehistoric forts on the upper Snake River plain may mark Numic expansion in this area, though their reporters prefer a deteriorating climate as a cause for defensive works (Henrikson and Pace 2006).

## Weapons

The appearance of the plain stave self bow in the Interior Northwest between 2,500 and 2,000 rcybp has been highlighted as an accelerant of collective violence (Chatters 2004:73–4). However, here as elsewhere, it may not be

**174** | Kenneth C. Reid

the bow itself so much as the type of stone point that best tracks military as opposed to homicidal violence. Thus, while a faith in notch orientation as a time marker continues to comfort regional culture historians, demonstrations of the overlapping time frames for side-, corner-, and basal-notched and pin-stemmed arrow points are by now so widespread (Draper 1991:649–73; Lohse and Schou 2008:191; Smith 1977:54–5) that behavioral explanations for this variability can no longer be ignored.

Ethnographic evidence confirms that stone arrow points were used for big-game hunting and war, not for smaller game (Ellis 1997:40–53). Surveys of arrow point form agree that side-notched points were favored for hunting game because they were easier to extract. Loosely hafted stemmed or corner-notched points with pronounced barbs were preferred for combat because the point either came off in the wound, or the barbs enlarged the wound still further upon extraction (Spier 1930:31–2; Keeley 1996:52; Loendorf 2010:116–18).

The abundance of stone arrow points at sites in Hells Canyon in the past 2,500 years distinguishes this area from other parts of the Interior Northwest. For example, at the Upper Landing village (10IH1017), five contemporaneous winter housepits were intercepted or completely exposed in block excavations (Gallison et al. 1996). Dating to between 1,700 and 1,400 rcybp, the floors and yards were littered with more than a thousand preformed, completed, and fragmentary arrow points (Draper 1991:693–722). When classified into 302 complete and 103 fragmentary preforms, 339 complete corner-notched/removed points, and 45 side- or unnotched points, only 11 percent of the sample would have been suitable for hunting, while 89 percent of the unbroken, corner-notched/removed points would have been suitable for fighting. Of the 258 arrow point fragments, nearly two-thirds were tips and only 14 (5 percent) were barbs. Remembering that what a weapon is designed for and how it was last used are two different questions, we might still guess that unbroken war points would not litter the village if they had been used to defend it. Similarly, the small number of intact hunting points suggests most of them broke and were discarded offsite. Among fragments, the abundance of tips and the scarcity of barbs are consistent with this interpretation.

The abundant, acutely barbed war points were not accompanied by any evidence of violence to the settlement. None of the houses show signs of burning, and the well-preserved mammalian fauna included no human remains. Comparably large samples (>10/cubic meter) of similar mixes of arrow point forms from nearby villages such as Hells Canyon Creek and McGraw Creek have not been classified in sufficient detail to explore this pattern at a regional scale (Pavesic 1986; Warren et al. 1999). Again, however, the well-preserved mammalian fauna at both sites did not include any evidence of human trauma.

Hunter-Gatherer Defensive Behavior in the Interior Northwest | **175**

The layout of all three settlements fits the soundscape-and-social cohesion model for hunter-gatherer villages outlined by Moore (2005:35). His cross-cultural analysis identified a threshold of 8 meters within which people living in sound-permeable structures can overhear one another's talk. Longer distances between houses reflected tensions and frictions within the community. Greater social solidarity, a precondition for successful defense, prevailed where houses clustered within less than 8 meters from one another.

Among these Hells Canyon villages, this measure of community cohesion, coupled with the abundance of war points, hints at bow-equipped populations capable of self-defense without recourse to fortifications. However, when compared with Middle Holocene assemblages in the same canyon reaches, the appearance of the bow corresponds to an abrupt increase in deer, bighorn sheep, and lagomorph remains rather than increased human skeletal trauma. The contemporaneity of barbed war points with hunting points reflects a robust capacity for self-defense, with big-game hunters able to transform themselves into warriors at short notice.

## Battlefield Cemeteries

Nez Perce graves capped by rock cairns are clustered in cemeteries near winter villages, often along a nearby eminence overlooking the village (Spinden 1908:181), a pattern typical of the Interior Northwest (Schulting 1995:176–7). When cairns cluster at some distance from a village, they suggest offsite and potentially collective mortality. An example reported by the missionary Samuel Parker in 1835 occurred on a tributary of the lower Clearwater River. Located 8 to 10 km from the nearest village, the cemetery marked the site of an ambush where 15 or 20 Nez Perce were killed by Numa raiders. Rock cairns a meter in height marked the spots where each man fell, leaving an unambiguous battlefield signature (Parker 1990:285–6). Archaeologists and oral historians have recorded similar clusters in nonresidential contexts at several places within and along the western rim of Hells Canyon.

The largest of these cairn clusters, Johnson Bar South (10IH1036), occupies an extensive Bonneville flood terrace in the heart of Hells Canyon (Figure 9.1). Spread over an area of 10 hectares, the site numbers at least 145 cairns with 151 nearby placed-rock features. The latter consist of single rocks positioned on outcrops near the cairns, and are a typical feature of ancestral Nez Perce cemeteries. No housepit cluster or other evidence of settlement occurs nearby. While the identity of the cairns as graves is hypothetical, several dismantled examples accompanied by shovel-cut holes are consistent with documented grave-looting behavior in the region. If the cairns do mark contemporaneous graves, the implied loss of life is not without precedent in Nez Perce oral tradition (Sappington et al. 1995:196).

IPC-RR0104. Site overview. View to northeast. 12 April 1999. Roll 42-Frame 3.

**Figure 9.1** Johnson Bar South, a probable battlefield cemetery in Hells Canyon, Idaho (view downstream and to the north). Author photograph.

Finally, the absence of sacked villages with traumatized skeletons, together with many unsacked villages with satellite cemeteries, is consistent with a prevailingly defensive posture in the region. Kelly (2000:174) suggests a frequency of 10 percent or more violent deaths in a cemetery population as an archaeological index for war. None of the late prehistoric cemeteries inventoried along the middle Columbia and Snake rivers approach this threshold for skeletal trauma (Chatters 1989, 2004; Schulting 1995; Sprague 1967).

## Rock Art

In the absence of skeletal trauma, rock art sometimes offers the most compelling clues to the trauma and drama of prehistoric warfare. In the Interior Northwest, shield-bearing warrior figures cluster along borderlands contested by Sahaptin, Numic, and Algonkian speakers (Boreson 2012:64–6; Merrell 2012:50). Depictions of warriors, casualties, and dueling champions sometimes resemble counterparts to the east, affording clues to weapons, wounds, and even ideologies. The imagery of pre-contact warfare (approximately AD 1400–1600/1700) in western Montana shows pedestrian combat at close quarters using clubs, spears, and shields (Keyser et al. 2012:338–44). Here and in our study area, bows are infrequent motifs and arrow wounds are scarce. Evidence of the heraldic imagery marking military identity and status so prominent on the northwestern Plains can also be seen in the Interior Northwest, perhaps representing western sorties or local imitations of "big men" from the northwestern Plains.

## Discussion

Archaeologists studying the record of collective violence in the Interior Northwest might begin with a close review of the scattered ethnographic and historic evidence for defensive works throughout the area. These features are probably more common, more detectable, and better indicators of organized shifts in labor than the record of skeletal trauma can provide. Increased use of remote sensing or LIDAR imagery could clarify the distribution of fortifications and defensive fieldworks by bringing larger scales of analysis into play than those afforded by pedestrian survey.

The relationships between warfare, wound patterns, and weapon systems explored by Chatters (2004) deserve more attention. For example, Schulting (1995:100, 109) cites several examples of speared and clubbed adult women from the same mid-Columbia region reviewed by Chatters, suggesting that some of the interpersonal violence played out between genders rather than warring communities. I have argued here that the immediate effect of the bow and arrow was to increase hunting success rather than to promote warfare. Among stone arrow points, variability in notch orientation, stem width, and barb angles plausibly reflects differences between hunting and fighting. Their contemporaneity suggests that violence covaries with access to big game, rather than fisheries or root meadows.

If remote battlefield cemeteries are the inverse of sacked and massacred villages, their tendency to occur in buffer zones far from settlements might be consistent with a defensive "wait and parry" regional posture (Clausewitz 1993:427). The clustering of shield-bearing figures in these contested borderlands is consistent with this hypothesis. Finally, iconographic evidence for heraldry, pennants, flags, bustles, distinctive headdresses, and hairstyles hints at the emergence of military sodalities as a measure for emergent social complexity. This path to war and increasing complexity was not explored in Kelly's (2000) model of segmentation and social substitution, but it might repay further study. For example, on the southern Plains, military sodalities promoted tribal integration among seasonally dispersed bilateral kindreds, without recourse to age-grades or unilineal affiliations (Meadows 1999:3–6, 369–74).

# Conclusion

Egalitarianism is a hard-won and precariously maintained achievement, not a blank slate or starting point that allows more complex arrangements to evolve later (Wiessner 2006:166–8). Keeping kin networks intact and negotiating balanced power relations promised participants greater rewards than land grabs or population subtractions in the Interior Northwest. Egalitarian norms may have been in constant tension with more hierarchical ambitions and expectations, but negative sanctions of ridicule and mockery constrained the blandishments of aggrandizing "big men" (Sappington et al. 1995:196). On balance, the bilateral/cognitive kinship patterns prevailing in the region seem to have checked any drift toward social substitution and self-perpetuating military violence.

Nevertheless, any one settlement node remains vulnerable to attack and plunder, and strong social webs spun from weak settlement strands can only benefit from deterrent capabilities. A visible capacity for self-defense instills confidence among both residents and potential kin and trading partners. Strongholds, refuges, and perhaps quivers bristling with barbed arrow points allowed the region's riverine residents to gauge their investments in a pan-plateau network more rooted in marriage and trade than glory and plunder. From this perspective, Ray's plateau pacifism might reflect a regional readiness to "trust but verify," one that sometimes erupted into episodic violence but more often forestalled it.

# Acknowledgments

I thank the editors and James C. Chatters for helpful comments on an earlier draft.

# References

Ackerman, Lillian A. 1994. Nonunilinear Descent Groups in the Plateau Culture Area. *American Ethnologist* 21:286–309.

Anastasio, Angelo 1975. *The Southern Plateau: An Ecological Analysis of Intergroup Relations.* University of Idaho Laboratory of Anthropology, Moscow.

Aoki, Haruo 1994. *Nez Perce Dictionary.* University of California Press, Berkeley.

Arnold, Jeanne E. 2004. A Transcontinental Perspective on the Evolution of Hunter-Gatherer Lifeways on the Plateau: Discussion and Reflection. In *Complex Hunter-Gatherers: Evolution and Organization of Prehistoric Communities on the Plateau of Northwestern North America*, edited by William C. Prentiss and Ian Kujit, pp. 171–81. University of Utah Press, Salt Lake City.

Boreson, Keo 2012. Shield Figure Petroglyphs at the Watson Site, Southeastern Oregon. In *Festschrift in Honor of Max G. Pavesic*, edited by Kenneth C. Reid and Jerry D. Galm, pp. 55–72. Journal of Northwest Anthropology Memoir No. 7, Richland, WA.

# Hunter-Gatherer Defensive Behavior in the Interior Northwest | **179**

Boyd, Robert T. 1985. The Introduction of Infectious Diseases among the Indians of the Pacific Northwest. Unpublished Ph.D. dissertation, Department of Anthropology, University of Washington, Seattle.

Chatters, James C. 1989. Pacifism and the Organization of Conflict on the Plateau of Northwestern America. In *Cultures in Conflict: Current Archaeological Perspectives*, edited by D. C. Tkaczuk and B. C. Vivian, pp. 241–52. University of Calgary, Alberta.

————— 2004. Safety in Numbers: The Influence of the Bow and Arrow on Village Formation on the Columbia Plateau. In *Complex Hunter-Gatherers: Evolution and Organization of Prehistoric Communities on the Plateau of Northwestern North America*, edited by William C. Prentiss and Ian Kujit, pp. 67–83. University of Utah Press, Salt Lake City.

Clausewitz, Carl von (edited and translated by Michael Howard and Peter Paret) 1993. *On War.* Everyman's Library, New York.

Drake, J. M. 1897. Report of the Commanding Officer, First Oregon Cavalry, dated November 6, 1865, submitted to Headquarters, District of Oregon, Fort Vancouver, Washington Territory. In *The War of the Rebellion: A Compilation of the Official Records of the Union and Confederate Armies*, Series I, Vol. L, Part 1, Reports, pp. 335–45. Government Printing Office, Washington, D.C.

Draper, John A. 1991. Upper Landing Lithics Data. In *Prehistory and Paleoenvironments at Pittsburg Landing: Data Recovery and Test Excavations at Six Sites in Hells Canyon National Recreation Area, West Central Idaho*, edited by Kenneth C. Reid, Vol. 2, Appendix D, pp. 649–753. Center for Northwest Anthropology Project Report No. 15. Washington State University, Pullman.

Ellis, Christopher J. 1997. Factors Influencing the Use of Stone Projectile Tips: An Ethnographic Perspective. In *Projectile Technology*, edited by Heidi Knecht, pp. 37–74. Plenum Press, New York.

Ewers, John C. 1944. The Blackfoot War Lodge: Its Construction and Use. *American Anthropologist* 46:182–92.

Gallison, James C., Kenneth C. Reid, and James C. Chatters 1996. *Results of Data Recovery and Impact Assessments at Upper Landing (10IH1017), Deep Gully (10IH1892), and the Kurry Terrace Sites, Pittsburg Landing, Hells Canyon National Recreation Area, Wallowa-Whitman National Forest, Western Idaho.* Rainshadow Research Project Report No. 25. Pullman, WA.

Gibbs, George 1978. *Indian Tribes of Washington Territory.* Ye Galleon Press, Fairfield, WA.

Goodale, Nathan, William C. Prentiss, and Ian Kujit 2004. Cultural Complexity: A New Chronology of the Upper Columbia Drainage Area. In *Complex Hunter-Gatherers: Evolution and Organization of Prehistoric Communities on the Plateau of Northwestern North America*, edited by William C. Prentiss and Ian Kujit, pp. 36–48. University of Utah Press, Salt Lake City.

Hayden, Brian 1997. *The Pithouses of Keatley Creek: Complex Hunter-Gatherers of the Northwest Plateau.* Harcourt Brace, Fort Worth, TX.

Henrikson, Lael 2002. Ponds, Rivers, and Bison Freezers: Evaluating a Behavioral Ecological Model of Hunter-Gatherer Mobility on Idaho's Snake River Plain. Unpublished Ph.D. dissertation, Department of Anthropology, University of Oregon, Eugene.

Henrikson, L. Suzann, and Brenda R. Pace 2006. *Between a Rock and a Hard Place: Late Holocene Defensive Structures on the Eastern Snake River Plain.* Paper presented at the 30th Great Basin Anthropological Conference, October 19–22, Las Vegas, NV.

Keeley, Lawrence H. 1996. *War Before Civilization.* Oxford University Press, New York.

Keeley, Lawrence H., Marisa Fontana, and Russell Quick 2007. Baffles and Bastions: The Universal Features of Fortifications. *Journal of Archaeological Research* 15:55–95.

Kelly, Raymond C. 2000. *Warless Societies and the Origin of War.* University of Michigan Press, Ann Arbor.

Kent, Susan 1980. Pacifism—A Myth of the Plateau. *Northwest Anthropological Research Notes* 14:125–34.

Keyser, James D., David A. Kaiser, George Poetschat, and Michael W. Taylor (editors) 2012. *Fraternity of War: Plains Indian Rock Art at Bear Gulch and Atherton Canyon, Montana.* Oregon Archaeological Society Press Publication No. 21. Portland, OR.

Loendorf, Chris 2010. *Hohokam Core Area Sociocultural Dynamics: Cooperation and Conflict along the Middle Gila River in Southern Arizona during the Classic and Historic Periods.* Unpublished Ph.D dissertation, Arizona State University, Tempe.

Lohse, E. S., and C. Schou 2008. The Southern Columbia Plateau Projectile Point Sequence: An Informatics Based Approach. In *Projectile Point Sequences in Northwestern North America*, edited by Roy L. Carlson and Martin P. R. Magne, pp. 187–208. Archaeology Press, Simon Fraser University, Burnaby, BC, Canada.

Lothson, Gordon A. 1989. A Model for Prehistoric Bighorn Sheep Procurement, Processing and Utilization along the Middle Reach of the Columbia River, Washington. Unpublished Ph.D. dissertation, Department of Anthropology, Washington State University, Pullman.

Marshall, Alan G. 1977. Nez Perce Social Groups: An Ecological Interpretation. Unpublished Ph.D. dissertation, Department of Anthropology, Washington State University, Pullman.

Meadows, William C. 1999. *Kiowa, Apache, and Comanche Military Societies.* University of Texas Press, Austin.

Merrell, Carolynn L. 2012. Our View for Understanding the Big Spring Pictographs. In *Festschrift in Honor of Max G. Pavesic*, edited by Kenneth C. Reid and Jerry D. Galm, pp. 37–54. *Journal of Northwest Anthropology* Memoir No. 7, Richland, WA.

Moore, Jerry D. 2005. *Cultural Landscapes in the Ancient Andes: Archaeologies of Place.* University Press of Florida, Gainsville.

Parker, Samuel 1990. *Journal of an Exploring Tour Beyond the Rocky Mountains.* University of Idaho Press, Boise.

Pavesic, Max G. 1986. *Descriptive Archaeology of Hells Canyon Creek Village.* Boise State University Archaeological Reports No. 14, Boise, ID.

Prentiss, William C., and Ian Kujit (editors) 2004. *Complex Hunter-Gatherers: Evolution and Organization of Prehistoric Communities on the Plateau of Northwestern North America.* University of Utah Press, Salt Lake City.

Ray, Verne F. 1933. *The Sanpoil and Nespelem: Salishan Peoples of Northeastern Washington.* AMS Press, New York.

————— 1939. *Cultural Relations in the Plateau of Northwestern America.* AMS Press, New York.

Sappington, Robert L., Caroline D. Carley, Kenneth C. Reid, and James D. Gallison 1995. Alice Cunningham Fletcher's "The Nez Perce Country." *Northwest Anthropological Research Notes* 29(2):177–220.

Schulting, Rick J. 1995. *Mortuary Variability and Status Differentiation on the Columbia-Fraser Plateau.* Simon Fraser University Archaeology Press, Burnaby, BC, Canada.

Smith, William 1977. *Archaeological Explorations in the Columbia Basin: A Report on the Mesa Project, 1973–1975.* Central Washington Archaeological Survey. Central Washington University, Ellensburg.

Spier, Leslie 1930. *Klamath Ethnography.* University of California Publications in American Archaeology and Ethnography 30. University of California Press, Berkeley.

Spinden, Herbert Joseph 1908. *The Nez Percé Indians.* Memoirs of the American Anthropological Association Vol. 2(3). Menasha, WI.

Sprague, Roderick 1967. *Aboriginal Burial Practices in the Plateau Region of North America.* Unpublished Ph.D. dissertation, Department of Anthropology, University of Arizona, Tucson.

Suttles, Wayne 1981. *Plateau Pacifism Reconsidered–Ethnography, Ethnology, and Ethnohistory.* Paper presented at the 34th Northwest Anthropological Conference, March 26–28, Portland, OR.

Teit, James A., and Franz Boas 1928. *The Salishan Tribes of the Western Plateaus.* 45th Annual Report of the Bureau of American Ethnology, Washington, D.C.

Walters, L. V. W. 1938. Social Structure. In *The Sinkaietk or Southern Okanogan of Washington*, edited by Leslie Spier, pp. 71–99. General Series in Anthropology No. 6, Contributions from the Laboratory of Anthropology No. 2. George Banta Publishing Co., Menasha, WI.

Warren, Claude N., Robert M. Yohe II, and Max G. Pavesic 1999. *The Archaeology of the McGraw Creek Site (35-WA-1), Hells Canyon, Oregon*. Idaho State Historical Society Special Publication, Boise.

Wiessner, Polly 2006. From Spears to M-16s: Testing the Imbalance of Power Hypothesis Among the Enga. *Journal of Anthropological Research* 62:165–91.

Wileman, Julie 2009. *War and Rumours of War: The Evidential Base for the Recognition of War in Prehistory*. BAR International Series 1984. Archaeopress, Oxford, UK.

# 10

## Scales of Violence across the North American Arctic

John Darwent and Christyann M. Darwent

Violent conflict among indigenous hunter-gather peoples across the North American Arctic occurred on two extremes. On the one end in northwestern Alaska, violent conflict was frequent, large-scale, pervasive, and brutal among the Iñupiat nations (e.g., Burch 1974, 1988, 1991, 1998, 2005, 2007) as well as adjacent groups in the southern Bering Sea areas (e.g., Funk 2010; Lantis 1946; Maschner and Reedy-Maschner 1998, 2007). On the other end of this scale, in the eastern Arctic of Canada and Greenland, the opposite was case: larger-scale conflicts, which some would characterize as warfare, were almost unheard of among Inuit peoples (e.g., Boas 1888; Briggs 1970; Irwin 1990). While violent interpersonal conflict leading to deaths either through murder or retribution certainly did occur, often cultural practices were set in place to stop such vengeance-driven feuding and violence from escalating to an intra- or intergroup level, and even at times at the level of an individual (Briggs 1970; Fossett 2001; Irwin 1990; Rasmussen [1927] 1999).

What is most intriguing about this dichotomy is why did a group of people who had a common ancestry—culturally, linguistically, and genetically—come to occupy two ends of a violence-scale spectrum? Although the specific origins and spread of the Thule culture, which is the ancestral archaeological culture of the modern Iñupiat and Inuit, are still under debate, clearly the Thule evolved in the Bering Strait–northwestern Alaska area by at least AD 1000 and spread to Greenland by AD 1300. And based on the archaeological record of northwestern Alaska (e.g., Mason 2009, 2012), it appears that when they departed Alaska they were engaging in endemic warfare.

---

*Violence and Warfare among Hunter-Gatherers*, edited by Mark W. Allen and Terry L. Jones, 182–203. ©2014 Taylor & Francis. All rights reserved.

Scales of Violence across the North American Arctic | **183**

The late Ernest Burch (1974, 1988, 1991, 1998, 2005, 2007) made the study of warfare among the Iñupiat people in northwestern Alaska prior to and during early contact with Euroamericans one of his lifelong academic pursuits. In his piece "From Skeptic to Believer," Burch (1991) provides an account of how he had to overcome his initial ethnographic presumptions that feuding had not escalated to the level of warfare among "Eskimo nations" as professed by such notable ethnographers as Spencer (1959). There is little that we can add here to Burch's voluminous and meticulous research, especially with the additional works of other authors on this topic, including Malaurie (1974), Maschner (1997; Maschner and Mason 2013; Maschner and Reedy-Maschner 1998, 2007), Mason (1998, 2009, 2012), and Sheehan (1995, 1997). Therefore, we take a different tack and approach the topic of warfare from the other side of the Arctic, partly to avoid redundancy but also to stop the spillage of assumptions about the nature of Alaskan warfare from being erroneously applied to the eastern Arctic.

It is our premise that the apparent absence of organized warfare in the eastern Arctic resulted from changes to group social structure needed to adapt to greater distances among reliable and sufficient food resources in the eastern Arctic (see Fitzhugh 1997). Distance has two effects: it renders boundaries among groups of people superfluous and inhibits communication, both of which erode group identity. However, the resource areas themselves, though dispersed, are still worth fighting over for control—if the costs of such conflicts are not overwhelmingly high. Jackson and Morelli (2011:35) surmise that one of the prerequisites for a war between two rational actors is that "the costs of war cannot be overwhelmingly high" and that at least one side of the conflict must see that the gains of the violent action outweigh the expected costs. In the case of the Inuit of the eastern Arctic, we concur with Irwin (1990) that there could be no winners in warfare in this region because the costs of war even to the winners are too high. Specifically, the loss of males through warfare could potentially diminish even the winning group's ability to hunt and therefore subsist.

## Ethnographic Evidence for Violence in the Arctic

There are numerous locations that have names signifying past violent encounters across the North American Arctic (e.g., Battle Rock in northwest Alaska [Giddings and Anderson 1986]; *Innuarfissuaq*, or "place of the bloody battle," in Inglefield Land, north Greenland [Holtved 1944]). It is also clear that Arctic peoples murdered and avenged each other. However, when it comes to discussing ethnographic accounts of larger-scale violence, what is often referred to as warfare, there are very few instances recorded in the eastern Arctic, particularly when it comes to Inuit-versus-Inuit group interactions.

## Western Arctic Iñupiat

Burch (1974, 1988, 1991, 1998, 2005, 2007; Burch and Correll 1972) has provided detailed and extensive accounts of raiding and warfare among Iñupiat nations in north and northwest Alaska (Figure 10.1); however, when Burch initiated his work in this region of Alaska in 1960, the prevailing notion about the Arctic was that hunter-gatherer violence never reached the "nation" scale and thus could not be considered "warfare" (e.g., Spencer 1959). In contrast to this notion, he was faced with evidence for large-scale violence in the historical and early ethnographic studies, exemplified by a gruesome photograph provided by Rasmussen ([1927] 1999:332) of a pile of human skeletal remains described as "Battlefields of Former Days": in this image, up to 70 different individuals are represented by broken skulls.

Modeled in part on the work of Dorothy Jean Ray (1975), Burch (1998:8) describes the socioterritorial organization of the early historical Iñupiat as akin to societies or nations operating as autonomous political units: "like modern nations, those of early nineteenth-century northern Alaska had dominion over separate territories, their citizens thought of themselves as being separate peoples, and they engaged one another in war and in trade." Ethnographic informants and historical accounts from the nineteenth century suggest at least 75 different raids or battles occurred in northern Alaska during this time (Burch 2005).

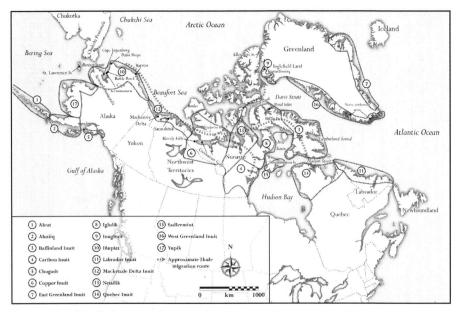

**Figure 10.1** North American Arctic with relevant locations mentioned in the text.

Scales of Violence across the North American Arctic | **185**

Men were conditioned as both hunters and warriors from a young age, with a considerable number of games and sports used to train and test skills of agility, strength, or endurance (Burch 2005). Surprise attacks or raids, as well as open combat battles, took place from late September to mid-November. The ground was frozen, thus making overland travel easier, and darkness had returned, but there was usually not much snow yet, which could be used to track in a retreat or spoil a sneak attack because of the crunch underfoot. Fall was also the time of year when women, children, and the elderly could be left on their own to eat off of summer stores or to fish. The ultimate form of combat was open battle and involved armies of dozens or even hundreds of men (a significant number in the north). These were undertaken either because tensions on both sides were high or because too many troops had assembled to launch a sneak attack (Burch 2005).

Victory meant annihilation of the enemy, including women and children, but without losses to one's own side—although the latter rarely occurred (Burch 2005). Hostages were never taken and prisoners or slaves were taken only on very rare occasions. Women were sometimes captured, but often not as a wife or slave; instead, she was typically raped, tortured, and killed before the captor returned home (Burch 2005). For the Iñupiat, it seemed, "armed conflict and threat of armed conflict were basic facts of life" (Burch 2005:57).

## Eastern Arctic Inuit

Most of what is ethnographically known about the Inuit was collected beginning in the late 1800s, and unlike many indigenous groups at the time that only lived in vestiges of their former lifeways, the Inuit were still more or less living in traditional societies on the land. Some of the more notable works include those of Kaj Birket-Smith (1929, 1936), Franz Boas (1888), Knud Rasmussen ([1927] 1999), and Edward Weyer (1932). Based on these works and others, 12 different groups (based on language and geography) of Inuktitut-speaking Inuit occupied regions of the Canadian and Greenlandic Arctic (Figure 10.1). For the most part, people in these groups lived in dispersed bands and had a marine-focused economy with the addition of terrestrial resources where available and abundant.

One of the aspects of Inuit societies in the eastern Arctic remarked upon the most was the near absence of larger-scale conflicts (war) and the presence of group behaviors aimed at curtailing violence within bands (e.g., Briggs 1970; Fossett 2001; Irwin 1990). Boas (1888:57) remarked for Baffin Island that "real wars or fights between settlements, I believe, have never happened, but contests have always been confined to single families." This lack of larger-scale external conflicts is underscored by the lack of an Inuit word for war (Irwin 1990:195) and the absence of mythological references for war (e.g., Boas 1888; Irwin 1990; Rasmussen [1927] 1999).

**186** John Darwent and Christyann M. Darwent

**Table 10.1** Incidences of male violence recorded by Knud Rasmussen ([1927] 1999) in the settlement of Kunajuk on the Ellice River (*Kuunnuaq*), near Queen Maud Gulf, Canada

| Name | Violent Act | Type of Murder |
|---|---|---|
| Angualik | Took part in murderous attack | Revenge killing |
| Erfana | Killed Kununassuaq; took part in killing of Kutdlaq | Revenge killing (×2) |
| Kingmerut | Killed Maggararaq; took part in murderous attack | Revenge killing (×2) |
| Tumaujoq | Killed Ailanaluk in revenge for killing Mahik | Revenge killing |
| Uakuaq | Killed Kutdlaq in revenge for killing Qaitsaq | Revenge killing |
| Pangnaq | 12-year-old; shot father for ill treatment of mother | Patricide |
| Ingoreq | Attempted murder of two men | |
| Kivggaluk | Father and brother both murdered by others | |
| Maneraitsiaq | Wounded a man in bow-and-arrow duel | |
| Angnernaq | One of his two wives stolen; not yet taken vengeance | |
| Erqulik | Two attempts made to steal his wife; not yet taken vengeance | |
| Portoq | Stole wife of another man | |

It cannot be said that Inuit societies were less prone to committing acts of violence than other societies. Interpersonal violence is well known from ethnographic accounts in the eastern Arctic, and the "motive was invariably some quarrel about a woman" (Rasmussen [1927] 1999:235) or an act of revenge (Table 10.1), which was the assumed reaction for another act of violence (Rink 1875:310). Stories existed from earlier times that disputes could arise between groups such that the level of violence or revenge raids continued for years until an entire village had been exterminated, though such events were not observed in modern times (Rasmussen [1927] 1999:45, 233). Such escalations were anathemas to be avoided. Another method of dealing with an individual who was particularly violent or mentally unstable and creating havoc within a given community was for the community to pressure a family member to dispatch the offender (Burch 2005:298; Rasmussen [1927] 1999:174–5), a form of group selection (Irwin 1990).

There were many different cultural practices/adaptations in place in Inuit societies to avoid such revenge-related retaliations from getting out of hand, some of which may or may not be conscious changes. Irwin (1990:207) notes that the linguistic changes (lack of warfare terminology) and lack of higher political organizations made planning and implementing warfare difficult: the Inuit reared children with attitudes of nonaggression and taught mythology that underscored the costs of murder; there was threat of retribution against killers (publically sanctioned executions); and Inuit societies encouraged intermarriage between bands as ways of reducing violent conflicts. Troublesome people were not tolerated. Often parties would break off from the original village or group and migrate long distances to avoid future conflicts. Just as Eric the Red was banished from Iceland after

## Scales of Violence across the North American Arctic | **187**

committing several murders and migrated to Greenland to establish a new colony, Qitdlarssuaq (or "the Great Qillaq") left Pond Inlet after committing a series of murders to avoid impending revenge by the remaining family members and headed north across Lancaster Sound, eventually landing in Inglefield Land, Greenland (Mary-Rouselliere 1991).

Rasmussen, in his travels across Arctic America ([1927] 1999), was particularly struck by the change he experienced from east to west in the level of trust and openness among Inuktitut-speaking peoples. There was much more distrust and propensity to warlike behavior in the west than the east, an observation that is supported by similar observations by Beechy (1831). What was striking to Rasmussen ([1927] 1999) was the cultural emphasis on war in the west: young men were specifically trained to be warriors, and there was admiration for those who participated in larger-scale violence and were good killers. This was in contrast to the east, where there was no preparation or training for war among the young men; rather, skill as a hunter was revered above all and there was no exaltation of men who killed others (e.g., Briggs 1970; Fossett 2001; Rasmussen [1927] 1999).

Although there appears to have been relatively little in the way of larger-scale conflicts between Inuit groups in the eastern Arctic, such encounters did occur between Inuit groups and their neighbors inhabiting the adjacent interior or forested regions (e.g., Chipewyan, Cree, Dene, Gwitch'in, Innu). The most famous of these was a massacre of Copper Inuit along the Coppermine River, which was witnessed by Hudson's Bay Company explorer Samuel Hearne (1795) in 1771. He was being guided by a group of Chipewyan, who, along with local Dene, traditional enemies of the Copper Inuit, attacked and slaughtered approximately 20 men, women, and children with arrows, knives, and spears. Hearne (1795) recorded the location of this attack as "Bloody Falls" (*Kugluk*).

Further to the east, D'Anglure (1984:477, 499) reported some 20 raids by the Eastern Cree on the Inuit between 1707 and 1794 that resulted in the taking of Inuit scalps and slaves (see also Friederici 1907). Tensions between these two groups remain high even to this day. A documentary recently produced by Zacharias Kunuk (Inuit) and Neil Diamond (Cree), titled *Inuit Cree Reconciliation* (2013, Isuma Productions), involves interviews with elders in two northern Québec communities about a 1770s war and the lingering impact. Although the examples of Inuit versus other groups listed here are of aggressions from forest-dwellers toward Inuit, the aggression was a two-way street.

Not all Inuit groups had frequent contact or even any contact with non-Inuit interior groups because of where their territories were located (e.g., Baffin Island and Greenland). In Greenland, Nansen (1893) reported that the Inuit considered larger-scale conflicts or war unthinkable and repugnant. Based on this and other accounts (Saabye 1818; Weyer 1932), Irwin (1990:194) suggests that violence was restricted to murder and feuds.

188 | John Darwent and Christyann M. Darwent

# The Archaeological Record

The archaeological record of northwest Alaska stretches back well over 11,000 years, but there is no substantive evidence for larger-scale conflict until the last two millennia. Obviously, this does not mean that there was a lack of violence, but due to poor preservation and rapid sea-level rise after 1000 BC (Mason and Jordan 1993), there is little of the early archaeological record of the region left. Presumably the movement of new peoples into the region would have created intergroup conflicts. For instance, when the first groups of Arctic Small Tool tradition (ASTt) people moved into Alaska from Siberia approximately 2500 BC, it is highly probable they encountered groups related to the Northern Archaic tradition, which had been residing in the interior since approximately 4000 BC (see Esdale 2008 for review). While it is unlikely that Northern Archaic peoples simply ceded their territory to ASTt peoples, if conflict arose it is now lost to time; this is largely because most ASTt and Northern Archaic sites consist of lithic scatters, but also because we lack any direct ethnographic analogs that would allow us to identify specific artifact classes associated with larger-scale conflict.

Beginning approximately AD 1 there was a marked increase in the complexity of the archaeological record along the Bering and Chukchi sea coasts. This intensification starts with the development of the Old Bering Sea (OBS) and Ipiutak cultures by AD 200 alongside the pre-existing Norton culture that had been present in the region since approximately 400 BC (Darwent and Darwent In Press; Dumond 1984, 2000; Mason 1998). At this time, Mason (1998) and others envision the Bering and Chukchi seas area as populated by various ethnic groups akin to a Mediterranean-like system of competing fledgling polities. Based on mortuary data—in particular from Point Hope (Larsen and Rainey 1948) and the East Cape area in Siberia (see Mason 1998:256–9 for review)—and new technological innovations that led to surpluses and societal stratification (e.g., large-scale walrus hunting [see Hill 2011]), Mason (1998, 2009, 2012; see also Maschner and Mason 2013) conjectures that there was an increase in larger-scale violence by AD 600, though the impacts of this conflict on the development of these societies were likely less than those associated with the acquisition of more "mundane items" such as wood and food resources (Mason 1998:288).

## Rise of Thule Culture

Beginning approximately AD 800, large economic changes occurred in the Bering and Chukchi seas region (Mason 1998, 2009). While at this time Ipiutak groups and OBS groups begin to dwindle and disappear, two new archaeological cultures developed or arrived in the region: Punuk (Collins 1929), located on St. Lawrence Island and the Chukchi Peninsula in Siberia, and Birnirk (Ford 1959; Mathiassen 1930), centered on the Barrow region but extending south to the Seward Peninsula. The role of Birnirk is not clear because sites associated with this archaeological culture are few and widely dispersed (e.g., Mason 1998; Whitridge 1999), but with Punuk came several developments: (1) intensification of whaling, which brought about social changes through establishment of whaling societies, (2) increase in trade networks, and (3) arrival of the Asian War Complex that reintroduced the bow and arrow to the region, specifically the sinew-backed recurved compound (Collins 1937; Maschner and Mason 2013; Mason 2012; Maxwell 1985; Whitridge 1999). It also brought with it slat armor (Figure 10.2), which is probably the most reliable artifact type to predicate the presence of larger-scale violence in the Arctic. While other artifacts linked through ethnographic analogy to warfare are present, such as bear-bone daggers (Figure 10.3) (Brown et al. 2012; Murdoch 1892) and war clubs (Rasmussen [1927] 1999), most of these could potentially be used in hunting contexts as well. Armor is different because it

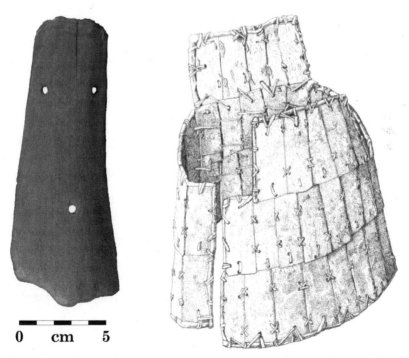

**Figure 10.2** Slat-armor piece carved from caribou antler recovered from KTZ-304, Feature 21, at Cape Espenberg, Alaska, which dates to ca. AD 1025–1398 (Photograph by Jeremy Foin). Hypothetical reconstruction of slat-armor vest illustrated by Mark Lutrell (Cooper and Bowen 2012: Fig. 3; reprinted with permission of the authors and Regents of the University of Wisconsin Press).

0     cm     5

**Figure 10.3** Large knife or dagger (*savik*) carved of polar bear bone used in close-contact fighting; recovered from midden deposit outside of KTZ-087, Feature 87, at Cape Espenberg, Alaska, and dating to ca. AD 1278–1475. Photograph by Jeremy Foin (Brown et al. 2012: Fig. 1).

is not necessary for hunting and is used only as defense for particular forms of warfare. Mason (2012) has summarized all the known examples of slat armor from the Bering and Chukchi sea areas, and the earliest well-dated examples come from approximately AD 900 (see also Cooper and Bowen 2012).

The Thule culture developed in northwest Alaska possibly as early as AD 1000 (Mason 1998, 2009; Maxwell 1985). Although ideas concerning its development are still evolving, the region "was a complex melting pot of peoples with diverse identities, interacting in complex networks of trade, alliance, and conflict" (Friesen and Arnold 2008:534). Thus, regardless from which particular group they derived most of their characteristics, the Thule culture was a hybrid that brought together a mix of effective hunting and survival methods that had not been seen previously in the Arctic (Maxwell 1985:297–8). These included the use of dogsled traction (Jenness 1940; Morey 2010), skin-covered boats (*umiat* and kayaks), float-based seal hunting, and organized large-whale hunting.

Keenleyside (1998) investigated bioarchaeological evidence for violence or trauma from at least AD 900 on 128 individuals from pre-contact sites at Barrow and Point Hope dating from the Birnirk to Late Thule periods. Cranial trauma was restricted to only 3 percent of the sample and consists of healed fractures of the mandible and facial bones. This is a much different pattern than observed on pre-contact Aleut skeletal remains, where cranial trauma was noted on 15 percent of the sample, and primarily on males. The type of trauma also differed from the north Alaskan sample in that the traumas were small, healed depression fractures of the frontal, parietal, and occipital bones. Unlike cranial trauma, comparison of postcranial trauma between the Birnirk/Thule and Aleut skeletal populations was statistically insignificant in that both had similar incidences (12–16 percent) of healed fractures to ribs, clavicles, scapulae, radii, tibiae, fibulae, and foot bones. Although falls could account for these injuries, they were more likely incurred from interpersonal violence. As discussed previously, warfare was widespread in prehistoric Aleut populations, and likely contributed to the higher incidence of depression fractures (Keenleyside 1998).

More recently, a detailed analysis was undertaken of a much larger sample of skeletal remains from Point Hope in north Alaska comparing the earlier Ipiutak to later Tigara (late Thule period) burial populations (Dabbs 2011). Although the sample size for Ipiutak (n=76) is considerably smaller than for Tigara (n=296), weapon wounds were noted on 4 percent of the Ipiutak compared with 2 percent of the Tigara individuals. Cranial trauma, which is a proxy for the level of violence within a population (Walker 1989, 2001), was significantly higher among the Tigara (11 percent) compared with the Ipiutak (2 percent), with the latter restricted to a single nasal fracture. Postcranial trauma to ribs and limbs dominated both sets of human remains; however, the amount of postcranial trauma doubled (11 percent to 22 percent) between the Ipiutak and Tigara populations. Given that the Tigara, unlike the Ipiutak, were participating in whale-hunting activities (Dabbs 2011; Sheehan 1995, 1997), the higher incidence of trauma may be a combination of risky hunting behaviors along with increased interpersonal violence.

Regardless of when the Thule departed Alaska, the speed at which they crossed the Arctic was undeniably rapid. Recent radiocarbon dates associated with Early Thule contexts in Inglefield Land, northwestern Greenland (see LeMoine and Darwent 2010, In Press), suggest that the Thule may have arrived in the region by the early AD 1200s but definitely by the early AD 1300s (see Friesen and Arnold [2008] for similar discussions related to populating of the western Canadian Arctic). Thus this movement of people, over a distance of more than 3,000 km, transpired in a century or less. This movement is not only impressive in terms of distance but also because great stretches of the expanse were essentially wasteland from which even the most industrious Arctic resident would have had trouble eking out a living.

# 192 | John Darwent and Christyann M. Darwent

## Early Thule Interaction with Other Groups

Who, if any, indigenous peoples the Thule encountered during their migration to the east is one of the most interesting and debated questions in eastern Arctic archaeology. Prior to the arrival of the Thule, the eastern Arctic was occupied by the Paleoeskimo, an offshoot of the ASTt peoples who migrated to Canada and Greenland between approximately 2500 and 2000 BC and undertook their own cultural evolution after this point. To our knowledge, there have been no reports of artifacts or mortuary remains from more than 3,000 years of occupation that would suggest any larger-scale conflicts occurred during their tenure.

When and how the last Paleoeskimo peoples, known as Late Dorset, disappeared is a mystery. Although some researchers have argued for their disappearance before the Thule arrived (Park 1993, 2000), most envision a scenario where Thule hunters encountered Late Dorset groups and outcompeted them with more effective hunting technology and group social organization (Maxwell 1985). The Late Dorset, though adapted to living in the high Arctic, do not appear to have used dogsleds or skin boats, and did not possess bow-and-arrow technology; thus, they could not compete with the new arrivals from the west. It is well known that the bow and arrow was highly effective in raiding events in southeastern Alaska and the Aleutian Islands (Maschner and Reedy-Maschner 1998; Maschner and Mason 2013), as well as northern Alaska (Burch 1998), and thus may have proved deadly against local Late Dorset populations.

While the jury is still out concerning Thule–Late Dorset interaction, it is certain that the Thule did encounter the Norse. There is, however, limited archaeological, written, or oral history evidence for direct encounters between the two in Greenland, Helluland (Baffin Island), or Markland (Labrador) (e.g., Fossett 2001). From one of the Norse Greenland sagas, the twelfth-century *Historia Norvegiae* (Jansen 1972:35), it is reported that "toward the North, hunters have found some little people whom they call *skraeling*; their situation is that when they are hurt by weapons their sores become white without bleeding, but when they are mortally wounded their blood will hardly stop running." Clearly, the passage is referring to some incident(s) of violent encounters between ancestral Inuit and Norse peoples; the discussion concerns mortal versus innocuous wounds, which implies conflict between the two groups.

Skraelings are not mentioned again in Norse sagas until the mid-fourteenth century (Gulløv 2000:321–2). In the *Icelandic Annals*, a hostile altercation was recorded between the Thule and Norse in AD 1379, which, by the date, likely occurred in the more southeasterly settlement (see Figure 10.1), where 18 Norse men were killed and two boys captured. However, for more than 200 years of writings on Greenland (see Gulløv 2000 for a review), it is difficult to characterize the eastern Thule as overly violent when so little is mentioned of their encounters.

Few Thule artifacts have ever made their way into Norse Greenlandic sites; however, Norse artifacts have turned up in Thule sites in Canada and Greenland (e.g., LeMoine and Darwent 2010; Schledermann 1980, 2000; Schledermann and McCullough 2003; see also Fitzhugh and Ward [2000], and references therein). Several theories exist to explain this disproportion, including that the Thule acquired these objects through scavenging Norse sites and shipwrecks, by trade, or in raids. On the latter, the possibility that the Thule-Inuit played a large role in the demise of the Norse Greenlandic colonies has been seized upon by many authors, with Jared Diamond's (2005) *Collapse* being one of the more notable. As Dugmore et al. (2007:19) point out, the newly arrived Thule were likely "far more experienced and skilled in low-intensity warfare than once believed and so might have had combat skills superior to those of the Norse Greenlanders, who by 1200 AD were neither Viking warriors nor medieval men at arms, but peasant farmers." However, while Dugmore et al. (2007:30–1) hold out the possibility that Thule-Norse conflict contributed to the Norse decline to a small degree, they find other issues—climate, lack of adaptation to new environmental conditions, trade, and politics—much more influential (see also McGovern 2000).

Other groups that the Thule may have encountered on their journeys east were forest-dwelling Indian groups, ancestors to present-day Dene, Gwitch'in, Innu, and Cree. With one possible exception, discussed later in this chapter, at the Saunaktuk site (Melbye and Fairgreive 1994), there is no evidence of violent interaction between these groups and Thule migrants.

## Taking Attitudes toward Violence East

From relatively low densities of Early Thule archaeological features across the Arctic compared with later "Classic" Thule (AD 1300–1500), it appears that the migration was not an en masse event but rather incursions by groups of up to several hundred people or smaller (Friesen and Arnold 2008). When these groups of Thule left Alaska, they took with them their material culture, housing, social system, language, and subsistence practices. Thus it is also likely they took their attitudes toward larger-scale conflict with them. If the appearance of slat armor (Figure 10.3) and other accoutrements of the Asian War Complex after AD 900 signals that larger-scale conflict was present in northwestern Alaska (Collins 1937; Maschner and Mason 2013; Mason 2009, 2012), it is probable that Thule groups departed with "warlike" tendencies to the east. There is no direct evidence, but clearly such a proclivity would not have impeded their acquisition of Late Dorset territory.

Friesen and Arnold (2008:534) suggest that for the first 150 to 200 years after the Thule arrived in the eastern Arctic they would have gone through

**194** | John Darwent and Christyann M. Darwent

a "settling-in" period (Classic Thule). This period would have included the process of adapting Alaska-based subsistence strategies to new areas, sometimes successfully and other times not (as large areas of abandonment of the high Arctic after AD 1400 would attest). It would also have been the point in time that attitudes toward actively participating in larger-scale violent acts would have changed. One of the first effects of such a rapid move would be the dispersal of populations; any sort of "nation" organization based on territorial boundaries would cease to operate, and political organization would have been reduced to a band level. This would have effectively ended larger-scale conflicts because the impetus for territorial acquisition through lethal raiding would be removed. But second, and more important, there likely would have been some sobering realizations of the consequences of unchecked violence in smaller-sized societies.

To our knowledge, there have been no discoveries of artifacts, features, or mortuary evidence that would signal the presence of larger-scale conflict in the Canadian and Greenlandic Arctic in the Thule period *east* of the Mackenzie Delta (more on this region in this chapter). One of the largest cemetery populations in the eastern Arctic, located on Southampton Island (n=183), records numerous pathological conditions related to subsistence and other related activities, but none appear to have evidence for cranial trauma or weapon wounds from interpersonal violence (Merbs 1983, 2002, 2004; Merbs and Wilson 1962). Additional studies from the Cumberland Sound region of Baffin Island (Salter 1984) likewise do not report violent trauma.

After AD 1400 there was a general collapse of the Classic Thule culture, which was coetaneous with a decline in bowhead whaling (McCartney 1977; Schledermann 1979). It was at this point that McGhee (1974) perceives that regionalization of the various Inuit groups seen at contact developed. For many of these groups, such as the Copper Inuit and the Inughuit, it is likely that the mechanisms in place to stop escalating conflict from occurring were in place. With the exception of one area, the larger-scale conflicts seen in Alaska had likely declined throughout the Canadian and Greenlandic Arctic (see Fossett [2001] for further discussion).

The exception is the Mackenzie Delta, where there is good evidence for larger-scale conflicts and the perpetuation of the same system of nations that Burch (1998, 2005) reconstructed for northwestern Alaska (Friesen 2012, 2013). Teeming with local resources, especially beluga whale and fish, this area is one of the richest in the Arctic and is able to support larger populations of people (e.g., Betts 2008). Evidence for increased conflict, reviewed by Friesen (2012:33), comes in the form of polar bear–bone daggers (Friesen and Hunston 1994; McGhee 1974), a large whalebone war club (Arnold and Pokiak 2011), and a dense concentration of butchered humans. This latter discovery is a particularly dramatic case of violence, which occurred at the archaeological site of Saunaktuk in the Mackenzie Delta region, ca. AD 1300 to

Scales of Violence across the North American Arctic | **195**

1400. Here, Melbye and Fairgreive (1994) describe a suite of human skeletal remains of at least 35 Thule-Inuit individuals that appear to represent women, children, and elderly. Nearly every identifiable skeletal element had knife cuts: these marks occurred in clusters associated with dismemberment, defleshing, scalping, and facial mutilation. Torture by piercing the distal femur appears to have been inflicted on at least two individuals. All but one infant long bone had been split longitudinally and splintered. Melbye and Fairgreive (1994) infer that the remains were the result of a conflict with interior "Indian" peoples, mainly because such violent incidents were documented ethnographically between Inuit and groups such as the Gwitch'in (Krech 1976, 1979, 1984; Slobodin 1960) in the Mackenzie Delta and Eskimo Lakes region. However, we posit that the age of this site might make such claims premature. If bands of violence-prone/warlike Thule were moving through the Mackenzie Delta region, the blame could be placed on conflicts between two Thule nations rather than "Indian" groups.

While the occupation of this area prior to AD 1400 appears to have been limited, after this point Friesen and Arnold (2008:534) conclude there were rapid changes in settlement systems and use intensity that essentially transformed the area to the Mackenzie Inuit pattern seen until the nineteenth century (Betts 2008; Friesen 2013). While there were in situ changes, there also were likely population influxes from the west. It cannot be said definitively that the migrants were refugees of sorts fleeing a violent west (though Mason [2012:77–8] sees an increase in the indications of warfare after AD 1300 in northwestern Alaska); however, these people would have no doubt brought similar attitudes toward larger-scale conflict with them to the Mackenzie Delta. Therefore, even if the original smaller populations in the delta region were beginning to shift to a pattern of more limited violence seen in other Inuit populations, these changes were likely negated.

## Discussion

Taking into account minor aberrations and those related to later European incursions (see Fossett [2001] for an extensive discussion), it is evident that violence was on a much greater scale in the western Arctic compared with that of the eastern Arctic, with the Mackenzie Delta region serving as rough demarcation as to where the divergence begins. Rasmussen ([1927] 1999) recorded this split ethnographically during his journey across the Arctic.

It is clear from Burch's (1974, 1988, 1998, 2005, 2007) work that larger-scale attacks were undertaken by Iñupiat nations on other Iñupiat nations and on adjacent "Indian" groups on a regular basis. Burch's concept of a nation most likely corresponds with the generally accepted classification of a tribe (as opposed to a chiefdom, which would be an overarching organization that

**196** | John Darwent and Christyann M. Darwent

controlled the nations). Based on Friesen's (2012, 2013) postulation that the Mackenzie Delta had or developed the same system of nations, it is likely that this level of violence extended to this region as well.

From the outset, it is impossible for the same levels of violence to exist in the east as in the west because nation organizations either never developed or disappeared. Athapaskan attacks (or vice versa) on Inuit villages aside (discussed later in this chapter), such large-scale violent encounters were never recorded of between Inuktitut-speaking groups in the eastern Arctic. Violence was, however, still prevalent in eastern Inuit societies. This lower scale of violence is because among the eastern Inuit there were societal mechanisms in place to stop violence from escalating into larger affairs (Briggs 1970; Fossett 2001; Irwin 1990; Rasmussen [1927] 1999). Attacks were made on Europeans (e.g., Frobisher, Davis), but it was made under the assumption that these would not escalate to long-term revenge feuds because they were "one-time visitors" (Fossett 2001:55). Further, as Fossett (2001:55) explains, "attacks on them did not involve breaking alliances and the subsequent destruction of partnerships, alienation of trade, and reduced access to spouses and adopted children. Not only were the costs of raiding Europeans considerably lower than the costs of attacking neighboring communities, the rewards—metal and wood—were significantly higher."

It is evident from ethnographic accounts that the cultural necessity to avenge the wrongful death of a family member was paramount among the Inuit and Iñupiat (e.g., Burch 2005; Fossett 2001; Mary-Rouselliere 1991; Rasmussen [1927] 1999; Rink 1875). Obviously, if vengeance killing went unchecked within a group, it could escalate to a larger conflict leading to internal blood feuds or worse. In the west, the nation organizations kept such intragroup conflicts at bay and sanctioned vengeance could only be undertaken by the deceased's closest male relative using specific killing rituals, though blood feuds did break out (Burch 2005:20–1). However, when it came to people outside of one's group, it was a different story. Burch (2005:20) noted: "To kill one's own countryman [tribe member] was murder (*iñuaq-*), whereas to kill a foreigner (*tuqut-*) [member of another tribe] was conceptually not much different from killing a mosquito."

In the east, similar rules were in place to stop the escalation of vengeance internally within groups, if not even more held to. As discussed, there were often societal attempts to head off further bloodshed before vengeance killings could occur (i.e., payments in kind for losses; provision of new spouses, both male and female). In addition, troublesome individuals were sometimes "disposed of" by their own families to bring conflict under control (Rasmussen [1927] 1999; see also Burch [2005:312, note 18] who notes this practice for the Iñupiat as well). However, there appears to have been a fundamental change from lauding warriors to revering hunters: societies did not train for war, and other cultural adaptations arose to curb internal group violence (Irwin 1990).

Also, at some point during their trek across the Arctic, the Thule that settled in the east lost their bellicose response to rival groups of other Thule and underwent a change from a complex to a simpler political system. Likely because of decreased population densities and reduced communication lines caused by increased distance between resource patches, and collapse of whale-hunting social structure after AD 1500, the nation or tribe systems that were likely in place before people ventured east decayed or were abandoned outright.

If one adheres to a distinct directionally based hierarchical scale of evolutionary achievement, where more complex is seen as more evolved, then the Thule underwent some form of devolution. However, we see the change as a move to a more evolved state of environmental exploitation, where environmental conditions make adherence to practices of maintaining nation-like organizations and engaging in larger-scale violence maladaptive. Bettinger (2013) makes a similar link between the changes from large-scale, communal-hunting social organizations to more individual hunting practices and family bands in the Great Basin as being more evolutionarily adaptive to the local environment.

While lower population densities might explain decreased large-scale violence, especially considering the increased distances between resources in the east, people had to change their inherent response to strike out against individuals from adjacent bands, and the reason for this need is that larger-scale conflict among Inuit in the eastern Arctic had no winners (Fossett 2001). In a twist of scale, Irwin (1990:189) equates the cost-benefit ratio of the choice to undertake larger-scale violent actions by the Inuit as being the same as those for a nuclear war: mutual destruction of both participant groups in the conflict. In the north, men undertook most violent conflict, and thus most of the immediate casualties in a conflict were hunter-aged males. While on a reproductive level a group can get by on a diminished number of males, in the eastern Arctic, where males of reproductive age provided the vast majority of the calories consumed by the group through hunting, a shortage of males would have meant dire consequences (Irwin 1990:206; Smith and Smith 1994). The only situation where there would be an advantage for one group to attack another would be if there was a guarantee that the aggressor would not lose any of its men during the attack. Even with triumph on the battlefield (so to speak), if the winning group lost even just one of its men, its capacity to survive is diminished dramatically. In the same light, this same requisite applies to the need to keep internal conflicts from escalating. Returning to the western Arctic, the Iñupiat nations and others to the south could continue to engage (some would say "forced" to continue [Mason 2012]) in persistent larger-scale violence because these groups could absorb the social (and subsistence) damage of the conflict. For instance, if a woman lost her husband during a raid on another group, she would have other social connections that would ensure that she did not starve. This might not have been the case in the east.

## 198 | John Darwent and Christyann M. Darwent

How quickly attitudes changed toward larger-scale conflicts during the initial Thule migrations into the eastern Arctic is unknown, assuming larger-scale violence was endemic in the west at the time of their departure. On one side of the argument, by the time that they encountered the Norse in the thirteenth century, it is possible that they were still very prone to and capable of aggressive actions against foreign groups (Dugmore et al. 2007), and the few passages available from the Norse sagas would appear to back this assumption. Similarly, if the massacre of Inuit at the Saunaktuk site (Melbye and Fairgreive 1994) was perpetrated by another Thule group in the thirteenth or fourteenth century instead of by forest dwellers, then it would appear that the Thule had not scaled down their level of violence.

On the other side of the argument, if one takes into account McGhee's (1984, 2000, 2004) arguments that the Thule migration was fueled by the quest for metal, then the Thule were more apt to engage in trade with Norse rather fight with them (Maxwell 1985). As the Norse were exporting large quantities of walrus ivory back to Europe, possibly traded from Thule hunters, it is likely that most Thule–Norse interactions were not violent (McGhee 1984; Maxwell 1985).

Conflicts between forest-dwelling groups and Inuit groups (and those with Europeans in the sixteenth and seventeenth centuries [Fossett 2001]) stand out as possible exceptions to the overall pattern of reduced larger-scale violence in the east. However, the magnitude of such raids appears to be considerably smaller than any recorded for northwestern Alaska. There were no political organizations that could plan attacks to the same extent in eastern areas. Irwin (1990) makes the case that friction between the Inuit and forest-dwelling groups likely only occurred when there was Inuit expansion into the forest. As is evident from northwestern Alaska, where the Iñupiat inhabit both interior and coastal areas, Inuit technology was perfectly suited to exploiting such environments. Conversely, forest-dwelling groups, while able to use the tundra and coast during the summer, could not make effective use of coastal areas during the winter. Thus land acquisition, which was at the root of conflicts among Iñupiat nations in western Alaska (Burch 2005), was not the goal of these raids. Also at stake is the issue of the antiquity of conflicts between forest dwellers and the Inuit, because it has been suggested that much of the conflict between these two groups may have been connected to the expansion of the fur-trade industry (i.e., Hudson's Bay Company), into the Arctic and Subarctic. If this is the case, then the most violent conflicts in the eastern Arctic are a product of Euroamerican contact and represent change to existing, possibly more peaceful, lifeways (e.g., Fossett 2001).

Shedding the use of definitions of warfare to study violence among hunter-gatherers to a system that examines the scale of violence allows for greater understanding of variations in violent conflicts. It is clear from the ethnographic record that during late prehistoric and early historic times in the western

Scales of Violence across the North American Arctic | **199**

Arctic the scale of violence was considerably higher than in the eastern Arctic. Although both populations are descendants of the Bering Strait/Chukchi Sea Thule culture, we believe that the Inuit adapted their social organization to the new reality of patchy resources in the eastern Arctic by evolving to less politically complex societies and undertaking cultural practices that sought to limit violence on all levels.

## References

Arnold, Charles D., and Myrna Pokiak 2011. *Inuvialuit Artifacts from Kuukpak*. Government of the Northwest Territories, Yellowknife, Canada.

Beechy, Frederick William 1831. *Narrative of a Voyage to the Pacific and Bering's Strait to Co-operate with the Polar Expeditions; Performed in his Majesty's Ship "Blossom" . . . in the Years 1825, 26, 27, 28*. Colburn and Bently, London.

Bettinger, Robert L. 2013. Effects of the Bow on Social Organization in Western North America. *Evolutionary Anthropology: Issues, News, and Reviews* 22(3):118–23.

Betts, Matthew W. 2008. *Subsistence and Culture in the Western Canadian Arctic: A Multicontextual Approach*. Canadian Museum of Civilization, Gatineau, Quebec, Canada.

Birket-Smith, Kaj 1929. *The Caribou Eskimos: Material and Social Life and Their Cultural Position*. Gyldendalske Boghandel, Copenhagen.

——— 1936. *The Eskimos*. Translated from Danish by W. E. Calvert. Methuen, London.

Boas, Franz 1888. *The Central Eskimo*. Annual Reports of the Bureau of American Ethnology, No. 6. Smithsonian Institution, Washington, D.C.

Briggs, Jean 1970. *Never in Anger: Portrait of an Eskimo Family*. Harvard University Press, Cambridge, MA.

Brown, Sarah K., T. Max Friesen, Owen K. Mason, and Christyann M. Darwent 2012. Ancient DNA Identification of a Polar Bear Bone Dagger from Cape Espenberg, Alaska. *Alaska Journal of Anthropology* 10:173–5.

Burch, Ernest S. Jr. 1974. Eskimo Warfare in Northwest Alaska. *Anthropological Papers of the University of Alaska* 16:1–14.

——— 1988. War and Trade. In *Crossroads of Continents: Cultures of Siberia and Alaska*, edited by William W. Fitzhugh and Aron Crowell, pp. 227–40. Smithsonian Institution Press, Washington, D.C.

——— 1991. From Skeptic to Believer: The Making of an Oral Historian. *Alaska History* 6:1–16.

——— 1998. *The Iñupiaq Eskimo Nations of Northwest Alaska*. University of Alaska Press, Fairbanks.

——— 2005. *Alliance and Conflict: The World System of the Iñupiaq Eskimos*. University of Nebraska Press, Lincoln.

——— 2007. Traditional Native Warfare in Western Alaska. In *North American Indigenous Warfare and Ritual Violence*, edited by Richard J. Chacon and Rubén G. Mendoza, pp. 11–29. University of Arizona Press, Tucson.

Burch, Ernest S., and Thomas C. Correll 1972. Alliance and Conflict: Inter-regional Relations in North Alaska. In *Alliance in Eskimo Society*, edited by Lee Guemple, pp. 17–39. Proceedings of the American Ethnological Society 1971 Supplement. University of Washington Press, Seattle.

Collins, Henry B. 1929. *Prehistoric Art of the Alaskan Eskimo*. Smithsonian Miscellaneous Collections 81(14), Smithsonian Institution, Washington, D.C.

——— 1937. *Archeology of St. Lawrence Island, Alaska*. Smithsonian Miscellaneous Collections 36(1). Smithsonian Institution, Washington, D.C.

## 200 | John Darwent and Christyann M. Darwent

Cooper, H. Kory, and Gabriel J. Bowen 2012. Metal Armor from St. Lawrence Island. *Arctic Anthropology* 50:1–19.

D'Anglure, Bernard Saladin 1984. Inuit of Quebec. In *Handbook of North American Indians, Vol. 5: Arctic*, edited by David Damas and William C. Sturtevant, pp. 476–507. Smithsonian Institution, Washington, D.C.

Dabbs, Gretchen R. 2011. Health Status among Prehistoric Eskimos from Point Hope, Alaska. *American Journal of Physical Anthropology* 146:94–103.

Darwent, Christyann M., and John Darwent, In Press. The Enigmatic Choris and Old Whaling "Cultures" of the Western Arctic. In *Handbook of Arctic Archaeology*, edited by T. Max Friesen and Owen K. Mason. Oxford University Press, United Kingdom.

Diamond, Jared 2005. *Collapse: How Societies Choose to Fail or Succeed*. Penguin Books, New York.

Dugmore, Andrew J., Christian Keller, and Thomas H. McGovern 2007. The Norse Greenland Settlement: Reflections on Climate Change, Trade and the Contrasting Fates of Human Settlements in the Atlantic islands. *Arctic Anthropology* 44:12–36.

Dumond, Don E. 1984. Prehistory of the Bering Sea Region. In *Handbook of North American Indians. Vol. 5, Arctic*, edited by David Damas and William C. Sturtevant, pp. 94–105. Smithsonian Institution Press, Washington, D.C.

—— 2000. *Henry B. Collins at Wales 1936: A Partial Description of Collections*. University of Oregon Anthropological Paper 56, Eugene.

Esdale, Julie 2008. A Current Synthesis of the Northern Archaic. *Arctic Anthropology* 45:3–38.

Fitzhugh, William W. 1997. Biogeographical Archaeology in the Eastern North American Arctic. *Human Ecology* 25:385–418.

Fitzhugh, William W., and Elizabeth Ward (editors) 2000. *Vikings: A North Atlantic Saga*. Smithsonian Institution Press, Washington, D.C.

Ford, James A. 1959. *Eskimo Prehistory in the Vicinity of Point Barrow, Alaska*. Anthropological Papers of the American Museum of Natural History 47(1), New York.

Fossett, Renée 2001. *In Order to Live Untroubled: Inuit of the Central Arctic, 1550 to 1940*. University of Manitoba Press, Winnipeg, Canada.

Friederici, Georg 1907. Scalping in America: Annual Report of the Board of Regents of the Smithsonian Institution for the Year Ending June 30, 1906. U.S. Government Printing Office, Washington, D.C.

Friesen, T. Max 2012. The Importance of Reading Ernest: Applying Burch's Study of Interregional Interaction to Inuvialuit Ethnohistory. *Arctic Anthropology* 49:29–40.

—— 2013. *When Worlds Collide: Hunter-Gatherer World-System Change in the 19th Century Canadian Arctic*. The University of Arizona Press, Tucson.

Friesen, T. Max, and Charles D. Arnold 2008. The Timing of the Thule Migration: New Dates from the Western Canadian Arctic. *American Antiquity* 73:527–538.

Friesen, T. Max, and Jeffrey Hunston 1994. Washout—The Final Chapter: 1985–86 NOGAP Salvage Excavations on Herschel Island. *In Bridges across Time: The NOGAP Archaeology Project*, edited by Jean Luc Pilon, pp. 39–60. Canadian Archaeological Association Occasional Paper No. 2, Ottawa.

Funk, Caroline 2010. The Bow and Arrow War Days on the Yukon-Kuskokwim Delta of Alaska. *Ethnohistory* 57:523–69.

Giddings, J. Louis, and Douglas D. Anderson 1986. *Beach Ridge Archaeology of Cape Krusenstern: Eskimo and Pre-Eskimo Settlements around Kotzebue Sound*. Publications in Archaeology No. 20. National Park Service, Department of the Interior, Washington, D.C.

Gulløv, Hans Christian 2000. Natives and Norse in Greenland. In *Vikings: The North Atlantic Saga*, edited by William W. Fitzhugh and Elizabeth I. Ward, pp. 318–26. Smithsonian Institution Press, Washington, D.C.

Hearne, Samuel 1795. *A Journey from Prince of Wales's Fort in Hudson's Bay to the Northern Ocean . . . in the Years 1769, 1770, 1771 and 1772*. Strahan and Cadell, London.

Scales of Violence across the North American Arctic | **201**

Hill, Erica 2011. The Historical Ecology of Walrus Exploitation in the North Paciûc. In *Human Impacts on Seals, Sea Lions, and Sea Otters: Integrating Archaeology and Ecology in the Northeast Paciûc*, edited by Todd J. Braje and Torben C. Rick, pp. 41–64. University of California Press, Berkeley.

Holtved, Erik 1944. *Archaeological Investigations in the Thule District, I-II.* Meddelelser om Grønland 141. C.A. Reitzels Forlag, Copenhagen, Denmark.

Irwin, Colin 1990. The Inuit and the Evolution of Limited Group Conflict. In *Sociobiology and Conflict: Evolutionary Perspectives on Competition, Cooperation, Violence and Warfare*, edited by Johan M. G. van der Dennen and Vincent S. E. Falger, pp.149–88. Chapman and Hall, London.

Jackson, Matthew O., and Massimo Morelli 2011. The Reasons for War: An Updated Survey. *Handbook on the Political Economy of War.* Edward Elgar Publishing, Cheltenham, UK.

Jansen, Henrik M. 1972. A Critical Account of the Written and Archaeological Sources' Evidence Concerning the Norse Settlements in Greenland. *Meddelelser om Grønland* 182(4):1–158.

Jenness, Diamond 1940. *Prehistoric Culture Waves from Asia to America.* U.S. Government Printing Office, Washington, D.C.

Keenleyside, Anne 1998. Skeletal Evidence of Health and Disease in Precontact Eskimos and Aleuts. *American Journal of Physical Anthropology* 107:51–70.

Krech, Shepard, III 1976. The Eastern Kutchin and the Fur Trade, 1800–1860. *Ethnohistory* 23:213–35.

——— 1979. Interethnic Relations in the Lower Mackenzie River Region. *Arctic Anthropology* 16:102–22.

——— 1984. "Massacre" of the Inuit. *The Beaver* Summer: 52–59.

Lantis, Margaret 1946. The Social Culture of the Nunivak Eskimo. *Transactions of the American Philosophical Society New Series* 35:153–323.

Larsen, Helge, and Froelich Rainey 1948. *Ipiutak and the Arctic Whale Hunting Culture.* Anthropological Papers of the American Museum of Natural History Vol. 42, New York.

LeMoine, Genevieve M., and Christyann M. Darwent 2010. The Inglefield Land Archaeology Project: Overview. *Geografisk Tidsskrift [Danish Journal of Geography]* 100:279–96.

——— In Press. Development of Polar Inughuit Culture in the Smith Sound Region. In *Handbook of Arctic Archaeology*, edited by T. Max Friesen and Owen K. Mason. Oxford University Press, UK.

Malaurie, Jean 1974. Raids et esclavage dan les sociétés autochtones du Détroit de Behring. *Inter-Nord* 13–14:129–55.

Mary-Rouselliere, Guy 1991. *Qitdlarssuaq: The Story of a Polar Migration.* Wuerz Publishing, Winnipeg, Canada.

Maschner, Herbert D. G. 1997. The Evolution of Northwest Coast Warfare. In *Troubled Times: Violence and Warfare in the Past*, edited by Deborah L. Martin and David W. Frayer, pp. 267–302. War and Society Series Vol. 4. Gordon and Breach, Langhorne, PA.

Maschner, Herbert D. G., and Owen K. Mason 2013. The Bow and Arrow in Northern North America. *Evolutionary Anthropology* 22:133–8.

Maschner, Herbert D. G., and Katherine L. Reedy-Maschner 1998. Raid, Retreat, Defend (Repeat): The Archaeology and Ethnohistory of Warfare on the North Pacific Rim. *Journal of Anthropological Archaeology* 17:19–325.

——— 2007. Heads, Women, and the Baubles of Prestige: Trophies of War in the Arctic and Subarctic. In *The Taking and Displaying of Human Body Parts as Trophies by Amerindians*, edited by Richard J. Chacon and David H. Dye, pp. 32 44. Springer, New York.

Mason, Owen K. 1998. The Contest between the Ipiutak, Old Bering Sea, and Birnirk Polities and the Origin of Whaling during the First Millennium A.D. along Bering Strait. *Journal of Anthropological Archaeology* 17:240–325.

——— 2009. Flight from the Bering Strait: Did Siberian Punuk/Thule Military Cadres Conquer Northwest Alaska. In *The Northern World A.D. 1100–1350: The Dynamics of*

**202** John Darwent and Christyann M. Darwent

*Climate, Economy and Politics*, edited by Herbert D. G. Maschner, Owen K. Mason, and Robert McGhee, pp. 76–128. University of Utah Press, Salt Lake City.

Mason, Owen K. 2012. Memories of Warfare: Archaeology and Oral History in Assessing the Conflict and Alliance Model of Ernest Burch. *Arctic Anthropology* 49:72–91.

Mason, Owen K., and James Jordan 1993. Heightened North Pacific Storminess and Synchronous Late Holocene Erosion of Northwest Alaska Beach Ridge Complexes. *Quaternary Research* 40(1):55–69.

Mathiassen, Therkel 1930. *Archaeological Collections from the Western Eskimos.* Reports of the Fifth Thule Expedition 1921–1924, Vol. 10, pp. 1–98. Gyldendalske, Copenhagen, Denmark.

Maxwell, Moreau S. 1985. *Prehistory of the Eastern Arctic.* Academic Press, Orlando, FL.

McCartney, Allen P. 1977. *Thule Eskimo Prehistory along Northwestern Hudson Bay.* National Museum of Man, Archaeological Survey of Canada Mercury Series Paper No. 70, Ottawa.

McGhee, Robert 1974. *Beluga Hunters: An Archaeological Reconstruction of the History and Culture of the Mackenzie Delta Kittegaryumiut, Newfoundland.* Social and Economic Studies No. 13. Institute of Social and Economic Research, Memorial University of Newfoundland, St. John's.

——— 1984. The Timing of the Thule Migration. *Polarforschung* 54:1–7.

——— 2000. Radiocarbon Dating and the Timing of the Thule Migration. In *Identities and Cultural Contacts in the Arctic*, edited by Martin Appelt, Joel Berglund, and Hans Christian Gulløv, pp. 181–91. Danish Polar Center, Copenhagen, Denmark.

——— 2004. *The Last Imaginary Place: A Human History of the Arctic World.* Key Porter, Toronto, Canada.

McGovern, Thomas 2000. The Demise of Norse Greenland. In *Vikings: The North Atlantic Saga*, edited by William W. Fitzhugh and Elisabeth I. Ward, pp. 327–39. Smithsonian Institution Press, Washington, D.C.

Melbye, Jerry, and Scott I. Fairgreive 1994. A Massacre and Possible Cannibalism in the Canadian Arctic: New Evidence from the Saunaktuk Site (NgTn-1). *Arctic Anthropology* 31:57–77.

Merbs, Charles F. 1983. *Patterns of Activity-Induced Pathology in a Canadian Inuit Population.* Archaeological Survey of Canada Mercury Series, Paper 119. Canadian Museum of Civilization, Ottawa.

——— 2002. Asymmetrical Spondylolysis. *American Journal of Physical Anthropology* 119:156–74.

——— 2004. Sagittal Clefting of the Body and Other Vertebral Developmental Errors in Canadian Inuit Skeletons. *American Journal of Physical Anthropology* 123:236–49.

Merbs, Charles F., and William H. Wilson 1962. Anomalies and Pathologies of the Sadlermiut Eskimo Vertebral Column. *National Museum of Man Contributions to Anthropology, 1960, Part I.* Bulletin No. 180, pp. 154–180. National Museum of Man, Ottawa, Canada.

Morey, Darcy F. 2010. *Dogs: Domestication and Development of a Social Bond.* Cambridge University Press, Cambridge, UK.

Murdoch, John 1892. *Ethnological Results of the Point Barrow Expedition.* Ninth Annual Report, Bureau of American Ethnology. Government Printing Office, Washington D.C.

Nansen, Fridtjof 1893. *Eskimo Life.* Longmans, Greens, London.

Park, Robert 1993. Approaches to Dating the Thule Culture in the Eastern Arctic. *Canadian Journal of Archaeology* 18:29–48.

——— 2000. The Dorset-Thule Succession Revisited. In *Identities and Cultural Contacts in the Arctic*, edited by Martin Appelt, Joel Berglund, and Hans Christian Gulløv, pp. 192–205. Danish Polar Center, Copenhagen, Denmark.

Rasmussen, Knud (1927) 1999. *Across Arctic America: Narrative of the Fifth Thule Expedition.* University of Alaska Press, Fairbanks.

Ray, Dorothy Jean 1975. *The Eskimos of Bering Strait, 1650–1898.* University of Washington Press, Seattle.

Rink, Henrik 1875. *Tales and Traditions of the Eskimo.* W. Blackwood, Edinburgh and London.

# Scales of Violence across the North American Arctic | **203**

Saabye, Hans E. 1818. *Greenland: Being Extracts from a Journal Kept in that Country in the Years 1770 to 1778*. A. S. Boosey and Sons, London.

Salter, Elizabeth M. 1984. Skeletal Biology of Cumberland Sound, Baffin Island. Unpublished Ph.D. dissertation, Department of Anthropology, University of Toronto, Canada.

Schledermann, Peter 1979. The "Baleen Period" of the Arctic Whale Hunting Tradition. In *Thule Eskimo Culture: An Anthropological Retrospective*, edited by Allen P. McCartney, pp. 134–48. Archaeological Survey of Canada Mercury Series Paper No. 88. National Museums of Canada, Ottawa.

———— 1980. Notes on Norse Finds from the East Coast of Ellesmere Island, N.W.T. *Arctic* 33:454–63.

———— 2000. Ellesmere: Vikings in the Far North. In *Vikings: A North Atlantic Saga*, edited by William W. Fitzhugh and Elizabeth Ward, pp. 248–56. Smithsonian Institution Press, Washington, D.C.

Schledermann, Peter, and Karen M. McCullough 2003. *Late Thule Culture Developments on the Central East Coast of Ellesmere Island*. Sila—The Greenland Research Centre at the National Museum of Denmark and the Danish Polar Center, Copenhagen, Denmark.

Sheehan, Glenn W. 1995. Whaling Surplus, Trade, War, and Integration of Prehistoric Northern and Northwestern Alaskan Economies, 1200–1826. In *Hunting the Largest Animals: Native Whaling in the Western Arctic and Subarctic*, edited by Allen P. McCartney, pp. 185–206. Canadian Circumpolar Institute, University of Alberta, Edmonton, Canada.

———— 1997. *In the Belly of the Whale: Trade and War in Eskimo Society*. Aurora Monograph Series 6. Alaska Anthropological Association, Anchorage.

Slobodin, Richard 1960. Eastern Kutchin Warfare. *Anthropologica* 2:76–94.

Smith, Eric Alden, and S. Abigail Smith 1994. Inuit Sex-Ratio Variation: Population Control, Ethnographic Error, or Parental Manipulation? *Current Anthropology* 35(5):595–659.

Spencer, Robert F. 1959. *The North Alaskan Eskimo: A Study in Ecology and Society*. Smithsonian Institution Press, Washington, D.C.

Walker, Phillip L. 1989. Cranial Injuries as Evidence of Violence in Prehistoric Southern California. *American Journal of Physical Anthropology* 80:313–23.

———— 2001. A Bioarchaeological Perspective on the History of Violence. *Annual Review of Anthropology* 30:537–96.

Weyer, Edward 1932. *The Eskimos*. Yale University Press, New Haven, CT.

Whitridge, Peter 1999. The Prehistory of Inuit and Yupik Whale Use. *Revista de Arqueología Americana* 16:99–154.

# 11

## The Spectre of Conflict on Isla Cedros, Baja California, Mexico

*Matthew R. Des Lauriers*

A rchaeologically observed markers for warfare are often indirect, especially with regard to settlement pattern, architecture, and the presence of weaponry. Obviously, when paleopathological studies identify an actual *incidence* of violence, we are looking at something that actually came to pass. However, many people conduct their daily lives, as well as their short- and long-term planning, based upon what they *anticipate* will happen. Human beings are quite capable of making proactive choices, but this means that they will sometimes plan for that which never comes to pass, or fail to adequately prepare for that which does occur. In her excellent analysis of the relationship between mobility strategies and site structure, Susan Kent (1991, 1992) observes that both site structure and architecture are strongly affected not by the actually observed length of residence at a site, but on the length of time the occupants *anticipate* dwelling there. Choices regarding the location and amount of labor and material expended in constructing houses were made when the site was initially occupied, not when it was abandoned. As such, when people develop strategies for defense or conflict avoidance, they are doing so based upon the anticipated potential of violence, rather than with the perfect vision of hindsight. Sometimes the wars in our minds can be as archaeologically visible as actual conflict.

### Accounts of a Guarded Landscape

On Isla Cedros, Baja California (Figure 11.1), ethnohistoric documents, including explorers' accounts and detailed Jesuit manuscripts, combine with

---

*Violence and Warfare among Hunter-Gatherers,* edited by Mark W. Allen and Terry L. Jones, 204–219. ©2014 Taylor & Francis. All rights reserved.

# The Spectre of Conflict on Isla Cedros, Baja California, Mexico | 205

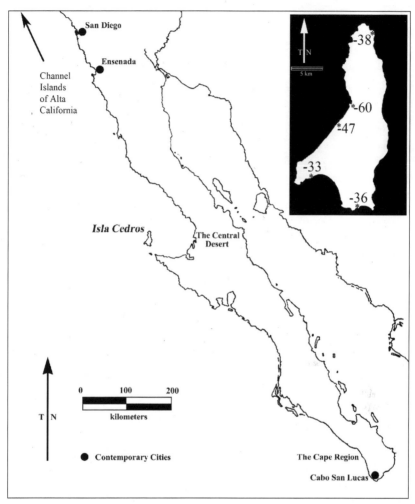

**Figure 11.1** Baja California and Isla Cedros. Inset shows the locations of Punta Chual (PAIC-33), Campo Quintero (PAIC-36), Punta Norte (PAIC-38), Vargas Village (PAIC-47), and El Coloradito (PAIC-60). These are some of the most prominent village sites, though the island is home to more than a dozen other sites with 20 or more house features.

more than a decade of archaeological research by the Proyecto Arqueologico Isla de Cedros (PAIC) to provide a still-improving image of indigenous society around the time of European contact (Des Lauriers 2010; Des Lauriers and García-Des Lauriers 2006). The island has an archaeological record that extends back more than 12,000 calendar years (Des Lauriers 2006a, 2008, 2010) and includes hundreds of Holocene-aged sites, most

**206** | Matthew R. Des Lauriers

of which can be described as exceptionally well preserved (Des Lauriers 2006b, 2010).

The earliest written historical accounts come from Capitán Francisco de Ulloa's voyage of 1539–1540. The accounts were penned by the captain and and one of his crew, Francisco Preciado. In the 1540 report to Hernán Cortez, Ulloa noted during some relatively peaceful dealings on the water near Punta Norte (Figure 11.2): "And in the boat with four paddlers, a man older than the others came, and he did not paddle, but was ordering them what to do, and he spoke to us, and took the things that we gave them; it seemed to us that he must be something more than the others" (Montané-Martí 1995:240; translation mine). Upon landing at this village—smaller than the one near the southeast corner of the island—Ulloa's men were surprised by a confrontation by a small fearless group of warriors, who painted themselves with cakes of white chalk and menaced the Spanish landing party. These same warriors had only the day before been trading fish and sea lion stomach bags of water in exchange for glass beads and other trinkets (Montané-Martí 1995:241). Two centuries later, the Jesuit Fr. Taraval, in charge of the new Mission San Ignacio near the very midpoint of the peninsula, mentioned the presence of "three communities" on Isla Cedros, who in "ancient times" had "among them some wars and battles, in which another population, which had lived there, perished completely" (Venegas 1979:408; translation from Des Lauriers and García-Des Lauriers 2006:141). The passage continues:

> There were two clans that were always enemies with each other. . . . [After the "destruction" of one clan in a war] there were three clans, all of which, although they were of the same language, they differed in the pronunciation, and in diverse words characteristic of each clan. With all this, these being distinct clans, they were all under the rule of one, who was he who came as leader of the north. He they obeyed and served, and after him, his successors were always governors of the island, as if by right. . . . [A]ll put themselves under [his] protection . . . who was, they say, the most accomplished and honored man that had lived on the island (Venegas 1979; translation from Des Lauriers and García-Des Lauriers 2006:141, brackets mine).

It is not clear when this apparent political unification of the island occurred. What is clear is that it was likely a recent historical event rather than one that took place in a legendary or mythological past. The combination of political and religious authority also seems to have emerged on the island, since Taraval wrote, "He who was their governor was also their priest, or wizard, though this did not prevent the existence of other subordinates, in such a way that in each clan there was a *capitán* for its government" (Venegas 1979:408; translation by Des Lauriers and García-Des Lauriers 2006:141). It is from the Jesuit manuscripts that we obtain the term *Huamalgua* as the indigenous name of the island, translated by the missionaries as meaning "island of fogs"

# The Spectre of Conflict on Isla Cedros, Baja California, Mexico

**Figure 11.2** Punta Norte Village (PAIC-38) aerial view.

(Des Lauriers 2010). As the only indigenous term preserved to the present day that might be close to their own self-referent, I have chosen here and in other publications to refer to the Late period (AD 1100–1732) inhabitants of Isla Cedros as *Huamalgüeños*.

Upon his first direct contact with the Huamalgüeños, Capitán Francisco de Ulloa was impressed with the speed and organization with which the native village was evacuated of women and children the moment the Spanish ship's boats were lowered into the water. The men of the village divided into three groups and took defensive positions: "part of them in the settlement, and part on the coast, and others on a hill" (Montané-Martí 1995:236; translation mine). The most likely location for this particular battle was the large village site near a spot today known as Campo Quintero (Figure 11.3). The islanders defended their settlement against the Spanish landing using bows, slings, and large, heavy wooden staves wielded as battle clubs.

Isla Cedros was not alone in the Baja California region in experiencing conflict between indigenous groups. In *Antigua California*, Harry Crosby observes,

> All seventeenth- and eighteenth-century accounts of California [the peninsula] that were based on extended Spanish contacts reported constant warfare or at least skirmishes between bands. These apparently had some bases in territorial disputes, but they often were of a more ritual character involving tests of

**Figure 11.3** Aerial view of village at Campo Quintero (PAIC-36).

manhood and solidarity of band members in carrying out what might best be called feuds, so small were the groups involved (Crosby 1994:180–1).

However, given the higher population density and greater geographic and/ or economic circumscription (Des Lauriers 2010) of Isla Cedros populations when compared with that of the mainland of Baja California (Aschmann 1959; Gutierrez and Hyland 2002), the Santa Barbara Channel region (Gamble 2008; Kennett and Kennett 2000), or the Northwest Coast (see Ames 1994; Ames and Maschner 1999; Blackman 1990; de Laguna 1990), I suspect that the disputes over territory and resources figured more prominently among the causes of conflict between island communities and clearly developed beyond simple feuding. Though in some cases the incidence of violence is blamed upon the disruptive effects of the colonial encounter, this does not explain the Isla Cedros situation. From the very first contact, early in the year 1540, Europeans encountered a people who quickly obtained a reputation for bravery and fearlessness. The Cabrillo expedition of 1542 paused briefly at the island, but the lack of detail inherent to the surviving documents of that voyage is at least partly due to the fact that the document usually referred to as a log of the expedition, the "Paez diary," is a "paraphrase of a copy of a copy" (Mathes 1994:248) and cannot be assumed to be either complete or entirely accurate in details such as locations where native peoples were sighted. Fr. Antonio

The Spectre of Conflict on Isla Cedros, Baja California, Mexico | **209**

de la Ascencion, the chronicler of the well-prepared and exceptionally well-documented Vizcaíno expedition in 1602, wrote, "We further pursued our journey until we reached Cedros Island, *which was recognized by everyone*. On it there were some *wild and warlike Indians* who did not wish us to be where we were, and who threatened us and by signs gave us to know that we should leave the locality" (translation from Aschmann 1974:178; emphasis mine).

The rapid deployment for combat and the surprising (to the Spanish) ferocity with which the Cedros Islanders resisted Ulloa's landings in 1540 (Montané-Martí 1995) may be another indication of a familiarity with conflict among Isla Cedros communities. Combined with the Jesuit documentation of native historical traditions in which conflict and warfare figure prominently, interpersonal and intergroup conflict was not alien to the Huamalgüeños. Particularly within the bounded space of Isla Cedros, tensions originating in resource competition and/or historic rivalry between communities could reach a breaking point. As discussed later in this chapter, this may partially explain the archaeological observation that visibility and elevation were more important criteria for locating villages than protection from the elements or immediate proximity to water. This is not a trend, but a fairly absolute pattern. None of the villages (settlements with more than 20 houses) are located within 500 meters of a flowing spring, and all are located on uplifted marine terraces. Even the uncommon clusters of a few houses (too small to be considered a village) located on terraces in major drainages share many of the same topographic features such as steep gully walls below the houses and approaches to the site limited by higher canyon and arroyo walls above. No Late period site with more than three house features is located more than 250 meters from the coast, while the flowing and pooling water sources are all located at least 1 km from the beach.

Given that the size of the coastal settlements on Isla Cedros was far larger than that described for any other part of Baja California outside of the Cape Region or the Colorado Delta, the intensity and nature of conflict by residents of this little-known island may not have been comparable with that of their relatives on the sparsely populated central part of the mainland peninsula, where conflicts as described throughout most of the peninsula by Jesuit chroniclers (i.e., del Barco [1776] 1988; Venegas 1979; and others) were generally of brief duration, small scale, and with low casualty rates. The concerns usually seem to have centered on blood feuds between kin groups and raids to capture sacred items belonging to enemy shamans (such as hair capes; see Meigs 1968). Despite the short duration of many actual conflict *events*, in some areas, the existence of a *state of conflict* between two or more groups could have a much longer duration, such as that described by the Spanish as existing between the Pericú of the La Paz area and the Guaycura to the west and south. This area was in a state of open hostility from at least 1596 to 1668, with the interior groups being described as the aggressors. All indications are that the "Guaicuro" were successful in dislodging the Pericú from the shores of Bahía La Paz sometime between 1668 and 1720, when the Jesuit mission was founded at that location (Mathes 1975). This provides another example of conflict that was not low intensity or of little consequence, and that intergroup violence on the peninsula—in terms of its impact on social interaction, economy, and territory—occasionally had some of the effects often attributed to "warfare" in the larger sense.

If we were able to examine the frequencies of these different kinds of conflict in pre-contact Baja California, we would most likely find that the vast majority of conflict *events* were of low intensity and relatively narrow in scope (e.g., blood feuds, raids, or ambuscades). Meanwhile, larger-scale conflicts of sustained duration and broad scope—involving entire communities (or even larger alliances of multiple communities) set against one another (see Crosby 1994; del Barco [1766] 1988; Venegas 1979)—occurred at a *much* lower frequency on the peninsula as a whole. Much of the Central Desert of Baja California had a very low population density, even when compared with adjacent areas of this exceptionally rugged peninsula (Aschmann 1959). In the Chumash region of Alta California, conflict seems to have existed at a consistently low level, particularly between interior and coastal groups, only rarely escalating to larger-scale, high-intensity conflict involving entire communities and destruction of homes and theft of stored resources (see Gamble 2008). This indeed makes sense, since a great deal of the local economic system depended upon reasonably stable social and economic relationships between neighboring groups. A constantly insecure and violent landscape could never have produced and maintained the shell bead exchange networks for which the region is widely known.

For Isla Cedros, the bounded landscape inherent to insular environments, combined with the remarkably high population density of the island relative to its adjacent mainland (see Aschmann 1959; Des Lauriers 2010), would have spurred much greater competition and territorial inertia among resident groups. The lack of a risk-buffering, economically integrated system like that of southern Alta California would have meant that resource imbalances would have to have been addressed through more effective local management practices. No sacks of craft-specialized goods could be exchanged in lean times, no shift of significant numbers of people could occur from island to mainland, and no significant surplus was produced on the mainland that could be transferred to the island. The Cedros Islanders were "on their own" in terms of dealing with the inevitable crises that beset successful human settlements of any landscape. More effective management depends first and foremost upon restriction of access to resources susceptible to overexploitation. This is the only means to avoid the "tragedy of the commons" (see McCay 1978, 1980, 1981; McCay and Acheson 1987; and others) for which fishing communities are especially at risk. Even the modern fishing *cooperativas* of Baja California

The Spectre of Conflict on Isla Cedros, Baja California, Mexico | **211**

depend upon restricting access to designated species of sealife, and have clearly demarcated boundaries which are monitored constantly by *vigilancia* patrols (Des Lauriers 2009, 2010). Both today and in the past, these boundaries and exclusive rights held at the community level are central to concepts of landscape, identity, and social interaction. Similar social and ideological structures are found among the peoples of the Northwest Coast of North America and are frequently associated with the concept of restricted use-rights to territories or at least restricted access to certain resources (Boas and Codere 1966; Drucker 1939; Earle 2000; Kroeber 1925). This landscape of guarded resources on Isla Cedros would have certainly resulted in some degree of inherent tension (though not constant open conflict) between resident groups, amply supported by the descriptions of conflict in the Jesuit manuscripts (del Barco [1776] 1988; Venegas 1979).

Incidentally, the posited bounded territories may also partly explain the surprising size of some of the major village sites on Isla Cedros, since one site contains 481 house features and the three largest villages together contain 668 house features in densely packed clusters (see Figures 11.2 and 11.3). Especially in geographic areas where population densities can be quite high, a major concern in any group's selection of habitation locales would be this anticipated potential for aggression. For most of the history of research, Alta California was treated as a peaceful "Garden of Eden," with low rates of violence and easy living, reminiscent of 1940s tourism posters. However, some scholars (Allen 2012; see also Brill, Eerkens et al., Pilloud et al., and Schwitalla et al., this volume) have now begun to question this image, suggesting that ". . . rates of violence in prehistoric California are far above most comparable North American sites; and within California, they show great variability in practice, and become more common going from earlier to later periods" (Ferguson 2013).

The holding of usufruct rights and layered strategies for avoiding the tragedy of the commons (see McCay and Acheson 1987) are much more common among maritime peoples than some traditional models have held (Durrenberger and Pálsson 1987). These use-rights, while held collectively by a community, can be a source of conflict *between* neighboring communities, while at the same time encouraging cohesion and solidarity *within* a community. Among of the many examples cited by Durrenberger and Pálsson (1987:516) is that of "conflicts between villages in Japan, whether in ancient or modern times, as each has tried to extend the area of its common village-fishing territory at the expense of other villages." This competition for resources is not and was not something that could be separated from kinship networks, nor community identity, and thus necessarily draws in the participation of larger and larger social units as boundary formation becomes more frequent and intense. Not all boundaries promote conflict; indeed, some can actually mitigate the frequency of violence by establishing

# 212 | Matthew R. Des Lauriers

agreed-upon limits and zones (e.g., Goldschmidt and Haas 1998). The usufruct rights to landscapes and/or specific resources vested in lineages, clans, and communities can be very clearly conceptualized and closely guarded by those vested in such a system (see Acheson and Gardner 2004). Jesús Rojo, one of Nabhan's informants in a wonderful examination of the ethnozoology of the Seri of Sonora (located just across the Sea of Cortez from central Baja California), reported:

> *Ihízitim*—that's *terreno*, homeground. For me, it's Punta Mala on Isla Tiburón; that's where my grandfather lived, where my father, *mi jefe*, was born. It's based around a camp, one that each family has, one that belongs to all of the descendants. It's only for them—those who live there are the only ones who can use the resources nearby the camp. All the descendants have rights there (Nabhan 2003:53).

For the ancient Cedros Islanders, like other island populations, further division of already bounded space into alternately competing and cooperating groups (Kennett and Kennett 2000) might also have provided strong incentives for the exploitation of such a diverse range of resources. Even if the territorial divisions were not absolutely geographic and pertained only to use-rights of particular resources such as sea mammal rookeries (Hildebrandt and Jones 1992), these would have been jealously guarded.

One example of this capacity and willingness to defend against encroachment comes from the first-contact accounts of Francisco de Ulloa and Francisco Preciado (Montané-Martí 1995). Upon seeing Ulloa's crew preparing to land on a beach in front of a village somewhere on the southeastern corner of the island, the Huamalgüeño men rapidly sent the women and children up the nearby arroyos by various routes into the uplands:

> And the men stayed, part of them in the village, some on the beach, and others on a hill. . . . [A]nd seeing the place at which we were landing, they moved toward us and began to speak in loud and serious voices and signaled to us that we shalt not pass. . . . [W]e landed against their will, and seeing this, they armed themselves with many stones and great staves that they used with both hands and prepared themselves with great energy and determination to contest our landing, which they did for a while. . . . [S]o determined were some of them to repel us that they waded into the water to receive us with their stones and staves, with which they gave such great blows that they could shatter our wooden shields. They fought with us toe-to-toe for a while before we finally broke their ranks (original Spanish in Montané-Martí 1995:236–238; my translation).

The rapidity with which the Huamalgüeños challenged the Spanish landing, wading into the surf to fight hand-to-hand (Montané-Martí 1995),

The Spectre of Conflict on Isla Cedros, Baja California, Mexico | **213**

suggests that the idea of group-versus-group conflict was not alien to them, and that they were capable of engaging in a significant degree of interpersonal violence. As such, there may have been an incentive to abide by the rules governing boundaries and resource use-rights. In addition, broad cross-cultural studies of the relationship between conflict and climate change (Hendrix and Salehyan 2012) have demonstrated that it is not only drought, but also unusually wet years that can be associated with violent events. It is not resource scarcity that leads to increased incidence of violence, but instability and uncertainty that actually tend to correlate with outbreaks of unrest and conflict (Theisen 2008). Populations occupying regions with long histories of scarcity are usually distributed at much lower densities and can accommodate the variability through mobility or otherwise more flexible human ecological relationships. It is rapid change and an inability to accurately predict near-term conditions that are most problematic (Des Lauriers 2009), especially among groups like aquatic hunter-gatherers (Ames 2002) for whom physical preparations and/or technology play a critical role. These environmental shocks to the economic and social systems can increase the potential for conflict and simultaneously the *anticipation* of intercommunity violence, potentially leading communities to prepare themselves for such even before the initiation of actual combat.

## Conflict and Territorial Clan Villages

Lambert (2002) succinctly lays out four lines of physical evidence for warfare in the archaeological record: "settlement data, injuries in human skeletal remains, war weaponry, and iconography" (Lambert 2002:209). Of these, the Isla Cedros record is uneven for several reasons. First, the evidence from Huamalgüeño period (AD 1100–1732) human remains is exceedingly sparse, not because they have not been located, but because cremation at very high temperatures was the social norm for the time, causing a great deal of the "forensic" evidence to be destroyed even prior to entering the archaeological record. Iconography is also currently a lacuna in our data from Isla Cedros, as rock art or other representative forms of creative expression have yet to be identified on the island. The neighboring mainland has abundant rock art, and the Sierra de San Francisco in the very center of the peninsula is a UNESCO world heritage area due to the massive and renowned Great Mural tradition (Crosby 1997; Gutierrez and Hyland 1994, 2002; and others). In those panels, representations of human figures pierced by fletched projectiles (whether darts or arrows) are not at all uncommon (Crosby 1997; Laylander 2005), though interpretations of these run from representations of actual conflict (Laylander 2005) to primordial ancestor figures (Gutierrez and Hyland 2002) to more esoteric ritually embedded artistic expressions.

**214** | Matthew R. Des Lauriers

For Isla Cedros itself, this leaves the settlement data and war weaponry. The weapons used by the Cedros Islanders against the Spanish in 1540 included bows and arrows, slings and stones, and heavy wooden staves. Problematically, all of these items are also useful in hunting otters, sea lions, deer, rabbits, and seabirds, all of which were components of the Huamalgüeño diet to greater or lesser degrees (Des Lauriers 2009, 2010). In addition, although preservation on Isla Cedros is good, our ability to distinguish slingstones from other beach pebbles deposited in sites for varied reasons is questionable. Staves would also likely have been burned with their owners, given the propensity for immolating the possessions of the dead, up to and including the house in which they died. Exceptionally well-made arrow points may provide some indication, since their frequency increases exponentially after about AD 1100; however, this by itself cannot be assumed to have a direct correlation to intergroup violence. Fortunately, as Lambert (2002:209) points out, "Settlement data is particularly useful for identifying both concern with defense and the consequences of failed (or absence of) defensive measures. The time and material resources people deem necessary for protection can help define *perceptions of threat*" [emphasis mine].

In keeping with this line of thought, the ethnohistoric data regarding territorial divisions, clan structure of society, and ancestor worship described in the Jesuit manuscripts (Venegas 1979; see Des Lauriers and García-Des Lauriers 2006) can be more completely understood within the context of the archaeological data from Campo Quintero (PAIC-36), Punta Norte Village (PAIC-38), Vargas Village (PAIC-47) and El Coloradito (PAIC-60) (Figure 11.1). On Isla Cedros, the four largest Late period village sites (and even most of the minor village sites) share the following characteristics: (1) they are located on elevated marine terraces with excellent view sheds that cover both the land and seascape; (2) they fall away on at least two sides due to steep beach cliffs or arroyo walls; and (3) they have excellent boat landings immediately below or adjacent to the village. All of these factors seem to be consistent with a need for large communities in defensible locations. Based on surface manifestations, Campo Quintero contains 481 house features, Punta Norte contains 50, Vargas Village contains 137, and El Coloradito contains at least 90. The dense clustering of structures reflects the strong tendency to meet these site standards, since not all stretches of coastline adequately fulfill the requirements. Locations that would have been more practical in terms of water source, access to a wider variety of coastal resources, travel corridors to the interior, and abundant plant resources are numerous, and yet seem to have been studiously avoided for use as residential sites during the time period between AD 1100 and 1732 (the Huamalgüeño or "Late" period of Isla Cedros history). Sometimes these "preferable" locales are less than a kilometer from the actual site of the major village, further underscoring the conscious and consistent selection of the defensible locales over other equally viable choices

# The Spectre of Conflict on Isla Cedros, Baja California, Mexico | **215**

in the immediate vicinity. While archaeological deposits dating to the latest period of island indigenous history are numerous, those with evidence for use as *residential* sites is limited to the proposed "nucleated" settlements, which never have fewer than approximately 20 house features (one example), usually have 30 to 50, and in three instances have more than 100. Many of the other sites are middens with evidence for processing of sea mammals, *agave* roasting, or collection of shellfish, but lack architecture and structured discard patterns characteristic of residential villages occupied for extended periods of time. Of the Huamalgüeño period (AD 1100–1732) villages containing more than 30 house features (n=9), none are located in low-lying areas; all are located above rocky shorelines, have narrow cove boat landings, and are bounded on at least two sides by vertical or near-vertical rock and soil walls at least 5 meters in height. This specific type of landscape feature played a major role in the combat against Ulloa's crew in 1540, when approximately half of the warriors from the first contact village near the southeast corner of the island remained on the beach cliff above the landing spot to rain arrows and slingstones down on the Spanish, while another portion of the defending force challenged the landing in hand-to-hand combat on the beach below. This clearly demonstrates that the Cedros Islanders made tactical use of the topography characteristic of these village sites, and did so in an organized fashion rather than simply by lucky accident.

Also noteworthy is the observation that for the stretch of coastline between La Colorada on the southwest corner of Isla Cedros to a major village site at El Coloradito (PAIC-60) on the central west coast, a pattern of discontinuous site distributions is clearly displayed. Surveys along the coast and up the various arroyos and canyons revealed that all Late period sites have greater densities in proximity to large village sites like PAIC-47 and PAIC-60 that decline in frequency as one moves away from the these locations. Even the space between these village sites (located less than 5 km from one another) displays a pattern of decreasing density and size of Huamalgüeño period midden and roasting feature deposits until one reaches a nadir at the approximate midpoint between the two (Des Lauriers 2010). This is suggestive of a pattern of land use that involved clearly defined territorial boundaries between these clan- and lineage-organized villages. Violation of these boundaries, or failure to abide by social norms recognizing the resource use-rights of a particular community or kin group, could have provided one justification for intergroup violence. Conversely, adherence to these intercommunity "agreements" regarding use-rights and boundaries—however formal or informal—would have been one way to reduce the frequency of violent events, even under a constant shadow of potential outbreak.

For Isla Cedros, these patterns cannot be confused with post-contact developments in Native American warfare. First contact was in January of 1540; by 1732, the island was entirely depopulated. It would be implausible to

**216** | Matthew R. Des Lauriers

argue that the admirable defense mounted by the inhabitants of the southern village on that bright winter morning 474 years ago was inspired by exposure to European battlefield tactics. The ethnohistoric accounts and archaeological data from Isla Cedros represent an entirely indigenous example of defensive settlement, organized deployment of warriors, and combat skill.

## A Landscape of Anxiety

The scale of warfare practiced would not have been sufficient to require a defensible water source, since the actual combat duration for punitive raids of this type seldom lasted long enough for water access to become a liability for defenders. Another notable feature is that the villages are often in locations rather exposed to the elements, even when more sheltered flat areas with good beach access and a reliable water source are available in the immediate vicinity. These factors seem to have been the defining considerations for village placement, even if defensibility was not the only motivation. Clearly, raiding on a small scale would not leave a dramatic mark on the archaeological record. "Nevertheless, there should be signs that a prehistoric tribal group was either engaged in conflict with foreign groups or was at least *concerned about potential conflict*. The latter may be objectified in the construction of defensive features, such as walls or moats, or the *deliberate selection of defensible site locations*." (Haas 1990:177; emphasis mine).

The question is, was the tension—the potential for violence—at least as important as actual warfare in pushing the islanders toward living in densely packed, defensively located settlements? Or was the incentive that by living on high, windswept coastal terraces (Figures 11.2 and 11.3), a community could discourage attacks by making them far too costly for an aggressor in terms of casualties to carry out except for the most extreme cases or circumstances? Obviously, this question will be answered differently in various times and places, but several things should be kept in mind.

*Defensive settlements are most often built to discourage rather than invite attack.* As such, they can be seen as an attempt to decrease the frequency or human costs of intercommunity conflict. Indeed, even when conflict occurs, it seldom resolves the crisis that precipitated it. The root problem of a drought-induced resource shortfall is not resolved when one village raids another. In fact, in a regional perspective, such disruption to systems of interaction and potential risk-sharing have the net effect of actually *reducing* the carrying capacity of a landscape, rather than increasing it. View, as an example, war-torn regions of our world today, regardless of the cause of the current conflicts. They universally experience economic depression, greater food insecurity, and lowered overall ability to support the resident communities in a stable fashion. This is something as true today as it was in the distant past.

The Spectre of Conflict on Isla Cedros, Baja California, Mexico | **217**

As President John F. Kennedy said in his remarks at West Point on June 6, 1962, ". . . the basic problems facing the world today are not susceptible of a final military solution."

*Cross-culturally, when violence becomes truly ubiquitous and endemic, it adversely affects all other aspects of social interaction.* In my view, a landscape of endemic intercommunity violence is most often part and parcel of the instability inherent in dramatic transitions or transformations of society rather than ever being a stable state in and of itself. As demonstrated by contemporary, empirical studies of such landscapes of insecurity and violence—with special attention to the effects such conditions have on health and community viability—such maladaptive behavior cannot be sustained indefinitely (Gray et al. 2003).

*Traditional societies have long memories, even across time periods of radical change* (e.g., Silliman 2009). As such, settlement patterns that emerge during periods of crisis may persist for some time after they have ceased to truly be necessary. Likewise, people may plan for the occurrence of violence that does not come to pass, situating themselves so defensively that no hostile group is ever able or willing to mount an assault. In archaeological data, we see what people in the past planned for, what choices they made in the face of a host of challenges and opportunities, but we cannot always tell whether they made the "correct" decision in some abstract sense of the term. People in the past, just like us, are left to deal with both the short- and long-term consequences of their choices.

## References

Acheson, James M., and Roy J. Gardner 2004. Strategies, Conflict, and the Emergence of Territoriality: The Case of the Maine Lobster Fishery. *American Anthropologist* 106:296–307.

Allen, Mark W. 2012. A Land of Violence. In *Contemporary Issues in California Archaeology*, edited by Terry L. Jones and Jennifer E. Perry, pp. 197–216. Left Coast Press, Walnut Creek, CA.

Ames, Kenneth M. 1994. The Northwest Coast: Complex Hunter-Gatherers, Ecology, and Social Evolution. *Annual Review of Anthropology* 23:209–29.

——— 2002. Going by Boat: The Forager-Collector Continuum at Sea. In *Beyond Foraging and Collecting: Evolutionary Change in Hunter-Gatherer Settlement Systems*, edited by Ben Fitzhugh and Junko Habu, pp. 19–52. Kluwer Academic and Plenum, New York.

Ames, Kenneth M., and Herbert D. G. Maschner 1999. *Peoples of the Northwest Coast: Their Archaeology and Prehistory*. Thames and Hudson, London.

Aschmann, Homer 1959. The Central Desert of Baja California: Demography and Ecology. *Ibero-Americana* 42:1–315.

——— 1974. A Late Recounting of the Vizcaíno Expedition and the Plans for the Settlement of California. *Journal of California Anthropology* 1:174–85.

Blackman, Margaret B. 1990. Haida: Traditional Culture. In *Northwest Coast*, edited by Wayne Suttles, pp. 240–60. Handbook of North American Indians, Vol. 7, William C. Sturtevant, general editor. Smithsonian Institution, Washington, D.C.

Boas, Franz, and Helen Codere 1966. *Kwakiutl Ethnography*. University of Chicago Press, IL.

Crosby, Harry W. 1994. *Antigua California: Mission and Colony on the Peninsular Frontier, 1697–1768*. University of New Mexico, Albuquerque.

**218** | Matthew R. Des Lauriers

Crosby, Harry W. 1997. *The Cave Paintings of Baja California: Discovering the Murals of an Unknown People.* Sunbelt Publications, San Diego.

del Barco, Miguel [1776] 1988. *Historia Natural y Crónica de la Antigua California [adiciones y correcciones a la noticia de Miguel Venegas].* 2nd edition. Universidad Nacional Autónoma de México, Instituto de Investigaciones Históricas, Mexico City.

de Laguna, Frederica 1990. Tlingit. In *Northwest Coast*, edited by Wayne Suttles, pp. 203–28. Handbook of North American Indians, Vol. 7, William C. Sturtevant, general editor. Smithsonian Institution, Washington, D.C.

Des Lauriers, Matthew R. 2006a. Isla Cedros. In *The Prehistory of Baja California: Advances in the Archaeology of the Forgotten Peninsula*, edited by Don Laylander and Jerry D. Moore, pp. 153–66. University Press of Florida, Gainesville.

—— 2006b. The Terminal Pleistocene and Early Holocene Occupation of Isla Cedros, Baja California. *Journal of Island and Coastal Archaeology* 1:255–70.

—— 2008. A Paleoindian Fluted Point from Isla Cedros, Baja California. *Journal of Island and Coastal Archaeology* 3:1–7.

—— 2009. "Good Water and Firewood": The Island Oasis of Isla Cedros, Baja California, Mexico. *Pacific Science* 63:649–72.

—— 2010. *Island of Fogs: Archaeological and Ethnohistorical Investigations of Isla Cedros, Baja California.* Salt Lake City, University of Utah Press.

Des Lauriers, Matthew R., and Claudia García-Des Lauriers 2006. The *Huamalgüeños* of Isla Cedros, Baja California, as Described in Father Miguel Venegas' 1739 Manuscript *Obras Californianas. Journal of California and Great Basin Anthropology* 26:123–52.

Drucker, Philip 1939. Rank, Wealth and Kinship in Northwest Coast Society. *American Anthropologist* 41:55–65.

—— 1965. *Cultures of the North Pacific Coast.* Chandler Publishing, New York.

Durrenberger, E. Paul, and Gísli Pálsson 1987. Ownership at Sea: Fishing Territories and Access to Sea Resources. *American Ethnologist* 14:508–22.

Earle, Timothy 2000. Archaeology, Property, and Prehistory. *Annual Review of Anthropology* 29:39–60.

Ferguson, R. Brian 2013. Pinker's List: Exaggerating Prehistoric War Mortality. In *War, Peace, and Human Nature: The Convergence of Evolutionary and Cultural Views*, edited by Douglas P. Fry, pp. 112–31. Oxford University Press, Oxford, UK.

Gamble, Lynn H. 2008. *The Chumash World at European Contact: Power, Trade, and Feasting Among Complex Hunter-Gatherers.* University of California Press, Los Angeles.

Goldschmidt, Walter R., and Theodore H. Haas 1998. *Haa Aani, Our Land: Tlingit and Haida Land Rights and Use.* University of Washington Press, Seattle.

Gray, Sandra, Mary Sundal, Brandi Wiebusch, Michael A. Little, Paul W. Leslie, and Ivy L. Pike 2003. Cattle Raiding, Cultural Survival, and Adaptability of East African Pastoralists. *Current Anthropology* 44(Supplement):3–30.

Gutierrez, Maria de la Luz, and Justin Hyland 1994. Arte Rupestre de Baja California Sur. *Arqueología Mexicana* 2:84–9.

—— 2002. *Arqueología de la Sierra de San Francisco.* Instituto Nacional de Antropología e Historia, Mexico City.

Haas, Jonathan 1990. Warfare and the Evolution of Tribal Polities in the Prehistoric Southwest. In *The Anthropology of War*, edited by Jonathan Haas, pp. 171–89. Cambridge University Press, Cambridge, United Kingdom.

Hendrix, Cullen S., and Idean Salehyan 2012. Climate Change, Rainfall, and Social Conflict in Africa. *Journal of Peace Research* 49:35–50.

Hildebrandt, William R., and Terry L. Jones 1992. Evolution of Marine Mammal Hunting: A View from the California and Oregon Coasts. *Journal of Anthropological Archaeology* 11:360–400.

## The Spectre of Conflict on Isla Cedros, Baja California, Mexico | **219**

Kent, Susan 1991. The Relationship between Mobility Strategies and Site Structure. In *The Archaeological Interpretation of Spatial Patterns*, edited by Ellen Kroll and T. Douglas Price, pp. 33–60. Plenum, New York.

———— 1992. Studying Variability in the Archaeological Record: An Ethnoarchaeological Model for Distinguishing Mobility Patterns. *American Antiquity* 57:635–60.

Kroeber, Alfred L. 1925. *Handbook of the Indians of California*. Bureau of American Ethnology Bulletin 78. Washington, D.C.

Kennett, Douglas J., and James P. Kennett 2000. Competitive and Cooperative Responses to Climatic Instability in Coastal Southern California. *American Antiquity* 65:379–95.

Lambert, Patricia M. 2002. The Archaeology of War: A North American Perspective. *Journal of Archaeological Research* 10:207–41.

Laylander, Donald 2005. Ancestors, Ghosts, and Enemies in Prehistoric Baja California. *Journal of California and Great Basin Anthropology* 25:169–86.

Mathes, W. Michael 1975. Some New Observations Relative to the Indigenous Inhabitants of La Paz, Baja California Sur. *Journal of California Anthropology* 2:180–2.

———— 1994. The Expedition of Juan Rodríguez Cabrillo, 1542–1543: An Historiographical Reexamination. *Southern California Quarterly* 76:247–53.

McCay, Bonnie J. 1978. Systems Ecology, People Ecology, and the Anthropology of Fishing Communities. *Human Ecology* 6:397–422.

———— 1980. A Fishermen's Cooperative, Limited: Indigenous Resource Management in a Complex Society. *Anthropological Quarterly* 53:29–38.

———— 1981. Optimal Foragers or Political Actors? Ecological Analyses of a New Jersey Fishery. *American Ethnologist* 8:356–82.

McCay, Bonnie J., and James M. Acheson (editors) 1987. *The Question of the Commons: The Culture and Ecology of Communal Resources*. University of Arizona Press, Tucson.

Meigs, Peveril, III 1968. Capes of Human Hair from Baja California. *Pacific Coast Archaeological Society Quarterly* 4(1):21–8.

Montané-Martí, J. C. 1995. *Francisco de Ulloa: Explorador de Ilusiones*. Coleccion Alforja del Tiempo No. 1. Universidad de Sonora, Hermosillo, Mexico.

Nabhan, Gary 2003. *Singing the Turtles to Sea: The Comcáac (Seri) Art and Science of Reptiles*. University of California Press, Los Angeles.

Silliman, Stephen, W. 2009. Change and Continuity, Practice and Memory: Native American Persistence in Colonial New England. *American Antiquity* 74:211–30.

Theisen, Ole Magnus 2008. Blood and Soil? Resource Scarcity and Internal Armed Conflict Revisted. *Journal of Peace Research* 45:801–18.

Venegas, Miguel 1979. *Obras Californianas*. Vol 4. Facsimile of handwritten manuscript, edited by Miguel Mathes. On file, Universidad Autonoma de Baja California Sur, La Paz.

# PART III

# Violence and Warfare among Semisedentary Hunter-Gatherers

# 12

## Foragers and War in Contact-Era New Guinea

Paul ("Jim") Roscoe

There are two basic narratives about the antiquity of war, each with profound implications for our understanding of the human species (Allen 2012:198–200). The long chronology, as we might call it, holds that we have been a warring species as far back as the hominin-chimpanzee split. In some versions of the long chronology, this disposition to coalitional lethal violence is the product—in males, if not also females—of genetic disposition (Le Blanc 2003; Wrangham 1999). In another, it is a function of a developed intelligence, one sufficient to formulate interests and advance them through lethal violence when such a strategy is advantageous (Roscoe 2007). Opposed to this long chronology, however, is a view that humans were comparatively peaceful for most of their time on earth, taking to war only recently—within the Holocene—either for materialist reasons or because increasing complexity outstripped the capacity of longstanding social mechanisms to control conflict (Ferguson 2006, 2013; Fry 2006, 2009).

These differences have yet to be resolved, not least because the evidence to evaluate them is slender compared with the social, political, and philosophical weight they must bear. Bone and skull fractures in Neanderthal skeletons, for instance, provide provocative evidence that lethal violence may date back tens of millennia. These data are tantalizing, but they are also suspect. True, they could be evidence of Neanderthal warfare, but they might be no more than the tribulations of a particularly rugged and hazardous lifestyle. Flint weapons embedded in human vertebrae may signify that lethal violence—perhaps even collective lethal violence—occurred 20,000 or more years ago, but they may

---

*Violence and Warfare among Hunter-Gatherers*, edited by Mark W. Allen and Terry L. Jones, 223–240. ©2014 Taylor & Francis. All rights reserved.

**224** | Paul ("Jim") Roscoe

instead indicate nothing more than an unfortunate accident. A perforation in a first thoracic vertebra can clearly index death at spear or dagger point, but perhaps the fatality resulted from an intragroup conflict that got out of hand rather than an extragroup killing in a raid (Ferguson 2006, 2013; Fry 2006:124–41; Trinkhaus and Buzhilova 2012). The evidence for war prior to the Holocene, in sum, remains ambiguous.

In his spirited and erudite volume, *The Human Potential for Peace*, Douglas Fry (2006; see also Fry 2009; Fry and Söderberg 2013) takes a different approach to the antiquity of war, advancing what is currently perhaps the most detailed theoretical and empirical defense of the short chronology. Fry's focus is ethnographically known "simple," mobile forager bands. Prior to the Holocene, all humans subsisted by hunting and gathering. We know hardly more about the social contours of these societies than we do of their inclination to war. Thanks to a century of anthropological fieldwork, however, we know an awful lot more about those hunter-gatherer societies that survived into recent times, and Fry's analytical strategy is to use what we know of contemporary foragers to develop an understanding of their pre-Holocene counterparts. He concludes that warfare is neither inevitable nor part and parcel of the human condition. Humans can be aggressive, he concedes, but as hunter-gatherers they have a profound potential for peace rather than violence, and until about 10,000 years ago they were peaceful.

Extant hunter-gatherers, Fry (2006: 22–40, 97–113, 146–61, 181–3, 200–16; Fry and Söderberg 2013) argues, exhibit several characteristics and deploy several key mechanisms that preempt conflict and aggression from erupting into lethal violence. First, they have little motive to go to war. People have too few material goods and no stored food to make plunder worthwhile, their mobility makes it difficult to abduct women or take slaves against their will, and their territories are too large and their populations too small for defensive warfare to be viable. Second, the structure and organization of their society do not lend themselves to war. Their bands are too small "to support warfare" (Fry and Söderberg 2013:271). Their social networks are egocentric, fluid, and bilaterally organized; their residence is multilocal; and their political organization is egalitarian, all features that hinder the formation of military coalitions. Finally, mobile foragers have several mechanisms to resolve conflict before it escalates to lethality. The first is *avoidance*, "ceasing or limiting interaction with a disputant, either temporarily or permanently" (Fry 2006:22). Disputants may simply refuse to speak or interact, or they may move away from one another. A second mechanism is *toleration*: the issue causing conflict "is simply ignored, and the relationship with the offending party is continued" (Fry 2006:26), one or both parties simply letting go of their frustration or umbrage. Third, there is *negotiation* or *settlement*. Disputants either reach a compromise or mutually agreeable, nonviolent solution themselves (negotiation), or they do so with the aid of third parties, who act as peacemakers, mediators, judges, etc.

# Foragers and War in Contact-Era New Guinea | 225

Last, there is *self-redress*, "taking justice into one's own hands . . . a person with a grievance takes unilateral action against another individual" (Fry 2006:108).

Prior to the Holocene, when humans still lived as hunter-gatherer bands, Fry argues, these characteristics and conflict management mechanisms were crucial in preempting human lethal violence. This is not to say that such violence was completely unknown. Occasionally, self-redress manifested itself in physical violence, and sometimes this violence escalated to lethality. But these incidences constituted "homicide" (or "revenge homicides," "individual self-redress homicide," or "manslaughter"), not war, because for the most part, they involved just one or two individuals seeking self-redress for personal reasons against another specific individual or two, often from within the same "local group" (Fry 2006:88, 90–1,111–13; Fry and Söderberg 2013:271–2).[1] Motives for these "homicides" included rivalry over women, the execution of an extreme deviant, or a killing to avenge a previous killing (see discussion of cases in Fry 2006:Chapter 16). What these societies did not have, however, was warfare.

So what happened? If humans were peaceful prior to the Holocene, what made them resort to war later? Fry's answer is that complex social organization emerged. About 10,000 years ago, the social complexity of some simple, nomadic hunter-gatherers began to increase, band society giving way to "tribal" society. With this transition, societies based on egocentric, bilateral kin networks developed more complex social forms based on lineages and clans, and lethal violence expanded to include a new form, feud: that is, small-scale, asymmetric lethal violence between "kin militias." In addition to "homicide"— one or two individuals acting out of personal motives to kill one or two others—*groups* (i.e., formal kin groups such as lineages and clans) also began to seek self-redress, targeting other like groups based on a principle of social substitutability (Kelly 2000). On this new principle, lethal violence could be targeted not just on particular malefactors to advance personal agendas, but on any member of a malefactor's family, lineage, or clan (Fry 2006:90, 97–113).

With further increases in social complexity, as tribes gave way to chiefdoms and then to states, the repertoire of lethal violence expanded yet further to include war. In contrast to homicide and feud, war is targeted not on particular individuals or specific kin groups but promiscuously against another community; its motives are not personal but stem rather from "general hostility toward other groups" (Fry and Söderberg 2013:272). It "is focused against nonspecified members of another community and it is geared towards either the killing of people or achieving some goal that makes the killing of people likely" (Fry 2006:91; see also Fry and Söderberg 2013).

Fry's argument that the hunter-gatherer lifestyle is inimical to lethal coalitionary violence is important because it is by far the most developed counterpoint to current theories that posit a long chronology of war. It is also valuable, though, because it moves the debate over the antiquity of war beyond

**226** | Paul ("Jim") Roscoe

the interpretive ambiguities of the current archaeological record. In this chapter, I evaluate his arguments that feuding and war are comparatively recent human innovations using data on a set of "simple" foragers that have been consistently overlooked: the hunters and gatherers of New Guinea. I argue that there are problems with some of the definitional and theoretical underpinnings to Fry's argument, and I show that, even if we set these reservations aside, we can plausibly infer from the New Guinea evidence that warfare could just as likely have predated the Holocene as emerged during its course.

## Early Forager Society and the Ethnographic Record

"Ethnographic data on simple nomadic hunter-gatherers," Fry proposes, "provide the best basis for drawing inferences about the lifeways of ancestral humans" (2006:181); in effect, they are "windows to the past" (2006:200–16). As Fry himself acknowledges, there is a problem in supposing that "if we want a window to the past, we should look for recurrent patterns among extant simple foragers." It is that "simple current-day hunter-gatherers are not identical to ancestral groups" (Fry 2006:182). This is a crucial point, and one that Fry fails to pursue. As a result, I fear he has greatly underestimated its implications for the antiquity of war.

Very few forager groups managed to survive into recent times, and those that did inhabited extremely marginal environments such as deserts, arctic wastes, and dryland tropical rainforests.[2] Anthropologists and archaeologists have long understood the reasons for this bias. To begin with, some of the ancient forager groups that inhabited richer environments evolved long ago into more complex sociopolitical forms, which in turn incorporated, annihilated, or displaced less complex forms in other niches. By the modern era, these more complex forms had expanded to embrace peoples inhabiting all but the most marginal of environments: those that were not worth the economic, political, or military costs of incorporation (Dickson 1990; Kelly 2000; LeBlanc 2003:105–6; Lee and DeVore 1968). As a result, it is likely that the suite of modern, ethnographically known foragers is highly unrepresentative of foragers 10,000 years ago. Either they are the descendants of ancient foragers long adapted to highly atypical environments, of refugee groups displaced by or splintered off from more complex societies, or both. What they are certainly not are reliable analogs for forager societies prior to the Holocene.[3] To use them as a window onto past forager lifeways is to view that past through a glass that is dark indeed.

This bias in the standard forager file toward groups in marginal environments is particularly likely to distort our view of lethal violence at the beginning of the Holocene. By definition, subsistence resources in these environments are both more depauperate and more unpredictable in their spatial and temporal occurrence than those in richer environments. As a result, forager groups in marginal environments are likely to have atypically low densities because their resource base is sparse, and to have strong interests in forging cooperative relations with other, neighboring groups so as to buffer fluctuations in what resources they do have. The combined effect is to create a social universe characterized by amity more than enmity. Because they are so thinly spread across the landscape, bands only rarely encounter one another; and because they depend reciprocally on one another for subsistence, they have every incentive to interact amicably rather than offensively.

Things would have been different at the beginning of the Holocene. The typical forager group would have had access to subsistence resources that were more abundant and predictable than those of contemporary foragers in their marginal environments. Ancient foragers would likely therefore have existed at higher densities than those of today, bringing their bands closer to one another. In addition, bands in these richer environments would have been less dependent on their neighbors for subsistence buffering than ethnographically described foragers in marginal environments. With their bands closer to and less dependent on one another, ancient foragers would therefore have had more opportunities and greater incentives to deploy lethal violence than those of today. If, as higher-density groups, they also had more developed status competition and were marginally better organized, they might have had an even greater incentive and capacity for war. In sum, we might expect the social world of ancient foragers to be biased more toward lethal violence than that of recent foragers, with implications for the forms of lethal violence they deployed. Violence may have occurred on a significantly greater scale than the simple "homicides" envisaged by Fry.

## The Hunters and Gatherers of New Guinea

So much for conjecture. But are there any ethnographically known forager groups left in the world that might help us test this hypothesis? There are. As I have argued elsewhere, hunter-gatherer scholars have overlooked a suite of ethnographically known forager groups that appear to have exploited considerably richer environments than those of the standard forager file: the hunter-gatherers and fisher-gatherers of New Guinea (Roscoe 2002, 2005, 2006).

It is a widely held misconception that "the subsistence base for all New Guinea societies is root crop horticulture. There are no societies in New Guinea which only hunt, forage, and collect; every society is dependent to some extent on horticulture" (Rosman and Rubel 1989:27). A detailed review of the Melanesian ethnographic record, however, turns up numerous references to "hunters and gatherers" (Roscoe 2002). At least 10 contact-era groups, in fact, appear to have subsisted almost entirely by wild resources (defined as resources that living members have not themselves intentionally bred or planted). Another 20 or so procured at least 90 percent of their calories from the wild, and a further 20 probably obtained 75 to 89 percent of their calories from foraging.

The flora mainstay in the diet of all these groups was the starch of the wild sago palm (*Metroxylon* sp.). Sago is an attractive subsistence resource because it is highly reliable and yields an abundance of calories for very little effort. A half-hour's work in the sago groves is usually adequate to furnish a forager's entire daily energy requirements (Roscoe 2005:558–60). The disadvantage of sago is that it provides almost no protein or fat (Ruddle et al. 1978:57, 61–7); as a consequence, New Guinea's contact-era hunter-gatherers were critically dependent on aquatic and terrestrial game to meet the rest of their nutritional needs.

The particular balance between aquatic and terrestrial game in the diet had major implications for forager density, settlement size, and mobility (Roscoe 2006). *Hunter*-forager groups procured the faunal component of their diet primarily from terrestrial and arboreal rather than aquatic resources; *fisher*-forager groups depended primarily on aquatic resources procured either directly through their own efforts or indirectly through trade.

New Guinea's fisher-foragers were remarkably similar in culture and social organization to the chiefdom foragers of the Northwest Coast. Most lived in large settlements, some of them the largest conurbations in New Guinea; they were largely sedentary; their ritual and artistic life was elaborate; and they conducted large amphibious raids, sometimes against one another but more commonly on small, hinterland settlements, often in a quest for heads. Most scholars would join Fry in assuming that hunter-gatherers preceded fisher-foragers in human prehistory, though evidence that fishing has great antiquity in the human species does raise questions of why this presumption is so readily accepted (Erlandson 2001). Suffice it to say, if pre-Holocene society included fisher-foragers, it would greatly complicate Fry's contention that feuding and war postdated the start of the Holocene because, as he himself points out, fisher-foragers typically have a complex social organization, in which feuding and war are "common" or "typical" features (2006:97–113).

Setting this issue aside, though, let us focus on those New Guinea forager groups most relevant to Fry's arguments, the island's "simple" hunter-foragers. We can identify 10 hunter-forager groups that depended for at least 90 percent of their caloric intake on wild resources, several of them apparently procuring 95 percent or more of their subsistence from the wild. These groups all lived in or on the margins of freshwater wetlands, the natural habitat of the sago palm. Their densities were among the lowest in New Guinea, and they appear to have inhabited a subsistence cul-de-sac, unable to intensify their production of food to support higher densities because their wetland environments were

Foragers and War in Contact-Era New Guinea | **229**

unsuited to either cultivation or pig production. Even so, their densities were more than six times higher on average than those in Fry's standard forager file (Tables 12.1, 12.2). Whereas the densities of the groups in Fry's sample averaged 0.126 per square km (median, 0.036/sq. km), ranging from 0.001 to 0.860 people per square km, those in New Guinea averaged 0.8 per square km (median, 0.5/sq. km), ranging between 0.2 and 2.0 per square km. (The difference between the two means is significant at the 0.05 level.) To put it another way, only 12 percent of Fry's sample were denser than the lowest-density group in the New Guinea sample.

**Table 12.1** Fry's "simple" nomadic forager file

| Group | Density per sq. km | Group Size | War? | Group | Density per sq. km | Group Size | War? |
|---|---|---|---|---|---|---|---|
| !Kung* | 0.1–0.2 | 25 | No | Siriono | 0.41** | NA | No |
| Hadza* | 0.15 | 18 | No | Slave* | 0.014 | NA | No |
| Mbuti* | 0.17 | NA | No | N. Paiute* | 0.013 | NA | No |
| Semang* | 0.05–0.19 | 20–30 | No | Yahgan* | 0.046 | NA | No |
| Andamanese* | 0.86 | 30–50 | No | Yolngu/Murngin | 0.05 | NA | No |
| Veda* | NA | NA | No | Walbiri | 0.01 | NA | No |
| Tiwi* | NA | 40–50 | No | Gilyak* | 0.192 | NA | Yes |
| Aranda* | 0.03 | NA | No | Yukagir* | 0.005 | NA | Yes |
| Gugadja | 0.057 | NA | No | Ingalik* | 0.025–0.040 | 50–100** | Yes |
| Copper Inuit* | 0.012 | 15 | No | Naskapi* | 0.004 | 100–300** | Yes |
| Mardu | 0.006 | 15–20 | No | Micmac* | 0.023 | NA | Yes |
| Netsilik | 0.005 | 24 | No | Kaska* | 0.001 | NA | Yes |
| Paliyan | 0.77 | NA | No | Botocudo* | 0.11 | NA | Yes |
| N. Salteaux* | 0.006 | 24 | No | Aweikoma* | 0.038 | NA | Yes |

*Cases also included in Fry and and Söderberg (2013:271). NA indicates not available. Sources: Fry 2006: Chapters 8,12,16. Density values from Kelly (1995:222–6). **http://dice.missouri.edu. Group sizes from Kelly (1995:211; 2013:171).

**Table 12.2** The hunter-gatherers of contact-era New Guinea

| Group | Density per sq. km | Group Size | Mobility |
|---|---|---|---|
| Alamblak | 1.6 | 17 | Sedentary |
| Arafundi (Lower) | 2.0 | 120 | Sedentary |
| Bahinemo | 0.2 | 40 | Semisedentary |
| Berik | 0.6 | 94 | Semisedentary |
| Bitara | 0.3 | 50 | Semisedentary |
| Bonerif | 0.4 | 45 | Semisedentary |
| Ittik | 0.4 | NA | Semisedentary |
| Kwerba (Ségar-Tor) | 0.5 | 55 | Semisedentary |
| Mander | 0.3 | 90 | Sedentary? |
| Sanio-Hiowe | 1.6 | 20 | Semisedentary |

NA indicates not available.

These differences in niche productivity and population density were associated with several significant social differences with implications for the deployment of lethal violence. To begin with, New Guinea foragers were more sedentary than those in the standard forager file. About half of Fry's sample was "fully nomadic or migratory bands," the other half comprising "seminomadic communities whose members wander in bands for at least half the year but occupy a fixed settlement at some season or seasons" (Fry 2006:105). This contrasts with the New Guinea sample, none of which were fully nomadic or migratory; 70 percent fell into the seminomadic category, and 30 percent were more or less sedentary. Most New Guinea foragers also lived in somewhat larger political communities than those in Fry's file. It can be difficult to judge what constitutes the political community among hunter-gatherers, and what ethnographic information there may be about its size can be even more difficult to evaluate. The evidence we have, though, indicates that only two polities in Fry's file had more than 50 people, while half of the New Guinea sample numbered or exceeded 50.

A third difference was that New Guinea forager communities typically lived much more closely to one another than did those in the "simple" nomadic forager file. Figure 12.1 models the relationship between population density and the spatial separation of centroids in a hexagonal array of political communities for communities with: (1) 25 members (the approximate median size of communities in Fry's file); and (2) 50 members (the median size of the

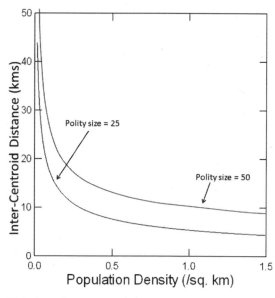

**Figure 12.1** Variation of intercentroid distance with density for polities of sizes 25 and 50.

Foragers and War in Contact-Era New Guinea | **231**

New Guinea forager file).[4] The model indicates that the centroids of a quarter of the communities in Fry's sample (densities ≤0.01/sq. km) were more than 50 km apart; almost two-thirds (densities ≤0.1/sq. km) were more than 20 km from one another; and just about one-third (densities >0.1/sq. km) had centroids 5 to 17 km apart. This compares to the New Guinea sample, where community centroids *all* lay between 5 km (for the Sanio-Hiowe) and 17 km (for the Bahinemo) apart.

All other things being equal, these differences lead us to expect the incidence of lethal violence to be greater among New Guinea foragers than those in more marginal environments. For one thing, the incentives for violence are greater. Living in a richer environment, they are less dependent on neighboring communities to buffer their subsistence; living more closely together, they are more likely to encounter them; and existing at higher densities, incentives to gain status through lethal violence may be greater. For another, the opportunity to deploy coalitional violence is also greater. With their greater densities and large settlements, they could organize coalitional violence on a larger scale and more rapidly; moreover, with neighboring communities closer to hand and more sedentary, there is less difficulty in locating and attacking them.

## Homicide, Feud, or War? Coalitional Violence in Contact-Era New Guinea

Whether or not we accept that there was a greater propensity to lethal violence in New Guinea than among foragers in more marginal environments, there remains the question of the form this violence took. Did New Guinea lethal violence rise to the level of feud or war, or was it nothing more than the "homicide" that, in Fry's view, prevailed among ethnographically known foragers?

Fry's definition of homicide as an interindividual act undertaken for personal motives is a little idiosyncratic. Many scholars define homicide not by the number of individuals involved and their motives but in terms of the communities to which they belong. If one US citizen kills another, or a UK citizen, for instance, this is defined as homicide and treated as a "crime," because killer and victim are members of the same nation-state in the former instance and of two closely allied nation-states in the latter. Were the United States and the United Kingdom at war with one another, though, US soldiers would be committing no homicide in killing UK citizens (within the bounds of the Geneva Convention). They would simply be doing their job and might be formally commended for doing so. The same attitudinal structure prevailed in New Guinea. Killing within a polity was generally abhorred as the grossest of antisocial acts, and a community went to great pains to preempt or deter it. Killings between allied political communities were similarly regarded, albeit to

## 232 | Paul ("Jim") Roscoe

greater or lesser degree, depending on the degree of interpolity amity. Killings of enemies beyond the alliance circle, however, were enjoined and celebrated as the finest male behavior.

There are problems also in Fry's definitional differentiation of feud from war. Recall that in Fry's lexicon, feuding is collective lethal violence targeted indiscriminately on a formal descent group. A malefactor may not pay for his or her misdeed, but someone in his or her descent group will. This contrasts with warfare, which is collective violence targeted promiscuously on "another community." Unfortunately, Fry fails to define what he means by a "community," and how it differs from a unilineal descent group. The point is important because, in several parts of contact-era New Guinea, the largest autonomous community was, in fact, a descent group. The large clans to which the people of the Central and Western Highlands belonged, for instance, constituted the autonomous polity. (Usually, they were allied to other clans to make up a "tribe" or "phratry," which was also conceptualized as a descent group, but it was the former, not the latter, that was the sovereign political unit.) The same was true for the Alamblak, a Sepik hunter-forager group. Here, the hamlet was the largest autonomous political community but, ideally at least, it was also a descent group, containing members of one or more "clan-sections" (i.e., sections of a single clan) (Haberland and Seyfarth 1974:274) or a "lineage" (Edmiston and Edmiston 1989:33). These descent-group polities generate some unhappy ambiguities for Fry's definitions of feud and warfare. We are obliged to conclude that the raids prosecuted and sustained by Alamblak hamlets and the open battles fought by Highland clans, with a hundred or more warriors on either side, were simultaneously both feud and warfare.

Setting these definitional concerns aside in favor of Fry's definitions, however, what can we say about the forms of lethal violence among New Guinea's foragers? Certainly, there were killings that Fry would define as homicide. Other instances of lethal violence, however, are more difficult to characterize in these terms because they involved a significant number of attackers, and they were targeted not on a particular malefactor but on a collectivity. These were probably not feuds as Fry would define them. The social organization of forager groups in the Upper Tor Valley (the Berik, Bonerif, Ittik, Kwerba, and Mander) was based on bilateral kinship (Oosterwal 1961:147–88). Lacking formal descent groups, therefore, they could no more have feuding than the groups in Fry's forager sample, where "bilateral or ambilineal descent" was likewise the "most typical" form of social organization (Fry 2006:167). The remaining groups in the New Guinea forager sample had patrilineal lineages, clans, or both,[5] but these units seem to have been too weak and unimportant to have incorporated the principle of social substitutability that Fry sees as critical to feuding. Among the Bahinemo, "[c]lan functions are rather vague and unimportant" (Dye and Dye 1967:12). Sanio-Hiowe organization was "a highly flexible, two-ply structure in which the patrilineal organization

Foragers and War in Contact-Era New Guinea | **233**

allocates hunting rights and helps assure male cooperation in intergroup conflict, while bilateral ties bind together small, internally harmonious residential groups whose composition is sensitive to changes in the productive capacity and needs of the members" (Townsend 1969:180). In the main, these structures of descent seem to have functioned to define either the territories within which their members could jointly hunt, fish, and gather, the social boundaries beyond which they had to marry, or both, but there is no indication that people targeted their enemies for lethal violence purely on the basis of their descent group membership.[6]

The evidence we have, in fact, suggests that lethal coalitional violence among New Guinea foragers targeted victims not on the basis of their lineage or clan affiliation but their *polity* or *community* affiliation. In Fry's terms, in other words, they were waging war. Consider, for instance, the most spectacular instance of hunter-forager raiding we know of in New Guinea, a large raid that the Bitara-speaking community of Bitara launched against the Palu, another Bitara-speaking community, somewhere between 1950 and 1960. The Palu had killed a woman of the Bitara community, so the Bitara recruited the Sanio of the Nakek and Sio communities to help them exact revenge. The force is said to have numbered a "hundred," though in all likelihood this should simply be taken to mean "a lot." It was flood season at the time, and the Palu had dispersed to their bush camps. The raiding party—some traveling in canoes, the rest making their way overland—had visited several known Palu camps to no avail when they heard the sound of sago logs being chopped open for sago grubs. The force began to converge on the sounds, and a few of the raiders stepped out into the open, pretending to be friendly to the Palu foragers. Once the rest of the force had filtered into position, the attack was launched on a prearranged signal. Some of the Palu managed to escape, but when the fighting was over, the raiders had killed three men and two women for the loss of just one of their own warriors (Bragge n.d.:401, 471).[7]

The crucial point here is that the Bitara and their Sanio allies went hunting for *any* Palu they could find to avenge the killing of the Bitara woman: in other words, they perpetrated what Fry would define as an act of war. We can observe much the same logic in the military ethnography of other New Guinea forager groups: the grievance instigating the attack might be personal, but the vengeance was targeted indiscriminately on another community. Although the Bahinemo rarely fought among themselves, for instance, several communities would combine to seek vengeance on neighboring groups, some of them foragers, others fisher-foragers. Sometime in the 1930s or 1940s, the Yerikai-speaking community of the same name attacked the Bahinemo community of Yigei, killing a woman and two men. Yigei mistakenly thought the attackers were the Kamasuit (a settlement that was annihilated before linguists could establish the language they spoke) and recruited warriors from the Bahinemo communities of Namu, Gahom, and Wagu to assist them in taking revenge.

**234** | Paul ("Jim") Roscoe

The raiders gathered at Yetesui and set off in the dark hours of the morning for a small Kamasuit camp of three houses. Once there, they broke into the houses and killed the inhabitants. In total, 11 Kamasuit died: three males and eight females, all promiscuously targeted for a killing they had nothing to do with. A Kamasuit boy, Bis, was abducted and taken back to Wagu, where he grew up and later died (Bragge n.d.:413).

A decade or two later, the Bahinemo community of Namu lost several members in two attacks by the communities of Mari and Yambi Yambi (groups that appear to have depended on wild resources for more than 75 percent of their calories [Roscoe 2002]). Not long after, a Namu man came across the tracks of five Mari and Yambiyambi hunters in the lower Bifa River area and hurried back to Namu to spread the news. The Namu had no way of knowing whether the tracks belonged to those who had killed their kinfolk, but seizing the opportunity for payback, they moved down the Bifa, located the hunters asleep in a bush house, and attacked, killing four of them (Bragge n.d.:413).

In other instances, the ethnographic record fails to clarify the motive behind forager attacks but reveals the same pattern of targeting a community at large rather than a descent group or a particular malefactor. This was the case in Alamblak fighting. The Alamblak were divided into six "communities" or "tribes." A community, in turn, comprised a set of small, hamlet-sized polities—lineage-based, as we have seen—that counted one another as allies. Relations among these "tribes" or alliances could change from enmity to friendship and back over time (Edmiston and Edmiston 1989:21; Haberland and Seyfarth 1974:273). This could create a treacherous situation. Members of alliances that had earlier been enemies might, after long years of peace, be invited as "'friends' to a large feast, in order to slaughter them treacherously—above all in the time shortly before sunrise, when everyone was fast asleep" (Haberland and Seyfarth 1974:353, my translation). More usually, it seems, the men of one or several hamlet-polities in one alliance combined to attack and kill a woman or old person from another alliance out at work in the sago groves. On occasion, however, the entire adult male complement of an alliance combined to launch an attack on a hamlet in another alliance. "Thus the Wagim, in a night attack on a hamlet of the Benaräm, had burnt the men's house and several houses and killed several men" (Haberland and Seyfarth 1974:354; my translation).

The Alamblak also conducted headhunting raids, a practice that hardly fits the limited violence that Fry ascribes to "simple" nomadic foragers. They launched these raids, it seems, not against other Alamblak but against more distant enemies—including the Bahinemo, Karawari, and Yimas (the latter two fisher-forager groups)—to avenge similar attacks on the Alamblak (Haberland and Seyfarth 1974:352–4). Headhunting raids were sometimes overnight affairs, launched usually on foot, though occasionally by canoe. The heads were brought back to be modeled, painted, and stored as trophies

Foragers and War in Contact-Era New Guinea | **235**

to be used in future "ritual preparation for warfare" (Edmiston and Edmiston 1989:24; Haberland and Seyfarth 1974:352–7; my translation).

Among the Lower Arafundi, every community seemed to count every other as a potential enemy, along with members of some other language groups (Roscoe and Telban 2004:105). The community of Awim counted as enemies—and fought—Wambramas, Yamandim, and Meakambut (all Lower Arafundi communities) and Namata (Upper Arafundi). In addition to the Awim, Yamandim fought against the people of Imanmeri (Lower Arafundi), the Yimas speakers of Yimas village (fisher-foragers), and the Kansimei (Awiakay speakers). In some of these fights, they were aided by the Ambonwari and Kundima, two fisher-forager Karawari groups. We have no details of the lethal violence involved in Lower Arafundi fighting, but we do know that, like the Alamblak, they carried out "head hunting assaults, mostly of the kind in which a heavily-armed war group assaulted a single woman at her sago work in the forest. The skull was kept as a trophy for a long time, allegedly also modelled and painted" (Haberland 1966:60). In addition, some communities cannibalized enemies whom they had killed (Roscoe and Telban 2004:106).

Of the groups in the New Guinea forager sample, only the tribes in the western half of the Upper Tor Valley (the Bora Bora, Ségar, Waf, and Daranto) approximated Fry's peaceful picture of relations among "simple" nomadic foragers. The Bora Bora had a reputation for abducting women, and several groups acknowledged that "marriages by capture frequently used to occur in former years" (Oosterwal 1961:118; compare with Fry 2006:181). "Very often wars were the result of such raids" (Oosterwal 1961:118). Nonetheless, most fighting in the upper reaches of the western Tor took a "ritualized" or restrained form (Oosterwal 1963:91–4).

> In their wars, it is not the aim to kill. The word, "war," also does not fit here. Everything that belongs to war is absent: one does not hate; one also does not want to steal land in order to increase one's own area; and one does not want to exterminate. . . . In the zeal of fighting, there are sometimes deaths, but that is deplored by both parties (Oosterwal 1963:93–4; my translation).

In the eastern sector of the Upper Tor, however, unrestrained lethal violence was more common. Some of it was instigated by the Warès, a group that may or may not have been foragers.[8] Prior to the Warès incursion, however, the Ittik, who we know were an Upper Tor forager group, had been "a rather war-minded tribe" (Oosterwal 1961:26), "the terror of the Tor district" (Oosterwal 1961:84). We have few details of their lethal predations, but they were sufficient that the Netherlands Administration compelled them to settle on the coast, the better to control their activities. Like the Bora Bora and the Warès, the Ittik were renowned as "women-abductors" (Oosterwal 1961:118). It was not

# 236 | Paul ("Jim") Roscoe

just the Ittik, though, who instigated lethal violence in the western part of the Upper Tor. In 1968, the Mander attacked the Berik, forcing a number to flee to the coast. This, however, was "the last known intergroup raid" in the Upper Tor (Westrum 1983:277).

## Conclusion

Like Fry, I believe that humans have a profound potential for peace. Indeed, it is as plausible on Darwinian grounds that humans have a genetic *aversion* to conspecific lethal violence as a genetic disposition *toward* it. The reason that, as a species, we do kill is attributable to our developed intelligence, a capacity that has allowed us to recognize when it is in our interests to kill, and to develop "psychological" (or "cultural") technologies that short-circuit this aversion when it is in our interests to kill (Roscoe 2007). If this argument is correct, then there is no reason why conspecific killing should not have been part of our behavioral repertoire for the 100,000 years or so that we have been *Homo sapiens sapiens*, if not considerably longer.

As a species with a developed intelligence, however, it follows also that we would have been as capable tens of millennia ago as we are today of recognizing not only when lethal, conspecific violence was in our interests, but also that it can be advantageous in some circumstances to project it maximally and promiscuously against other communities. In other words, there are no *a priori* reasons why feuding and war, as Fry define them, should not have existed long before the Holocene.

This conclusion runs counter to Fry's argument, based on the ethnography of recent forager groups, that lethal violence among forager groups was limited to "homicide," and that feuding and war emerged during the Holocene. The sample from which he derives this conclusion, however, is heavily biased toward low-density foragers exploiting marginal environments, and it is therefore plausible that the generally peaceful lifeways that Fry observes in this sample is a function of their marginal environment rather than any human potential for peace. What I have tried to show in this chapter is that in looking at hunter-forager groups that existed in more productive environments and at higher densities, we find ample evidence of lethal violence that, even by Fry's restrictive definitions, amounts to warfare.

Just as Fry's ethnographic file has its drawbacks, so too the New Guinea data are not without their flaws as analogs for human society in the deep past. Most if not the entire New Guinea forager file indulged in desultory incipient cultivation, although this probably provided less than 3 percent of dietary calories in about half of the cases and only about 4 to 10 percent in the rest. Several foragers raised piglets they had captured from the wild, though the degree to which this was a post-contact innovation is unclear. In addition, New Guinea's foragers existed within a matrix of other societies

Foragers and War in Contact-Era New Guinea | **237**

that relied to varying degrees on cultivation and pig production. Many of the same flaws, however, bedevil the standard forager file from which Fry draws his ethnographic inspiration. New Guinea foragers may have depended on domesticated resources for up to 10 percent of their calories, but Fry's sample procured up to 5 percent of their diet from such resources, and some appear to have obtained far more. When Lee (1993:156) first began to study the !Kung in 1963, they were procuring some 15 percent of their diet from other sources than the wild, and there has been a long-running debate about their relationship with pastoralist neighbors. As much as 60 percent of the Mbuti diet came from crop foods that they obtained in trade from neighboring Bantu agriculturalists (Bailey et al. 1989). Nor were New Guinea foragers unusual in being embedded within a matrix of more complex cultivators and pastoralists: the same was true for many if not most ethnographically known hunter-forager groups in Africa, North America, South America, India, and southeast Asia.

To misquote a former US Secretary of Defense, we enter debates about human prehistory with the hunter-forager analogs we have, not the forager analogs we want or wish we might have. Neither the standard nor the New Guinea forager files are perfect analogs for prehistory, but with their richer environments and greater densities, New Guinea forager groups would seem to be the more representative of prehistoric foragers. That being the case, warfare is likely to be of greater antiquity than Fry contends.

Oddly enough, Fry's own data and argument indicate precisely this. According to his own data (see Table 12.1), at least 29 percent of the 28 "simple" forager groups in his standard forager file practiced war (2006:104). Indeed, he and Söderberg concede as much: "most incidents of lethal aggression can aptly be called homicides, a few others feud, *and only a minority warfare*" (Fry and Söderberg 2013:272; emphasis added); "if the actual circumstances of lethal aggression are examined," foragers "*are not particularly warlike*" (Fry and Söderberg 2013:272; emphasis added). But if, as Fry argues, ethnographically known foragers are "windows into the past," then it follows that prior to the Holocene at least some foragers *did* practice warfare: perhaps as many as 29 percent if we are to rely on his data!

There is a tantalizing hint that Fry actually agrees. Despite the overall gist of his argument, he nonetheless summarizes it as "a series of compelling, logical reasons that explain why *warfare was only a rare anomaly* during all but the last tiny fraction of human prehistory" (Fry 2006:140–1; emphasis added). We might quibble over whether war was but a rare anomaly prior to the Holocene, but we agree, it seems, that it did exist prior to the Holocene.

At this point in human history, we cannot hope to add many more ethnographic analogs to our file of foragers. Thus, going forward, we shall mainly need to rely on archaeology if we are to resolve the issue of the antiquity of war. Where Fry is almost surely right is that warfare did increase dramatically in scale and frequency with the transition from foraging to farming and pastoralism, and

# 238 | Paul ("Jim") Roscoe

it is this development that has the greater importance to humanity. As I noted at the beginning of this chapter, though, the antiquity of war is also a question with major political and philosophical consequences for our understanding of humans as a species. On this question, the scale and incidence of war are irrelevant. What matters is how long humans have been warring. The New Guinea data are congruent with a long rather than a short chronology of war: a conclusion with which, in the ultimate analysis, Fry might actually agree.

## Notes

1. Surveying 135 lethal events among ethnographically known, mobile foragers, Fry and Söderberg (2013:271) found that 55 percent involved just one killer and one victim; 23 percent involved more than one participant killing a single individual; and 22 percent involved more than one person killing more than one person. They also found that 36 percent of all lethal events occurred within the same "local group," while only 15 percent occurred "across societal lines" (Fry and Söderberg 2013:272).

2. Based on calculations of the net primary productivity (NPP) of 186 forager, pastoralist, horticulturalist, and agriculturalist environments, Porter and Marlowe (2007) question the claim that ethnographically described foragers inhabit marginal environments. They find that NPP levels in forager environments to be only slightly (and not significantly) more marginal than those of agriculturalists worldwide. The glaring problem with their claim is that most of the forager populations with high NPPs in their sample are located in dryland tropical rainforests, a biome that Bailey and his colleagues (Bailey et al. 1989; Bailey and Headland 1991; Headland 1987) have argued at length cannot by itself support a forager adaptation. Although it is doubtful that Bailey et al.'s argument can be applied to *wetland* tropical rainforests that support sago (Roscoe 2005), *dryland* tropical rainforests do seem to be marginal environments for foraging. Suffice it to say, Porter and Marlowe's figures show that NPP levels in the environments of foragers that do not exploit rainforest environments are much lower than those of pastoralists, horticulturalists, and agriculturalists.

3. As LeBlanc (2003:105–6) points out, the same circumstance also biases the *archaeology* of forager groups. Foragers leave an ephemeral footprint to begin with, and in nonmarginal environments, millennia of farming and industrial activity have tended to obliterate these traces. As a result, much of the surviving archaeological evidence of forager lifestyles comes from marginal environments.

4. The relevant equation is $d = \sqrt{(1.1547 \times P / D)}$, where $d$ is the intercentroid separation of hexagonally arranged political communities, $P$ is political community size, and $D$ is density.

5. For the Alamblak, see Edmiston and Edmiston (1989:18) and Haberland and Seyfarth (1974:270–4); for the Arafundi (Lower), Haberland (1966:60) and Roscoe and Telban (2004:103); for the Bahinemo, Dye and Dye Bakker (1991:3); and for the Sanio-Hiowe, Townsend (1969:71,136–8).

6. For the Alamblak, see Edmiston and Edmiston (1989:33); for the Bahinemo, Dye and Dye Bakker (1991:3–5); and for the Sanio-Hiowe, Townsend (1969:142, 173).

7. During the first half of the twentieth century, Bitara people also "fought back and forth" with the Bahinemo of Wagu, Yigei, Gahom, and Wagu. Sababok, a famous Bitara ancestor of the Guria clan, in Kagiru polity, had been killed in an attack on the Gahom community (Bragge n.d.:401–2).

8. The Warès came from the Lake Plains, an area that seems to have been populated by forager groups (Roscoe 2002). Sometime between 1917 and 1947, they started a push down through the Foja Pass, reducing the Foja to a handful of people and wiping out the Soebar and the Broemia (Oosterwal 1961:22, 26).

# References

Allen, Mark W. 2012. A Land of Violence. In *Contemporary Issues in California Archaeology*, edited by Terry L. Jones and Jennifer E. Perry, pp. 197–215. Left Coast Press, Walnut Creek, CA.

Bailey, Robert C., Genevieve Head, Mark Jenike, Bruce Owen, Robert Rechtman, and Elzbieta Zechenter 1989. Hunting and Gathering in Tropical Rain Forest: Is It Possible? *American Anthropologist* 91:59–82.

Bailey, Robert C., and Thomas N. Headland 1991. The Tropical Rainforest: Is It a Productive Environment for Human Foragers? *Human Ecology* 19:261–85.

Bragge, Laurie n.d. ca. 1970s. Interview Notes. Bragge Archives, Koetong, NSW, Australia.

Dickson, D. Bruce 1990. *The Dawn of Belief.* University of Arizona Press, Tucson.

Dye, T. Wayne, and Sally Dye 1967. Gahom Essentials for Translation, Part 2: Anthropology. Manuscript on file, Summer Institute of Linguistics, Ukarumpa, Papua New Guinea.

Dye, T. Wayne, and Edith Dye Bakker 1991. The Response of Bahinemo Foragers to Imposed Land Tenure Changes: An Emic Perspective. Paper presented at the Annual Meeting of the American Anthropological Association, Denver, CO.

Edmiston, Patrick, and Melenda Edmiston 1989. Alamblak Background Study. Manuscript on file, Summer Institute of Linguistics, Ukarumpa, Papua New Guinea.

Erlandson, Jon M. 2001. The Archaeology of Aquatic Adaptations: Paradigms for a New Millennium. *Journal of Archaeological Research* 9:287–350.

Ferguson, R. Brian 2006. Archaeology, Cultural Anthropology, and the Origins and Intensifications of War. In *The Archaeology of Warfare: Prehistories of Raiding and Conquest*, edited by Elizabeth N. Arkush and Mark W. Allen, pp. 470–523. University Press of Florida, Gainsville.

――― 2013. The Prehistory of War and Peace in Europe and the Near East. In *War, Peace, and Human Nature: The Convergence of Evolutionary and Cultural Views*, edited by Douglas P. Fry, pp. 191–240. Oxford University Press, New York.

Fry, Douglas P. 2006. *The Human Potential for Peace: An Anthropological Challenge to Assumptions about War and Violence.* Oxford University Press, New York.

――― 2009. *Beyond War: The Human Potential for Peace.* Oxford University Press, New York.

Fry, Douglas P., and Patrik Söderberg 2013. Lethal Aggression in Mobile Forager Bands and Implications for the Origins of War. *Science* 341:270–3.

Haberland, Eike 1966. Zur Ethnographie der Alfendio-Region (Südlicher Sepik-Distrikt, Neuguinea). *Jahrbuch des Museums für Völkerkunde zu Leipzig* 23:33–67.

Haberland, Eike, and Siegfried Seyfarth 1974. *Die Yimar am Oberen Korowori (Neuguinea).* Franz Steiner, Wiesbaden, Germany.

Headland, Thomas N. 1987. The Wild Yam Question: How Well Could Independent Hunter-gatherers Live in a Tropical Rain Forest Ecosystem? *Human Ecology* 15:463–91.

Kelly, Raymond C. 2000. *Warless Societies and the Origin of War.* University of Michigan Press, Ann Arbor.

Kelly, Robert L. 1995. *The Foraging Spectrum: Diversity in Hunter-Gatherer Lifeways.* Washington, D.C., Smithsonian Institution Press.

――― 2013. *The Lifeways of Hunter-Gatherers: The Foraging Spectrum.* New York, Cambridge University Press.

LeBlanc, Stephen A. 2003. *Constant Battles: The Myth of the Peaceful, Noble Savage.* St Martin's, New York.

Lee, Richard B. 1993. *The Dobe Ju/'hoansi.* Harcourt Brace, Fort Worth, TX.

Lee, Richard B., and Irven DeVore 1968. Problems in the Study of Hunters and Gatherers. In *Man the Hunter*, edited by Richard B. Lee and Irven DeVore, pp. 3–12. Aldine, Chicago.

Oosterwal, Gottfried 1961. *People of the Tor: A Cultural-Anthropological Study on the Tribes of the Tor Territory (Northern Netherlands New-Guinea).* Royal van Gorcum, Assen, the Netherlands.

――― 1963. *Die Papua: Von der Kultur eines Naturvolks.* W. Kohlhammer Verlag, Stuttgart, Germany.

240 | Paul ("Jim") Roscoe

Porter, Claire C., and Frank W. Marlowe 2007. How Marginal Are Forager Habitats? *Journal of Archaeological Science* 34:59–68.

Roscoe, Paul 2002. The Hunters and Gatherers of New Guinea. *Current Anthropology* 43:153–62.

——— 2005. Foraging, Ethnographic Analogy, and Papuan Pasts: Contemporary Models for the Sepik Ramu Past. In *Papuan Pasts: Cultural, Linguistic and Biological Histories of Papuan-speaking Peoples*, edited by Andrew Pawley, Robert Attenborough, Jack Golson, and Robin Hide, pp. 555–84. Pacific Linguistics No. 572. Research School of Pacific and Asian Studies, The Australian National University, Canberra.

——— 2006. Fish, Game, and the Foundations of Complexity in Forager Society: The Evidence from New Guinea. *Cross-Cultural Research: The Journal of Comparative Social Science* 40:29–46.

——— 2007. Intelligence, Coalitional Killing, and the Antecedents of War. *American Anthropologist* 109:485–95.

Roscoe, Paul, and Borut Telban 2004. The People of the Lower Arafundi: Tropical Foragers of the New Guinea Rainforest. *Ethnology* 43:93–115.

Rosman, Abraham, and Paula G. Rubel 1989. Stalking the Wild Pig: Hunting and Horticulture in Papua New Guinea. In *Farmers as Hunters: The Implications of Sedentism*, edited by Susan Kent, pp. 27–36. Cambridge University Press, Cambridge, UK.

Ruddle, Kenneth, Dennis Johnson, Patricia K. Townsend, and John D. Rees 1978. *Palm Sago: A Tropical Starch from Marginal Lands*. University Press of Hawaii for the East-West Center, Honolulu.

Townsend, Patricia Kathryn Woods 1969. *Subsistence and Social Organization in a New Guinea Society*. Ph.D. dissertation, Department of Anthropology, University of Michigan, Ann Arbor. University Microfilms, Ann Arbor.

Trinkhaus, E., and A. P. Buzhilova 2012. The Death and Burial of Sunghir 1. *International Journal of Osteoarchaeology* 22:655–66.

Westrum, Peter 1983. An Update on Berik Social Organization. In *Gods, Heroes, Kinsmen: Ethnographic Studies from Irian Jaya, Indonesia*, edited by William R. Merrifield, Marilyn Gregerson, and Daniel C. Ajamiseba, pp. 272–88. Cenderawasih University and the International Museum of Cultures, Jayapura, Indonesia, and Dallas, TX.

Wrangham, Richard W. 1999. Evolution of Coalitionary Killing. *Yearbook of Physical Anthropology* 42:1–30.

# 13

## Middle and Late Archaic Trophy Taking in Indiana

*Christopher W. Schmidt and Amber E. Osterholt*

In the archaeological record, trophy taking is the removal of body parts from living or recently deceased people. Although documented for some time in the Eastern Woodlands, only recently has it been described in sites from Indiana. In this chapter, we describe this phenomenon as it is expressed during the Middle and Late Archaic periods (MLAP) in the southern part of the state along the Ohio River; all of the sites are located either on the river or nearby on one of its small tributaries or sloughs. The sites are Bluegrass in Warrick County (Mayes 1997; Stafford et al. 2000), Kramer Mound and Meyer in Spencer County (Bader 2011; Bergman et al. 2013), 12Fl73 in Floyd County, 12Hr6 in Harrison County, and Firehouse in Dearborn County (Schmidt et al. 2010); all date from approximately 6,500 to 3,000 years ago (see Figure 13.1 for site locations and Table 13.1 for dates).

In the Ohio River valley, the MLAP are characterized by kin-based groups that lived in semisedentary villages and subsisted on wild resources including nuts, seeds, mussels, fish, and deer (e.g., Fortier 1983; Johannessen 1980; Schmidt 2001). Mortuary data suggest that the sociopolitical organization was band level; there are no diagnostic "Big Man" burials known. But the size of the sites and the complexity of the material culture suggest a sociopolitical organization that is beyond band level and akin to that of tribes (Emerson and McElrath 2009). Evidence of interpersonal violence (i.e., embedded projectile points and depressed cranial fractures) appear in approximately 3 percent of skeletons, a value that is similar to contemporary sites in the

---

*Violence and Warfare among Hunter-Gatherers,* edited by Mark W. Allen and Terry L. Jones, 241–256. ©2014 Taylor & Francis. All rights reserved.

Christopher W. Schmidt and Amber E. Osterholt

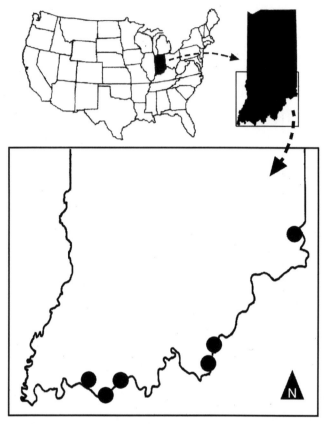

**Figure 13.1** Southern half of Indiana (north is up). Sites from left to right: Bluegrass, Kramer Mound, Meyer, 12Hr6, 12Fl73, and Firehouse.

**Table 13.1** Dates from Indiana sites

| Sites | Date, y BP | Method | Source |
|---|---|---|---|
| Bluegrass | 5,600–7,000 (cal) | Radiocarbon | Stafford and Cantin (2009) |
| Kramer | 5,700–6,200 (cal) | Radiocarbon | Bergman et al. (2013) |
| Meyer | 5,300 (conventional) | Radiocarbon | Bader (2011) |
| 12Hr6 | ~3,000 | Artifact association | Unpublished |
| 12Fl73 | ~5,000–6,000 | Artifact association | Unpublished, personal communication, Sheldon Burdin |
| Firehouse | ~3,000 | Artifact association | Unpublished |

Eastern Woodlands but somewhat lower than what is found later in prehistory, especially after AD 1000 during late prehistory (Lockhart and Schmidt 2007, 2008; Osterholt 2013).

Middle and Late Archaic Trophy Taking in Indiana | **243**

In southern Indiana, trophy taking tended to involve the removal of entire forearms and heads, although MLAP people also took soft tissue–only trophies such as scalps and tongues. In Indiana, only a single individual was found with its legs removed, yet lower limbs were commonly taken as trophies in Kentucky (Webb 1946). Thus, there are local nuances in MLAP trophy taking that warrant further investigation. This chapter is part of a continuing effort to describe and contextualize trophy taking in the Ohio River valley, where it is a persistent yet poorly understood component of MLAP skeletal assemblages.

## Prehistoric Warfare in Indiana

Warfare prior to European contact is little known in Indiana. Presumably warfare played an important role during late prehistory, particularly during the Mississippian period. The largest Mississippian site in Indiana is Angel, located in Vanderburgh County on the Ohio River deep in the southwest corner of the state. Population estimates for Angel are between 3,000 and 5,000; it had a large central platform mound, a central plaza, and palisade (Black 1967). Evidence for warfare at Angel includes eight instances each of scalping and blunt force trauma (Ausel 2013). Milner et al. (1991) report warfare during the late prehistoric at the Oneota site Norris Farms in Illinois. There, multiple people were scalped and a few were buried in shared graves as if they were killed at the same time (Milner et al. 1991). A contemporary site in northern Indiana is Woodland Ridge in Carroll County, which is not terribly far from Norris Farms. Its cultural affiliation is not clear, but it too has evidence of scalping and has at least one grave with multiple people. In addition, one individual had an arrow point embedded in an upper thoracic vertebra, an injury that was clearly perimortem (Schmidt et al. 2010).

Early/Middle Woodland warfare in Indiana is ambiguous. There are no described burials with scalping or embedded points dating to this period, but there are a number of sites that have trophy-taking evidence. Some have suggested that the Early and Middle Woodland are part of the so-called *Pax Hopewelliana*, a stretch of decreased conflict brought about by a region-wide religious movement that established long-distance trade routes and social alliances; under this model, the trophies are seen as ancestor veneration. The idea of long-term peace, however, is not universally accepted; Seeman (2007) views the various trophy sites as clear evidence of violence. Two prominent Early/Middle Woodland sites in Indiana include Windsor Mound and GE Mound: the former consists of 44 trophy heads arranged within an earthen mound (McCord and Cochran 1996); the latter was a very large mound containing the burial of what must have been a Big Man accompanied by 21 ground human mandibles (see Schmidt 1998 for discussion). It is unclear whether the Windsor or GE Mound remains are trophies of war or venerations, but it is interesting that the mandibles from GE are perforated for display on a necklace or similar accoutrement.

## Middle and Late Archaic Violence in the Eastern Woodlands

Archaic period violence is usually associated with trophy taking, evidence for which is widespread in the Eastern Woodlands. Along the Green River in Kentucky, Indian Knoll, Ward, Barrett, and Carlston Annis have individuals with clear evidence of trophy taking. At Indian Knoll the trophies include arms, legs, heads, scalps, and a torso (Snow 1948; Webb 1946). At Ward, trophy taking includes upper and lower limbs, heads, and isolated mandibles and teeth (Mensforth 2001). Ward also has a single grave with the skeletons of five young to middle adult males, four of which have projectile point injuries (Mensforth 2007). The Barrett site in Kentucky does not have evidence of scalping or trophy taking, but at least two individuals have projectile point injuries and 12 have healed cranial depressed fractures.

Ross-Stallings (2007) describes a Late Terminal Archaic site in Tennessee that has at least 12 decapitated skulls as well as fragmented cranial remains with evidence of scalping. Likewise, Smith (1993, 1995, 1997) reports scalping and decapitation and forelimb removal in several sites from Tennessee. Jacobi (2007) reports a grave containing three individuals who "were thrown into a burial pit with no regard or concern as to how the bodies should be positioned" (Jacobi 2007:320). Two of the bodies have points embedded in their vertebrae; one individual has seven points associated with his remains including four in the thoracic cavity, two in the spinal column (one embedded ventrally, one dorsally), and one in his mouth; he also has his forearms removed. In Alabama, Mensforth (2007) notes that five sites have evidence of violence including perimortem projectile point injury and head removal.

In Ohio, scalping was found at two very late MLAP sites, Clifford Williams and Stratten-Wallace. At the former, the victim was a young adult female; at the latter, it was a male (Mensforth 2007). The Frontenac Island site in New York has evidence for decapitation and dismemberment; in fact, two burials consist only of torsos. All told, 11 people were victimized by trophy taking, including adult males and females as well as two children (Mensforth 2007). At Robeson Hill in Illinois, Winters (1969) found a young adult male buried in an extended position with his left leg slightly akimbo. A projectile point was found in the distal end of the left femur. There was a separate burial at that site missing its head, although Winters was unable to determine what caused its absence.

## Indiana Middle and Late Archaic Trophies

Three Indiana sites bear evidence of limb and head removal. The oldest example dates to roughly 6,000 years ago and comes from the Bluegrass site, where an adult female was found missing her left forearm and head. Cut marks were on the ventral, medial, and lateral aspects of the distal humerus and on cervical vertebrae 3 through 5; the first two cervical vertebrae were missing along with the head (Lockhart and Schmidt 2007). A second adult individual from Bluegrass was missing both arms, both legs, and its head. Cut marks were found on the ribs near where the scapulae were positioned in life, and on the pelvis. No cervical vertebrae were recovered. This second individual, which is represented by only a thorax and pelvis, is unlike any other trophy victim yet found and, in fact, may represent a trophy itself rather than a trophy victim.

The most recent Late Archaic dismemberment/decapitation victim comes from the Firehouse site and dates to the height of the Riverton culture around 3,000 years ago. The victim was a young adult male who had his right forearm and head removed. Cut marks were located on the distal humerus in the same locations as they were on the Bluegrass female. Also similar to the Bluegrass female were the presence of cut marks on cervical vertebrae 3 through 5 and the absence of the first and second vertebrae. This individual had perimortem trauma that included stab and puncture marks in the chest, and five projectile points were found among the ribs. A sixth point was found adjacent to the second lumbar vertebra, which had a healed puncture on its spinous process. The point entered the victim from his right posterior side, traveled through the base of his second thoracic vertebral spine, and came to rest at the left transverse process. The point is Riverton and may represent the earliest example of an atlatl being used as a weapon in Indiana (Schmidt et al. 2010). However, the atlatl point damage is fully healed, indicating that the individual survived the first attack only to succumb some time later to a subsequent violent event.

A third site with evidence of limb removal is 12F173, which is roughly contemporary with Bluegrass. This site bears a particularly idiosyncratic expression of trophy taking in Indiana. A partial adult male skeleton in a flexed position was found eroding out of the Ohio River bank. Next to this individual was a cache of five left and right forelimbs representing five victims (i.e., the left and right limbs matched up). There were 10 radii and 10 ulnae, all of which had lengths indicating that they came from males; most of the forearms were missing their hands. Some of the forelimbs were curated because they were placed in the cache after their soft tissues had decayed; the bones were not positioned anatomically correctly. One forearm did have its hand present at the time of burial; the scaphoid and lunate were articulated with

**Figure 13.2** Cache of forelimbs from site 12F173.

the radius. No cut marks were found on these bones, and none of the other six skeletons found at the site had either trophies or evidence of trophy taking. The orientation of the cache was parallel to the body and perpendicular to the riverbank. The distal or hand ends of the forearms were placed toward the river (Figure 13.2).

The 12F173 cache is unique in Indiana. In fact, the only other cache known in the state consists of crania from the Early/Middle Woodland Windsor Mound, located in the far east-central portion of the state (McCord and Cochran 1996). Late Archaic caches from outside of Indiana include a large cluster of human crania at the Collegedale site in Tennessee (Ross-Stallings 2007) and a small collection of human teeth at Ward in Kentucky (Mensforth 2001).

Scalping is present at two mortuary sites in Indiana, both of which come from commingled contexts. The skeletal remains from the Terminal Late Archaic 12Hr6 site were damaged by looting activities and erosion of the Ohio River bank. The site produced at least 20 people, although it has yet to be osteologically studied. The Middle Archaic Kramer site also was damaged by oil company exploration. The human remains there were highly commingled and broken into thousands of fragments, most of which were less than 15 cm in length. It has a minimum number of individuals (MNI) of 41, nearly half of which were children (Bergman et al. 2013).

Both sites produced a single cranial fragment with cut marks. The fragment from 12Hr6 is a left temporal with parallel cuts along the squama. The

**Figure 13.3** Scalping marks on cranial fragment from Kramer Mound. Cuts are at the top left; coronal suture is at bottom right.

fragment from Kramer was from the frontal bone adjacent to the coronal suture. The cuts on it are highly diagnostic for scalping, running obliquely across the fragment and indicating a circumferential orientation. Several cuts overlap creating marks that are more than a millimeter wide (Figure 13.3). Detailed analysis of the cuts indicates that they are wide and shallow, and may have been created by a large bifacial chert blade or a ground stone tool (Schnellenberger 2013).

Tongue removal is found at the Meyer site, which is the only site known to have such evidence. Burial 42 is a 12- to 15-year-old probable male found in situ buried on his right side and loosely flexed; his head had been cut off and placed in his right hand. A semicircular, internally beveled fracture on the base of the cranium indicates that he suffered a perimortem blow to the head. Moreover, there were possible stab marks on the thorax, although taphonomic damage to the right shoulder, thorax, and pelvis obscure them.

On the mandible, there were cut marks on the distal aspect of the right ramus, the inferior aspect of the right corpus, and on the lingual aspect of the

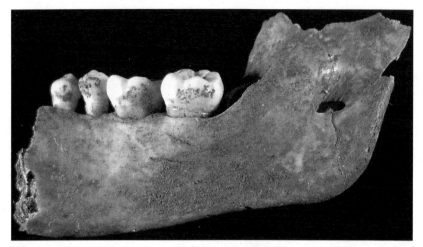

**Figure 13.4** Mandible from B.42 at the Meyer Site. Note deep cut marks in the middle of the right corpus, and notch cut into inferior corpus border.

right corpus on and nearly parallel to the mylohyoid line (Figure 13.4). The lingual cuts were particularly deep and wide. The lingual corpus cuts were not secondary to the obviously percussive cuts created on cervical vertebrae 3 through 5 (the first two accompanied the skull). In fact, it is clear that the breadth of the scratches resulted from a sawing action that is perpendicular to the direction of the cervical cuts (Lockhart et al. 2009). The mandible was in proper anatomical position, and there were no cut marks around the articular condyles or the temporal bones; thus, there was no attempt to remove it.

The most parsimonious explanation for the placement of these cut marks is that the mylohyoid muscle and other muscles at the base and lateral aspects of the tongue were cut from the right corpus. That mass of soft tissue was pulled inferiorly, and the musculature anchoring the left side of the tongue was severed without hitting bone. This technique is similar to that used by hunters to remove animal tongues, and may have been the technique used at Crow Creek (Willey 1990). Similarities between trophy taking and animal butchery have been documented elsewhere (e.g., Andrushko et al. 2005).

## Trophy-Taking Procedure

Middle and Late Archaic people used stone tools in both incisive and percussive manners to take trophies in Indiana. This determination comes from an analysis of scalp, humeral, and cervical cuts. Cut mark analysis commenced with the aid of a white light confocal profiler (WLCP) housed at the University of Indianapolis, which is able to convert surfaces into three-dimensional data clouds suitable for quantitative analysis (Schmidt et al. 2012). Cuts were magnified 20 times and studied in both profile and plan views. Results of the study indicate that steel tools did not create the cranial and humeral cuts; their kerf shapes were far too wide relative to their depths for steel tools, including trowels (Schmidt et al. 2012; Schnellenberger 2013). In fact, most of the cuts were so wide that they could have been made with sharpened ground stone tools like axes. However, large bifacial chert tools, particularly those with jagged blades, also create wide, shallow cuts (Schmidt et al. 2012).

Attempts were made to replicate forelimb removal by the lead author and a colleague using chert and slate flakes on cadavers. The cuts were made incisively, meaning we sliced through the soft tissues as if we were using modern knives and performing a dissection. We hypothesized that the cuts on the humeri (medial, lateral, and ventral aspects) represented all of the necessary incision locations to remove the limb. This did not prove to be the case. The ventral cut at the elbow joint quickly severed the tendons of the long and short heads of the biceps brachii muscle. The medial and lateral cuts were made just above the epicondyles and those severed the origins of the flexors and extensors of the hand, respectively. At this point we hoped that the ulna could then be dislodged from the humerus and the triceps muscle cut without affecting the bone. That was impossible. We realized that the fascial bands around the joint required cuts around the head of the ulna to separate the forearm from the humerus. We determined that flexing the elbow and tracing around the ulnar head with the cutting implement freed it. That final cut sometimes nicked the articular cartilage, but did not leave cuts on the dorsal aspect of the distal humerus or the ulna. After just a few attempts at removing forearms, we were able to completely remove one in approximately 90 seconds leaving cuts only in those places where they were located archaeologically (Lockhart and Schmidt 2008). Certainly, practitioners of limb removal in the past would have been more expeditious. Interestingly, the cuts that we left on the bones using flake tools in an incisive manner were very small compared with those on the MLAP skeletons, supporting the idea that their limbs were removed with larger implements using firmer or percussive strokes.

Cuts on the lateral aspects of the cervical vertebrae are clearly percussive chop marks that have large, deep, V-shaped kerfs created by large implements. The chopping strokes are in the medial-lateral plane, affecting the vertebrae primarily on their lateral aspects. Head-removal chop placement was determined by the location of the mandible, which limited access to the first two cervical vertebrae. Each decapitated individual described here had the first

250 | Christopher W. Schmidt and Amber E. Osterholt

two cervical vertebrae either missing, as at the Firehouse and Bluegrass sites, or accompanying the removed head, as at Meyer. The removal ended once the second and third vertebrae were separated, a process that often lacked precision as cervical vertebrae as far down as C5 were cut.

## Discussion

Recent research by Osterholt (2013) indicates that the trophy taking found in Indiana is part of a regional phenomenon. Trophy taking is ubiquitous throughout North America (e.g., Chacon and Dye 2007), but some regions appear to have practiced it more intensively than others. During the MLAP, one of those regions of concentration extended from the northern bank of the Ohio River down to the Tennessee River. In addition to the sites from Indiana, the area of concentration includes several sites along the Green, Cumberland, and Tennessee rivers (e.g., Carlston Annis, Indian Knoll, and Ward in Kentucky [Webb 1946, 1950; Mensforth 2001] and Big Sandy, Collegedale, Eva, and Robinson in Tennessee [Ross-Stallings 2007; Smith 1993, 1995, 1997]). The frequency and types of trophy taking in this region of concentration indicate that it was prevalent in this area but not standardized. For example, in the Green River region, burials were sometimes accompanied by entire limbs (e.g., Webb 1946), a phenomenon not found in Indiana or along the Tennessee River. What was similar, however, was the manner in which trophies were taken. For example, cut marks associated with forelimb removal were similarly placed in Indiana, Kentucky, and Tennessee, and the technique remains the same for at least the 2,000 years that separate Bluegrass and Firehouse.

Within the area of concentration, it is common to find both small and large sites with trophy-taking evidence. Indian Knoll has more than 1,000 skeletons, while Firehouse has only five individuals; yet, both have excellent examples of trophy taking. Outside of the area of concentration, the presence of trophy taking is less predictable. For example, Black Earth is a large site in southern Illinois with substantial MLAP components (Jefferies and Butler 1982). Based upon data from sites along the Ohio and Green rivers, one would expect to find between one and three trophy victims among the more than 150 MLAP burials. Yet, none were found in a recent survey of the skeletal remains specifically targeting evidence of trophy taking. Black Earth has bone pins that stylistically link it with sites in Indiana, particularly Bluegrass (Jefferies 1997). Despite its material culture connection to sites with trophy taking, Black Earth is not positioned on the Ohio River or one of its tributaries, and it is not a shell midden site; it is now thought to mark a boundary between the region of trophy-taking concentration and its hinterlands (Osterholt 2013).

# Middle and Late Archaic Trophy Taking in Indiana | **251**

Osterholt's research indicates that trophy taking was not a random violent act, but a phenomenon that was part of a cultural system within particular areas. Currently, there is no evidence that trophies were traded, but their appearances in burials indicate that they were meaningful to the deceased, the deceased's family, or both. That some were curated (as seen at 12F173) indicates that the meaning or value of the trophy could be maintained for a period of time before they were added to a grave.

The relationship of trophy taking to conflict is difficult to discern. By late prehistory it is clear that trophy taking was associated with significant violence (e.g., Willey 1990). In 2010, Schmidt et al. compared MLAP trophy taking to that of the late prehistoric sites of Norris Farms and Woodland Ridge. Oneota trophy taking focused almost exclusively on scalping; multiple people were killed. In addition, it appears that several of the killed and scalped were buried in common graves (Milner et al. 1991), indicating that during late prehistoric trophy taking accompanied attacks on groups of people. In contrast, MLAP trophy taking focused primarily on large trophies like entire heads and limb segments. MLAP victims were almost always buried individually. In Indiana, no site had more than two victims; most had just one. This suggests that MLAP trophy taking was not associated with group-level attacks; rather, it appears that attacks targeted single individuals. In fact, it may have been that the trophy was the reason for the attack. An example of this comes from the ethnographic record. The Jivaro of South America seek out vulnerable individuals in rival tribes to attain heads, which they "shrink" and use as protective magical amulets (Harner 1972). There is no attempt to attack the victim's group; in fact, there may be no hostility toward the group from which the victim came (Harner 1972). The MLAP trophies were used in graves, indicating that their value may have been in their magical powers where, for example, they could protect the dead or allow the dead to control the trophy victim in the afterlife. Therefore, trophies are not exclusive indicators of military prowess and may reflect cosmological concerns (e.g., Harner 1972).

There is no doubt that taking trophies accompanied violence: recall the stab wounds and projectile point damage on the young adult male from the Firehouse site who eventually lost his head and forelimb. However, there has been a tendency to sweep nearly all violent acts under the rug of the general term "warfare" without a detailed effort to understand the circumstances of the violence as indicated osteologically. Emphasizing the presence of warfare in prehistory has been a laudable response to postprocessual movements that questioned its existence in ancient North America, but it is important not to forget the osteological evidence of violence to elucidate important nuances that distinguish different types of warfare (see Lambert 1997, 2002, 2008; Milner 1995, 2007; Milner et al. 1991; Walker 2001 for excellent discussions regarding the bioarchaeology of warfare).

## 252 | Christopher W. Schmidt and Amber E. Osterholt

To a certain extent, Mensforth (2001, 2007) has done just this by discussing varieties of warfare, each with distinctive motivations and differing means of execution (i.e., mourning war and shame aggression). In fact, he notes that shame aggression assault, which occurs when an individual is motivated to kill to regain social prestige, would not constitute warfare because the act is perpetrated by an individual against an individual (Mensforth 2007:225). Drawing from Kelly (2000), Mensforth adds that sociopolitical organization affects how violence against a person or people in a particular group is viewed by members of that group and in some ways determines the response they will have. Coupling warfare types with aspects of culture such as sociopolitical organization provides a theoretical foundation for interpreting osteological evidence of violence. This approach is necessary because couching MLAP trophy taking as "warfare" without clarifying what is meant by the term ignores any number of explanations that are indicated by the MLAP skeletal data. In other words, it does not help to clarify what is going on if we describe the violence in the MLAP and late prehistoric as simply "warfare" when we know that for each the type of warfare is distinct, based on the differences they have in their osteological profiles.

Briefly, the osteological distinctions between the MLAP and late prehistory include the following: head removal is far more common in the MLAP than scalping; the opposite is true in late prehistory. For the MLAP, it is usually one or just a few individuals who are trophy victims in any one cemetery. During the late prehistoric it is common to have multiple victims of violence within a single cemetery and evidence that several were killed at one time. Finally, most MLAP trophy victims are usually buried individually; during the late prehistoric, it is common to have graves containing more than one violence victim (for details regarding the osteological distinctions between MLAP and late prehistoric trophy victims, see Lockhart 2008; Schmidt et al. 2010).

By looking specifically at its osteological and mortuary manifestations, it is clear that trophy taking was not static in prehistory; its association with warfare changed over time. Understanding trophy taking requires that it be studied within the contexts from which it came. Thus, MLAP trophy taking has to be considered within its very particular frame of reference within the MLAP and recognized as a culturally specific phenomenon in addition to or even beyond the violence that begat it. The most direct indications from the remains themselves are that MLAP trophies had meaning and power that was transferred to or seized by those who acquired trophies and/or those who either deposited them or had them deposited into their graves. It was not important to victimize numerous people at once, and complete heads or limb segments were preferred.

## Conclusion

Detailed study has revealed that trophy taking was an important phenomenon in southern Indiana during the MLAP. Trophies concentrated on the bony elements of the extremities, including the head, although at times soft tissue trophies were taken. The techniques for trophy taking changed little, but the types of trophies varied somewhat even within geographic areas where trophy taking was common. MLAP trophy taking likely had motivations that were distinct from the motivations of those taking trophies during late prehistory. Important nuances of the MLAP trophy taking may have been associated with magic inherent to human body parts that served to address cosmological views of death. MLAP trophies were not necessarily indicators of prowess in conflict and reflect beliefs and practices unique to those people of the MLAP.

## Acknowledgments

The authors would like to thank Rebecca Van Sessen and Anna Casserly for their assistance with various aspects of this study. The WLCP analysis was supported by a grant from the National Science Foundation (to CWS).

## References

Andrushko, Valerie A., Kate Latham, Diane Grady, Allen Pastron, and Phillip Walker 2005. Bioarcheological Evidence for Trophy-Taking in Prehistoric Central California. *American Journal of Physical Anthropology* 127:375–84.

Ausel, Erica L. 2013. Migration, Violence and Depopulation: Recent Bioarchaeological Investigations at Angel Mounds. Paper presented at the Annual Meeting of the Midwest Archaeological Conference, Columbus, OH, October 24–27.

Bader, Anne T. 2011. Evidence of Ritualized Mortuary Behavior at the Meyer Site: An Inadvertent Discovery in Spencer County, Indiana. *Indiana Archaeology*, Indiana Department of Natural Resources, Indianapolis, IN.

Bergman, Christopher, Tanya P. Lemons, and Christopher W. Schmidt 2013. *Scientific Recovery Investigations at the Kramer Mound (12Sp7): Prehistoric Artifact Assemblages, Faunal and Floral Remains, and Human Osteology.* Report submitted to the Department of Natural Resources, Division of Historic Preservation and Archaeology, Indianapolis, IN.

Black, Glenn A. 1967. *Angel Site*. Indiana University Press, Bloomington.

Chacon, Richard J., and David H. Dye 2007. *The Taking and Displaying of Human Body Parts as Trophies by Amerindians.* Springer, New York.

Emerson, Thomas E., and Dale L. McElrath 2009. The Eastern Woodlands Archaic and the Tyranny of Theory. In *Archaic Societies: Diversity and Complexity Across the Midcontinent*, edited by Thomas E. Emerson, Dale L. McElrath, and Andrew C. Fortier, pp. 23–38. State University of New York Press, Albany.

Fortier, Andrew C. 1983. Settlement and Subsistence at the Go-Kart North Site: A Late Archaic Titterington Occupation in the American Bottoms. In *Archaic Hunter and Gatherers in the American Midwest*, edited by James L. Phillips and James A. Brown, pp. 243–60. Academic Press, New York.

**254** | Christopher W. Schmidt and Amber E. Osterholt

Harner, Michael J. 1972. *The Jivaro: People of the Sacred Waterfalls.* University of California Press, Berkeley.

Jacobi, Keith P. 2007. Disabling the Dead: Human Trophy Taking in the Prehistoric Southeast. In *The Taking and Displaying of Human Body Parts as Trophies by Amerindians,* edited by Richard J. Chacon and David H. Dye, pp. 299–338. Springer, New York.

Jefferies, Richard W. 1997. Middle Archaic Bone Pins: Evidence of Mid-Holocene Regional Scale Social Groups in the Southern Midwest. *American Antiquity* 62:464–87.

Jefferies, Richard W., and Brian Butler 1982. *The Carrier Mills Project: Human Adaptation in the Saline Valley, Illinois.* Research Paper 33. Center for Archaeological Investigations, Southern Illinois University at Carbondale.

Johannessen, Sissel 1980. Floral Resources and Remains. In *The Dyroff and Levin Sites: A Late Archaic Occupation in the American Bottom,* edited by Thomas A. Emerson, pp. 120–30. FAI-270 Archaeological Mitigation Project Report No. 24. Department of Anthropology, University of Illinois, Urbana.

Kelly, Raymond C. 2000. *Warless Societies and the Origin of War.* University of Michigan Press, Ann Arbor.

Lambert, Patricia M. 1997. Patterns of Violence in Prehistoric Hunter-Gatherer Societies of Coastal Southern California. In *Troubled Times: Violence and Warfare in the Past,* edited by Debra L. Martin and David W. Frayer, pp. 77–110. Gordon and Breach Publishers, Amsterdam, the Netherlands.

——— 2002. The Archeology of War: A North American Perspective. *Journal of Archaeological Research* 10:207–41.

——— 2008. The Osteological Evidence for Indigenous Warfare in North America. In *North American Indigenous Warfare and Ritual Violence,* edited by Richard J. Chacon and Ruben G. Mendoza, pp. 202–21. The University of Arizona Press, Tuscon.

Lockhart, Rachel A. and Christopher W. Schmidt 2007. Evidence of Decapitation and "Trophy Taking" During the Late Archaic in Southern Indiana [abstract]. *American Journal of Physical Anthropologists* 44(Supplement):158.

——— 2008. Patterns in Head and Forearm Removal Trauma during the Late Archaic in Southern Indiana [abstract]. *American Journal of Physical Anthropologists* 46(Supplement):141.

Lockhart, Rachel A., Christopher W. Schmidt, and Stephen A. Symes 2009. Understanding Middle and Late Archaic Forearm Removal [abstract]. *American Journal of Physical Anthropologists* 48(Supplement):177.

Mayes, Leigh Ann 1997. The Bluegrass Site (12W162): Bioarchaeological Analysis of a Middle-Late Archaic Mortuary Site in Southeastern Indiana. Unpublished Master's thesis, Department of Anthropology, University of Southern Mississippi, Hattiesburg.

McCord, Beth K., and Donald A. Cochran 1996. Windsor Mound: A Synthesis of an Adena Mound in Randolph County. Report submitted to the Department of Natural Resources Division of Historic Preservation and Archaeology. Report of Investigations 37. Ball State University, Muncie, IN.

Mensforth, Robert P. 2001. Warfare and Trophy Taking in the Archaic Period. In *Archaic Transitions in Ohio and Kentucky Prehistory,* edited by Olaf H. Prufer, Sara E. Pedde, and Richard S. Meindl, pp. 110–40. Kent State University Press, Kent, OH.

——— 2007. Human Trophy Taking in Eastern North America during the Archaic Period: The Relationship to Warfare and Social Complexity. In *The Taking and Displaying of Human Body Parts as Trophies by Amerindians,* edited by Richard J. Chacon and David H. Dye, pp. 222–77. Springer, New York.

Milner, George R. 1995. An Osteological Perspective on Prehistoric Warfare. In *Regional Approaches to Mortuary Analysis,* edited by Lane Anderson Beck, pp. 221–44. Plenum Press, New York.

Milner, George R. 2007. Warfare, Population, and Food Production in Prehistoric Eastern North America. In *North American Indigenous Warfare and Ritual Violence,* edited by Richard J. Chacon and Ruben G. Mendoza, pp. 182–201. The University of Arizona Press, Tuscon.

Milner, George R., Eve Anderson, and Virginia G. Smith 1991. Warfare in Late Prehistoric West-Central Illinois. *American Antiquity* 56:581–603.

Osterholt, Amber E. 2013. Defining a Region of Trophy Taking Concentration in the Eastern Woodlands. Unpublished Master's thesis, Department of Anthropology, University of Indianapolis, IN.

Ross-Stallings, Nancy 2007. Trophy Taking in the Central and Lower Mississippi Valley. In *The Taking and Displaying of Human Body Parts as Trophies by Amerindians,* edited by Richard J. Chacon and David H. Dye, pp. 339–70. Springer, New York.

Schmidt, Christopher W. 1998. Dietary Reconstruction in Prehistoric Humans from Indiana: An Analysis of Dental Macrowear, Dental Pathology, and Dental Microwear. Unpublished Ph.D. dissertation, Department of Anthropology, Purdue University, West Lafayette, IN.

——— 2001. Dental Microwear Evidence for a Dietary Shift between Two Nonmaize-Reliant Prehistoric Human Populations from Indiana. *American Journal of Physical Anthropology* 114:139–45.

Schmidt, Christopher W., Christopher R. Moore, and Randy Leifheit 2012. A Preliminary Assessment of Using a White Light Confocal Imaging Profiler for Cutmark Analysis. In *Forensic Microscopy for Skeletal Tissues: Methods and Protocols,* edited by Lynne S. Bell, pp. 235–48. Springer Press, NY.

Schmidt, Christopher W., Rachel A. Lockhart, Christopher Newman, Anna Serrano, Melissa Zolnierz, Anne T. Bader, and Jeffrey A. Plunkett 2010. Skeletal Evidence of Cultural Variation: Mutilation Related to Warfare and Mortuary Treatment. In *Human Variation in the Americas: the Integration of Archaeology and Biological Anthropology,* edited by Ben M. Auerbach, pp. 215–37. Occasional Paper No. 38. Center for Archaeological Investigations, Carbondale, IL.

Schnellenberger, Jack 2013. Confocal Microscopy of Cut Marks on a Middle Archaic Cranial Fragment. Paper presented at the Annual Meeting of the Indiana Academy of Science, Indianapolis, IN, March 9.

Seeman, Mark F. 2007. Predatory War and Hopewell Trophies. In *The Taking and Displaying of Human Body Parts as Trophies by Amerindians,* edited by Richard J. Chacon and David H. Dye, pp. 167–89. Springer, New York.

Smith, Maria O. 1993. A Probable Case of Decapitation at the Late Archaic Robinson Site (40SM4), Smith County, Tennessee. *Tennessee Anthropologist* 182:131–42.

——— 1995. Scalping in the Archaic Period: Evidence from the Western Tennessee Valley. *Southeastern Archaeology* 14:60–8.

——— 1997. Osteological Indications of Warfare in the late Archaic Period of the Western Tennessee Valley. In *Troubled Times: Violence and Warfare in the Past,* edited by Debra L. Martin and David W. Frayer, pp. 241–65. Gordon and Breach Publishers, Amsterdam, the Netherlands.

Snow, Charles 1948. Indian Knoll Skeletons of Site Oh2, Ohio County, Kentucky, Part II. *Reports in Anthropology and Archaeology* 4(3):371–556. University of Kentucky, Lexington.

Stafford, C. Russell, Ronald L. Richards, and C. Michael Anslinger 2000. The Bluegrass Fauna and Changes in Middle Holocene Hunter-Gatherer Foraging in the Southern Midwest. *American Antiquity* 65:317–36.

Stafford, C. Russell, and Mark A. Cantin 2009. Archaic Period Chronology in the Hill Country of Southern Indiana. In *Archaic Societies: Diversity and Complexity Across the Midcontinent,* edited by Thomas E. Emerson, Dale L. McElrath, and Andrew C. Fortier, pp. 287–316. State University of New York Press, Albany.

Walker, Phillip L. 2001. A Bioarcheological Perspective on the History of Violence. *Annual Review of Anthropology* 30:573–96.

**256** | Christopher W. Schmidt and Amber E. Osterholt

Webb, William S. 1946. Indian Knoll Site Oh2 Ohio County, Kentucky, Part I. *Reports in Anthropology and Archaeology* 4:115–356. University of Kentucky, Lexington.

——— 1950. The Carlston Annis Mound. *Reports in Anthropology and Archaeology* 7:266–354. University of Kentucky, Lexington.

Willey, P. 1990. *Prehistoric Warfare on the Great Plains: Skeletal Analysis of the Crow Creek Massacre Victims.* Garland Publishing, Inc., New York.

Winters, Howard D. 1969. *Riverton Culture.* Illinois State Museum, Springfield.

# 14

## The Bioarchaeological Record of Craniofacial Trauma in Central California

*Marin A. Pilloud, Al W. Schwitalla, and Terry L. Jones*

B ased on ethnographic accounts and archaeological research, warfare among the indigenous populations of California was neither rare nor infrequent, and a great deal of research has been done on this topic for southern California, primarily by Lambert (1994, 1997) and Walker (1989, 1997). As research of warfare and violent behavior in prehistoric populations has grown, studies in California have also expanded to include the northern and central parts of the state (Andrushko et al. 2005, 2010; Bartelink et al. 2013; Chelotti 2013; Jurmain et al. 2001, 2009; Jurmain and Bellifemine 1997; Willits 2011). Here, we contribute to this research by considering patterns in a large set of central California burial data compiled by one of us (Schwitalla) over the last 13 years. Specifically, we evaluate variation related to sex, age, location and timing of injury (antemortem or perimortem), and size of wound in one particular form of violence—craniofacial trauma—with the goal of quantifying the relative frequency and cultural importance of this type of violence among these prehistoric hunter-gatherer populations.

The seminal studies of cranial trauma by Lambert (1994) and Walker (1989) identified a peak in cranial vault fractures during the Early Middle period (1400 cal BC–cal AD 580) in southern California. Walker (1989) suggested that the unusually high frequency of nonlethal cranial injuries on the Channel Islands reflected extreme demographic pressure and intense competition over resources that was diffused via ritualized sublethal fighting (Walker 1989:313). A later peak (ca. AD 900) in projectile violence was attributed to resource scarcity

---

*Violence and Warfare among Hunter-Gatherers*, edited by Mark W. Allen and Terry L. Jones, 257–272. ©2014 Taylor & Francis. All rights reserved.

258 | Marin A. Pilloud, Al W. Schwitalla, and Terry L. Jones

during the Medieval Climatic Anomaly and the introduction of the bow and arrow (Schwitalla et al. 2014). Our evaluation of prehistoric cranial trauma data from central California used these findings as a starting point; specifically, we sought to compare findings from the south with the more recently available data from further north to determine whether similar patterns might exist and if they warranted a similar explanation. In this study we have examined patterns in the temporal, spatial, and sexual distribution of this form of trauma in central California relative to the Santa Barbara Channel with the hope that such comparisons might clarify the behaviors and motivations behind the interpersonal aggression that resulted in these types of cranial injuries.

## Materials and Methods

Data were taken from the Central California Bioarchaeological Database (CCBD), which includes information on more than 16,000 individuals excavated between the 1880s and 2012 (Schwitalla 2013; Schwitalla et al. 2014). The CCBD was created from pre-existing archaeological site reports housed at regional repositories, including published and unpublished archaeological site reports, osteological appendices, burial records, and NAGPRA (Native American Graves and Repatriation Act) inventories. In some cases, the principal analysts that conducted the field investigations provided additional data. None of the studies reported here were specifically undertaken for the purposes of this chapter. Results from earlier versions of this database have been reported previously (Andrushko et al. 2010; Jones and Schwitalla 2008; Schwitalla 2010, 2013; Schwitalla and Jones 2012; Schwitalla et al. 2014). The version of the database used for current study includes information on 16,820 individuals.[1] Basic demographic information is available for each of these individuals, including age and sex. Temporal assignments were based on artifact associations, obsidian hydration values, radiocarbon dates, and stratigraphic superposition at sites with delineated temporal components.

Although the database is quite large, the current study was limited to analysis of a subset of individuals with intact skulls and for whom relative age and sex assessments were available (Table 14.1). The archaeological sites were grouped into three well-established geographic and cultural regions—San Francisco Bay,

**Table 14.1** Demographic profile of the skeletal sample

|  | Adolescent (12–18 y) | Young Adult (18–35 y) | Middle Adult (35–45 y) | Old Adult (45+ y) | Adult (18+ y) | Total |
|---|---|---|---|---|---|---|
| No. females | 91 | 1089 | 485 | 513 | 402 | 2580 |
| No. males | 51 | 1227 | 519 | 368 | 392 | 2557 |
| No. Indeterminate | 226 | 290 | 51 | 66 | 432 | 1065 |
| Total | 368 | 2606 | 1055 | 947 | 1226 | 6202 |

The Bioarchaeological Record of Craniofacial Trauma | 259

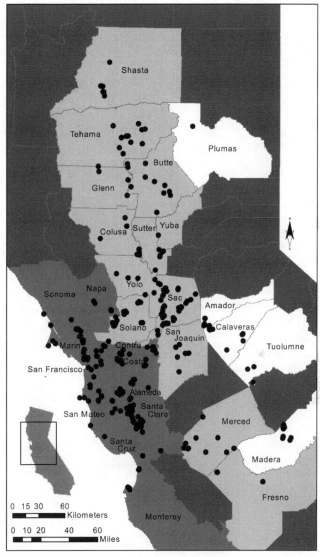

**Figure 14.1** Location of sites used in study by geographic region: San Francisco Bay (dark gray), Central Valley (light gray), Sierra Nevada (white).

Central Valley, and Sierra Nevada (Figure 14.1)—and were further assigned to one of six time periods based on the recent updates to the Central California Taxonomic System (CCTS) made by Groza (2002), Hughes and Milliken (2007), and Schwitalla (2013). These time periods are: Early (3050–500 cal BC), Early Middle (500 cal BC–cal AD 420), Late Middle (cal AD 420–1010),

**Figure 14.2** A 45-year-old adult male (Burial 131) with antemortem depressed cranial fracture to the right parietal from CA-CCO-548. Burial dates to the Early period (3050–500 BC) (Photograph courtesy of Randy S. Wiberg).

Middle-Late Transition (cal AD 1010–1390), Late Prehistoric (cal AD 1390–1720), and Protohistoric/Historic (cal AD 1720–1899).

Data were compiled on craniofacial trauma to include fracture type (depressed, comminuted, linear) and timing of injury (antemortem or perimortem), resulting in a total of six possible fracture types (Figures 14.2 and 14.3). Notations were also made on general location of the trauma on the skull: frontal, parietal, occipital, temporal, facial, nasal, and mandible. Data were also available in some instances on the size of the injury resulting from the blunt

**Figure 14.3** A 23-year-old adult male (12-3562) exhibiting multiple perimortem depressed cranial fractures from CA-ALA-309. Burial dates to the Late Middle period (AD 420–1010) (Photograph by Sally R. Evans).

force trauma. Statistical analyses were conducted in SPSS 21.0 and include chi-square, correspondence analysis, and one-way analysis of variance (ANOVA).

## Results

### Sex and Age

A total of 264 (4.3 percent) of 6,202 adult individuals with crania exhibited evidence for some type of blunt force craniofacial trauma. That is, 103 (4.0 percent) of 2,580 females, 141 (5.5 percent) of 2,557 males, and 20 (1.9 percent) of 1,065 individuals of indeterminate sex. While the percentages between males and females are similar, this difference was found to be statistically significant ($\chi^2$=6.58; $p$=0.01).

Males and females show some patterned differences in terms of age and presence of craniofacial trauma (Figure 14.4). Females appear to have experienced trauma increasingly through age, whereas males show a peak during middle adulthood. However, overall, the trend is for the presence of trauma to increase with age. Statistically significant differences were only noted between female age groups ($\chi^2$=20.89; $p$=0.00), and between males and females only in the young adult demographic ($\chi^2$=13.62; $p$=0.00), during which time males exhibit nearly twice the amount of craniofacial trauma as females.

It should be noted that antemortem trauma would have been acquired through one's lifetime, representing cumulative healed wounds. As a result, older adults should have higher rates of these types of injuries than younger individuals. Therefore, the presence of antemortem and perimortem trauma were evaluated separately. In looking at antemortem trauma, the same patterns are evident; female frequencies rise through age, and there is a statistically significant difference between males and females only during the young adult period (Table 14.2). When only perimortem trauma is considered, rates are much lower, indicating that people generally survived these types of trauma. In terms of male–female differences, no statistically significant differences exist in any age group, and both groups show a decrease in these types of traumas as age increases (Table 14.3).

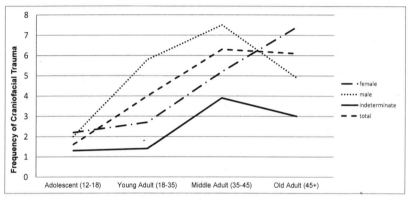

**Figure 14.4** Distribution of craniofacial trauma divided by age and sex.

**Table 14.2** Distribution of antemortem craniofacial trauma by sex

|  | Female |  | Male |  | Chi-square |  |
|---|---|---|---|---|---|---|
| Age | N | % | N | % | $\chi^2$ | $p$ value |
| Adolescent (12–18 y) | 1/91 | 1.1 | 1/51 | 2.0 | 0.18 | 0.68 |
| Young Adult (18–35 y) | 17/1089 | 1.6 | 42/1228 | 3.4 | 8.04 | 0.01 |
| Middle Adult (35–45 y) | 21/485 | 4.3 | 31/520 | 6.0 | 1.36 | 0.24 |
| Old Adult (45+ y) | 33/513 | 6.4 | 16/368 | 4.3 | 1.77 | 0.18 |

**Table 14.3** Distribution of perimortem craniofacial trauma by sex

|  | Female |  | Male |  | Chi-square |  |
|---|---|---|---|---|---|---|
| Age | N | % | N | % | $\chi^2$ | $p$ value |
| Adolescent (12–18 y) | 1/91 | 1.1 | 1/51 | 2.0 | 0.18 | 0.68 |
| Young Adult (18–35 y) | 11/1089 | 1.0 | 21/1228 | 1.7 | 2.08 | 0.15 |
| Middle Adult (35–45 y) | 4/485 | 0.8 | 7/520 | 1.3 | 0.63 | 0.42 |
| Old Adult (45+ y) | 3/513 | 0.6 | 2/368 | 0.5 | 0.01 | 0.93 |

## Type and Location of Trauma

Males and females show quite similar patterns of injury location (Table 14.4). Females exhibit a slightly higher frequency of trauma in the parietal region, whereas males exhibit high frequencies in both the frontal and parietal bones. A statistically significant difference was only found on the frontal, with males showing trauma in this location at almost twice the frequency of females. In a consideration of both sexed and unsexed individuals, the most commonly affected bone is the parietal, followed closely by the frontal. In a correspondence analysis (Figure 14.5), sex-related patterns can be further

**Table 14.4** Distribution of craniofacial trauma by location and sex

| Location | Female N/2580 | % | Male N/2557 | % | Indeterminate N/1065 | % | Total N/6202 | % | Chi-square* $\chi^2$ | $p$ value |
|---|---|---|---|---|---|---|---|---|---|---|
| Frontal | 33 | 1.3 | 53 | 2.1 | 8 | 0.8 | 93 | 1.5 | 4.49 | 0.03 |
| Parietal | 45 | 1.7 | 50 | 2.0 | 13 | 1.2 | 108 | 1.7 | 0.31 | 0.58 |
| Occipital | 7 | 0.3 | 8 | 0.3 | 1 | 0.1 | 16 | 0.3 | 0.08 | 0.78 |
| Temporal | 7 | 0.3 | 8 | 0.3 | 0 | 0 | 15 | 0.2 | 0.08 | 0.78 |
| Facial | 3 | 0.1 | 3 | 0.1 | 0 | 0 | 6 | 0.1 | 0.00 | 0.99 |
| Nasal | 9 | 0.3 | 13 | 0.5 | 1 | 0.1 | 23 | 0.4 | 0.77 | 0.38 |
| Mandible | 7 | 0.3 | 6 | 0.2 | 0 | 0 | 13 | 0.2 | 0.07 | 0.79 |

* Chi-square is only between males and females.

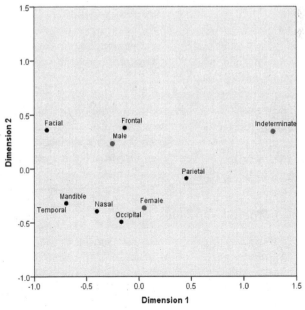

**Figure 14.5** Correspondence analysis of craniofacial trauma location and sex.

**264** | Marin A. Pilloud, Al W. Schwitalla, and Terry L. Jones

**Table 14.5** Distribution of fracture types

| | Frontal | | Parietal | | Occipital | | Temporal | | Facial | | Nasal | | Mandible | |
|---|---|---|---|---|---|---|---|---|---|---|---|---|---|---|
| | N | % | N | % | N | % | N | % | N | % | N | % | N | % |
| AM Depressed | 75 | 22.6 | 98 | 29.1 | 11 | 3.3 | 3 | 0.9 | 5 | 1.5 | 0 | 0 | 1 | 0.3 |
| AM Comminuted | 1 | 0.3 | 1 | 0.3 | 0 | 0 | 0 | 0 | 1 | 0.3 | 2 | 0.6 | 0 | 0 |
| AM Linear | 5 | 1.5 | 0 | 0 | 0 | 0 | 4 | 1.2 | 0 | 0 | 31 | 9.2 | 11 | 3.3 |
| PM Depressed | 15 | 4.5 | 20 | 5.9 | 5 | 1.5 | 1 | 0.3 | 0 | 0 | 0 | 0 | 0 | 0 |
| PM Comminuted | 10 | 3.0 | 14 | 4.2 | 2 | 0.6 | 4 | 1.2 | 2 | 0.6 | 0 | 0 | 4 | 1.2 |
| PM Linear | 3 | 0.9 | 2 | 0.6 | 1 | 0.3 | 4 | 1.2 | 1 | 0.3 | 0 | 0 | 0 | 0 |

AM indicates antemortem; PM, perimortem.

visualized. In multivariate space, males cluster with the frontal and facial region, whereas females group with the parietal, occipital, and nasal bones.

For the purposes of this study there were 42 potential types of fractures, originating from seven recorded locations and six fracture types. Of these possible 42, only 29 were observed. In Table 14.5 each fracture type is considered as a percentage of the total fractures (n=337). Within this sample, antemortem depressed fractures of the parietal bones are the most common (29.1 percent), followed closely by antemortem depressed fractures of the frontal bone (22.6 percent). The next most common fracture is antemortem linear fracture of the nasal bones (9.2 percent), which is found at a significantly lower rate than the other two types. These are followed by perimortem depressed fractures of the parietal (5.9 percent) and frontal (4.5 percent) bones. The other fracture types occur at much lower frequencies.

When examining the most common fracture type per bone element, antemortem depressed fractures are the most common type among the frontal, parietal, occipital, and facial bones, whereas antemortem linear fractures are the most common type in the nasal bones and mandible. In the temporal bone, three fracture types are seen in similar frequencies: antemortem linear, perimortem linear, and perimortem comminuted.

## Spatial and Temporal Variation

No difference was found between males and females within each individual geographic region (Figure 14.6); however, significant differences were apparent between regions. The Central Valley was found to have the highest incidence of craniofacial trauma, followed by the San Francisco Bay and the Sierra Nevada.

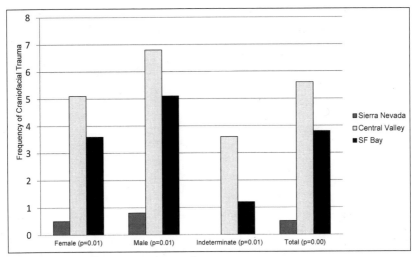

**Figure 14.6** Distribution of craniofacial trauma by region and sex. *P* values are the result of a chi-square analysis between regions.

**Table 14.6** Temporal distribution of craniofacial trauma

|  | Female |  | Male |  | Indeterminate |  | Total |  | Chi-square* |  |
|---|---|---|---|---|---|---|---|---|---|---|
| Time Period | N | % | N | % | N | % | N | % | $\chi^2$ | *p* value |
| 3050–500 BC | 12/247 | 4.9 | 14/278 | 5.0 | 1/97 | 1.0 | 27/622 | 4.3 | 0.01 | 0.93 |
| 500 BC–AD 420 | 18/545 | 3.3 | 31/550 | 5.6 | 1/213 | 0.5 | 50/1308 | 3.8 | 3.49 | 0.06 |
| AD 420–1010 | 20/665 | 3.0 | 24/695 | 3.5 | 7/298 | 2.4 | 51/1654 | 3.1 | 0.22 | 0.64 |
| AD 1010–1390 | 26/627 | 4.1 | 34/597 | 5.7 | 10/286 | 3.5 | 70/1510 | 4.6 | 1.57 | 0.21 |
| AD 1390–1720 | 15/349 | 4.3 | 16/310 | 5.2 | 0/130 | 0 | 31/789 | 4.1 | 6.69 | 0.04 |
| AD 1720–1899 | 12/147 | 8.2 | 22/127 | 17.3 | 1/45 | 2.2 | 35/319 | 11.0 | 5.26 | 0.02 |
| Chi-square |  | 9.64 |  | 39.91 |  | 9.66 |  | 41.96 |  |  |
| *p* value |  | 0.09 |  | 0.00 |  | 0.09 |  | 0.00 |  |  |

* Chi-square is only between males and females.

Rates of temporal variation were very steady through the strictly prehistoric periods, but show a dramatic increase during Protohistoric/Historic times (Table 14.6). The sexes are broadly comparable throughout time, except during the Early Middle (500 cal BC–cal AD 420) and Protohistoric/Historic (cal AD 1720–1899) periods, when males show higher rates of craniofacial trauma.

Evaluating the temporal patterns by region, the Sierra Nevada region shows a peak in craniofacial trauma between cal AD 1010 and 1390 (Table 14.7), whereas the other regions only show a significant increase during the Protohistoric/Historic period. Significant differences between the groups are only evident during the Late Middle period (cal AD 420–1010), at which time the Central Valley had the highest rate of craniofacial trauma.

**266** | Marin A. Pilloud, Al W. Schwitalla, and Terry L. Jones

**Table 14.7** Temporal and regional distribution of craniofacial trauma

| | Sierra Nevada | | Central Valley | | San Francisco Bay | | Chi-square | |
|---|---|---|---|---|---|---|---|---|
| Time Period | N | % | N | % | N | % | $\chi^2$ | $p$ value |
| 3050–500 BC | 0/56 | 0 | 21/389 | 5.4 | 6/177 | 3.4 | 3.98 | 0.14 |
| 500 BC–AD 420 | 0/99 | 0 | 16/352 | 4.5 | 34/857 | 4.0 | 4.48 | 0.11 |
| AD 420–1010 | 1/118 | 0.8 | 35/776 | 4.5 | 15/760 | 2.0 | 10.39 | 0.01 |
| AD 1010–1390 | 1/43 | 2.3 | 19/351 | 5.4 | 50/1116 | 4.5 | 1.06 | 0.59 |
| AD 1390–1720 | 0/54 | 0 | 8/212 | 3.8 | 23/523 | 4.4 | 2.53 | 0.28 |
| AD 1720–1899 | 0/27 | 0 | 33/269 | 12.3 | 2/23 | 8.7 | 3.91 | 0.14 |
| Chi-square | 4.3 | | 26.41 | | 10.60 | | | |
| $p$ value | 0.50 | | 0.00 | | 0.06 | | | |

**Table 14.8** Dimensions of antemortem depressed fractures by element in central California

| | | Males | | | Females | | | Indeterminate | | | Total | | | | |
|---|---|---|---|---|---|---|---|---|---|---|---|---|---|---|---|
| Cranial | Element | n | $\bar{x}$ | $\sigma$ | n | $\bar{x}$ | $\sigma$ | n | $\bar{x}$ | $\sigma$ | n | $\bar{x}$ | $\sigma$ | F | $p$ value* |
| Parietal | Diameter | 6 | 12.18 | 7.43 | 8 | 10.69 | 5.75 | 4 | 18.38 | 2.80 | 18 | 12.90 | 6.39 | 0.18 | 0.68 |
| | Depth | 11 | 2.42 | 2.41 | 18 | 1.85 | 1.09 | 4 | 1.38 | 0.25 | 33 | 1.98 | 1.60 | 0.74 | 0.40 |
| Frontal | Diameter | 7 | 19.39 | 10.67 | 8 | 12.18 | 3.18 | 1 | 9.56 | – | 16 | 15.17 | 8.09 | 3.34 | 0.09 |
| | Depth | 6 | 2.15 | 1.81 | 6 | 2.51 | 2.50 | 2 | 0.65 | 0.71 | 14 | 2.09 | 2.03 | 0.08 | 0.78 |
| Occipital | Diameter | 2 | 15.15 | 3.74 | 3 | 6.28 | 5.68 | 0 | — | — | 5 | 9.82 | 6.57 | 3.61 | 0.15 |
| | Depth | 1 | 1.60 | — | 1 | 2.00 | — | 0 | — | — | 2 | 1.80 | 0.28 | — | — |

All measurements are in millimeters.
*ANOVA is only between males and females.

## Dimensions of Antemortem Depressed Fractures

In several instances data were recorded on the dimensions of antemortem depressed fractures on the parietal, frontal, and occipital bones (Table 14.8). In a one-way ANOVA of mean diameter and depth of trauma, no significant differences were found between males and females, although the difference in diameter size of antemortem trauma to the frontal was significant at the $\alpha$=0.1 level.

These dimensions were compared to those reported by Walker (1989) from southern California. Overall, the central California cranial injuries were larger and deeper than those in southern California (Table 14.9). Exceptions to this pattern were found in the female sample, where diameters of the parietal and occipital were larger in southern California. One-way ANOVA was used to evaluate differences between dimensions. In cases where the dimensions were larger in central California, statistical significance was achieved (Table 14.10).

The Bioarchaeological Record of Craniofacial Trauma | **267**

**Table 14.9** Dimensions of antemortem depressed fractures by element in southern California

| Cranial | Element | Males | | | Females | | | Total | | |
|---|---|---|---|---|---|---|---|---|---|---|
| | | n | $\bar{x}$ | $\sigma$ | n | $\bar{x}$ | $\sigma$ | n | $\bar{x}$ | $\sigma$ |
| Parietal | Diameter | 33 | 11.61 | 6.36 | 18 | 14.39 | 6.34 | 61 | 12.39 | 6.21 |
| | Depth | 33 | 0.95 | 0.55 | 18 | 0.54 | 0.58 | 60 | 0.83 | 0.60 |
| Frontal | Diameter | 45 | 10.71 | 5.21 | 24 | 10.71 | 6.49 | 78 | 11.05 | 6.01 |
| | Depth | 45 | 0.96 | 0.74 | 23 | 0.74 | 0.58 | 77 | 0.88 | 0.66 |
| Occipital | Diameter | 1 | 7.00 | — | 1 | 22.00 | — | 2 | 14.50 | 10.61 |
| | Depth | 1 | 1.00 | — | 1 | 0.12 | — | 2 | 0.56 | 0.62 |

All measurements are in millimeters. Data from Walker (1989).

**Table 14.10** Results of one-way ANOVA of dimensions of antemortem depressed fractures between southern and central California

| Cranial | Element | Males | | Females | | Total | |
|---|---|---|---|---|---|---|---|
| | | F | $p$ value | F | $p$ value | F | $p$ value |
| Parietal | Diameter | 0.04 | 0.85 | 1.99 | 0.17 | 0.09 | 0.76 |
| | Depth | 11.05 | 0.00 | 20.26 | 0.00 | 24.84 | 0.00 |
| Frontal | Diameter | 12.16 | 0.00 | 0.37 | 0.54 | 5.51 | 0.02 |
| | Depth | 9.08 | 0.00 | 10.41 | 0.00 | 17.81 | 0.00 |
| Occipital | Diameter | — | — | — | — | 0.55 | 0.49 |
| | Depth | — | — | — | — | 6.65 | 0.12 |

## Discussion

Males and females show very similar patterns in the type, frequency, and location of blunt force craniofacial trauma. While males show a statistically higher frequency of craniofacial trauma, the difference is not marked. This is similar to what Bartelink et al. (2013) found in their study of a more limited sample of central California burials; they reported cranial vault trauma in 2.0 percent of males and in 0.7 percent of females. They report these results to be statistically insignificant, and sexual differences to be minor. Such findings appear to be somewhat unusual, as several other California studies have found that males tend to have higher rates of cranial trauma in both the San Francisco Bay Area (Jurmain et al. 2009; Jurmain and Bellifemine 1997) and in southern California (Lambert 1997; Walker 1997).

While our findings suggest that the sexes were broadly similar in terms of craniofacial trauma in central California, some areas of difference were discernible. A significant difference was found in antemortem depressed fractures of the parietal, which occur at higher frequencies among females. This suggests that females may have engaged in more nonlethal warfare affecting the sides of their cranium, whereas males appear to have a higher frequency of cranial trauma on the frontal bone, suggesting more face-to-face combat. However, females may have also engaged in similar types of activities as they still show high frequencies in the frontal, particularly when compared with other bones in the skull.

It is also clear that males tend to show evidence for antemortem trauma at a young age. These results suggest that younger males were more heavily engaged in activities that lead to antemortem craniofacial trauma. Among females, antemortem trauma is seen at higher rates in older women, which may be related to two things: (1) older women were freer to engage in violent behaviors or may have felt more invested in their community, whereas younger women may have avoided such activities perhaps due to childbearing and -rearing; or (2) women tended to survive these traumas more commonly, suggesting a "milder" form of combat such that this higher frequency is actually representative of the fact that these healed wounds are cumulative. Alternatively, it is also possible that these age patterns suggest that males who avoided aggressive behavior in their youth were preferentially able to survive to old adulthood; conversely, females that *did* engage in such behaviors tended to survive later. This interpretation would have broader implications for the motivations and consequences of interpersonal aggression for each of the sexes. In terms of perimortem trauma, males show higher rates than females in every age group, and both groups show a general decrease as one matures. These results suggest that seemingly lethal types of aggression tended to occur at younger ages in both males and females.

In terms of trauma location and type, antemortem depressed fractures of the frontal and parietal are the most common, with the remainder of locations and fracture types occurring at much lower frequencies. These findings are somewhat similar to those of Walker (1989) from southern California. Within his sample, most antemortem depressed cranial fractures were found on the frontal.

No statistical difference was found between males and females in injury size in central California, except perhaps in frontal bone diameter, where males show larger injuries than females. In addition, males were found to have craniofacial trauma in the frontal nearly twice as often as females. Overall, the dimensions of wounds from central California are larger than those reported from southern California by Walker (1989). Walker argued that based on the high frequency (18.6 percent in the Channel Islands) of these sublethal types of injuries of the cranial vault, this type of interpersonal violence may have been highly ritualized. The finding of larger injuries in central California at a lower frequency (4.3 percent) speaks to differences in the type of combat and likely the instruments used to inflict trauma. These results suggest that this behavior was not as ritualized in central California as it apparently was in southern California, and that larger weapons could

The Bioarchaeological Record of Craniofacial Trauma | **269**

have been used with the intent of inflicting great bodily harm. This seems consistent with the greater frequency of trophy-taking features in central California as opposed to southern California (Andrushko et al. 2010; Schwitalla et al. 2014, and this volume).

The highest rates of craniofacial trauma for both sexes and in each time period are from the Central Valley, which also had the highest ethnographic population density, suggesting relative demographic pressure may have been an influence on the rates of interpersonal violence in this region. Over time both the Central Valley and the San Francisco Bay fluctuate in terms of craniofacial trauma frequency (Figure 14.5); however, both regions show dramatic increases during the Protohistoric/Historic period, whereas the Sierra Nevada shows no increase during that time. While not statistically significant, there is a peak in craniofacial trauma frequency during the Middle-Late Transition period (cal AD 1010–1390) in the Sierra Nevada, which corresponds to a period of extreme drought during the Medieval Climatic Anomaly (Stine 1994). This drought and its effects on native populations have been extensively studied throughout California (Jones et al. 1999; Jones and Schwitalla 2008; Pilloud 2006; Raab and Larson 1997; Weiss 2002). There is some evidence to suggest that these climatic changes had marked effects on populations in the Sierra Nevada (Hull 2007); this may be reflected in the increase in craniofacial trauma as competition for resources increased. The San Francisco Bay area also shows high frequencies of craniofacial trauma during the Middle-Late Transition, albeit not as high as the Protohistoric/Historic period. Almost undoubtedly the latter can be attributed to the presence of Europeans, who had established themselves in Mexico and the American Southwest 200 to 300 years earlier. Problems experienced by people who were in direct conflict with Europeans probably had a rippling effect throughout indigenous western North America as people tried to migrate away from the zones of direct contact and conflict. Certainly these movements and their effects are fairly well documented in eastern North America (e.g., Worth 1995). This same process has been argued to explain the spread of diseases throughout the New World in advance of the Europeans themselves (e.g., Erlandson and Bartoy 1995; Preston 1996).

## Conclusions

Our results indicate that blunt force craniofacial trauma was prevalent throughout central California during the Prehistoric, Protohistoric, and Historic periods. Males and females display evidence for this form of trauma at comparable rates through time and across regions. Differences are apparent in the location of trauma by sex; males have trauma most commonly on the frontal, and females on the parietal. There are also age differences between sexes in terms of antemortem trauma; males acquire trauma predominantly

# 270 | Marin A. Pilloud, Al W. Schwitalla, and Terry L. Jones

during young adulthood, and females show higher rates of antemortem trauma as middle-aged to old adults.

In the Santa Barbara Channel, Walker (1989) suggested that a high frequency of cranial trauma was the result of sublethal ritualized combat. In central California, blunt force cranial injuries are less frequent but show wider and deeper wounds, suggesting there was more intent to inflict serious harm. If Walker's (1989) assessment is accurate for southern California, it suggests that warfare in central California was more serious, but also less frequent and not ritualized.

In the San Francisco Bay Area and Central Valley, the frequency of cranial trauma increased dramatically during the Protohistoric/Historic period (AD 1720–1899), but this trend was not apparent in the Sierra Nevada, where trauma was found at higher rates (albeit not statistically significant) during the Medieval Climatic Anomaly, a period marked by severe droughts. In general, however, craniofacial trauma occurred at the lowest rates in the Sierra Nevada, which also had the lowest population density. This seems to indicate that interpersonal violence in central California was at least partially related to resource availability, but also increased with the arrival of the Europeans in southwestern North America.

## Note

1. The database used here is a slightly earlier version (n=16,820) than the more recent version used in Chapter 15 (n=17,898).

## References

Andrushko, Valerie A., Kate Latham, Diane Grady, Allen Pastron, and Phillip L. Walker 2005. Bioarcheological Evidence for Trophy-Taking in Prehistoric Central California. *American Journal of Physical Anthropology* 127:375–84.

Andrushko, Valerie A., Al W. Schwitalla, and Phillip L. Walker 2010. Trophy-Taking and Dismemberment as Warfare Strategies in Prehistoric Central California. *American Journal of Physical Anthropology* 141:83–96.

Bartelink, Eric J., Valerie Andrushko, Viviana Bellifemine, Irina Nechayev, and Robert J. Jurmain 2013. Violence and Warfare in the Prehistoric San Francisco Bay Area, California: Regional and Temporal Variations in Conflict. In *The Routledge Handbook of the Bioarchaeology of Human Conflict*, edited by Christopher Knüsel and Martin Smith, pp. 285–307. Oxford University Press, Oxford, UK.

Chelotti, Kristin L. 2013. Temporal Analysis of Craniofacial Trauma in Prehistoric California's Central Valley. Unpublished Master's thesis, Department of Anthropology, California State University, Chico.

Erlandson, Jon M., and Kevin Bartoy 1995. Cabrillo, the Chumash, and Old World Diseases. *Journal of California and Great Basin Anthropology* 17:153–73.

Groza, Randy 2002. *An AMS Chronology for Central California Olivella Shell Beads.* Unpublished Master's thesis, Department of Anthropology, California State University, San Francisco.

## The Bioarchaeological Record of Craniofacial Trauma | 271

Hughes, Richard E., and Randall T. Milliken 2007. Prehistoric Material Conveyance. In *California Prehistory: Colonization, Culture, and Complexity*, edited by Terry L. Jones and Kathryn A. Klar, pp. 259–72. AltaMira Press, Walnut Creek, CA.

Hull, Kathleen 2007. The Sierra Nevada: Archaeology in the Range of Light. In *California Prehistory: Colonization, Culture, and Complexity*, edited by Terry L. Jones and Kathryn A. Klar, pp. 177–90. Altamira Press, Walnut Creek, CA.

Jones, Terry, Gary M. Brown, L. Mark Raab, Janet L. Mcvickar, W. Geoffrey Spaulding, Douglas J. Kennett, Andrew York, and Phillip L. Walker 1999. Environmental Imperatives Reconsidered: Demographic Crises in Western North America During the Medieval Climatic Anomaly. *Current Anthropology* 40:137–210.

Jones, Terry L., and Al Schwitalla 2008. Archaeological Perspectives on the Effects of Medieval Drought in Prehistoric California. *Quaternary International* 188:41–58.

Jurmain, Robert, Eric J. Bartelink, Alan Leventhal, Viviana Bellifemine, Irina Nechayev, and Robert D. Jurmain 2001. Paleoepidemiological Patterns of Trauma in a Prehistoric Population from Central California. *American Journal of Physical Anthropology* 115:13–23.

Jurmain, Robert, and Vivienne Ines Bellifemine 1997. Patterns of Cranial Trauma in a Prehistoric Population from Central California. *International Journal of Osteoarchaeology* 7:43–50.

Jurmain, Robert D., Vivienne I. Bellifemine, Melynda Atwood, and Diane Digiuseppe 2009. Paleoepidemiological Patterns of Interpersonal Aggression in a Prehistoric Central California Population from CA-ALA-329. *American Journal of Physical Anthropology* 139:462–73.

Lambert, Patricia M. 1994. War and Peace on the Western Front: A Study of Violent Conflict and Its Correlates in Prehistoric Hunter-Gatherer Societies of Coastal California. Unpublished Ph.D. dissertation, Department of Anthropology, University of California, Santa Barbara.

—— 1997. Patterns of Violence in Prehistoric Hunter-Gatherer Societies of Coastal Southern California. In *Troubled Times: Violence and Warfare in the Past*, edited by Debra L. Martin and David W. Frayer, pp. 77–110. Routledge, New York.

Pilloud, Marin A. 2006. The Impact of the Medieval Climatic Anomaly in Prehistoric California: A Case Study from Canyon Oaks, CA-ALA-613/H. *Journal of California and Great Basin Anthropology* 26:57–69.

Preston, William P. 1996. Serpent in Eden: Dispersal of Foreign Diseases into Pre-Mission California. *Journal of California and Great Basin Anthropology* 18:3–37.

Raab, L. Mark, and Daniel O. Larson 1997. Medieval Climatic Anomaly and Punctuated Cultural Evolution in Coastal Southern California. *American Antiquity* 62:319–36.

Schwitalla, Al W. 2010. The Medieval Climatic Anomaly in Central California: Environmental Imperatives Reconsidered from a Bioarchaeologial Perspective. Unpublished Master's thesis, Department of Anthropology, California State University, Sacramento.

—— 2013. *Global Warming in California: A Lesson from the Medieval Climatic Anomaly (A.D. 800–1350)*. Center for Archaeological Research at Davis No. 17. University of California, Davis.

Schwitalla, Al W., and Terry L. Jones 2012. A Land of Many Seasons: Bioarchaeology and the Medieval Climatic Anomaly Hypothesis in Central California. In *Contemporary Issues in California Archaeology*, edited by Terry L. Jones and Jennifer A. Perry, pp. 93–114. Left Coast Press, Walnut Creek, CA.

Schwitalla, Al W., Terry L. Jones, Marin A. Pilloud, Brian F. Codding, and Randy S. Wiberg 2014. Violence among Foragers: The Bioarchaeological Record from Central California. *Journal of Anthropological Archaeology* 33:66–83.

Stine, Scott 1994. Extreme and Persistent Drought in California and Patagonia during Mediaeval Time. *Nature* 369:546–49.

Walker, Phillip L. 1989. Cranial Injuries as Evidence of Violence in Prehistoric Southern California. *American Journal of Physical Anthropology* 80:313–23.

## 272 | Marin A. Pilloud, Al W. Schwitalla, and Terry L. Jones

Walker, Phillip L. 1997. Wife Beating, Boxing, and Broken Noses: Skeletal Evidence for the Cultural Patterning of Violence. In *Troubled Times: Violence and Warfare in the Past*, edited by Debra W. Frayer and David L. Martin, pp. 145–63. Routledge, New York.

Weiss, Elizabeth 2002. Drought-Related Changes in Two Hunter-Gatherer California Populations. *Quaternary Research* 58:393–6.

Willits, Nikki Ann 2011. Temporal Patterns of Skeletal Trauma among Native Americans in Prehistoric Central California. Upublished Master's thesis, Department of Anthropology, California State University, Chico.

Worth, J. E. 1995. *The Struggle for the Georgia Coast: An 18th-Century Spanish Retrospective on Guale and Mocama*. Anthropological Papers of the American Museum of Natural History No. 75. American Museum of Natural History, New York.

# 15

## Archaic Violence in Western North America: The Bioarchaeological Record of Dismemberment, Human Bone Artifacts, and Trophy Skulls from Central California

Al W. Schwitalla, Terry L. Jones, Randy S. Wiberg, Marin A. Pilloud, Brian F. Codding, and Eric C. Strother

> They showed themselves to be some-what crafty and thievish, for as soon as one stolen thing was taken from their hands they stole another, and we did not have eyes enough to watch and care for everything. So we resorted to the expedient of putting them out of camp and telling them goodbye in a good natured way, but this did not succeed, and one of them even became impudent with the commander who thus far had shown great patience with them. So, half angry, he took from the Indian a stick which he had in his hands, gave him a light blow with it and then threw the stick far away, thereupon all departed, talking rapidly and shouting loudly, which I suspected was a matter of threatening. Some of them came to see us, carrying bows and arrows, for all had very good ones and well made, the bow of good wood, small and wound with tendons like those we saw on the Channel (Santa Barbara), and the arrows of little reeds, very smooth, well made, and with flints, transparent and very sharp. One came with a scalp hanging from a pole. This did not please me, for it suggested war (Pedro Font, member of the Anza expedition, in Bay Miwok territory 1776 from Bolton [1930:376–7]).

When California began to embrace the New Archaeology in the 1970s, violence, with a few key exceptions (e.g., James and Graziani 1975; McCorkle 1978; Pastron et al. 1973), was often pushed

---

*Violence and Warfare among Hunter-Gatherers*, edited by Mark W. Allen and Terry L. Jones, 273–295. ©2014 Taylor & Francis. All rights reserved.

aside as a focus of anthropological research. In extreme cases (e.g., Margolin 1978) authors sought to consciously ignore this more unseemly aspect of the bioarchaeological and ethnographic record to promote unrealistically sublime portraits of the indigenous past. In most cases, however, neglect was more benign as researchers began to focus on issues of environment, subsistence, and ecology that de-emphasized the role of violence in the region's hunter-gatherer prehistory.

Popular in North America and beyond, the paradigmatic blinders of the 1970s and 1980s (see Keeley 1996) belied the fact that California ethnography attests to intergroup conflict and trophy taking (Johnson 2007; review by Lambert 2007a), andthat archaeologists had recognized evidence for violence and apparent trophies of conflict since the 1930s when several skull cache features, human calvarium bowls, and modified postcranial human bone elements were recovered from Early period cemeteries in the Sacramento–San Joaquin Delta region (Figure 15.1). Archaeologists interpreted these artifacts and features at the time as trophies of war (e.g., Heizer and Hewes 1938; Lillard and Purves 1936; Lillard et al. 1939; Schenck and Dawson 1929), and the sites that produced them (CA-SAC-107, CA-SJO-56, CA-SJO-68, and CA-SJO-142) also yielded human interments with multiple signs of violent perimortem trauma. As a result of these cumulative observations, the practice of trophy taking figured prominently in the early regional cultural taxonomy, more specifically as a characteristic attribute of the Early Horizon or Windmiller Pattern (Beardsley 1948, 1954; Heizer 1949; Ragir 1972), which is a distinctive complex centered around the Sacramento–San Joaquin Delta marked by ventrally extended burials with westerly orientation, and certain types of charmstones, stemmed and concave base projectile points, and square and rectangular *Olivella* shell beads. Windmiller is now recognized as one of several complexes that date between 3000 and 1000 cal BC (the Early period) in central California. Most researchers associate this period with diverse, broad-based, subsistence modes (e.g., Moratto 1984:201–2) that Fredrickson (1974) classified as "Middle Archaic." The latter featured increased sedentism and use of acorns, but lacked the intensive acorn focus and complex political structures that would appear later.

Following the lead of southern California archaeologists (e.g., Lambert 1994, 1997, 2007b; Walker 1989), recent studies have resurrected the evidence for violence in prehistoric central California, beginning first with site-specific bioarchaeological studies (e.g., Jurmain 2001; Jurmain and Bellifemine 1997; Jurmain et al. 2009; Reid 2010) and culminating most recently in multisite overviews (Allen 2012; Andrushko et al. 2005, 2010; Bartelink et al. 2013; Schwitalla et al. 2014) that have included attempts to reevaluate the temporal and spatial distribution of trophy taking and dismemberment (Andrushko et al. 2005, 2010; Lambert 2007a).

Archaic Violence in Western North America | 275

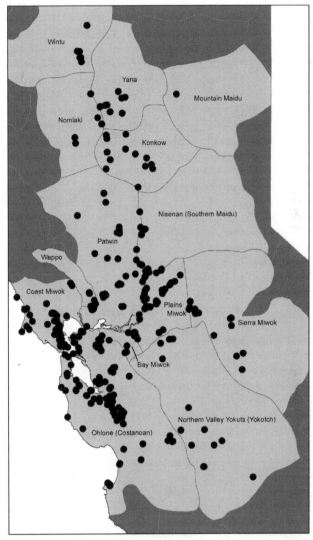

**Figure 15.1** Archaeological sites in the most recent version of the Central California Bioarchaeological Database.

Schwitalla et al. (2014) in particular delineated 87 cases from 37 sites in central California of modified human bones and/or limb dismemberment. These findings showed that this form of violence was not restricted to the Windmiller Culture, and that its apex occurred during the Early Middle period (500 BC–AD 420) or Fredrickson's (1974) Upper Archaic. These

## 276 | Al W. Schwitalla et al.

recent studies considered only a restricted range of evidence for trophy taking, specifically cases with cut and/or chop marks on bone as definitive physical evidence of the human bone manipulation. They did not take into consideration additional contextual evidence for violence and trophy taking. More specifically, the earlier studies did not consider cases of extra crania (or other body elements) recovered in situ from graves of completely articulated individuals or individual skeletons missing crania or other elements that were otherwise fully articulated. While these remains (or lack thereof) do not exhibit the physical evidence that has been highlighted in the previous studies, their context nonetheless suggests trophy-taking behavior, particularly when, as we show here, burials with these traits tend to co-occur at sites that also show physical evidence of trophy taking. Here, we redress the shortcomings of the earlier studies by summarizing both cases with physical evidence of human bone manipulation and contextual cases of skulls and other body elements interpreted as trophies from central California. In this manner, we attempt to demonstrate a connection between these various manifestations of violent interpersonal behavior.

## Materials and Methods

Evidence of trophy taking and trophies of war were reassessed with the most recent (2014) version of the Central California Bioarchaeological Database (CCBD) compiled by the lead author over the last 13 years. The CCBD is a meta-database created from both pre-existing archaeological site reports and current data generated by the principal analysts conducting the research. None of the studies reported here were specifically undertaken for the purposes of the current study, although four of us (Pilloud, Schwitalla, Strother, and Wiberg) have analyzed and reported on many of the burials (n=4,059) in the database in the past 35 years as part of cultural resource management (CRM) investigations. Results from earlier versions of the CCBD have been reported previously (Jones and Schwitalla 2008; Schwitalla 2010, 2013; Schwitalla and Jones 2012; Schwitalla et al. 2014). The database now includes information on 17,898 individuals from 355 archaeological sites and 19 ethnographic tribal territories compiled from published and unpublished archaeological site reports, osteological appendices, burial records, and NAGPRA (Native American Graves Protection and Repatriation Act) inventories. The geographic and ethnographic distribution of sites in the database is summarized in Tables 15.1 and 15.2, and Figure 15.1.

From the overall database we have identified all cases of four seemingly interrelated but distinctive forms of evidence for trophy taking and/ dismemberment: (1) human bones with physical evidence of scalping, decapitation, and/or dismemberment in the form of cut marks and/or

**Table 15.1** Summary of geographic and ethnographic distribution of burials in the Central California Bioarchaeological Database with evidence of trophy taking

| Ethnographic Territory | Geographic Region | N Sites | N Sites with Evidence of Trophy Taking | N Burials | Burials with Butchering | Human Bone Artifacts | Burials with Missing Elements | Burials with Extra Elements |
|---|---|---|---|---|---|---|---|---|
| Bay Miwok | SF Bay | 24 | 7 | 1,681 | 0 | 9 | 2 | 15 |
| Coast Miwok | SF Bay | 42 | 3 | 1,078 | 6 | 0 | 4 | 0 |
| Costanoan | SF Bay | 104 | 27 | 6,826 | 53 | 13 | 34 | 17 |
| Wappo | SF Bay | 2 | 0 | 26 | 0 | 0 | 0 | 0 |
| Hill Nomlaki | Sacramento Valley | 2 | 1 | 553 | 1 | 0 | 1 | 0 |
| Hill Patwin | Sacramento Valley | 5 | 2 | 317 | 2 | 2 | 0 | 0 |
| Konkow | Sacramento Valley | 10 | 1 | 256 | 0 | 0 | 0 | 4 |
| Maidu | Sacramento Valley | 1 | 0 | 14 | 0 | 0 | 0 | 0 |
| Nisenan | Sacramento Valley | 17 | 2 | 432 | 0 | 0 | 1 | 1 |
| River Nomlaki | Sacramento Valley | 4 | 0 | 31 | 0 | 0 | 0 | 0 |
| Plains Miwok | Sacramento Valley | 36 | 8 | 2,406 | 2 | 6 | 8 | 13 |
| River Patwin | Sacramento Valley | 9 | 4 | 344 | 4 | 0 | 14 | 2 |
| Southern Patwin | Sacramento Valley | 23 | 2 | 1,279 | 0 | 0 | 0 | 2 |
| Northern Valley Yokuts | San Joaquin Valley | 20 | 1 | 1,232 | 2 | 1 | 0 | 5 |
| Wintu | Sacramento Valley | 9 | 0 | 418 | 0 | 0 | 0 | 0 |
| Yana | Sacramento Valley | 10 | 1 | 91 | 1 | 0 | 0 | 0 |
| Central Sierra Miwok | Sierra Nevada | 3 | 0 | 27 | 0 | 0 | 0 | 0 |
| Northern Sierra Miwok | Sierra Nevada | 16 | 2 | 377 | 3 | 1 | 0 | 2 |
| Southern Sierra Miwok | Sierra Nevada | 18 | 1 | 510 | 1 | 0 | 0 | 0 |
| **Total** | | **355** | **62** | **17,898** | **75** | **32** | **64** | **61** |

# 278 | Al W. Schwitalla et al.

**Table 15.2** Summary of central California archaeological sites with trophy-taking evidence

| Site | Ethnographic Territory | N Cut Marks | N Human Bone Artifacts | N Missing Skeletal Elements | N Extra Skeletal Elements |
|---|---|---|---|---|---|
| ALA-12 | Costanoan | 0 | 1 | 2 | 0 |
| ALA-13 | Costanoan | 0 | 0 | 0 | 2 |
| ALA-42 | Costanoan | 0 | 0 | 1 | 1 |
| ALA-309 | Costanoan | 5 | 0 | 2 | 1 |
| ALA-328 | Costanoan | 6 | 0 | 5 | 1 |
| ALA-329 | Costanoan | 0 | 0 | 3 | 0 |
| ALA-343 | Costanoan | 3 | 1 | 1 | 2 |
| ALA-509 | Costanoan | 1 | 0 | 0 | 0 |
| ALA-613 | Costanoan | 9 | 2 | 4 | 0 |
| SBN-35 | Costanoan | 0 | 2 | 0 | 0 |
| SCL-6 | Costanoan | 0 | 0 | 1 | 0 |
| SCL-12 | Costanoan | 1 | 0 | 1 | 2 |
| SCL-38 | Costanoan | 1 | 0 | 1 | 0 |
| SCL-137 | Costanoan | 0 | 1 | 1 | 0 |
| SCL-194 | Costanoan | 2 | 0 | 0 | 1 |
| SCL-478 | Costanoan | 6 | 0 | 3 | 0 |
| SCL-674 | Costanoan | 12 | 6 | 5 | 0 |
| SCL-690 | Costanoan | 0 | 0 | 1 | 0 |
| SCL-732 | Costanoan | 3 | 0 | 0 | 0 |
| SCL-806 | Costanoan | 0 | 0 | 0 | 1 |
| SFR-4 | Costanoan | 1 | 0 | 0 | 0 |
| SMA-23 | Costanoan | 0 | 0 | 0 | 1 |
| SMA-110 | Costanoan | 0 | 0 | 0 | 1 |
| SMA-125 | Costanoan | 1 | 0 | 0 | 0 |
| SMA-335 | Costanoan | 0 | 0 | 0 | 2 |
| CCO-235 | Costanoan | 2 | 0 | 0 | 2 |
| CCO-474 | Costanoan | 0 | 0 | 3 | 0 |
| **Subtotal** | | **53** | **13** | **34** | **17** |
| MRN-5 | Coast Miwok | 1 | 0 | 1 | 0 |
| MRN-67 | Coast Miwok | 5 | 0 | 2 | 0 |
| MRN-242 | Coast Miwok | 0 | 0 | 1 | 0 |
| **Subtotal** | | **6** | **0** | **4** | **0** |
| CCO-138 | Bay Miwok | 0 | 0 | 0 | 1 |
| CCO-139 | Bay Miwok | 0 | 0 | 0 | 2 |
| CCO-141 | Bay Miwok | 0 | 0 | 1 | 0 |
| CCO-250 | Bay Miwok | 0 | 0 | 0 | 1 |
| CCO-309 | Bay Miwok | 0 | 7 | 0 | 0 |

(*Continued*)

## Archaic Violence in Western North America | **279**

**Table 15.2** (*Continued*)

| Site | Ethnographic Territory | N Cut Marks | N Human Bone Artifacts | N Missing Skeletal Elements | N Extra Skeletal Elements |
|---|---|---|---|---|---|
| CCO-548 | Bay Miwok | 0 | 2 | 1 | 10 |
| CCO-696 | Bay Miwok | 0 | 0 | 0 | 1 |
| **Subtotal** | | **0** | **9** | **2** | **49** |
| SAC-29 | Plains Miwok | 1 | 1 | 1 | 0 |
| SAC-67 | Plains Miwok | 1 | 0 | 0 | 0 |
| SAC-107 | Plains Miwok | 0 | 1 | 2 | 4 |
| SAC-151 | Plains Miwok | 0 | 0 | 0 | 1 |
| SJO-56 | Plains Miwok | 0 | 1 | 2 | 0 |
| SJO-68 | Plains Miwok | 0 | 2 | 0 | 6 |
| SJO-112 | Plains Miwok | 0 | 0 | 1 | 2 |
| SJO-142 | Plains Miwok | 0 | 1 | 2 | 0 |
| **Subtotal** | | **120** | **50** | **88** | **111** |
| CAL-14 | N. Sierra Miwok | 3 | 0 | 0 | 2 |
| CAL-99 | N. Sierra Miwok | 0 | 1 | 0 | 0 |
| **Subtotal** | | **3** | **1** | **0** | **2** |
| MAD-117 | S. Sierra Miwok | 1 | 0 | 0 | 0 |
| **Subtotal** | | | | | |
| MER-215 | N. Valley Yokuts | 0 | 0 | 0 | 3 |
| SJO-91 | N. Valley Yokuts | 2 | 1 | 0 | 2 |
| **Subtotal** | | **2** | **1** | **0** | **5** |
| SOL-364 | Hill Patwin | 1 | 2 | 0 | 0 |
| YOL-70 | Hill Patwin | 1 | 0 | 0 | 0 |
| **Subtotal** | | **2** | **2** | **0** | **0** |
| SOL-2 | S. Patwin | 0 | 0 | 0 | 1 |
| SOL-11 | S. Patwin | 0 | 0 | 0 | 1 |
| **Subtotal** | | **0** | **0** | **0** | **2** |
| COL-2 | River Patwin | 2 | 0 | 5 | 1 |
| COL-247 | River Patwin | 0 | 0 | 1 | 0 |
| YOL-13 | River Patwin | 1 | 0 | 8 | 1 |
| YOL-27 | River Patwin | 1 | 0 | 0 | 0 |
| **Subtotal** | | **4** | **0** | **14** | **2** |
| SAC-99 | Nisenan | 0 | 0 | 0 | 1 |
| YUB-1 | Nisenan | 0 | 0 | 1 | 0 |
| **Subtotal** | | **0** | **0** | **1** | **1** |
| TEH-10 | Hill Nomlaki | 1 | 0 | 1 | 0 |
| **Subtotal** | | **1** | **0** | **1** | **0** |
| BUT-90 | Konkow | 0 | 0 | 0 | 4 |
| **Subtotal** | | **0** | **0** | **0** | **4** |
| BUT-294 | Yana | 1 | 0 | 0 | 0 |
| **Subtotal** | | **1** | **0** | **0** | **0** |
| **Grand Total** | | **20** | **32** | **32** | **28** |

**Sources:** Schwitalla et al. (2014); Strother (2008); Waechter and Stevens (2013).

chop marks (Figure 15.2); (2) human bones modified into formal artifacts (Figure 15.3); (3) missing or repositioned cranial and/or postcranial skeletal elements from an otherwise articulated skeleton that suggest scalping, decapitation, or dismemberment by their context (Figure 15.4); and (4) crania

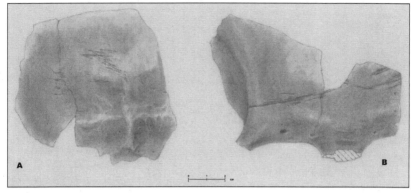

**Figure 15.2** Butchering marks as evidence of scalping from CA-MRN-67: (A) clustered incising cutmarks on the occipital region of the cranium, Burial 478; (B) clustered incising cutmarks on the frontal, right parietal region of the cranium, Burial 478. This young adult of indeterminate sex was interred during the Early period (2526 cal BC) (Illustrations by Phillip D. Schmidt).

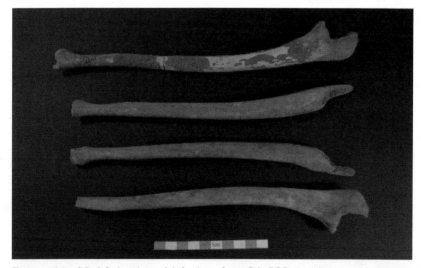

**Figure 15.3** Modified right and left ulnae from CA-SOL-364 (center two elements modified, and pictured alongside two unmodified right and left ulnae from the same Early Middle period site [210 cal BC–cal AD 420]) (Photograph courtesy of Al W. Schwitalla).

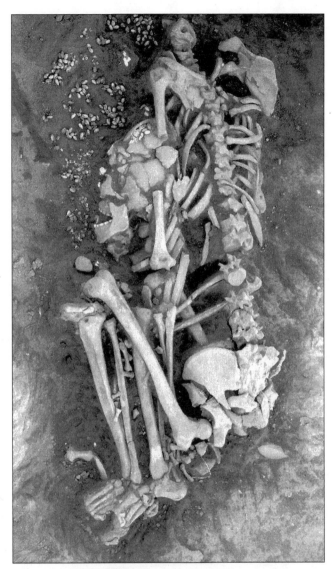

**Figure 15.4** Burial 44, an adult male, in situ, with a trophy skull at CA-ALA-42. Note: all cervical vertebrae are present and articulated for both Burial 44 and the trophy skull found next to and within the chest cavity of Burial 44 (Wiberg 1997), dating to the Middle-Late Transition (cal AD 1010–1210) (Photograph courtesy of Randy S. Wiberg).

and/or articulated postcranial elements found in contexts that suggest their use as trophies, either as isolates (Figure 15.5) or as additional skeletal segments associated with individual skeletons (Figure 15.6).

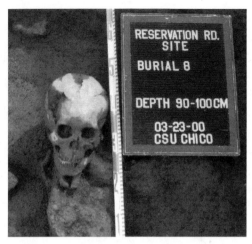

**Figure 15.5** Burial 8, a young adult female (20 years old), interred as an isolated skull, and deliberately oriented on a rock platform in association with other individuals that exhibited evidence of perimortem trauma at CA-COL-247 during the Early period (3050–500 cal BC) (White 2003). Placard reads "Reservation Rd. Site/Burial 8/Depth 90–100 cm/03-23-00/CSU Chico" (Photograph courtesy of Greg G. White).

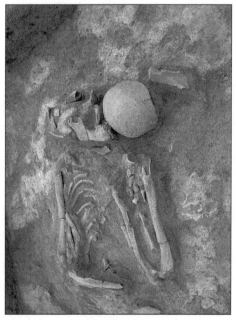

**Figure 15.6** Burial 137, adult male, interred with a trophy skull at CA-CCO-548, sometime during the Early period (3050–500 cal BC) (Photograph courtesy of Randy S. Wiberg).

Archaic Violence in Western North America | **283**

# Results

Among the 17,898 burials in the current database, 12,694 (70.9 percent) are adults (18 years or older at the time of death): 4,240 adult males, 4,437 adult females, and 4,017 adults of indeterminate or undetermined sex (Table 15.3). A total of 4,078 individuals (22.8 percent) are subadults of indeterminate sex, and 279 (1.6 percent) are older subadults/late adolescents for whom sex could be determined. A total of 847 (4.7 percent) burials have neither sex nor age determinations. Of the 355 sites in the database, a total of 62 (17.5 percent) show evidence for at least one of the four forms of trophy taking/dismemberment violence that we highlight here: 28 sites (7.9 percent) produced remains with cut or chop marks indicating butchering; 16 sites (4.5 percent) produced human bones fashioned into formal artifacts; 30 sites (8.5 percent) produced burials with missing elements; and 30 sites (8.5 percent) produced burials with extra elements or isolated skeletal segments. Many sites produced examples of multiple forms of trophy-taking–related violence; only one site, CA-ALA-343, produced examples of all four types, but 11 sites produced examples of three types, and 14 produced examples of two types. The following is a more detailed description of the findings for each of these forms of trophy-taking–related violence.

## Human Bones with Evidence of Butchering

Butchering is the most common form of trophy-taking–related violence in the database, with 75 cases from 28 sites (Figure 15.7A). The largest number from any single site was 12 (4.9 percent of 243) from CA-SCL-674 (Grady et al. 2001), though a nearby site, CA-SCL-478, also produced six examples (6.7 percent of 90) (Wiberg 2002). The ethnographic territory that produced the greatest number of examples was Costanoan (n=53) in the San Francisco Bay region, the area where the greatest amount of excavation has taken place. It was absent from nine ethnographic territories, although some are represented by small samples. The overall crude prevalence rate for the entire central California sample is 0.42 percent.

Interestingly, the majority of burials with butchering marks (n=44) were identified in mass graves containing two or three individuals. In all cases, the other individuals in the mass grave also exhibited physical evidence of violence. Mass graves with three individuals showing physical evidence of violence were uncovered at CA-ALA-309, CA-CAL-14, CA-MRN-67, and CA-SAC-67 (Missioni 1981; Skelton 1989; Strother 2004, 2013). Graves with two individuals with physical evidence were reported from CA-ALA-309, CA-ALA-328, CA-CCO-474, CA-MRN-5, CA-MRN-67, CA-SCL-194, CA-SCL-478 (n=3), CA-SCL-674 (n=6), CA-SCL-732, and CA-SJO-91 (Cambra et al. 1996; Evans et al. 2009; Grady et al. 2001; Johnson 1971; McW. Bickel 1976; Ryan 1972; Strother 2003, 2004, 2013; Wiberg 1993, 2002).

**Table 15.3** Demographic breakdown of burials in the Central California Bioarchaeological Database by ethnographic territory

| Ethnographic Territory | N Burials | | | | | | |
|---|---|---|---|---|---|---|---|
| | Adult Female | Adult Male | Adult Indeterminate (Sex) | Subadult Indeterminate (Sex) | Subadult Determinate (Sex) | Indeterminate for Age and Sex | Total |
| Bay Miwok | 375 | 370 | 624 | 276 | 14 | 22 | 1,681 |
| Coast Miwok | 232 | 281 | 277 | 222 | 5 | 61 | 1,078 |
| Costanoan | 1,746 | 1,888 | 1,179 | 1,627 | 148 | 238 | 6,826 |
| Wappo | 2 | 11 | 0 | 3 | 0 | 10 | 26 |
| Hill Nomlaki | 128 | 123 | 47 | 236 | 4 | 15 | 553 |
| Hill Patwin | 42 | 36 | 135 | 97 | 0 | 7 | 317 |
| Konkow | 55 | 50 | 85 | 52 | 8 | 6 | 256 |
| Maidu | 4 | 6 | 0 | 4 | 0 | 0 | 14 |
| Nisenan | 90 | 70 | 104 | 67 | 7 | 94 | 432 |
| River Nomlaki | 9 | 8 | 8 | 5 | 1 | 0 | 31 |
| Plains Miwok | 564 | 582 | 650 | 467 | 32 | 111 | 2,406 |
| River Patwin | 83 | 107 | 48 | 83 | 9 | 14 | 344 |
| Southern Patwin | 321 | 370 | 171 | 292 | 24 | 101 | 1,279 |
| Northern Valley Yokuts | 258 | 283 | 323 | 290 | 15 | 63 | 1,232 |
| Wintu | 44 | 52 | 142 | 95 | 0 | 85 | 418 |
| Yana | 27 | 24 | 15 | 23 | 2 | 0 | 91 |
| Central Sierra Miwok | 4 | 3 | 14 | 6 | 0 | 0 | 27 |
| Northern Sierra Miwok | 117 | 65 | 90 | 84 | 7 | 14 | 377 |
| Southern Sierra Miwok | 139 | 108 | 105 | 149 | 3 | 6 | 510 |
| **Total** | **4,240** | **4,437** | **4,017** | **4,078** | **279** | **847** | **17,898** |

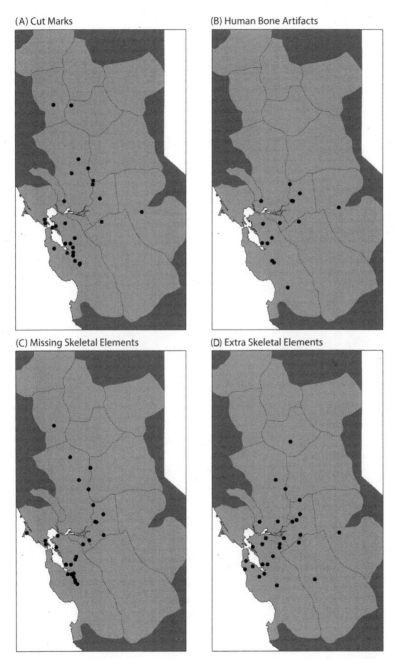

**Figure 15.7** Sites with skeletal evidence for trophy taking in central California: (A) burials with butchering/chop marks; (B) human bone artifacts; (C) missing elements; (D) extra or isolated elements.

286 | Al W. Schwitalla et al.

**Table 15.4** Human bones with evidence of butchering over time in central California

| | N Human Bones | | | |
|---|---|---|---|---|
| Time Period | Females | Males | Indeterminate | Total |
| 3050–500 BC | 0 | 3 | 3 | 6 |
| 500 BC–AD 420 | 7 | 30 | 4 | 41 |
| AD 420–1010 | 4 | 7 | 1 | 12 |
| AD 1010–1390 | 1 | 7 | 1 | 9 |
| AD 1390–1720 | 1 | 4 | 1 | 6 |
| AD 1720–1899 | 1 | 0 | 0 | 1 |
| Totals | 14 | 51 | 10 | 75 |

The sample exhibits demographic patterns similar to those reported previously by Andrushko et al. (2010) and Schwitalla et al. (2014): of 75 individuals, 51 (68 percent) are male; 14 (18.7 percent) are female; and 10 (13.3 percent) are indeterminate for sex. This suggests that males were at least three times more likely to be subjected to this type of violent behavior than females. Temporal patterning is also consistent with previously identified trends. The highest frequency of this form of violence was during the Early Middle period (500 cal BC–cal AD 420), representing a substantial increase from the preceding Early period (Table 15.4). Following this peak, the frequency of this form of violence generally declined; only two burials from the Protohistoric/Historic period (cal AD 1720–1899) showed this form of violent trauma.

## Human Bone Artifacts

Human bone artifacts and modified human elements have been considered previously as possible evidence for violence by Andrushko et al. (2010) and Schwitalla et al. (2014). These are the most uncommon examples of trophy-taking–related behavior, with total of only 32 specimens documented in the current version on the database from 16 sites (Figure 15.7B). All but five were associated with human burials. Seventeen artifacts were associated with eight male burials; seven were associated with five female burials, and three were associated with three indeterminate burials. The specific elements include eight femora, seven modified ulnae, seven radii, four calvaria, three tibiae, two fibulae, and one rib. Formal artifacts as defined by the typology of nonhuman bone implements for central California (Gifford 1940) include six femur daggers, four calvarium containers or skull bowls, one radius whistle, one tibia whistle, one femur whistle, one femur atlatl, one fibula pin, and one fibula dagger. The remaining artifacts exhibited various combinations of drilling, polishing, grinding, and asphaltum and/or shell bead applique. These artifacts were represented in only six ethnographic territories: Costanoan (n=13), Bay

# Archaic Violence in Western North America | **287**

**Table 15.5**  Human bone artifacts by burial association over time in central California

| | N Human Bone Artifacts | | | | |
|---|---|---|---|---|---|
| Time Period | Females | Males | Indeterminate | Isolate (nonassociated) | Total |
| 3050–500 BC | 1 | 11 | 1 | 3 | 16 |
| 500 BC–AD 420 | 5 | 6 | 1 | 0 | 12 |
| AD 420–1010 | 1 | 0 | 0 | 2 | 3 |
| AD 1010–1390 | 0 | 0 | 0 | 0 | 0 |
| AD 1390–1720 | 0 | 0 | 1 | 0 | 1 |
| AD 1720–1899 | 0 | 0 | 0 | 0 | 0 |
| **Totals** | **7** | **17** | **3** | **5** | **32** |

Miwok (n=9), Plains Miwok (n=6), Hill Patwin (n=2), Northern Sierra Miwok (n=1), and Northern Valley Yokuts (n=1). This spatial distribution extends well beyond the limits of the Windmiller Culture in that nearly half of the examples were recovered from the southern San Francisco Bay Area, which has never produced complete or definitive Windmiller assemblages. The temporal distribution of these modified elements, however, is chronologically consistent with the Early or Middle Archaic period in that highest frequency of these artifacts date to the Early period (n=16; 50 percent), followed by the Early Middle period (n=12; 37.5 percent), with only four (12.5 percent) examples recovered from contexts postdating cal AD 420 (Table 15.5). The production of human bone artifacts was clearly a pre–AD 1000 (Middle and Late Archaic) cultural activity that was not pursued by ethnographically observed groups.

While these artifacts have the least certain connection with violence—they could have been produced for a number of reasons and in a variety of cultural-behavioral contexts—nearly a third of them (n=10; 32.3 percent) were interred with burials that also showed physical signs of violence (butchering marks). In tandem, it is difficult to escape the conclusion that these artifacts were related to acts of war or violence.

## Burials with Missing or Repositioned Cranial and/or Postcranial Skeletal Elements from Otherwise Articulated Skeletons

Because prehistoric cemetery sites in central California have in most instances been subject to a variety of taphonomic disturbances (e.g., bioturbation, geomorphological shifting and deposition, and prehistoric, historic, and contemporary disturbance), it is generally accepted that a certain amount of post-interment movement of skeletal elements will occur. In light of these disturbances, this form of trophy-taking–related behavior

**288** | Al W. Schwitalla et al.

has been overlooked in studies that have emphasized only the physical evidence of violence. However, careful excavation and documentation of both skeletal articulation and zones of stratigraphic disturbance make it possible to distinguish taphonomic signatures from products of intentional human behavior. Archaeological field documentation for the 64 cases we have identified from 30 sites in the current database (Figure 15.7C) provides compelling evidence that these features are not the result of postmortem disturbance, but rather result from trophy taking. These features were recorded at 30 sites; the largest number from any single site was eight from CA-YOL-13 (6.5 percent of 124). The ethnographic territory that produced the greatest number of examples was Costanoan (n=34) in the San Francisco Bay region, but again this is the area that has experienced the most excavation. Burials of this type were absent from 12 ethnographic territories. The overall crude prevalence rate for the entire central California sample is 0.36 percent.

These burials show a range of missing elements; most common were instances of missing crania and mandibles (n=18); five had mandibles without crania. Also common were burials missing bones of the forearm (radius and ulna) (n=16) or lower legs (tibia, fibula and/or feet) (n=14). There were four cases where a cranium and mandible were present, but the position of the skull showed that it had been severed from the body and placed in an unnatural position, or articulating cervical vertebrae indicated that the skull belonged to a different individual entirely (see Figure 15.4). Importantly, many of the burials with missing elements also showed butchering marks on a different limb (n=21; 32.8 percent). Nineteen (29.7 percent) of these burials also showed evidence of projectile point/sharp force trauma. Twenty-four of the individual burials occurred as part of a mass grave containing two to four individuals. Eerkens et al. in Chapter 16 discuss this type of grave, demonstrating that the individuals in a mass grave had extralocal origins. The co-occurrence of the different types of evidence in a mass burial indicates fairly conclusively that the individuals were victims of violence/trophy taking related to some form of intergroup conflict/warfare.

The majority of the sample represented males (n=38; 59.4 percent); 15 (23.4 percent) were females, and the remainder was indeterminate. These percentages compare favorably with the physical evidence in suggesting that males were considerably more likely to be subjected to this type of violence than females. Temporal patterning is also consistent with the other indicators. The highest frequency of this form of violence was during the Early Middle period (500 cal BC–cal AD 420) (Table 15.6). Following this peak, the frequency of this form of violence initially declined during the Late Middle period, and then increased during the Middle-Late Transition. It was nearly absent during the Protohistoric/Historic period (n=1).

Archaic Violence in Western North America | **289**

**Table 15.6** Burials with missing or repositioned cranial or postcranial skeletal elements

| Time Period | N Burials | | | |
| --- | --- | --- | --- | --- |
| | Females | Males | Indeterminate | Total |
| 3050–500 BC | 3 | 5 | 2 | 10 |
| 500 BC–AD 420 | 6 | 11 | 3 | 20 |
| AD 420–1010 | 1 | 8 | 1 | 10 |
| AD 1010–1390 | 1 | 10 | 4 | 15 |
| AD 1390–1720 | 3 | 4 | 1 | 8 |
| AD 1720–1899 | 1 | 0 | 0 | 1 |
| **Totals** | **15** | **38** | **11** | **64** |

## Cranial and Postcranial Elements Found as Isolates or in Other Contexts Suggesting Use as Trophies

This form of trophy-taking–related violence was represented by 61 examples from 30 sites (Figure 15.7D). The largest number from any single site was 10 (4.9 percent of 243) from CA-CCO-548 (Wiberg 2010). The ethnographic territory that produced the greatest number of examples was Costanoan (n=17); however, this form of violence does not show a connection to the southern San Francisco Bay area, as do burials with physical evidence. Unlike the other indicators, the examples in Costanoan territory do not represent the majority of the overall sample, but rather a smaller proportion (27.9 percent). The overall crude prevalence rate for the entire central California sample is 0.34 percent.

By far the most common isolated element was the skull, represented by 47 examples; these included 23 isolated skulls, 20 skeletons interred with extra skulls, and four skull caches (containing 2 to 15 skulls each). In nearly all cases, archaeologists in the field described these features as "trophy skulls," and noted the absence of stratigraphic disturbances in the vicinity of the interment. In many cases the skulls were discovered atop or below artifacts, on platforms of stones, or oriented in certain ways that make them unmistakable as intentional features rather than products of disturbance or intrusion. Other isolated skeletal elements included four hands, two feet, two tibiae, and one fibula, all associated as extra elements in graves.

The majority of the trophy skulls and other elements were indeterminate (n=42; 68.9 percent) for sex; 12 (19.7 percent) could be identified as males, and the remainder (n=7; 11.5 percent) was female. Temporal patterning is similar to the other indicators, but not identical; the highest frequency of this form of violence was during the Early period (3000–500 cal BC) (Table 15.7). Following this peak, this form of violence declined during the Middle period, and then increased again during the Middle-Late Transition. It was nearly absent during the Late Prehistoric and Protohistoric/Historic periods.

**Table 15.7** Summary of cranial and postcranial elements found as isolates or in other contexts suggesting use as trophies from central California

| Time Period | N Cranial and Postcranial Elements | | | |
|---|---|---|---|---|
| | Females | Males | Indeterminate | Total |
| 3050–500 BC | 0 | 1 | 20 | 21 |
| 500 BC–AD 420 | 1 | 5 | 3 | 9 |
| AD 420–1010 | 1 | 1 | 6 | 8 |
| AD 1010–1390 | 4 | 3 | 11 | 18 |
| AD 1390–1720 | 0 | 2 | 2 | 4 |
| AD 1720–1899 | 1 | 0 | 0 | 1 |
| **Totals** | 7 | 12 | 42 | 61 |

## Summary and Conclusions

Archaeologists who conducted seminal excavations in central California in the 1930s and 1940s noted what to them seemed to be clear evidence of trophy taking in the form of isolated human skulls, extra skulls, repositioned skulls and other skeletal elements, and formal artifacts fashioned from human bone. At the time, these features and artifacts seemed to be most common in the Sacramento–San Joaquin Delta area during the Early Horizon or Early period (subsequently renamed the Windmiller Culture of the Middle Archaic period [Fredrickson 1974]). Following these early discoveries, violence and apparent products of violent behavior disappeared as foci of archaeological research in central California for several decades, only to reemerge in the early 2000s following the seminal studies of Lambert (1994, 1997) and Walker (1989) from the southern coast. The renewed interest in violence has included multiple studies of the evidence for trophy taking (Andrushko et al. 2005, 2010; Bartelink et al. 2013; Lambert 2007a; Schwitalla et al. 2014), to which the ethnographic and historic record attests. Until now, all of these more recent studies, including our own, have emphasized only the physical evidence for trophy taking in the form of skeletons exhibiting butchering marks and/ or formal artifacts made from human bones. Here we have resummarized those findings and combined them with the other signatures of trophy taking recognized in the 1930s and 1940s: (1) burials with missing or repositioned cranial and/or postcranial elements, and (2) crania and postcranial elements found as isolates or in other contexts suggesting use as trophies. By far the most common form of the latter are what can most simply be described as "trophy skulls."

Virtually all of the previous trophy-taking studies have concluded that this behavior was most common not during recent times, but rather during earlier periods of central California prehistory. Our compilation of four types of evidence from the regional database of 17,898 burials confirms that pattern,

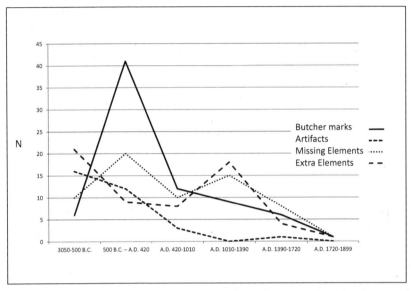

**Figure 15.8** Trends through time in trophy-taking features and artifacts in central California.

albeit with some important variations. All four forms of violence were at their highest frequencies during the Early (3000–500 cal BC) and/or Early Middle (500 cal BC–cal AD 420) periods, declining thereafter (Figure 15.8). Burials with physical evidence (butchering) show a distinctive apex during the Early Middle period, as do burials with missing elements. However, human bone artifacts and trophy skulls were at their all-time highest levels during the Early period, and declined thereafter. None of these signs of trophy taking are restricted to the Sacramento–San Joaquin Delta area; indeed, most show concentrations in the southern San Francisco Bay area. The exceptions to this are trophy skulls, which, although not absent from the San Francisco Bay area, do not show the same concentration in the south Bay as the other indicators. Burials with missing skulls and trophy skulls also appear to increase during the Middle-Late Transition (cal AD 1010–1390), but decrease afterwards. This later but less dramatic resurgence in trophy-related violence may reflect increased intergroup conflict related to the appearance of the bow and arrow between approximately cal AD 1000 and 1200 and/or drought-related resource scarcity during the Medieval Climatic Anomaly, as we have argued previously (Schwitalla et al. 2014).

Trophy-taking violence peaked in central California before serious economic intensification began. The latter is generally attributed to the Late Middle and Late periods. Lambert (2007a) and others (Andrushko et al. 2010;

## 292 | Al W. Schwitalla et al.

Schwitalla et al. 2014) have suggested that this violence is related to the intrusion of new groups into central California as indicated by the linguistic record (see Moratto 1984). Lambert (2007a) in particular reported some at least modest ethnographic support for the notion that head-taking was largely introduced into California by incoming Penutian language–speaking peoples, and that it was absent or much less common among speakers of Hokan languages who had settled California earlier. Almost certainly, ethnic conflict between residents and incoming migrants represents at least part of the explanation for the early evidence for trophy taking in central California, although our database, which contains information almost exclusively from the ethnographic territories of Penutian speakers, does not allow us to evaluate the Hokan-Penutian hypothesis directly. However, more attention also needs to be paid to the nature of economic and sociopolitical transitions between cal AD 420 and 1390 to sort out ethnic identities more clearly and develop a better understanding of the context of the diachronic variation in violence.

## References

Allen, Mark W. 2012. A Land of Violence. In *Contemporary Issues in California Archaeology*, edited by Terry L. Jones and Jennifer E. Perry, pp. 93–114. Left Coast Press, Walnut Creek, CA.

Andrushko, Valerie A., Kate Latham, Diane Grady, Allen Pastron, and Phillip L. Walker 2005. Bioarcheological Evidence for Trophy-Taking in Prehistoric Central California. *American Journal of Physical Anthropology* 127:375–84.

Andrushko, Valerie A., Al W. Schwitalla, and Phillip L. Walker 2010. Trophy-taking and Dismemberment as Warfare Strategies in Prehistoric Central California. *American Journal of Physical Anthropology* 141:83–96.

Bartelink Eric J., Valerie Andrushko, Viviana Bellifemine, Irina Nechayev, and Robert J. Jurmain 2013. Violence and Warfare in the Prehistoric San Francisco Bay Area, California: Regional and Temporal Variations in Conflict. In *The Routledge Handbook of the Bioarchaeology of Human Conflict*, edited by Christopher Knüsel and Martin Smith, pp. 285–307. Oxford University Press, Oxford, UK.

Basgall, Mark E. 1987. Resource Intensification among Hunter-Gatherers: Acorn Economies in Prehistoric California. *Research in Economic Anthropology* 9:21–52.

Beardsley, Richard K. 1948. Culture Sequences in Central California Archaeology. *American Antiquity* 14:1–28.

———— 1954. Temporal and Areal Relationships in Central California Archaeology. *University of California Archaeological Survey Reports* 24:1–62; 25:63–131.

Bolton, Herbert E. (editor) 1930. *Anza's California Expeditions*. 5 volumes. University of California Press, Berkeley.

Cambra, Rosemary, Alan Leventhal, Laura Jones, Julia Hammett, Les Field, Norma Sanchez, and Robert Jurmain 1996. Archaeological Investigations at Kaphan Umux (Three Wolves) Site, CA-SCL-732: A Middle Period Prehistoric Cemetery on Coyote Creek in Southern San Jose, Santa Clara County, California. Ohlone Families Consulting Services and the San Jose State Academic Foundation. Submitted to Santa Clara County Traffic Authority and the California Department of Transportation, District 4.

Evans, Sally R., Craig P. Smith, and Cassandra Chattan 2009. Results of an Archaeological Monitoring Program for the Construction of the Fireside Inn Affordable Housing Project, at

## Archaic Violence in Western North America | **293**

the Site of CA-MRN-05/H 115 Shoreline Highway, Mill Valley, Marin County, California. Archaeological Resource Services, Petaluma, California. Copies available from California Historic Resources Information Center, Sonoma State University, Rohnert Park.

Fredrickson, David A. 1974. Cultural Diversity in Early Central California: A View from the North Coast Ranges. *Journal of California Anthropology* 1:41–54.

Gifford, Edward W. 1940. Californian Bone Artifacts. *University of California Anthropological Records* 3:153–237.

Grady, Diane L., Kate A. Latham, and Valerie A. Andrushko 2001. *Archaeological Investigations at CA-SCL-674, the Rubino Site, San Jose, Santa Clara County, California.* Coyote Press Archives of California Prehistory, Salinas, CA.

Heizer, Robert F. 1949. The Archaeology of Central California I: The Early Horizon. Anthropological Records Vol. 12:1. University of California Press, Berkeley.

Heizer, Robert F., and Gordon W. Hewes 1938. Animal Ceremonialism in Central California in Light of Archaeology. *American Anthropologist* 42:587–603.

James, Steven R., and S. Graziani 1975. California Indian Warfare. *Contributions of the University of California Archaeological Research Facility* 23:47–109.

Johnson, Jerald J. 1971. Preliminary Report on the French Camp Slough Site (CA-SJO-91). Report on file at the Department of Anthropology, Archaeological Study Center, California State University, Sacramento.

Johnson, John R. 2007. Ethnohistoric Descriptions of Chumash Warfare. In *North American Indigenous Warfare and Ritual Violence*, edited by Richard J. Chacon and Rubén G. Mendoza, pp. 74–113. University of Arizona Press, Tucson.

Jones, Terry L., and Al W. Schwitalla 2008. Archaeological Perspectives on the Effects of Medieval Drought in Prehistoric California. *Quaternary International* 188:41–58.

Jurmain, Robert D. 2001. Paleoepidemiological Patterns of Trauma in a Prehistoric Population from Central California. *American Journal of Physical Anthropology* 115:13–23.

Jurmain, Robert D., and Vivienne I. Bellifemine 1997. Patterns of Cranial Trauma in a Prehistoric Population from Central California. *International Journal of Osteoarchaeology* 7:43–50.

Jurmain, Robert, Eric J. Bartelink, Alan Leventhal, Viviana Bellifemine, Irina Nechayev, Melynda Atwood, and Diane DiGiuseppe 2009. Paleoepidemiological Patterns of Interpersonal Aggression in a Prehistoric Central California Population from CA-ALA-329. *American Journal of Physical Anthropology* 139:462–73.

Keeley, Lawrence H. 1996. *War Before Civilization.* Oxford University Press, New York.

Lambert, Patricia M. 1994. War and Peace on the Western Front: A Study of Violent Conflict and its Correlates in Prehistoric Hunter-Gatherer Societies of Coastal Southern California. Unpublished Ph.D. dissertation, Department of Anthropology, University of California, Santa Barbara.

———— 1997. Patterns of Violence in Prehistoric Hunter-Gatherer Societies of Coastal Southern California. In *Troubled Times: Violence and Warfare in the Past*, edited by Debra L. Martin and David W. Frayer, pp. 77–109. Gordon and Breech Publishers, Amsterdam, the Netherlands.

———— 2007a. Ethnographic and Linguistic Evidence for the Origins of Human Trophy Taking in California. In *The Taking and Displaying of Human Body Parts as Trophies by Amerindians*, edited by Richard J. Chacon and David H. Dye, pp. 65–89. Springer, New York.

———— 2007b. The Osteological Evidence for Indigenous Warfare in North America. In *North American Indigenous Warfare and Ritual Violence*, edited by Richard J. Chacon and Rueben G. Mendoza, pp. 202–21. University of Arizona Press, Tucson.

Lillard, Jeremiah B., and Wiliam K. Purves 1936. *The Archaeology of the Deer Creek-Cosumnes Area Sacramento County, California.* Sacramento Junior College, Department of Anthropology, Bulletin No. 1. Sacramento Junior College, Board of Education. Sacramento, CA.

Lillard, Jeremiah B., Robert F. Heizer, and Franklin Fenenga 1939. *An Introduction to the Archeology of Central California.* Sacramento Junior College, Department of Anthropology, Bulletin No. 2. Sacramento Junior College, Board of Education. Sacramento, CA.

294 | Al W. Schwitalla et al.

Margolin, Malcom 1978. *The Ohlone Way*. Heyday Books, Berkeley, CA.

McCorkle, Thomas 1978. Intergroup Conflict. In *California*, edited by Robert F. Heizer, pp. 694–700. Handbook of North American Indians, Vol. 8, William C. Sturtevant, general editor. Smithsonian Institution Press, Washington, D.C.

McW. Bickel, Polly 1976. Toward a Prehistory of the San Francisco Bay Area: The Archaeology of Sites CA-ALA-328, ALA-13, and ALA-12. Unpublished Ph.D. dissertation, Department of Anthropology, Harvard University, Cambridge, MA.

Missioni, Sandie 1981. Human Skeletal Analysis of Burial 1 at CA-SAC-67, The Brown Site, Accession Number 81-74. Department of Anthropology, Archaeological Study Center, California State University, Sacramento.

Moratto, Michael J. 1984. *California Archaeology*. Academic Press, Orlando, FL.

Pastron, Allen G., Carl William Clewlow, and Paul T. Atkinson 1973. Aboriginal Warfare in Northern California. *The Masterkey* 47:136–42.

Ragir, Sonia 1972. The Early Horizon in Central California Prehistory. *Contributions of the University of California Archaeological Research Facility* No. 15. Department of Anthropology, University of California, Berkeley.

Reid, Phillip G. 2010. Osteological Evidence of Trauma and Interpersonal Violence at CA-ALA-343 in Fremont, California. Unpublished Master's thesis, Department of Anthropology, California State University, San Francisco.

Ryan, Dennis J. 1972. The Paleopathology of Ala-328: The Relationships among Disease, Culture, and Environment in a California Indian Population. Unpublished Master's thesis, Department of Anthropology, San Francisco State College, San Francisco, CA.

Schenck, Egbert W., and Elmer J. Dawson 1929. Archaeology of the Northern San Joaquin Valley. *University of California Publications in American Archaeology and Ethnology* 23:123–46.

Schwitalla, Al W. 2010. The Medieval Climatic Anomaly in Central California: Environmental Imperatives Reconsidered from a Bioarchaeological Perspective. Unpublished Master's thesis, Department of Anthropology, California State University, Sacramento.

—— 2013. *Global Warming in California: A Lesson from the Medieval Climatic Anomaly (A.D. 800–1350)*. Center for Archaeological Research at Davis Publication No. 17. Department of Anthropology, University of California, Davis.

Schwitalla, Al W., and Terry L. Jones 2012. A Land of Many Seasons: Bioarchaeological Signatures of the Medieval Climatic Anomaly in Central California. In *Contemporary Issues in California Archaeology*, edited by Terry L. Jones and Jennifer E. Perry, pp. 93–114. Left Coast Press, Walnut Creek, CA.

Schwitalla, Al W., Terry L. Jones, Marin A. Pilloud, Brian F. Codding, and Randy S. Wiberg 2014. Violence among Foragers: The Bioarchaeological Record from Central California. *Journal of Anthropological Archaeology* 33:66–83.

Skelton, Randall R. 1989. Osteological Analysis at CA-CAL-14/405. In Data Recovery of CA-CAL-14/405, A Prehistoric Period Site at Vallecito, Calaveras County, California, by Neal Neuenschwander and Ann S. Peak, pp. 142–209. Unpublished report prepared for Calaveras County Water District, San Andreas, California. Peak and Associates, Inc. Sacramento, CA.

Strother, Eric C. 2003. Songs of Insult: Study of Perimortem Cutmarks on Human Bone at CA-CCO-474/H. Unpublished Master's thesis, Department of Anthropology, California State University, Hayward.

—— 2004. Osteological Analysis at CA-ALA-309. In Report on the Madison Marquette Bay Street Project Burial Removal and Construction Monitoring CA-ALA-309 and CA-ALA-310, Emeryville, Alameda County, California, prepared by Heather Price, Eric Strother, Jennifer Price, Aimee Arrigoni, Marin Pilloud, Lisa Valkenier, James Allan, and William Self, pp. 120–79. Unpublished report prepared by William Self and Associates, Inc. Orinda, CA.

—— 2008. Osteological Analysis at CA-SCL-12. In Data Recovery, Burial Removal and Construction Monitoring at the Moffett Towers Project, CA-SCL-12/H Sunnyvale, Santa

# Archaic Violence in Western North America | **295**

Clara County, California, edited by Aimee Arrigoni, Drew Bailey, David Buckley, Angela Cook, Allen Estes, Paul Farnsworth, Melinda Hickman, and Eric Strother, pp. 87–122. William Self and Associates, Inc., Orinda, CA.

Strother, Eric C. 2013. Preliminary Analysis of Mortuary and Trauma Patterns at CA-MRN-67. Holman and Associates, San Francisco, California.

Waechter, Sharon A., and Nathan E. Stevens 2013. Report On Archaeological Monitoring And Salvage Excavations At CA-SBN-35/H Near San Juan Bautista, California. Far Western Anthropological Research Group, Inc., Davis, CA. Report submitted to Pacific Gas & Electric Company, San Ramon, CA.

Walker, Phillip L. 1989. Cranial Injuries as Evidence of Violence in Prehistoric Southern California. *American Journal of Physical Anthropology* 80:313–23.

White, Gregory G. 2003. Final Report of Testing and Mitigation at Four Sites on the Level (3) Long Haul Fiber Optic Alignment, Colusa County, California. Unpublished report prepared for Kiewit Pacific Corporation, Concord, CA. California State University, Chico Archaeological Research Program Reports No. 42, California State University, Chico.

Wiberg, Randy S. 1993. Archaeological Impact Mitigation at CA-SCL-194: Report of Native American Burials and Archaeological Data Recovered during Construction Monitoring at the AvenidaEspana Senior Housing Project, San Jose, Santa Clara County, California. Unpublished report submitted to the Housing Authority of the County of Santa Clara, San Jose, CA. Holman and Associates Archaeological Consultants, San Francisco, CA.

—— 1997. Archaeological Investigations at Site CA-ALA-42, Alameda County, California: Final Report. Report prepared for Standard Pacific of Northern California, Pleasanton, CA. Holman and Associates Archaeological Consultants, San Francisco, CA.

—— 2002. Archaeological Investigations: Skyport Plaza Phase I (CA-SCL-478), San Jose, Santa Clara County, California. Unpublished report prepared for Spieker Properties, San Jose, CA. Holman and Associates Archaeological Consultants, San Francisco, CA.

—— 2010. Archaeological Investigations at CA-CCO-18/548: Final Report for the Vineyards at Marsh Creek, Contra Costa County, California. Report prepared for Shea Homes, Brentwood, CA. Holman and Associates, San Francisco, CA.

# 16

## Stable Isotope Perspectives on Hunter-Gatherer Violence: Who's Fighting Whom?

*Jelmer W. Eerkens, Eric J. Bartelink, Karen S. Gardner, and Traci L. Carlson*

The study of the human capacity for violence has been a major area of anthropological interest for more than a century (Chagnon 1988; Ember and Ember 1995; Ferguson 1984; Ferguson and Whitehead 1992; Gat 2000; Haas 1990; Keeley 1996; Lambert 2002; Martin and Frayer 1997; Otterbein 1994; Turney-High 1971; Walker 2001; Wrangham and Peterson 1996). The study of the origins and causes of interpersonal violence has drawn heavily from the ethnographic record (Ember and Ember 1995; Keeley 1996) and comparative studies of primates (Boesch et al., 2008; Knauft 1991; Wrangham and Glowacki 2012; Wrangham and Peterson 1996; Wrangham et al. 2006).

Archaeologists have more recently addressed the importance of interpersonal violence and warfare in prehistory, including among hunter-gatherers (Arkush and Allen 2006; Keeley 1996; LeBlanc 1999; Martin and Frayer 1997; Martin et al. 2012). Bioarchaeological studies in particular have played an important role in this field (Andrushko et al. 2005, 2010; Chacon and Dye 2007; Keeley 1996; Lambert 2002; Maschner and Reedy-Maschner 1998; Milner 1995; Walker 2001). By contrast, stable isotope analysis has played just a minor role in such studies. In this chapter, we aim to demonstrate the tremendous potential for this line of investigation to inform our understanding of violence in prehistory.

---

*Violence and Warfare among Hunter-Gatherers*, edited by Mark W. Allen and Terry L. Jones, 296–313. ©2014 Taylor & Francis. All rights reserved.

In California, ethnohistoric and ethnographic accounts (e.g., Cook 1976a; Font [1776] 1930; Langsdorff 1968) are suggestive of intermittent warfare and at least a moderate level of interpersonal violence (Lambert 2007; Milliken 1995). These accounts indicate that ambushes and raids resulted from disputes over territory, access to food and raw materials, for revenge, and for acquiring marriage partners, typically females (James and Graziani 1975). Archaeological studies show that evidence of prehistoric interpersonal violence is relatively common (Allen 2012; Andrushko et al. 2005, 2010; Bartelink et al. 2013; Broughton et al. 2010; DiGiuseppe 2009; Grady et al. 2001; Jurmain 1991, 2001; Jurmain and Bellifemine 1997; Jurmain et al. 2009; Lambert 1994, 1997; Nelson 1997; Schwitalla 2013; Walker 1989; Weiss 2006; Wiberg 2002). The factors behind such violence have been debated. For example, high rates of projectile point injury between approximately AD 300 and 1500 in the Santa Barbara Channel area occur alongside severe drought conditions corresponding to the Medieval Climatic Anomaly (Jones and Schwitalla 2008; Jones et al. 1999).

Although studies of antemortem trauma on human remains are of interest for reconstructing patterns of skeletal injury in a past society, evidence of perimortem trauma is most likely to reflect the death event and provide a possible context, for example, where a nonlocal individual may have been killed and subsequently buried outside their natal territory. It is within this context in particular that stable isotopes can be used to determine whether victims of violence are most likely foreign or local to the area where they were buried. Because stable isotope ratios in human tissues reflect diet and migration history, they can be used as tracers for determining where particular individuals are from. Here we examine three archaeological cases studies from central California, each representing multiple victims of violence likely tied to a single event. We use a multi-isotope approach to assess whether the victims are likely local or nonlocal to the area where they were interred. We then highlight the potential of isotope studies to answer much broader questions regarding the nature of interpersonal violence in prehistory in future research.

## Stable Isotopes

Humans synthesize biological tissues, including bone and teeth, from the food and water they consume. A wide range of biomolecules (e.g., lipids, amino acids, sugars, water) are extracted from food and water and used to synthesize new biomolecules and, eventually, human tissues. Many of the elements comprising these biomolecules have multiple stable isotopes, the ratios of which can be measured today using mass spectrometers.

Various physical and biological processes fractionate the stable isotopes of elements. As a result, the ratios of stable isotopes can vary across geological formations, geographic regions, and/or biological systems. When humans eat foods from a particular region, isotopic signatures are incorporated into

**298** | Jelmer W. Eerkens et al.

bones and teeth. In the analyses in this chapter, we examine isotopic signatures preserved in human bone. Bone is a living tissue that continually remodels during life, and includes organic (collagen) and inorganic (apatite) components, each of which can be analyzed for their stable isotope composition. Estimates of elemental—and hence isotopic—turnover in human bone vary depending on the particular bone and bone tissue (e.g., cortical versus cancellous). Generally, human bone records a signature representing the last 10 to 20 years of life (Schwarcz and Schoeninger 1991), giving us an averaged signal of where a person was living during that window of time. Our main aim in the study is to compare isotopic signals preserved in the bones of victims of violence against signals preserved in either local rodents or other humans lacking evidence of violence. Analyses focus on five different stable isotope ratios of the elements carbon (C), nitrogen (N), oxygen (O), sulphur (S), and strontium (Sr).

Stable C and N isotopes are typically used to study the paleodiet of individuals (Schoeninger 1985); however, because different foods vary in their spatial distribution, they can also provide data on paleogeography. In central California, carbon isotopes ($^{13}C/^{12}C$, expressed as $\delta^{13}C$) can provide a signature of the consumption of marine versus terrestrial foods (Bartelink 2006, 2009; DeNiro and Schoeninger 1983; Eerkens et al. 2013; Kellner and Schoeninger 2007; Schwarcz and Schoeninger 1991), and thus acts as a tracer of individuals living in coastal or estuarine environments.

Nitrogen isotopes ($^{15}N/^{14}N$, expressed as $\delta^{15}N$) reflect the general trophic level of consumed foods (Ambrose 1993; DeNiro and Epstein 1981; Schoeninger 1985). In terrestrial systems in central California, there are essentially three trophic levels: plants, herbivores, and carnivores. By contrast, in aquatic environments, including fresh, brackish, and marine, there are more trophic levels, resulting in greater enrichment of $^{15}N$ at the top of the food chain (typically large fish, predatory birds, and aquatic mammals). Thus, $\delta^{15}N$ values can help discriminate the spatial location of individuals living near large aquatic systems. In central California, such systems include the Pacific Coast, San Francisco Bay, the brackish-water Suisun Marsh, the California Delta, and the Sacramento River (Eerkens et al. 2013).

The oxygen needed to synthesize apatite in bone and teeth is derived mainly from imbibed water (Bryant et al. 1996; Kohn 1996; Longinelli 1984; Sponheimer and Lee-Thorp 1999). Oxygen isotope ratios ($^{18}O/^{16}O$, expressed as $\delta^{18}O$) in water are not constant around the world and vary greatly with latitude, elevation, and distance from large bodies of water. In central California there is a steep east-west gradient in $\delta^{18}O$ in surface waters due to fractionation effects on water during precipitation (Kendall and Coplen 2001; Unnikrishna et al. 2002). This high contrast assists in bracketing different geographic regions for $\delta^{18}O$ and, again, allows us to trace the approximate location of an individual while different tissues were forming.

The ratio of $^{87}Sr$ to $^{86}Sr$ varies as a function of geologic age in sediments (Capo et al. 1998; Faure 1986; Faure and Hurley 1963). Plants take up Sr from the soil and pass it up the food chain with little to no modification. Because most small-scale societies obtain the majority of their food from locations near their residence, Sr signatures in biological tissues generally reflect the geographic residence of an individual. Our studies are focused on Sr isotope signatures in bone, hence tracing the geographic location of an individual in the last 10 to 20 years of their life. In central California, there is a general north-south gradient in Sr isotope ratios in bedrock in the Sierra Nevada, though Sr isotopes in the coastal ranges are more complex.

Finally, sulfur isotopes ($^{34}S/^{32}S$, expressed as $\delta^{34}S$) have only recently been used in archaeology (Craig et al. 2006; Nehlich et al. 2010; Richards et al. 2003). Sulfur is passed up the food web from the soil to plants and animals with little fractionation. $\delta^{34}S$ varies in nature from −20 to +22 per mil, with high values reflecting heavy marine diets and lower values reflecting greater input from terrestrial organisms. Although less is known about underlying bedrock $\delta^{34}S$ distributions in central California, we use this isotope ratio to compare victims of violence with others buried in the cemetery.

## Three Case Studies

Using this isotopic approach, we examine three case studies from central California (Figure 16.1). Each represents a clear case of violent death, where a group of males had been killed and placed in a single pit in what are

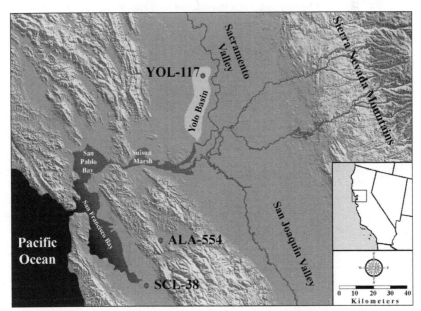

**Figure 16.1** Location of the three central California case studies discussed in the text.

distinctively nontraditional burial styles. Our goal in each case is to ascertain whether these males were "locals" to the site, and thus likely affiliated with the rest of the population, or whether they represent outsiders who came from another region. For a baseline comparison for the stable isotopes, we use either archaeological rodents from the region, or other humans from the site.

## CA-YOL-117

The archaeological site CA-YOL-117 is located within the Yolo Basin, a major spillway of the Sacramento River in central California (see Figure 16.1). The site is a small elevated mound and includes a range of habitation debris consistent with occupation during the last 700 years of prehistory. Unfortunately, in spite of small-scale excavations, a report was never written, and little is known about the site in general.

In 1964, a farmer was modifying the mound and discovered human bone. Subsequently, the skeletal remains and associated artifacts of three individuals were salvaged by Martin Baumhoff of the University of California at Davis Anthropology Department, prior to additional bulldozing disturbance. The three individuals were not buried in flexed positions, in what would have been a "traditional" style. Instead, they appear to be more haphazardly placed into a single pit in a semi-extended position. Figure 16.2 represents a reconstruction of the mass burial based on field sketch map made in 1964.

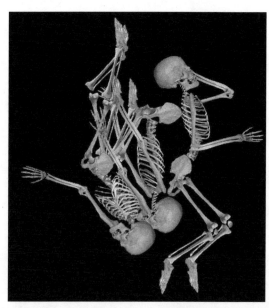

**Figure 16.2** Mass burial pit from CA-YOL-117, reconstructed from 1964 field sketch.

Stable Isotope Perspectives on Hunter-Gatherer Violence | **301**

All three individuals were young adult males, with little evidence of pathological conditions or indicators of nutritional stress. Multiple projectile points consistent with arrows were found in the ribcages of all three individuals (but not embedded in the bone). In addition, one had obsidian embedded in the vertebral column and another had cut marks on the vertebral column consistent with perimortem wounds caused by a projectile point. Together, the data strongly suggest all three individuals died as part of a single violent event.

Radiocarbon dates were obtained on all three of the burials from collagen extracted from bone. Uncalibrated, these dates are $460 \pm 25$, $395 \pm 25$, and $480 \pm 25$ years before present (BP) (Burials 2, 3, and 4, respectively). The dates were calibrated using the online version of CALIB 5.1 (Stuiver et al. 2005). Assuming these individuals lived contemporaneously, as suggested by the single pit, then overlap in the calibrated radiocarbon dates should provide the most likely interval during which the individuals were killed. The three calibrated radiocarbon dates overlap in their 95 percent confidence intervals between AD 1440 and 1450, suggesting the three men were killed close to this window of time.

## Stable Isotope Results

Lacking other human burials from this site for comparison, we resort to using seven prehistoric rodent bones associated with four sites within 20 km of CA-YOL-117 (CA-SAC-43, CA-SOL-271, CA-YOL-197, and CA-YOL-229), to establish a "local" isotopic signature. Sr and O stable isotope ratios were measured on hydroxylapatite from these faunal samples as well as the three males from CA-YOL-117. In addition, C and N isotopes were measured on bone collagen from the three males.

The Sr and O data are presented in Figure 16.3. The local rodents appear as open circles near the lower middle area of the graph. By comparison, the CA-YOL-117 males appear as open diamonds below the local rodents. As seen in the graph, although there is overlap in $\delta^{18}O$ values, the Sr isotope values clearly distinguish the humans from the local signature. This suggests these males were not local to the Yolo Basin region.

Instead, based on comparisons with data from Jorgenson et al. (2009), Eerkens et al. (2014), and unpublished data, it appears that these individuals were living to the north of the Yolo Basin. Further, $\delta^{13}C$ data indicate that these individuals did not live on the coast, though they may have been consuming minor amounts of marine-derived protein (e.g., anadromous salmon; see Figure 16.4). $\delta^{15}N$ values indicate they probably consumed significant amounts of protein derived from an aquatic environment where the food chain is lengthened.

All together, we believe these individuals were not local to CA-YOL-117, and were living to the north of the Yolo Basin, most likely along the Sacramento River. If so, the minor marine carbon signature present in bone collagen could represent consumption of small amounts of migrating anadromous salmon

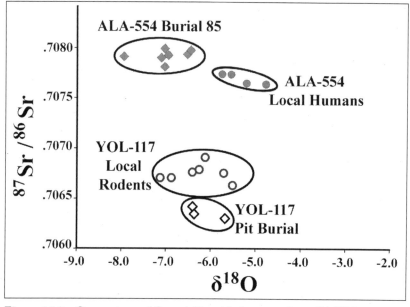

**Figure 16.3** Comparison of Sr and O stable isotopes from CA-YOL-117 and CA-ALA-554 samples.

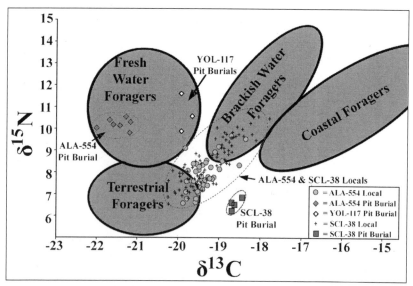

**Figure 16.4** $\delta^{13}C$ and $\delta^{15}N$ in bone collagen for pit burials ("nonlocals") from CA-ALA-554, CA-SCL-38, CA-YOL-117, and "locals" from CA-ALA-554 and CA-SCL-38, and expected ranges for central California environmental zones.

available in that region. We do not know why they were in the Yolo Basin, away from their homeland, but now know they were killed and buried there.

## CA-ALA-554

CA-ALA-554 is located in the north-south–trending Amador Valley in the modern-day city of Pleasanton. A large and perrennial water source, Arroyo Creek, runs just to the west of the site and would have provided inhabitants a range of foods and water. Amador Valley lies between San Francisco Bay (20 km to the west) and the Central Valley (35 km to the east). Judging by the high density of archaeological sites, the valley was home to high population densities in prehistoric times.

Excavation of the burials discussed here took place in 2011 as part of a salvage project for a strip mall and parking lot. During excavation, a range of domestic features, midden, and other materials were found, indicating the presence of a significant habitation site. Moreover, 160 burials containing the skeletal remains of nearly 200 individuals were discovered.

Included among the burials is a mass burial (Burial 85; see Figure 16.5) containing the remains of seven young adult males. These males were buried

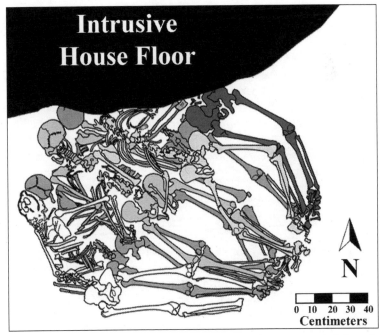

**Figure 16.5** Seven males from CA-ALA-554 and intrusive housepit (adapted and modified from William Self Associates, Inc. 2012).

**304** | Jelmer W. Eerkens et al.

in an extended position with the heads oriented roughly toward the northwest and without associated grave goods; again, an unusual burial style for the region and time period. The bodies were placed side by side or on top of one another in an oblong pit, with their ankles and feet positioned on top of one another. A perimortem fracture to the cranial vault on one of the burials and a fragment of a chert biface or point was found near the thorax of another. Based on these data, excavators concluded these individuals had been killed as part of a single violent event.

Bone collagen from two of the burials produced radiocarbon dates of 1,180 ± 20 years BP and 1,170 ± 20 years BP, in good concordance with one another. Based on temporally diagnostic artifacts, radiocarbon dates, and stratigraphic position, it appears that this part of the site was not in use when the seven males were buried, though other contemporaneous interments do occur in other parts of the site. Thus, it appears that these individuals were buried on the outskirts of the active part of the site.

At some point more recent in time, a house floor was excavated into the burial pit, resulting in the removal of the skulls and upper torsos of three individuals. Charcoal from this house floor was radiocarbon dated to 940 ± 30 years BP (William Self Associates, Inc. 2012). Other burials were placed near the mass grave later in time, as the active part of the site migrated northward.

### Stable Isotopic Results

C and N isotope ratios were measured on bone collagen (Figure 16.4) and Sr and O isotopes on bone apatite (see Figure 16.3). The seven males from Burial 85 were compared with a sample of other burials from the site interred in typical styles (i.e., flexed). To date, just four individuals have been evaluated for Sr and O isotopes, while a much larger sample has been measured for C and N.

Isotopic results shown in Figures 16.3 and 16.4 demonstrate that the Burial 85 males are distinct from the rest of the CA-ALA-554 population. Again, this strongly supports the interpretation that they are not local to the site. More important, the stable isotope data point to a potential homeland of the Burial 85 males. The $\delta^{18}O$ data indicate a geographic source to the east of the Amador Valley. Further, $^{87}Sr/^{86}Sr$ values indicate a source in the San Joaquin Valley, to the southeast. These values are consistent with the $\delta^{13}C$ and $\delta^{15}N$ values reported in Figure 16.4, which indicate a noncoastal source, but one with high dietary protein input from aquatic environments. This is consistent with a homeland close to or along the San Joaquin River or southern Delta.

In sum, it appears these males were in the Amador Valley away from their homeland to the east, killed as part of a single violent event, and buried at CA-ALA-554.

## CA-SCL-38

CA-SCL-38, also known as the Yukisma Mound, is located in the Santa Clara Valley, approximately 2 miles southeast of the San Francisco Bay, and within the modern city of Milpitas. CA-SCL-38 was first recorded by Clement Meighan in 1952 and was principally excavated between 1993 and 1994 (Bellifemine 1997). A recent master's thesis (Gardner 2013) and two published articles (Gardner et al. 2011; Jurmain 2001) summarize these findings.

Excavation of the Yukisma Mound was part of a salvage project in support of an expansion of the prison now located on the site. In contrast to the evidence found at CA-YOL-117 and CA-ALA-554, there was no clear evidence of house floors or domestic debris at CA-SCL-38. Rather, the excavated portion of the site suggests that it was used exclusively for mortuary and ceremonial purposes. Radiocarbon dates, obsidian hydration measurements, and temporally sensitive artifacts indicate that the site was used between about AD 1010 and 1720.

During the 1993–1994 excavations, 243 gravelots were identified, containing the remains of 248 individuals. One of these burials was different from the rest: it contained the remains of four young males, buried in progressively disorganized positions. While the first in the grave was positioned in the traditional flexed posture (B141), the next two were extended and stacked together (B142 and B143), and the fourth appears to have been flung on top of the others (Figure 16.6).

The four males in this burial were all between 15 and 30 years old, with no evidence of pathology. Two of them had embedded obsidian points (B142 in the distal left femur, B143 in a left lower rib). B144 had an associated projectile point, and was the only one of these four with associated artifacts (three bird bone tubes near his right hip). A note in an unpublished osteological report indicates that narrow, linear indentations were observed on his distal right humerus and proximal ulna, which might suggest an incomplete attempt at trophy taking. A calibrated radiocarbon date from bone collagen of B144 places this burial at $245 \pm 50$ years BP, around AD 1705 (Gardner 2013).

### *Stable Isotope Results*

C and N stable isotope ratios were measured in the bone collagen of 128 individuals and the bone apatite of 122 individuals. In addition, stable S isotope ratios were measured in the bone collagen of 11 adult males and two faunal samples. The individuals in the unusual burial were included in each group. While their $\delta^{13}C$ values from both bone collagen and apatite were similar to others from SCL-38, their $\delta^{15}N$ values were significantly lower, indicating that these individuals ate a diet of low-trophic-level foods, with little to no input from marine resources (see Figure 16.4). The $\delta^{34}S$ values for

**Figure 16.6** Excavation photo of B141, B142, B143, and B144 from CA-SCL-38. Placard reads "CA SCL 38/Burial Feature 141–144/OFCS Dec 9 1993." Courtesy of Ohlone Families Consulting Services, used with permission of the Muwekma Ohlone Tribal Council.

these individuals were elevated relative to other adult males and fauna from the site, again suggesting they were not part of the local population.

The combination of low $\delta^{15}N$ values and elevated $\delta^{34}S$ values does not match local values, nor does it match the pattern seen in any site yet measured in central California. The low nitrogen values suggest that these males were from an inland area, likely to the south or east, where marine or other aquatic resources were not regularly consumed. However, they were buried within this ancestral Ohlone mortuary site, among members of the local population. Additional isotopic analyses, including O and Sr, may help identify their place of origin, but must await future research.

An interesting twist is presented by new mitochondrial DNA (mtDNA) evidence (Monroe et al. 2013). These studies reveal that the mtDNA haplogroups of these four individuals are very consistent with the local Santa Clara Valley population, including a rather unique variant of Haplogroup C, found only at this point in the San Francisco Bay area. Because mtDNA is maternally inherited, these results suggest that the mothers of these males may have been part of the local population, and perhaps married exogamously into other regions. The males may have been returning to visit kin, to fight a common enemy, or for trade negotiations. This affiliation might explain their burial within the cemetery and the more respectful positioning of B141. However, the haphazard positions of the other three individuals, the lack of grave goods, and the possible cut marks on B144 suggest a less amicable relationship with the local population.

## Discussion

In all three case studies, the males buried in the pits were hypothesized to have been nonlocal victims of violence based on contextual and osteological data. In all three cases, stable isotope data strongly support these interpretations. We argue that these men most likely entered a foreign territory, and were killed and subsequently buried outside of their native homeland. We do not know, of course, the reasons why they were away from their native villages or why they were killed. Were they actively engaging in warfare or a raiding party as members of an outside group? Were they caught crossing a territorial boundary without permission? Were they ambushed during a trading session or other planned visit? Was this retribution for a prior crime (also perhaps violent)? Answers to these questions may come from greater in-depth contextual analyses of particular cases, as well as ancient DNA studies.

In any case, stable isotope data provide a powerful tool for gaining information about the spatial location of native homelands of victims of violence. This allows us to evaluate who is fighting with whom in prehistory, at least in a geographic sense. Importantly, such information allows us to test hypotheses about the nature of warfare, not just among hunter-gatherers, but a wide range of societies.

Our sample of case studies in central California is small. However, we note several items that we think relate to violence in general among the hunter-gatherers of this region. These could be points of departure for future research. First, the males buried in these mass graves appear to be coming from some distance away, enough so that their stable isotope values are significantly different than the local signature (based on human or rodent data). If these mass graves were the result of aggression between neighboring villages (e.g., within 5 km), in most cases there would be little to no difference in the isotopic

**308** | Jelmer W. Eerkens et al.

signatures. Indeed, it may be the distance between the homeland and ultimate burial location that drives the existence of such mass graves. That is, adult males are heavy, and—lacking alternative modes of transportation—carrying multiple bodies over long distances may not have been possible. Moreover, if no survivors escaped to report the event, contacting living relatives for repatriation may have amounted to an admission of guilt by the perpetrators and been cause for retribution. It is also possible the bodies were intentionally retained and perhaps put on display as a sign of victory prior to burial. In any case, the victims did not receive "normal" burial treatment. They seem to have been placed into pits, perhaps to avoid the foul smell of decomposition (and the attraction of scavengers), or perhaps to quickly dispose any evidence (i.e., bodies) of the violent event.

Second, in all three cases the victims were not from coastal areas of California. Ethnographic and archaeological evidence suggests population densities were lower in these regions (Baumhoff 1963; Cook 1976b; Kroeber 1939). Instead, the victims seem to have come from inland areas with much higher population densities, such as the Sacramento–San Joaquin Valley. One hypothesis to be tested in future research, thus, is whether the frequency of intergroup violence in late prehistoric central California was positively correlated with population density, perhaps as part of competition over land and resources.

Third, mass burials with evidence for violence (e.g., embedded projectile points indicating dismemberment) appear to be related to inter- rather than intragroup violence. Again, the violence in these cases seems to be between groups living at greater distances from one another, rather than neighboring groups. In the future we plan to analyze samples from victims of violence who were buried in single graves, rather than as part of mass graves, and in more traditional burial styles. We hypothesize that such burials may inform more on intragroup violence; that is, isotopic data will indicate they are locals rather than foreigners.

## Conclusions

The presence of multiple burials showing evidence of violence from prehistoric sites is an important component of our understanding of ancient violence among hunter-gatherers. The presence of such pits has been used to reconstruct information around the frequency of interpersonal violence in California (Schwitalla 2013). As we have shown here, stable isotope data can add important contextual information to such cases, and can show whether they are the byproduct of inter- versus intragroup violence. We have not discussed the data here, but complementary isotopic analyses on teeth from the same individuals can add valuable information. For example, in the CA-YOL-117 case, isotopic analyses of the teeth of all three individuals indicates they had historical ties to the place where they were ultimately buried, even though

Stable Isotope Perspectives on Hunter-Gatherer Violence | **309**

they did not live there as adults (Eerkens et al. 2014). Likewise, ancient DNA analyses in the CA-SCL-38 case indicate a potential genetic connection to the place those males were buried.

Our sample of just three case studies is obviously small, but it is easy to envision that with additional examples, including both mass and individual graves, we can begin to work out the prevalence of intra- versus intergroup violence. Furthermore, we may be able to determine where particularly contentious "boundaries" existed in the past; that is, isotopically distinctive areas on the landscape across which violence was markedly higher (e.g., Allen 2012). In all these respects, stable isotopes can offer a unique perspective on ancient violence that complements osteological and other studies.

## Acknowledgments

We thank Chris Peske for drafting Figure 16.2. We thank the UC Davis Museum of Anthropology for providing access to the CA-YOL-117 remains; Ramona Garibay, William Self Associates, Kari Lentz, and Jennifer Blake for supporting the CA-ALA-554 analyses; and Alan Leventhal (San Jose State University), Rosemary Cambra, and the Muwekma Ohlone tribe for supporting the CA-SCL-38 research. We thank Gina Jorgenson, Gry Barfod, Justin Glessner, Susan Talcott, Alex Greenwald, and Greg Burns for help with isotopic analyses and sample preparation. We thank Olaf Nehlich, Benjamin Fuller, and Michael Richards of the Max Planck Institute for Evolutionary Anthropology for running the stable sulfur isotope analysis; Joy Matthews of the Stable Isotope Facility at UC Davis for the collagen analyses; and Howie Spero of the Stable Isotope Laboratory at UC Davis for running apatite samples.

## References

Allen, Mark W. 2012. A Land of Violence. In *Contemporary Issues in California Archaeology*, edited by Terry L. Jones and Jennifer E. Perry, pp. 197–216. Left Coast Press, Walnut Creek, CA.

Ambrose, Stanley H. 1993. Isotopic Analysis of Paleodiets: Methodological and Interpretive Considerations. In *Investigations of Ancient Human Tissues: Chemical Analyses in Anthropology*, edited by Mary K. Sandford, pp. 59–129. Gordon and Breach Science Publishers, Langhorne, PA.

Andrushko, Valerie A., Kate A. S. Latham, Diane L. Grady, Allen G. Pastron, and Phillip L. Walker 2005. Bioarchaeological Evidence for Trophy-Taking in Prehistoric Central California. *American Journal of Physical Anthropology* 127:375–84.

Andrushko, Valerie A., Al W. Schwitalla, and Phillip L. Walker 2010. Trophy-Taking and Dismemberment as Warfare Strategies in Prehistoric Central California. *American Journal of Physical Anthropology* 141:83–93.

Arkush, Elizabeth N., and Mark W. Allen 2006. *The Archaeology of Warfare*. University Press of Florida, Gainesville.

Bartelink, Eric J. 2006. Resource Intensification in Pre-Contact Central California: A Bioarchaeological Perspective on Diet and Health Patterns among Hunter-Gatherers from the Lower Sacramento Valley and San Francisco Bay. Ph.D. dissertation, Texas A&M University, College Station. University Microfilms, Ann Arbor, MI.

Bartelink, Eric J. 2009. Late Holocene Dietary Change in the San Francisco Bay Area: Stable Isotope Evidence for an Expansion in Diet Breadth. *California Archaeology* 1:227–52.

Bartelink Eric J., Valerie Andrushko, Viviana Bellifemine, Irina Nechayev, and Robert J. Jurmain 2013. Violence and Warfare in the Prehistoric San Francisco Bay Area, California: Regional and Temporal Variations in Conflict. In *The Routledge Handbook of the Bioarchaeology of Human Conflict,* edited by Christopher Knüsel and Martin Smith, pp. 285–307. Oxford University Press, Oxford, UK.

Baumhoff, Martin A. 1963. Ecological Determinants of Aboriginal California Populations. *University of California Publications in American Archaeology and Ethnology* 49:155–235.

Bellifemine, Viviana 1997. Mortuary Variability in Prehistoric Central California: A Statistical Study of the Yukisma Site, CA-SCL-38. Unpublished Master's thesis, Department of Interdisciplinary Studies, San Jose State University, CA.

Boesch, Christophe, Catherine Crockford, Ilka Herbinger, Roman Wittig, Yasmin Moebius, and Emmanuelle Normand 2008. Intergroup Conflicts among Chimpanzees in Tai National Park: Lethal Violence and the Female Perspective. *American Journal of Primatology* 70:519–32.

Broughton, Jack M., Michael D. Cannon, and Eric J. Bartelink 2010. Evolutionary Ecology, Resource Depression, and Niche Construction Theory in Archaeology: Applications to Central California Hunter-Gatherers and Mimbres-Mogollon Agriculturalists. *Journal of Archaeological Method and Theory* 17:371–421.

Bryant, J. Daniel, Paul L. Koch, Philip N. Froelich, William J. Showers, and Bernard J. Genna 1996. Oxygen Isotope Partitioning between Phosphate and Carbonate in Mammalian Apatite. *Geochimica et Cosmochimica Acta* 60:5145–8.

Capo, Rosemary C., Brian W. Stewart, and Oliver A. Chadwick 1998. Strontium Isotopes as Tracers of Ecosystem Processes: Theory and Methods. *Geoderma* 82:197–225.

Chacon, Richard J., and David H. Dye 2007. *The Taking and Displaying of Human Body Parts as Trophies by Amerindians.* Springer, New York.

Chagnon, Napoleon A. 1988. Life Histories, Blood Revenge, and Warfare in a Tribal Population. *Science* 239:985–92.

Cook, Sherburne F. 1976a. *The Conflict between the California Indian and White Civilization.* University of California Press, Berkeley.

——— 1976b. *The Population of the California Indians, 1769–1970.* University of California Press, Berkeley.

Craig, O. E., R. Ross, Søren H. Andersen, N. Milner, and G. N. Bailey 2006. Focus: Sulphur Isotope Variation in Archaeological Marine Fauna from Northern Europe. *Journal of Archaeological Science* 33:1642–6.

DeNiro, Michael J., and Samuel Epstein 1981. Influence of Diet on the Distribution of Nitrogen Isotopes in Animals. *Geochimica et Cosmochimica Acta* 45:341–51.

DeNiro, Michael J., and Margaret J. Schoeninger 1983. Stable Nitrogen Isotope Ratios of Bone Collagen Reflect Marine and Terrestrial Components of Prehistoric Human Diet. *Science* 220:1381–3.

DiGiuseppe, Diane M. 2009. Assessing Forearm Fractures from Eight Prehistoric California Populations. Unpublished Master's thesis, Department of Interdisciplinary Studies, San Jose State University, CA.

Eerkens, Jelmer W., Gry H. Barfod, Gina J. Jorgenson, and Chris Peske 2014. Tracing the Mobility of Individuals using Stable Isotope Signatures in Biological Tissues: "Locals" and "Non-Locals" in an Ancient Case of Violent Death from Central California. *Journal of Archaeological Science* 41:474–81.

Eerkens, Jelmer W., Madeline Mackie, and Eric J. Bartelink 2013. Brackish Water Foraging: Isotopic Landscapes and Dietary Reconstruction in Suisun Marsh, Central California. *Journal of Archaeological Science* 40:3270–81.

Stable Isotope Perspectives on Hunter-Gatherer Violence | **311**

Ember, Carol R., and Melvin Ember 1995. Warfare, Aggression, and Resource Problems: SSCS Codes. *World Cultures* 9:17–57.

Faure, Gunter 1986. *Principles of Isotope Geology*. Wiley, New York.

Faure, G., and P. M. Hurley 1963. The Isotopic Composition of Strontium in Oceanic and Continental Basalts: Application to the Origin of Igneous Rocks. *Journal of Petrology* 4:31–50.

Ferguson, R. Brian (editor) 1984. *Warfare, Culture, and Environment*. Academic Press, Orlando, FL.

Ferguson, R. Brian, and Neil L. Whitehead (editors) 1992. *War in the Tribal Zone: Expanding States and Indigenous Warfare*. School of American Research Press, Santa Fe, NM.

Font, Pedro (1776) 1930. *Font's Complete Diary of the Second Anza Expedition. Anza's California Expeditions*, Vol. IV. University of California Press, Berkeley.

Gardner, Karen S. 2013. Diet and Identity among the Ancestral Ohlone: Integrating Stable Isotope Analysis and Mortuary Context at the Yukisma Mound (CA-SCL-38). Unpublished Master's thesis, Department of Anthropology, California State University, Chico.

Gardner, Karen S., Alan Leventhal, Rosemary Cambra, Eric J. Bartelink, and Antoinette Martinez 2011. Mothers and Infants in the Prehistoric Santa Clara Valley: What Stable Isotopes Tell Us about Ancestral Ohlone Weaning Practices. *Proceedings of the Society for California Archaeology* 25:1–14.

Gat, Azar 2000. The Human Motivational Complex: Evolutionary Theory and the Causes of Hunter-Gatherer Fighting. Part 1. Primary Somatic and Reproductive Causes. *Anthropological Quarterly* 73:20–34.

Grady, Diane L., Kate A. Latham, and Valerie A. Andrushko 2001. *Archaeological Investigations at CA-SCL-674, the Rubino Site, San Jose, Santa Clara County, California*. Coyote Press Archives of California Prehistory, Salinas, CA.

Haas, Jonathan (editor) 1990. *The Anthropology of War*. Cambridge University Press, Cambridge, UK.

James, Steven R., and Suzanne Graziani 1975. California Indian Warfare. *Contributions of the University of California Archaeological Research Facility* 23:47–109.

Jones, Terry L., and Al W. Schwitalla 2008. Archaeological Perspectives on the Effects of Medieval Drought in Prehistoric California. *Quaternary International* 188:41–58.

Jones, Terry L., Gary M. Brown, L. Mark Raab, Janet L. McVickar, W. Geoff Spaulding, Douglas J. Kennett, Andrew York, and Phillip L. Walker 1999. Environmental Imperatives Reconsidered: Demographic Crises in Western North America during the Medieval Climatic Anomaly. *Current Anthropology* 40:137–70.

Jorgenson, Gina A., Jelmer W. Eerkens, Gry H. Barfod, and Eric J. Bartelink 2009. Migration Patterns in the Prehistoric California Delta: Analysis of Strontium Isotopes. *Proceedings of the Society for California Archaeology* 23:1–7.

Jurmain, Robert D. 1991. Paleoepidemiology of Trauma in a Prehistoric Central California Population. In *Human Paleopathology: Current Syntheses and Future Options*, edited by Donald J. Ortner and Arthur C. Aufderheide, pp. 241–8. Smithsonian Institution Press, Washington, D.C.

———— 2001. Paleoepidemiolgical Patterns of Trauma in a Prehistoric Population from Central California. *American Journal of Physical Anthropology* 115:13–23.

Jurmain, Robert D., and Vivienne I. Bellifemine 1997. Patterns of Cranial Trauma in a Prehistoric Population from Central California. *International Journal of Osteoarchaeology* 7:43–50.

Jurmain, Robert, Eric J. Bartelink, Alan Leventhal, Viviana Bellifemine, Irina Nechayev, Melynda Atwood, and Diane DiGiuseppe 2009. Paleoepidemiological Patterns of Interpersonal Aggression in a Prehistoric Central California Population from CA-ALA-329. *American Journal of Physical Anthropology* 139:462–73.

Keeley, Lawrence H. 1996. *War Before Civilization: The Myth of the Peaceful Savage*. Oxford University Press, Oxford, UK.

Kellner, Corina M., and Margaret J. Schoeninger 2007. A Simple Carbon Model for Reconstructing Prehistoric Human Diet. *American Journal of Physical Anthropology* 133:1112–27.

## 312 | Jelmer W. Eerkens et al.

Kendall, Carol, and Tyler B. Coplen 2001. Distribution of Oxygen-18 and Deuterium in River Waters across the United States. *Hydrological Processes* 15:1363–93.

Kohn, Matthew J. 1996. Predicting Animal $\delta^{18}O$: Accounting for Diet and Physiological Adaptation. *Geochimica et Cosmochimica Acta* 60:4811–29.

Knauft, Bruce M. 1991. Violence and Sociality in Human Evolution. *Current Anthropology* 32:391–428.

Kroeber, Alfred E. 1939. Cultural and Natural Areas of Native North America. In *University of California Publications in American Archaeology and Ethnology* Vol. 38. University of California, Berkeley.

Lambert, Patricia M. 1994. War and Peace on the Western Front: A Study of Violent Conflict and its Correlates in Prehistoric Hunter-Gatherer Societies of Coastal Southern California. Unpublished Ph.D. dissertation, Department of Anthropology, University of California, Santa Barbara.

—— 1997. Patterns of Violence in Prehistoric Hunter-Gatherer Societies of Coastal Southern California. In *Troubled Times: Violence and Warfare in the Past,* edited by Debra L. Martin and David W. Frayer, pp. 77–109. Gordon and Breech Publishers, Amsterdam, the Netherlands.

—— 2002. The Archaeology of War: A North American Perspective. *Journal of Archaeological Research* 10:207–41.

—— 2007. Ethnographic and Linguistic Evidence for the Origins of Human Trophy Taking in California. In *The Taking and Displaying of Human Body Parts as Trophies by Amerindians,* edited by Richard J. Chacon and David H. Dye, pp. 65–89. Springer, New York.

Langsdorff, Georg Heinrich von 1968. *Voyages and Travels in Various Parts of the World during the Years 1803, 1804, 1805, 1806, and 1807 [1813–1814].* Bibliotheca Australiana 41. Da Capo Press, New York.

LeBlanc, Steven A. 1999. *Prehistoric Warfare in the American Southwest.* University of Utah Press, Salt Lake City.

Longinelli, Antonio 1984. Oxygen Isotopes in Mammal Bone Phosphate: A New Tool for Paleohydrological and Paleoclimatological Research. *Geochimica et Cosmochimica Acta* 48:385–90.

Martin, Debra L., and David W. Frayer (editors) 1997. *Troubled Times: Violence and Warfare in the Past.* Gordon and Breach, Amsterdam, the Netherlands.

Martin, Debra L., Ryan P. Harrod, and Ventura R. Pérez (editors) 2012. *The Bioarchaeology of Violence.* University Press of Florida,

Maschner, Herbert D. G., and Katherine L. Reedy-Maschner 1998. Raid, Retreat, Defend (Repeat): The Archaeology and Ethnohistory of Warfare on the North Pacific Rim. *Journal of Anthropological Archaeology* 17:19–51.

Milliken, Randall 1995. *A Time of Liittle Choice: The Disintegration of Tribal Culture in the San Francisco Bay Area, 1769–1810.* Ballena Press Anthropological Papers Vol. 43, Menlo Park, CA.

Milner, George R. 1995. An Osteological Perspective on Prehistoric Warfare. In *Recent Approaches to Mortuary Analysis,* edited by Lane A. Beck, pp. 221–44. Plenum Press, New York.

Monroe, Cara, Karen S. Gardner, Eric L. Lenci, Alan Leventhal, Rosemary Cambra, Eric J. Bartelink, and Brian M. Kemp 2013. Mystery Men of Yukisma: Ancient DNA and Stable Isotope Data Used to Deduce the Origin and Relationship of an Unusual Group Burial at CA-SCL-38. Paper presented at the 47th Annual Meeting of the Society for California Archaeology, Berkeley, CA, March 7–10.

Nehlich, Olaf, Dušan Borić, Sofija Stefanović, and Michael P. Richards 2010. Sulphur Isotope Evidence for Freshwater Fish Consumption: A Case Study from the Danube Gorges, SE Europe. *Journal of Archaeological Science* 37:1131–9.

Nelson, James S. 1997. Interpersonal Violence in Prehistoric Northern California: A Bioarchaeological Approach. Unpublished Master's thesis, Department of Anthropology, California State University, Chico.

## Stable Isotope Perspectives on Hunter-Gatherer Violence | **313**

Otterbein, Keith F. (editor) 1994. *Feuding and Warfare: Selected Works of Keith F. Otterbein.* Gordon and Breach, Amsterdam, the Netherlands.

Richards, Michael P., Ben T. Fuller, M. Sponheimer, T. Robinson, and L. Ayliffe 2003. Sulphur Isotopes in Palaeodietary Studies: A Review and Results from a Controlled Feeding Experiment. *International Journal of Osteoarchaeology* 13:37–45.

Schoeninger, Margaret J. 1985. Trophic Effects on $^{15}N/^{14}N$ and $^{13}C/^{12}C$ Ratios in Human Bone Collagen and Strontium Levels in Bone Mineral. *Journal of Human Evolution* 14:515–25.

Schwarcz, Henry P., and Margaret J. Schoeninger 1991. Stable Isotope Analyses in Human Nutritional Ecology. *Yearbook of Physical Anthropology* 34:283–321.

Schwitalla, Al W. 2013. *Global Warming in California: A Lesson from the Medieval Climatic Anomaly (A.D. 800–1350).* Center for Archaeological Research at Davis No. 17, University of California, Davis.

Sponheimer, Matt, and Julia A. Lee-Thorp 1999. Oxygen Isotopes in Enamel Carbonate and their Ecological Significance. *Journal of Archaeological Science* 26:723–8.

Stuiver, Minze, Paula J. Reimer, and Ron W. Reimer 2005. CALIB 5.0. (WWW program and documentation). http://calib.qub.ac.uk/

Turney-High, Harry H. 1971. *Primitive War: Its Practice and Concepts.* University of South Carolina Press, Columbia.

Unnikrishna, Padinare V., Jeffrey J. McDonnell, and Carol Kendall 2002. Isotope Variations in a Sierra Nevada Snowpack and their Relation to Meltwater. *Journal of Hydrology* 260:38–57.

Walker, Phillip L. 1989. Cranial Injuries as Evidence of Violence in Prehistoric Southern California. *American Journal of Physical Anthropology* 80:313–23.

——— 2001. A Bioarchaeological Perspective on the History of Violence. *Annual Review of Anthropology* 30:573–96.

Weiss, Elizabeth 2006. Facial Trauma in a Prehistoric California Population: Patterns and Comparisons. *Journal of Paleopathology* 18:107–16.

Wiberg, Randy S. 2002. Archaeological Investigations: Skyport Plaza Phase I (CA-SCL-478), San Jose, Santa Clara County, California. Report on file, California Historical Resources Information System, Northwest Information Center, Sonoma State University.

William Self Associates, Inc. 2012. Report on Archaeological Data Recovery at CA-ALA-554, Pleasanton, California. Edited by Allen Estes, Melanie Medeiros, and James Allan. Submitted to Property Development Centers and Safeway, Inc. Report on file, California Historical Resources Information System, Northwest Information Center, Sonoma State University.

Wrangham, Richard W., and Luke Glowacki 2012. Intergroup Aggression in Chimpanzees and War in Nomadic Hunter-Gatherers: Evaluating the Chimpanzee Model. *Human Nature* 23:5–29.

Wrangham, Richard, and Dale Peterson 1996. *Demonic Males: Apes and the Origins of Human Violence.* Houghton Mifflin, New York.

Wrangham, Richard W., Michael L. Wilson, and Martin N. Muller 2006. Comparative Rates of Aggression in Chimpanzees and Humans. *Primates* 47:14–26.

# 17

## The Technology of Violence and Cultural Evolution in the Santa Barbara Channel Region

*James M. Brill*

The study of violence among hunter-gatherer societies is challenging in many ways. While the weaponry used by hunter-gatherers is often the same as that used for hunting, it is possible that projectile points were specialized for use against human targets (Keeley 1996:52). For example, points with extreme barbs might be used in warfare because they are nearly impossible to extract. These observations, however, have seldom been systematically investigated. In this study, I explore morphological differentiation in tool types through the lens of specialization for violence in the Santa Barbara Channel region of southern California. As noted by Allen (2012:208), there is a significant body of both ethnographic and archaeological literature on specialized points used against humans in California, including the Santa Barbara Channel (Gamble 2008:260; Glassow 1997; Hudson and Blackburn 1982). Here, I examine this possibility directly through a model based on theories of technological investment. Specifically, I hypothesize that there was a recognizable investment in the technology of violence (tools used in violent interactions) in this region at a time when there is a peak in evidence for violence in burials (projectile points embedded in skeletal remains). A coefficient of variation ($CV$) has been used to gauge standardization in dimensions of spear, dart, and arrow projectile point types found in these skeletons with a particular focus on those dating to the Medieval Climatic Anomaly (MCA),

---

*Violence and Warfare among Hunter-Gatherers,* edited by Mark W. Allen and Terry L. Jones, 314–332. ©2014 Taylor & Francis. All rights reserved.

The Technology of Violence and Cultural Evolution | **315**

a time associated with drought-related resource stress in the Santa Barbara Channel and elsewhere in California (Arnold 1992; Johnson 2004; Jones et al. 1999; Kennett 2005; Kennett and Kennett 2000; Lambert 1994). Using this methodology, a relationship emerges between violence and technology in the Malaga Cove projectile point type, which helps to advance more general theories of specialization, violence, and cultural change related to the spread of the bow and arrow.

To link specialization and violence, theories of specialization (specifically Arnold 1987, 1992, 1995; Arnold and Graesch 2001; Arnold and Munns 1994) and artifact standardization (Eerkens and Bettinger 2001), as well as theories of technological investment (specifically Bettinger et al. 2006; Ugan et al. 2003), are explored, with *specialization* defined as the application of standardized artifact attributes or characteristics for a perceived advantage, and *standardization* defined as the control or minimization of variation. *CV* is used to quantify the rate of variation observed.

## Cultural History of the Santa Barbara Channel

The Santa Barbara Channel includes the northern coast of California's southern "Bight" along with the northern Channel Islands (Figure 17.1). The prehistoric climate of the Channel and its effects on human populations have been heatedly debated over the last two decades (e.g., Arnold 1992; Arnold et al. 1997; Gamble 2005; Jones and Schwitalla 2008; Jones et al. 1999 and comments; Kennett and Kennett 2000; Lambert 2002; Raab and Larson 1997), with most of the focus on the impact of the MCA. This period, spanning roughly between AD 800 and 1400 (Jones et al. 1999), was marked by cool sea-surface temperatures and anomalously prolonged droughts (Kennett and Kennett 2000; Stine 1994). While the timing of the droughts is generally accepted, their severity and especially their relative impact on people have been the points of contention (Gamble 2005; Jones and Schwitalla 2008).

Kroeber's ethnographic work with the Chumash ([1925] 1976) extolled the extreme environmental productivity of the region, with its high productivity due to the low-cost marine resource base. Johnson (2004) explains that this productivity is because the Santa Barbara Channel was composed of several ecological transition zones that produced a high abundance of terrestrial and marine food resource. As a result, the Chumash population grew very large, with an estimated peak of 10,000 (Arnold et al. 1997). The Chumash are considered one of the most complex examples of a hunter-gatherer group in California, although when this complexity reached such high levels is debated (Gamble 2008).

Santa Barbara Channel prehistory is generally divided into three major cultural periods based on the sequence refined by King (1990): an Early period

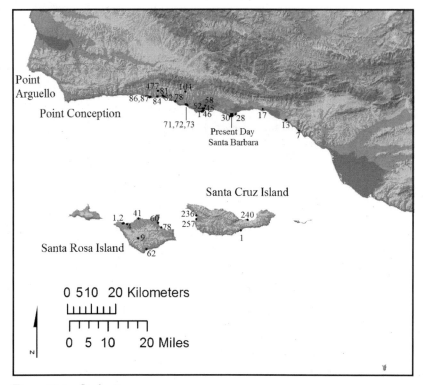

**Figure 17.1** Study sites.

from 6000 to 1400 cal BC; a Middle period from 1400 cal BC to cal AD 100, and a Late period from cal AD 1100 through contact. The time period of interest for the research reported here is the Middle-Late period Transition (ca. cal AD 1100–1300), which many scholars (Arnold 1992; Arnold et al. 1997; Jones et al. 1999; Kennett and Kennett 2000; Lambert 2002; Raab and Larson 1997) have noted as a time of intense cultural and ecological change for the Chumash. In summarizing the skeletal data from the Channel, Lambert (1994:62) used a slightly modified cultural chronology in which she merged the latter portion of the Middle period with Middle-Late Transition into a period she referred to as the Late Middle, dated between cal AD 580 and 1380.

Some scholars believe that the MCA had a significant impact on the resources available to the Chumash (Jones and Schwitalla 2008; Jones et al. 1999; Raab and Larson 1997), and that this caused stress for resident human populations in the Channel region. Jones et al. (1999) argued for particularly devastating effects of these droughts, pointing to a dramatic increase in aridity and a rapid decline in already limited freshwater. Several investigations by Arnold

The Technology of Violence and Cultural Evolution | **317**

and others postulated a decline in marine resources (Arnold 1992, 2004; Arnold et al. 1997), but Kennett and Kennett (2000) found evidence for productive marine environments coincident with aridity and decreased terrestrial vitality during the MCA.

Perhaps the best evidence for of stress is in skeletal remains. Arnold (1992), following Walker and Lambert (1989), noted that there are high rates of cribra orbitalia during her Transitional period (cal AD 1150–1300), which she attributed to malnutrition. Lambert (1993) noted that health greatly declined in this period, and also identified a higher frequency of periosteal lesions and decreased stature (Lambert 1994). Walker (2007) confirmed these findings, and argued that the skeletal evidence suggested high rates of infectious disease, possibly related to contaminated water sources, as well as high rates of congenital diseases, which is also indicative of severe resource stress.

Lambert (1994) and Kroeber ([1925] 1976) have posited that violence in the Santa Barbara Channel has a long history that continued into the mission era. Kroeber ([1925] 1976) considered the Chumash to be one of the first Native American groups to have recorded historic contact with Europeans. Lambert (1994) noted that the descriptions resulting from these early contacts, which began in the 1540s, vacillate between affectionate accounts of peaceful traders to bitter narratives of savage and godless bands of aggressive heathens. Johnson summed up these accounts and the reasoning behind them:

> Warfare was endemic among the Chumash. Virtually every Spanish visitor commented on raiding and feuding between mainland communities. Ethnohistoric sources record that the causes for intercommunity violence were competition for hunting, gathering, and fishing territories; failure to respond to invitations to fiestas; retribution for suspected witchcraft; and retaliation for previous attacks (Johnson 1988; Landberg 1965; Lambert 1994; L. King 1982). In a cross-cultural study, warfare frequency was shown to result from unpredictable natural disasters that destroy food supplies and spawn mistrust of others (Ember and Ember 1992). Ethnographic and ethnohistoric texts show that these causal factors appear to have been present among the Chumash (Johnson 2004:151).

Bioarchaeological analysis has demonstrated that violent injury in the form of depressed cranial fractures, ulnar shaft "parry" fractures, and projectile point wounds were the most prevalent types of the injuries in the Santa Barbara Channel (Lambert 1994, 1997, 2002, 2001; Walker and Lambert 1989). Lambert (1994, 1997, 2002) provided the greatest insight into the violence of this area before, during, and after the Middle and Late periods. She stated that projectile point trauma is one of the most important aspects of studies on prehistoric violence, as it is highly unlikely to be accidental (Lambert 1994, 2002). Further, she found that the rate of violence greatly increased during the

Middle period (1490 cal BC–cal AD 1380), with projectile injury peaking in the Late Middle period (cal AD 1170–1380) (Lambert 1994).

## Models of Technological Investment

To demonstrate technological change, models of technological investment provided insight into the notions explored in this study. Investment in a technology can be seen as an essential step in the process of specialization as defined here. A model of this process can be perceived as follows:

1. An individual determines technology *x* is lacking efficiency at a task.
2. The individual *invests* in that technology by either refining it, or changing to a differing technology, which accomplishes the desired task.
3. The refinement or change made by the individual will lead to standardization in form, as alluded to by Arnold (1987) and defined by Eerkens and Bettinger (2001).

The application of this standardization in this model is the main aspect of specialization as defined here (*specialization* as the application of standardized artifact attributes or characteristics for a perceived advantage). A more simple statement of this idea is that investment leads to standardization, and standardization leads to specialization. This formulation can be seen as an operationalization illustrated by the "Continuum of Innovation" (Figure 17.2).

Models by Ugan et al. (2003) and Bettinger et al. (2006) further illustrate investment and technological change. The premise behind these models is simple: to discover when technology should be *refined* or *replaced* to increase the returns of a technology. The Ugan et al. (2003) model is better suited

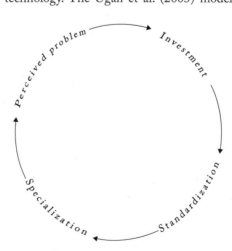

**Figure 17.2** Continuum of innovation.

The Technology of Violence and Cultural Evolution | **319**

to explore changes within a category of technology—such as when a finely made fishhook replaces a crudely made one—which I classify as a *refinement*. Bettinger et al. (2006) demonstrate what I call their *replacement investment model*: a technology will replace another if the time spent making the technology is less than the amount of returns it produces.

## Investing in Violence: When Is Violence Worth the Trouble?

How can a seemingly maladaptive activity such as violence be integrated into a model that requires a conscious focus on adaptation for survival? First, it must be assumed that violence can have a positive benefit, making it a worthwhile investment of energy. This is not a new idea in Human Behavioral Ecology, but one that is much muted and often dismissed. Jochim best expresses the idea of the potential benefits from violence:

> Competition, of course, may not be avoided at all, but rather might result in direct confrontation through warfare or its threat. Such a solution might be one of the only options available in a situation with little possibility of differentiation of activities or few refuges. Conflict, on the other hand, may be an attractive solution even when many alternatives are available, since its benefits seem to include, in addition to resource acquisition or removal of competitors, other reinforcements such as prestige allotment or the enhancement of the power or authority of a decision making elite. The benefits would have to be weighed against the cost of mortality, labor, and organization involved in both offensive and defensive aggregations. (Jochim 1981:63).

The idea of conflict related to resources here is paramount, as both of these models focus on resource acquisition. As Jochim states, violence in some cases cannot be completely divorced from resource acquisition or procurement. Two probable connections of violence to resource acquisition are conflict for areas producing resources, and conflict over collected resources. Furthermore, Jochim (1981) refers to the benefit of the "removal of competitors," an idea also explored by Harris. Harris postulates that this removal can reduce population pressure on carrying capacity in the short term, which can be an added benefit of violence (Harris [1977] 1991).

## A Model of Weapon Specialization for the Santa Barbara Channel

When preliminary research revealed that projectile and spear points used in violent contexts were not visually different from utilitarian points, I attempted to determine what differences in form related to function could

**320** | James M. Brill

be elucidated, and if evidence of specialization could be found. The guiding questions were: What technologies were used in violence along the Santa Barbara Channel? Is there evidence for a change in the technologies used in violence that accompanies observed increases of skeletal injuries linked to violence? Can we find evidence of technological specialization through the technology of violence? Did the Chumash use violence as an adaptive response to resource stress?

Based on the high rates of violence and disease in the skeletal record from the Santa Barbara Channel, the Middle-Late Transition appears to have been an interval of high stress. Furthermore, the swiftness of environmental change represented in the climatic record (Jones and Schwitalla 2008; Jones et al. 1999; Kennett and Kennett 2000; Raab and Larson 1997) suggests that diet breadth could not be successfully expanded only by investment in traditional procurement technology or practice.

With this theoretical framework in place, an overarching hypothesis was formulated: rapid environmental change during the Middle and Late periods resulted in direct competition in the form of violence as the only method for raising carrying capacity. Carrying capacity was augmented by eliminating competition for the remaining limited resources. Procurement tools were specialized to be more effective for violence. This increased investment would be represented by standardization of point and spear forms, and/ or advent or borrowing of a new technology, such as the bow and arrow. This overarching hypothesis was tested by formulating three data-focused hypotheses:

- *Hypothesis 1–Task Specialization*: Tools used in violence will show less metric variation because they are directly related to a focused, specialized task.
- *Hypothesis 2–Temporal Specialization*: Tools used in violence show less metric variation during periods of observed increases in skeletal injuries linked to violence, as pressure to specialize would be greatest at these times.
- *Hypothesis 3–Punctuated Specialization*: the reduction in variation in the tools of violence, if observed, will be limited to periods of high violence, supporting Lambert's (1994) and Jones et al.'s (1999) "punctuated" views of violence, which is contrary to Gamble's views (2005, 2008) of consistently high levels of violence.

## Methods

For this study, I examined 779 projectiles and 94 spear points from 34 sites in the Santa Barbara Channel region dating from the Early to Late periods (Figure 17.1, Table 17.1). I considered both points embedded within skeletons and projectiles in good association with human remains as points marking interpersonal violence in contrast with points used only for hunting. Of these, the embedded points provided the clearest evidence of a technology of violence.

## The Technology of Violence and Cultural Evolution | 321

**Table 17.1** Summary of the projectile point sample

| Site | Burial Association | Vandenberg | Malaga Cove | Canaliño | Spears | Reference |
|---|---|---|---|---|---|---|
| | | | | | | |
| | | LATE EARLY | | | | |
| SBA-1 | Nonassociated | 6 | 0 | 0 | 0 | Lambert 1994 Corbett 2007 Gamble 2008 |
| | Cemetery | 3 | 1 | 0 | 0 | |
| | Burial Associated | 0 | 0 | 0 | 1 | |
| SBA-30 | Nonassociated | 1 | 0 | 0 | 1 | Lambert 1994 |
| SBA-52 | Nonassociated | 20 | 0 | 2 | 2 | Lambert 1994 Corbett 2007 |
| SBA-58 | Nonassociated | 11 | 0 | 1 | 0 | Lambert 1994 Breschini et al. 1996 |
| | Burial Associated | 2 | 0 | 0 | 0 | |
| SBA-78 | Nonassociated | 3 | 18 | 13 | 0 | Breschini et al. 1996 |
| | Cemetery | 0 | 3 | 7 | 1 | |
| SCRI-236 | Nonassociated | 1 | 1 | 0 | 0 | Breschini et al. 1996 |
| | Burial Associated | 1 | 0 | 0 | 0 | |
| SRI-41 | Burial Associated | 5 | 0 | 0 | 1 | Kennett 1997 Corbett 2007 SBMNH 2008 |
| | PIGA | 8 | 0 | 0 | 0 | |
| Subtotal | | 61 | 23 | 23 | 6 | |
| | | EARLY MIDDLE | | | | |
| SBA-71 | Burial Associated | 1 | 2 | 0 | 2 | Breschini et al. 1996 Corbett 2007 |
| SBA-81 | Nonassociated | 37 | 32 | 8 | 0 | SBMNH 2008 |
| | Burial Associated | 12 | 3 | 2 | 12 | |
| | Embedded | 0 | 1 | 0 | 0 | |
| SBA-84 | Nonassociated | 46 | 38 | 32 | 4 | Breschini et al. 1996 Corbett 2007 |
| SCRI-1 | Nonassociated | 6 | 3 | 0 | 0 | SBMNH 2008 |
| | Burial Associated | 1 | 4 | 0 | 0 | |
| SCRI-257 | Nonassociated | 3 | 7 | 0 | 5 | Breschini et al. 1996 Corbett 2007 |
| | Burial Associated | 6 | 0 | 0 | 0 | |
| SRI-1 | Burial Associated | 2 | 0 | 0 | 0 | Kennett 1997 SBMNH 2008 |
| SRI-62 | Nonassociated | 0 | 1 | 0 | 0 | Kennett 1997 SBMNH 2008 |

*(Continued)*

## 322 | James M. Brill

**Table 17.1** *(Continued)*

| | | Types | | | | |
|---|---|---|---|---|---|---|
| Site | Burial Association | Vandenberg | Malaga Cove | Canaliño | Spears | Reference |
| | Burial Associated | 1 | 0 | 0 | 0 | |
| Subtotal | | 115 | 91 | 42 | 23 | |
| | | LATE MIDDLE | | | | |
| SBA-13 | Nonassociated | 1 | 0 | 0 | 0 | Breschini et al. 1996 |
| SBA-17 | Burial Associated | 0 | 1 | 0 | 0 | SBMNH 2008 |
| SBA-28 | Nonassociated | 60 | 3 | 0 | 7 | SBMNH 2008 Gamble 2008 |
| SBA-46 | Nonassociated | 1 | 8 | 0 | 2 | King 1990 Lambert 1994 SBMNH 2008 Gamble 2008 |
| | Cemetery | 1 | 1 | 6 | 0 | |
| | Burial Associated | 0 | 10 | 0 | 0 | |
| | PIGA | 0 | 15 | 0 | 0 | |
| SBA-72 | Nonassociated | 4 | 5 | 0 | 0 | Breschini et al. 1996 Corbett 2007 Gamble 2008 |
| | Burial Associated | 14 | 7 | 0 | 33 | |
| | Embedded | 0 | 0 | 0 | 5 | |
| SBA-73 | Nonassociated | 76 | 46 | 12 | 2 | Corbett 2007 |
| | Burial Associated | 2 | 0 | 0 | 0 | |
| SBA-82 | Nonassociated | 15 | 12 | 13 | 1 | Lambert 1994 |
| | Burial Associated | 0 | 0 | 7 | 0 | |
| SBA-86 | Nonassociated | 0 | 0 | 0 | 1 | Breschini et al. 1996 |
| | Burial Associated | 0 | 0 | 0 | 6 | |
| | Embedded | 1 | 4 | 0 | 0 | |
| SRI-2 | Nonassociated | 1 | 1 | 2 | | Breschini et al. 1996 |
| | Cemetery | 0 | 4 | 5 | 0 | |
| | Burial Associated | 2 | 1 | 0 | 0 | |
| | Embedded | 0 | 1 | 0 | 0 | |
| SRI-4 | Nonassociated | 0 | 1 | 0 | 0 | Kennett 1997 SBMNH 2008 |
| SRI-9 | Nonassociated | 0 | 1 | 0 | 0 | Kennett 1997 SBMNH 2008 |
| | Burial Associated | 0 | 1 | 0 | 0 | |
| NA | Nonassociated | 0 | 0 | 0 | 1 | SBMNH 2008 |
| Subtotal | | 178 | 122 | 45 | 58 | |

*(Continued)*

# The Technology of Violence and Cultural Evolution | 323

**Table 17.1** *(Continued)*

| Site | Burial Association | Vandenberg | Malaga Cove | Canaliño | Spears | Reference |
|------|--------------------|------------|-------------|----------|--------|-----------|
| | | | | LATE | | |
| SBA-7 | Nonassociated | 6 | 3 | 0 | 2 | SBMNH 2008 |
| | Burial Associated | 0 | 1 | 1 | 2 | |
| SBA-28 | Nonassociated | 0 | 0 | 8 | 0 | SBMNH 2008 Gamble 2008 |
| SBA-45 | Nonassociated | 0 | 1 | 1 | 0 | SBMNH 2008 |
| | Burial Associated | 0 | 3 | 1 | 0 | |
| SBA-87 | Nonassociated | 3 | 2 | 0 | 0 | SBMNH 2008 |
| | Burial Associated | 4 | 1 | 0 | 0 | |
| SBA-104 | Burial Associated | 0 | | 1 | | SBMNH 2008 |
| SBA-477 | Nonassociated | 3 | 0 | 3 | 0 | SBMNH 2008 |
| | Burial Associated | 0 | 0 | 1 | 0 | |
| SCRI-1 | Nonassociated | 0 | 0 | 1 | 0 | SBMNH 2008 |
| SCRI-236 | Nonassociated | 0 | 0 | 1 | 0 | Breschini et al. 1996 |
| SCRI-240 | Nonassociated | 2 | 2 | 0 | 0 | Gamble 2008 |
| | Burial Associated | 0 | 0 | 3 | 0 | |
| SRI-60 | Nonassociated | 2 | 3 | 5 | 1 | Kennett 1997 SBMNH 2008 |
| | Cemetery | 0 | 0 | 0 | 1 | |
| | Burial Associated | 2 | 8 | 4 | 0 | |
| SRI-62 | Nonassociated | 0 | 0 | 1 | 0 | Kennett 1997 SBMNH 2008 |
| SRI-78 | Nonassociated | 2 | 0 | 0 | 1 | SBMNH 2008 |
| Subtotal | | 24 | 24 | 31 | 7 | |
| Grand Total | | 378 | 260 | 141 | 94 | |

**Notes:** SBMNH indicates Santa Barbara Museum of Natural History; PIGA, projectiles in good association with violent confrontation (Lambert 1994); cemetery, points or Spears found in known cemeteries, but not attributed to an individual burial (based on original field notes).

The coefficient of variation ($CV$) was used because it is an easily calculable measurement and allows for artifact variability within samples to be scaled and compared with a baseline (Eerkens and Bettinger 2001). In addition, because $CV$ is not greatly affected by sample size, the rate of variation can be compared across samples. Eerkens and Bettinger (2001) combined the concept of Weber fractions (limits of human ability to detect differences) and the limits of variation in normally or uniformly distributed populations. From these studies, a scale was established to accurately evaluate the degree of variation in artifact measurements using *CV*.

Data collection was conducted at the Santa Barbara Museum of Natural History, where sites dating from the Early period through Late period (6630 BC–AD 1804) containing projectile and spear points were identified (Table 17.1). Three point types were chosen for measurement because they are the most prevalent, represent consecutive periods of time, and have been recovered from the entire region: Vandenberg Contracting-stemmed (considered an atlatl dart; Justice 2002), Malaga Cove and Canaliño Triangular (both considered arrow points; Justice 2002) (Figure 17.3), and spears. The artifacts were measured on site at the Santa Barbara Museum.

The sampled points were divided by association (nonassociated, burial-associated [artifacts associated with defined burials], projectiles in good association with violent contexts, cemetery [points found in known cemeteries], and points and spears embedded in human remains). Metric data were collected (for a full description of methodology and unabridged data, see Brill 2012). Attributes were measured on the points and spears, with *CV* percentage calculated for each measurement (see Tables 17.2, 17.3). All measurements were averaged to create a *CV* percentage that characterized each grouping in the sample through context and time, and allowed for comparison across samples.

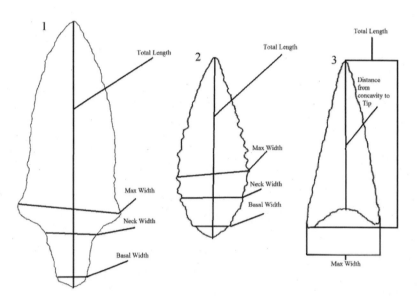

**Figure 17.3** Point measurements. Point 1 is a Vandenberg Contracting Stem; Point 2 is a Malaga Cove; Point 3 is a Canalino Triangular. Points not to scale and idealized in morphology.

# The Technology of Violence and Cultural Evolution | **325**

**Table 17.2** Definitions of projectile point measurements

| Measurement | Definition |
|---|---|
| Total length | Total length of the point, from the very end of the base to the terminus of the tip. |
| Basal width | The width of the base at its widest point. |
| Neck width | On notched points, this is "the measurement between the most distal points in the notch" (Yohe 2002:52). |
| Total width | The width of the projectile from its widest points. |
| Maximum thickness | The thickness of the projectile from its thickest point. |
| Weight | The total weight the projectile. |
| Distance from concavity to tip | Taken on concave based points, measures the distance from the interior point of the concavity to the tip of the point. |


**Table 17.3** Chronology of the Santa Barbara Channel

| Calibrated Dates (Erlandson and Colten 1991) | Modified ETP Chronology | Predominant Point Type |
|---|---|---|
| AD 1782–1804 | | |
| AD 1670–1782 | L (Late) | Canaliño Triangular |
| AD 1380–1670 | ETP | |
| AD 1170–1380 | (Extended Transitional Period) | Malaga Cove |
| AD 980–1170 | LM (Late Middle) | Vandenberg and Malaga |
| AD 580–980 | | |
| 800 BC–AD 580 | EM (Early Middle) | |
| 1490–800 BC | | Vandenberg Contracting Stem |
| 2850–1490 BC | LE (Late Early) | |
| 5350–2850 BC | | |
| 6630–5250 BC | EE (Early Early) | Earlier Forms |

Points were assigned to time periods based on the established cultural chronology for the Santa Barbara Channel, with the exception that I distinguished an Extended Transitional period dating from cal AD 1000 to AD 1400 (Figure 17.3). This was done to clarify the differing thoughts on the Middle to Late period transition (see Arnold 1992; Gamble 2008; Jones and Schwitalla 2008). This designation combines Arnold's (1992) chronology with King's (1990) typology along with the current paleoclimate sequence developed by Kennett and Kennett (2000).

## Results

For the Vandenberg Contracting-stemmed sample, the differences in *CV* percentage between the levels of association were minimal, suggesting that violence and, to a greater extent, other tasks did not require specialization of

**326** | James M. Brill

this dart point type. The Malaga Cove type yielded *CV* percentage values that were lower for the group of specimens associated with violence, and showed lower variation than most samples, supporting specialization for that task. A small sample size for Canaliño Triangular points did not allow for meaningful interpretation. The embedded spear sample displayed a much lower total *CV* percentage than samples from other contexts, again suggesting specialization for violence.

*CV* percentage was also calculated across time periods. For Vandenberg Contracting-stemmed points, variation was minimal, indicating no apparent specialization related to time. In the Malaga Cove sample, violence-associated points showed the lowest *CV* percentage among all samples, suggesting a relationship between specialization for violence and the high levels of violence indicated from the bioarchaeological record for that period (Lambert 1994). For Canaliño Triangular points, small sample size did not allow for temporal analysis. For spears, the embedded examples did not have a lower *CV* percentage in the Late Middle period compared with the other Late Middle period spear examples, suggesting no apparent specialization relative to time.

Building upon specialization for violence, temporal specialization becomes the key issue in evaluating the alternate hypotheses developed for this study. Temporal specialization would be supported if *CV* percentage were lower in the Late Middle and Extended Transition periods. Only the Malaga Cove points used in violence showed evidence of specialization during periods with higher bioarchaeological evidence of violence (Table 17.3). While nonassociated Malaga Cove points from the Late Middle period exhibited the lowest *CV* percentage, the nonassociated Malaga Cove points from the Extended Transition period do not show a reduction in *CV* percentage. Ideally, the samples from both periods would exhibit a clear decline in *CV* percentage to support the hypothesis. The points in good association and embedded examples showed the lowest *CV* percentage for all samples from the Extended Transition period, and across all time periods. From a strictly temporal perspective, this reduction of *CV* percentage in tools used in violence during the Extended Transition period is supportive of a focus on implements of war during times of increased violence. However, the other projectiles, including Vandenberg Contracting-stemmed points and spears, do not show specialization during the period of elevated violence. No Canaliño Triangular points were found in contexts related to violence.

The notion of punctuated specialization would be supported if there were a reduction of *CV* percentage restricted to the Late Middle and Extended Transition periods. This hypothesis differs from the notion of temporal specialization, as it would not be supported if there were a reduction in variation outside of the periods of high violence. A modicum of support was noted only for Malaga Cove points, but was not substantive enough to be meaningful. The Vandenberg sample shows a reduction of *CV* percentage in the Early

The Technology of Violence and Cultural Evolution | **327**

Middle period, which is not a time associated with high levels of violence. For Malaga Cove points, support for the hypothesis was inconclusive, as there is a reduction of $CV$ percentage outside of time periods of violence. However, as the violence-associated and embedded points are only found during periods of violence, and have the lowest $CV$ percentage across samples, the hypothesis is generally supported. The small sample sizes of Canaliño Triangular points and spears excluded them from testing this hypothesis.

## Discussion and Conclusion

Task specialization was one of the actions tested in this study. Task specialization is supported only for Malaga Cove points, as the points in good association and embedded samples had a lower $CV$ percentage than the samples unrelated to violence. The $CV$ percentage for projectiles in good association and embedded examples is lower, although not to a level of extreme standardization as described by Eerkens and Bettinger (2001). Reduced $CV$ percentage was not observed for Vandenberg points related to violence, and the sample of Canaliño points was too small for analysis. This supports the notion that Malaga Cove points found in violent contexts were made specifically for that task.

Thus, I found that the technologies of violence in the Santa Barbara Channel were Vandenberg Contracting-stemmed points, Malaga Cove points, and spears. These artifacts were found embedded in individuals and in good association connecting them with individuals who died by these weapons. The evidence also suggests that there was a change in technology related to violence. The increase in violence observed during the Late Middle and Extended Transition periods corresponds to the replacement of Vandenberg Contracting-stemmed points with Malaga Cove points (Justice 2002). While this change is part of a larger-scale technological change in the form of the introduction of the bow and arrow (Blitz 1988), the increased violence at the time, combined with the lower $CV$ percentage of embedded and violence-associated Malaga Cove points, as well as the lower $CV$ percentage of all Malaga Cove points during the Late Middle and Extended Transition periods, suggests that violence could be a contributing factor to the adoption of the bow and arrow in this area, as has been posited before (Allen 2012:208; Blitz 1988; Bradbury 1997; Keeley 1996:52). It is also interesting to note that when the high rates of violence in the area subsided during the Late period, Malaga Cove points were generally replaced by Canaliño Triangular points (Justice 2002). No Canaliño Triangular points were found in embedded or violence-associated contexts. The spear sample is also most prevalent in burial-associated contexts from the Early Middle and Late Middle periods, with few examples appearing after the Late Middle period. This small representation

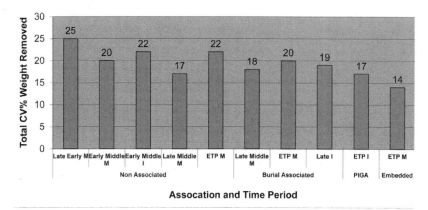

**Figure 17.4** Total $CV$ percentages with weight removed for each Malaga Cove sample divided by time. M indicates mainland samples; I, island samples.

could also be an indication that Malaga Cove points became the dominant technology used in violence. These findings are also supported by Lambert's (1994) findings (see Figure 17.4) that showed a dramatic peak in individuals with projectile wounds in the Late Middle period, which is when Malaga Cove points became the dominant point form (Justice 2002).

Using the Continuum of Innovation (Figure 17.2), a *refinement* and *replacement* can be observed with the emergence of Malaga Cove points. As violence continued to increase and reached its peak during the Late Middle and Extended Transition periods, the Chumash invested in Malaga Cove points as another tool of violence. Because spear and Vandenberg points were found throughout time and used in violence, the emergence and continued focus on Malaga Cove points (represented by a lower $CV$ percentage in violent contexts) indicates a refinement of this technology for violence. The eventual abandonment of Vandenberg point forms can be interpreted as a replacement. Furthermore, Malaga Cove points show evidence of a specialization for violence. For Malaga Cove points, the reduction in variability (along with a decrease in size) of the points is directly associated with violence, and the timing of the reduction of variation of the Malaga Cove points corresponds to evidence of an increase in violence in the region (Arnold 1992; Arnold et al. 1997; Jones et al. 1999; Kennett and Kennett 2000; Raab and Larson 1997).

Finally, determining whether the Chumash used violence as an adaptive response during the MCA is a complex task. An evaluation of artifact change found that Malaga Cove points were adopted and showed the most evidence of specialization during the Extended Transition period, which includes the intervals of the most severe climate during the MCA (Jones and Schwitalla 2008; Jones et al. 1999; Kennett and Kennett 2000). The timing of this artifact change during the Extended Transition period supports the

**Figure 17.5** Sex distribution of people with projectile wounds (from Lambert 1994:137).

hypothesis associating environmental stress with innovation. If traditional procurement practices were sufficient, technology would not need to change (Ugan et al. 2003). Because this innovation is linked to a rise in violence, this rise must be examined.

The degree to which violence in the Channel area was directly related to environment and ecology, however, has been challenged by Gamble (2005, 2008), who argued that violence in this region was unrelated to environmental change, and was instead a component of exchange relationships (Johnson 2007). In the current study, I found that projectile points embedded in skeletons include Vandenberg Contracting-stemmed and Malaga Cove types as well as spears. These artifacts span the full regional culture history (Justice 2002). Examples found in good association with skeletons and embedded examples were found in the Late Early, Early Middle, Late Middle, and Extended Transition periods. This evidence and the ethnography of violence documented in the region (Lambert 1994) also lend some support to Gamble's (2008) notion that violence did not correlate with environment. However, I also found that change was punctuated. The evidence of specialization for violence during the Extended Transition period indicates an increased focus on the technology of violence during a time of increased aggression and large-scale environmental change. Because this evidence corresponds to changes in technology (the adoption of the bow and arrow) and specialization of form (observed in $CV$ percentage reduction

## 330 | James M. Brill

in Malaga Cove points), it suggests a period of punctuated change. Change in the technology of Malaga Cove points during the Extended Transition period supports the idea that environmental change was a factor in a rise in violence and in cultural change. The results of this study support the idea of an investment in violence as a replacement investment (Bettinger et al. 2006) of atlatl darts by projectiles, as well the refinement (Ugan et al. 2003) of Malaga Cove points used in violent interactions.

In sum, violence was an adaptive response during a time of resource stress, and when environmental productivity improved, violence declined. The lack of points embedded in skeletons and violence-associated points later in time supports this notion. Violence was ever-present among the Chumash, but a punctuated rise is also apparent during the Extended Transition period. The observed change in metrics and $CV$ percentage in the Malaga Cove samples shows a purposeful change in a technology for improvement in a task, in this case violence. When considered in the context of environmental change, and the lack of alternative nonviolent adaptations for survival, the turn to improvement in the technology of violence is logical. For Malaga Cove points, the reduction of variation of the points is directly associated with violence, and the timing of the reduction of variation of the Malaga Cove points corresponds to evidence of an increase in violence in the region (Arnold 1992; Arnold et al. 1997; Jones et al. 1999; Kennett and Kennett 2000; Raab and Larson 1997). This change and refinement of Malaga Cove points can be seen as the driving force behind the adoption of the bow and arrow in this region, with violence as the prime motivator.

This application lays the groundwork for more sophisticated quantifiable and testable metric attributes that can be used to better answer larger cultural questions. $CV$ can be applied to other metric features to delve deeply into artifact attributes, further illuminating the relationship between violence and technology.

## References

Allen, Mark W. 2012. A Land of Violence. In *Contemporary Issues in California Archaeology*. edited by Terry L. Jones and Jennifer E. Perry, pp. 197–216. Left Coast Press, Walnut Creek, CA.

Arnold, Jeanne 1987. *Craft Specialization in the Prehistoric Channel Islands*. University of California Press, Berkeley.

—— 1992. Complex Hunter-Gatherer-Fishers of Prehistoric California: Chiefs, Specialists, and Maritime Adaptations of the Channel Islands. *American Antiquity* 57:60–84.

—— 1995. Transportation Innovation and Social Complexity among Maritime Hunter-Gatherer Societies. *American Anthropologist* 97:733–47.

—— (editor) 2004. *Foundations of Chumash Complexity*. Cotsen Institute of Archaeology, University of California, Los Angeles.

Arnold, Jeanne, and Anthony P. Graesch 2001. The Evolution of Specialized Shellworking among the Island Chumash. In *The Origins of a Pacific Coast Chiefdom: The Chumash of the Channel Islands*, edited by Jeanne Arnold, pp. 71–112. University of Utah Press, Salt Lake City.

Arnold, Jeanne, and Ann Munns 1994. Independent or Attached Specialization: The Organization of Shell Bead Production in California. *Journal of Field Archaeology* 21:473–89.

Arnold, Jeanne E., Roger H. Colten, and Scott Pletka 1997. Contexts of Cultural Change in Insular California. *American Antiquity* 62:300–18.

Bettinger, Robert, Bruce Winterhalder, and Richard McElreath 2006. A Simple Model of Technological Intensification. *Journal of Archaeological Science* 33:538–45.

Blitz, John H. 1988. Adoption of the Bow in Prehistoric North America. *North American Archaeologist* 9:123–45.

Bradbury, A. 1997. The Bow and Arrow in the Eastern Woodlands: Evidence for an Archaic Origin. *North American Archaeologist* 18:207–33.

Breschini, Gary S., Trudy Haversat, and Jon M. Erlandson 1996. *California Radiocarbon Dates.* Eighth edition. Coyote Press, Salinas, CA.

Brill, James 2012. Violent Adaptations: Technology of Violence and Cultural Evolution along the Santa Barbara Channel. Unpublished Master's thesis, Department of Anthropology, California State University, Chico.

Corbett, Ray 2007. The Grammar and Syntax of the Dead: A Regional Analysis of Chumash Mortuary Practice. Unpublished Ph.D. dissertation, Department of Anthropology, University of California, Los Angeles.

Eerkens, Jelmer, and Robert L. Bettinger 2001. Techniques for Assessing Standardization in Artifact Assemblages: Can We Scale Material Variability. *American Antiquity* 66:493–504.

Ember, Carol R., and Melvin Ember 1992. Resource Unpredictability, Mistrust and War: A Cross-Cultural Study. *Journal of Conflict Resolution* 36:242–62.

Erlandson, J. M., and R. H. Colten (editors) 1991. *Hunter-Gatherers of Early Holocene Coastal California.* Perspectives in California Archaeology, Vol. 1. UCLA Institute of Archaeology, Los Angeles.

Gamble, Lynn 2005. Culture and Climate: Reconsidering the Effect of Paleoclimatic Variability among Southern California Hunter-Gatherer Societies. *World Archaeology* 37:92–108.

——— 2008. *The Chumash World at European Contact: Power, Trade, and Feasting Among Complex Hunter-Gatherers.* University of California Press. Berkeley.

Glassow, Michael A. 1997. Middle Holocene Cultural Development in the Central Santa Barbara Channel Region. In *The Archaeology of the California Coast during the Middle Holocene,* edited by Jon M. Erlandson and Michael A. Glassow, pp. 73–90. Cotsen Institute of Archaeology, University of California, Los Angeles.

Harris, Marvin (1977) 1991. *Cannibals and Kings: The Origins of Cultures.* Random House, New York.

Hudson, Travis, and Thomas C. Blackburn 1982. Food Procurement and Transportation. In *The Material Culture of the Chumash Interaction Sphere, Vol. I,* edited by Thomas C. Blackburn, pp. 1–387. Ballena Press and Santa Barbara Museum of Natural History, Santa Barbara, CA.

Jochim, Michael 1981. *Strategies for Survival: Cultural Behavior in an Ecological Context.* Academic Press, New York

Johnson, John R. 1988. Chumash Social Organization: An Ethnohistoric Perspective. Unpublished Ph.D. dissertation, Department of Anthropology, University of California, Santa Barbara.

——— 2004. Social Responses to Climate Change among the Chumash Indians of South-Central California. In *Prehistoric California: Archaeology and the Myth of Paradise,* edited by L. Mark Raab and Terry Jones, pp. 149–59. University of Utah Press, Salt Lake City.

——— 2007. Ethnohistoric Descriptions of Chumash Warfare. In *North American Indigenous Warfare and Ritual,* edited by Richard Chacon and Ruben Mendoza, pp. 74–113. University of Arizona Press, Tucson.

Jones, Terry, Gary Brown, L. Mark Raab, Janet McVicker, W. Geoff Spaulding, Douglas J. Kennett, Andrew York, and Phillip Walker 1999. Environmental Imperatives Reconsidered, Demographic Crises in Western North America During the Medieval Climatic Anomaly. *Current Anthropology* 40:137–70.

# 332 | James M. Brill

Jones, Terry, and Al Schwitalla 2008. Archaeological Perspectives on the Effects of Medieval Drought in Prehistoric California. *Quaternary International* 188:41–58.

Justice, Noel 2002. *Stone Age Spear and Arrow Points of California and the Great Basin.* Indiana University Press, Bloomington.

Keeley, Lawrence 1996. *War Before Civilization.* Oxford University Press, Oxford, UK.

Kennett, Douglas J. 1997. Late Holocene Shifts on Santa Rosa Island, Southern California. Paper presented at the Annual Meeting for the Society for California Archaeology, Sonoma, CA.

———— 2005. *The Island Chumash: Behavioral Ecology of a Maritime Society.* University of California Press, Berkeley.

Kennett, Douglas J., and James Kennett 2000. Competitive and Cooperative Responses to Climatic Instability in Coastal Southern California. *American Antiquity* 65:379–95.

King, Chester 1990. *Evolution of Chumash Society: A Comparative Study of Artifacts Used for Social Systems Maintenance in the Santa Barbara Channel Region before AD 1804.* Garland, New York.

King, Linda B. 1982. Medea Creek Cemetery: Late Inland Chumash Patterns of Social Organization, Exchange, and Warfare. Unpublished Ph.D. dissertation, Department of Anthropology, University of California, Los Angeles.

Kroeber, Alfred (1925) 1976. *Handbook of the Indians of California.* Dover Press, New York. Originally published as Bulletin 78 of American Ethnology of the Smithsonian Institute.

Lambert, Patricia 1993. Health in Prehistoric Populations of the Santa Barbara Channel Islands. *American Antiquity* 58:509–22.

———— 1994. War and Peace on the Western Front: A Study of Violent Conflict and Its Correlates in Prehistoric Hunter-Gatherer Societies of Coastal Southern California. Unpublished Ph.D. dissertation, Department of Anthropology, University of California, Santa Barbara.

———— 1997. Patterns of Violence in Prehistoric Hunter-Gatherer Societies of Coastal Southern California. In *Troubled Times: Violence and Warfare in the Past*, edited by Debra L. Martin and David W. Frayer, pp. 77–109. Gordon and Breach Publishers, Amsterdam, the Netherlands.

———— 2002. Archaeology of War: A North American Perspective. *Journal of Archaeological Research* 10:207–41.

Landberg, Leif C. W. 1965. *The Chumash Indians of Southern California.* Southwest Museum Papers No. 19. Southwest Museum, Los Angeles.

Raab, L. Mark, and Daniel Larson 1997. Medieval Climatic Anomaly and Punctuated Cultural Evolution in Evolution in Coastal California. *American Antiquity.* 62:319–36.

Santa Barbara Museum of Natural History 2008. *NAGPRA and Associated Funerary Objects Inventory.* Manuscript on file, Department of Anthropology, Santa Barbara Museum of Natural History, Santa Barbara, CA.

Stine, Scott 1994. Extreme and Persistent Drought in California and Patagonia during Medieval Time. *Nature* 369:546–9.

Ugan, Andrew, Jason Bright, and Alan Rodger 2003. When Is Technology Worth the Trouble? *Journal of Archaeological Science* 30:1315–29.

Walker, Phillip 2001. A Bioarchaeological Perspective on the History of Violence. *Annual Review of Anthropology* 30:573–96.

———— 2007. Skeletal Biology: California. In *Environment, Origins, and Population,* edited by David H. Ubelaker, pp. 548–56. Handbook of North American Indians, Vol. 3, William C. Sturtevant, general editor. Smithsonian Institution, Washington, D.C.

Walker, Phillip, and Patricia Lambert 1989. Skeletal Evidence for Stress during a Period of Cultural Change in Prehistoric California. In *Advances in Paleopathology*, edited by Luigi Capasso, pp. 207–12. Marino Solfanelli, Chieti, Italy.

Yohe II, Robert 2002. Analysis of Flaked Stone Artifacts. In *Archaeological Laboratory Methods, an Introduction. Third Edition*, edited by Mark Sutton and Brooke Arkush, pp. 37–67. Kendall/Hunt, Dubuque, IA.

# 18

## Updating the Warrior Cache: Timing the Evidence for Warfare at Prince Rupert Harbour

Jerome S. Cybulski

The "warrior cache" is a clustered assemblage of weaponry and related items—16 pieces in total—that was found during excavations at the Boardwalk site, Prince Rupert Harbour, British Columbia, Canada, in 1968 (MacDonald and Cybulski 2001:8–9). It is one piece of evidence that has stimulated debate on the antiquity and duration of Northwest Coast warfare prior to the time of European contact (e.g., Ames 2001; Angelbeck 2007:267–8; Marsden 2001; Maschner 1997). Direct additional evidence consists of human burials from multiple sites in the region that show the hallmarks of warfare in terms of skeletal trauma. Characteristic for this group are cranial depression fractures from club blows, facial skeleton and tooth fractures (likely also from club blows and, perhaps, fists), defensive fractures of the forearm and hand, boxer's fractures of the hand, and, perhaps most definably, cut marks in the neck vertebrae of headless skeletons, particularly at the Lachane site across the Harbour from Boardwalk (Cybulski 1992:142–58; 2006:540; 2014:421–38).[1] The headless remains and cut marks signal decapitation, a not-infrequent consequence of Northwest Coast warfare as reported in the oral histories of the various groups that inhabit the British Columbia segment, including the Coast Tsimshian, whose territories encompass Prince Rupert Harbour (Boas 1916:373, 410–11; Marsden 2001).

---

*Violence and Warfare among Hunter-Gatherers,* edited by Mark W. Allen and Terry L. Jones, 333–350. ©2014 Taylor & Francis. All rights reserved.

**334** | Jerome S. Cybulski

On the basis of indirect evidence from radiocarbon-dated human remains nearby, different estimated ages of around 500 BC and AD 200 have been proposed for the warrior cache (Ames 2005:248; Cybulski 1993; MacDonald 1983). Among the items in the cache were six copper tubes, four of which contained dowels or pegs made of western red cedar (Ames 2005:209–13). Nearby in the same cultural pit and likely associated lay a copper-stained articulated human cranium and lower jaw believed to be a war trophy (Cybulski 1993, 2014). Accelerator mass spectrometry (AMS) radiocarbon dates have now been obtained directly from the cranium and one of the cedar dowels, and are reported here. They define an age of around cal AD 1000 for the deposition of these items, an age that is similarly shown for a clustering of headless skeletons at the Lachane site and two possible decapitations at Garden Island, a third burial site at Prince Rupert Harbour. These data may provide catastrophic end markers following a long period of warfare that ultimately resulted in the abandonment of the Prince Rupert Harbour region as a viable living area. Collagen-based radiocarbon dates obtained from more than 80 sets of human remains at a total of six Prince Rupert Harbour sites indicate warfare in the region for a period of about 2,000 years, 1000 cal BC to cal AD 1000.

## Materials and Methods

Boardwalk (GbTo-31), Lachane (GbTo-33), and Garden Island (GbTo-23) are three of eight Prince Rupert Harbour shell middens from which human burials were excavated and collected in the 1960s and 1970s as part of a National Museum of Canada, National Museum of Man field project (MacDonald and Inglis 1981).[2] The others were Dodge Island (GbTo-18), Parizeau Point (GbTo-31), Baldwin (GbTo-36), Grassy Bay (GbTn-1), and Ridley Island (GbTn-19). All told, a minimum of 271 individuals was counted for the osteological analysis; 11 were later added from salvage excavations at the Lachane site in 1987 (Simonsen 1988). Details of the site excavations may be found in MacDonald and Inglis (1981), MacDonald and Cybulski (2001), and Ames (2005). All of the sites, shown in Figure 18.1, are within a 20-square-km area in Prince Rupert Harbour with five separated by no more than 2 or 3 km, situated almost across from one another on Kaien and Digby Islands. It is apparent that the sites were used for both habitation and human burial concurrently or, perhaps, at different times.

I personally studied and interpreted all of the skeletal remains. Relevant patterns for the interpretation of warfare (i.e., trauma incurred through interpersonal violence rather than accident) have been described and illustrated in detail elsewhere (Cybulski 1992:142–58; 2006:539–42; 2014:421–34); some examples are discussed here.

# Timing the Evidence for Warfare at Prince Rupert Harbour | 335

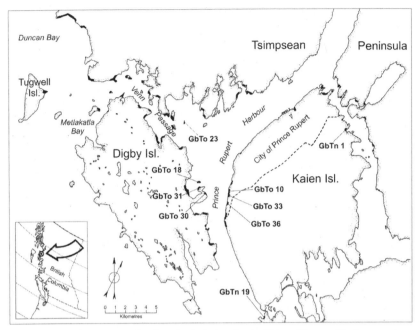

**Figure 18.1** Locations of archaeological sites in the Prince Rupert Harbour region, modified from a drawing by David W. Laverie (Courtesy of the Canadian Museum of Civilization).

## Radiocarbon Dating

The 1966 through 1987 field excavation record, on file in the Archives of the Canadian Museum of Civilization (e.g., Inglis 1973; MacDonald 1968), was studied as part of the osteological analysis. From 1966 to and including 1979, 71 radiocarbon dates were obtained by the archaeologists from samples of charcoal (n=64), blocks or pieces of wood (n=3), peat (n=3), and humus (n=1). Two additional charcoal dates were later obtained as part of the Lachane site salvage excavation (Simonsen 1988). Only five samples were reportedly associated with human burials, and at least one of the associations was questionable. Hence, in 1977, I began selecting bone samples from burials that were then submitted for dating by me or by Richard Inglis, excavator of the Lachane and Baldwin sites (Inglis 1974). In total, 39 samples were tested, largely in 1977 and 1979, by traditional radiocarbon dating techniques requiring usually 80 to 85 grams of bone in each case. Most of the samples were tested by the Saskatchewan Radiocarbon Dating Laboratory ("S" in the text and tables here) and two by the Geological Survey of Canada ("GSC").

**336** | Jerome S. Cybulski

In 2004, I began to obtain AMS dates from human bone collagen, a procedure that requires significantly smaller amounts of bone and provides greater precision in the results. Ultimately, 54 samples were tested by Beta Analytic Inc., including five from skeletons previously tested at the Saskatchewan laboratory and two by the Geological Survey of Canada. Included in the AMS testing was a bone sample from XVII-B:338, the copper-stained trophy head believed to have been placed with the warrior cache. AMS dates were also obtained for one of the cedar dowels with the warrior cache that had originally been wrapped in copper.[3]

## Calendar Calibration

All radiocarbon dates were calibrated and are reported here in AD and BC years, as well as BP years. The calibrations were completed using CALIB 6.11 (Stuiver and Reimer 1993; Stuiver et al. 2011). Calibration curve "2" (Northern Hemisphere terrestrial calibration dataset) was used for all the charcoal and other terrestrial plant assays, while calibration curve "4" (Mixed Northern Hemisphere and marine dataset) was applied to the bone dates to allow for compensation of the marine reservoir effect.

## Marine Reservoir Effect

Human bone dates from proximate seaside inhabitants are variably influenced by the marine reservoir effect (e.g., Arneborg et al. 1999; Yoneda et al. 2002). Because of a high marine protein content in Northwest Coast diets (Chisholm et al. 1983), it is probable that radiocarbon dates from directly tested Northwest Coast human remains may be off by as much as 600 to 800 calibrated calendar years on average depending on local fluctuations in oceanic deep water upwelling (Richards et al. 2007; Southon and Fedje 2003). To correct for the marine reservoir effect in CALIB 6.11, Delta R years ($\Delta R$) and Delta R standard deviation ($\sigma R$) values were obtained from the online Marine Reservoir Correction Database, which is intended for use with the CALIB and OxCal calibration programs. No values are provided for Prince Rupert Harbour, but five values are available for nearby Haida Gwaii (the Queen Charlotte Islands), yielding a weighted mean $\Delta R$ of 265 and standard deviation of 80.

The percentage of marine protein for each sample was calculated wherever possible from the $^{13}C/^{12}C$ ratio ($\delta^{13}C$) provided by the radiocarbon dating laboratory or otherwise directly obtained from the skeletal contributor. For each sample that did not have a ratio reported with the date, either a site or regional average was used. The percentage of marine protein was separately calculated for each sample by means of linear interpolation with end points for the $\delta^{13}C$ values of $-21.0$ (=100 percent terrestrial protein) and $-12.5$

(=100 percent marine protein). The end points were selected using published sources as guides (Arneborg et al. 1999; Chisholm et al. 1983), but weighed also against the relative proportions of marine and terrestrial protein that might have been available to the Prince Rupert Harbour population as indicated by the archaeological distribution of faunal remains. Only one of the Prince Rupert sites, Boardwalk, could be considered unbiased in its collection protocol because of recent testing of the site rather than from the excavations that yielded the human burials. My interpretation of data reported by Stewart et al. (2009) indicates, on the basis of minimum number of individuals (MNI) counts, that 83.3 percent of the faunal remains represented marine dietary potential.[4] A second northern Northwest Coast site unbiased in its faunal collection protocol is Greenville (GgTj-6) on the Nass River (Balkwill and Cybulski 1992). In this instance, 86.3 percent of relevant faunal remains suggested marine dietary potential.

An average marine dietary potential for the two North Coast sites, Boardwalk and Greenville, and, presumably, a prehistoric North Coast population, would be about 85 percent from the distribution of faunal remains. On the interpolation scale, this value provides a $\delta^{13}C$ value of $-13.75$, which is the unrounded average for the dated Boardwalk burials accompanied by laboratory-determined stable carbon isotope ratios (n=15). The average for Greenville samples (n=6; Cybulski 1992, 2010:97) was $-13.93$; this value compares with 84 percent on the interpolation scale. Chisholm et al. (1983) provided a $\delta^{13}C$ average of $-13.3$ for the prehistoric British Columbia coast as a whole that prompted them to estimate an average marine dietary protein intake of 91 percent. Their $\delta^{13}C$ average corresponds to 90.6 percent on my interpolation scale. Overall, this scale provides a suitable proxy for the determination of marine protein dietary potential from $\delta^{13}C$ values for each sample calibration.

## Context

### The Warrior Cache

The original Boardwalk site (GbTo-31) excavations were carried out over three field seasons (1968–1970) in six areas labeled A through F (MacDonald and Inglis 1981; see Figure 4 in MacDonald and Cybulski 2001:7). Most of the human remains recorded in the site were in Areas A and C, large back-ridge shell dumps determined to be definable cemetery locations (Cybulski 1992:42–3).

The initially proposed 500 BC date for the warrior cache (MacDonald 1983:111) appears to have come from its depth-below-datum concordance with a nearby dated human burial in the same excavation unit, one of eight in Area A opened in 1968. The date reported for a femur from XVII-B:319, submitted for testing in 1977, was 2,610 ± 65 years BP (S-1285).[5] Careful

**338** | Jerome S. Cybulski

study of the field record, however, indicates that the cache was not in the same stratigraphic layer but rather in a pit intrusive from the layer above, the basis for the AD 200 estimate mentioned in the introduction (Cybulski 1993).

## Trophy Head

There is good reason to suspect that XVII-B:338 was associated with the artifact cluster and not the remnant of an intentional burial. The cranium and mandible were fully articulated and well preserved, and could not be associated with any nearby human remains that would suggest the deposition of a complete corpse. These observations suggest that XVII-B:338 was placed as a near fully or partially fleshed separate head, although no remnant neck vertebrae were present as might be expected in a case of decapitation (see section in this chapter on decapitation at Lachane).

The possible occurrence of a trophy head was not unusual for the Boardwalk site. Two other isolated crania, one with and one without a lower jaw, were found with a complex of burials in a nearby excavation unit, while portions of two human crania were found alongside the pelvic bones of Burial XVII-B:375, an articulated skeleton in Area C, as if they had adorned a belt or skirt.

Besides its proximity, the association of XVII-B:338 with the artifact cluster was indicated by blue-green copper salt stains throughout the right side of the cranial vault, facial skeleton, mandible, and teeth. The closest copper artifacts, the only ones in the excavation unit and general region, were bracelets and wrapped cedar pegs in the warrior cache.

## Decapitation at the Lachane Site

The Lachane site (GbTo-33) was principally excavated in 1973 but briefly tested in 1970 and revisited for a partial salvage operation in 1987 (Inglis 1974, 1976; Simonsen 1988). Human remains were uncovered and collected on all three occasions, presenting a minimum of 73 individuals for study (Cybulski 1996). Like Boardwalk, Lachane was partitioned into excavation areas in 1973, in this case labeled A through H. Three headless skeletons in Area B were identified as "decapitated" and "definitely associated" in that year's field record. Area B was not given a structural label, although it included house features and served as a cemetery area, perhaps at different times (Ames 2005:89–91). The headless skeletons were located in the west section of Trench III, one of seven excavation trenches that defined Area B. At least 30 individuals were identified from the area, and 17 skeletons, over and above the headless ones, appeared positioned as intentional burials.

Two of the posited decapitations, XVII-B:467 and XVII-B:481, were confirmed in the laboratory. The skeletons lacked first through fourth cervical (neck) vertebrae, as well as the crania and mandibles, and had cut marks in the

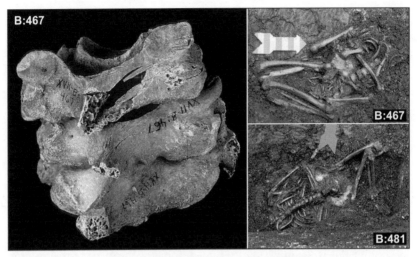

**Figure 18.2** Two of three headless individuals found within 2 to 3 meters of one another at the Lachane site (GbTo-33). Fine and larger cuts can be seen in the neck vertebrae of XVII-B:467. XVII-B:467 and B:481 present unconventional burial attitudes (described in the text). Cervicals photo by the author; burial photos by field personnel under the direction of Richard I. Inglis (Courtesy of the Canadian Museum of Civilization).

fifth cervicals (Figure 18.2). In XVII-B:467, the sixth cervical was also marked with cuts. In each instance, the cuts were old and discolored, unlike those that might have resulted from excavation trauma or other recent disturbance.

The remaining cervical and upper thoracic (ribcage) vertebrae of XVII-B:481 had been subjected to postmortem damage that left only the neural arches preserved. In the fifth cervical, fine cuts were faintly visible in the superior edges of the right lamina. In both individuals, the fineness of all the cuts suggested they could have been made with a "shell knife," an implement used to remove the head of an enemy slain in battle, according to local native oral tradition as related to me by the site's excavator, Richard I. Inglis.

The third postcranial skeleton in the complex, XVII-B:466, lacked all upper vertebrae to and including the fifth thoracic. It was therefore not possible to examine neck bones for cuts. Complicating the interpretation was the fact that the skeleton had been partly disturbed prior to its 1973 discovery, possibly accounting for loss of vertebrae as well as a few other skeletal parts. The skeleton also lacked a sternum, several hand and foot bones, and a left patella.

Judging from available field photographs and hand sketches, the three skeletons were in unusual body positions relative to those shown by most other intact or partly intact burials in the Prince Rupert Harbour middens. Burials XVII-B:466 and XVII-B:467 lay beside one another, and the dispositions of the skeletons suggested those of individuals who had collapsed on the spot of

**340** | Jerome S. Cybulski

their demise or decapitation, or of corpses that had otherwise been discarded rather than carefully placed in burial (Figure 18.2). The least disturbed of the two, XVII-B:467, appeared collapsed from a kneeling position, with lower legs folded under the thighs, upper spine sharply curved forward and to the right, and at least one arm flexed on top of a hip. The skeleton of XVII-B:481, located about 60 cm to the southeast of XVII-B:467, was on its back with knees raised, lower legs flexed beneath and to the right of the thighs, and forearms flexed with hands together, apparently behind the lower back.

A third headless skeleton with cut marks in a cervical vertebra was identified in the laboratory. It was XVII-B:454, one of four designated burials collected during a test excavation at the Lachane site in 1970. Burial XVII-B:454 was poorly represented skeletally, and there was no information on the attitude of the body. Besides the cranium and mandible, the first through third cervical vertebrae were missing. The fourth cervical was incomplete but clearly showed fine cuts like those in XVII-B:467 and XVII-B:481. Although the exact location of the skeleton was not recorded, some of the 1970 test excavation activity was in the vicinity of what later became the west section of Trench III.

There may, in fact, have been five decapitated persons in and about the west section of Trench III. A fifth possibility is XVII-B:483, a sparsely represented postcranial skeleton that had been documented as a "scattered incomplete human" after the collapse of the north excavation wall of Trench III West. The remains were earlier reported in level notes as a possible burial extending into the wall at excavation level 10 about 14 inches (approximately 36 cm) higher than the elevation of the in situ decapitations reported in level 11.

There was no information on the original attitude of the body. Evidence that it could have been a decapitation was circumstantial. There were no cervical vertebrae to show cuts, and many other postcranial skeletal elements were also missing. However, there were no disturbed cranial parts (or full crania) collected in or near the west section of Trench III for possible assignment to the postcranial skeleton. Only one small cranial fragment was identified among 67 scattered or isolated skeletal elements collected from the west section of Trench III, and less than 5 percent of all disturbed skeletal elements collected from Area B were cranium parts. The probability that one or more of the cranial elements could have belonged to XVII-B:483 was quite low. The proximity of this person to the others and the absence of cranium and mandible suggested that it might have been a decapitation. This premise is supported by radiocarbon dating (see below).

## Other Skeletal Evidence for Warfare

Outside of the decapitations, 54 adults in the Prince Rupert Harbour series exhibited trauma likely due to interpersonal violence. The most common indicator, in 30 instances, was a depressed fracture of the cranial vault.

As detailed and illustrated elsewhere, those injuries likely resulted from a blow to the head with a stone club (Cybulski 2014). In most instances, the lesion was healed, but in two cases unhealed perimortem injuries indicated that the blows could have been the manner if not the cause of death (see Figure 4 in Cybulski 2006:540; Figure 22.5 in Cybulski 2014:425). It seems that at least three different types of stone clubs could have been responsible for the range of lesions in the Prince Rupert Harbour crania (Cybulski 2014:426–7).

Other trauma likely due to interpersonal violence included fractures of the upper facial skeleton and teeth (17 individuals), fractures of the mandible (3 cases), forearm shaft fractures (12 individuals; one had both forearms broken), fractures of the medial rays of the hand (usually the fourth or fifth metacarpal or both (8 individuals, all male), fractures of the clavicle (collar) bone (6 individuals, all left side, all male), and rib wounds (at least one arguable instance). These were not all separate individuals; at least 19 sustained multiple injuries due to violence. For example, Burial XVII-B:396 from the Boardwalk site had a funnel-shaped depressed fracture of the frontal bone and a massive healed fracture of the facial skeleton, a parry-type fracture of the left forearm, and fractured third and fourth metacarpals of the right hand. As described in terms of mechanics elsewhere, the depressed fracture and the facial fracture (both healed) may have occurred at the same time by means of two rapid blows by a club-wielding assailant (Cybulski 2014:426–7). Four other individuals, including one from the Boardwalk site and three from Lachane, exhibited both depressed fractures of the cranial vault and fractured forearm shafts. For all instances of skeletal trauma due to interpersonal violence, seven Prince Rupert Harbour sites were represented.

## Chronology

Table 18.1 reports the radiocarbon dates and resulting calendar calibrations for the warrior cache and decapitations. The warrior cache is represented by the trophy crania, XVII-B:338, and a cedar dowel. The date for the latter is not likely to be influenced by the marine reservoir effect; this is indicated by the low $\delta^{13}C$ ratio. The fact that that ratio is at the bottom of the interpolation scale used in this study to estimate the proportion of marine protein intake appears to justify the value of −21 per mil as the appropriate end point for 100 percent terrestrial protein. There is clear overlap of the calibrated calendar ages of the trophy cranium and cedar dowel, strongly supporting their likely association in the warrior cache.

Burial XVII-B:481 was originally radiocarbon dated in 1979 at 1,750 ± 40 years BP (S-1663; Cybulski 1996). Assuming that date was acceptable for the in situ decapitation complex suggested by Burials XVII-B:481, B:467, and B:466, I later obtained AMS dates for the out-of-context Burials XVII-B:454 and B:483 to test their presumed association. The returned

# 342 | Jerome S. Cybulski

**Table 18.1** Laboratory-provided radiocarbon dates for the warrior cache and associated trophy head, and the decapitated (or presumed or possibly decapitated) individuals in the Prince Rupert Harbour sites

| Burial | Laboratory No. | Measured age, y BP | Conventional age, y BP | $\delta^{13}C$ | Calibrated age range |
|---|---|---|---|---|---|
| Boardwalk Warrior Cache | | | | | |
| Trophy head[1] | Beta-200548 | 1390 ± 40 | 1550 ± 40 | −15.0 | cal AD 730–1060 (cal BP 1220–890) |
| Cedar dowel[2] | Beta-245147 | 950 ± 40 | 1010 ± 40 | −21.3 | cal AD 900–1160 (cal BP 1050–790) |
| Decapitations | | | | | |
| Lachane | | | | | |
| XVII-B:454 | Beta-227184 | 1480 ± 40 | 1660 ± 40 | −13.9 | cal AD 720–1040 (cal BP 1230–910) |
| XVII-B:466 | Beta-241035 | 1450 ± 40 | 1650 ± 40 | −12.8 | cal AD 790–1190 (cal BP 1160–760) |
| XVII-B:481 | Beta-283861 | 1410 ± 40 | 1590 ± 40 | −14.1 | cal AD 780–1150 (cal BP 1170–800) |
| XVII-B:483 | Beta-227183 | 1540 ± 40 | 1730 ± 40 | −13.7 | cal AD 680–1010 (cal BP 1270–940) |
| Garden Island | | | | | |
| XVII-B:165 | Beta-283862 | 1390 ± 40 | 1570 ± 40 | −13.8 | cal AD 810–1180 (cal BP 1140–770) |
| XVII-B:192 | Beta-200549 | 1390 ± 40 | 1580 ± 40 | −13.7 | cal AD 810–1180 (cal BP 1140–770) |

**Notes:** The calibrated ages for the human bone dates are corrected for the marine reservoir effect. The $\delta^{13}C$ values are those provided by Beta Analytic Inc.
[1] Canadian Museum of Civilization human remains catalog XVII-B:338.
[2] Canadian Museum of Civilization artifact catalog GbTo-31:267.

measured ages were close to one another, but notably younger than the original measured age for XVII-B:481. I then tested Burial XVII-B:466: it too presented a substantially younger age, raising the possibility that either a second decapitation event was represented at Lachane or that the date initially provided for XVII-B:481 was inaccurate. Burial XVII-B:481 was retested by AMS and, as seen in Table 18.1, provided an age comparable with the results for XVII-B:454, B:466, and B:483. According to CALIB 6.11, the four tested AMS radiocarbon ages are statistically the same at the 95 percent probability level, and the calibrated age ranges minimally overlap by 250 years. The sum of the calibrated probability distributions indicate the apparently one-time decapitation event took place somewhere in the range of cal AD 700 to 1130 (1,250–820 years cal BP).

In Table 18.1, I have included two sets of remains from Garden Island (GbTo-23), XVII-B: 165 and XVII-B:192. Both were well-represented skeletons that lacked crania and mandibles and might be considered examples of decapitation. However, in both cases, the seven cervical vertebrae were missing so that possible cuts could not be discerned. The radiocarbon information, particularly the calibrated age ranges, draw attention because these data are very much the same as those for the decapitations at Lachane. Burial XVII-B:165 is of particular interest because the skeleton was reasonably well articulated in situ but in an unconventional way. The body lay torso on front laterally twisted to the left, legs irregularly half-flexed to the left, right forearm flexed up under the chest, and left upper arm abducted with the forearm half-flexed at the elbow and partly beneath a large rock. The remaining skeleton was largely complete except for the hands, which could not be found during laboratory study and were presumably missing on site. Of particular interest is that the calibrated age range of this AMS-dated individual is very similar to that of the decapitation complex at Lachane, and that the radiocarbon age is statistically the same. The second headless skeleton at Garden Island, XVII-B:192, produced an identical calibrated age range; unfortunately, the position of the body was not recorded in situ. It was not associated with XVII-B:165 but was found at the opposite end of the site, 60 meters away.

## The Chronology of Warfare

Summed probability distributions were obtained for the warrior cache and for the Lachane decapitation complex using CALIB 6.11. For the trophy head, XVII-B:338, and cedar dowel, the two-sigma start and end points were cal AD 790 and cal AD 1150 (1,160–800 years cal BP). The two-sigma start and end points for the sampled Lachane complex was cal AD 700 and cal AD 1130 (1,250–820 years cal BP). Thus, the two events appear to correspond with an overlapping range of about 350 years. In the big picture, both events came late in the chronological evidence for warfare as presented by the Prince Rupert Harbour sites.

Figure 18.3 is an attempt to provide an overall view of the timing of warfare at Prince Rupert Harbour against a background of what is known about the sites. The chart summarizes the calibrated chronology of the shell middens (as determined by dated terrestrial samples), the burial program, and the duration of warfare based on the mortuary evidence, skeletal data, and evidence of the warrior cache. The vertical gray bands illustrate the calibrated age ranges for the six sites that had skeletal evidence for trauma due to interpersonal violence as well as dated terrestrial samples.[6] Superimposed on the gray bands, which cover the calibrated age ranges of the terrestrial samples, are the calibrated age ranges of those dated burials with skeletal trauma due to interpersonal violence (dark squares), the collagen-dated burials with suspected indicators of warfare (light or white squares), and all other collagen-dated burials (circles).

344 | Jerome S. Cybulski

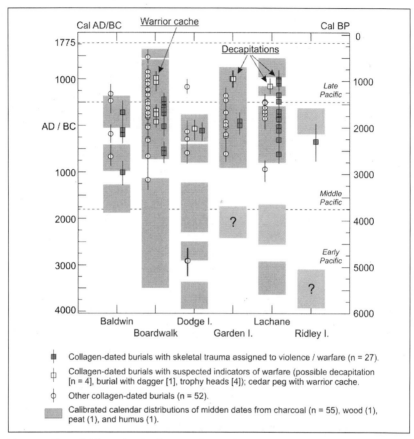

**Figure 18.3** Calibrated calendar ages for six Prince Rupert Harbour middens, including site ages based on dated terrestrial samples, dated human burials with skeletal trauma due to interpersonal violence, dated materials with contextual evidence for warfare, and other dated burials. The human bone ages have been adjusted for the marine reservoir effect. The horizontal dotted lines demarcate the Early (cal 4400–1800 BC), Middle (cal 1800 BC–AD 200/500), and Late Pacific (cal AD 200/500–1775) cultural periods or phases in use for the Northwest Coast as calibrated by Kenneth Ames and Herbert Maschner (1999). Drawing by the author.

Specifics are detailed in the legend of Figure 18.3. The squares and circles are the median probability estimates of the calibrations and are included to better visualize the calibration sets; it is the ranges, however, that are important.

The calibration ranges for the sites (gray bands) were derived from 55 dated charcoal samples, one wood sample, one peat sample, and one humus sample obtained by the archaeologists. Not included in this analysis were a very few charcoal dates that had been rejected by the archaeologists as being out of

# Timing the Evidence for Warfare at Prince Rupert Harbour | **345**

sequence or possibly contaminated (see Cybulski 1992:228–9). I also did not include any of five dated shell samples from the Boardwalk site, although their inclusion would not have changed Figure 18.3.

It will be noted that gaps exist in the age calibration record of each site as depicted by the gray bands. Perhaps most notable is the relatively consistent and apparently persistent gap across all of the sites at about the 3,000-year cal BP level. One might interpret this as possibly reflecting a general abandonment of sites in the Harbour at that time, or merely an artifact of the data at hand associated with so-called "plateaus" in the $^{14}C$ calibration curve (Gajewski et al. 2011:388–9). The haphazardness or temporal inconsistency of gaps above this level across the sites probably simply means that the period was not fully sampled.

Of general interest is that the ages for almost all of the human burials excavated from the Prince Rupert Harbour middens fall between 1390 cal BC and cal AD 1640 (3,340–310 years cal BP), but that the sites themselves are much older as determined by the terrestrial sample dates. The only known exceptions were two individuals at Dodge Island with almost identical age ranges of 3180/3240 to 2630 cal BC (5,190/5,130–4,580 years cal BP). The conventional age for XVII-B:160a, an early young adult female (16–18 years), was 4,880 ± 40 years BP (Beta-202019); for XVII-B:160b, an older male, it was 4,870 ± 40 years BP (Beta-202020). The two individuals were almost certainly buried together, although they were not recognized as two individuals in the field record. Only the younger individual was described; the second, older male skeleton was apparently eroding from an excavation wall of the same excavation unit. The two were separated and identified during laboratory analysis. They were dated for confirmation because the recorded individual was reported to be associated with a charcoal sample that had been dated at 4,875 ± 125 years BP (S-1409).

The earliest dated skeleton with trauma due to interpersonal violence (a perforating upper facial fracture below the left orbit and a fractured tooth) was at the Baldwin site, 1290 to 770 cal BC (3,240–2,720 cal BP). The most recent were the two decapitations at Lachane with cut cervicals; their summed probability distribution was cal AD 720 to 1100 (1,230–850 years cal BP). Only the decapitations (at Lachane and the possible Garden Island cases) and the warrior cache and trophy head at Boardwalk make up the latest indicators of warfare at Prince Rupert Harbour. There was one indicator of skeletal trauma due to violence at Dodge Island, a perimortem club blow to the cranium of XVII-B:166. However, a second suspected indicator, approximately contemporary, was a young male buried with a slate dagger on his chest, positioned in line with his sternum (XVII-B:170 in Table 1 of MacDonald and Cybulski 2001:11; indicated as a light square on Figure 18.3). Burials XVII-B:166 and B:170 ranged from 340 cal BC to AD 130 (2,290–1,820 years cal BP).

**346** | Jerome S. Cybulski

## Discussion

At the outset of this research, it was not my intention to interpret or assess the chronology of the Prince Rupert Harbour sites per se, but simply to give context to the human burials in terms of warfare. Ames (2005:49–112) has diligently addressed the chronology of Prince Rupert Harbour in great detail in his assessment of the artifacts from many of the same middens. Hence, it seems natural to compare notes. We each looked at Boardwalk, Baldwin, Lachane, and Garden Island. He did not consider Dodge Island in the same detail as the other sites because GbTo-18 had previously been reported by another archaeologist (Sutherland 1978). I did not consider a midden at Grassy Bay (GbTn-1) since it provided only one human burial, that of a child aged 5 to 7 years, which was not relevant to the question of warfare. I did not consider Kitandach, GbTo-34, because it yielded no burials, only a few fragmentary pieces of human bone including a culturally modified parietal (Cybulski 1978). I also did not consider GbTp-1 on Lucy Island in part because it is located outside the Harbour area and in part because it did not provide any warfare-relevant human skeletal material. It is, however, significant from the standpoint of burials chronology and is mentioned here.

Notwithstanding these differences, the general patterns provided by Ames' Figure 5.29 (2005:102) and my Figure 18.3 are the same for the midden chronology, which is not too surprising given that we used the same dated charcoal, wood, peat, and humus samples with basically the same calibration schemes. The Prince Rupert Harbour middens were in use beginning at or close to 4000 cal BC (5,950 years cal BP; although Ames gives cogent arguments for a considerably earlier beginning occupation of the Harbour), with terminal dates at about cal AD 1600 (350 years cal BP). Neither of us had much confidence with the earliest dates for Garden Island (n=1) and Ridley Island (n=2), and their calibration ranges are qualified by question marks in my Figure 18.3 (see Ames 2005:58, 103).

Where Ames and I differ is in the chronology of the burial program. Ames used 37 dated burial samples that were available prior to 2004, when I began obtaining AMS dates and he was putting the finishing touches on his manuscript (Ames 2005:iii). Six of those samples were redated by AMS (including, for example, XVII-B:481 as noted earlier). Ames did not adjust for the marine reservoir effect when calibrating the dates. His conclusions about the burial program at Prince Rupert Harbour terminating in the back-ridge of Boardwalk by approximately AD 1 and generally (apparently in the Harbour as a whole) by AD 600 (Ames 2005:294) would therefore prove premature. One of his final conclusions, however, is that the Harbour may have been totally abandoned as a settlement area around AD 800 to 1000 (Ames 2005:295). The chronological data presented here seem to suggest that 2,000 years of warfare in the region could have been responsible, either in whole or in part, for that proposed abandonment.

It seems reasonable to conclude from the present analysis that the burial program in Prince Rupert Harbour truly began at about 1000 cal BC and continued unabated until about cal AD 1000 plus or minus a couple hundred years. The most recently dated burial, at the Boardwalk site, appears to be an outlier, as its calibrated range does not overlap with the next latest burial. The former, XVII-B:386, was not in the back-ridge cemetery area but in Area D, a "platform" area at the front or beach side of the site. The next latest burial indicating termination of the Boardwalk site burial program was XVII-B:520 in Area A, coeval with other dated burials from Boardwalk and Lachane, the warrior cache, and the decapitations (see Table 18.1). XVII-B:386 appears to have been an isolated interment after the close of warfare in the Harbour, the latter perhaps signaled by the decapitations and deposition of the warrior cache.

It is interesting that almost no human burials occur during the first almost 3,000 years of midden buildup at the Prince Rupert Harbour sites, approximately 4000 to 1100 cal BC (5,950–3,050 years cal BP). It cannot be said that they are among the undated burials excavated from the Harbour sites since those dated were carefully selected to test for potential early, middle, and late depositions based on stratigraphic positions and depths below datum. It is difficult to account for the two exceptions at Dodge Island. Recent evidence indicates, however, that XVII-B:160a and XVII-B:160b are not the only earliest burials in the vicinity of Prince Rupert. The sparse remains of three individuals were collected from a disturbed deposit at site GbTp-1 on the Lucy Islands, outside the Harbour about 19 km west of Prince Rupert, in the winter of 1984–1985 (Cybulski 1986; see also Cui et al. 2013). While I originally thought they would be contemporary with the bulk of the burials in the Harbour sites, a fragment from a cranium, XVII-B: 938, provided an AMS measured age of 5,330 ± 40 years BP (conventional age of 5,530 ± 40 years BP) ($\delta^{13}$C=−12.9) or 3920 to 3530 cal BC (5,870–5,480 years cal BP) when calibrated for the marine reservoir effect. A second dated individual, represented by a mandible, XVII-B:939, provided an adjusted age range of 4310 to 3940 cal BC (6,260–5,890 years cal BP). Perhaps other early human burials may yet be found in the Harbour and surrounding area.

The aboriginal people of the Northwest Coast have been characterized as *complex* hunter-gatherers or fisher-gatherers (Ames 1994; Moss 2011). While linguistically and, in some measures, socioculturally diverse, they shared in a marine- and riverine-oriented subsistence base and outlook that supported a highly complex and stratified social system that emphasized property and wealth, individual and kin group ranking, title-holding, and hereditary rights and ownership (Donald 1997). It is, perhaps, not unexpected under such circumstances that intertribal and intervillage warfare may have been a way of life.

**348** | Jerome S. Cybulski

## Acknowledgments

Most of the research on which this paper is based was completed while I was Curator of Physical Anthropology at the Canadian Museum of Civilization, Gatineau, Quebec, Canada. I thank the museum for funding my research and for its support over the years. I thank Dr. George MacDonald for giving me the opportunity to do field work at Prince Rupert Harbour during the North Coast Prehistory Project and for encouraging my study of the human remains over the subsequent decades. My museum colleague Dr. Janet Young served as a receptive sounding board for various aspects of this research in its later stages as the project underwent several permutations and combinations since I first updated the warrior cache in 1993. David Archer at Northwest Community College provided comments on an earlier version of this chapter, for which I am grateful.

## Notes

1. Such injuries are generally indicative of the human osteological evidence for warfare in prehistoric societies (Lambert 2002:210, 2007).
2. The National Museum of Canada, National Museum of Man, was subsequently renamed the Canadian Museum of Civilization and is currently known, at the time of this writing, as the Canadian Museum of History in Gatineau, Quebec.
3. The human remains are reported in this paper by their Canadian Museum of Civilization (CMC) catalog numbers (e.g., XVII-B:338).
4. Cogent arguments for the use of MNI rather than number of identified specimens (NISP) in interpreting dietary potential from archaeological faunal remains are provided by Friesen and Arnold (1995).
5. It is assumed in this paper that all Saskatchewan dates were reported by the laboratory as measured ages.
6. The seventh site with an example of skeletal trauma due to interpersonal violence, Parizeau Point (GbTo-30), is not included in Figure 18.3 inasmuch as no charcoal, wood, or humus samples were dated from that site. Two burials without trauma were collagen-dated, providing age ranges of cal 170 BC to AD 350 (2,120–1,600 years cal BP) and cal AD 710 to 1150 (1,240–800 years cal BP). These ranges closely match the middle and terminal calibrated ranges of the Prince Rupert Harbour burial program as shown by the other sites.

## References

Ames, Kenneth M. 1994. The Northwest Coast: Complex Hunter-Gatherers, Ecology, and Social Evolution. *Annual Review of Anthropology* 23:209–29.

———— 2001. Slaves, Chiefs and Labour on the Northern Northwest Coast. *World Archaeology* 33:1–17.

———— 2005. *The North Coast Prehistory Project Excavations in Prince Rupert Harbour, British Columbia: The Artifacts.* British Archaeological Reports (BAR) International Series 1342, John and Erica Hedges Ltd., Oxford, UK.

Ames, Kenneth M., and Herbert G. Maschner 1999. *Peoples of the Northwest Coast: Their Archaeology and Prehistory.* Thames and Hudson, London.

Angelbeck, Bill 2007. Conceptions of Coast Salish Warfare, or Coast Salish Pacificism Reconsidered: Archaeology, Ethnohistory, and Ethnography. In *Be of Good Mind: Essays on the Coast Salish*, edited by B. G. Miller, pp. 260–3. UBC Press, Vancouver and Toronto, Canada.

Arneborg, Jette, Jan Heinemeier, Niels Lynnerup, Henrik L. Nielson, Niels Rud, and Árný E. Sveinbjörnsdóttir 1999. Change of Diet of the Greenland Vikings Determined from Stable Carbon Isotope Analysis and $^{14}$C Dating of Their Bones. *Radiocarbon* 41:157–68.

Balkwill, Darlene, and Jerome S. Cybulski 1992. Faunal Remains. In *A Greenville Burial Ground: Human Remains and Mortuary Elements in British Columbia Coast Prehistory*, edited by Jerome S. Cybulski, pp. 75–111. Archaeological Survey of Canada Mercury Series Paper 146. Canadian Museum of Civilization, Gatineau.

Boas, Franz 1916. Tsimshian Mythology, Based on Texts Recorded by Henry W. Tate. In *31st Annual Report of the Bureau of American Ethnology to the Secretary of the Smithsonian Institution 1909–1910*. Government Printing Office, Washington, D.C.

Chisholm, Brian S., D. Erle Nelson, and Henry P. Schwarcz 1983. Marine and Terrestrial Protein in Prehistoric Diets on the British Columbia Coast. *Current Anthropology* 24:396–8.

Cui, Yinqiu, John Lindo, Cris E. Hughes, Jesse W. Johnson, Alvaro G. Hernandez, Brian M. Kemp, Jian Ma, Ryan Cunningham, Barbara Petzelt, Joycelynn Mitchell, David Archer, Jerome S. Cybulski, and Ripan S. Malhi 2013. Ancient DNA Analysis of Mid-Holocene Individuals from the Northwest Coast of North America Reveals Different Evolutionary Paths for Mitogenomes. *PLOS ONE* 10.1371/journal.pone.0066948. Available online at http://www.plosone.org/article/info:doi/10.1371/journal.pone.0066948.

Cybulski, Jerome S. 1978. Modified Human Bones and Skulls from Prince Rupert Harbour, British Columbia. *Canadian Journal of Archaeology* 2:15–32.

——— 1986. Human Remains from Lucy Island, British Columbia, Site GbTp 1, 1984/85. Library and Archives Archaeology Ms. 2360, Canadian Museum of Civilization, Gatineau.

——— 1992. *A Greenville Burial Ground: Human Remains and Mortuary Elements in British Columbia Coast Prehistory*. Archaeological Survey of Canada Mercury Series Paper 146, Canadian Museum of Civilization, Gatineau.

——— 1993. Notes on the Cache in Area A of the Boardwalk Site (GbTo 31). Library and Archives Archaeology Ms. 4222, Canadian Museum of Civilization, Gatineau.

——— 1996. Context of Human Remains from the Lachane Site, GbTo 33 (Including Evidence for Decapitation). Library and Archives Archaeology Ms. 3973, Canadian Museum of Civilization, Gatineau.

——— 2006. Skeletal Biology: Northwest Coast and Plateau. In *Environment, Origins, and Population*, edited by David H. Ubelaker, pp. 532–47. Handbook of North American Indians, Vol. 3, William C. Sturtevant, general editor. Smithsonian Institution, Washington, D.C.

——— 2010. Human Skeletal Variation and Environmental Diversity in Northwestern North America. In *Human Variation in the Americas: The Integration of Archaeology and Biological Anthropology*, edited by Benjamin M. Auerbach, pp. 77–112. Occasional Paper No. 38, Center for Archaeological Investigations, Southern Illinois University, Carbondale.

——— 2014. Conflict on the Northern Northwest Coast: 2000 Years Plus of Bioarchaeological Evidence. In *The Routledge Handbook of the Bioarchaeology of Human Conflict*, edited by Christopher Knüsel and Martin J. Smith, pp. 415–51. Routledge, New York.

Donald, Leland 1997. *Aboriginal Slavery on the Northwest Coast of North America*. University of California Press, Berkeley.

Friesen, T. Max, and Charles D. Arnold 1995. Zooarchaeology of a Focal Resource: Dietary Importance of Beluga Whales to the Precontact Mackenzie Inuit. *Arctic* 48:22–30.

Gajewski, Konrad, Sam Muñoz, Matthew Peros, André Viau, Richard E. Morlan, and Matthew Betts 2011. The Canadian Archaeological Radiocarbon Database (CARD): Archaeological $^{14}$C dates in North America and Their Paleoenvironmental Context. *Radiocarbon* 53:371–94.

Inglis, Richard I. 1973. Burial Forms, GbTo-33, 1973 Season. Library and Archives Archaeology Ms. 2265, v. 5, Canadian Museum of Civilization, Gatineau.

**350** | Jerome S. Cybulski

Inglis, Richard I. 1974. Contract Salvage 1973: A Preliminary Report on the Salvage Excavations of Two Shell Middens in the Prince Rupert Harbour, B.C. GbTo-33/36. In *Archaeological Salvage Projects 1973*, edited by William J. Byrne, pp. 64–73. National Museum of Man Mercury Series, Archaeological Survey of Canada Paper 26, National Museums of Canada, Ottawa.

———— 1976. Wet Site Distribution—The Northern Case GbTo 33–The Lachane Site. In *The Excavation of Water-Saturated Archaeological Sites (Wet Sites) on the Northwest Coast of North America*, edited by Dale R. Croes, pp. 158–85. National Museum of Man Mercury Series, Archaeological Survey of Canada Paper 50, National Museums of Canada, Ottawa.

Lambert, Patricia M. 2002. The Archaeology of War: A North American Perspective. *Journal of Archaeological Research* 10:207–41.

———— 2007. The Osteological Evidence for Indigenous Warfare in North America. In *North American Indigenous Warfare and Ritual Violence*, edited by Richard J. Chacon and Ruben G. Mendoza, pp. 202–21. The University of Arizona Press, Tuscon.

MacDonald, George F. 1968. GbTo-31 Field Notes, Burial Forms, Catalogue, 1968 Season. Library and Archives Archaeology Ms. 6, v. 4, Canadian Museum of Civilization, Gatineau.

———— 1983. Prehistoric Art of the Northern Northwest Coast. In *Indian Art Traditions of the Northwest Coast*, edited by Roy L. Carlson, pp. 99–120. Archaeology Press, Simon Fraser University, Burnaby, Canada.

MacDonald, George F., and Jerome S. Cybulski 2001. Introduction: The Prince Rupert Harbour Project. In *Perspectives on Northern Northwest Coast Prehistory*, edited by Jerome S. Cybulski, pp. 1–23. Archaeological Survey of Canada Mercury Series Paper 160, Canadian Museum of Civilization, Gatineau.

MacDonald, George F., and Richard I. Inglis 1981. An Overview of the North Coast Prehistory Project (1966–1980). *BC Studies* 48:37–63.

Marsden, Susan 2001. Defending the Mouth of the Skeena: Perspectives on Tsimshian Tlingit relations. In *Perspectives on Northern Northwest Coast Prehistory*, edited by Jerome S. Cybulski, pp. 61–106. Archaeological Survey of Canada Mercury Series Paper 160, Canadian Museum of Civilization, Gatineau.

Maschner, Herbert D. G. 1997. The Evolution of Northwest Coast Warfare. In *Troubled Times: Violence and Warfare in the Past*, edited by Debra L. Martin and David W. Frayer, pp. 267–302. Gordon and Breach, Amsterdam, the Netherlands.

Moss, Madonna L. 2011. *Northwest Coast: Archaeology as Deep History.* Society for American Archaeology Press, Washington, D.C.

Richards, Michael P., Sheila Greer, Lorna T. Corr, Owen Beattie, Alexander Mackie, Richard P. Evershed, Al von Finster, and John R. Southon 2007. Radiocarbon Dating and Dietary Stable Isotope Analysis of Kwaday Dän Ts'inchí. *American Antiquity* 72:719–33.

Simonsen, Bjorn O. 1988. Final Report on Archaeological Salvage Excavations and Construction Monitoring at the Lachane Site (GbTo-33) Prince Rupert, B.C. Library and Archives Archaeology Ms. 3033, Canadian Museum of Civilization, Gatineau.

Southon, John R., and Daryl Fedje 2003. A Post-Glacial Record of $^{14}$C Reservoir Ages from the British Columbia Coast. *Canadian Journal of Archaeology* 27:95–111.

Stewart, Kathlyn M., Frances L. Stewart, and Gary Coupland 2009. Boardwalk, Northern Northwest Coast, Canada—A New Face to an Old Site. *Canadian Journal of Archaeology* 33: 205–33.

Stuiver, Minze, and Paula J. Reimer 1993. Extended $^{14}$C Database and Revised CALIB Radiocarbon Calibration Program. *Radiocarbon* 35:215–30.

Stuiver, Minze, Paula J. Reimer, and Ron Reimer 2005. CALIB $^{14}$C Radiocarbon Calibration. Available online at http://calib.qub.ac.uk/calib/ (accessed September 3, 2012).

Sutherland, Patricia D. 1978. Dodge Island: A Prehistoric Coast Tsimshian Settlement Site in Prince Rupert Harbour, British Columbia. Library and Archives Archaeology Ms. 1345, v. 1, Canadian Museum of Civilization, Gatineau.

Yoneda, Minoru, Atsushi Tanaka, Yasuyuki Shibata, Masatoshi Morita, Kazuhiro Uzawa, Masashi Hirota, and Masao Uchida 2002. Radiocarbon Marine Reservoir Effect in Human Remains from the Kitakogane site, Hokkaido, Japan. *Journal of Archaeological Science* 29:529–36.

# PART IV

## Synthesis and Conclusion

# 19

## The Prehistory of Violence and Warfare among Hunter-Gatherers

Terry L. Jones and Mark W. Allen

Rarely in the course of a career does an archaeologist become involved with a topic that is profoundly relevant to a modern audience. Certainly, most prehistorians can justify the importance of their research, and it often attracts at least some interest from members of the curious public, typically when they deal with things that are very ancient or very unusual. Violence and warfare, of course, are far from unusual in the modern world and have also been the subject of centuries of writing and theorizing by philosophers, anthropologists, psychologists, and other social scientists. At some level, most of this research has been undertaken to better understand violence and warfare with the hope of discovering some way to end it or—at the very least—to reduce its impacts. This long history of self-interested research has resulted in a stalemate between two opposing perspectives: (1) the Hobbesian view that violence and warfare were the norm for most of humanity's past prior to the establishment of civilizations, and (2) the Rousseau-based contention that the roots of violence and warfare lie in civilizations themselves, and that simpler, earlier societies were marked by peace. Of late, there has been a frenzy of discourse on violence and warfare, much of which can still be sorted into these two basic camps. This most recent spike has brought with it an increasingly intense focus on the past, particularly the prehistory of warfare (e.g. Arkush and Allen 2006; Chacon and Mendoza 2007a, 2007b; Fry 2013; Gat 2006; Haas and Piscitelli 2013; Keeley 1996; Kelly 2002, 2005; Lambert 2002; LeBlanc 1999; LeBlanc and Register 2003, among others). As noted in the volume's introduction, consideration of the

---

*Violence and Warfare among Hunter-Gatherers,* edited by Mark W. Allen and Terry L. Jones, 353–371. ©2014 Taylor & Francis. All rights reserved.

**354** | Terry L. Jones and Mark W. Allen

past has been further narrowed to a specific focus on violence and warfare among hunter-gatherers. Because the hunting and gathering adaptation characterized the vast majority of humanity's past, the question boils down to whether we can trace an unbroken chain of violence and warfare from the earliest hominins through a long prehistory of hunting and gathering up to the appearance of urban communities, or whether the many millennia of hunting and gathering were marked by relative intergroup harmony, with warfare emerging only very recently and suddenly with chiefdoms or civilizations (Otterbein 2004), or with complex forms of hunting and gathering (Fry and Söderberg 2013; Kelly 2002), or with the historic intrusion of Europeans into indigenous societies (Ferguson 1992). In Chapter 1, Allen framed this as a debate between a long chronology of war and a short one, and in Chapter 2, Steven LeBlanc outlined issues in the debate in greater detail, summarizing the previously available archaeological and ethnographic information that supports a long chronology, foretelling the basic and inescapable conclusion that emerges from nearly all of the 16 case studies presented in this volume: that the archaeology and ethnography of hunter-gatherers support a long chronology for violence and warfare.

It is also apparent that a multitude of variables seems to influence the quality and frequency of warfare among foraging societies over time and space, as well as our ability to recognize it. Among the latter are several patterns that can be seen in much of the literature on warfare, including the studies in this volume. First, a certain a degree of overzealousness—if not hostility—can often be detected in writing about warfare. Scholars seem to rarely approach the topic without predisposition, and frequently assemble and interpret empirical evidence with certain outcomes in mind. "Peaceniks" or "doves" seem to feel justified in supporting their biases because of their ultimate goal of forcing modern societies to see themselves as the root of their own dilemmas. "Hawks" seem inflamed by the empirical liberties seemingly taken by the politically motivated social critics, and therefore feel justified in taking liberties of their own. This process is best illustrated by the use of varied definitions of warfare that can automatically either recognize or exclude the types of smaller-scale, intergroup, violent conflicts that occur among and between low-population hunter-gatherer communities. In our discussion here we accept the definition proposed by LeBlanc and many other scholars on the subject—*socially sanctioned lethal conflict between independent polities*—since, as he points out, nearly any other definition would rule out most of the violent acts described in the chapters in this book, and would drive us quickly (and incorrectly) to a conclusion that hunter-gatherers did not engage in war.

Another tradition in the long discourse on warfare has been a tendency to rely nearly exclusively on ethnography and/or history rather than archaeology because while the latter can provide unequivocal evidence for interpersonal violence (e.g., embedded projectile points or craniofacial trauma on skeletons),

The Prehistory of Violence and Warfare among Hunter-Gatherers | **355**

the context of the violent acts cannot be known with certainty. Many recent works of the last two decades have sought to reverse this trend and have embraced the archaeology of warfare (e.g., Arkush and Allen 2006; Keeley 1996; Lambert 1994, 1997, 2002; LeBlanc 1999; Martin et al. 2012; Milner 2005; Milner et al. 1991), recognizing that only the archaeological record can provide a deep temporal perspective on this issue. Nonetheless, recent highly influential papers (e.g., Fry and Söderberg 2013) and books (Fry 2006, 2007) have continued to eschew archaeology in favor of ethnography. In the current volume we have included both.

We have divided this volume into noncomplex and complex forager societies to reflect the recent suggestion that the short chronology of warfare began with the emergence of sociopolitically complex hunter-gatherers. Nine case studies in Part II consider mobile foragers from Europe, North America, South America, and Australia. In Part III we consider seven case studies from New Guinea, the Midwest, California, and the Northwest Coast of North America.

## Violence and Warfare among Mobile Foragers

Among the nine case studies considering mobile foragers, three deal exclusively with archaeological findings, two rely mainly on ethnographic information, and four use combinations of archaeology and ethnography. The archaeological case studies that are by far most damning to the short chronology are the treatments of the European Mesolithic (versus Paleolithic) (Estabrook) and North American Paleoindian (Chatters), but the persistent problem with bioarchaeological evidence is that it can never be unequivocally attributed to warfare. Short-chronology proponents might well argue that these two studies demonstrate violence, but not warfare. However, the complementary ethnographic data from other studies in Part II also offer clear cases of warfare among foragers. The detailed ethnographic information summarized by Allen, Pardoe, Sutton, Reid, and Darwent and Darwent also seriously undermines the short chronology of war.

Estabrook's consideration of the Mesolithic relative to the Paleolithic in Europe strikes at the heart of several key issues in the archaeology of hunter-gatherer warfare. As is often the case with the archaeological record, the sample of burial data available for the more recent Mesolithic era is considerably more robust than that from the preceding Paleolithic era due to issues of preservation and taphonomy. Estabrook takes a novel approach to this problem, pooling all injures for the Middle Paleolithic, the Upper Paleolithic, and the Mesolithic, then ranking them according to severity. She then employs a contingency table analysis to make direct comparisons between the small Paleolithic samples and the considerably larger Mesolithic sample. Results suggest a lower-than-predicted frequency of perimortem injuries during the Middle Paleolithic

**356** | Terry L. Jones and Mark W. Allen

and a much higher frequency of this type of wound in the Mesolithic, which she attributed to an escalation of violence during the Mesolithic, a time generally associated with greater sedentism and complexity in Europe. She acknowledges that the trend could simply reflect better preservation of bone for the Mesolithic or sampling bias due to one site, Ofnet, which produced an unusually large number of trophy heads with perimortem trauma. She further suggests increased contact with unfamiliar groups, shrinking territories, and/ or climate change could account for the increased evidence for lethal violence during the Mesolithic. While the study demonstrates an increase in violence during the Holocene coincident with increased sociopolitical complexity, it documents an unbroken line of violence between the Middle Paleolithic and the Mesolithic.

Chatters' extremely important compilation of information on nearly all of the oldest (more than 9,000 years BP) reported skeletons from North America (including Mexico) shows unexpected patterns that simply do not square with a short chronology for high levels of conflict. While there are some 50 total skeletons known, only 28 (12 male, 16 female) individuals are complete or well preserved enough to detect signs of violent trauma. A total of 10 (38 percent) of the 28 exhibit traumas consistent with violent injury. As with the Middle Paleolithic in Europe, the sample size is obviously small, but it reveals distinct patterns. Traumas consistent with (but not necessarily due exclusively to) violence are present on more than half of the males, with several exhibiting multiple signs. The majority of these were nonlethal blows to the front of the head with clubs or fists, but there were also penetrating wounds, including the famous dart point in Kennewick Man's pelvis, and a young male stabbed twice in the chest. Only three (18 percent) of the females exhibited violent trauma, and Chatters speculates that their injuries could be due to violent abuse. He recognizes that the high levels of violence represented among these highly mobile, sparsely distributed earliest American populations is antithetical to any notion of population or complexity-driven violence. He suggests that the high level of violence and injury among the early North American groups may reflect innate male aggression and competition for scarce females. He makes a case for considerable sexual dimorphism among the early Paleoamericans, and a much longer life span for males due to high female mortality exacerbated by a high degree of mobility. By comparison with skeletons from Europe and Asia and other biological studies, Chatters makes a case that male robusticity and aggression were advantageous traits in colonizing situations, and further argues that these colonizing populations can be considered "wild" as opposed to the later, more subdued "domesticated" groups.

Allen and Pardoe report a combination of archaeological and ethnographic information from Australia: Allen summarizes the continent as a whole,

# The Prehistory of Violence and Warfare among Hunter-Gatherers | 357

and Pardoe provides a detailed examination of one region, Murray River. Despite extreme differences in ecology, population density, mobility, and social organization, there is abundant evidence of warfare over long spans of time in Australia. It also clearly varied through time and space. Pardoe finds that the despite the fact that the Central Murray River region is the most densely inhabited region in Australia, it does not show higher levels of skeletal violence than areas with lower population density. This is an intriguing finding in that it suggests a more complex relationship between resources, population, and violence than is often assumed; it supports other studies that have found a lack of correlation between population density and intensity of violence (Kelly 2013).

The Australian cases are critical to an overall conceptualization of violence in hunter-gatherer societies because they have so often been held up as models of peaceful societies where war was very rare. Most recently this was done by Fry (2006:16–161), who titled a book chapter "Aboriginal Australia: A Continent of Unwarlike Hunter-Gatherers." The incongruence between his interpretation and the ethnographic, historic, and bioarchaeological data summarized by Allen and Pardoe in this volume comes from Fry's reliance on a handful of ethnographies collected late in the twentieth century, and clearly represents a classic example of the "Peacenik" approach to violence research. Allen and Pardoe, on the other hand, consulted a wider range of ethnographic sources with greater time depth, and combined them with other sources, including bioarchaeological evidence, the latter of which shows extremely high frequencies of cranial depressions (23 percent of males and 36 percent of females).

Gordón's paper presents seminal findings from Patagonia. Relying mainly on evidence of skeletal trauma, she points out that violent conflict clearly escalated in later prehistory, but that it was unequivocally present prior to European contact. It also varied by region, with the highest levels in northern Patagonia. Her findings clearly debunk Ferguson's contention that violence in indigenous South America was a product of European intrusion.

Sutton's chapter is a reprint from an article that first appeared in the *Journal of California and Great Basin Anthropology* in 1986, at a time when the vast majority of California and Great Basin anthropologists were turning a blind eye to violence. Swimming against this theoretical tide, Sutton provided a well-documented ethnohistorical examination of the apparent conflict between expanding Numic-speaking groups and their surrounding neighbors in the Great Basin of the western United States. Sutton's accounts illuminate fighting on all fronts, with the Numa generally as the aggressor. This evidence is entirely congruent with other archaeological data that support a "Numic Spread," when after 1,000 years ago a new archaeological culture rapidly replaced others throughout the Great Basin (Simms 2008). In an example of

**358** | Terry L. Jones and Mark W. Allen

the "pacified past," Sutton's argument for Numic warfare fell largely on deaf ears in the Great Basin, but in the context of the current volume, it appears as a strong case of aggressive forager warfare that resulted in territorial expansion over a large area at the expense of other groups.

Reid's chapter examines the nature of conflict in the adjacent area of the Interior Northwest, particularly the Colombia and Snake river basins, where he and others have compared the regional ethnographic accounts of relative peace by the "dovish" Verne Ray (1933, 1939) with the archaeological record. One of the surprising archaeological findings from the region is a large number of fortified mesas and other high-ground locations, as well as the common clustering of households and caches of specialized war projectile points for what appears to be mutual defense. He argues, however, that there is not much evidence that these fortified sites were often attacked. Instead, he points to burial cairns marking battlefield cemeteries and rock art featuring club- and shield-bearing warriors (rarely shown with bows) that are found in the buffer zones between different groups. He sees the conflict as fairly limited and focused mostly on access to hunting areas. Since fortifications are "game-changers" in warfare (see Allen 2008; Arkush 2011) and rare among foragers, further areal excavations of fortified settlements in the Interior Northwest would be most desirable.

Darwent and Darwent make well-supported interpretations of the variation in conflict in the Arctic region. The evidence for violence prior to 2,000 years ago is rare, but this is likely a product of poor preservation. For the past two millennia, however, there is clear evidence for warfare in the Alaskan area that included brutal annihilation of entire communities, the use of specialized weapons, and armor. However, there is also evidence for strong cultural/geographic variation; war was a major part of western Arctic culture, but Darwent and Darwent note its general absence from the Inuit regions east of the Mackenzie Delta, although there were some limited conflicts between the Inuit and their boreal forest neighbors, and, most famously, with the Norse. Darwent and Darwent make the case that in the eastern Arctic, populations were so small and key resources were so widely separated that there could be no winners in war; the death of even one man could be catastrophic for a group, as each hunter was inordinately important in acquiring marine resources. Their chapter does suggest at least in this case a correlation between higher frequencies of warfare (western Arctic) and more complex political organization.

Des Lauriers focuses on the defensive posturing of the inhabitants of Cedros Island in Baja California, and further also notes widespread forager conflict in the adjacent desert interior of the peninsula. He notes that Cedros Island had large villages that seemed to be positioned more with the needs of defense in mind than access to fresh water or the ocean, an interpretation supported by encounters with early European visitors.

The Prehistory of Violence and Warfare among Hunter-Gatherers | **359**

## Violence and Warfare among Semisedentary Hunter-Gatherers

The chapters in Part III consider forager societies from regions generally associated with greater levels of sedentism, reliance on stored foods, higher population densities, and complex (non-band) forms of sociopolitical organization: New Guinea, California, the Midwest Archaic, and the Northwest Coast of North America. Only one chapter, however—Paul Roscoe's treatment of New Guinea—is actually based on ethnographic information; the remainder deal with the archaeological past, where the problem of whether these prehistoric societies matched the ethnographic ones in terms of levels of complexity cannot be completely ignored. Nonetheless, all of these studies reveal the presence of significant violence and conflict between social groups and contribute to the perception of an unbroken line of violence between early hominins and historic hunter-gatherers, indicating a long chronology for warfare.

Roscoe's ethnographic study is noteworthy for several reasons. First, it defies the stereotype that traditional New Guinea was made up solely of horticulturalists. He documents a number of rather sedentary hunter-gatherer groups that rely heavily on the sago palm. These cases, he argues, are highly problematic for advocates of the short chronology of war who consistently choose ethnographic examples of mobile foragers in marginal landscapes to emphasize a lack of warfare. Roscoe points out the inconsistencies of the Fry (2006, 2007) definitions, and makes a strong case that hunter-gatherers in New Guinea are a far better analogy for hunter-gatherers of the distant past, and that they suggest the likelihood of warfare during the Mesolithic or Paleolithic.

Schmidt and Osterholt present an analysis of trophy taking of human body parts, mainly heads and complete limbs, from the Middle Archaic of southern Indiana (ca. 6,500–3,000 years ago). Scalps and tongues were also apparently taken as trophies. Among the tribal level hunter-gatherers of the Eastern Woodlands during this period, violence is evident (from embedded projectile or trauma) in about 3 percent of human skeletons. They note that there are usually one or a few trophy victims (many of whom clearly died violently from other wounds or embedded weapons) in any particular cemetery, and that such victims are usually found in association with burials of other individuals, sometimes showing evidence of curation. Schmidt and Osterholt emphasize that while the practice of taking trophies was widespread geographically and temporally, it varied considerably in terms of the types of trophies taken and their context. Experimental studies with various cutting tools on cadavers allowed the authors to develop a reasonable reconstruction of how limbs and/ or heads were removed. Analysis of cut marks on limbs and vertebrae show consistency in technique across time and space, suggesting that there was a

**360** | Terry L. Jones and Mark W. Allen

specific tradition for engaging in this practice. The authors further point out that trophies and their context are not in themselves a sufficient source of information for understanding the level or nature of Middle Archaic violence or warfare.

Four chapters deal with California, which—following the seminal work of Lambert (1994, 1997) and Walker (1989)—has become a hotbed for archaeological research on violence. While the ethnography of violence in California was summarized as early as 1978 (McCorkle 1978) and has since been treated more extensively (Allen 2012; Johnson 2007; Lambert 2007a, 2007b), violence was generally a taboo subject in California between the 1960s and the 1980s, when dovish views such as those of Margolin (1978) were especially influential. The initial wave of bioarchaeological research on violence focused on the complex maritime chiefdoms of the Chumash and Gabrielino of southern California (Johnson 2007; Lambert 1994, 1997, 2002). The chapter by Brill in the current volume continues the focus on that area, but with an emphasis on weaponry (projectile points) rather than skeletal remains. More recent work, however, has focused on central California, which was occupied by semisedentary hunter-gatherers with acorn-based economies (Bartelink et al. 2013; Jurmain 2001; Jurmain et al. 2009: Schwitalla 2013; Schwitalla et al. 2014). Three of the four chapters on California focus on this region, the first two of which rely on the unusually large database compiled by Al Schwitalla over the last 13 years. Pilloud et al. report on incidences of craniofacial trauma from a version of the Central California Bioarchaeological Database (CCDB) compiled through 2012 that includes information on 16,820 burials. Schwitalla et al. report on evidence for dismemberment, human bone artifacts, and trophy skulls in the most up-to-date (2014) version of the database (n=17,898).

Pilloud et al. show that antemortem and perimortem craniofacial trauma was fairly common across the prehistoric, protohistoric, and historic periods in central California for both males (5.5 percent) and females (4.0 percent). Unlike data from Australia, which showed a lack of correlation between trauma frequency and population density (Pardoe, this volume), the central California data show the highest rates of this form of trauma in the most densely populated Central Valley, and the lowest in the more sparsely populated Sierra Nevada. A partial correlation with resource stress was also revealed, as higher levels of violence were evident in the Sierra Nevada during the droughts of the Medieval Climatic Anomaly. There is also a clear increase in craniofacial trauma after European contact. Pilloud et al. also compare the severity of blows as measured by the size and depth of injuries with data from southern California and found evidence for more lethal intent in central California. Perimortem cranial traumas are found in about 1.1 percent of the sample, with males (approximately 1.4 percent) being likelier than females (approximately 0.87 percent) to have received their death wound in this way. Males also took

The Prehistory of Violence and Warfare among Hunter-Gatherers | **361**

more blows to the frontal bone than females, suggesting they were more likely to have engaged in face-to-face encounters.

Schwitalla et al. summarize archaeological evidence for trophy taking in central California, an ethnographically attested behavior, the apparent products of which were recognized by archaeologists as early as the 1930s, but were subsequently understudied. Four seemingly interrelated forms of evidence for trophy taking and/dismemberment were summarized: (1) human bones with physical evidence in the form of cut marks and/or chop marks; (2) human bones modified into formal artifacts; (3) missing or repositioned cranial and/ or postcranial skeletal elements from otherwise articulated skeletons; and (4) crania and/or articulated postcranial elements found in contexts that suggest their use as trophies. All four show their highest frequencies not during recent times, but rather during earlier periods of central California prehistory, specifically during the Early (3000–500 cal BC) and/or Early Middle (500 cal BC–cal AD 420) periods, declining thereafter. Schwitalla et al. agree with others (e.g., Andrushko et al. 2010) that the early peak in trophy taking seems related to the intrusion of new ethnolinguistic groups into central California. There is also evidence for a modest resurgence in trophy taking during the Medieval Climatic Anomaly.

Eerkens et al. introduce a compelling new methodology for studying hunter-gatherer violence in central California that has great potential for application elsewhere. Looking at cases of mass (n=3, 4, 7) burials within larger cemeteries, they compared findings of multiple stable isotopes from the skeletal remains of victims in the mass graves with those from the rest of the cemetery. The individuals in the mass graves were victims of violence who were dispatched simultaneously and buried together. The stable isotope findings from both the mass graves and the other individual burials were compared with the isotopic signatures associated with the local area, which allowed the authors to distinguish individuals who lived locally from those who were outsiders. In all three case studies (all postdating cal AD 1000), they found strong evidence that the multiple young male victims in the mass graves had different isotope profiles from the rest of the cemetery and were therefore not local residents, but rather outsiders who died far from their home territories. Eerkens et al. interpret this pattern as a reflection of intergroup conflict, which speaks to the importance of ethnic differentiation as a variable influencing hunter-gatherer violence. The ability to assess whether victims of violent death were local or extralocal provides crucial information for better understanding the context of prehistoric violence or warfare and how it varies across regions and through time.

In the chapter on coastal southern California, Brill tests a hypothesis ultimately derived from human behavioral ecology that increased conflict would lead to standardization and subsequent specialization of projectile points. Research on the weapons of hunter-gatherer warfare is important as

## 362 | Terry L. Jones and Mark W. Allen

another line of evidence that can complement the skeletal record. It is common to see arguments for specialized war points in different areas, but often these are based on assumptions that particular forms such as barbs would be harder to extract from wounds (Keeley 1996). Brill's approach has rarely been applied to hunter-gatherer weaponry. His analyses suggest that one likely Chumash arrow point type does seem to have been specialized for war during a period of high conflict.

The final chapter of the book focuses on warfare among some of the most well known complex hunter-gatherers in the world, the native inhabitants of the Northwest Coast of North America. Cybulski examines the evidence of violence in one particular location, Prince Rupert Harbour of British Columbia, with the aim of better understanding the temporal context of evidence for warfare in the region. Through a program of bone collagen dating, he refines the chronology of numerous burials and trophy skulls at several sites, and argues for a sustained era of warfare from approximately 3,000 to 1,000 years BP. The primary evidence supporting this prolonged period of conflict is skeletal, with trauma likely caused by violence from such weapons as stone clubs. Trophy taking of heads was common. Cybulski posits that his findings support the argument that warfare in Prince Rupert Harbour was at such a high level that it resulted in virtual abandonment of this resource-rich region. His work demonstrates that careful documentation of archaeological context, including reanalysis of collections excavated decades ago, is required to make inferences about the nature of prehistoric violence and warfare, even in a region where there is abundant evidence from ethnohistory, ethnography, and previous archaeological research.

## The Long Chronology and Variation in Hunter-Gatherer Warfare

In our view it is hard to escape the conclusion from the ethnographic and archaeological evidence from Europe, North America, South America, Australia, and New Guinea that hunter-gatherers both simple and complex engaged in socially sanctioned lethal conflict between independent polities, suggesting an extremely long history of warfare that can ultimately be traced back to early hominins. To accept the long chronology of war, therefore, is to acknowledge that humans likely do have an innate biological propensity to engage in conflict, as has been argued most cogently by Wrangham and Peterson (1996). However, it is equally clear that levels of warfare have not been constant through time, nor are they evenly distributed through space. Humans may possess this biological inclination, but they do not act on it constantly. Wars by their very nature are episodic events of intense violence that occur sporadically, not continuously. Important subthemes that emerge

## The Prehistory of Violence and Warfare among Hunter-Gatherers | 363

from the chapters in this volume therefore represent attempts to cope with and explain variation through time and space in hunter-gatherer warfare. Here there is no consensus among the authors, but rather several alternative themes.

## Sociopolitical Complexity as a Bridge to Organized Intergroup Violence

Our volume is organized to facilitate comparison between relatively simple and complex hunter-gatherers. The most strident claim on this issue is by Fry and Söderberg (2013), whose study of ethnographic foragers found evidence for low levels of warfare among mobile, noncomplex hunter-gatherers, albeit by using a definition of warfare that excluded most of the types of warfare that foragers engage in, and applying it to a narrow range of ethnographic sources. Chapters in the current volume do not provide a definitive statement on this hypothesis, but several do suggest elevated levels of violence with more complex forms of sociopolitical complexity. Foremost among these is Estabrook's study in which she found a higher frequency of perimortem injuries during the Mesolithic than the Middle Paleolithic, which she attributed to an escalation of violence during the Mesolithic, a period typically associated with greater sedentism among European hunter-gatherers. In the Arctic, Darwent and Darwent document considerably lower levels of violence in the eastern half of the continent where political structure was less complex. Although the study of violence and warfare has hardly begun in Australia, Pardoe's chapter points out that despite having perhaps the densest population and most complex social organization on the continent, the Central Murray region does not reveal correspondingly higher relative levels of violence. Roscoe's New Guinea findings show high levels of violence among foragers with simple political organization but high population density.

California's archaeological record, unfortunately, is somewhat ambiguous on this issue due to preservation issues that limit the number of available early Holocene burials, as well as a lack of consensus on exactly when sociopolitical complexity emerged. In southern California, most researchers in the Santa Barbara Channel argue for a relatively punctuated jump toward chiefdom-like political structure sometime between cal AD 500 and 1150, and Lambert (1994) documented a coincident peak in projectile violence. However, she suggested that the proximate cause for the increases was drought-related resource scarcity and/or the introduction of a new weapon system, the bow and arrow. Lambert's study did show the lowest frequency of projectile violence (1.4 percent) in her sample of 70 skeletons predating 3500 BC, a time she associates with low population density, high mobility, and band-like political organization. In central California, there are no burials in the Schwitalla database that predate 3050 cal BC, even though the artifact record indicates human presence as early as 13,000 years ago. Craniofacial trauma represents approximately 5.0 percent of the male population from 3050 cal BC onward, with little variation except for a dramatic increase during protohistoric/historic times. Trophy taking was a phenomenon that peaked relatively early (between 3050 cal BC and cal AD 420). Projectile violence, summarized in another study (Schwitalla et al. 2014), showed two periods of high frequency: one during the Early Middle period (500 cal BC–cal AD 420), and a latter increase beginning around cal AD 1000. With high levels of projectile violence and trophy taking, the Early Middle period seems to stand out as a time of interest. Fredrickson (1974:49) classified this period as Upper Archaic, which he defined as being marked by "increased sociopolitical complexity, development of status distinctions based on wealth . . . [and] greater complexity of exchange systems." This characterization would seem to also provide support for some correlation between complexity and increased levels of violence.

Kelly's (2002) model of segmentation and social substitution, mentioned in several chapters, can be considered a more specific elaboration on the idea of warfare emerging hand in hand with sophisticated sociopolitical organization. As compelling as the model may be in terms of its applicability to ethnographic data, it is extremely difficult to test archaeologically because of the difficulty in recognizing lineage-based social organization in the archaeological record. Nearly all societies in California, for example, had lineage-based kin organization at the time of contact, but there is a widely held assumption that the earliest prehistoric colonists did not reckon kin lineally, and that lineages emerged sometime later. One of us, years ago (Jones 1996), speculated that lineal kin group organization may have evolved in California around 3500 BC. If this was so, the apparent increase in violence after that date in California could provide support for Kelly's model, but the increase may also be a reflection of taphonomic realities and the near absence of pre-3500 BC burials in California. Furthermore, lineage-based kin organization may well have been imported into western North America from the Old World so that a segmented situation could have existed from the very beginning. We simply do not know.

Standing in contradiction to patterns that support a correlation between complexity and violence, however, are the skeletal data reported by Chatters for North American Paleoindians. While sample size is not robust, these are the oldest skeletons in North America, and they exhibit startlingly high frequencies of evidence for conflict, including projectile violence. These populations have always been thought to represent the antithesis of sociopolitical complexity with exceptionally high mobility. The degree to which the figures for violent injury among these populations shatter many preconceptions about complexity and violence cannot be overstated, and Chatters' suggestion that these colonizing populations may have been profoundly different biologically and culturally from later populations can certainly be understood in light of such findings.

## The Prehistory of Violence and Warfare among Hunter-Gatherers | 365

## Ecology, Carrying Capacity, Resource Scarcity, and Competition

The use of basic ecology to explain episodes of hunter-gatherer warfare is a theme represented in a number of chapters in this book and one with a long history in anthropological archaeology. LeBlanc lays out the basic principles fairly clearly in Chapter 2, where he suggests that hunter-gatherer populations tend to grow to limits of environmental carrying capacity, which puts them in situations of near-constant resource stress and potential competition. Additional population growth or environmental deterioration could upset the carrying capacity–population balance, creating stress and providing a basis for competition over resources and, ultimately, war. In other words, a primary cause for war is resource scarcity that can be brought on by demographic imbalance.

Chapters that suggest the possibility that rapid climate change and resource scarcity contributed to increased warfare include Estabrook's, where it is mentioned as a potential contributing factor to Early Holocene violence among Mesolithic populations of Europe, and California, where droughts of the Medieval Climatic Anomaly have long been argued to have prompted resource stress and violence in the Santa Barbara Channel (Jones et al. 1999; Kennett and Kennett 2000; Lambert 1994). Brill's contribution in Chapter 17 adds a new dimension to the long-acknowledged correlation between high violence and the Medieval droughts in the Channel area. He shows at least a hint of specialization in weaponry geared toward intergroup conflict during this same time. Schwitalla et al.'s (Chapter 15, this volume; 2014) findings, along with Pilloud's et al.'s in Chapter 14, however, suggest a much more muted response to droughts in central California with a pattern of regional variability in which some areas show no meaningful change in violence.

The population component of the ecological equation, as alluded to in a number of chapters, is complex. LeBlanc asserts in Chapter 2 that hunter-gatherer populations tend to grow simply and quickly to near carrying capacity so that the potential for resource stress would be omnipresent, making them sensitive (if not vulnerable) to any sudden changes in climate, technology, or the surrounding cultural milieu. As appealing as that argument may seem, it is unlikely that prehistoric California provides much of a match for its predictions. Walker (1989) suggested that a major contributing factor in the high levels of cranial trauma in the Santa Barbara Channel was the extreme demographic pressure on the Channel Islands. But elsewhere in California, the sophisticated ecological analysis of native demography by Baumhoff (1963) suggested that populations at contact were still below carrying capacity after 13,000 years of residence. Others have suggested that human numbers reached a point where they impinged upon (depressed) local game populations by approximately 500 BC (Broughton 1994, 1999). Even if the latter scenario is true (and many scholars now question it; see Jones 2013; Whitaker 2008),

**366** | Terry L. Jones and Mark W. Allen

the period of growth toward carrying capacity simply does not seem to have been a short one.

Spatial patterns evident in the current volume give no clear consensus on the role of population density in precipitating resource competition and violence. In Australia, Pardoe and Allen see no obvious correlation between population and violence. In California, Pilloud reports the highest levels of craniofacial violence in the densely populated Central Valley. Darwent and Darwent report considerably lower levels of violence in the eastern Arctic, where population density was lower than in the west. Chatters' findings from North America are again critical, in this case contradicting any simple equation between population density and violence since there is no reason to think that human populations were high in North America between 13,000 and 9,000 years ago.

The ecological/demographic conclusions from Roscoe's New Guinea study are also of critical importance. He makes the case that generalizations about foragers residing in marginal environments cannot be extrapolated to the whole of hunter-gatherer prehistory in that many places in the world where hunter-gatherers resided were resource-rich environments (like California, the Northwest Coast, and the Murray River in Australia), and that these would inevitably support higher, more crowded populations with more resource competition, regardless of the level of sociopolitical complexity.

## Sex, Warfare, and Individual Incentives

Yet another dimension of the biological inclination toward war and explanations for variation involves views on the incentives of individual actors to engage in violence. Such evolutionary perspectives have a long history in anthropology beginning with Darwin (1873), who suggested that warfare could have actually encouraged the evolution of altruistic behavior (involved with group defense and protection) among humans when groups who effectively cooperated in defense expanded their numbers at the expense of those who did not. Bowles (2009) recently evaluated Darwin's hypothesis with a combination of archaeological and ethnographic data not unlike the information we have assembled here, and tentatively concluded in favor of Darwin's hypothesis. He suggested that frequent lethal warfare may actually have kept a check on human population growth between 100,000 and 20,000 years ago.

Perhaps not surprisingly, contemporary evolutionary theorists, operating within human behavioral ecology, have of late also sought to evaluate the possible role of violence in humanity's past (see Cashdan and Downs 2012). These efforts begin with recognition that chimpanzees engage in war as part of territorial competition for food for themselves, their mates, and offspring, which suggests potential evolutionary payoffs for males who are successful in violent aggression (Wrangham and Glowacki 2012). Chagnon (1988) argued that reproductive variables must be considered in potential explanations for warfare among human societies, based on findings from the Yanomomo that showed that males who had killed had more wives and offspring than those who had not. Several authors have suggested that high-mobility foragers may have few additional incentives beyond these basic ones to resort to violence, and that risks had to be carefully weighed against potential gains (Glowacki and Wrangham 2013; Wrangham and Glowacki 2012). Chatters suggests that evolutionary incentives may be a contributing explanation for the high level of violence among Paleoindian populations, with males competing not for food resources but for scarce females.

Findings in the current volume also suggest that sex roles in violence may vary considerably among hunter-gatherers, and that such roles need to be considered more seriously in evolutionary ecological models. Pardoe's research from Australia shows that females had startlingly high frequencies of depression fractures (17–71 percent), and in nearly all regions showed higher frequencies than males. In California, Pilloud's data on craniofacial trauma shows males (approximately 1.4 percent) with only slightly higher frequencies than females (approximately 0.87 percent), with males taking more blows to the frontal bone than females. California ethnography includes accounts of females fighting fiercely alongside males (Schwitalla et al. 2014) in historic times.

## Ethnic Warfare

A theme in the current volume that is touched upon only briefly, but which cannot be overlooked, is the apparent correlation between increased warfare and in-migrations of new groups into regions. Estabrook suggests that such migrations were yet another factor that contributed to increased lethal warfare during the Mesolithic in Europe. In California, a region marked by startlingly high ethnolinguistic diversity at the time of contact, a very early (ca. 3000–500 BC) peak in trophy taking seems to co-occur with the intrusion of new groups into the central part of the state. Sutton's documentation of Numic expansion in the Great Basin through conflict is also an apparent case of prehistoric ethnic aggression.

Of course, the intrusion of Europeans into the New World can be considered the ultimate case of ethnically defined violence. Archaeological evidence from North America (California and the Northwest Coast), Australia, and Europe all show that foragers were engaging in violent intergroup attacks prior to the arrival of Europeans. Findings from California and South America show that violence increased after the arrival of Europeans, but that it was well established prior to that time.

## Technology

A final contributing factor in the escalation and decline of forager warfare is the technology of war. Nowhere was the influence of a single intrusive prehistoric weapon system so influential as the bow and arrow in North

America, an event considered in detail in a series of recent studies (Bettinger 2013; Kennett et al. 2013; Milner et al. 2013). In the current volume, Brill's study shows an apparent specialization in arrow points produced for warfare, one of many lines of evidence that suggest this new weapon system effected an increase in violence when it appeared suddenly in North America late in the Holocene. Reid also notes specialized war points in the Interior Northwest. Allen discusses the specialized "Death Spear," which evidently has a history of at least 4,000 years in Australia. Hunter-gatherer technology of warfare is not limited to the offense. Darwent and Darwent describe armor in the Arctic, and there are similar examples from elsewhere, including California (Allen 2012), as illustrated by the image on the cover of this volume. Shields were ubiquitous and always near to hand in Australia (Allen, this volume). Fortifications, perhaps contrary to common knowledge, are not precluded among hunter-gatherers, as illustrated by Reid.

## New Directions to Address Old Questions

Analysis of hunter-gatherer violence and warfare is not an easy task. This volume illustrates that significant progress can be made through the comparative studies of both ethnographic and archaeological case studies through multiple lines of evidence. This might be thought of as a strategy for the study of hunter-gatherer conflict. Methodological innovations are also on display in the chapters assembled here, and these might be viewed as tactical approaches to the study of early violence and war. Estabrook uses a novel approach to accommodate the limited data from the Paleolithic and Mesolithic, as does Chatters in his analysis of the earliest Americans. In comparison, the Central California Bioarchaeological Database assembled by Schwitalla represents an embarrassment of riches in terms of sample size, as evidenced by the detailed studies reported here by Pilloud et al. and Schwitalla et al. While samples of this size may not be possible elsewhere, it does point to the potential this approach could offer for other hunter-gatherer cases. Rock art holds promise as a means of better understanding conflict among mobile foragers as noted by Allen for Australia, and the Interior Northwest by Reid. Reid also uses the distribution of burial cairns to identify the locations where warriors fell. Eerkens et al. reveal a technique that can identify the "homelands" of combatants through signature isotopes. This approach will no doubt be applied elsewhere and will provide exceptional contextual information so crucial for analysis of prehistoric violence and warfare. Cybulski reveals yet another way to improve the context of archaeological cases as he reanalyzed data collected over decades to tease out detailed chronological control in Prince Rupert Habour. Trophy taking has garnered much attention in recent years (Andrushko et al. 2010; Chacon

The Prehistory of Violence and Warfare among Hunter-Gatherers | **369**

and Dye 2007; Lambert 2007b), but Schmidt and Osterholt report on experimental archaeological approaches to dismemberment, and this not-for-the squeamish approach reveals both longstanding traditions and unique cultural practices of trophy taking in the Eastern Woodlands. Brill employs a new approach to the study of war weaponry, one that draws heavily from human behavioral ecology.

The antiquity of violence and warfare and what they reveal about human nature are compelling issues, as is evidenced by their long hold on discourse across specialties. It is hoped that this volume reveals a productive line of research on these topics as well as a variety of promising methodological approaches, since there can be little doubt that the long intellectual war over war is yet to be concluded.

# References

Allen, Mark W. 2008. Hillforts and the Cycling of Maori Chiefdoms: Do Good Fences Make Good Neighbors? In *Global Perspectives on the Collapse of Complex Systems,* edited by Jim A. Railey and Richard Martin Reycraft, pp. 65–81. Maxwell Museum of Anthropology Anthropological Papers No. 8, Albuquerque, NM.

―――― 2012. A Land of Violence. In *Contemporary Issues in California Archaeology,* edited by Terry L. Jones and Jennifer E. Perry, pp. 93–114. Left Coast Press, Walnut Creek, CA.

Andrushko, Valerie A., Al W. Schwitalla, and Phillip L. Walker 2010. Trophy-Taking and Dismemberment as Warfare Strategies in Prehistoric Central California. *American Journal of Physical Anthropology* 141:83–96.

Arkush, Elizabeth N. 2011. *Hillforts of the Ancient Andes: Colla Warfare, Society, and Landscape.* University Press of Florida, Gainesville.

Arkush, Elizabeth N., and Mark W. Allen (editors) 2006. *The Archaeology of Warfare: Prehistories of Raiding and Conquest.* University of Florida Press, Gainesville.

Bartelink Eric J., Valerie Andrushko, Viviana Bellifemine, Irina Nechayev, and Robert J. Jurmain 2013. Violence and Warfare in the Prehistoric San Francisco Bay Area, California: Regional and Temporal Variations in Conflict. In *The Routledge Handbook of the Bioarchaeology of Human Conflict,* edited by Christopher Knüsel and Martin Smith, pp. 285–307. Oxford University Press, Oxford, UK.

Baumhoff, Martin A. 1963. Ecological Determinants of Aboriginal California Populations. *University of California Publications in American Archaeology and Ethnology* 49:155–336.

Bettinger, Robert L. 2013. Effects of the Bow on Social Organization in Western North America. *Evolutionary Anthropology* 22:118–23.

Bowles, Samuel 2009. Did Warfare among Ancestral Hunter-Gatherers Affect the Evolution of Human Behaviors? *Science* 324:1293–8.

Broughton, Jack M. 1994. Declines in Mammalian Foraging Efficiency during the Late Holocene, San Francisco Bay. *Journal of Anthropological Archaeology* 13:371–401.

―――― 1999. Resource Depression and Intensification during the Late Holocene, San Francisco Bay: Evidence from the Emeryville Shellmound Vertebrate Fauna. *University of California Anthropological Records* 32. University of California, Berkeley.

Cashdan, Elizabeth, and Stephen M. Downs 2012. Evolutionary Perspectives on Human Aggression: Introduction to the Special Issue. *Human Nature* 23:1–4.

Chacon, Richard J., and David H. Dye (editors) 2007. *The Taking and Display of Human Body Parts as Trophies by Amerindians.* Springer, New York.

## 370 Terry L. Jones and Mark W. Allen

Chacon, Richard J., and Rubén G. Mendoza 2007a. *North American Indigenous Warfare and Ritual Violence*. University of Arizona Press, Tucson.
——— 2007b. *Latin American Indigenous Warfare and Ritual Violence*. University of Arizona Press, Tucson.
Chagnon, Napoleon 1988. Life Histories, Blood Revenge and Warfare among a Tribal Population. *Science* 239:985–92.
Darwin, Charles 1873. *The Descent of Man*. D. Appleton and Company, New York.
Ferguson, R. Brian 1992. Tribal Warfare. *Scientific American* 266:108–16.
Fredrickson, David A. 1974. Cultural Diversity in Early Central California: A View from the North Coast Ranges. *Journal of California Anthropology* 1:41–54.
Fry, Douglas P. 2006. *The Human Potential for Peace: An Anthropological Challenge to Assumptions about War and Violence*. Oxford University Press, New York.
——— 2007. *Beyond War: The Human Potential for Peace*. Oxford University Press, New York.
——— (editor) 2013. *War, Peace, and Human Nature*. Oxford University Press, New York.
Fry, Douglas P., and Patrik Söderberg 2013. Lethal Aggression in Mobile Forager Bands and Implications for the Origins of War. *Science* 341:270–2.
Gat, Azar 2006. *War in Human Civilization*. Oxford University Press, New York.
Glowacki, L., and Richard W. Wrangham 2013. The Role of Rewards in Motivating Participants in Simple Warfare. *Human Nature* 24:444–60.
Haas, Jonathan, and Matthew Piscitelli 2013. The Prehistory of Warfare: Misled by Ethnography. In *War, Peace, and Human Nature*, edited by Douglas P. Fry, pp. 168–90. Oxford University Press, Oxford, UK.
Jones, Terry L. 1996. Mortars, Pestles, and Division of Labor in Prehistoric California: A View from Big Sur. *American Antiquity* 6:243–64.
——— 2013. Archaeological Perspectives on Prehistoric Conservation in Western North America. *International Journal of Environmental Studies* 70:350–7.
Jones, Terry L., Gary Brown, L. Mark Raab, Janet McVickar, Geoffrey Spaulding, Douglas J. Kennett, Andrew York, and Phillip L. Walker 1999. Environmental Imperatives Reconsidered: Demographic Crises in Western North America during the Medieval Climatic Anomaly. *Current Anthropology* 40:137–56.
Johnson, John R. 2007. Ethnohistoric Descriptions of Chumash Warfare. In *North American Indigenous Warfare and Ritual Violence*, edited by Richard J. Chacon and Rubén G. Mendoza, pp. 74–113. University of Arizona Press, Tucson.
Jurmain, Robert D. 2001. Paleoepidemiological Patterns of Trauma in a Prehistoric Population from Central California. *American Journal of Physical Anthropology* 115:13–23.
Jurmain, Robert, Eric J. Bartelink, Alan Leventhal, Viviana Bellifemine, Irina Nechayev, Melynda Atwood, and Diane DiGiuseppe 2009. Paleoepidemiological Patterns of Interpersonal Aggression in a Prehistoric Central California Population from CA-ALA-329. *American Journal of Physical Anthropology* 139:462–73.
Keeley, Lawrence H. 1996. *War before Civilization*. Oxford University Press, New York.
Kelly, Raymond C. 2002. *Warless Societies and the Origin of War*. University of Michigan Press, Ann Arbor.
——— 2005. The Evolution of Lethal Intergroup Violence. *Proceedings of the National Academy of Sciences* 102:15294–8.
Kelly, Robert L. 2013. From the Peaceful to the Warlike: Ethnographies and Archaeological Insights into Hunter-Gatherer Warfare and Homicide. In *War, Peace, and Human Nature*, edited by Douglas P. Fry, pp. 151–67. Oxford University Press, Oxford, UK.
Kennett, Douglas J., and James P. Kennett 2000. Competitive and Cooperative Responses to Climate Instability in Coastal Southern California. *American Antiquity* 65:379–95.
Kennett, Douglas J., Patricia M. Lambert, John R. Johnson, and Brendan J. Culleton 2013. Sociopolitical Effects of Bow and Arrow Technology in Prehistoric Coastal California. *Evolutionary Anthropology* 22:124–32.

## The Prehistory of Violence and Warfare among Hunter-Gatherers | 371

Lambert, Patricia M. 1994. War and Peace on the Western Front: A Study of Violent Conflict and Its Correlates in Prehistoric Hunter-Gatherer Societies of Coastal California. Unpublished Ph.D. dissertation, Department of Anthropology, University of California, Santa Barbara.

——— 1997. Patterns of Violence in Prehistoric Hunter-Gatherer Societies of Coastal Southern California. In *Troubled Times: Violence and Warfare in the Past*, edited by Debra L. Martin and David W. Frayer, pp. 77–110. Gordon and Breach, Amsterdam, the Netherlands.

——— 2002. The Archaeology of War: A North American Perspective. *Journal of Archaeological Research* 10:207–41.

——— 2007a. The Osteological Evidence for Indigenous Warfare in North America. In *North American Indigenous Warfare and Ritual Violence*, edited by Richard J. Chacon and Reuben G. Mendoza, pp. 202–21. The University of Arizona Press, Tucson.

——— 2007b. Ethnographic and Linguistic Evidence for the Origins of Human Trophy Taking in California. In *The Taking and Displaying of Human Body Parts as Trophies by Amerindians*, edited by Richard J. Chacon and David H. Dye, pp. 65–89. Springer, New York.

LeBlanc, Steven A. 1999. *Prehistoric Warfare in the American Southwest*. University of Utah Press, Salt Lake City.

LeBlanc, Steven A., and Kathleen E. Register 2003. *Constant Battles: The Myth of the Peaceful, Noble Savage*. St. Martin's Press, New York.

McCorkle, Thomas 1978. Intergroup Conflict. In *California*, edited by Robert F. Heizer, pp. 694–700. Handbook of the North American Indians, Vol. 8, William C. Sturtevant, general editor. Smithsonian Institution, Washington, D.C.

Margolin, Malcom 1978. *The Ohlone Way*. Heyday Books, Berkeley, CA.

Martin, Debra L., Ryan P. Harrod, and Ventura R. Pérez (editors) 2012. *The Bioarchaeology of Violence*. University Press of Florida, Gainesville.

Milner, George R. 2005. Nineteenth-Century Arrow Wounds and Perceptions of Prehistoric Warfare. *American Antiquity* 70:144–56.

Milner, George R., Eve Anderson, and Virginia G. Smith 1991. Warfare in Late Prehistoric West-Central Illinois. *American Antiquity* 56:581–603.

Milner, George R., G. Chaplin, and E. Zavodny 2013. Conflict and Societal Change in Late Prehistoric Eastern North America. *Evolutionary Anthropology* 22:96–102.

Otterbein, Keith F. 2004. *How War Began*. Texas A&M University Press, College Station.

Ray, Verne F. 1933. *The Sanpoil and Nespelem: Salishan Peoples of Northeastern Washington*. AMS Press, New York.

——— 1939. *Cultural Relations in the Plateau of Northwestern America*. AMS Press, New York.

Schwitalla, Al W. 2013. *Global Warming in California: A Lesson from the Medieval Climatic Anomaly (A.D. 800–1350)*. Center for Archaeological Research at Davis Publication Number 17. Department of Anthropology, University of California, Davis.

Schwitalla, Al W., Terry L. Jones, Marin A. Pilloud, Brian F. Codding, and Randy S. Wiberg 2014. Violence among Foragers: The Bioarchaeological Record from Central California. *Journal of Anthropological Archaeology* 33:66–83.

Simms, Steven R. 2008. *Ancient Peoples of the Great Basin and Colorado Plateau*. Left Coast Press, Walnut Creek, CA.

Walker, Phillip L. 1989. Cranial Injuries as Evidence of Violence in Prehistoric Southern California. *American Journal of Physical Anthropology* 80:313–23.

Whitaker, Adrian R. 2008. The Role of Human Predation in the Structuring of Prehistoric Prey Populations in Northwestern California. Unpublished Ph.D. dissertation, Department of Anthropology, University of California, Davis.

Wrangham, Richard, and Dale Peterson 1996. *Demonic Males: Apes and the Origins of Human Violence*. Hougton Mifflin, Boston.

Wrangham, Richard W., and L. Glowacki 2012. Intergroup Aggression in Chimpanzees and War in Nomadic Hunter-Gatherers: Evaluating the Chimpanzee Model. *Human Nature* 23:5–29.

# Index

12Fl73, 241–242, 245–246
12Hr6, 241–242, 246

## A

Aché, 37
acorns, 274, 360
Aeta, 28
age grades, 177
Agta, 28
Alabama, 71, 244
Alaska, 71, 182, 184, 188, 190, 193–194, 358
   Barrow Region, 184, 189
   Cape Espenberg, 189–190
   ethno-linguistic groups (tribes)
     Aleut, 34, 184
     Birnirk, 189
     Ingalik, 229
     Iñupiaq (Eskimos), 29, 32–35, 38
       Western Eskimo, 33
     Ipiutak, 188
     Kobuk, 26–27
     Kotzebue Sound Eskimo (see Iñupiaq)
     Noataker, 26
     Nuataagmiut, 26
     Punuk, 188
   Prince of Wales Island, 71
   Seward Peninsula, 189
Algonkians, 171–172
alliances, 18, 36, 42, 137, 143, 153, 159, 164, 234

altruism, 18
ambush, 27, 34, 169, 297, 307
American Southwest, 18, 158
Americans, 159
Andamanese, 28, 32, 33, 35, 229
Angel, 243
animal resources, 336–337, 365
   aquatic, 228, 301, 306
   big game, 170, 174, 177, 214
   caribou, 26
   eels, 98
   fish, 98, 114, 170, 227–228, 347
   fowl, 114
   salmon, 28, 172, 301
   small game, 117, 214
Apache, 151, 158–159, 162–164
Arch Lake, 72–73
Archaic (North America)
   California, 23, 274–275, 287, 364
   Eastern, 71, 85
   general, 90
   Midwest, 23, 79, 241–253, 359
   Northern, 188
Arctic (see also Alaska), 23, 32, 182–199, 358, 363, 366
   Baffin Island, 184, 185, 187, 192, 194
   Bering Sea, 182, 184, 188
   Bering Strait, 182, 184, 199
   Chukchi Sea, 184, 188
   ethno-linguistic groups (tribes)
     Athapaskan, 195
     Birnirk, 189
     Gwitch'in, 187, 195

Innu, 187
Inughuit, 194
Inuit, 182–199
   Copper Inuit, 187, 194, 229, 358
   Iñupiaq (Eskimo), 28–29, 32–35,
     39, 182–199
   Ipiutak, 188
   Netsilik, 39–40, 229
   Punuk, 188
   Greenland, 182–183, 187, 191, 193
   Mackenzie Delta, 194–195, 358
Arctic Small Tool Tradition, 188, 192
Arkansas River, 159
Arlington Spring, 71, 73
armor, 32, 33, 189–190, 358, 368
Arroyo Seco 2, 138
Ashworth Shelter, 72–75, 78–79, 89
Asia, 88, 90, 356
   Siberia, 188
Asian War Complex, 189, 193
assassinations, 124
Australia, 23, 97–107, 112–130,
   356–357, 363, 368
   Adelaide Plains, 124
   aborigines, 26, 28–30, 32, 35, 38–40,
     90, 97–132
   Aranda, 229
   Bangerang (Yorta Yorta), 118
   Barapa Barapa (Wemba Wemba),
     117, 121
   Dreamtime, 104–105, 116
   Gugadja, 229
   Kaurna, 124
   kidney fat excision, 120
   Loddon Tribe (Gunbowers), 119
   Mallee, 119
   Mardu, 229
   Millegundeet, 119
   Minatogawa, 88
   Ngarrindjeri, 124
   Ngooraialum, 118
   Pitjantjatjara, 104, 106
   Tiwi, 229
   Walbiri, 229
   Wathaurung, 103
   Yolngu/Murngin, 229
   Yorta Yorta, 112

arid zone, 113, 124, 126
Arnhem Land, 104, 113, 122
   Botany Bay, 101
   Darling River, 40
   Dimboola, 119
   Hay Plain, 99
   Kimberley Region, 105
   King George's Sound, 102
   Melbourne, 103
   Murray-Darling River, 37
   Murray River, 99, 112–132, 357, 363,
     366
   Murrumbidgee River, 99
   New South Wales, 99
   Port Jackson, 101
   Queensland, 105
   semiarid zone, 126
   Swan River Colony, 102
   Torres Strait, 105
   Victoria, 99, 103, 105, 124
   Western Desert, 105, 113
Australian Small Tool Tradition, 99, 103
Aweikoma, 229
axes, 35
   as trade commodity, 121

## B

backed blades, 99, 100
Baldwin, 334–335, 344–346
Bantu, 32
Barrett, 244
Battle Rock, 183
battlefield cemeteries, 170, 175–177,
   358, 368
big-game hunting, 31, 159, 188, 212
Big Sandy, 250
Birsmatten-Bassigrotte 1, 53, 61–62
Black Earth, 250
Bloody Falls (Kugluk), 187
Bluegrass, 241–242, 245
Boardwalk, 333–335, 337, 342, 344–347
boats, 32, 34, 39
   canoes, 233–234
   kayak, 32
   rafts, 33
   skin, 192

## 374 | Index

Bøgebakken, 53, 61–62
Botocudo, 229
boundary maintenance, 105, 115, 128, 129, 211
British Columbia, 71, 333–348
  Digby Island, 334–335
  ethno-linguistic groups (tribes)
    Coast Tsimshian, 333
    Kaska, 229
    Kaien Island, 334–335
    Nass River, 337
    Prince Rupert Harbour, 333–348
    Queen Charlotte Islands, 336
Brown's Valley, 73–74, 86
Buckley, William, 26, 33, 103
buffer zones, 35, 177, 358
Buhl, 71, 73, 85
Burch, Ernest, 183–185, 195–196
Bushmen (see !Kung), 38, 39

## C

CA-ALA-12, 278
CA-ALA-13, 278
CA-ALA-42, 278, 281
CA-ALA-309, 261, 278, 283
CA-ALA-328, 278, 283
CA-ALA-343, 278, 283
CA-ALA-509, 278
CA-ALA-554, 299–309
CA-ALA-613, 278
CA-BUT-90, 279
CA-BUT-294, 279
CA-CAL-14, 279, 283
CA-CAL-99, 279
CA-CCO-138, 278
CA-CCO-139, 278
CA-CCO-141, 278
CA-CCO-235, 278
CA-CCO-250, 278
CA-CCO-309, 278
CA-CCO-474, 278, 283
CA-CCO-548, 260, 279, 282, 289
CA-CCO-696, 279
CA-COL-2, 279
CA-COL-247, 279, 282
CA-MAD-117, 279

CA-MER-215, 279
CA-MRN-5, 278, 283
CA-MRN-67, 278, 280, 283
CA-MRN-242, 278
CA-SAC-29, 279
CA-SAC-43, 301
CA-SAC-67, 279, 283
CA-SAC-99, 279
CA-SAC-107, 274, 279
CA-SAC-151, 279
CA-SBA-1, 321
CA-SBA-7, 323
CA-SBA-13, 322
CA-SBA-17, 322
CA-SBA-28, 322–323
CA-SBA-30, 321
CA-SBA-45, 323
CA-SBA-46, 322
CA-SBA-52, 321
CA-SBA-58, 321
CA-SBA-71, 321
CA-SBA-72, 322
CA-SBA-73, 322
CA-SBA-78, 321
CA-SBA-81, 321
CA-SBA-82, 322
CA-SBA-84, 321
CA-SBA-86, 322
CA-SBA-87, 323
CA-SBA-104, 323
CA-SBA-477, 322
CA-SBN-35, 278
CA-SCL-6, 278
CA-SCL-12, 278
CA-SCL-38 (Yukisma Mound), 278, 299–309
CA-SCL-137, 278
CA-SCL-194, 278, 283
CA-SCL-478, 278, 283
CA-SCL-674, 278, 283
CA-SCL-690, 278
CA-SCL-732, 278, 283
CA-SCL-806, 278
CA-SCRI-1, 321, 323
CA-SCRI-236, 321, 323
CA-SCRI-240, 323
CA-SCRI-257, 321

CA-SFR-4, 278
CA-SJO-56, 274, 279
CA-SJO-68, 274, 279
CA-SJO-91, 279, 283
CA-SJO-112, 279
CA-SJO-142, 274, 279
CA-SMA-23, 278
CA-SMA-110, 278
CA-SMA-125, 278
CA-SMA-335, 278
CA-SOL-2, 279
CA-SOL-11, 279
CA-SOL-271, 301
CA-SOL-364, 279, 280
CA-SRI-1, 321
CA-SRI-2, 322
CA-SRI-4, 322
CA-SRI-9, 322
CA-SRI-41, 321
CA-SRI-62, 321, 323
CA-SRI-78, 323
CA-THE-10, 279
CA-YOL-13, 279, 288
CA-YOL-27, 279
CA-YOL-70, 279
CA-YOL-117, 299–309
CA-YOL-197, 301
CA-YOL-229, 301
CA-YUB-1, 279
California
    Alta, 23, 28, 32–35, 38, 40, 71, 97,
        151, 160, 210, 359–362, 366
    Amador Valley, 303–304
    Catalina Island, 34
    central, 257–270, 296–309,
        360–361, 363
    Central Valley, 264–266, 269–270,
        303, 360, 366
    Channel Islands, 257, 265, 268,
        314–330
    culture history, 259–260, 273–292,
        314–330, 364
    ethno-linguistic groups (tribes)
        Achumawi, 151, 153
        Atsugewi, 32, 153
        Chumash, 82, 210, 314–330, 360,
            362

Costanoan, 277–278, 283–284,
    288–289
Gabrieleno, 360
Halchidhoma, 160, 162
Hokan, 153
Konkow, 277, 279, 284
Maidu, 152, 277, 284
Miwok, 152, 277–279, 284
Mohave, 151, 160–162
Monache, 150–152, 163
Nisenan, 277, 279, 284
Nomlaki, 277, 279, 284
Ohlone, 306
Patwin, 277, 279, 284
Takic speakers, 34
Wappo, 277, 284
Wintu, 32, 284
Yana, 277, 279, 284
Yokuts, 150–152, 277, 279, 284
Yuman, 160
Sacramento River, 298, 300–301
Sacramento–San Joaquin Delta,
    274, 290–291, 298
San Francisco Bay, 264, 266, 270,
    283, 287–288, 291, 298, 303,
    305, 307
San Joaquin River, 304
Santa Barbara Channel, 208, 258,
    270, 297, 314–330, 363, 365
Santa Clara Valley, 305, 307
southern, 266
Yolo Basin, 300–301
Baja, 23, 204–217, 358
    Central Desert, 205, 210
    Isla Cedros, 204–217
Calusa, 28, 39
camp fights
    men versus women, 117
    women versus women, 117
Camp Quintero, 207–208, 214
Canada, 154, 182, 193
cannibalism, 168, 235
Carlston Annis, 224, 250
carrying capacity, 29, 30, 39, 41, 70, 320,
    365–366
cemeteries, 81, 194, 252, 274, 305–307,
    324

**376** | Index

Central California Bioarchaeological
Database, 258–270, 275–292, 360,
368
Chagnon, Napoleon, 366–367
Chamalhuacan, 71, 73, 86
Chatters, James, 173, 177, 356, 366–368
Chevalier de la Verendrye, 156
children, 35
abduction, 151
killed, 185
rearing, 186
chimpanzees, 17, 89
Chippewa, 35, 187
Clifford Williams, 244
climate, 30
change (*see also* Medieval Climatic
Anomaly), 50, 66, 114, 134
Clovis, 74
Collegedale, 246, 250
Colombres, 53, 61–62
colonialism, 19, 137
Colorado, 159–160
Colorado River (North America),
160–162
Columbia Plateau (*see also* Interior
Northwest), 81
Columbia River, 168–169, 172, 176–177,
358
competition, 18, 22, 31 (*see also* resource
competition)
for females, 82–83
contact period, 22–23, 354, 367
Arctic, 195
Australia, 100–101
California,
Alta, 269, 317, 360
Baja, 204–210, 358
Northwest Coast, 333
Patagonia, 136–137, 143
Plains, 157
cooperation, 31, 42, 212
Cordilleran ice sheet, 70
cranial morphology, 86, 137, 139–140
Cree (Dene), 154, 156, 187
cribra orbitalia, 85, 317
Culoz sous Balme, 53, 61–62
cycad palms, 98

**D**

dances, 102
De Bruin, 53, 61–62
death rates, 34
decapitation (*see also* trophy taking), 67,
244
defense, 32, 34
positioning, 71, 137, 156, 170, 207,
209, 214
successful, 175
demography, 22, 71, 113–114
Australian, 114
New Guinea, 229–231
Patagonia, 143
descent groups, 19, 232
digging sticks, 116
dingo, 99, 128
Dinka, 136
disease, 29
epidemics, 29, 158
infectious, 136, 269
malaria, 40
Dodge Island, 334–335, 344–347
domestication, 27, 137
domestic violence (*see also* camp fight),
117, 124, 127, 129
Donkalnis, 53, 61–62
Dorset, 192–193
doves, 17, 354, 358, 360
duel
stylized, 118, 127
Dust Cave, 72–74
Dye, David, 20
Dynamic Phase, 100

**E**

Eastern Woodlands (North America),
20, 359, 369
ecology, 49, 70
basis for war, 41
economy, 170
economic networks, 22, 189
exchange, 143, 168
marine focus, 185
egalitarian society, 178

El Coloradito, 214
enculturation, 17
environments
  Australian, 114
  marginal, 38–40, 149, 226–227, 231, 236
  richness of, 114
Epullán Grande Cave, 134
Escalante, 159–160
ethnic conflict, 292, 367
Europeans (*see also* Norse)
  captives sold to, 163
  expansion of, 105, 136–137, 143
  use of breech loaders, 121
  use of muskets, 121
  violence against, 121, 196, 198
Eva, 250
evolution (*see also* genetic factor), 31, 50
execution, 169, 186, 196, 225

**F**

face-to-face violence, 82, 124, 212
farmers, 28, 30, 32, 35, 40, 160, 359
females (*see* women)
Ferguson, R. Brian, 20, 136, 357
feuding, 19, 20, 169, 182, 187, 209, 231–232, 317
firearms, 136, 154–157, 159, 162, 164
Firehouse, 241–242, 245
Florida, 28, 39
flour, 121
fortifications, 136, 170–173, 177–178, 358, 368
  fortified mesas, 168–169
  Fuertes, 136–137
Franchthi, 53, 61–62
Francisco de Ulloa, 206–207, 209, 212
French and Indian War, 158
Fry, Douglas, 19, 38, 106, 224–227, 229–233, 236–237, 357, 359, 363

**G**

Garden Island, 334–335, 342–346
Gat, Azar, 18
GbTp-1 (Lucy Island), 346

genetic factors, 17, 38, 42–43, 115, 223, 236, 356, 362
Gilyak, 229
Gøngehusvej, 53, 61–62
Gordon Creek, 72–73
Gore Creek, 73, 84
Goughi Cave, 53, 61–62
Grassy Bay, 334–335, 346
Great Basin (North American), 23, 30, 32, 149–164, 357
  ethno-linguistic groups (tribes)
    Kawaiisu, 150–151
    Northern Shoshoni, 151, 154–157
    Numic (Numa), 151, 171–172, 357–358
      as raiders, 175
      expansion, 149–164, 173, 357, 367
      language family, 23, 32
    Paiute, 32
      Northern (Snake), 150–157, 229
      Southern (Chemehuevi), 150–151, 160–163
      Surprise Valley, 152
    Panamint, 151
    Shoshone, 32, 151
    Ute, 32, 151, 158–160, 162
    Washo, 152
  Great Salt Lake, 159
  Honey Lake Valley, 152
  Humboldt Sink, 153
  Providence Mountains, 161
  Soda Lakes, 161
  Warner Valley, 152
Great Plains (North American), 79–80, 154, 156–159, 163–164, 168, 177
  Black Hills, 154
  Dakotas, 154
  ethno-linguistic groups (tribes)
    Arapaho, 157
    Arikara, 156
    Assiniboine, 156
    Caddoans, 158
    Cheyenne, 156–157
    Comanche, 151, 157–159, 162
    Crow, 156–157
    Gens de Chevaux, 156
    Kwqaharis, 158

**378** | Index

Sioux, 35
Yamparikas, 158
Red River, 158
Green River, 244
Greenville, 337
Grinos Point, 75–78, 82, 84
group selection, 31, 185

**H**

Haas, Johnathan, 20
Hadza, 32, 37, 229
Harris lines, 85
hawks, 17
health, 71
herders, 29, 31–32, 136
herding, 38
Hiwi (South America), 37
Hobbes, Thomas, 16, 353
Hoëdic, 53, 61–62
Holocene, 205, 226–227, 237, 356, 363, 365
Early, 18, 134, 138
Late, 98, 100, 133–136, 138, 168
mid, 98–100, 134, 138, 175
Homicide (*see* murder), 19–20, 84, 169, 182–183, 225, 227, 231
*Homo* (genus), 18
*Homo sapiens*, 50, 87, 89
Hopi, 151
Hopkins, Sarah Winnemucca, 153
Horn Shelter, 72–77, 85–87
horses, 137, 154–159, 162–164
Hottentot, 33
Hourglass Cave, 74, 84–85
Hoyo Negro, 72–73, 75, 77, 79, 84, 86
human behavioral ecology, 319, 360, 366, 369
human biology
Australian, 114–115
human bone artifacts, 273–275, 280, 360

**I**

Idaho, 158
Illinois, 244, 250
India, 37–38

Indian Knoll, 85, 244, 250
Indiana, 241–253
Indonesia, 105
injuries (*see also* trauma)
treatment of, 119
Innuarfissuaq (Place of the Blood Battle), 183
insults
as cause for violence, 118
intensification
Australian, 98
Californian, 291
economic, 98–100
violence, 50–51
Interior Northwest (North America), 168–178, 358, 368
Clearwater River, 175
ethno-linguistic groups (tribes)
Bannock, 152
Blackfoot, 151, 154–157, 164
Flathead, 154, 157
Gros Ventres, 156
Klamath, 151–153, 169–170
Modoc, 153
Molale, 153
Nez Perce, 154, 170, 172, 175
Sahaptian, 151, 153–154, 164, 171
Salish, 154, 169, 171
Interior Salish, 173
Spokane, 172
Waiiatpuan, 153–154
Warm Springs Indians, 153
Yakama, 173
Hell's Canyon, 174–176
Hell's Canyon Creek, 174
Snake River, 168, 173, 176, 358
Yakima River, 171
investments, 32
technological models, 318–330
Iron Gate, 53–54, 61–62
island refuge, 169

**J**

J.C. Putnam, 71, 73
Johnson Bar South, 175–176
Jomon, 28, 39

## Index | 379

## K

Keeley, Lawrence, 15–16, 19–20
Kelly, Raymond, 21, 169–170, 176–177, 364
Kelly, Robert, 20
Kennewick Man, 71, 75–76, 78, 81, 85, 356
Kentucky, 71, 243, 246, 250
kidney fat excision, 120
kinship
 bilateral kinship groups, 170, 177–178, 225, 232
 clans, 169, 206, 215, 225, 232
 kin groups as communities, 20, 241
 lineages, 169, 215, 225, 232, 364
 non-unilineal, 169
 ranked kin groups, 347
 unilineal, 177
Kitandach, 346
Korsør, 54, 61–62
Kramer Mound, 241–242, 246–247
Krapina (Neanderthal site), 51
Kroeber, Alfred, 150, 160–161
KTZ-087, 190
KTZ-304, 189
!Kung 28, 30–31, 40, 229, 237

## L

La Brea, 72–73, 85
Lachane, 333–335, 338–339, 342–347
Lamb, Sydney, 149–150
Lambert, Patricia, 82, 257, 290, 317–318, 360, 363
Las Palmas Woman, 72–73, 83
Laurentide Ice Sheet, 70
leadership, 20
 hereditary, 168
 in war, 159
LeBlanc, Steven, 18, 238, 354, 365
Levant, 28
lineal descent, 98
linguistics, 39
 California, 292
 groups, 27, 103
 loan words, 152

speech communities, 170
 warfare vocabulary, 117
livestock, 29, 236–237
long chronology, 17–18, 21, 223–226, 238, 354, 362
loot, 159
Lucy Island, 346–347

## M

Magdalenian, 90
malaria (*see* disease)
Mannlefsen, 54, 61–62
Maori, 15, 136
marine reservoir effect, 336–337
Marmes, 71–73, 75–76, 81
marriage patterns, 115, 297
massacre, 33, 105, 168–169, 177, 187, 198
Mbuti, 38, 229, 237
McGraw Creek, 174
meat, 173
 as trade commodity, 121
mediation, 224
Medieval Climatic Anomaly, 134, 258, 269–270, 291, 297, 314–316, 328, 360–361, 365
Mesa Complex, 172–173
Mesolithic, 23, 49–69, 90, 355–356, 359, 363, 368
metal, 29, 196, 198, 338
Meyer, 241–242, 247–248
Micmac, 229
microliths
 Australia, 99–100
 Middle East, 39
Minnesota, 71
missionaries, 29, 103
Mississippian, 243
mitochondrial DNA (mtDNA), 307
mobility, 28, 32, 70, 83, 89–90, 159, 213, 230, 356, 363
Mojave Desert, 160–161, 163
Møllegabet, 54, 61–62
Montana, 177
moths, 98
mounds, 115, 128, 241–244, 246–247, 300, 305

**380** | Index

shell, 99
temple, 39
Mountain West (North America), 33
mtDNA (*see* mitochondrial DNA)
Muge, 54–55, 61–62
murder (*see also* homicide), 37, 119, 187
mutilation, 153, 195
mythology of war, 185

**N**

NAGPRA (*see* Native American Graves
 Protection and Repatriation Act)
Naharan, 72–73, 84
Narabeen Skeleton (*see also* Octavia
 Man), 101, 128
Naskapi, 229
Nassau Bay, 33
Native American Graves Protection and
 Repatriation Act (NAGPRA), 258
Natufians, 28, 39
Navajo, 159
Nayaka, 28
Neanderthals, 52, 90, 223
Nebraska, 154
Neo-Marxism, 100
Neolithic, 49
New Guinea, 23, 28, 34, 39–40,
 223–238, 359–363
 Bifa River, 234
 ethno-linguistic groups (tribes)
  Alamblak, 229, 232, 234
  Ambonwari, 235
  Arafundi, 229, 235, 238
  Bahinemo, 229, 232–234, 238
  Benaräm, 234
  Berik, 229, 232, 236
  Bitara, 229, 233, 238
  Bonerif, 229, 232
  Bora Bora, 235
  Daranto, 235
  Foja, 238
  Gidra, 40
  Ittik, 229, 232, 235
  Kamasuit, 233–234
  Karawari, 234
  Kundima, 235

Kwerba, 229, 232
Mander, 229, 232, 236
Mari, 234
Meakambut, 235
Namata, 235
Palu, 233
Sanio-Hiowe, 229, 232–233, 238
Ségar, 235
Waf, 235
Wagim, 234
Wambramas, 235
Warès, 235, 238
Yamandim, 235
Yambi Yambi, 234
Yerikai, 233
Yimas, 234–235
 Sepik, 232
 Upper Tor Valley, 232
New Mexico, 158–159
New York, 244
New Zealand, 15, 136
noble savage, 17–18, 70, 116
Norse, 192–193, 198, 358
North Dakota, 156
Northwest Coast (North America), 23,
 28, 34, 39, 80, 82, 168, 208, 211, 228,
 359, 362, 366
 ethno-linguistic groups (tribes)
  Chinook, 169
  Coast Tsimshian, 333
  Tlingit, 39
Northwest Interior (*see* Interior
 Northwest)
Norton, 188
Nuer, 136
Nunu, 40
nutritional stress, 85

**O**

ochre, 104
Octavia Man (*see also* Narrabeen
 Skeleton), 101, 128
Ofnet, 55–56, 61–62, 66, 356
Ohio, 244
Ohio River, 241, 243, 245, 250
Old Bering Sea, 188

Old Woman Mountain, 161
On-Your-Knees Cave, 72–73, 84
Oregon, 153–154
Otterbein, Keith, 17

## P

Pacific Coast, 163, 298
Paleoeskimo, 192
Paleoindian (North America), 23, 70–96,
  356, 364, 367
Paleolithic, 23, 359, 368
  Middle, 49–69, 355–356, 363
  Upper, 21, 49–69, 88, 355
paleopathology (*see also* trauma), 100–101
Paliyan, 28, 229
Parizeau Point, 334–335, 348
Peacenik, 354, 357
Pecos, 158
Pelican Rapids (*see also* Minnesota
  Woman), 72–73, 75–77, 79, 85–86
Penon, 72–73
Penutian, 153
Pinker, Steven, 18, 20
pioneers, 80, 89
Plateau (North America), 35
Pleistocene, 49
  Late, 18, 87, 107
Point Hope, 191
political organization
  bands, 19, 22, 104, 185, 197, 224–225,
    227, 241, 363
  chiefdoms, 37, 137, 195, 225, 228,
    360, 363
  small-scale, 142
  tribes, 37, 104, 120, 162, 177, 195,
    197, 225, 232, 241, 359
Polynesia, 15, 89
population, 29–30
  density, 170, 208, 308, 359
    influence on rates and violence, 129
  growth, 30
  movements, 160, 191, 193, 198
  pressure, 116, 365
  sinks, 40
psychology, 17
  evolutionary, 42

Punta Norte, 207, 214
Pygmies, 28

## R

raiding (*see also* surprise attack), 27, 34,
  36, 158–159, 162, 169, 184, 192, 194,
  233, 297, 317
  after European contact, 136
  against Spanish, 162
  night, 103, 120, 122, 129, 232
  parties, 33
  slave, 29, 185
  taking captives, 163
  to capture sacred items, 209
Ray, Verne, 168–169, 171, 178, 358
resource competition, 36, 39–40, 70,
  97–99, 183
resource stress, 29–31, 170
revenge, 36, 183, 185–186, 196, 297
  killings, 120–121, 128
rhizome, 114
Ridley Island, 334–335, 344, 346
Rio Grande, 159
risk, 33–34
  among males, 87
  vs. benefit, 18
ritual, 16
ritual conflict, 118, 169
Robeson Hill, 244
Robinson, 250
rock art, 98, 100, 136, 157, 170–171,
  176–177, 213–214, 258, 368
roots, 170, 227
Roscoe, Paul, 18, 359, 366
Rousseau, Jean Jacques, 16, 70, 143, 353
rule of 10, 37

## S

sago palm, 228, 234
Salteaux, 229
San Julian (Fuerte), 137
San Luis Valley, 159
San Miguel skeleton, 75–77
Saukamappee (Cree), 155
Saunaktuk, 193, 198

## 382 | Index

Schela Cladovei, 56, 61–62
Secoy, Frank, 154–156, 163
sedentism, 28, 50, 90, 99
   Australia, 115
   California, 274
seeds, 98
segmented societies, 21, 364
Semang, 28, 229
sex roles in violence, 367
sexual dimorphism, 85–86, 88–89, 91
sham fights
   Australian, 116, 119, 127
shaman, 152, 209
shields, 32, 33, 118, 124, 176–177, 358, 368
short chronology, 17, 19–20, 223–226,
   238, 354–355, 359
Sierra Nevada, 150–151, 163, 264–266,
   270, 299, 360
Siriono, 229
Skateholm, 56, 61–62
skeletal evidence (*see* trauma)
Slave (tribe), 229
Smith, David Livingston, 18
social stratification, 347
South Africa, 30, 31
South America, 35, 37, 251
   Amazonia, 32
      ethno-linguistic groups (tribes)
         Jivaro, 251
         Yanomami, 28, 39, 82, 366–367
   Andes, 134–135
   ethno-linguistic groups (tribes)
      Onas, 136
      Kaweskar, 142
      Yaghan, 33, 229
      Magallanes region, 138
      Magellan Strait, 134, 138
   Pampean Region, 137
   Patagonia, 133–145, 357
      Colorado River, 133, 135, 137–138,
         142–143
      Chubut, 135, 137–138
      Chubut River, 137
      Negro River, 135, 137, 142
      Santa Cruz, 135, 138
   Tierra del Fuego, 32–34, 135–136, 142
   Valdivia, 137

Spirit Cave, 71–73, 75–76, 81
stable isotopes, 296–309, 360, 368
starvation, 31
Stick Man, 74–77, 81
storage, 16, 22, 28, 39, 169, 173, 359
Stova Bjers, 56, 61–62
strangers, 32
Stratten-Wallace, 244
stylized combat (*see* sham fights), 235
surplus, 22, 188
surprise attack, 104, 151, 154–156, 185
Surprise Valley, 152

## T

tactics, 162
Tägerup, 56, 61–62
Tasmania, 32
technology, 30, 49
   Arctic, 188, 190, 192
   basketry, 163
   fish traps, 39
   hot rock cooking, 91
   of violence, 314–330
   procurement tools, 320
   projectile, 50
   tools, 29
Teit, James, 153–154
Tench, Watkin, 101–102
Tennessee, 79, 244, 246, 250
territoriality, 35, 66, 70, 98–100,
   104–106, 115–116, 128, 143, 297,
   307–309, 317, 333
testosterone, 89
Téviec, 56, 61–62
Thule, 182–199
Tlapacoya, 74–75
torture, 185, 195
trace element analysis, 22
trade
   Norse, 192, 198
   Spanish, 158
training for war, 184–185, 187, 196
trauma (*see also* skeletal evidence), 22,
   49–69, 112–113, 137–142
   analysis, 140–142
   Australian, 122–128

blunt force, 52, 63–69, 115, 243
British Colombia cranio-facial, 333–348
California cranio-facial, 257–270, 304, 317, 360, 363, 366
cranial, 51, 58, 79, 139, 169, 191, 260, 263–264, 333
classification of, 139–140
cranial depressions, 122, 125–127, 129
from steel weapons, 141
parrying fractures, 82, 122–124, 129, 317, 333, 341
penetrating, 356
projectile, 63–69, 138, 169, 174, 301, 304, 317
skeletal, 49–92, 169, 173, 176, 191, 333–348
violent, 80, 137–138, 194–195
trial by ordeal, 117–118
Le Tron Violet, 56, 61–62
trophy taking, 35, 168, 368–369
as part of cultural system, 251
caches, 245–246, 274, 289
experimental replication, 248–250, 359, 369
forearms, 243–245, 359
hands, 289, 359
headhunting, 234–235, 251
in British Colombia, 333–334, 338, 362
in California, 269, 273–292, 305, 361, 363
in Indiana, 245–250
legs, 243, 289, 359
Mesolithic, 356
scalps, 243–244, 247, 251, 359
similarities with animal butchery, 248
skulls, 67, 243–244, 274, 359–360
tongues, 243, 247, 359
tubers, 117
Tybrind, 57, 61–62

**U**

United States military, 158
unsegmented societies, 21
Upper Landing, 174

**V**

Valle di Zambaua, 57, 61–62
Vargas Village, 214
Vasilyevka, 57, 61–62
Vayda, Andrew, 15
Veda, 229
Voloshkoe, 57, 61–62

**W**

Walker, Philip, 257, 266, 268–270, 290, 360, 365
war lodge, 172
Ward, 244, 246, 250
"warrior gene," 89
Washington, 168, 172
weapons (*see also* firearms), 32–33, 98
atlatl, 35, 51
boomerangs, 116, 118, 120
bow and arrow, 35, 169, 177, 207, 214, 233, 291, 327, 330, 367–368
effectiveness, 192
self bow, 173–174
sinew-backed recurved compound, 189
changes in, 170
clubs, 35, 116, 118, 177, 194, 207, 212, 214, 341, 356, 362
daggers, 32–33, 35, 189–190, 194
darts, 78
death spears, 99, 102, 116, 368
kidney-fatting cords, 116
knives, 35, 78
projectiles, 71, 360, 363
California types, 314–330
changes in, 66
Desert series, 173
embedded, 50, 127–128, 244–245, 305, 314, 326, 359
hunting versus war, 174–175, 177–178, 214, 314–330, 362, 368
nulla nullas, 118
slings, 207, 212, 214
spears, 21, 78, 120–121, 128, 138, 177, 327
waddies, 112, 120

## 384 | Index

western goods, 136
Western Stemmed Tradition, 71
Whaling, 189–190, 194, 197
White, John, 101–102
Whitewater Draw, 72–73
"wild type," 89–91, 356
Wilson-Leonard, 74, 86, 87
Wizard Beach, 71, 75, 84
women
  capture, 36, 151, 156, 235
  involvement in violence
    as combatants, 161
    cranial depressions, 125–127, 129, 367
    parrying fractures, 123–124, 129
    relative to males in violence, 117, 141
    speared and clubbed, 177

  killed, 185, 233
  theft of, 118
Woodland Period, 243
Wrangham, Richard, 17, 19, 362
Wyoming, 80, 89, 158

### Y

Yakagir, 229
yam stick, 117
yams, 114
Yucatan Peninsula, 71, 83

### Z

Zhoukoudian, 88
Zvejnieki, 57, 61–62

# About the Editors and Contributors

## About the Editors

**Mark W. Allen** earned his Ph.D. in anthropology at UCLA, with a dissertation focused on Maori warfare conducted through close partnership with the *Iwi* (tribe) Ngati Kahungunu. He is currently Professor of Anthropology at California State Polytechnic University, Pomona. His research interests include the archaeology of warfare, complex pre-state societies, and hunter-gatherers. He has conducted archaeological fieldwork in Kentucky, Illinois, California, the Great Basin, Guatemala, Fiji, New Zealand, Hawai'i, and New Mexico. His previous employment includes teaching stints at UCLA and Pomona College, and working as an archaeologist at the U.S. Army's National Training Center at Fort Irwin in the Mojave Desert. He is coeditor of *The Archaeology of Warfare: Prehistories of Raiding and Conquest* (Arkush and Allen 2006, University Press of Florida) and *Burnt Corn Pueblo: Conflict and Conflagration in the Galisteo Basin, A.D. 1250–1325* (Snead and Allen 2010, Anthropological Papers of the University of Arizona), and author of *Living on the Edge: The Archaeology of Two Western Mojave Desert Landscapes* (2013, Maturango Museum Press).

**Terry L. Jones** is Professor of Anthropology and Chair of the Department of Social Sciences at California Polytechnic State University, San Luis Obispo, where he has taught for the last 16 years. He received his Ph.D. in anthropology from the University of California, Davis, in 1995 and he also holds an M.A. in Cultural Resources Management from Sonoma State University (1982). He has worked as a professional archaeologist for 30 years mostly on the central California coast, where he studies hunter-gatherer ecology and maritime adaptations. He has published more than 60 articles and book chapters on California prehistory as well as monographs and edited volumes, including *Prehistoric California: Archaeology and the Myth of Paradise* (with L. Mark Raab), *California Prehistory: Colonization, Culture, and Complexity* (with Kathryn Klar), and *Contemporary Issues in California Archaeology* (with Jennifer Perry). Jones is the founding editor of the journal *California Archaeology*.

## About the Contributors

**Eric J. Bartelink** is an associate professor at California State University, Chico, and the director of the Human Identification Laboratory and co-coordinator of the Certificate in Forensic Identification. He received his Ph.D. from Texas A&M University in 2006. His research interests include taphonomy, paleopathology, paleodiet, trauma analysis, and the application of stable isotope analysis to human skeletal remains. He has conducted research on prehistoric and historic human skeletal remains from California, American Samoa, and Nevada.

**James M. Brill** received his B.A. in anthropology from the University of California, Davis, in 2006 and his M.A. in anthropology from California State University, Chico, in 2012. His research focuses on the interaction of technology and violence, as well as human behavioral ecology. He is currently pursuing interests outside of academia.

**Traci L. Carlson** received her B.S. in biology from Colorado State University in 2011 with minors in biomedical science and criminology. She went on to earn her M.S. in forensic science from University of California, Davis, in 2014. Her research interests include applying forensic science to the field of human rights, and increasing access to forensic science services for countries where the field is not as developed.

**James C. Chatters** received his Ph.D. from the University of Washington in 1982 and has conducted extensive research in hunter-gather prehistory in the North American Northwest, paleoanthropology of the earliest Americans, theory of cultural macroevolution, and late Quaternary palynology and mammalian paleontology. Best known for his discovery of Kennewick Man, he has been involved in recovery and first studies of 10 of the continent's 50 oldest skeletons. His work has been published in *World Archaeology, Journal of World Prehistory, Quaternary Research, American Antiquity, Current Anthropology, Journal of Anthropological Archaeology, Journal of Archaeological Science,* and *Science,* as well as numerous books, including *Macroevolution in Human Prehistory* (2010, Springer) and *Ancient Encounters: Kennewick Man and the First Americans* (2002, Simon & Schuster). He is currently working on submerged late Pleistocene human and animal remains in Quintana Roo, Mexico.

**Brian F. Codding** is an Assistant Professor of Anthropology at the University of Utah. He received his B.S. from the Social Sciences Department at California Polytechnic State University, San Luis Obispo, and his M.A. and Ph.D. from the Department of Anthropology at Stanford University. His research examines variability in human-environment interactions across ethnographic and archaeological contexts in western North America and Australia, particularly through the framework of behavioral ecology.

## About the Editors and Contributors | 387

**Jerome S. Cybulski** is a Research Associate with the Canadian Museum of History in Gatineau, Quebec, and Adjunct Research Professor in Anthropology at the University of Western Ontario. His studies include environmental adaptation, paleopathology, dietary isotopes, and DNA variation in ancient and living peoples, as well as warfare and violence among the ancients. He has done archaeological fieldwork and analyzed human remains throughout Canada's West Coast and in the Canadian Plateau, and studied the bones of mummies in Egyptian tombs. He is the author, coauthor, or editor of several books, including *Perspectives on Northern Northwest Coast Prehistory* (2001, Canadian Museum of History), and many conference papers and journal articles. Recent publications include "The China Lake and Big Bar Burials" in *A Human Voyage* (2011, Nelson Education); "Canada" in *The Routledge Handbook of Archaeological Human Remains and Legislation* (2011, Routledge); and "Human Skeletal Variation and Environmental Diversity in Northwestern North America" in *Human Variation in the Americas* (2010, Center for Archaeological Investigations, Southern Illinois University Carbondale). Cybulski has a B.A. and M.A. from the State University of New York at Buffalo and a Ph.D. in physical anthropology with a minor in human genetics from the University of Toronto.

**Christyann M. Darwent** is associate Professor of Anthropology at the University of California, Davis. She earned her Ph.D. from the University of Missouri in 2001. Darwent has conducted archaeological fieldwork in the Arctic for the past 22 years and codirected projects in western Alaska and northwestern Greenland funded through the National Science Foundation's Polar Programs. She has published more than 30 articles on zooarchaeology and High Arctic ecosystems, her main areas of interest. Most recently she has been collaborating with colleagues in veterinary genetics to investigate Arctic dogs, using them as a proxy to examine human migrations and interactions. Since 2012 she has served as Editor of the University of Wisconsin Press journal *Arctic Anthropology*.

**John Darwent** received his B.A. from the University of Calgary, an M.A. from Simon Fraser University, and a Ph.D. from the University of Missouri in 2005. He has conducted fieldwork across western North America, as well as in Missouri, the Canadian Arctic, and Greenland, and is currently a Research Associate/Lecturer at the University of California, Davis. His research interests are related to lithic technology and the use of seriation and cladistics to investigate cultural transmission and change. Most recently he has been collaborating with the Greenland National Museum to investigate a unique stratified site that is under threat of coastal erosion. In addition to articles in *American Antiquity, Antiquity, Journal of Archaeological Science*, and *Journal of Theoretical Biology*, his extensive archaeological and experimental research on nephrite was published as *Prehistoric Nephrite Use on the British Columbia Plateau* (1998, Simon Fraser University Press).

**388** | About the Editors and Contributors

**Matthew R. Des Lauriers** is associate Professor of Anthropology at California State University, Northridge, where he has taught since 2006. He received his Ph.D. in anthropology from the University of California, Riverside, in 2005. He has worked as a professional archaeologist for 20 years throughout California and the Great Basin. His current research program is focused on Isla Cedros, Baja California, Mexico. He has developed strong collaborative relationships with the Instituto Nacional de Antropologia e Historia de Mexico as well as the local institutions on Isla Cedros. His work emphasizes ethnoarchaeology, experimental approaches, the Peopling of the New World, and the human ecology of maritime hunter-gatherers. His book *Island of Fogs: Archaeological and Ethnohistorical Investigations of Isla Cedros, Baja California* (2010, University of Utah Press) won the 2012 Society for American Archaeology Scholarly Book of the Year award. He has also published more than 20 other articles and book chapters in national and regional journals.

**Jelmer W. Eerkens** received his Ph.D. from the University of California, Santa Barbara, in 2001, and is currently Professor of Anthropology at the University of California, Davis. He is interested in the evolution and transmission of cultural practices and information in small-scale societies, and in the application of archaeometric techniques to recover novel information about ancient societies. He conducts fieldwork in California and southern Peru.

**Virginia Hutton Estabrook** is currently a Visiting Assistant Professor of Anthropology at the University of California, Riverside. Her background is in paleoanthropology and bioarchaeology. She holds degrees from Bryn Mawr College (A.B. summa cum laude, 2000) and from the University of Michigan, Ann Arbor (M.A., 2001 and Ph.D., 2009). Her dissertation, "Sampling Biases and New Ways of Addressing the Significance of Trauma in Neandertals," is available for download on the Paleoanthropology Society website. Her research is focused on Paleolithic trauma and the origins of human violence, skeletal indicators of obesity, and improving methodology for the analysis of fragmentary human skeletal remains. She divides her time between the United States and Portugal, where she is working on a project examining changes in health and nutrition in Lisbon during the period of Portuguese global exploration (fifteenth to nineteenth centuries).

**Karen S. Gardner** works as a consulting osteologist and archaeologist in the San Francisco Bay Area. She completed her B.A. in anthropology at the University of California, Santa Cruz, and her M.A. in anthropology at California State University, Chico. Her primary research interests are social identity in the archaeological record, paleodietary studies, and stable isotope analysis, with focus on populations from prehistoric California and Peru.

**Florencia Gordón** received her undergraduate degree in anthropology (2005) and Ph.D. in natural sciences (2011) from the National University of La Plata (UNLP), Buenos Aires, Argentina. Her doctoral research focused on the bioarchaeological patterns of interpersonal violence and conflict in hunter-gatherer populations from Patagonia during the Late Holocene. She is now a Researcher at Consejo Nacional de Investigaciones Científicas y Técnicas (CONICET), and divides her time between scientific research and teaching anthropology at the University (UNLP). She is currently extending the scope of her investigations to the influence that environmental factors may play in the evolution process of human populations through the paleodiets of human groups who lived in northern Patagonia during the Holocene in relation to the ecological niche construction.

**Steven A. LeBlanc** received his B.A. from Pomona College, his M.A. from the University of California, Santa Barbara, and his Ph.D. from Washington University in St. Louis. He did a postdoctoral fellowship at the University of Michigan. He was a curator at the Southwest Museum in Los Angeles and was most recently Director of Collections at the Peabody Museum of Archaeology and Ethnology at Harvard University. His research interests include archaeological theory, and he jointly authored *Explanation in Archaeology* (1971, Columbia University Press). His interests also include Mimbres pottery and archaeology, and he is the author of *The Mimbres People* (1983, Thames and Hudson), *The Galaz Ruin* (1984, University of New Mexico Press), and *Painted by a Distant Hand* (1984, Peabody Museum). His interest in warfare is both regional and global; he has published *Prehistoric Warfare in the American Southwest* (1999, University of Utah Press), and coedited *Deadly Landscapes: Case Studies in Prehistoric Southwestern Warfare* (2001, University of Utah Press) and *Constant Battles: The Myth of the Peaceful, Noble Savage* (2003, St. Martin's Press), as well as numerous papers on the topic.

**Amber E. Osterholt** is a Ph.D. student at the University of Nevada, Las Vegas; she received her M.S. in anthropology from the University of Indianapolis in 2013. Her research focuses on performative and cultural violence and trophy taking in prehistoric North American communities.

**Colin Pardoe** is a bio-anthropologist and archaeologist based in Australia. A B.Sc. from the University of Toronto and an M.A. from the University of Manitoba placed him in an anthropological tradition that studied skeletal remains in their archaeological context, with a strong focus on population distribution and evolutionary processes. He received his Ph.D. from The Australian National University, examining patterns of biological variation across the continent. Since 1984, he has worked as a research fellow, museum curator, and private consultant. In addition to ongoing research in Aboriginal Australia, he has undertaken research on gene flow in Europe and along the

**390** | About the Editors and Contributors

northeast coast of the Indian Ocean. Current interests include prehistoric transitions and continuities in Europe.

**Marin A. Pilloud** is a forensic anthropologist at the Central Identification Laboratory, Joint POW/MIA Accounting Command. She received her B.A. from the University of California, Berkeley, and her M.A. and Ph.D. from The Ohio State University. Her research interests include dental anthropology (metrics, morphology, development, adaptation, and population variation) and the bioarchaeology of central Anatolia and prehistoric California.

**Kenneth C. Reid** received his B.A. in journalism from the University of Missouri. Following military service with the Vietnamese Army, he traveled widely in Asia before earning graduate degrees in anthropology from the University of Kansas. Since 2000, he has been the State Archaeologist and Deputy State Historic Preservation Officer for Idaho. His work has appeared in *American Antiquity, North American Archaeologist, Plains Anthropologist, Journal of California and Great Basin Anthropology, Journal of Northwest Anthropology*, and several academic and university presses and museum monograph series. His current research interests include the colonization dynamics of hunter-gatherers, "tribal zone" or contact-era archaeology, and cultural chronologies of the Intermountain West.

**Paul ("Jim") Roscoe** is Professor of Anthropology at the University of Maine, where he has taught since 1984. He received his Ph.D. in social anthropology from the University of Rochester and holds a M.A. in social anthropology and a M.Sc. in liberal studies in science. He has conducted two and a half years of fieldwork in Papua New Guinea and specializes in the anthropology of war, political and cultural evolution, and the human dimensions of climate change. His articles have appeared in *American Anthropologist, American Ethnologist, Journal of Anthropological Archaeology, Journal of Archaeological Method and Theory, Journal of the Royal Anthropological Institute, Man (N.S.)*, and *World Archaeology*.

**Christopher W. Schmidt** is Professor of Anthropology, Director of the Indiana Prehistory Laboratory, and Director of the Anthropology Graduate Program at the University of Indianapolis. He received his Ph.D. from Purdue University in 1998. His research efforts focus on the relationships between diet and pathology. He has published 30 articles and book chapters, coedited the volume *The Analysis of Burned Human Remains* (2008, Academic Press) and is editor of the journal *Dental Anthropology*.

**Al W. Schwitalla** is a consulting archaeologist with more than 25 years of experience, primarily in central California. He is currently the principal of Schwitalla Cultural Consulting and Millennia Molding and Casting Company in Sacramento. He earned both his B.A. and M.A. in anthropology from California State University, Sacramento. His research interests include Native American health and behavioral trends, artifact typological analysis, and the historic contact era in California. Schwitalla is best recognized for his artifact reproduction and interpretation work in cooperation with California tribal groups from throughout the state.

**Eric C. Strother** has 16 years of professional archaeological experience working throughout central California and southern Nevada, and is currently a senior archaeologist and physical anthropologist at Garcia and Associates in Marin County. Strother holds an M.A. in anthropology from California State University, East Bay, with an emphasis in human and nonhuman osteology. His research interests have included pre-contact violence in central California and skeletal health as reflected in the archaeological record. Strother has also taught physical anthropology and field archaeology at California State University, East Bay, and assisted Sonoma County law enforcement with forensic assessments. He is listed on the Register of Professional Archaeologists.

**Mark Q. Sutton** began his career in 1968, working at a site with the local community college while still in high school. He went on to earn a B.A. (1972), an M.A. (1977), and a Ph.D. (1987) in anthropology. He has worked for the US Air Force, the US Bureau of Land Management, various private consulting firms, and taught at a number of community colleges and universities. He taught at California State University, Bakersfield, from 1987 to 2007, where he retired as Emeritus Professor of Anthropology. He now works for Statistical Research, Inc. in San Diego. From 1986 to 2000, Sutton served as Editor of the *Journal of California and Great Basin Anthropology*. Sutton has investigated hunter-gatherer adaptations to arid environments, entomophagy, prehistoric diet and technology, and the prehistory of California. Sutton has worked at more than 120 sites in western North America, has presented some 126 papers at professional meetings, and has published some 190 books, monographs, articles, and reviews on archaeology and anthropology, including the textbooks *Introduction to Native North America, A Prehistory of North America, Archaeology: Science of the Human Past, Introduction to Cultural Ecology, Paleonutrition*, and *Laboratory Methods in Archaeology*.

**Randy S. Wiberg** earned his M.A. in anthropology from San Francisco State University in 1984, and was a senior archaeologist with Holman & Associates for 34 years. His main research interests include archaeological study of central California mortuary practices and the identification of pathological conditions in human skeletal remains. He has coauthored journal articles and book chapters on California prehistory, structural cemetery evolution, remote sensing, and hunter-gatherer warfare.